BEHIND THE SCREEN

ALSO BY WILLIAM J. MANN

Wisecracker: The Life and Times of William Haines
The Men from the Boys
The Biograph Girl

BEHIND THE SCREEN

HOW GAYS AND LESBIANS SHAPED HOLLYWOOD

1910–1969

William J. Mann

VIKING

VIKING

Published by the Penguin Group
Penguin Putnam Inc., 375 Hudson Street,
New York, New York 10014, U.S.A.
Penguin Books Ltd, 27 Wrights Lane,
London W8 5TZ, England
Penguin Books Australia Ltd, Ringwood,
Victoria, Australia
Penguin Books Canada Ltd, 10 Alcorn Avenue,
Toronto, Ontario, Canada M4V 3B2
Penguin Books (N.Z.) Ltd, 182–190 Wairau Road,
Auckland 10, New Zealand

Penguin Books Ltd, Registered Offices:
Harmondsworth, Middlesex, England

First published in 2001 by Viking Penguin,
a member of Penguin Putnam Inc.

1 3 5 7 9 10 8 6 4 2

LIBRARY OF CONGRESS CATALOGING IN PUBLICATION DATA
Mann, William J.
Behind the screen : how gays and lesbians shaped Hollywood,
1910–1969 / William J. Mann.
p.   cm.
ISBN 0-670-03017-1 (alk. paper)
1. Gay motion picture actors and actresses—United States—Biography.
2. Gay motion picture producers and directors—United States—Biography. I. Title.

PN2286.5 .M36   2001
791.43'028'08664—dc21   2001017984

This book is printed on acid-free paper. ∞

Printed in the United States of America
Set in Bembo
Designed by Jaye Zimet

For Tim Huber
and
Miles White

CONTENTS

•

INTRODUCTION

•

"Tell me anywhere else in America where you could have found it."

Across from me, the blue eyes of the eighty-year-old man shone sharply in the Palm Springs sun. His fingers tapped hard upon the glass surface of the table.

"You *can't,* can you?" He sat back in his chair and gave me a satisfied smile. "Because there *was* nowhere else. Not unless you were in Café Society or some bigwig on Broadway. But in Hollywood . . . gays had power, gays were 'in.'"

He was remembering the Friday night bridge games he and his friends used to throw in the Hollywood hills during the 1950s—bridge games where the gray smoke hung low, where the whiskey flowed fast and the repartée even faster—where Rock Hudson often did the honors mixing the drinks, where a cabal of off-duty publicists would swap news of the studios, where deals were struck and history was made—and where everyone, man and woman, was gay.

He savored the memory. "Nowhere else in America did gays have such a way of being together, of not worrying about their jobs, of just being who they were," he insisted. "I came from a small town in the Midwest. My father was a postal worker. I could never have imagined the kind of gay life that I would find in Hollywood."

Suddenly he leaned across the table, passionate. "This book of yours," he said. "Don't repeat all that *crap* about how tough Rock Hudson had it. You know—how he had to pretend to be straight and live a lie and all that. That was just surface. Rock Hudson had it *easy.* You just ask any Joe from Peoria what life was like for *him.* Who *didn't* have to lie? Who *didn't* have to pretend? The difference was, in Hollywood, our bosses lied *for* us. They protected us. We had a whole *community,* for God's sake. We had—dare I say it?—*power.* Where else in America did gays have such a thing?"

Sitting there that afternoon, early on in my research for this book, I knew that there had, in fact, been gay communities of the kind he described in places other than Hollywood, that gays and lesbians in certain areas of New York and San Francisco, for example, had had "such a thing" as early as the nineteen-teens—but I didn't tell him that. His point about Hollywood remained valid nonetheless.

The prevailing image of the studio era, both on and off the screen, has been one of hostility toward homosexuals. The assumption has been that Hollywood's classical period, from roughly the 1920s to the 1950s, was a time of repression and conformity, and that only with the end of the studio era (and the arrival of the modern gay movement) did gays in Hollywood find free expression and association. Certainly references to "the Hollywood closet" have become ubiquitous, with a sense that it has always existed, and in the same form, and for everyone. Yet over and over again, I'd ask survivors what it was like—what the experience of gay men and lesbians in the Hollywood studio era had been—and I was nearly always told the same thing: "We had no problem." "No one cared that we were gay." "It just wasn't an issue."

Could it be true? Certainly they must be repressing something, I thought. If I'd asked the same question of someone from any other industry during the period, surely I'd have gotten a very different answer. Homosexuals didn't have it easy in the first three-quarters of the twentieth century, even if the last quarter was often not much better: they were fired, purged, harassed, ostracized, made invisible. So it was difficult to take these old men at their word. Surely they weren't suggesting that tolerance and progressive thinking had been prized in the capitalist oligarchy of the Hollywood studio system, an enterprise fiercely committed to the defense and propagation of traditional middle-class American values.

But over and over, the same answer: "They didn't care," insisted Robert Shaw, a writer for Fox. "If you gave them the right image, they didn't care what you did when you left the studio."

Ah, yes, there it was: the catch I was suspecting. The *image*. Ever since the pioneer moviemakers first blazed a trail to the West, it has been *image* that has sustained Hollywood. The studios were called *dream factories,* after all—the makers of myths. That was their commodity, the goods they sold: the image translated into dollars. So long as you held up the image, so long as you made the dollars, there was indeed no problem.

Here is where, if I pressed, a darker side to the gay experience emerged. Ask those who contradicted the image what it had been like in the studios, and another reply was offered. "It could be awful," admitted Alan Cahan, a onetime publicist for Universal. "You had to be vigilant at all times."

Ask anyone who hadn't played by the rules—like William Haines, if he were still alive, the biographical subject of my previous book, *Wisecracker,* who lived openly with his male partner in defiance of studio wishes and who had little time for fostering a heterosexual image. Haines was fired for his disregard of image; he spent the rest of his life reviling his boss, Louis B. Mayer, only too glad to burst balloons of studio-era nostalgia. Ask others: actress Lizabeth Scott, perhaps, who received no help from her studio when *Confidential* slandered her in print and thus sullied the image. Ask even behind-the-scenes people, like set decorator Howard Bristol, who— gay-bashed in a Santa Monica park in 1953—found work hard to get for several years. Ask legendary costume designer Travis Banton, who hoped marriage might persuade studio moguls to take a second chance on a career ruined by drink and homosexual carousing. (It didn't.) Ask director Dorothy Arzner, who tried to be an independent woman, not to mention lesbian, in a club run by old straight boys.

"It was the best and the worst of times," said the costume designer Miles White of the gay experience in the studio era. "On the one hand, they didn't care, and you had extraordinary freedom, but on the other, of *course* they did, and you weren't free at all."

• • •

Yet this is not a book about exposing the lies of the Hollywood image. That can be fun for a while, contrasting the publicity (Tab Hunter and Anthony Perkins double-dating with a couple of bright-eyed starlets) with the reality (Tab and Tony dropping the girls off and going home together), but really that's just a game, the way things were done. Far more interesting than how Hollywood *lied* is how it told the *truth*—a truth that manifested itself in those bridge games in the Hollywood hills where publicists Alan Cahan and Pat Fitzgerald and Lynn Bowers drank whiskey and smoked cigarettes with agents Henry Willson and Dick Clayton, where journalists like Mike Connolly and stars like Rock Hudson swapped tricks. All of them gay. All of them part of the system. All with their own share of power. This was as much a truth of gay Hollywood as any movie star fired for bad press or any photo-op date between Ramon Novarro and Myrna Loy.

Just as Neal Gabler explored the Jewish experience in Hollywood in his groundbreaking *An Empire of Their Own: How the Jews Invented Hollywood,* and just as various studies have looked at the parts played by women, African Americans, and Latinos, the time has come when we can seriously and without sensationalism assess the gay and lesbian experience of studio-era Hollywood. The research for this book began as a logical outgrowth of my work on *Wisecracker;* much material contained in interviews for that project proved germane to this one. Yet it quickly became apparent that the story of gays in Hollywood could not focus solely on movie stars. You'll find Cary Grant, Tyrone Power, Charles Laughton, Marlene Dietrich, Montgomery Clift, and Rock Hudson in these pages, but only as context. In truth, the sagas of actors, while flashy, are hardly representative of the experience of most Hollywood homosexuals. Even as William Haines was booted out by Mayer, gays would continue to rule the roost in the MGM costume and property departments for the next twenty years.

For this book, then, I wanted to look at the *totality* of the gay experience, something that has never before been attempted: a thoughtful examination of what it was like for gay men and lesbians in *all* areas of the studio system—writing, directing, editing, costumes, sets, technical, publicity. Where exactly did gays work in the studios? What did they do? Were they treated any differently? What power did they have? What were their personal lives like? Did many play straight? Did they express their sexuality on the job in any way? Did their gayness influence at all the work that they did?

In their study of homosexuality in the American theater, Robert Schanke and Kim Marra wrote that "sexuality permeates people's beliefs, actions and social relations." Their survey of leading theatrical figures examined not only *how* but *why* they created the works they did. "Far from irrelevant," Schanke and Marra wrote, "these questions, in acknowledging sexuality as a historical force, inquire into the very fabric of the past."

In other words, sexuality should not be treated merely as fodder for gossip writers or celebrity tattlers—although books on gay Hollywood have too often gone that sensational route in the past. By seeing these cinema pioneers not only as actors, directors, writers, and designers, but also as *gay men and lesbians,* we can hopefully cast new light not only on their experiences but also on the very history of American film itself.

Much of the serious writing on gay Hollywood in the past decade has centered around the concept of "spectatorship," or the experience of the audience. Various studies have explored how the films of Hollywood's classical period have shaped the consciousness of gay and lesbian viewers, and how a queer read can be as valid as any other for many of these films. "Cinema is public fantasy that engages spectators' particular, private scripts of desire and identification," the critic and theorist Patricia White has written. Yet as fascinating and useful as this approach is, it is *not* the approach I am taking here. Rather than images shaping the audience, I am concerned with how gay men and women shaped Hollywood itself. While I do consider how the gayness of particular figures may have manifested in their films, this is—first and foremost—a social history. While such historians as Allan Berubé, George Chauncey, and Esther Newton (to name just a few) have documented social histories for homosexuals in other walks of life, the same has been almost studiously avoided for gays in the film colony. Until now.

Here, for the first time, the story of gay men and lesbians in Hollywood is chronicled in context with their times: the freedom of the Roaring Twenties, the Production Code clampdown of the 1930s, the wartime revival of the gay subculture, the ferocious backlash and inquisitions of the 1950s, the liberation of the 1960s. Back and forth the pendulum swung; no gay story can be seen outside of its era. Rock Hudson lived in a Hollywood far different than did Ramon Novarro.

Of course, each narrative, each life, remains unique unto itself. No person can be put easily into a box; human relationships have always been complex, fluid, and as different as the individuals involved. There are those who truly live bisexually without claiming that sexuality as a basis for their identity; there are also those, then as well as now, who never fully accept their essential same-sex orientation. Not every figure profiled in this book is therefore on the same emotional page. Screenwriter Gavin Lambert wrote that his friend, director Lindsay Anderson, felt "isolated by guilt over his sexuality," a condition Lambert said wasn't uncommon. Lindsay "never got over it," while Lambert and other contemporaries moved on to healthy acceptance and integration of sexuality into their lives. Lambert also wrote of the director Nicholas Ray, who, despite affairs with men, never acknowledged either homosexuality or bisexuality. Others, like Charles Laughton, began by compartmentalizing sexuality from the rest of their lives, only to become more accepting of it as they got older: Laughton would, late in life, tell his wife Elsa Lanchester he preferred spending time with Christopher Isherwood and Don Bachardy because they were of his "own kind."

Yet even within very different narratives, I frequently discovered continuity. The early lives of Hollywood's gays tended to follow a similar pattern, one that echoes down familiarly through the generations: square pegs born into families of round holes, yearning from a very young age to escape their communities of origin, often rejecting career paths chosen by their parents and leaving home to redefine themselves elsewhere. Again, not all fit the formula: the writer Charles Brackett was a son who *didn't* rebel, who *didn't* want to be different, who obediently followed the course set down by his family. Still, it remains striking how many of Hollywood's gay stories *do* match the pattern, from the last decades of the nineteenth century to the middle decades of the twentieth.

One thing is certain for all of them: to have stayed in their hometowns would have meant forfeiting many of the choices they found in Hollywood. In Tecumseh, Nebraska, and Naugatuck, Connecticut, they wouldn't have known the freedom to speak openly about their lives with similarly undisguised colleagues. Living openly with a same-sex partner would have been next to impossible. It's difficult to imagine a field outside the movie studios where the very gayness of these individuals would actually carry some professional advantage. In any other setting except screenland, to define themselves even implicitly as homosexual would have been a radical act. Yet all of these things were possible—and common—in Hollywood.

Life in the film capital offered alternatives. In certain studio departments, such as costume and set decoration, being gay could actually be seen as *beneficial,* given the perceived talent of homosexuals for those fields. In addition, within these departments, gay men actually held positions of power, often using their own social networks as hiring pools. The result was homosexuals and heterosexuals working side by side with a degree of openness not seen nearly anywhere else; clashes occurred, but were far fewer than might be expected elsewhere.

True, a similar integration also existed in the world of the New York theater and in the more bohemian environments of Greenwich Village and San Francisco—but the studios weren't based on the theater model, and Hollywood, a small town with small-town values, was certainly far from bohemian. In fact, from the start there existed a divide in Hollywood, a split that helped define its often schizophrenic attitude toward gays. Cinema's peculiar hybrid of theater and science allowed for not only the mixing of gay and straight, but also East Coast and West Coast, sophisticate and traditionalist, university and trade school, rich and poor. The clash between the middle-class values of industry leaders and the nonconformist ideals of the artists forms much of the narrative of this book.

Meanwhile, the very structure of the studios themselves—approximations of middle-class corporate America—lent itself to the uniqueness of the gay experience in Hollywood. The movies were, after all, an *industry:* with production policies and procedures, departments headed by middle management who reported up the line to bosses who reported to a board. In such a structure in any other industry, homosexuality would not have been tolerated. But in the studios, within certain proscribed parameters and within specific departmental boundaries, gay employees lived and worked openly, without fear of reprisal or harassment.

In setting out to tell their stories, it was also important to recognize what historian Sam Abel has called the "shifting social constructions of same-sex desire." (John Loughery has suggested that American homosexuality is "a concept fashioned anew every twenty-five years or so.") I would need to surrender modern-day notions of what it means to be "in" or "out" of "the closet." The closet, in fact, is not an appropriate construct to use in analyzing studio-era Hollywood; to make sense, it needs the opposing construct of "openly gay"—an idea that really only began to evolve in this country during the 1950s with the Mattachine Society, and in truth, for most North Americans, not until after the Stonewall Riots of 1969. Rather, the terms used here are "overt" and "circumspect," words taught to me by the survivors themselves. ("Overt" was also the term used by psychologists and sociologists documenting gay life in the 1940s and 1950s, particularly Maurice Leznoff and Evelyn Hooker.) Alan Cahan explained "circumspect" this way: "Although people might have known someone was gay, if he was circumspect it meant he was *careful*. He might even live with another man, but he brought a woman to functions. He behaved properly. He didn't put the makes on someone on the set."

It follows, then, that someone who was overt *did* put the makes on: William Haines, for example, or many of the costume designers, who could be as campy as they liked and "get away with it," according to survivors. Yet the simple breakdown between "circumspect" and "overt" is still too stark, too close to being "in" or "out." As I discovered, within this spectrum there were roughly three expressions, and of course they often overlapped. At one extreme were those who were *very* overt, like Haines, who didn't care what people knew, while at the other end of the spectrum there were those who were *so* circumspect, like Charles Brackett, that even close friends often did not know the truth.

Most of Hollywood's known homosexuals, however, occupied a middle space, and this is the condition most of the survivors described to me. "People just knew, they accepted it, and nobody talked about it," said Arthur Laurents. It was a space that definitely had its rules and boundaries, yet still offered a lifestyle unimaginable in its authenticity to most homosexuals in other parts of the country. Eve Kosofsky Sedgwick has called this condition "the imponderable open secret," and it is the degrees within that openness that prove fascinating.

Most striking is the pattern that emerged when class background was considered. While nearly all the studio workers were white, even those in the most menial positions, they were quite eclectic in class. The most overt gays tended to have come from working-class backgrounds, while those from the middle classes invariably were more circumspect. Once again the example is Brackett, scion of an upper-middle-class Eastern family, who would treat his homosexuality in Hollywood as a dark secret. Even within the largely queer environment of costume design, class distinctions held: the middle-class, status-conscious Adrian was far less apt to be "obvious" than the working-class Howard Greer or Orry-Kelly.

The whiteness of the studios makes this, with very few exceptions, a study of the *white* gay experience; likewise, the prevailing patriarchy of the studios kept women (for the most part) in proscribed roles within the studio structure. Still, it's intriguing that of the women who *did* manage to achieve a degree of power—becoming directors, writers, or producers—a number were lesbian: Dorothy Arzner, Zoe Akins, Harriet Parsons, all of whom are herein profiled. The female survivors of the era are few, unfortunately, and only two agreed to be interviewed, anonymously.

The number of gay Jews in the studio did, however, allow me to make some interesting observations about the diversity of the gay experience: the more open about their Jewishness, for example, the more likely they were to be overt sexually. Parallels between the Jewish and the gay experiences in Hollywood are apparent. Both were seen as antithetical to the middle-class American dream; both could and sometimes *did* try to "pass." Both were susceptible to self-hatred: the gay agent John Darrow was known to publicly berate his lover, the director Charles Walters, as a "stupid faggot," while Dore Schary remembered being horrified by "top-drawer Jewish studio executives" whose first pejorative when provoked was always "dirty kike."

Yet the two experiences diverge rather sharply as well. Neal Gabler chronicled how the founders of the movie industry came from Jewish traditions to create in Hollywood a larger "American" myth. Gays, on the other hand, came from heterosexual traditions; they would first have to shape their *own* subculture before becoming partners in the enterprise of myth-making. Their talents in design and fashion proved useful to the moguls in creating the image of Hollywood they sent out across the globe. At the same time, however, many gays were also constructing a kind of "flip side" to the Hollywood American myth: the subtly subversive films of George Cukor, Dorothy Arzner, James Whale, and Mitchell Leisen; the queer characterizations of the Hollywood sissies; the sexual underground of the film colony that more than once drew the wrath of reformers. It is this tradition of both collaboration and contradiction that makes the story of gay Hollywood so fascinating.

• • •

Inaugurating my research, I cast my net wide, going through each and every obituary in *Variety* from 1905 to 1995, collecting those that contained the usual gay flags: "Lifelong bachelor"; "Survived by a sister and a nephew"; or, most typical and most inaccurate, "There are no immediate survivors." For, of course, there *were* survivors—lovers, friends, gay families who knew these people far better than any brother or sister might have. I was fortunate in some instances to find these people, often listed as the informants on death certificates. Frequently younger than their partners, they were still alive and willing to be interviewed.

From this original *Variety* list—numbering close to one thousand—I compiled the names that, after a process of elimination, would eventually form the heart of this book: actors, directors, writers, editors, costumers, decorators, publicists, journalists, and others. To discern their sexuality, I searched out friends, relatives, letters, oral histories, mentions in the memoirs of others. I'd look for "queer markers": lack of marriage, lack of children, marriage to known homosexuals, arrests on moral charges, association with other gays in articles and columns. Census records revealed same-sex partners living together; death certificates offered the indicative "never married" status; probate files and wills documented a figure's true (and not merely his blood) family. I'd run their names past survivors: *Oh, yes,* they'd say, *he was gay; he'd come to brunch with his boyfriend.* Or else, *Sorry, never heard of him.* In this way, the portrait of gay Hollywood began to unfold itself.

I admit to some reverse bias upon commencement, assuming, for example, that most of those fabulous art directors of Hollywood's golden age must have been gay. But, to my surprise, most of them left wives and children and grandchildren. No proof, necessarily, of heterosexuality, but the absence of any "lifelong bachelors" among them was telling in itself. Discovering that the changeover to sound had required an architectural background for art directors led me toward the answer for this conspicuous absence of gays. It introduced me to the concept of "queer work," the idea that some fields are strongly associated with one gender (like architecture with men) and therefore often hostile to new arrivals who are either of the opposite gender or homosexual. An occupation associated with a particular gender becomes "queer" when entered by a number of workers of the other gender. Hairdressing, for example, has been considered women's work; when men work in the field, it is considered queer (likewise when women work at the loading dock). That distinct gay and straight enclaves existed in the studios soon became obvious to me when my file on "sound technicians" remained thin and the one on "costume designers" bulged so much I had to create a second one, and then two, and then three. "Queer work" is a construct that informs a good deal of the discussion in this study.

Of course, it is a study that could never be exhaustive. Undoubtedly there were many gays whose identities will never be known, their presence in certain departments mere speculation. I was also careful about who I pulled back in after casting my net wide. To profile an individual for this study, I needed more than just hearsay or innuendo. In recent years there has been a tendency to attach labels to figures for whom such labeling would have been meaningless. Barbara Stanwyck, for example, may well have been gay as some allege, but in truth I have seen no evidence nor heard any anecdote that makes such a description certain. Yet it is important to say, at the same time, I have seen very little evidence of *hetero*sexuality on her part either—with the exception of her well-known attachment to Robert Taylor, which itself is enigmatic.

There is a balance that must be found in writing about the perceived gayness of historical figures. The "burden of proof" for homosexuality has traditionally been held far higher than that for heterosexuality. The historian Neil Miller has written: "To insist on evidence of genital sex or the discovery of some lost 'coming out' manifesto to prove that someone was gay or lesbian sets up a standard of proof that cannot be met." Such isn't the case, of course, for heterosexuality. Popular wisdom presumes a romantic, sexual relationship between Katharine Hepburn and Spencer Tracy—despite the fact that neither ever claimed such. Many acquaintances insist the relationship was a devoted yet platonic friendship, at least for most of its duration, but that hasn't prevented numerous writers from spinning romantic fairy tales about it—which few ever challenge.

Meanwhile, angry debate and hot denials still meet any discussion of a homosexual relationship between Cary Grant and Randolph Scott—despite the photographs in *Modern Screen,* the double entendres in their contemporary press, the references in the papers of Hedda Hopper and others, and the testimony of many survivors. A television profile of Cesar Romero in the year 2000 can still sound like a fan-magazine article from the 1940s, never mentioning his gayness and citing his "devotion to his sister" as the reason he never married. *Vanity Fair*—of all things—has run recent articles endeavoring to situate Claudette Colbert and Adrian (Adrian!) as heterosexual. (Who's next? Liberace?) Even the author of a recent book on Ramon Novarro is notably hesitant to suggest a romantic, sexual relationship between the star and the journalist Herbert Howe, despite Howe's gushing prose and the recollections by others of a romance. Yet at the same time, the author speculates comfortably on a possible *hetero*sexual affair Novarro may have had because, after all, he must have been "curious."

Why this reticence? This double standard? It would appear that in an attempt to counterbalance the excesses of some writers, others have gone too far in the opposite extreme. But the pervasiveness of heterosexual presumption is a far greater threat to the truth than the occasional posthumous mislabeling of a celebrity as homosexual.

Discussing gay identity in a historical context must always be done with both fairness and consistency. The writer must remember that identities—while perhaps reflecting innate desires and sensibilities—are nonetheless overwhelmingly constructed socially. "The invocation of identity is always a risk," the writer Judith Butler has warned, and she's right. John Loughery observed that "it is doubtful that anyone has ever viewed himself or herself solely as a gay man, a lesbian, a Jew, an African-American, a southerner." Yet he also cautioned against that very same "never-to-be-summarized 'personhood,'" for it "carries with it a disconnectedness that is apt to fail us in critical moments."

Considering historical figures in the context of any of their multiplicity of labels can offer a unique and special understanding, but it is a consideration that, until very recently, has not often encompassed sexuality. For while "few people regard a Jew's embrace of his religious or cultural background as a limitation on his individuality," Loughery has pointed out that "many people—gay and straight—[still] think it absurd or quaint that sexuality should be an issue of equivalent profundity." Thus, while it is important not to reduce a figure's life experiences and motivations to any one part of her or his identity, it is equally as important not to disregard or dismiss as trivial any of those parts either.

Identity is of course the result of many forces, from class and culture to personal experience, geography, and the tenor of the times. (As we've seen, Lindsay Anderson, Nicholas Ray, and William Haines were hardly cut from the same cloth.) There needs therefore to be a recognition of the fluid complexity of sexual and gender identity and experience. Persons not easily classified—gay, straight, bisexual—then become appropriate figures of study for projects such as these, and often end up proving the most instructive of all.

In fact, Blanche Weisen Cook has famously suggested a continuum for the lesbian experience that may or may not even include "consciously-desired genital experience with another woman." She wrote: "Women who love women, who choose women to nurture and support and to create a living environment in which to work creatively and independently, are lesbians." Maybe Claudette Colbert—or Janet Gaynor or Zoe Akins, all discussed herein—never used the word "lesbian," and maybe they never even engaged in sexual activity with another woman, but under Weisen Cook's definition they remain suitable for inclusion in this book.

Yet the reluctance of some historians to even *consider* the possibility of sexual expression has been a barrier in the attempt to fully understand these people's lives. Despite the fact that the only evidence of an ongoing, committed, intimate relationship in Hattie McDaniel's life is with another woman, her biographer categorically dismissed any suggestion that McDaniel might have been anything other than absolutely, positively, 100 percent heterosexual. Until fairly recently, some insisted that poet Hart Crane's close friendships with several men were strictly nonsexual; the publication of more explicit letters forever disproved that theory.

We may never have such explicit "proof" of the homosexuality of Hollywood figures. Indeed, many of the subjects I profile in this book were careful to conceal the specifics of their lives. Although in several cases I had access to correspondence and personal papers, much appears to have been purged of any personal references. The Zoe Akins collection actually states that this was done by Akins herself, and the mind-numbing innocuity of Edward Everett Horton's letters suggests such an explanation as well. To a lesser extent, the same is true about the George Cukor correspondence at the Academy of Motion Picture Arts and Sciences library. Yet even this purging is telling: like Thomas Mann and Walt Whitman, both of whom burned personal papers they deemed too gay-explicit, the Hollywood gays fit a historical pattern.

I have chosen therefore not to waste valuable space trying to "prove" the unprovable: who had genital contact with whom. Rather, I examined the *relational* or "homosocial" aspects of sexuality, using Christopher Isherwood's credo to consider as gay "those men who live together for years and make homes and share their lives and their work." Indeed, the historian Robert Padgug used as a guide the idea that "sexuality consists of active social relations, and not simply sexual acts." Most of my subjects were in fact part of a larger "gay" community within Hollywood. They were the "sophisticates" in the press of the 1930s, singled out from the traditionally "married with children"; later they were part of specific gay circles as identified to me by survivors.

Given this frequent lack of hard historical evidence, I determined early on that I would need to look for answers in places often ignored or marginalized in the past. Writing gay histories requires a revaluation of traditional rules of "evidence." Learning to read between the lines *without reading into them* is an acquired skill, as is learning to discern the truth as much by what *isn't* said as what *is*. The Hollywood press of the studio era is loaded with information on the gay subculture, and I suggest that much of it is there consciously. One of my most intriguing discoveries was how many of the reporters and publicists were themselves gay. Use of such phrases as "temperamental," "sensitive bachelor," and "rebelliously unfeminine" by a straight reporter might seem merely coincidental, yet when penned by Herbert Howe or Jerry Asher or Herb Sterne perhaps a deeper meaning is intended. In this way, gays were shaping the myth themselves.

Researching gay history also requires weighing the vast body of gossip, film lore, and legend—too often high-handedly dismissed without even cursory consideration by writers consumed by their own seriousness of purpose. Yet as critic and historian Andrea Weiss has pointed out, "Rumor and gossip constitutes the unrecorded history of the gay subculture"—an assessment expanded upon by B. Ruby Rich: "If oral history is the history of those denied control of the printed record, gossip is the history of those who cannot even speak in their own first-person voice." While insufficient on its own as a basis for sweeping conclusions, such oral traditions *do* often point the way toward understanding the truth of gay history.

And while it is always important not to employ modern interpretations of experiences or identities, it's also vital that evidence not be overlooked in that attempt: sometimes the obvious is indeed telling us something. The word "gay," for example, was used in the Hollywood press both to describe "cheerful exuberance" *and* as a marker of something more. It was attached too often to homosexual figures for it to be merely coincidental. Certainly by the early 1950s it had become a standard euphemism for homosexual in the scandal magazines. If not holding the ascendancy it has today, "gay" has meant "homosexual" for at least a hundred years: historian Gary Schmidgall, biographer of Walt Whitman, found it used in such a way in the first years of the twentieth century. He observed that "spoken in the right company, 'gay' may long have had something of its familiar post-Stonewall ring." All one has to do is view the film *My Weakness* (1933) to see this in action: Charles Butterworth and Sid Silvers, both incurably in love with Lillian Harvey, come up with a solution. "Let's be gay!" Butterworth suggests. The Hays Office demanded the line be obscured by a soundtrack, but few in the audience who heard it could have missed its meaning.

• • •

The stories in this book are almost entirely new. These are not figures who have been written about at great length before. The movie stars who *do* appear here—J. Warren Kerrigan, Lilyan Tashman, Franklin Pangborn, Clifton Webb, George Nader—are those whose stories have never been fully told. A few whom I discuss at some length—Cukor, Arzner, Leisen, Adrian—*have* been the subjects of previous biographies, and excellent ones. But in each case there were gaps: Cukor in terms of the gay subtext of his work, the other three in terms of biographical material.

Each of my profiles also had to somehow inform the larger gay experience. Yes, Anna Q. Nilsson may have been a lesbian, and so might have Jean Arthur. Burt Lancaster may have had affairs with men, and Henry Wilcoxon may have routinely picked up male hitchhikers for sex. But beyond a few anecdotes, their stories offer little to illuminate what life was like for gay men and lesbians in Hollywood. A full-scale biography of someone like Arthur might offer considerable insight, but as such, it was beyond what I could do here.

For in truth, this work, while using biography as a tool, is a chronicle not so much of individual lives as individuals as part of a subculture. Those whose connection to the larger gay community was tangential at best are not examined; rather, I have sought to explore the ways in which gay men and lesbians "gravitated" (in the words of director Curtis Harrington) toward each other in the studios. Frank Lysinger, who worked in the music department at MGM, remembered, "My being gay and knowing all these people—the doors were always open. It was all this 'understood' business. They knew I knew, I knew they knew. It was kind of a brotherhood. You'd meet each other through one and you'd see each other out."

It's the "brotherhood" I'm interested in. The homosexuals of the Hollywood studios forged their own distinctive culture with their own language, customs, and folk histories. George Chauncey has demonstrated that vibrant queer communities in pre-Stonewall New York disproved the myths of isolation, invisibility, and internalization (the idea that they uncritically accepted the dominant culture's view of them). Likewise, what I discovered in Hollywood—with its teeming nightlife and gay-dominated units within the studios—lays to rest those myths in regard to screenland as well.

One of the most stirring of the questions I posed in this study was how the gayness of these individuals came through in their work. Admittedly, this is the most subjective aspect of the book: George Cukor's habit of using gay outsiders like Oliver Messel and George Hoyningen-Huene on his films in place of straight studio personnel; Dorothy Arzner's collaboration with Zoe Akins on films offering surprisingly feminist messages; the gay aesthetic recognized in certain set decorators; the elusive "gay sensibility" of such diverse figures as writer DeWitt Bodeen, costume designer Travis Banton, producer Ross Hunter, and the entire Freed unit at MGM. It is, in effect, proposing a "queer cinema" some fifty years before the term was coined—created by men and women whose lives, in the words of critic Matthew Tinkcom, "predate the political act of self-naming themselves as gay." Tinkcom argued that we face a "historical and theoretical vacuum" when we attempt to reconcile the traditional perception of Hollywood hostility to gays with the reality of gay creativity in many Hollywood films.

In filling that vacuum, then, is it possible to see the gay influence in *The Wizard of Oz,* for example, because Adrian created the Munchkins and Jack Moore the Yellow Brick Road? Can we reflect upon the gayness of the narrative of *Cat People,* written by DeWitt Bodeen? Might we consider the queerness of the very *look* of *Casablanca,* whose fantastic sets were designed by George James Hopkins? Or detect the gay soul of *Meet Me in St. Louis,* because its direction was staged by Vincente Minnelli, its score orchestrated by Conrad Salinger, and its production arranged by Roger Edens? Might we reconsider the entire body of work of such directors as George Cukor or Dorothy Arzner or Edmund Goulding or James Whale, seeing their films as the creations of artists *who were gay?*

It is of course impossible to offer here all the analyses, comparisons, and impressions that the work of such myriad artists demands and deserves. It is my hope that this book will encourage others to look anew at the work of many of these individuals from this perspective. As Schanke and Marra pointed out, the awareness of a historical figure's gayness "does not just add to but *transforms* the record."

• • •

It's been lamented that so many of my subjects are dead. Many times I heard the wish that I'd undertaken this project ten years ago. True, I wish I'd gotten to some folks earlier: set decorator Jack Moore, still alive when I began my research, died in December 1998. Yet I doubt he or any of the others, had they lived, would have shared as much as people like to imagine they might have.

"My uncle would never have agreed to come out in your book," said Michael Grace, the nephew of MGM set director Henry Grace. Despite being comparatively undisguised about his gayness during his career, and despite taking a progressive lead in organizing the groundbreaking industry strikes in 1945–46, Grace drew a zone of privacy around his personal life, especially as he got older and homosexuality became a more explicit topic of discussion. From the retrospective vantage point of his nephew, Henry Grace—one of the least circumspect figures in the studios—seems "very closeted." Even those we consider the most likely to have openly shared their stories might well have proven intractable.

My experience with the handful of prominent names still alive suggests this as well. My letters to them usually went unanswered; follow-up phone calls were met with polite but firm refusals. Leonard Gershe, a writer in MGM's legendary Freed unit and a close friend of one of my primary profiles, Roger Edens, was at least gracious enough to respond with a note, turning me down with the explanation that he had never felt comfortable discussing sexuality—his or anyone else's. (A second letter offering to forgo any talk of sexuality and concentrate just on what it was like to work in the Freed unit was unanswered.) A few months later, however, Gershe was apparently comfortable enough to affirm *hetero*sexuality for Claudette Colbert in the pages of *Vanity Fair.*

I came to understand that it's not so much *sexuality* these people are uncomfortable discussing: it's *homo*sexuality. For them, it's as if the studio era hasn't ended; the old concern for *image* remains frozen in time. That's not to condemn them: they lived and worked in an era much different from this one, and to judge anyone without living their experience would be unjust.

Still, I cannot help but admire those who *have* embraced a more contemporary way of interacting with the world. I am grateful for those who did share their stories with me in some way, notable among them Arthur Laurents, Gavin Lambert, George Nader, Mark Miller, Curtis Harrington, and Miles White. Equally important are those whose fame never reached the height of Laurents or Nader or White, the dozens of writers, publicists, costumers, actors, and others who shared with me their experiences in the studios. I was also aided immensely by the cooperation of surviving lovers, friends, and family of the many who had already passed on.

Movies, and in particular the movies produced during Hollywood's classical studio age, have immeasurably shaped popular culture and the way we see ourselves and our world. *The Celluloid Closet,* both book and film, has documented how the images on the screen taught gay people about themselves. It's my hope that this book takes that process one step further: to understand where those images came from, who put them there, and what kinds of experiences their creators needed to go through to get them onto the screen. Gays and lesbians have been shaping Hollywood in all of its manifestations from the very beginning. Can we discern them at last? Can we see their gifts, their contributions? Nietzsche wrote that "the degree and kind of a person's sexuality reach up into the ultimate pinnacle of his soul." If that is true, Hollywood's gays, behind the screen and between the lines, offer a glimpse into our own.

BEHIND THE SCREEN

GREAT GODS

THE FIRST GAY IDOLS

1910-1925

The handsome hero couldn't breathe: there was water up his nose. The villain held him by the back of his neck, keeping him facedown in the flume. Behind him, the crew slapped their knees in laughter, and the director, barely able to conceal his own mirth, ticked off the extra seconds in his mind. When finally he called "cut," up from the flume staggered the Great God Kerrigan—cursing, spitting, gasping for air.

Right from the start, Hollywood has been predicated on illusion, on things being not quite what they seem. That day in 1910, at the dawn of Hollywood filmmaking, the wilderness of La Mesa, California, passed for a sagebrush canyon of Arizona, and the perfumed, effeminate J. Warren Kerrigan posed as a fast-shooting, buckskin-wearing cowboy. Not today would Kerrigan, idol of forty million, pose for publicity photographers. Not today would he sit haughtily in his make-up chair, with studio beautician Loiz Huyck using her eyebrow pencil and mascara to turn him into the handsomest of all movie cowboys. Rather, today he would spit and gag and cough water from his nose; this day, as many days, he'd endure the mocking laughter of the crew.

Director Allan Dwan would later admit to prolonging the scene in this little one-reeler called *The Poisoned Flume* to keep Kerrigan's face submerged in the water for as long as possible. He wanted to give the company a good laugh at the expense of their effete leading man. It's a tale as old as time and as familiar as any childhood playground: the bullies taunting the queer.

Right from the beginning, it was a divide that defined Hollywood: the sissies and the he-men, the theater people and the technicians, the artists and the cowboys. And the cowboys didn't much care for the artiste Kerrigan. These were scrappy pioneers, after all, with *warrants* on their heads: the Edison Company, alleging Dwan and the American Film Company were infringing on the Great Man's patents, had sent out spies and thugs to stop them. To survive, they had to be *fierce*. Forging through sagebrush and desert, they were ready for anything. Dwan hired authentic cowboys armed with Winchesters, and it didn't take much to induce the director himself—a former football coach—to pull out his own sidearm and shoot up tin cans in the arroyo. "The word got out," he'd remember, "that we were *tough*."

But Jack Kerrigan—their hero, their star, their linchpin for success at the box office—was anything but tough. He was pampered, powdered, and "pretty fond of himself at the time," said Dwan. The cowboys had Kerrigan's number: "Make us *handsome* like him," they'd implore Loiz Huyck with a wink, but she knew it was impossible. They were a breed apart from each other, these rough-and-tumble All-Men and the comely star in his velvet smoking jacket, who lived with his mother when they weren't out shooting and who told the fan magazines he liked the girls best "when they leave me alone."

Since his first picture with the Chicago-based Essanay company two years earlier, Kerrigan had become the most recognized male face on the screen: the first true superstar of the movies. "The Great God Kerrigan," the fan magazines called him. To him came unprecedented fame and fortune and—perhaps more importantly—the ability to live as he pleased, and with *whom* he pleased. In the comfortable home he built for himself near the Cahuenga Pass, not only was there a room for Mother but also one for his lover, James Vincent, a handsome young actor for whom Kerrigan would secure bit parts and walk-ons in his pictures.

But, as ever, such advantage came with a price—and for Kerrigan, he paid for it on the set that day in La Mesa, where his much-photographed, much-recognized, much-adored face was held underwater for the kick it gave to the rowdy crew.

Score one for the he-men. Kerrigan, facedown in the flume, sums up the gay experience in American cinema for many decades: the best and the worst of times, for as long as the studio era lasted.

• • •

Yet while Jack Kerrigan might not have been tough like a cowboy, he wasn't without his own resources. By 1912, he commanded enough star power to install his twin brother, Wallace, as business manager at American, better known as "Flying A." With his standing in the fan-magazine polls unchallenged, he could now strike—and seventy years later his revenge still rankled Allan Dwan. "Kerrigan put a knock into the company saying I was getting out of hand," Dwan told Peter Bogdanovich. "Unless I was replaced, he was going to leave the company."

In Hollywood, moneymaking star—nine times out of ten—trumps director. And so Dwan was out. "It was terrifying," he admitted, "to suddenly find myself out of work."

Rack this one up for the sissies. Of course, it wasn't the end of Dwan; he'd go on to an important career, even directing Kerrigan again at Universal. But Kerrigan's victory shows that as far back as 1912, gays—within their given niche—could wield power within the studio system. His story demonstrates as well that Hollywood's gays were present from the beginning, helping to mold the very system that would prove both their bane and their beneficence.

J. Warren Kerrigan's homosexuality, no doubt as obvious to his industry contemporaries as it is to us, was never secret: not to crew, not to costars, not to employers, not even to his mother, who from 1910 on never moved from under her son's roof. In the theater, of course, where Kerrigan had his start, homosexuality was hardly novel. To be sure, many of the perfumed, pomaded leading men of the stage were gay, not to mention the countless scenic designers, costumers, scenarists, and librettists. Even several well-known managers and producers straddled the conventions of heterosexuality: Morris Gest and Charles Frohman, to name just two. Gay historian Michael Bronski has pointed out that a homosexual association with the theater has existed since Elizabethan times, calling the theater a rare "port of safety for homosexuals." He added that "nowhere else in popular culture were, and are, gay men so accepted."

But in the movies, it was different. These were cowboys and frontiersmen, inventors and electricians, working-class Jews and Irishmen with backgrounds as hucksters and crafty capitalists, with wives and children and immigrant dreams to support. No perfume here.

These were the years of the Great Migration, when only the strong survived. As the days got shorter and the Chicago winds began to blow, Flying A—like so many others throughout the East and Midwest—set off for California. With Edison's henchmen hot on their heels, these little bands of filmmakers and their ragtag companies ventured into the Wild West, which promised not only freedom but—just as importantly—*sunshine*. In the days before arc lamps and indoor studios, the sun was the West's biggest premium, holding the industry in place even after Edison's Trust withered up and died.

The story of gay men and lesbians in Hollywood—and how they shaped their industry and art—only really begins here, in California, when they settled down among the cowboys and con men and began spinning the illusion that would transform a nation. "Came the dawn," wrote one scribe of the early days, "lavender and gold . . . from all walks they came to colonize the land of dreams."

It was a fascinating, volatile mix: on the one hand, actors and writers (many of whom were women), accustomed to the traditions to the theater; and on the other, directors and cameramen, nearly all men, who (like Allan Dwan) would rather have shot up tin cans on the fence than reminisce about Lillian Russell trodding the boards. The two camps had markedly different temperaments. As early as 1913, *Variety* was filled with reports of movie directors and crews harassing actresses in their stock companies. In December 1915 the district attorney even threatened to turn over to a Los Angeles grand jury accusations by several women that "liberties had been taken with them." It was always directors and crew singled out as culprits; in fact, at least one account says the actors were specifically *not* to blame.

It would be unfair—as well as inaccurate—to define the schism too specifically. Certainly there were lecherous actors and gentlemanly directors, and straight men have no particular patent on promiscuity. No generalization, no matter how helpful or insightful, is ever absolute: there were likely homosexual cameramen who kept their preferences quiet, and there was at least one director, William Desmond Taylor, who led a discreet gay life in the film colony as early as 1915.

But the divide was there, nonetheless, between two shifting, occasionally overlapping populations. It was a divide that would be variably and successively defined as East versus West, as New York versus Hollywood, as liberal versus conservative, as sophisticated versus rube, as artistic versus technical, as gay versus straight. That shouldn't suggest one side had talent and ability and the other didn't. The story of Hollywood is, in fact, the story of colliding forces influencing and melding and seducing each other. What emerged from these collisions was what we've come to know as classic American cinema—and the place where the magic first coalesced was a little boom town called Hollywood.

• • •

Whereas the Flying A company settled first in San Juan Capistrano, moving later to La Mesa and finally to Santa Barbara, other independents chose Los

Angeles. Even Edison Trust members came to L.A.: Selig Polyscope in 1908 and the famous Biograph Company, led by director D. W. Griffith, in 1910. Soon the city, and in particular its neighboring development of Hollywood, would become the preferred destination of the Eastern moviemakers.

Again, a culture clash. "Los Angeles," wrote historian Reyner Banham, "is the Middle West raised to a flashpoint." Indeed, the Midwest farmers who had settled the area in the previous century brought with them their solid, stoic Bible-Belt values. Yet already by the time the movie folk arrived, oilmen had begun transforming the bucolic conservatism of the place. Downtown Los Angeles was a potpourri of saloons, nickelodeons, and burlesque halls. The original farmers moved outward, into places like Hollywood.

The metropolitan area bustled at close to 800,000, but Hollywood, "the quiet suburb of stately residences built among the lemon groves of the foothill frostless belt," had a population of only 4,000 in 1909. Four years later, as steady hordes of movie people flooded in from the East, that figure nearly doubled. Hollywood real estate became gold: lemon groves that had sold for $700 in 1903 zoomed to $10,000 per acre by 1913. By then, movie profits could absorb such costs: the huge barnlike structures springing up overnight were, in truth, factories—*film* factories, churning out the celluloid dreams of a nation.

Hollywood the *illusion* was conjured in Hollywood the *place,* and no individual story makes sense without the context that place provides. This was never New York, where the sheer multitude of populations guaranteed both anonymity and a tolerance bordering on indifference. Hollywood was, and has remained, a small town, with small-town mores and values. Most of the workers in its chief industry were like workers in any other field in any other town across America: punching a time clock, doing their jobs, returning home at night to their families in the Valley.

"The movie men are real men," one defensive industry insider told *The New York News* a few years later, at a time when the film colony's morals were being challenged. "We are good family men, decent and honorable. I'll take on anyone who says otherwise. Who says we aren't he-men? I'm not afraid to fight."

And so they weren't. The fault line was drawn, as it ever has been.

THE GREAT GOD KERRIGAN

Jack Kerrigan's mother would recall her son's first fight, well before any cameras were rolling. "His stockings were down, his face was covered with blood and tears and sweat and dirt. Finally between sobs he confided to me that one of the bigger boys had told him he was too pretty for a boy." Little Jacky Kerrigan was six years old.

He was born July 25, 1882, one of twin sons of John and Sarah (McLean) Kerrigan, christened George Warren but always known as Jack. Father hailed from Ireland, mother from Canada. Settling in Louisville, Kentucky, immigrant John found a job as a clerk in a warehouse, and Sarah bore six children before the twins came. They moved across the Ohio River to New Albany, Indiana, in 1880, where John took over as superintendent of a local wholesale warehouse, and where Jack and his brother Wallace were born.

"For a year I carried this boy around on a pillow," recalled Sarah Kerrigan, "for he was delicate and I never knew when I might lose him."

Delicate. Imaginative. A *dreamer,* he was called. "I often went into the woods and acted and declaimed to my heart's content," Jack Kerrigan would remember, "thinking all along what a shame it was there was no one around to appreciate my talent."

No one, that is, but Mother. From a very early age, Jack would call Sarah "his dear one," and the bond between mother and son was fierce and impenetrable. "If there was ever a mother so completely wrapped up in her son," wrote *Photoplay* in 1916, "or a son so thoroughly in love with his mother, the romance is unchronicled."

It was Sarah who, lone among the clan, supported Jack's desire to be an actor, although early on she hoped he'd become a man of God. His more practical father, on the other hand, wanted his boy to follow in his footsteps at the warehouse. After attending the University of Illinois, Jack was dutifully installed as a clerk at his father's company. He survived the tedium by building "dens and tunnels among the empty dry-goods boxes, where no one could find me, and there spent most of my time reading."

He escaped with the intervention of his sister Kathleen and brother-in-law Clay Clement, who had their own stock company touring through the Midwest. Clement offered the stagestruck youth a part in their production of "Sam Houston." Kerrigan would recall later, without the slightest restraint of modesty, that his brother-in-law had wanted him for his "unlimited ambition and unusually good physique." In truth, he *was* attractive, with that tall (six-foot-one) classic matinee idol stature. His chest was of the puffed-up pigeon sort that lent itself well to strutting about onstage. That, of course, was the fashion: that and sharp, Barrymore-esque profiles and grand theatrical gestures. Jack, soon billing himself as the more thespian-sounding J. Warren Kerrigan, was made to order for the turn-of-the-century stage.

Yet when he played in "Brown of Harvard" in his hometown of Louisville in December 1908, the august critics at the *Louisville Post* were qualified in their support: "Warren Kerrigan was the recipient of considerable applause from his numerous friends in the audience, and although not an experienced actor, at times forcing an effect, has an excellent stage presence and will in time develop his natural talent."

It was left for the motion-picture camera to truly discover that natural talent. Film transformed J. Warren Kerrigan from yet another strutting, posturing stage actor into a *movie star*—the first male superstar of the cinema, in fact. If Kerrigan was a typical turn-of-the-century thespian, he was *transcendent* as a movie star. The camera offered an intimacy far greater than even front row center. Here it wasn't so much Jack's physique that mattered, but his eyes and his smile. Today, watching him on-screen in one of his few surviving films, one is struck first by his apparent girth: the barrel chest so prized in 1900 looks ungainly to modern audiences. But then he smiles: his eyes are dazzling. In that moment, it's easy to understand how he became the most popular star in the world.

Like so many of his contemporaries, he'd looked down at the "flickers." "Upstage Attitude" it was called. "Somehow," he said, "I thought it cheapened a man to be seen entering a five-cent house." Yet he took the job because it offered a chance to quit touring and settle in with Mother, now a widow. In Chicago, they lived together in a rooming house at 4631 Racine Street. Mother and son were a rare combination: their fellow roomers were mostly single young men—salesmen, shoe clerks, bookkeepers, and typewriters.

But the flickers didn't keep him long in one place either. This time it was out to California in search of sun and freedom from Edison's spies. Mother proved a valuable asset, being held up by the Flying A executives to the Santa Barbara community as a symbol of their homespun values. Once again, it is *image* that mattered, as far back as 1912. In Santa Barbara, Flying A built screenland's first real movie studio, with stages and cutting rooms and back lots—a stunning granite-and-glass palace funded largely on profits made by Kerrigan. Word to the trades was that Kerrigan had become so popular that he'd soon appear in other than "wild and woolley West plays."

Ever since another independent, Carl Laemmle, had broken the Trust taboo of naming stars—he'd hyped his theft of the Biograph Girl by publicizing her name, Florence Lawrence, in 1910—movie stars had become the driving force of the business. Upstarts like Flying A realized the tremendous value of star publicity for a suddenly film-conscious press, and began identifying their players. The newspapers and fan magazines elevated movie stars into royalty for the democracy—even more: into gods and goddesses. *Photoplay* dubbed Kerrigan "The Great God," and it stuck.

Readership was enormous for the movie publications, solidifying their influence almost from the start: by 1914, the champ, *Motion Picture Story* magazine, already had a circulation of 270,000. The nation's newspapers, sensing the public interest, quickly hired writers of their own to produce illustrated articles on the movies. The press helped create the phenomenon of the movie star. "It has come to the point," wrote Mrs. C.L.H., a fan from Charleston, South Carolina, "where we no longer go to see the picture, but the players." And her number-one player: "Warren J. [sic] Kerrigan of the American."

What made Kerrigan more appealing than other cowboys, allowing him to transcend the genre, was an elusive appeal that some historians have called "boyish" and others "light and breezy." His cowboys are gentler than most, sensitive, refined. Sure, he could still look pretty mean gazing down the barrel of a gun, but he smiled more than William S. Hart, and Broncho Billy Anderson never had that twinkle in his eyes.

Kerrigan's offscreen manner—described by at least one producer, Albert Smith, as "effeminate"—may have actually influenced his on-screen persona. Other gay actors, like William Haines and Clifton Webb, would also infuse their celluloid character with personal temper. If one is looking for what set Kerrigan apart as a movie cowboy, one needs to understand what first set him apart from his real-life peers.

Whereas Anderson and Hart stayed put in their spurs and ten-gallon hats, by 1912 Kerrigan was playing light comedy, historical parts, and drawing-room melodrama with equal reward. Such flexibility skyrocketed him to fame. When *Photoplay* conducted its first popularity poll in 1913, Kerrigan took the top slot, racking up 195,550 votes—30,000 more than his nearest competitor, James Cruze (later a prominent director). In a *Motion Picture* poll in May of the next year, Earle Williams edged him out by a mere handful of votes; but in June, Kerrigan again placed first in the more prestigious *Photoplay* contest, winning big (367,050) over his nearest male rival, Arthur Johnson (276,750).

His popularity was never just with the testosterone set. That same year, according to an item in *Moving Picture World,* he also placed first in a poll conducted by the curiously named Pansy Motion Picture Correspondence Club of Buffalo, New York. Was this an industry in-joke or a real club, formed by fans unconscious of—or unafraid of—the label?

With stardom also came the spotlight. "In spite of his good looks," opined the *Motion Picture Blue Book* in May 1914, "Warren Kerrigan does not care for girls. He is seldom seen with women. He says he loves the ladies devotedly—and then adds, 'when they leave me alone.'"

When he signed for better money with Universal's Victor studios in 1913, Kerrigan moved to Hollywood. Mother, brother Wallace, and now widowed sister Kathleen were all in tow, along with James Vincent. Around this time, a reporter visited "the Kumfy Kerrigan Kottage," as the clan dubbed it. The house was filled with red, white, and yellow roses. Kerrigan, then appearing on-screen as Samson, arrived for the interview in a soft white silk shirt, red smoking jacket, and "artistically disarranged" hair. Prior to answering any question, he'd look to Mother, who would nod permission before he'd proceed.

Mrs. Sarah Kerrigan had become an industry fixture, the first in a long line of film-star mothers to become characters almost as well known as their sons. To them their offspring could pledge undying devotion and thus avoid the nuptial noose. "[Kerrigan] has managed to reach the age of twenty-six [sic] without being married," wrote William Henry for *Photoplay* in February 1916. (Jack was, in fact, thirty-three.) "I never really had time to consider it," the star explained, "and anyway, I don't think I would be very likely to find a woman as good as my mother."

"In his home in Hollywood there is the little mother," wrote Elizabeth Petersen for *Motion Picture Classic* in December 1916, "the head of the house, ruled by and at the same time ruling her big, handsome son, who treats her with the same deference that he manifested as a boy. They read his coming roles together; they discuss his interpretation, his make-up, the details of his action." Reluctant, he said, to dispel fans' illusions, Kerrigan nonetheless admitted he looked forward to taking off his guns and chaps at the end of each day to head home and work in his flower garden, "where my best friend in the world—my dear mother—is waiting for me."

Even in 1916 there were readers savvy enough to pick up the markers of Kerrigan's queerness. Mother. Flower beds. Smoking jackets and disdain for the girls. Yet for a time, it was an image that worked. *Moving Picture Weekly* still cited him as tops in their 1916 popularity poll, and on the East Coast, only his rival Earle Williams could best him in a *New York Telegraph* contest.

Marriage, in those days, was actually anathema to star publicity. Even manufactured romances, so beloved by a later breed of studio publicists, were practically nonexistent in the first years of the star system. If the public knew their hero Francis X. Bushman actually had a wife and child, the dreams of millions would be dashed. So long as the stars remained single and theoretically "available," their fans could continue to fantasize that they might be the one to capture their idol's heart. The movie magazines were filled with stories of actors longing for the right woman, for the love that always seemed so tantalizingly just beyond their grasp. "Might it be *you?*" the writers asked. "Might *you* fill the empty place in his heart?"

Kerrigan, however, spoke of no empty place. For him, there was *Mother.* It was the perfect strategy, some thought. A writer for the *Columbus Dispatch* was especially observant:

> Does Warren Kerrigan's popularity as matinee film idol set the style for other players to shun matrimony? A man prominent in film circles says that ever since Kerrigan started to distribute photographs of himself and his sweet-faced, gray-haired mother, the other stars, those budding and those already arrived, have realized this pretty bit of sentiment is a strong campaign argument for popularity. . . .
>
> The photoplay actor's place in the film world is like the political candidate's position with the public. He must put forth his best foot and let the world see all his highest attributes and most valuable personality assets. If marriage is an argument against his popularity, then he feels he must keep the news of his wife and child hidden.
>
> Warren Kerrigan has no wife and no child. When he answers the questions of the fans by saying he is not married, he is telling the truth. . . . Perhaps there will come a time some day when the marriage issue will not be so important to the fans. Then, and not till then, can we hope to see our favorites acknowledge their husbands and wives.

By default, Jack Kerrigan becomes the honest man. Of course, he didn't tell the whole truth—that the room downstairs reserved for his "secretary" was actually occupied by his male lover—but he really *was* unmarried, and in 1916, that was a decided plus. The irony is fascinating: that a gay star, living with his mother, would be the paradigm on which other stars would model their images, while a straight star like Bushman would, by necessity, have to lie and pretend and create an illusion of being something he wasn't.

THE EARLY GAY FRATERNITY

Kerrigan wasn't alone. From Kerrigan to Tyrone Power to Rock Hudson, a large percentage of screen actors have always been homosexual. The actual number, of course, is impossible to determine, but even from the limited evidence that exists, the number is disproportionate, far greater than the general population estimate of 10 percent. From the very start of the studio era, there seems to have existed an unspoken queer fraternity, the embryonic beginnings of the gay subculture that would blossom in the 1920s and flourish through the 1960s.

Edwin August got his start with the old Biograph company, coming west with them in 1910. Rather than return to New York, he put down roots in Hollywood, moving over to Universal, where he met Kerrigan. They shared the same kind of theatrical background, and not a few other traits as well. "He was a homo," said his plain-talking Biograph costar, Blanche Sweet, who lived to ninety-one and pulled no punches.

The reclusive August had few people out to his chicken ranch at 648 South Figueroa, but Jack Kerrigan was one of them, which the fan magazines noted without further comment, besides mentioning "the hours of time and fun" it took to prepare August's signature dish, pimento haricots. Mused Dorothy Donnell of *Motion Picture* in 1914: "Few people know much of Edwin August's private life." Indeed, about all reporters got out of him was his recipe for haricots.

Born Edwin August Phillip von der Butz in St. Louis, he'd been educated at the Christian Brothers College and then joined several stock companies. Dark, brooding, and Germanic whereas Kerrigan was bright, dazzling, and Celtic, August never achieved the heights Jack did, but he was nonetheless very popular. He had an easier time than most getting over Upstage Attitude toward the flickers, working with Biograph in New York as early as 1908. Perhaps because he never had great success on the stage—his one Broadway appearance in the racy "Mr. and Mrs. Daventry" prompted a review that called him "quite as wooden as it is possible for an actor to be"—he was game for pictures. Besides, he was working with the very best at Biograph, in that halcyon period when D. W. Griffith was revolutionizing the art form. August was in many of the master's early works: *The Welcome Burglar, The Cardinal's Conspiracy, White Roses, A Blot on the 'Scutcheon, The Girl and Her Trust.*

Griffith's first wife, Linda Arvidson, a member of the Biograph company, left a saucy memoir of those early years, and there's enough double entendre in her pages to suggest August wasn't the only "homo" in the ranks. Actor Dell Henderson, whose wife later began traveling with the company, would often "cop little Jack Pickford as his bedfellow" in the early days. Arvidson writes of the "maidenly" character actress Kate Bruce frequently accommodating ingenue Dorothy West at her home. Even Mack Sennett gets a mention by Arvidson—"We wondered about Mack Sennett. Would he ever buy a girl an ice-cream soda?"—an implication perhaps seconded by the actor Ralph Graves, who told the historian Anthony Slide he'd had an "unholy relationship" with the king of silent comedy.

More obvious were the actors J. Jiquel Lanoe and Harry Hyde, whom

Blanche Sweet also identified as gay to Slide; they lived together in a hotel on Hollywood Boulevard. Lanoe, who came to the United States with the French Company of Players and appeared on Broadway in 1907 in "Iron Master," would play the campy, effeminate eunuch in Griffith's celebrated *Judith of Bethulia* (1913)—the first but hardly the last time a swish would play a swish in the movies.

It's no surprise that a movie company would have its share of gay men and lesbians. Drawn from stock companies and vaudeville houses across the country, actors were used to unconventional lifestyles. They lived on the edge, from town to town and theater to theater. It was only when they settled down, in the land of orange groves and middle-western values, did the gays among them become notable.

Edwin August seems to have sensed this dichotomy soon after arriving in Los Angeles. He wasn't asked for as many interviews as Kerrigan, but in each and every one he gave he comes across as resentful and sullen. This changed little in 1916 when August moved to New York and, stunning the industry, tossed his hat into the presidential campaign.

"Let those unlettered minds that sneer at the idea of a great photoplayer becoming President," wrote his campaign chairman Arthur Leslie to the *New York Star,* "remember that the motion picture stands first and alone of all great industries in the hearts of the people. Why should it not be represented in the Executive chair in the White House?"

Why not indeed. Some sixty years before Ronald Reagan, Edwin August put forward his name, partly tongue-in-cheek, but also because he seemed fed up with what he saw his industry, and his nation, becoming. In a year that had witnessed rising cries of censorship against movies—D. W. Griffith's *The Birth of a Nation,* Cecil B. DeMille's *The Cheat*—August took a stand. "He believes Federal Censorship sounds a death knell of free speech and of human freedom," read his campaign literature. "If speech is free, then let us have Free Silence." In other words, let the silent drama have the same freedoms the legitimate stage enjoyed.

"The danger of the motion picture," August told reporters, "is not the danger of immorality but *morality.* The motion picture is the poor man's university. Under censorship, one man can dictate the thought of millions."

A prophetic character, that Edwin August. And contradictory, too: by launching this campaign, he placed himself squarely in the public eye he had avoided for so long. But that was part of his platform, too. In June he came down squarely against the rise of press agents, those pesky early spin-meisters who were forever trying to make him say and do things he objected to.

"Have you not found their work the very quintessence of vulgarity?" he wrote to the *Star*. "They create false theatrical values. They stultify the artistry of the player and impede the cultural progress of the motion picture. They erect a colossus, *but with feet of clay* [emphasis his]."

Not much was heard of August's political ambitions after that—what press agent was going to write him up now? That summer *Photoplay* dismissed the whole "clever idea," saying that if August *were* to run, he'd be compelled to use his own name. With the World War raging in Europe, "Edwin August Phillip von der Butz" wouldn't sound very mellifluous to a nation increasingly anti-German.

Still, August is an interesting character: a gay actor who both loathed the personal publicity moviemaking required, and one so opposed to censorship that he took a very public stand against it. Perhaps that partly explains why his career sputtered to a close by the end of the decade. Although he'd play bit parts in films right up to 1947, he ended up having to play Santa Claus in a Beverly Hills department store to pay the bills.

If Hollywood was fair—and no one's ever claimed it was—Edwin August would have gone much farther. He was a talented man, much more talented than Kerrigan. Early on with Griffith, he began writing scripts as well as acting, including the lovely *The Mender of Nets* (1912) with Mary Pickford. When he jumped ship to Universal, it was as writer-director. He seems to have been a competent, if possibly even innovative, filmmaker. The trades praised his split-screen effects in *A Stolen Identity* (1913), for which he not only served as writer and director but also as actor in the two leading parts. Reportedly, he filmed his two characters in a double exposure walking and talking together along a street. Since the film, like so many of the period, has not survived, it's impossible to know for certain whether this might have also meant a tracking shot, a rarity in early cinema. If it did, the technique would have made his accomplishment even more impressive.

Writer, director, actor. Activist. Politician. In those topsy-turvy early days, when the final blueprints of the studio system had yet to be determined, it was easier to move around, to do what one wanted, to be what one wanted to be. It was a period when women writers often dominated companies, and when several women—rather than the lone Dorothy Arzner of the 1930s and 1940s—barked orders through megaphones as directors. Work ghettos did not yet exist: no "queer" work or "straight" jobs.

The dividing walls were there, but they were easier to scale. Edwin August managed, for a time. But even then there was a game to be played. Kerrigan helped write the rules; so long as they held, he stayed on top. But August had no patience for games. Rather than help mold the embryonic studio system, he challenged it—and found himself forever outside.

GAY HOLLYWOOD AND THE GREAT WAR

The First World War was supposed to have been the war to end all wars. Instead, all it seems to have ended was Jack Kerrigan's career.

At the start of it, he was still the country's number-one box-office star, having come in first (yet again) in fan-magazine polls held in May 1916, beating out Bushman and Earle Williams and his replacement at Flying A, Wallace Reid. He'd left Universal to launch his own J. Warren Kerrigan Feature Film Corporation. To promote the new venture, his publicist dreamed up a personal-appearance tour, one of the first ever for a motion-picture star. "Meet him face to face and shake his hand," read the hoopla in the press. "This is not a motion picture; it is Jack Kerrigan himself!"

From Hollywood he traveled to Texas, then to New Orleans and Atlanta and up along the East Coast. He enjoyed a triumphant return to New York, then headed up to Canada, back down through the Midwest, and ended up, tired and a bit cranky, in Denver. During the tour, he was under strict orders from his new distributors, the Paralta Company, not to show himself at all except at the theater. That meant no dinners, no walks, no sightseeing. It meant hotel suites and curtained windows on his automobile. So that day, meeting with the reporter from *The Denver Times,* he was one cross old queen, and the scribe asked him the one question that would throw four months of good press right out the window:

"Are you going to join the war?"

It was only natural to ask. It was May 1917; President Wilson had declared hostilities the previous month, and all over the country young men were enlisting to fight the Kaiser's Huns.

But the Great God Kerrigan huffed. "I am not going to war," he declared. "I will go, of course, if my country needs me, but I think that first they should take the great mass of men who aren't good for anything else, or are only good for the lower grades of work. Actors, musicians, great writers, artists of every kind—isn't it a pity when people are sacrificed who are capable of such things—of adding to the beauty of the world."

His words reverberated through the nation like a thunderbolt tossed down from Mount Olympus. Picked up and reprinted in papers across the nation, Kerrigan's statement stunned his legion of fans. America, predictably, didn't take kindly to its hero's arrogance, and in 1917 there were no spin doctors to backtrack for him, to feverishly offer *mea culpas* at press conferences and explain "what he *really* meant to say." It was a moment into Kerrigan's soul—into what the Gods thought of the little people who'd made them.

The Great War was the first major test for Hollywood in its relationship with America. Since the previous year, when Nazimova's popular *War Brides* had made the urgent appeal for peace, public sentiment had turned strikingly in the other direction. The loss of American life aboard the *Lusitania* had been enough to transform Germans into beasts in the popular press and the British into God's chosen people. The movies stood at a crossroads: would they be shaper or follower of public opinion? In the end, as ever, they were both.

The film industry, despite the hordes of free thinkers and free lovers who increasingly made up a large segment of its workforce, remained a conservative fortress. It was run by Jewish immigrants who desperately sought middle-class status for both themselves and their industry, who wanted nothing less than to codify the American dream. "What is amazing," Neal Gabler wrote in *An Empire of Their Own,* "is the extent to which they succeeded in promulgating this fiction throughout the world . . . one which idealized every old glorifying bromide about the country . . . so powerful that, in a sense, they colonized the American imagination."

Garth Jowett called the war "the ideal opportunity [for the film industry] to consolidate its role in American society." Kerrigan's comments, of course, flew directly in the face of what the industry was trying to become. Working in tandem with the government's Division of Films, the studios were turning out not only pro-war newsreels but propaganda fiction narratives designed to keep patriotism alive for the duration. Wallace Reid, Kerrigan's rival, made *The Firefly of France;* newer stars like Charles Ray jumped on the war bandwagon with such pictures as *The Claws of the Hun.* Chaplin made *Shoulder Arms;* Griffith made *Hearts of the World;* Pickford made *The Little American* and *Johanna Enlists.*

Writing eighteen years later, in the pacifist lull between the wars, Creighton Peet looked back on the era with disdain. "There are several lines of procedure in getting a population steamed up to the point of war. You show them glamorous and thumping (if silly) fiction, you show them jolly newsreels from the front with all the ghastly details carefully cut out, and you yell 'coward' at all those who don't fall into line quickly enough."

Kerrigan, to the industry, was a coward. The buzz flew across telegraph wires: Kerrigan—the hero—the top star in the land—was too good to fight. The talk continued all through the spring and into the summer, with *Photoplay,* in its August issue, taking Kerrigan to task under the headline "The Beautiful Slackers." Editor James Quirk pointed to high-profile Americans who had made the war "glorious," men like the poet Alan Seeger (killed fighting with the French Foreign Legion in 1916), the dancer Vernon Castle, and the movies' own Wallace McCutcheon, the actor-

dancer husband of screen star Pearl White, who was now a decorated officer in the British Army.

"The villains and character men," Quirk wrote, "are in the officers'
training camps right now, and we fear that our slackly beautiful heroes are
to be quite lonely."

Of course, Kerrigan took the hit for everybody else: unlike World War
II a generation later, none of the big stars were trooping off to war. Perhaps
the biggest name to serve was William Desmond Taylor, who, as a British
citizen, was drafted into the Royal Army, serving from August 1918 to
April 1919. A few character players did make news: Norman Kerry, in pictures just a year and yet to reach stardom, was training in North Carolina.
But Earle Williams stayed home, and Wallace Reid, and Chaplin and Fairbanks and William S. Hart.

Kerrigan, at age thirty-five, was actually too old for the draft in 1917, although he could have volunteered. What made it doubly tricky for him was
that for the past couple of years, he had been playing around with his true
age. In 1916, he told one reporter he was twenty-six. The very next year,
after war was declared and the draft took men up to age thirty, he started
claiming an 1879 birthdate, which would have made him thirty-eight.
When the draft was enlarged to take all able-bodied men aged eighteen to
forty-five, Kerrigan shrugged and went back to being twenty-six. In the
1920 Census he told the enumerator he was twenty-nine. But the year 1879
stuck, and several later articles—and even a few obituaries—would put him
three years older than he really was.

He never backtracked from his comments about the war, although as the
bad press escalated, he tried to offer alternative explanations for staying out
of the conflict. Soon after the *Photoplay* editorial, he fell on the set of a picture (ironically entitled *A Man's Man*). His leg was broken, said the reports—and *badly,* he insisted. The implication was clear: a soldier couldn't
march into battle on a badly broken foot.

Things just got worse for Kerrigan. In February 1918, Universal won a
lawsuit against him for breaking his contract. That same month, he dropped
dramatically in the popularity polls: *ninth,* with just 16,953 votes from *Motion Picture* magazine readers. Douglas Fairbanks, with close to 75,000 votes,
was on top. Old rivals like Reid, Bushman, and Williams were way ahead.
It's as precipitous a fall as any star ever experienced, matched only by
William Haines twelve years later.

Desperate to reclaim his position, Kerrigan invited Fritzi Remont from
Motion Picture over to his house. There she found the star and his mother
wrapping gifts for the "soldier boys and sailor lads." Said Mrs. K.: "Every
night we wrap until twelve o'clock." About his broken leg, the star com-

plained every chance he got, blaming himself for doing away with the crutches too early. "I grinned cheerfully for the camera while I endured my agony," he told Remont. "Nineteen interminable weeks!" he groused— during which time his distributor, Paralta, stopped paying him, and he lost his contract.

By the time the war was over, Kerrigan's leg was better. But his career had taken a fatal shot, as sure as if he'd been stationed on the Western Front.

That the war precipitated the end of Kerrigan's career has been alleged before, yet it always seemed too pat. There were certainly other factors—for one, the fickle taste of the public, especially in these early years—but the record *does* support the war theory. Kerrigan was number one in popularity polls one year and ninth the next, with the infamous Denver interview in between. His press changed from adulation to snotty asides like this one from the reviewer Laurence Reid: "'Ain't he jus' grand?' will be the thought of more than two impressionable maids as the star knits his brows together and gazes appallingly at them." For *The Drifters,* one reviewer captioned a photograph of the star: "Exit J. Warren with pretty curls and a dress-suit manner while entering is J. W. Kerrigan as a bold man of the hard-boiled Yukon region. With cudgel and gun he puts up a pretty fight for the right."

Of course, Kerrigan's homosexuality had nothing to do with his avoidance of the war, but many in the industry were surely only too happy to make the link. In the wake of the war fiasco, Kerrigan tried to butch it up and play it straighter: in October 1919, "all the way from stricken Poland," came a nine- (some sources say six-) year-old boy to be adopted by the star into the Kumfy Kerrigan Kottage. The child, Stephen Myronoff, crossed the country alone, under the auspices of the French Reconstruction Bureau in Paris. He spoke no English and had seen no moving pictures, but reporters swarmed around him when he arrived at Union Station, asking what he thought of his new home and his new father. The boy just stared blindly at them. Kerrigan, his arm draped paternally around the child's shoulders, explained that little Stephen's parents had lost their lives during the Polish uprising that followed the signing of the Armistice. The publicity went: "What more natural than that Kerrigan, being denied by Providence a son of his own, should take one by adoption?"

Providence indeed. There's no further mention of the little lost Polish boy in the press; the adoption isn't even alluded to in fan-magazine articles a year later. In the 1920 Census, taken just a few months after the adoption hoopla, little Stephen is not listed as living with Kerrigan and family. Was it all a sham? Did Kerrigan tire of the child? Had he served his purpose? Did adoption officials have questions about James Vincent's presence in the house?

It's a cynical view, and maybe Kerrigan genuinely tried to help the boy. But a sense of desperation comes through in the publicity. His pictures weren't doing well; he hinted to reporters he might go back to the stage. He seemed adrift, dispossessed.

In truth, there was a shift going on: whereas in 1914 and 1915, marriage and romance were considered taboo in star publicity, by 1918 and 1919 it had become common, even expected. As early as 1917, *Photoplay* began running its series "Who's Married to Who," replete with happy photos of such wedded stars as Wallace Reid and Dorothy Davenport. Thomas Meighan, a fast-rising box-office favorite, was reported to be "married and unashamed."

Filmdom's new icon, Douglas Fairbanks, was not only married, but quite widely rumored to be having an affair with America's Sweetheart Mary Pickford. When Mary and Doug asked screenwriter Frances Marion to rate their chances for career survival if they divorced their respective spouses and remarried each other, Marion gave them "better than even"— a remarkable sea change in public attitude. Indeed, Pickford and Fairbanks would march into new heights of fame as husband and wife.

Breathless reports of star weddings suddenly became great copy for the fan magazines (such as the nuptials of Tom Moore and Renee Adoree in the May 1921 *Photoplay*). By the early 1920s, marriage (and divorce) had not only become permissible, but actually the paradigm for movie stars to follow for the next several decades.

That shouldn't imply that the gay stars needed to fall into lockstep: not yet. The Roaring Twenties would still allow enough space in the margins for mavericks like Ramon Novarro and Eugene O'Brien. But the model, so painstakingly played in the sound era, was actually seeded here, in the post-war years. With the studios now coalescing into the highly organized structures they'd soon become, it's not surprising: the middle-class American dream—which included husband, wife, and children—would finally be codified by Hollywood.

Kerrigan could offer none of that. He'd try, with increasing pathos: for the first time, his publicity became filled with stories of marriage proposals ("He's been engaged six times . . . more than three hundred women have proposed to him") and the soon-to-become-standard line of "looking for the right woman" (compared to his old "I prefer Mother") began its refrain.

In the press, there were a few brave hearts who bought none of it, however. "Kerrigan's [publicity] man has been very efficient in making sure we know he's received fifteen marriage proposals in the last month," wrote one scribe, "two by cable from London society, one radiogram from a Parisian singer, and numerous calls from fair Hollywood damsels. We're a little weary of his attempts to persuade." The piece was headed: "Leap Year and Lavender Heroes." Kerrigan's cowardice, as it was perceived, was forever linked to his queerness.

POST-WAR GAY HOLLYWOOD

But not all gay stars avoided the war, and certainly the industry could see that. Most notable was pretty little Gareth Hughes, just five-feet-five and 125 pounds, who starred in *Every Mother's Son* for Fox in 1918, playing a pacifist. When his on-screen father calls him a "slacker"—surely reminding many of the *Photoplay* censure—Gareth has a change of heart and marches off to fight the Huns.

Hughes, not even an American citizen, didn't just *play* a soldier, he really *was* one: a private in the U.S. Army, stationed at Camp Wadsworth, Spartanburg, South Carolina. Though he never saw action, he came to Hollywood fully credentialed as having the "right stuff." Never mind that everyone knew he was a flaming little queen, having been the darling of Broadway: he had enlisted, he had done his part.

Born in Llanwelly, Wales, in 1897, Gareth Hughes was a dreamy boy. At thirteen, he left home to tour with a Welsh Shakespearean company, in which he played Desdemona. He arrived in America in 1913 with another Welsh company, and after a series of small roles on Broadway, broke into the big time with August Stridberg's "Easter." The *New York Times* said he "can touch with beauty all his playing . . . he has the rare genuine fire."

James Barrie's "The New Word" and then Oscar Wilde's "Salome" established Hughes as a bona fide Broadway sensation. Barely twenty, he danced the nights away with Isadora Duncan and got Mrs. Fiske roaring drunk. Producer Ryszard Ordynski brought Hughes out to Los Angeles in 1917 to play in a revival of "Everyman," and Hughes set about conquering Hollywood as well. He moved with the gay crowd of Ordynski and his lover, Famous Players set designer George James Hopkins, and was pals with Nazimova. The writer Fulton Oursler called Hughes "the charm boy to end all charm boys."

For a while, it was indeed a love affair between Hollywood and Gareth Hughes, who sent reviewers into rapture. Lillian Montanye actually compared him to the Boy Jesus in *Shadowland:* "The young actor has a rarely spirituelle face . . . the face of one who dreams dreams and sees visions." Actress Viola Dana remembered him less reverentially, telling historian Anthony Slide that most leading ladies refused to kiss him because he was so sexually active.

His star blazed bright and fast and by the mid-1920s had burned itself out. Hughes would later write of problems with alcohol and a growing sense of discontentment in his life. He made a popular return to the stage in "The Dunce Boy" in 1925, but had no follow-up. After a series of smaller and smaller roles on-screen and onstage, he joined an Episcopal monastery and spent the remaining years of his life working with the Paiute Indians in Nevada as a lay missionary. He died in 1965.

The difference between Hughes and Kerrigan is that Hughes opted out on his own, dispirited with Hollywood rather than Hollywood becoming dispirited with him. Hughes' popularity at the time of Kerrigan's downfall also demonstrates that homosexuality alone could hardly be blamed on his own career trouble. Only when it rubbed up against the image the industry was so desperately trying to cultivate—in this case, Kerrigan's perceived queerness as based on his war statements—would it prove problematic.

In fact, by the early 1920s, the gay subculture in Hollywood was expanding rapidly. There were the gatherings of "sophisticates" at Nazimova's home on Sunset Boulevard. At the Pasadena Playhouse, Gilmor Brown acted as a kind of godfather to many rising male stars, escorting them to important theater and film-industry functions. But most significant was the new gay blood regularly pumped into screenland by the burgeoning local theatrical companies of Oliver Morosco and Thomas Wilkes. For Morosco, San Jose–born Edmund Lowe became a sensation in 1916 playing the detective in "The Argyle Case," leading to a New York stage career and a highly successful run in the movies, starting with *The Wild Olive* in 1915. By 1922, Lowe was one of the movies' busiest leading men, appearing in pictures for Pathe, First National, Goldwyn, and Metro. He became popular offscreen, too, with one gossip columnist writing about Lowe's penchant for purple ties (identified by many historians as gay code). According to the columnist, in the wink-wink style that had become popular, when a sailor showed up at Lowe's door one day, the actor "wrapped his emerald suasette nightie around his perfect 36 and toddled to the door," welcoming the man inside.

In Wilkes' company at the Majestic Theatre, gay talent was even more abundant. Leading man Edward Everett Horton was well known to be homosexual, and Franklin Pangborn, whose name would forever be linked with Horton's in their later movie careers, also top-lined Majestic shows. Both Horton and Pangborn began appearing infrequently in movies at this time as well.

What had been pretty lonely terrain for J. Warren Kerrigan and Edwin August in 1911—getting together for a dinner of haricots at August's chicken ranch—had been transformed into a sizable community of gay players and industry workers in the years after the war. The war had nearly obliterated European filmmaking, so Hollywood stepped up production to fill the gap, and increased productivity meant a larger workforce—which in turn meant more actors, writers, and designers flooding in from New York. The movies promised them regular work (unlike the theater's sporadic schedules) and increasingly good pay.

Some gay actors, like Edmund Lowe, began by making pictures in New York. Harrison Ford (no relation to the current actor) was also originally based at the Famous Players Studio in Astoria, Queens. Like Lowe, Ford was known for his sartorial tastes, but whereas Lowe was ebullient, Ford was reserved, almost taciturn when it came to interviews. He came west with Constance Talmadge as her leading man in a series of comedies and later starred opposite her sister Norma, then the screen's top female draw, in such hits as *Love's Redemption* (1921) and *Smilin' Through* (1922). Both films were produced for First National by Talmadge's husband, Joseph Schenck, who reportedly *preferred* his wife's costars to be homosexual: he wouldn't have to worry that way about any resulting affairs.

Ford alternated in Norma's arms with Eugene O'Brien, a buff, bluff Irishman who Schenck liked and trusted, and who fulfilled the homo requirement quite easily. Offscreen, O'Brien and the Schencks were close friends, frequently socializing in each other's homes. The friendship may have held a secret, however: Schenck, walking past his wife's dressing room and hearing her peals of laughter, was reassured knowing it was O'Brien inside with her. But O'Brien—obliging and flexible—reportedly confided later that he often gave in and got it up when Norma was insistent.

O'Brien is a good example of the industry's attitude toward gays by the early 1920s. Not just tolerated, they were actually *integrated* into the very structure of the burgeoning studio system. If the moguls were attempting to re-create middle-class values and ideals, they knew gays were an important ally in doing so. It didn't matter who or what they were *off* the screen: all that counted was that they knew how to get it right for the finished product. Whether that be designing sets or clothes (discussed later in the careers of George James Hopkins, Howard Greer, and others) or acting the stalwart hero opposite Norma Talmadge, gays understood the middle-class dream as well as—or better—than anyone else.

Like the Jews, the early Hollywood gays also aspired to a certain social respectability. *Unlike* the Jews, however, most of the gays we can identify (with some significant exceptions) came from comfortable middle-class backgrounds: O'Brien, Ford, Lowe, George James Hopkins, Dorothy Arzner, William Desmond Taylor. To the rough-hewn immigrant moguls, homosexuals had the breeding and social experience they lacked. In Hollywood the gays were actually *needed*—whether it be to escort the ladies to social functions or to design sets and costumes to awe middle America. Their usefulness ensured a tolerance of their lifestyles, giving them a freedom to conduct their lives with a degree of integrity, authenticity, and social acceptance that they never would have found had they remained in their hometowns and pursued other occupations.

Certainly Eugene O'Brien might have had a good life staying put in Boulder, Colorado. He might have followed in his father's successful confectionery business, or he might have become a physician, as his parents had hoped. The O'Briens were *making it* in Colorado; only a generation away from their Irish immigrant parents, by 1880 John and Kate O'Brien employed a servant and lived in a middle-class mercantile neighborhood of engineers, business owners, and legal abstractors. Young Eugene stood to benefit from their hard work.

But the old longing—the wanderlust described in so many gay narratives, past and present—struck him early. Born Francis Eugene O'Brien in 1879, he was the third of four boys. While his brothers were rowdy and rambunctious, Eugene was more inclined to imaginative pursuits. Fascinated by a local stock company, he dreamed of going on the stage, but his father insisted he go to medical school. He gave it a shot, despised it, and persuaded his parents to consent to a switch in studies: civil engineering at a school in New York. But civil engineering wasn't what he was *really* after in New York: after class, he got a job as a chorus boy.

Eugene worked his way up to parts in musical comedy before Charles Frohman made him a star in 1914 with "Kitty MacKay." From then on, O'Brien was on top, imported to Hollywood in 1917, making a splash opposite Talmadge in *Poppy* and *Her Only Way.*

Like Kerrigan, O'Brien had been the "different" child, defying family to leave home and pursue his dream. But unlike the working-class Kerrigan, whose Hollywood home was known more for its "kumfiness" than any style, O'Brien brought to his new environment a highly defined sense of *class,* one that producers were only too glad to exploit. One reporter called O'Brien's home "plutocratic," the "sort of place to smoke his pipe and drink his drink, in mingled fumes, with cronies chosen well." A grand piano, a fire burning, a *Winged Victory,* Russian classics, and Kipling on his shelf—everything "jolly and masculine," the epitome of what the middle class imagined for an upper-class gentleman squire.

"Eugene O'Brien," added the writer, "is a good sort. He is the sort society takes by the right hand and the Bowery by the left. He makes the world very safe for democracy." O'Brien in the middle, linking rich and poor—just the image the middle-class movies wanted to emulate.

In many ways, the gays were the moguls' salvation, and they made their contribution conspicuously. This was not yet the era of Tyrone Power or Rock Hudson, when not even their publicists always knew for sure. In the freer, less aggressive media of the Teens and early Twenties, gay Hollywood could only have been more visible if the pages of the fan magazines had been printed in lavender. Not to the average moviegoer, of course—but to more sophisticated readers, even Kerrigan's devotion to Mother is a gay marker—a flag—a clue to those "in the know." (O'Brien, too, would talk of his commitment to his widowed mother, and so would countless gay stars through the decades.)

There were other markers as well. In one article, Harrison Ford was spied buying costumes and fabrics for Norma Talmadge; he was described as being "as enthusiastic as a young debutante planning her first party dress." (Perhaps items like these were why Ford was usually distrustful of the press.) Eugene O'Brien, being Irish, had more of the gift of gab. "I'm having an awful time with my hair," he confessed to writer Patty Doyle. "I belong to a bald-headed family, you know, but I don't want it to happen to me yet. I'm taking treatments, and you know, after one of them, my hair is as straight as a Mexican Indian's."

That was surely all that was straight about him. Known for his wavy hair, O'Brien had heard the jokes. He told Doyle: "I suppose they'll say now, 'O'Brien curls his hair, poor sis!'"

Reviewing the press accounts today, the most fascinating interviews are those written by male scribes who seemed "in the life" themselves. John Ten Eyck was a press agent in New York who had known O'Brien during the run of "Kitty MacKay." When *Photoplay* sent him to interview the star at his New York apartment (in the Fifties near Fifth Avenue), Ten Eyck was accompanied by a photographer. While reporter and star enjoyed tea together, discussing Laura Hope Crews and Clara Kimball Young, the photographer grew uncomfortable in such fancy surroundings—"chintz-hung," Ten Eyck described them, "with yellow flowers and the tang of sandalwood." Noticing the photographer's unease, O'Brien gave him a shot of Scotch. More background was provided by Ten Eyck:

> We are so used, here in America, to consider a man utterly incapable of making a home. The photographer, a person of no imagination, looked at the flowers and the pictures, and the tea, as much to say, "I wonder where he hides her . . . ?" Alas for customs which make us believe that the three essentials of a man's room were an iron bed, a college pennant, and a picture of a chorus girl in tights! We're emerging from that period—all of us except motion picture property men.

Ten Eyck writes *volumes* in that paragraph. It was November 1918. The war was over. The free-spirited, rule-breaking Twenties were on the horizon. Gender roles were being challenged. There was no reason, to Ten Eyck, to hide the kind of man O'Brien was—cultured, sophisticated, and obviously homosexual. The straight photographer—as most camera operators still were, being considered a technical and not yet an "artistic" field—was uncomfortable in a gay world. It was the same with "motion picture property men"—men of "no imagination" who still chose college pennants and chorus girls as props for the sets of men's rooms.

Significantly, the gay art director George James Hopkins, then designing sets at Fox and Paramount, would use similar language in his memoirs to disdain the property men he (and others with a more "artistic" bent) would eventually replace (see next chapter). And the lesbian Dorothy Arzner, then a script girl, would use the same word as Ten Eyck—"imagination"—to separate herself from other women whose adherence to traditional gender roles she found appalling (see Chapter 3, "Girls with Imagination").

O'Brien offers still more markers for the sophisticated reader. He lived in hotels: in New York at the Royalton, "a great midtown apartment house for men only." In Hollywood he took up residence at the Athletic Club, a legendary gay sexual cruising site. In the *Photoplay* interview, Ten Eyck asked him enigmatically if he'd "been to any enjoyable places lately." O'Brien answered that he had: "The shower-room in the gymnasium I frequent. After an hour's work with the gloves, or on the floor, if there's anything in the world more enjoyable than a long leisurely shower that soaks you until you think you have deep-sea ancestry, I'd like to know what it is!"

Such reportage is an example of a kind of "intertextual" understanding of films and film players. No one, then or now, views movies in a vacuum. Chon Noriega has argued that film reviews often allowed a "frame of reference" that "put the question of homosexuality" before the audience, even if Hollywood itself was silent on the subject. A similar intertextual recognition was administered through gossip columns and fan-magazine articles like Ten Eyck's, which offered audiences a prism through which they could view and interpret certain stars. For the average jane who read the fan magazine, O'Brien emerges as a cultivated man who is nonetheless athletic, enjoying a boxing match and a long, invigorating shower. For an urban homosexual, however, the references to all-male hotels and gymnasium shower rooms carried very specific implications. Ten Eyck—and O'Brien—and ultimately Hollywood—were spelling out the truth for those who could spell.

Hand-in-glove with such "sophisticated" reporting came, ironically enough, the Marriage Question. Absent from most interviews up until this point, it would become commonplace now that Mary and Doug and others had made romance and wedded bliss good copy.

O'Brien told Ten Eyck he was too busy to think of it, and besides, there was Mother. But reporter Patty Doyle asked him point-blank: "Do you like women?"—to which he replied he "had lots of pals among women." Pressed on why he hadn't *married* one of them—O'Brien was then forty-three, older than most of his peers—the star hedged, saying he couldn't get the one he wanted.

O'Brien never did get married, and the press would enjoy finding ways to play with his situation. Much that was written about him as the decade wore on could be taken two ways. "Eugene O'Brien says he is convinced that just because a blonde hair is found on a man's coat does not necessarily mean he is a gentleman," went one item. Another one openly laughed at a suggestion that the star was romancing a married actress: "I know it's absurd because I know Gene O'Brien pretty well. I've been up to his bachelor home on Whitley Heights."

Eugene O'Brien retired in 1928 after a series of accidents in which he broke his foot, his knee, and his leg. And those hair treatments didn't help: by the end of the decade he was pretty much bald. He lived in comfortable obscurity with his lover in Hollywood until his death in 1966.

The Marriage Question, however, would go on. The gay stars who followed would become more polished in their answers, yet they'd contain the same basic elements as O'Brien's first attempts: Mother; some variation on "the-one-I-want-didn't-want-me"; Mother; women as pals; the old "one-is-not-enough" response; Mother; and one other that O'Brien apparently hadn't yet thought up, that an actor—like a priest—is married to his work.

Meanwhile, Kerrigan, still clinging tenaciously to his film career, could never adjust to the new paradigm, and the Marriage Question eventually did him in. He'd been off the screen nearly three years when director James Cruze (a former rival in the popularity polls) hired him for his comeback in *The Covered Wagon*. Kerrigan admitted he knew Hollywood considered him "passé." The spin went out that he was being the dutiful son, as ever: "Warren Kerrigan spent his three years of idleness as the devoted companion and nurse of his invalid mother. . . . Her death some months ago has left the little white house very lonely."

Ironically, Kerrigan's *Covered Wagon* character, cowboy Will Banion, has lost his army commission for stealing cattle. The film's plot turns on the discovery that he's no thief at all, that in fact he'd had a noble purpose in commandeering those cows: to keep his battalion from starving. Kerrigan had to appreciate the message, and hope his public would give him a second chance the way Lois Wilson gives Will Banion in the picture.

They seemed to—for *The Covered Wagon* was a giant hit. But in the end it was a triumph for Cruze and Western pictures—and, within the industry, for Dorothy Arzner, its cutter—and not for Kerrigan. It was too late to change the image. Without his Dear One at his side, what could the fan magazines write about? Kerrigan seemed lost, a relic from another time. He managed to land a couple more big parts in big movies, due to the success of *The Covered Wagon,* but they, too, were dead ends. Albert E. Smith, one of the chiefs at Vitagraph, hired him reluctantly for *Captain Blood* in the spring of 1924, after he failed to obtain the lustier John Barrymore. He was disappointed with Kerrigan, who he felt was "a little too effeminate for the role." While the picture was a moderate success, critics seemed to share Smith's dissatisfaction: *Variety* called Kerrigan "listless."

It's a pitiful picture that emerges of Kerrigan in these final years. In need of cash, he started hawking Murad Turkish cigarettes in print ads. In 1925 he took out a remarkable ad of his own in *Motion Picture.* Under a photograph of himself, his open letter to the industry read:

> From the time I was 13, I had the support of a family on my hands. Later, my mother and I were so very close that I didn't feel the need of any other companion. It is only since I have been alone that I have had time and opportunity to think of marriage and—so far—I haven't found any girl who would think about it with me!
>
> But I'll fool 'em! I'm going to catch one, one of these days—you'll see!
>
> [Signed] J. Warren Kerrigan.

For Kerrigan to write an open letter "explaining" his bachelorhood is extraordinary evidence of how important the Marriage Question had become by this time. Yet his attempt to remake his image came too late. *Captain Blood* was the last film for which he received credit. Although he was said to have invested well and retired contentedly, in truth, like so many of the earliest stars, he was forced to do walk-ons in the 1930s. An item from 1934 said that "despite his previous statements," Kerrigan had recently done extra work on a Jimmy Durante film.

He never did "catch one" either. He remained a bachelor, continuing to live on and off with James Vincent into the next decade. When reporter Rosalind Shaffer asked him the Marriage Question in 1930—by then standard practice—he reflected back on his glory days and said, perhaps honestly: "I never did because all the girls seemed to get wise to me."

He died, forgotten, on June 9, 1947.

DESIGNING MEN

SETS, COSTUMES, AND THE GAY-STRAIGHT SPLIT

1916–1933

George James Hopkins was, in his own words, "a New York sophisticate" when he reported to work at the Fox studios in 1916, hired
as costume and set designer for megastar Theda Bara. He was
barely twenty-one, but already a veteran of Broadway spectaculars—
Ziegfeld, no less—and he was frankly aghast at what he discovered in Hollywood.

"At the time of my first studio experience," he'd sniff, years later, "most
sets were being constructed out of painted canvas. No one had ever heard
of a set decorator. Prop men scraped together what furniture they could lay
their hands on, and stuck it in front of the painted walls."

With all the arrogance of privileged youth, Hopkins was appalled by the
crude movie technicians, those men he said "lived in the Valley with their
wives and children," painters and carpenters and bricklayers recruited by
the fledgling industry. One observer at the time called the early cinema art
directors "glorified carpenters" whose talent consisted mainly in "setting
up a couple of flats at right angles." Hopkins quickly discovered, shudder-

ing all the while no doubt, that this was what passed for an "art department" in the early days of the studios.

And the *cameramen!* In his memoirs, Hopkins reserved his harshest judgment for them. Designing a gown of brilliant colors for Bara—for the sheer *aesthetics* of it—he found himself opposed at every turn by the "unimaginative" men behind the camera. With their primarily technical, mechanical backgrounds, they proved his biggest obstacles. "Cameramen," he said, "felt for some strange reason that color was distracting, that it would detract from the actors." But—he added incredulously—"This was *black-and-white* film."

Movie producers weren't much better in his eyes. After all, he was used to the extravagant tastes of a Charles Frohman—or better yet, Morris Gest, whose office, Hopkins recalled, had "resembled a Pasha's cozy corner, filled with couches, pillows, Oriental rugs, and the stifling odor of incense." He'd have known: while in New York, he'd had an affair with Gest.

But William Fox was about as far as one could get from Broadway. "What kind of place was *this,*" Hopkins asked himself upon arriving in Hollywood, "for someone like *me?*"

For *someone like him.* Hollywood, unclaimed and untamed, was still a blank slate upon which the various pioneers could make their mark. Neal Gabler has written of the opportunity that California offered the new and predominately Jewish movie moguls: "Unlike in the East, the social structure was primitive and permeable. One could even have said that California was the social equivalent of the movies themselves, new and unformed. . . . There was no real aristocracy in place and few social impediments obstructing Jews."

While the largely unclaimed Los Angeles wilderness may have been fertile ground for the Jews to invent the Hollywood film industry, it was a bit trickier when it came to gays. The cowboys shooting tin cans weren't completely gone, and the flamboyant (read, *gay*) sensibility that exuded even from heterosexual Broadway managers (Hopkins wrote of Ziegfeld receiving him in red silk pajamas on a chinchilla spread surrounded by potted pink azaleas and Pekingese dogs) was nowhere to be found among the new moguls. Just a few years away from their haberdasheries and jewelry shops, the new movie leaders were shaping the industry as a distinctly middle-class milieu, where the goal was always to approximate as closely as possible the bourgeois American ideal.

But such an ideal, everyone within the industry knew, was make-believe, an illusion. And wasn't that what movies were *supposed* to do—create illusions? Behind the façade, there was the reality: Jews making films about Christ, women writing men's adventure tales, gays pretending to be straight. Unlike the theater, where the magic wasn't about faking reality—

everyone knew a painted backdrop was a painted backdrop—the magic in Hollywood always depended upon the audience believing what they saw was *real*.

Interestingly, while both the Broadway theater managers and the new movie moguls were disproportionately Jewish, they were worlds apart in temperament, style, and taste. "Isn't this really the difference between the long-established, culturally paramount, and in part elitist world of the stage, and the new and disreputable movies?" suggested Broadway historian Ethan Mordden. "Theater men were confident, famous, admired. Movie men were cheesy, subversive—worst of all, former junk dealers, salesmen, and opportunists."

Like the theater managers, the movie men were attempting to sell glamour to the public, but they were never really part of that glamour themselves, at least not in the way a Charles Frohman was. "It's about style," said Mordden. "Men whose personal style was supposed to reflect the style of their productions—Frohman, classy; Ziegfeld, expensive. Movie producers didn't share this, for, from the start, there was the feeling that movies were real and plays were artificial."

To the Jews, the East may have represented a highly rigid social structure, exclusive of anyone not white, Anglo-Saxon, and Protestant. But—at least in New York theatrical circles—it also represented a world of fluid sexual and gender definitions, and that's what made the Hollywood experience so different for gays. What came together in Hollywood was that mix: an often uneasy pairing of West and East, of straight and gay, of convention and nonconformity.

Gays flocked to the new movie mecca, as did everyone, but for them it was not to be the overt power of the Jews. Of course, "gay" overlaps all categories, but in the beginning the ones we know of are all Wasps: even Kerrigan wasn't Irish-Catholic, but Irish-Anglican. Gay Jews had first to wait perhaps for straight Jews to claim power, and there simply were *no* nonwhites, gay or straight, in the industry as yet. That's not to say we know all. The closet can prove very deep, and who's to say what secrets some of the presumably heterosexual pioneers took to their graves?

Class, however, proves a far more useful classification. Like most of the industry's first known homosexuals, George James Hopkins came from the middle class—even the *upper* middle class, the rarefied world of Pasadena's affluent. He grew up with servants and automobiles and multiple homes. That partially explains his air of superiority recalling the "ignorant" working-class studio employees who "just could not grasp [his] artistic vision."

He was raised to be a Renaissance man. His mother was Una Hopkins, an interior designer in the tradition of Elsie de Wolfe. She wrote for *Cos-*

mopolitan and *Ladies' Home Journal,* extolling her personal, modernist design theory, and was hired by many wealthy Pasadenans to redecorate their homes and gardens. His father had died before he was born, leaving mother and son well-off, with investments in Pasadena real estate. Una used their affluence to encourage her son in his own artistic interests, giving him lessons in design and music.

The upper crust of Pasadena society may have been their friends, but the young George was more fascinated by their gardener, John Oakman. "He certainly wasn't young," he recalled, "half-black and half-white, an aging satyr." At age ten, George would sit in rapture listening to Oakman's tales of "Rabelesian adventures of sex with women." The gardener would expose his "rather wrinkled member" and urinate in front of the fascinated boy. "I'd return home shaken," George remembered. "You might say John Oakman introduced me to sex."

In 1911, at the age of fifteen, George was sent to the New York School of Fine and Applied Art (later Parsons). He had been a pampered prodigy at home; in the City of Bachelors he was high-strung and terrified. But *cute:* thin, long-lashed, with a perky nose and delicate smile. It was likely this combination that encouraged several prominent men to take him under their protective wing.

Charles Frohman, called by Gavin Lambert "the most powerful showman of his time," was the first of these. Controlling most of Broadway's theaters as well as the largest theatrical chain across the country, Frohman was a homely man of fifty, notorious for always having cream patties in his pudgy hand. His taste in plays was equally saccharine. For many years, he lived quite openly with a male companion, Charles Dillingham, whom he helped become a producer in his own right. The sixteen-year-old George Hopkins would often find himself the dinner guest of Frohman and Dillingham, and through them met some of Broadway's most famous names before Frohman drowned aboard the *Lusitania* in 1915.

Later mentors included Morris Gest, the brilliant theatrical impresario who brought, among others, Geraldine Farrar to the stage, and Melville Ellis, the dashing and influential costume designer for the Shuberts and—according to a rather surprising claim by Hopkins—Lee Shubert's lover. Sexual favors would certainly help explain Hopkins' extraordinary rise from art student to Broadway designer while still in his teens.

The New York theater was drenched in gay culture, but Hopkins said it was a truth not articulated. "Homosexuality wasn't the casual topic of conversation it is today," he wrote in the 1970s. But then, it didn't need to be, not on Broadway. It was just *there*—from the offices of Gest to the alliance between Frohman and Elisabeth Marbury, legendary theatrical agent and lover of Elsie de Wolfe.

Through Gest, Hopkins got a job with Ziegfeld, designing racy costumes for the world-famous "Follies." He also designed gowns for the play "An Unchastened Woman." Beaming over her son's success, Una convinced Oliver Morosco, the Los Angeles theatrical magnate, to hire George to design costumes for Morosco's film productions. This way, mother and son could be reunited, as Una was decorating Morosco's sets. They were later hired as a pair to work at the Realart Studios, one of Adolph Zukor's companies, releasing under the Paramount banner.

But it was with Theda Bara that Hopkins first made his mark. In early 1917 he began taking assignments at Fox in addition to his duties at Realart; one-studio contracts had not yet become standard for behind-the-scenes workers. It's likely that the Fox connection came through a new lover, Polish-born writer Ryszard (Richard) Ordynski, who had worked as a producer for Max Reinhardt on the Berlin stage and come to the U.S. in 1912. It was Ordynski who led Hopkins onto the set that first day to meet the enigmatic Bara. Hopkins would recall, "The set inside the tent was supposed to be Cleopatra's throne room. To reach it one had to wade through dust half a foot deep. There were hundreds of extras blocking our way. What I could see from a distance surprised me. Cleopatra didn't seem to have a particularly good figure. . . . Her costume consisted of a beaded shirt and two brass serpents entwined around not particularly impressive breasts."

As Ordynski made the introductions, Hopkins was struck by the sweat running down the screen goddess's face. "Remarkably self-possessed and not at all glamorous," he said. "I don't remember what we said but I immediately liked her. The liking was to become mutual for many years."

Theda Bara. The name alone conjures up the era. Black-ringed eyes, come-hither stares. The full-figured vamp squatting over the skeleton of a man. "Kiss me, my fool!" read the subtitles. *A Fool There Was. The Devil's Daughter. The Vixen. Sin.* These were Theda's films. She was billed as an Egyptian mystic, her name an anagram of "Arab Death." Part Elvira, Mistress of the Dark, part Mae West, she gave erotic, exotic expression to the taboo of female sexuality. Woman as aggressor. Woman as master. Woman as death.

In truth, she was plump and jolly, bored to tears with the whole publicity rap. After scraping off the mascara and putting on some clothes, she went back to being Theodosia Goodman, a tailor's daughter from Cincinnati. "She was just so bored, bored, bored by the whole 'woman of mystery' theme," Hopkins said. "She couldn't go out to nightclubs, couldn't be seen outside of the publicity, because that would have destroyed it all. She wanted company *desperately,* and the company turned out to be me."

Bara. Crawford. Lombard. Liz Taylor. A long, honorable, select tradition of female stars forging fierce, devoted friendships with gay men. Hopkins would go back to her hotel almost every night with Bara. She'd slip into an elegant dressing gown with a long train and happily entertain Hopkins and Ordynski for hours. After consulting her vibrations, she rechristened George "Neje," which he began using as screen credit. Two syllables, it was pronounced with its first "e" like a long "a," its second "e" as a short "u."

"Neje" also began writing her scenarios: among them *The She-Devil* (1918) and *A Woman There Was* (1919). Again, taking off one hat and putting on another was common in this early period. "Aside from the painters and carpenters," Hopkins recalled, "none of us were subject to union restrictions. I designed sets, dressed them, supervised costuming, and even wrote original screenplays and titles. I forgot to mention the art of acting—in which we all indulged upon occasion."

His Renaissance education paid off. "Writing scenarios comes as easy to George as designing costumes," wrote a reporter. "But one always suspects him of doing the costumes first and then fitting a story to them."

The fan magazines concurred that he was indeed "a sophisticated New York man," inherently possessing the kind of taste and style the new industry wanted desperately to emulate. "He has twinkling blue eyes and a quick friendly smile, and wears shell-rimmed glasses and a leather-lined overcoat," wrote *Picture Play*. He also had very specific ideas about film style: "Costumes have motif, as much as music or drama," he said. "For [Bara's] sirens, I use flame colors, for sirens are burning fountains of passion." A vampire, on the other hand, "sucks at emotions," he explained. "She feeds upon her victims . . . the lines must be long and slinky."

He admitted to being idiosyncratic. "I'm afraid I pay very little attention to historical detail. [On *Madame DuBarry*] I just got the silhouette correctly and filled in the rest myself. I hope I caught the spirit of that time, the luxurious abandon."

It's a queer take—appropriately—on the design theory of Griffith or DeMille, who considered historical accuracy synonymous with quality. But Hopkins marched to a different drummer. "I would be held back having to think of technicalities," he said, "instead of giving my imagination free rein."

That free rein also enabled him to move into designing sets. George James Hopkins was one of the first important influences on the *look* of Hollywood cinema, although he hasn't received much credit, the lion's share going to Wilfred Buckland, designer for DeMille. Part of the neglect comes from the simple fact that few of Hopkins' early films have survived. But by 1916, when *Photoplay* commented on the sudden rise of the "artistic executive" (or art director), Hopkins was already working at Realart. He would certainly have been grouped as part of the new "artistic breed of sophisticates" that *Photoplay* observed arriving in Hollywood. Critic Frank Webster wrote at the time that the maturation of pictures "has brought into the industry men thoroughly conversant with architecture and interior decorating." Whether other early pioneers in cinema art direction were gay is unknown. Yet all were part of a theatrical world that was rapidly replacing the "glorified carpenters" as movie set designers.

Again, what is significant is the movies' attempt to create an ever-more realistic illusion in place of the obvious theatrical artificiality of the stage. It might be suggested that homosexuals knew something about casting illusions, about making what wasn't real seem authentic. Hopkins quickly surpassed the old carpenters and bricklayers he'd disdained so much. By 1919, an article in *Picture Play* called him "one of the brightest and most influential figures behind the camera." His first set, for Bara's *Salome,* might not have been as awesome as Griffith's re-creation of Babylon in *Intolerance,* but it was certainly the most majestic the Fox lot had ever seen. A giant peacock throne towered over a reflecting pool, with jets of water flowing from the eyes of the tail feathers. Below, "nubile young maidens" reclined seductively amid satin pillows and chinchilla spreads (an homage perhaps to Ziegfeld and Gest?).

Hopkins' interiors—or at least his descriptions of them, as so many are lost forever—have what might today be called "camp" appeal. But it is the series of pictures he did with the director William Desmond Taylor that best exemplify his signature style.

HOPKINS, TAYLOR, AND AN EARLY GAY SENSIBILITY

Forty years later, Hopkins would still remember his heart "racing" the day the tall, handsome, aristocratic William Desmond Taylor first strode onto the lot. It was a crush his mother Una encouraged, adoring Taylor for his talent and his knowledge of period design. It wasn't long before director and set designer were lovers.

Taylor will forever be remembered more for his death than for his life: his murder in 1922 remains one of Hollywood's great unsolved mysteries and (as will be discussed in Chapter 4, "Sex Without Sin"), the first public-relations nightmare for the studios involving gay issues. But Taylor, a remarkably talented man, should be recalled for more than just lurid headlines. In the brief span of his career he directed some of Hollywood's biggest moneymakers and—if the few that survive are representative—they were as well crafted as they were popular.

Taylor was a company man. The industry admired him as much as they admired his profits. Like Eugene O'Brien, his sexuality was not an impediment to access into the power circles. Born in Ireland, he had impeccable manners, an ease with money men, and a romantic history of imprisonment in Dublin and adventures in Mexico. Whether all the stories were true or not didn't matter. This was Hollywood. All that mattered was the *perception* of truth.

In 1917, Taylor was named head of the newly formed Motion Picture Directors' Association, a social club that met at the Hotel Alexandria for beefsteak dinners and games of pinochle and to "tell each other how much they like their pictures." Such a thing Allan Dwan likely could never have imagined foraging through the wilderness just six years earlier. But the remarkable growth of the industry had, in a strikingly short time, created the framework of the system that would dominate production of the movies for the next forty years.

While most companies still had "home offices" in New York, their "factories" (production facilities or studios) were largely in Hollywood by 1920. Carl Laemmle, at Universal, promoted the idea of a "scientifically balanced program," with its film production "designed and equipped to roll out [pictures] like so many Model-Ts off the assembly line." Other studios followed the basic structure, and increasingly, scattered outfits were merging into larger concerns. Famous Players joined with Lasky, then Famous Players-Lasky combined with Morosco, Hobart Bosworth, and others to become Paramount. In 1924, Metro, Goldwyn, and Mayer merged into Metro-Goldwyn-Mayer. The result of these mergers was an efficient hierarchical system of production, with stars and writers reporting to directors reporting to producers reporting to studio chiefs.

Within this system, William Desmond Taylor stood tall. As a director of note in the most noteworthy of studios, Famous Players-Lasky, he commanded respect and attention, and at his Directors' Association meetings he was routinely clapped on the back by his pinochle-playing friends. "Taylor was a man of extreme courtesy," wrote Henry Dougherty of the *Los Angeles Express*. "He addressed those under him with the same courtesy with which he conversed with those who wrote his contracts and paid his salary."

Even Edward Doherty of the scandal sheet *New York News,* one of Taylor's shrillest critics in the post-murder brouhaha, would admit, "He made the average director look like what he is—a brainless mechanism braying through a microphone."

These scribes knew Taylor was different from the others. Always referred to as a "gentleman," he was a breed apart from the kinds of directors being charged with rape and sexual harassment. Yet even then there were whispers about his own nocturnal activities. Doherty, who regularly criticized the film colony's "licentiousness" in language worthy of fire-and-brimstone

preachers, would later suggest that even before Taylor's death, there had
been suspicion of the "gentleman" director's "unmanly" associations.

Taylor was indeed a gentleman—every account bears this out—but such
refinement didn't preclude an apparently wide-ranging enjoyment of sex.
He was romantically involved with the actress Neva Gerber, his costar from
his days as an actor at Vitagraph, and several other women, but his most sustained relationship was with George James Hopkins. In his memoirs, Hopkins wrote that as time went on, the two men became less secretive. In April
1921, they attended together Mary Garden's opening in Verdi's "Otello" at
the Philharmonic. While they did not walk in together, they sat beside each
other in the front orchestra, in full view of Mr. and Mrs. Cecil B. DeMille,
Mr. and Mrs. Jesse Lasky, and many other key industry figures. It was highly
unusual, two men accompanying each other to a public function; the protocol, even for those homosexuals in fairly "open" relationships, was to arrive with dates of the opposite sex. Hopkins, writing about their attendance
at the Philharmonic, believed it must have elicited comment.

Certainly it did from Mary Miles Minter. According to Hopkins, the
young actress—then completely besotted with Taylor—cried out, "So *this*
is what is going on!"

Hopkins may have been attempting some melodrama with this anecdote,
with himself as the star, implying that Minter shot Taylor some ten months
later in a jealous fury over George. But whatever the truth to that old who-
dunit, it's beyond the scope here. What's important is the fact that the industry surely knew that Taylor had relationships with both men and
women, and still he was afforded great influence, authority, and prestige. He
could risk sitting with another man in the front row applauding Mary Garden. The industry tolerated and protected his "secret."

Indeed, some of his best work was the result of his personal and professional collaboration with Hopkins. Historians looking for that elusive "gay
sensibility" in the work of gay directors can perhaps start here, with *The
Soul of Youth* (1920). Taylor enlisted Hopkins' help in livening up a mawk-
ish tale of a do-gooder judge who reforms wayward boys. The script implied the boys had whored themselves, so Hopkins convinced Taylor to
depict a scene in a whorehouse. In the days before the Hays Code existed
to prohibit such a thing, Taylor agreed. For good measure, they also threw
in a scene where the sixteen-year-old star (Lewis Sargent) is sold into sexual slavery.

Just to make sure they got their details correct, Hopkins wrote that he
and Taylor visited an actual male brothel in Los Angeles. Later, after Taylor's
death, there would be reports in the *New York Times* of the director's visits
to an all-male "love cult" in Chinatown, where "the men would lie in silk

kimonos, smoke the essence of the poppy flower and so commence their ritual, old as Sodom. . . . The members of the cult were held together by a bond, unthinkable, unnameable, unbelievable, and that each had sworn an oath of undying affection for the others."

Hopkins doesn't mention any of this, but he does say that after their visit to the brothel, they hired several attractive teenage boys to appear in *The Soul of Youth*. This is significant stuff: a noted director and his scenic designer patronizing the homosexual underworld and consciously bringing its influence into their work. To further give the picture its appropriate decadence, Hopkins bought up antiques and odd remnants, discovering several "erotic panels" with paintings of sailors cavorting with bare-breasted mermaids. Photographed and enlarged, they made a suitably audacious (and presumably outrageously campy) backdrop for the whorehouse scenes.

Julia Crawford Ivers, screenwriter on many of the Taylor-Hopkins pictures, may have clued into the reason for Hopkins' distinct (and what she viewed as "superior") style: "He has a weird touch," she admitted to one reporter, "which makes his work stand out."

That it certainly did. In *The Furnace* that same year, Hopkins designed a scene right out of Dante: a writhing, slinky, sadomasochistic Hell, with bodybuilders preening as they received their eternal torture. Hopkins wrote that studio workers gaped at the spectacle through a glass wall at the top of the stage. The actors were all nude, and only later, with flames added as special effects, were the forbidden body parts concealed. Although it was Wilfred Buckland who was credited as art director, Hopkins was manager of production, presumably in charge of the details of the scene.

One film that *has* survived, *Nurse Marjorie*, starring Mary Miles Minter, shows just how far Hopkins had come as a set designer, and indeed how far the art of cinematic set design had progressed. Hopkins built a replica of the Houses of Parliament that was a wonder to behold. The literal pinnacle of the Taylor-Hopkins partnership came with *The Top of New York,* in which George—once again "Neje"—wrote the screenplay and built fifteen-feet-tall replicas of New York rooftops. It would be Taylor's last film before his death.

In their five years of collaboration, Hopkins and Taylor created a body of work whose loss is inestimable. It was here that Hollywood came into being; the collaborative nature of filmmaking that would dominate in the studios was brilliantly manifested between director and designer. That Taylor and Hopkins were also romantically involved, partaking of Hollywood's gay subculture and bringing it deliberately into their films, makes the loss of their work even more tragic. They remain perhaps the brightest of the "New York sophisticates" who were transforming the medium into art. "It shouldn't be left up to the crew to put a set together," Hopkins would write. "It was time for *artists* to start designing the entire *look* of pictures."

THE NEW BREED: MITCHELL LEISEN AND HAROLD GRIEVE

Mitchell Leisen wasn't an artist; he was an architect, a man of formulas and fixtures, of numbers and equations. But from all accounts, he wasn't happy at his drafting table. This despite being part of a top Chicago architectural firm, designing such gems as the Drake Hotel. But from the time he was a young boy it had been his love of the theater—not hotels and office buildings—that had aroused his passion. Architecture school had been an effort to please his mother, who'd been determined her son would rise above his humble origins. Mitchell was born with a club foot in Menominee, Michigan, in 1898. His father ran a brewery. It wasn't long before mother Mabel had left her husband in search of a better life for her son.

In St. Louis, she found both corrective surgery and schooling for young Mitch, who'd go on to graduate from Washington University. He was anything but content, however, with his mother's choice of a career. To offset his boredom on the job, he'd design costumes for the local Playshop Players. On a whim, he took a vacation to Hollywood in 1919, thinking maybe he'd like to act. As would happen to many in this chronicle time and time again, it was Leisen's network of gay acquaintanceships that secured his connections. He was a friend (and possibly lover) of the famed dancer Ted Shawn, who was then doing choreography on a Gloria Swanson picture. Through Shawn, Leisen met Jeanie MacPherson, scenarist to Cecil B. DeMille, who persuaded the director to offer Leisen a job designing costumes. Leisen gladly accepted, creating Swanson's Babylonian wardrobe for *Male and Female,* being paid $125 a week. Enchanted with his new work, Leisen wired the firm in Chicago not to expect him back.

With his architectural background, Leisen quickly expanded his duties into set design, conceiving and executing the sets for some of DeMille's most lavish spectacles, including *The Road to Yesterday* and *The King of Kings.* Just as Hopkins was doing at Fox and Paramount, Leisen created fabulous, outsized monuments to the exuberant spirit of the new decade.

In 1922, he was loaned to Douglas Fairbanks to do the costumes for *Robin Hood.* He also took over many duties that should rightfully have fallen to art director Wilfred Buckland. It was Leisen who rigged up the seventy-foot slide that served as Fairbanks' getaway from the balcony, covering it with an enormous drape so that when shot, it looked as if Robin Hood were sliding magically down the fabric. So impressed with Leisen's ingenuity and insight was director Allan Dwan—Jack Kerrigan's old nemesis—that he turned over increasing responsibilities to the designer. When the women set out to chase Fairbanks, they hoisted their skirts in a way Dwan felt was inauthentic to the medieval period. He called Leisen and instructed him, "Teach them how to move."

Such directorial reliance on Leisen's innate sensibility—indeed, his very *gayness*—is echoed in a story told by Harold Grieve, another gay designer contemporary with Leisen. Los Angeles–born, Grieve was a recent graduate of Los Angeles High School when he got a job at the old Brunton Studios in the prop department. He wanted to be an artist, but his father had insisted he'd pay only for dental school. Faced with a such a future, Grieve opted out of college altogether; the studios became his higher education. In 1920 he moved over to Metro, where he drew perspective drawings for sets. It wasn't called the art department then, he'd recall; it was the "technical" department, and soon Grieve was doing everything from sketching to hanging drapes and building stages.

Director Rex Ingram, a man noted for his tolerance and open-mindedness, took a liking to Grieve during *The Prisoner of Zenda*. At one point, Ingram expressed dissatisfaction with the props, especially a box that was supposed to be very valuable in the script. The director turned past the seasoned prop men to look at the young Grieve.

"*You* know what I'm asking for, don't you?" he asked. Grieve responded that he believed he did. Ingram nodded. "I *know* you do," he said.

Such confidence was vindicated when Grieve returned, an antique jewel box in his hands. Ingram proclaimed it perfect for the scene. Grieve hadn't found it in the prop department, but rather in the shop of local interior decorator Raymond Gould. "So that kind of brushed me up for the studio," Grieve recalled, "as being one who would know what he was talking about."

Grieve doesn't say it, but it's clear from his telling that Ingram recognized something *different* in him, something he felt might be useful for the picture. Once again, gays were helping to shape the Hollywood magic for their studio bosses: they knew, as Grieve pointed out, what they were talking about.

The studio-educated Grieve would go on to construct the surrealistic sets for Nazimova's *Camille;* although credit went to Natacha Rambova, Grieve claimed much of the design was his work. ("I didn't feel hurt because all my crew, all my gang, knew who was doing what.") He faced such enforced anonymity again when Fred Niblo took over from Charles Brabin on MGM's epic *Ben-Hur.* Although new designers were hired, Grieve's notes indicate he believed much of his work remained intact in the finished picture. He took more public acclaim for *Dorothy Vernon of Haddon Hall,* *Lady Windemere's Fan,* and *So This Is Paris,* doing a mix of costumes and sets.

Hopkins, Leisen, and Grieve were part of a vibrant development in cinema art of which they were likely not the only gay men. But as the studio structure solidified, the gay presence would become increasingly compartmentalized, a breakdown here documented for the first time.

HOWARD GREER AND THE FORMATION OF THE LADIES' WARDROBE DEPARTMENT

By the early part of the 1920s, a division of labor began to emerge within the studios. Whereas in the Teens it had been common practice for a designer to handle both costumes and sets, the trend by mid-decade was for each studio to have its own star couturier: a high-fashion artiste specifically in place to create extravagant wardrobes for the studio's leading actress.

Howard Greer was the first of these, hired in 1922 by Famous Players-Lasky to design costumes for the tempestuous Pola Negri. Greer was the first costume designer to be given a contract to head a specific Wardrobe Department. (Just for women—the male actors still supplied their own clothes, except for historical epics.) In truth, the mass production of pictures by the studio film factories necessitated such a change. Greer was to preside over a department that grew to include more than a hundred employees: pattern makers, fitters, seamstresses, milliners, furriers, and embroiderers.

While women were employed for most of the menial work—sewing, cutting fabric—higher-paid positions like sketch artists and designer assistants were filled by men. And, in most every case, by *gay* men. From New York, Paris, and London they came, almost every one of them as gay as jaybirds, as Anita Loos used to say. There is no more direct example of an obvious, undiluted gay influence in film than in the area of costume design, especially in the early years, when *all* of the leading costume designers—Greer, Travis Banton, Ernst Dryden, Andre-ani, Adrian, just to name a few—were homosexual.

"All of the great film costume designers were gay," said Tony Award–winning and Oscar-nominated designer Miles White. "And yes, I think it's true that you can see [their gayness] in the great designs of a Howard Greer or Adrian. I think one's sexuality does make a difference. I would not have been the same designer I am today had I been straight. Gay designers have a feel for not only the design, but for the clothes themselves and how they'll be worn. We aren't *afraid* of them. We can imagine *wearing* them. . . . I know how to *wear* what I'm drawing. Straight men don't know how twenty layers of chiffon move in contrast to one."

Howard Greer certainly knew. Born in 1886 on a farm in Rushville, Illinois (not Nebraska as has often been stated), he was from an early age fascinated by fashion and design. The son of Sam and Hattie Greer, poor farmers who barely made a living, Greer was an exception among Hollywood's first gays: drawn from the dirt-poor working class, he seems to have always understood that he was different, and made no attempt to hide the fact.

Never very handsome, he was thin, with a long face and pinched features: the look of an old maid even as a young boy. When he was three, the family moved to the little town of Tecumseh, Nebraska. Investing the family's savings in a hobby that had long obsessed him, Sam Greer opened a florist shop. But while his roses were stunning, the enterprise failed, and the collapse of his dream left Sam Greer "taciturn and disillusioned." In the 1900 Census, he listed his occupation as house painter; he'd been out of work four months. To supplement their income, Hattie took in lodgers.

Young Howard learned about dreams from his father. He vowed never to surrender, never to become defeated as Sam had. Despite "Methodist taboos" that would occasionally "rear their ugly heads," Howard's mother allowed her son great leeway in his rather unorthodox tastes. Once he accompanied one of their lodgers—"a personable young bachelor who had no truck with loose women"—to the theater. Although the actual play receded from his memory, Howard would never forget one of the actresses, "a ravishingly beautiful female bedecked and bedizened as I'd never before envisioned. Her neck and shoulders were shamelessly naked, but no one seemed to mind. She was encased in a glittering redness, and I don't have to lie on a psychoanalyst's couch today to be told why I still love spangles, and any color at all so long as it's red."

Once again, it is the story of a gay child recognizing his difference and wanting more than what his society can offer. Like Kerrigan and O'Brien, had Howard Greer not been a *different* child—the kind that swooned over actresses "bedecked and bedizened"—he might have accepted his lot and stayed put. He could have taken over his father's farm, maybe even made a go of his floral business. But he wanted something more: he wanted to be an *artist*. Just what kind didn't matter: he wanted, as he said, to make "beauty out of life."

In a delicious mix of youthful chutzpah and naivete, he began writing to famous people, begging them to rescue him by giving him a job. He'd find their names in *Vanity Fair* and *Harper's Bazaar,* then sit down to pen letters "sincere, convincing, and heart-rending." It was an act borne out of desperation, but soaked with an utter confidence that his destiny awaited. Most of his letters went unanswered—only Florenz Ziegfeld was courteous enough to at least dictate an answer ("no")—but eventually his pluck paid off. A few weeks later a telegram arrived from the designer Lady Duff Gordon, also known as Lucile:

"Meet me in Chicago Thursday. Will give definite answer then."

Howard immediately cabled back: "Death alone will keep me from you."

Lucile was considered the greatest living artist when it came to fabric and color. With her sister, Elinor Glyn, the author of *It,* she helped define *fabulous* in the first decades of the century. Howard had read all about Lucile's salons in New York, Paris, London, and Chicago, mooning over her exquisite designs draped over equally exquisite models. "A fine business for a man to be in!" Sam Greer harumphed, but Howard paid him no mind.

In Chicago, he worked for Lucile as a sketch artist. He soon transferred to her New York salon, where he lived with Hubert Stowitts, a ballet star in Pavlova's company. Into this new world, Hattie came to visit. On a stroll through Central Park, she was aghast at lovers kissing publicly on park benches. But Howard "was beyond being affected by old-fashioned morals," he remembered. Indeed, "old-fashioned morals" were what pushed many of Hollywood's gays away from their homes in the first place.

"Howard was always at ease with what he was," said his friend Satch LaValley. "He never had a problem and couldn't understand anyone who did."

Drafted into World War I, he took shrapnel on the fields of France and survived twice being gassed. His most memorable experience, however, was forming the Argonne Players, a theatrical troupe, where he designed costumes for the "leading lady," played (of course) by a male soldier. At war's end, he arranged to be discharged abroad, and took an apartment in Paris. Writing for *Theatre* magazine, he became a regular with Isadora Duncan at the salons of Cecile Sorel, "the most famous, the most fascinating, and the most triumphant courtesan of Paris."

He returned to New York in 1921. "This was the Village of bathtub gin, speakeasies, tearooms marked by bottles hidden under pyramids of candlewax, and long-haired free-love." It was also the Village of William Haines, Edmund Goulding, Lilyan Tashman, and numerous other gay men and lesbians who would bring its bohemian values with them to Hollywood. Working again for Lucile, he also moonlighted, designing costumes for "The Greenwich Village Follies," starring famed female impersonator Bert Savoy. Never far economically from his working-class roots, Greer worked on such revues to make ends meet: the autocratic Lucile paid him just twenty-five dollars a week. So it was that when Hollywood came knocking, Greer was only too glad to open the door. "For money I would have gone to Timbuktu or Tibet," he said, "and if I knew nothing about the machinations of pictures, I had at least heard they paid fabulous salaries to their initiates."

He'd actually been Famous Players' *second* choice: Gilbert Clarke, another Lucile alumnus, had been approached first. Disdaining the movies, Clarke suggested Greer. "He disposed of a rival," Greer recalled, "and I—well, I found my life's work."

By the late 1920s, other studios had their own Greers. Ernst Dryden designed for Universal and Columbia, and MGM hired René Hubert, Andreani, and Gilbert Clarke (who, having seen the error of his ways, now happily accepted an offer from Hollywood). Homosexuals all, a fact acknowledged, even embraced, by studio moguls. In 1925, MGM also imported the dazzling Erté with much pomp and circumstance. The celebrated Russian designer arrived with his lover, Nicholas Ouroussoff, whose expenses were also picked up by the studio. Louis B. Mayer, whose antipathy to homosexuals was well known, nonetheless invited Erté and Ourossoff to dinner with his family.

"On the basis of my own relationship with him," Erté would recall, "I could never understand how the legend of his quick temper and difficult character had developed. In all my dealings with him I never saw any sign of either." When Erté left the studio, Mayer expressed his deep regret and gave the designer a personal photograph, inscribed with his warmest wishes.

Mayer's enthusiastic sponsorship of Erté is significant, especially given his later treatment of actors and directors known to be gay. Of course, Erté was a highly regarded name in fashion, but Mayer feared no one: he had been rude to people far more prestigious than the eccentric Russian designer. But Erté's homosexuality, however obvious, didn't offer the kind of threat that movie star William Haines' did, or director Edmund Goulding's: it was the homosexuality of a costume designer—who was, after all, *supposed* to be gay.

For gays in the studio wardrobe departments, there existed an extraordinary environment of freedom and tolerance, found virtually nowhere else in American industry. In fact, it's not quite accurate to say that homosexuality was merely *tolerated* in wardrobe. Given that all of the leaders in the field were gay, it's more correct to say that it was *expected*—that being gay actually carried with it some cachet.

There's a scene in the film *Myrt and Marge,* an early talkie (and later a radio program), where a group of chorus girls toss their costumes over to the designer. It's apparent to the audience—and to the other characters in the film—that the designer is gay. He banters with one of the girls about the man she's dating, and comments about buying a kimono for himself. There's no hiding or pretense. One of the girls hands the designer her boa, then turns back to add sharply, "And don't *wear* it." To which he replies sheepishly, *"Selfish."*

It's as good an illustration as any of the experience of the costume designer in the studio era. Both confidant and scapegoat, he was the most overtly queer presence in the studio. Exalted for his talent, he was still the butt of jokes from the "he-men" in other departments. Samuel Goldwyn's secretary would write to a friend in 1926 about the designer Adrian: "He is very effeminate. The men here kid him so."

Despite the kidding, it could actually be a career *advantage* to be homosexual in the wardrobe department. Shortly after Howard Greer arrived at Famous Players, he hired as an assistant a mousy little college girl by the name of Edith Head. Boyish and bespectacled, Edith had a husband, but from the start she adopted an ambiguous image of gender and sexuality. Of Mr. Head, she rarely spoke, fueling speculation throughout her life that she was a lesbian. Even a second marriage, to the set designer Wiard Ihnen, failed to derail the rumors; in fact, it was assumed by some that both were gay.

"Edith liked to give the impression that it was a marriage of convenience, but it was a loving partnership," said costume historian and Head's longtime friend David Chierichetti. "I think Edith may have rather enjoyed, even encouraged, the speculation. It was helpful for designers to be gay. There was a fraternity of designers, all homosexual. Edith may have actually *wanted* to be considered gay, or at least to give that impression."

Indeed, there is no anecdotal evidence of romantic or sexual relationships between Head and other women. There is considerable logic, however, to the idea that she may have cultivated a gender-ambivalent image within a field that was considered queer. She was embraced by Greer and later by Travis Banton, who helped boost her into a career that lasted until the 1980s. "I studied everything Howard Greer and Travis Banton did," she wrote. "They taught me constantly. I couldn't have stayed on a week without them."

By cultivating such an image, Head might be accepted within the fraternity of designers, which otherwise was an exclusively gay club, at least until the late 1930s. "They were all rivals, but they were friends," recalled Chierichetti of the costume designers he knew. Photographs often show Greer and Banton socializing together; they were known to be close friends. Even the reclusive Adrian joined them occasionally.

THE TRANSCENDENT TRAVIS

Travis Banton quickly outpaced Howard Greer at Paramount, becoming by the end of the 1920s one of the legendary Hollywood designers. Hired in late 1924 during Paramount's expansion of its wardrobe department, he was, like Greer, a New York couturier, having worked for the famed Madame Frances. His crowning claim to fame was his design of Mary Pickford's wedding dress for her marriage to Douglas Fairbanks.

Even more than Greer, Banton carried with him an aura of prestige. From a more affluent background than his friend and colleague, Banton was quickly embraced by Paramount as their arbiter of style and taste. He was born in Waco, Texas, on August 18, 1894, but his parents also lived part of the year in Manhattan, where his uncle, Joab Banton, was a district attorney and one of the chief forces behind the shutdown of Mae West's play "Sex." When Travis was two, the family began living full-time in New York, where Margaret Banton indulged her son's penchant for all things dramatic. As a very young boy, his idols were not nickelodeon cowboys but rather Julia Marlowe and Hazel Dawn, whom his mother had taken him to see on Broadway in "Cleopatra" and "The Pink Lady."

Rentfro Banton may have been more worldly than Sam Greer, but he still chafed at his teenaged son's desire to pursue a career in art and fashion. He enrolled Travis at Columbia University, setting him on a business course, but the boy rebelled and, with his mother's influence, was transferred to the Art Students League of the New York School of Fine and Applied Art (later Parsons). There he was a pupil of the esteemed teacher Robert Kalloch, who encouraged Banton's drawings of the female form. But to everyone's surprise, the young artist embellished his sketches with extravagant gowns and jewelry.

He was a small man, standing just about five-feet-eight, thin, boyishly handsome, with thick, dark hair, a drooping eyelid, and slightly uneven shoulders. Later, he'd bulk up somewhat, with one reporter commenting that his physique looked like a prizefighter's. But prizefighting was about as far away from Travis' goals as one could get. In 1917, encouraged by Kalloch and other teachers, Banton presented some sketches to Norma Talmadge, whose production company was still based in New York. He'd later tell *Photoplay* writer Julie Lang Hunt he was "a nervous, awkward youngster and there were probably plenty of mistakes in the drawings," but Talmadge was enthusiastic. She commissioned him to design one of her gowns for her picture *Poppy,* costarring Eugene O'Brien.

Travis' schoolwork was interrupted by service in the navy during the

World War; he enlisted in December 1917. From his military records, he doesn't appear to have been sent overseas, being stationed at the New London, Connecticut, naval base as a seaman second-class. He was, however, awarded a Victory Medal after the war, and was honorably discharged in September 1921.

Back in civilian life, he found work with the famed Madame Frances, and his reputation as a couturier rose rapidly. He was hired by Ziegfeld to do costumes for the "Follies," where one of his creations—a dress made almost entirely of black *coq* feathers—caused a sensation, and predicted his later work with Marlene Dietrich.

Producer Walter Wanger at Paramount got wind of Banton's style and brought him to Hollywood to design the gowns for the film *The Dressmaker from Paris,* starring Leatrice Joy. It was a tale of haute couture that climaxed with a fabulous fashion show, and Banton had a field day with dozens of costumes. On the basis of this, Paramount gave him a contract as the wardrobe department's second-in-command.

He seemed instinctively to understand the role costume played in cinema: it wasn't simply window-dressing, but an integral part of the narrative. "Clothes are used to tell a story," he told one reporter, "to further an impulse, or stress a desired purpose in the life of the character in question." Indeed, he was the first of the Hollywood designers to see costume in this way (although as far back as 1917, George James Hopkins was espousing a similar philosophy before moving into set design), and his influential approach became standard for all those who followed.

"The rest of us always watched Banton," admitted Walter Plunkett, the celebrated designer for *Gone With the Wind* and countless other classics, "because he was always a couple of years ahead of the fashion trend."

The designs he created around Paramount's leading female players in the late 1920s and early 1930s dazzled not only movie audiences but also the fashion houses of New York and Paris. Banton and his colleagues—Greer, Andre-ani, and especially Adrian at MGM—were often called upon to write fashion-tip columns and critiques for both movie magazines and the general press. Reporters began turning to them for fashion advice in the way they might once have turned to Schiaparelli or Chanel. The press even speculated that Hollywood would vanquish New York and Paris as the world's style-setter.

"Slowly but surely the Hollywoods are becoming the style center of the world," wrote the *New York Evening Journal* in 1935. "Travis Banton, recently returned from an extensive European tour, says that as far as Parisian styles are concerned, he will just go along glibly whipping up little creations out of his mind and not follow any dictate."

Banton's actresses loved him for setting them apart—for creating individual, distinct images they could exploit in their pictures and the press. Like Greer, Banton had little time for "old-fashioned morality," convincing a nervous Leatrice Joy and Pola Negri to hike up their hemlines. Joy had insisted that as a serious "dramatic actress" she couldn't be seen in trendy above-the-knee fashions, but Banton's scanty miniskirts only pushed her career to new heights. He admitted to getting drunk before going head-to-head with Negri, but once again he prevailed, and Negri became a fan for life.

Clara Bow proved less tractable. Insisting on wearing ankle socks with high-heel shoes, the lusty redhead both exasperated and enchanted Banton. "He finds it almost impossible to describe his mixed feelings for her," observed *Photoplay*. "She made him suffer, she caused him endless anxiety and worry, and yet there will always be a glowing place in his heart for her."

Part of his fondness for Bow may have sprung from a shared love of high living. Already by the mid-1920s Banton had a reputation around Hollywood, partying late into the night with Howard Greer. "I remember the talk," said one observer, who had friends in both the set and costume departments at several studios, many of whom had worked with Banton and Greer. "They were big drinkers and carousers. They'd pick up sailors, bring them back for parties. Everyone knew about it. They carried on with abandon."

Their carousing caused some concern in the Paramount front office. Underlying the seemingly structured and tolerant system, the old fault line remained: the moralists versus the sophisticates—men like Howard Greer and Travis Banton, who came to Hollywood to be as free from tradition and "old-fashioned morals" as possible.

Greer would leave Paramount by 1927. His end can't be simplified into a clash between opposing forces—his alcoholism certainly affected his job performance, and Paramount was right to can him—but from the start, anyone could have predicted Greer wouldn't last long. He seemed overwhelmed by it all, intoxicated by the indulgence of liberty. Despite the freedom the studio system offered him—or perhaps, *because* of it—he drank too much, slept around too much, became just "too much" in general for the studio to bear. His contract was not renewed: although Greer would continue to freelance in the movies, most of his time was spent running a very fashionable salon on Sunset Boulevard.

Promoted to top dog, Banton, for a time, managed to keep his own carousing in check. Possibly with his colleague-in-crime gone, he was able to better focus on his work, for it's in the 1928–1935 period that Banton reached his creative apex.

Looking back, Norman Norrell, a critic for *Women's Wear Daily*, commented, "Banton never got the recognition he deserved. Personally, I think Banton was a better designer than Adrian—better for modern dress, although he had great drama too. There's a timelessness about this man."

Nowhere does that timelessness appear more evident than in the costumes Banton designed for Marlene Dietrich, at the dawn of the sound era. Dietrich, who had emerged from the lesbian demimonde of Berlin, did not try to disguise her relationships with women or her penchant for traditionally male attire. Enchanted with Banton's design of a tuxedo for her in *Morocco,* she asked him to design a male suit for her personal use: broad shoulders, smart lapels, collar shirt, and necktie. Travis gladly obliged.

"To design for Marlene was a designer's dream," he'd recall. "I was never afraid to try something new and daring on her, knowing she would give it distinctive style."

That style has become legend: Dietrich in *Dishonored* in a coat of monkey-fur trim, feathered hat, and long black dotted veil. Dietrich in *The Devil Is a Woman* in angled hat, black satin ruffles, sequins, lace, and carnations. Such costuming took chances: in lesser hands, the exotic star might have come off looking ridiculous.

In a scene indelibly etched in the memories of generations of moviegoers, Dietrich emerges from the shadows in *Shanghai Express,* the enigmatic play of light and dark causing one's breath to catch in the throat. But it's not simply the striking chiaroscuro of her face that prompts such a reaction. When we first see her, as the debased siren of the East ("It took more than one man to change my name to Shanghai Lily"), she is wearing a black silk crepe dress, a black cloche of intricately woven feathers, and a spidery veil obscuring all but her lips. Around her shoulders swells a boa of *coq* feathers, while strands of jet beads dangle from her neck to her waist.

It is testimony to Banton's genius that the sublimity of the moment is not lost amid such a swirl of disparate and excessive elements. His was a touch that was highly individual: he found what was natural for his subject, and went from there. Feathers and veils rested comfortably on Dietrich; they would have been incongruous draped over Carole Lombard.

Although Dietrich proved his *pièce de résistance,* Banton worked successfully with Paramount's other actresses as well. "Carole Lombard was just a tootsie when she came to Paramount," said one colleague, "but Travis saw things in her even she didn't know she had." Lombard, who counted many gay men among her close friends (at least before her marriage to Clark Gable), called Banton "Teasie," and accepted without question whatever he designed for her. He dressed her in simple yet sensual lines, emphasizing her common-sense intelligence and good-natured sexuality. He was also close friends with Lilyan Tashman, who was about as open a lesbian as the film colony ever knew, admiring her "frank and lusty interest in clothes."

For Mae West, he ordered "diamonds—lots of 'em," as well as huge hats, boas, fox stoles, and tight sequined gowns to showcase her hourglass figure. For Dietrich, sublimity; for West, camp. West was duly pleased that Banton understood her sensibility as well as he did. Recalling her run-in with his district attorney uncle, she told him, "Wish I'd known you when the fireworks were going off."

GOWNS BY ADRIAN

By the late 1920s, Paramount and Metro-Goldwyn-Mayer were rival courts, with their prima donna designers often set up in opposition to each other. Travis Banton and Gilbert Adrian—the latter more commonly known simply by his surname—were the rival queens constantly being compared and contrasted in the press.

They had their similarities, but significant differences, too. Like Banton, Adrian came from a comfortable, middle-class family—but his was a *Jewish* family in the small Catholic industrial town of Naugatuck, Connecticut. Born Adrian Adolph Greenberg in 1903, his origin was a fact the world-famous single-named couturier preferred as few people to know as possible.

On Church Street the Greenbergs were the only Jews, surrounded by Irish Catholics and German Wasps, with names like Murphy and Warner and Andrews and St. John. That awareness of being different, of being apart from the ruling majority, seems to have stayed with him: in later life, Adrian's version of his family and background was not so much untrue as it was incomplete.

"His parents were middling well-to-do," wrote Hedda Hopper some years later, when the Adrian image was paramount. "His mother was an artist. His grandfather ran an art gallery. Many people think Adrian is a foreigner but his antecedents are deeply rooted in America. There is Bohemian blood far back in the family tree, which may be why he is a nonconformist."

That far-back "Bohemian blood" was as close as Adrian would ever get to publicly acknowledging his Jewishness. In his press, the "nonconformist" often referred to himself as a New Englander, with all the Wasp culture and Mayflower descent that implied. He'd give his full name, when pressed, as *Gilbert* Adrian; his father, he said, was Gilbert Adrian Sr. (Even when his parents came out to Hollywood, their names were retroactively changed to match their son's.)

But it was Gilbert *Greenberg* who ran a milliner's shop in downtown Naugatuck and who wanted nothing more than to see his son graduate from Yale Law School. Gilbert and Helena Greenberg inspired Adrian with dreams of social ascendance that Sam and Hattie Greer could never have imagined. The Greenbergs' successful business gave them the means with which to support their aspirations. They regularly took the train into New York to buy up stocks of French ribbons and willow plumes, keeping up with the orders placed at their shop for motoring hats and Easter bonnets.

There's the hint of some cultural ambivalence on their parts, a trait perhaps passed on to their son. Gilbert Greenberg always made clear that his father was born in England and his mother "at sea." In 1920, Helena Greenberg told a census enumerator that both her parents were native-born, when in truth they were German-born Jews. What's fascinating is that the Greenbergs were probably better off financially than most of their Christian neighbors, who were mostly unskilled laborers in Naugatuck's rubber factories and woollen mills. It must have been an odd dichotomy, a feeling of being both superior and inferior to the community at the same time.

Their hopes were pinned on their son, who, even by the age of three, was proving not to be a typical boy. He'd collect scraps of lace, satin, and felt from his father's shop, reveling in their look and feel. He'd remember sketching, on the wallpaper and in the flyleaves of books, "rather weird, imaginative things that terrified my mother." Some of these sketches survived: queer little people in pointed shoes, who'd provide the basis for Adrian's design of the Munchkins in *The Wizard of Oz*.

In school, he eschewed athletics and was known as a quiet, sensitive boy. Like Banton, he drew sketches that surprised his teachers: sinewy, erotic women in lavish costumes emulating the style of Aubrey Beardsley. At age twelve he illustrated the stories of Edgar Allan Poe. He was fortunate, he'd recall later, to have had such indulgent parents. As terrified as Helena might have been initially, she and Gilbert encouraged Adrian's peculiar art. When he was sixteen, they enrolled him in the New York School of Fine and Applied Art.

During his brief tenure at the school, Adrian formed a close relationship with one of his teachers, the twenty-six-year-old Robert Kalloch, the same man who had taught Travis Banton several years earlier. Also homosexual, Kalloch was known professionally by just his surname, and he proved influential on Adrian. Despite his student's low grades, Kalloch recommended Adrian to the summer Gloucester Playhouse as a costume designer. It was there that the youngster decided to drop the Greenberg—as Kalloch had dropped the Robert—and become simply *Adrian*.

Robert Riley, Adrian's biographer and friend, said that Gilbert Greenberg was understandably upset by the name change and what it implied: "that his son was becoming fancy, that he was trying to avoid a Jewish name." In fact, he wasn't just avoiding it, he was *obliterating* it. Needing a response to the question of whether "Adrian" was a first or last name, he made it the *surname,* and for his given name, he appropriated his father's. To him it was the only solution: whereas Kalloch could safely admit "Robert" without disturbing the sophisticated image he sought for himself, it wouldn't do for Adrian to admit "Greenberg." So he became Gilbert Adrian from New England from then on.

He wasn't much of a scholar, chafing under the rigid discipline of academia. Something happened; it was never clear what; but within months his teachers decided he'd be better off transferred to their Paris branch. He'd fit in better there, they told his parents.

Gay Paree. At the Bal du Grand Prix at the Opera House, where "the young, the raffish, the artists, everyone but the properly respectable" gathered to show off their finery, Adrian watched as Erté, then some years before his MGM contract, was carried in on a platter, his hair and body powdered white and covered with pearls. Erté would remain a fascination. When the flamboyant designer arrived in the United States in 1925, Adrian presented him with a photograph of himself inscribed: "From one who feels like squealing."

Soon afterward, hired by Hassard Short to design costumes for Irving Berlin's "Music Box Revue," Adrian dropped out of school, thus ending his formal education. His brilliance was never in traditional technique but always in his idiosyncrasies—a maverick style that left other designers both dismissive and envious. Seeing Adrian's work back in New York, Berlin's chief designer, Charles LeMaire, called them "very nice drawings," but predicted they'd never work as costumes. Consequently he vetoed much of Adrian's contributions to the show.

LeMaire is the only older gay man on record who seemed impervious to Adrian's spell. "He was a charming, slim, elegant boy with a very long face lit up by strange eyes," Erté would recall. Indeed, Adrian had matured into a strikingly handsome, debonair young man, and many were glad to take him under their wings. He became friendly with the producer Charles Dillingham, although once again LeMaire scuttled any chance of professional advancement from the relationship. Adrian charged that LeMaire was trying to keep him off Broadway. The haughty LeMaire only scoffed. "The trouble is," he said, "you don't design what people want. You design to suit yourself."

Precisely. Soon that peculiar, particular style would be *exactly* what people wanted. After designing for "The Greenwich Village Follies" and George White's "Scandals," Adrian was hired by Natacha Rambova, who adored Adrian's eccentricities and considered him perfect to design costumes for her husband, Rudolph Valentino. Moving to Hollywood, the twenty-year-old prodigy became a flamboyant presence. He decorated the walls of his apartment on Highland Avenue with silver tea papers and was soon seen all over town in a white suit and black cape lined in red satin.

His film work was equally as dramatic. For Valentino's costumes in *The Eagle,* he interpreted a Russian cossack uniform, and the tall astrakhan hats were copied by fashion designers nationwide. So pleased was Adrian with his work on the film that when Valentino's estate was auctioned after his death in 1926, he bought for himself one of the flaring cossack coats he'd designed for the star.

Choosing not to go back to New York with Valentino after their first pictures were completed, he instead entertained job offers from the studios. Once again, it was a gay man who provided the link: Mitchell Leisen, who seemed as taken with Adrian's looks as he was by his talent. Just five years older, Leisen would nonetheless remember Adrian as "just out of high school . . . I liked his sketches and so did DeMille and he was hired."

There was probably a bit more to it than that. According to David Chierichetti, "Leisen told me he once traveled from Los Angeles to New York in a stateroom on a train with his costume-designing protege Gilbert Adrian. Adrian woke him up in the middle of the night by tickling his nose with a feather, and Leisen's raised eyebrows conveyed to me the idea that he and Adrian subsequently had sex."

On Leisen's recommendation, Adrian took over wardrobe duties for De-Mille. He would go on to design several DeMille pictures, including the Biblical extravaganza *The King of Kings* in 1927. The film marked the first time Adrian could lavish his female characters with the kind of attention he once gave his exquisite childhood sketches. Jacqueline Logan's Mary Magdalene looks more like a Babylonian princess than a peasant prostitute, with her embroidered velvets and a bouffant skirt of leopard skin, her breasts barely covered with a spiral of strategically placed jewels. Onto the quintessential Christian epic, Adrian Adolph Greenberg had placed his unmistakable stamp.

When DeMille moved over for a brief tenure producing for MGM, Adrian followed. But whereas DeMille would be gone within a couple years, Adrian settled in for an astonishing career at the studio he'd help transform. "The MGM look" owes as much to Adrian's costumes as it does to Cedric Gibbons' interiors. He ruled the wardrobe department like a prince, and was treated as such: his contract promised one trip per year to New York, expenses fully paid. His screen credit, reflecting his preference to design only for women, would read "Gowns by Adrian," rather than the more crass "wardrobe" or "costumes." He made $1,000 a week.

He signed his first, seven-year contract during a momentous period. In that time sound came to moving pictures; fashions changed; the influence of Art Deco swept the cinema. But Adrian remained steadfast in his own iconoclasm. It's not surprising that his most successful professional relationship would be with another iconoclast: Garbo.

Banton had Dietrich; Adrian had Garbo. Legend has it that when he first saw her, done up by Andre-ani as a flapper, he became livid. "It's all wrong," he said, instinctively. "She's a tree, rooted to the ground." For their first collaboration, *A Woman of Affairs,* Adrian designed clothes that became Garbo trademarks: the famous slouch hat and the loosely belted trenchcoat. *Women's Wear Daily* featured the look, and it took off across America.

For Joan Crawford, who was definitely *not* a tree, he designed clothes fast and furious. With Crawford, Adrian could play with ruffles and frills, with short, sassy modern skirts perfect for dancing the Charleston atop tables. She had broad shoulders, a long waist, and short legs—a designer's nightmare. But not for Adrian. He simply made her shoulders even broader, which in turn made her hips seem smaller. Padded shoulders became the rage: Adrian would remark, "Who would ever believe my whole career would rest on Joan Crawford's shoulders?"

For *Madam Satan* (1930), one of his last collaborations with DeMille before the director left MGM, less was more. A quirky, extravagant, definitely pre-Code film, it climaxes in a bacchanalian costume party aboard a dirigible. Kay Johnson enters in a black velvet cloak, a serpent's head etched in mother-of-pearl sequins on the back. "Which one of you is man enough to go to hell with Madam Satan?" she asks, throwing off the cloak to reveal an ingenious costume of flesh-colored mesh that gives, at first glance, the impression of nudity.

"Adrian often disregarded what many considered 'appropriate' or 'good taste,'" said Robert Riley. "Those who lived by rigid standards were outraged." They were confounded, too, by a personal style that was surprisingly contemporary. "To add excitement to his own wardrobe," Riley said, "he'd wear ties that matched shirts that in turn toned in with the offbeat color of his suits. Everything was done for effect—*his* effect. As Charles LeMaire had said, Adrian designed to please himself. His costumes, his dinner parties, his paintings, were as much an extension of himself as the ideas he could express so persuasively."

Such freedom of expression was a rare gift for a gay man in 1930. Adrian likely wouldn't have found it had he followed his father's early wish that he become a lawyer. He wouldn't have found it in practically any other profession, not even within certain areas of the film industry. But in costume, the walls might have been painted lavender, as a character remarks in the film *The Broadway Melody* (1929). Adrian was never as indiscreet in his personal life as Howard Greer or Travis Banton over at Paramount, where the climate was more tolerant than at MGM. But stories still got around, probably apocryphal: a night out with Joan Crawford, both of them picking up men at the Montmarte; attractive young sketch artists being hired more for their looks than for their talent.

"Certainly, in the beginning, when I first met him," recalled his friend, Los Angeles socialite Mignon Winans, "he was with this very tall, handsome, young blondish man. He was open about it."

He was far from the only one. In the days before the Production Code profoundly changed the political climate in Hollywood, Adrian was less inclined to disguise his homosexuality than his Jewishness: recall the letter describing his effeminacy and how the men kidded him. His camouflage as a New England Yankee with a European flair deflected any attention from his Jewish origins. His employers might have all been Jews, but better for the *image* to align himself not with the crudity of a Louis B. Mayer but with the refinement of an Erté—or even, for that matter, a Travis Banton.

Yet while Adrian, in the beginning, may not have obscured his gayness to the extent he did his Jewishness, neither was he as nonchalant about it as Greer or Banton. Adrian, the most disciplined of all the great costume designers, also had the greatest success: he would set the style not only for the screen but for popular fashion as well. That success came with some cost, however. If Greer had been too indiscreet, Adrian honed discretion to a fine art. Just as he had with his Jewish last name, he would increasingly move to distance himself from any homosexual association. In that, he was hardly the iconoclast—but rather perfectly in step with the changing times.

A DIVISION OF LABOR:
THE ART DEPARTMENT OF THE SOUND ERA

By the early talkie era, Wardrobe was undeniably gay, but it remained a ghetto within a rapidly changing Art Department—one that bore little resemblance to the silent days of Hopkins, Leisen, and Grieve. By bringing a greater realism to the cinema, sound had outdated the stylized, stage-like aesthetic of silent pictures. "This [had been] the era of beautiful women and handsome male stars disporting themselves against lavish backgrounds in perfect escapist fashion," George James Hopkins said of the silent era. "With the advent of sound came reality."

For talkies, sets needed to be designed with the microphone in mind, with perfect acoustics that allowed pristine recording and prevented any outside noise. In this new realism, sets were constructed so that they might be viewed from many different angles. The art director of the sound era, therefore, was far more likely to be an architect than a painter or a decorator, and few would come in as green as Harold Grieve.

The changeover in the Art Department between silent and sound eras was striking. In 1921 the *Motion Picture Annual* listed just three art directors with a background in architecture; the rest were painters, stage designers, and costumers. By the late 1920s, however, nearly *all* were architects. MGM unit art director Arthur Lonergan told an interviewer that when he arrived on the lot in the 1930s, knowledge of architecture was an absolute requirement for the job, because "ninety percent" of what they did involved architectural work.

There is further significance to the architect–art director model: the new designers tended to be heterosexual, far more so than their silent-era counterparts. Given that the ranks of architects and draughtsmen were traditionally less populated with homosexuals (at least overt ones), it's not surprising to read the names of the sound-era art directors and observe that, as far as we can know, they were all straight: Lonergan, Boris Leven, Robert Haas, Frank Hotaling, Stephen Goosson, Van Nest Polglase, Robert Odell, just to name a few. In effect, the changeover to sound split the old art department into two: wardrobe, which was gay, and set design, which was straight.

"Hardly any of the art directors were gay," said Michael Grace, who made the acquaintance of many of them through his uncle Henry, supervising set decorator at MGM, and his father, Saunders Grace, who did the sets for dozens of films and television programs. "Most of them were draughtsmen and didn't know chintz from chenille." There were exceptions, he said: Paramount art director Hans Dreier, who dated Grace's aunt, was "very elegant but straight . . . unlike many of the art directors, he also knew decor and had taste regarding interiors. I think he was the minority, though. Most of the art directors just drew plans."

In the theater—where nearly all of the silent movie designers had hailed from—there wasn't as much of a need for technical backgrounds. Stage designer Stewart Chaney, who learned design basics doing window displays for Lord & Taylor, was no architect—but he *did* design an entire house on the stage for Broadway's "The 49th Cousin." The difference, of course, was that Chaney's house was viewed only from the single perspective of the traditional proscenium theater. Chaney was one of the stage's leading set designers; like his early film cousins, he also did costumes. Like them, too, he was gay, as were most of the theater's great scenic designers.

Not so cinema's masters of design. By the time of the "talkers," Harold Grieve recalled, he felt he no longer fit in. "When I was there [working in the studios] you were a complete identity," he said. "I'd been spoiled. I did everything, and there were very few art directors who had the privilege of doing what I had done, because it was always split up." Grieve left the in-

dustry to go into private interior decoration. (He'd also marry former actress Jetta Goudal.) Likewise, George James Hopkins, finding himself increasingly out of step in the studio, got a job decorating theater interiors for
the Fox chain. Leisen, with his architecture background, continued for a
time, although he shared Grieve's discomfort with the new field and soon
moved into direction.

Under the new paradigm, gays designed the costumes; straights designed
the sets. On the surface, it had nothing to do with homosexuality. The fact
that gays were infrequent architects speaks to sociocultural limitations and
assumptions, not to any specific studio policy. But the transformation of art
direction from "artistic" to "architectural" work—in effect, from "queer
work" to "straight work"—was nonetheless dramatic.

From the early 1930s on, art direction became the near-exclusive do-
main of heterosexuals. A survey of MGM's art department personnel taken
in 1943 for the Selective Service revealed that of 108 employees, a whop-
ping 84 percent were married, and of the remaining eighteen single employees, six were under the age of twenty-two. Art direction became, like
cinematography, a family business: Ralph Berger, art director at Universal
and RKO, was one of several unit art directors who trained his sons to follow in his career. They became known as "he-men," often the chums of the
director. Art direction could be *dangerous* work, after all: unit art directors
David Townsend and Harrison Wiley were both killed, in separate accidents for different studios, scouting locations for their films in 1935.
Machismo was in; the effeteness of a Hopkins or Grieve was out.

That's not to suggest that *all* the artists were winnowed out of the departments. Those who could fit in and keep up survived. Jack Okey was an
artist, and had a long career as an art director. But Okey was also straight—
a well-liked, slap-on-the-back kind of guy. And certainly many of the architects developed an artistic sensibility: one only needs view the work of a
Charles D. Hall or Richard Day to be convinced of this.

Then there was Cedric Gibbons, perhaps the most famous art director of
all time. As supervising art director of MGM, he carried great authority,
and was always seen as different from the others, a man apart. Inspired by
the landmark Exposition des Arts Décoratifs in Paris in 1925, Gibbons had
brought the Art Deco style to MGM films, and consequently, to American
architecture. Yet, although he was the son of an architect, he wasn't one
himself. Rather, like Banton and Adrian, he studied art and commercial design at the Art Students League. At MGM, he supervised the unit art directors—nearly all architects—but had little say over their designs. Arthur
Lonergan would remember he "pretty much left us alone."

Design historian John Hambley observed, "Gibbons' influence on film
design was gigantic, but where other key figures led by the example of their

personal creative will, Gibbons simply imposed his own taste and standards and demanded that his art directors achieve them."

Indeed, whereas other studio art department heads were known to fraternize with their unit art directors, Gibbons stood apart, different from the men under him. Scenic art chief George Gibson—like most of Gibbons' colleagues, a married man with children—worked in rolled-up sleeves and a smock. He'd recall Gibbons, always resplendent in suit, tie, and flower in his lapel, chiding him for his sartorial sloppiness. "George, goddamn it," Gibbons would say. "Why don't you get yourself a jacket!"

Rumors were perhaps inevitable about Gibbons. Extraordinarily handsome and well dressed, he was, for many years, a bachelor. His secretary, according to MGM research chief Elliot Morgan, was a very obvious lesbian. Finally, in 1930, at the age of thirty-seven, Gibbons married the actress Dolores Del Rio. The gay screenwriter DeWitt Bodeen, who made it a point to know the stories of everyone in Hollywood, would later write about the Gibbons-Del Rio match. "He was a shy man, twelve years older than she, but their engagement was announced only a few weeks after they had met, and shortly thereafter they were married in the chapel of the historic Santa Barbara Mission. Gibbons' marriage to one of Hollywood's most beautiful women took many by surprise."

"Shy man." "Took many by surprise." This is code, especially as written by a gay writer (who would himself comment on the "cryptic" quality of reporter Herbert Howe's work). Shortly after the marriage, Del Rio (about whom there were also rumors) suffered a nervous breakdown. She'd only say enigmatically that "tragic, terrifying things . . . cross-currents of human purposes" had crashed around her.

They were married for many years; it was reportedly a passionate coupling, with Gibbons playing Romeo to Del Rio's Juliet on the stairs of their house in Santa Monica Canyon. They weren't shy to admit to reporters, however, that they slept in separate bedrooms. In most cases, Gibbons loathed the press: life was too short, he told them, to waste on interviews. After their divorce, Gibbons married again, to another beautiful actress, but neither marriage produced any children.

Gibbons lived and died a very private man. Certainly such privacy, if he *were* gay, would have been understandable, given the nature of his occupation—far more understandable than Adrian's, for example, in a department universally perceived as queer. Art direction, on the other hand, required membership in a kind of "old boys' club," where actual artists were in short supply. Gibbons was never one of the old boys, but he commanded their respect; and because of that, he endured until the 1950s, leaving his incomparable mark on the American cinema.

• • •

According to Frank Lysinger, the companion of set dresser Richard Pefferle, most of the property department considered Gibbons to be homosexual. They would know: what gay presence remained in the art department by the early sound era was found here, among the set dressers. They would eventually achieve greater influence and recognition in the filmmaking process, but in the early Thirties, they were used primarily by the art director to select the right carpeting, curtains, or antiques to complement their sets.

At MGM, the set dressers were under the immediate supervision of property chief Edwin B. Willis. Born in 1893 in Illinois, Willis was briefly married and adopted a daughter. By 1920, however, he shared a home with his sister, helping to raise her children, one of whom was Lionel Lindon, later a well-known cameraman. Starting as an actor, Willis would move over to the prop department at Goldwyn by the late Teens, remaining through the 1924 merger. His staff knew he was gay, but, like Gibbons, he rarely fraternized with them. "I always found him very attractive," said Frank Lysinger. "Not handsome. Sexy. Big and masculine."

Departmental records do reveal a close working relationship between Gibbons and Willis, however. In September 1931, for example, Gibbons sent the prop department chief a note with a torn-out magazine page featuring a miniature silver locomotive. Thinking they might look pretty nifty in an upcoming picture, Gibbons requested that Willis have several of them cast. Willis apparently looked into the matter, determined the cost to be about $60 each, and sent a memo back up to the boss. There's no further communication on the matter; perhaps the high cost dampened Gibbons' enthusiasm.

The role of the set dresser would develop in importance as the decade went on. By the late 1930s, they'd be officially designated as "set decorators" (see Chapters 7, "Queer Work," and 8, "War Spirit"), a small gay enclave in the midst of a very macho-oriented Art Department. What was already obvious by the early Thirties was that the breakdown in the department had created distinct areas of "queer work," forever impacting the experience of homosexuals in the Hollywood studios.

GIRLS WITH IMAGINATION

HOLLYWOOD'S FIRST LESBIANS

1919-1935

I t's a fitting confluence that Dorothy Arzner began her career as a script girl to Nazimova: the most famous lesbian of the silent era mentoring the young woman who would go on to become the "sole distaff-side director" of Hollywood's Golden Age.

Herbert Cruikshank, whose frequent byline in the fan magazines suggests he knew the score, wrote of Arzner's beginnings: "With the nerve of a movie trade paper ad solicitor at Christmas time, she invaded the sacred precincts of Alla Nazimova's dressing room. And she came out a full-fledged script-girl."

Such code isn't hard to decipher: Dorothy Arzner had an affair with Madame Nazimova during the making of *Stronger Than Death* in 1919. Some have expressed skepticism; Nazimova, after all, was known to be very involved with the actress Jean Acker at the time. But Gavin Lambert, Nazimova's biographer, believed the story to be true. He sourced George Cukor, who was friends with both Nazimova and Arzner, and who scrupulously "separated falsehood from truth before passing on a story."

In any event, it would have been a short affair, a diversion for Nazimova, but no doubt a great thrill for the young, ambitious Arzner. Nazimova was, after all, one of the most powerful women in Hollywood, and her sophisticated soirees were the buzz of the town.

She was also an unapologetic lesbian. Tiny, with enormous purple (yes, *purple*) eyes and a shock of dark unruly hair, she would become a sexual aggressor of legend. When the director Erich Von Stroheim's daughter confided to George James Hopkins that she'd once knocked the great Nazimova to the floor after an unwelcome grope, Hopkins believed her. "I knew this was not idle gossip," he recorded, "having seen with my own eyes Nazimova in action in New York."

She was often billed Nazimova (Herself). Born in Russia, she became a giant of Broadway, even having a theater named after her. She was *the* interpreter of Ibsen—achingly, outrageously, and unavoidably tragic. When she transferred to film, her magnetic persona nearly melted the celluloid. Never before had there been anything like her. When Metro brought her to Hollywood—at an unheard-of salary of $13,000 per week—it was as a rival to Theda Bara, but Nazimova *decimated* poor Theodosia. She represented a new, hipper, more *sophisticated* view of sex. In her films, she pursued men not just for control but out of *desire*—an undisguised lust no woman had ever before exhibited on the screen.

"Nazimova," mused Darryl F. Zanuck, looking back. "The quintessential queen of the movie whores. It was the only time Hollywood let a star come near to orgasm on the screen."

What made Nazimova different from Bara? From other vamps like Louise Glaum or Valeska Suratt? Talent, for one, obviously: Nazimova's was gigantic. But Theodosia Goodman was happy chatting the night away with her pals Hopkins and Ryszard Ordynski, modeling new outfits for their oohs and ahhs in her hotel room. Nazimova would have had no time for such parlor games. Her passion was barely contained, in life or on the screen.

And—at least after 1918, after a passionate affair with Mercedes de Acosta—it was *lesbian* passion. In her few films that survive, what's preserved for all time is *lesbian passion*—passion that breaks rules, defies tradition, reverses gender roles, challenges assumptions—lesbian passion, even though it's ostensibly directed at a man.

Some reviewers seemed to catch it. "Her vogue," wrote one, "is based not so much on the perfection of productions as on her own bizarre personality and artistry, and seemingly an overwhelming appeal for the feminine sex."

In *Camille* (1921) she is cold and aloof to her Armand—Rudolph Valentino, then just breaking into stardom—and only really comes alive in the scenes with her friend Nichette, played by the young ingenue Patsy

Ruth Miller. Here Nazimova displays the kind of passion she'd become known for, but this time makes the lesbian impulse obvious, *blatant*— fondling and caressing the young girl, kissing her on the mouth four times. (In this she anticipates both Dietrich and Garbo.) Nazimova's twist on Dumas was heralded in an opening intertitle—"Why not a Camille of today?"—her idea—but the interpretation was *so* twisted that even Eva LeGallienne, herself a lesbian, was reported to be "shocked."

As Madame became more bold and eccentric, audiences began to fall away. Still, she persisted. Encouraged by her associate, the maverick costume and set designer Natacha Rambova, with whom she likely fell in love and had an affair, she produced *Salome* (1923). Today the stylized film is high camp and has gone down in legend as an "all-gay" production, supposedly Nazimova's homage to its author, Oscar Wilde. Gavin Lambert, in his biography of Nazimova, quoted one of the extras, who said some of the cast were gay and others weren't, adding, "There's nothing surprising or unusual about that." What *is* unusual was the casting of drag queens to mix in among the court ladies, and the gay sexual subplot: the lust between a Roman soldier, in a sleeveless lamé armor, and a Syrian captain with painted nipples and black tights.

By this time, Nazimova had become too outré for movie audiences, but she remained a powerhouse socially. In 1918 she bought a spectacular house at 8080 Sunset Boulevard, remodeled the interior, built a swimming pool, and transformed the three and a half acres into a lush tropical garden. "The Garden of Alla," she proclaimed—and the "8080 Club" soon became a gathering place for the trendiest, smartest, most adventuresome of the Hollywood set.

Despite the fact that she pretended to be married to a man, which allowed her to trade with some social currency, Nazimova in truth disregarded the manners and mores of Hollywood's middle-class guardians. No longer just a town of rednecks and cowboys, the film colony had come to accommodate an increasing number of New York and European theater émigrés whose tastes, values, and sexual habits were defiantly not middle class.

"There is no question," one well-placed industry figure told Thoreau Cronyn of the *New York Herald* in 1922, "that some of the well-known stage people who were brought out here a few years ago raised the deuce. They could not get over that Hollywood was either a one-night stand or a pleasure resort with the sky the limit."

At the Garden of Alla even the sky was too low. They lived on the cutting edge: playwrights, royalty, poets, fashion designers—all in Hollywood to pay court to Nazimova. Her regulars at the Garden of Alla included the flamboyant Mae Murray and her husband-director Robert Z. Leonard; screenwriter June Mathis; pianist Leopold Godowsky and his daughter Dagmar; the Talmadge sisters; and the Mdvani brothers, who were adamant in their claim to be Georgian princes.

At the heart of the Garden of Alla's sophistication, however, was lesbianism. Nazimova fashioned a West Coast complement to the lesbian salons of Elisabeth Marbury and Elsie de Wolfe that she had known in New York. Everyone in Hollywood understood that occasionally Nazimova's parties were only for girls. Madame even admitted to *Photoplay* that most of her friends were "young girls," and she enjoyed fostering the image of the foreign sexual sophisticate. To the soirees at the 8080 Club she invited intelligent young actresses who had intrigued her—"usually of a somewhat masculine type," recalled her sister. "She would take up with one 'pet' and that person would be for a short time exclusively hers. . . . I recall her sitting like a Goddess surrounded by these adoring neophytes, usually insignificant actresses."

Nazimova and her pets. It's impossible to overstate the impact they made on the nascent film industry. She was one of the first to define the publicity and the imagery herself. If by the Roaring Twenties Hollywood had become a haven for people who lived on the edge, much of the credit for that evolution must go to Madame Nazimova and her dazzlingly defiant personality, and the sophistication and sensibility she fostered at the 8080 Club.

THE LESBIAN NETWORK OF THE EARLY STUDIOS

If Madame liked her girls "somewhat masculine," then Dorothy Arzner more than fit the bill. Perennially in trousers and neckties, her short hair combed like a teenage boy's—complete with cowlick—Arzner was a femme's baby-butch dream. Just twenty-one when Nazimova met her, she was to older lesbians what George James Hopkins had been to Frohman and Gest, and Adrian to Dillingham and Leisen.

Born Emma Dorothy Arzner in San Francisco on January 3, 1897, she was the daughter of Louis and Jenette (Young) Arzner. Louis had been born in Munich, Germany, emigrating to the United States in 1882; Jenette was born in Scotland. Dorothy lost her mother early. After the disastrous earthquake and fire of 1906, Louis moved his motherless children south to Los Angeles, where he remarried Mabel Gorsuch. Dorothy would write that she was raised mostly by her grandmother; this was likely her *step*-grandmother, Mabel's mother, Lizzie Holmes, who lived with them.

Louis was a "loving father," Dorothy remembered, but he was busy as the proprietor of the bustling, popular Hoffman Cafe at 215 South Spring Street in downtown L.A. "It smelled of garlic and spices and beer," recalled the writer Ivan St. Johns. "It was a small place, with dark panelled walls and dim, warm lights. The kind of place where folks went for dinner and left at two o'clock in the morning—and there was no dancefloor and no music."

It was the Sardi's of the Teens on the West Coast: D. W. Griffith, Charlie Chaplin, Mack Sennett, Mickey Neilan, William S. Hart—often at the same time—might be found around the special "movie table," separated from the main dining room by a velvet drape. "They loved the Hoffmans and they loved old Louis Arzner," remembered St. Johns. "And they all knew his daughter, little Dorothy, who used to come and walk about the tables with big serious blue eyes, never saying a word but always looking."

Early movie folklorists couldn't resist the romance of it, imagining the young Dorothy with chin in hands, mooning over the pioneers' descriptions of their days on the set. But Dorothy, who grew to detest sentiment, would have none of it. "Not true!" she scrawled on a student dissertation, submitted for her comments, when the author described a starstruck young Arzner listening raptly to the stories of Griffith and Chaplin.

She wasn't the sort to moon around and daydream. She was a girl of action, serious and independent. She'd dress up as a male alter ego, "Garth," and, in a series of photographs taken at the time (one wonders by whom), looks supremely at ease in her boy's attire. Early on, she determined she'd be a doctor, and developed a reputation among her friends as "a modern girl." In 1911, Mabel Arzner, concerned that her stepdaughter was becoming too much of a tomboy, enrolled Dorothy at the prestigious Westlake School for Girls. She was an above-average student: her report cards show her best grades in mathematics (algebra, economics) and lowest in languages (French and Latin, for which she received IIIs, the equivalent of Cs.)

Graduating from Westlake in 1915, she began studies that fall at the University of Southern California, where medicine was still her goal. When President Wilson declared war on Germany in April 1917, Arzner joined a local ambulance corps, headed by movie director William de Mille, in the hopes of being sent overseas. She doesn't say what Munich-born Louis Arzner felt about the war, but *she* was raring to go. Her hopes proved in vain, however: although later publicity implied she had tended to soldiers wounded on the battlefield, in truth she never left L.A.

She was indeed an unusual girl, wanting to march off to war when even the Great God Kerrigan didn't want to go. William de Mille was certainly impressed with her; as a favor, he gave her and some friends a tour of the Famous Players-Lasky studios. Her pals, dazzled, told Dorothy that since she was a "modern girl" and motion pictures a "modern business," then it was a match made in heaven.

Dorothy, intrigued herself, had to agree.

The typical story of the young woman infatuated by the movies usually has her wanting to become a star. But not *all* girls wanted to dress up in fabulous gowns and pose pretty in front of the camera; *some* had other interests. Right from the start, what fascinated Dorothy Arzner was the mechanics *behind* the scenes, and she determined to learn everything she could.

It was good-bye, Dr. Arzner. Once again, in detailing Arzner's rise to the top, Herbert Cruikshank writes less than he knows. He reports Dorothy telling de Mille that she was willing to start at the bottom to get a job in the industry. "My dear young lady," Cruikshank quotes de Mille as responding, "where, pray, do you believe the bottom of the motion picture industry to *be?*"

Here Cruikshank winks at his reader: "Now Dorothy could have pulled a lot of nifties right there. But she knew that would be out of character. Maybe, however, there was a bit of an unconscious wisecrack when she smiled up at the big, strong mans [sic] and replied in her best Westlake manner: 'Why, the rock-bottom of the motion picture industry is the scenario department.'"

She wasn't wisecracking about that. In the silent era, the scenario department certainly *was* rock-bottom. Important screenwriters (many of them women) tended not to work at the studio. They composed their stories at home in longhand, then sent them in to be translated into correct form by typists in the scenario department—in truth, a highly efficient stenographers' office, but one trained in the specialized craft of scenarios. Dorothy walked in blind; if not for the kindness of colleagues, she'd have been out on her ear the next week.

"She used to sit up nights retyping her work," Cruikshank reported, "and another girl in the office (ah, there was a pal) used to put Dorothy's initials on some of her own pages." The first script she worked on was *The Valley of the Giants,* starring Wallace Reid.

For three months she typed scripts, learning what separated a good script from a bad one. "The script is the blueprint of the structure," she said. "Some might think that a stenographer typing scripts is pigeon-holed for life, but it's a motion picture education to a girl with imagination."

A girl with imagination. It was a phrase she'd use often about herself and about other women she admired in the industry, women who didn't merely accept their lot but rather challenged themselves and their employers. Women had, in fact, made considerable inroads through most areas of the film industry by the mid-Teens. In 1915 Robert Grau observed, "In no line of endeavor has woman made so emphatic an impress than in the amazing film industry. . . . The gentler sex is now so active a factor that one may not name a single vocation in either the artistic or business side [of the industry] in which women are not conspicuously engaged."

Indeed, Arzner had every reason to expect that although she might start at the bottom, she wasn't obligated to stay there. Women were directors (Cleo Madison, Alice Guy, Lois Weber) and screenwriters (Frances Marion, Jeanie MacPherson, Anita Loos) and editors (Mary O'Connor, Hetty Gray Baker) and even executives (Melodile Garbutt at Realart and Agnes Egan Cobb at Eclair). The suffrage movement had allowed a generation of women to consider options they may never have recognized before. In addition, the adolescent industry—still not entirely tamed nor hammered into place—offered opportunities for people of ambition and "imagination." Over and over, Arzner would use that word to explain how she managed to get ahead in a man's world: she had "imagination." Translation: she thought without regard to gender or convention. Dorothy Arzner, in the parlance of today, thought outside of the box.

• • •

Gay historian and critic Michael Bronski has argued that gays and lesbians, by nature, have an advantage in mastering such attitudes. "They've already repudiated a major social definition in regards to their sexuality," he postulated. "Transgressing other boundaries can be a logical step." Popular culture—in this case, the movies—offers a place to be different, "to express non-traditional and non-acceptable desires," thus attracting, according to Bronski, "those already outside the mainstream." Lesbians, especially, had a leg up: "Theater and film were places where women who weren't married could actually get work. And of those who weren't married, many were lesbians." It follows that, traditionally, large numbers of the women who have broken into "men's fields" have in fact been lesbian.

The sexuality of many of Hollywood's early women of influence is, of course, unknown. Weber, Marion, and Loos were all apparently heterosexual, but that's not taking into account the army of women in middle-line positions. Frederica Sagor Maas worked as a story editor at Universal in the 1920s, and in her memoirs recalled hiring assistants, all young women. Later, at MGM, she worked with Fred de Gresac, a self-styled Hungarian countess and an overt lesbian. "Sixtyish, with short, cropped, flaming red hair, Fred wore pants and men's shirts and ties," Maas recalled. "Soon enough I discovered she had designs on females younger than herself, and she aimed her guile in my direction. Since this was my first encounter with a lesbian, I didn't understand what was going on. I found mysterious little gifts on my desk when I came in, with beguiling notes: 'Your liquid brown eyes sear my soul.'" It took fellow writer Ray Doyle to clue Maas in: "That woman is a *les,* stupid. Shake her and tell her to go fly a kite."

It's one more retelling of the old "predatory lesbian" myth, but de Gresac certainly wielded enough influence to safeguard her boldness. There was no need for pretense here: Maas said de Gresac "knew the right people in the front office." Certainly she had a prestigious enough background. Married to the French singer Victor Maurel, de Gresac wrote "La Passerelle" for the great Mme. Rejane on Broadway in 1904 and collaborated with Victor Herbert on the light opera "Sweethearts" in 1913. Coming to Hollywood in 1915 to adapt "La Passerelle" as a film for Fannie Ward, de Gresac stayed on to write *La Boheme* for Lillian Gish, *Son of the Sheik* for Valentino, and *Camille* for Norma Talmadge. Her last picture was a remake of *Sweethearts* for Nelson Eddy and Jeanette MacDonald in 1938. She died in 1943.

Surely Fred wasn't alone. With so many women in the writing pool of the Teens and Twenties, there was bound to be a good number of lesbians among them. Certainly there's an undeniable lesbian read to Arzner's reminiscences of her days in the scenario department. She was taught and encouraged by a fellow typist named Agnes "Mike" Leahy, "a large red-haired girl"—presumably the "pal" of whom Cruikshank writes—who helped her keep up until she became proficient. In fact, it was Mike Leahy who had a contact among Nazimova's company and who helped Arzner secure the script-girl position on the *Stronger Than Death* set.

The lesbian network proved good to little Dorothy. Soon after her experience with Nazimova, she graduated to "cutter," or assistant to the film editors. She was glad for more creative control: "I felt a yearning to get a pair of scissors in my hands and hack film into pieces."

Editing, too, had its share of women. Arzner was trained by Nan Heron, a veteran: "I watched her work on one reel and she let me do the second, while she watched and guided every cut. On Sunday I went into the studio and assembled the next reel. On Monday I told her about it and she looked at it and approved. I finished the picture under her guidance." Impressed with her young charge, Heron got Arzner a job both cutting and holding script on another picture. She would cut thirty-seven pictures in one year.

Time and again, Arzner's story illustrates how women created avenues of access within the early studio structure, often helping each other along. Mike Leahy, Nan Heron, even Nazimova, offered important links to Dorothy as she moved forward.

Within clearly defined fields—editing being one—women could rise through the ranks. Margaret Booth started her illustrious career cutting at the Mayer studios in 1921 and continued editing into the 1980s. Cutting was at first seen as a menial profession; cutters, after all, simply followed the dictates of others. But as they developed their skill into its own particular art form, editors began to contribute their own imprint onto a finished picture. Katherine Eggleston, an editor at Mutual, described how she would view "the different scenes with an eye to clearness of story-construction and dramatic value, establishing sequence and ridding the picture of all that does not contribute to its effectiveness."

That's just what Arzner did editing James Cruze's epic *The Covered Wagon* (1923). So proficient was her work on the film that she was given a full-time contract, reportedly the first time an editor had been so awarded. Cruze took his company into the wilds of Utah for three months of shooting. The crew took bets on how long the little editor would last in the "exposure and real pioneering." She not only lasted, but dazzled Cruze with her ability. "I learned more about pictures in the cutting room than anywhere else," she told Adela Rogers St. Johns.

Watching *The Covered Wagon* today one is struck by how modern its construction feels: it moves swiftly, effortlessly, with none of the seemingly interminable footage of so many silent films. For such a sweeping epic—the story of a pioneer wagon train crossing the country, forging rivers and fending off Indian attacks—it holds to a reasonable time: just about ninety minutes. There is nothing superfluous, not one extraneous frame. Even the long panoramic sweeps of the breathtaking mountainous scenery last only as long as they should. The story proceeds smartly, efficiently. Arzner knew how to create real tension: the fight scene between the upstanding hero and nefarious villain is cut sharply and seamlessly, giving its violence a realism rarely managed even in talkies.

Her achievement is made even more extraordinary when one realizes who played the hero: J. Warren Kerrigan, who could barely punch his way out of a paper bag. There is no documentation of a meeting between Kerrigan and Dorothy Arzner during the filming of *The Covered Wagon*, though as part of the company off in the Utah mountains, they certainly would have known each other. There's no record, either, of what Arzner thought of Kerrigan's performance as she snipped and spliced his scenes.

But this intersection of two key figures, one on his way down and the other on her way up, marks the end of one era and the beginning of another. As the studio system slid its last nuts and bolts into place, those with imagination could chart careers quite remarkable in both their profit and probity. But those unable to recognize the changes in the unwritten rules of the game would simply not be allowed to play.

DOROTHY ARZNER, DIRECTOR

Arzner played, all right—moving next from editor to scenarist. She wrote the script of *Old Ironsides,* a tale of pirates on the high seas—a man's picture if ever there was one. A familiar sight climbing around the ship in her white trousers, Arzner became well liked by cast and crew. She confided to Laurence Stallings, on whose story she'd written the scenario, that next she wanted to direct. It was her belief, she said, "that woman's dramatic sense is invaluable to the motion picture industry."

Yet in the eight years since Arzner's first job in the scenario department, a sea change had occurred for women in the industry. As the mechanics of the studio system became more fixed, the number of female directors had dwindled. Lois Weber hadn't made a picture since 1923 (though she'd have a minor comeback in 1927), and Alice Guy had directed her last film in 1920. Arzner, surely cognizant of this change, told Stallings she was prepared to leave Paramount to accept a job writing scenarios at Columbia. There, at a smaller studio, she believed her chances of getting a directorial assignment were better. Stallings reportedly told her she was too good for Paramount to lose, and the next day spoke with *Old Ironsides* director James Cruze, who'd been Dorothy's champion ever since her expert cutting job on *The Covered Wagon.*

Here the story becomes fuzzy through endless reworkings in mimeographed accounts from the Paramount publicity department. According to some stories, Cruze put in a good word to B. P. Schulberg, and that was enough: Dorothy was tapped to helm her first picture, *Fashions for Women* (1927), starring Esther Ralston. In another version—one that Arzner preferred—she was on her way out, her desk and belongings packed, when she encountered production chief Walter Wanger, who asked her to stay. She agreed, on the condition that within two weeks she was directing an "A" picture: "I'd rather do a picture for a small company [like Columbia] and have my own way than a 'B' picture for a Paramount."

Regardless of how she got there, there was much hoopla in the press about Arzner's promotion. Schulberg turned himself into a pretzel patting himself on the back, calling Arzner the "first woman behind the megaphone in motion picture history"—completely disregarding the pioneering work of Weber, Guy, and others. The publicity department attempted to milk the novel idea of a female director for all it was worth—for who knew how long it might last?

"If I could tell you half the prejudice there has always been in Hollywood against women directors," Ivan St. Johns wrote in *Photoplay,* "you would understand a little of what it means to have Paramount deliberately hand over a megaphone to a woman. Yes, it's something unusual."

It's become Hollywood legend that Arzner would forever need to battle the male hierarchy of the studios, a contention perhaps confirmed by her friend, the screenwriter DeWitt Bodeen, who much later wrote to a friend how he "resented [Dorothy] being pushed around professionally because everybody knew she was a lesbian." But Arzner's own comments usually suggested otherwise. In the first years of her directorial career, she was gracious in her interviews. She told Herbert Cruikshank that her gender had "neither aided nor injured her chances," that in fact she'd never been conscious of her sex in her career. Many times, she expressed the belief that other "women with capabilities" could do what she had done, "providing she is willing to begin at the bottom and *work*." Which, of course, was exactly what (male) studio executives would want her to say.

In fact, Arzner could sometimes sound downright sexist. "Women are too easily diverted from their goal," she said in 1932. "They all carry in their minds the realization that someday someone else will have to worry about supporting them. Men, on the other hand, know that they are going to have to support themselves, and therefore work to build something for themselves."

She would, however, acknowledge the necessity of being at least a little canny. "A woman's intuition isn't worth two hoots in Hollywood," she wrote for *The Hollywood Reporter* in 1932, in an article called "How to Become a Woman Director." (Her wry opening: "There is only one way to become a woman director. You have to be a woman.") She went on: "A director has to think analytically. . . . All fish swim in water; men swim in water; therefore, men are fish. There's a little problem in logical thinking that most women know is wrong through intuition, but men find the answer by determining that everything that swims isn't a fish. I had to learn to reach my conclusions like a man."

She may have *acted* like a man, too—a *straight* man—on the set of her first film, starring the very femme Esther Ralston. "I began to resent some of the sexy scenes Arzner was asking me to do," Ralston recalled, decades later. "The photographing of my backside and the display of my legs just wasn't me!" She marched in to complain to Schulberg, who told Arzner to tone things down. "Arzner never forgave me," Ralston said.

Yet on the set of their next picture, *Ten Modern Commandments,* Arzner seemed *very* forgiving and friendly—*too* friendly, according to Ralston, who was complaining again. "With Arzner trying to get me to sit on her lap between takes and insisting on patting and fondling me, I began to freeze up and resent her attentions. After the picture was finished, I had a long talk with Jesse Lasky about Arzner, and I never had to do another film with her again."

While the anecdote may reveal more about Ralston than it does Arzner—a more extroverted star like Clara Bow found Arzner a delight, and was happily photographed sitting in her lap—historian Anthony Slide admits, "There is no question that by today's standards, such behavior would be labeled sexual harassment." Of course, in a culture that viewed lesbians as predatory, *any* attention from Arzner might have been (mis)interpreted as a sexual advance. Still, directors from the beginning of film history had been notorious for putting the moves on their leading ladies; in this instance, Dorothy Arzner was perhaps being just one of the boys.

With the boys of the crew, in fact, she got along famously, far better than effete gay men like George James Hopkins ever did. The (largely straight) technicians and grips liked Arzner, and she quickly adjusted to their irreverent slang. As she'd point out, the head electrician didn't say politely to his assistant, "Please light that small lamp, third from the left." He just barked: "Hit the baby." Arzner laughed: "I've seen a number of timid visitors start for the exits when they heard the electricians talk like that. But such slang is developed because of the need for clear, fast thinking." She became fluent: "cans" meant the earphones used by sound technicians; "frier," a Technicolor lamp; "tonsil doctor," a technician taking a voice test; and, most ironically, "Kill the broad!"—an order to extinguish a large boxy lamp.

Her approach to direction was far more collaborative than many of her peers. "In the studios, they call her type of direction 'the Dorothy Arzner system,'" Marky Dowling wrote for *Movie Classic*. "She works with the writer upon the script. She directs. Then she supervises the cutting. And the whole becomes a Dorothy Arzner production throughout."

Those productions were hardly typical Hollywood fare. Several studies have examined her films' "preoccupations with communities of women [and] the fragility of the heterosexual couple." In this, Arzner was defiantly *not* one of the boys, and producers had to recognize that. Despite her apparent graciousness in interviews and her insistence that no barriers existed for women in the industry, she crafted a series of films that subvert traditional gender roles and challenge male authority. The women in Arzner's films always confront basic life choices of marriage and career. As critic Myron Meisel wrote, "Arzner deplores the necessity to choose, but if pressed, she unhesitatingly chooses the latter."

The Wild Party (1929) was Arzner's first talking picture, starring Clara Bow, then tops at the box office. Based on a novel by Warner Fabian, it was set in a women's college dormitory. Whereas the novel warns of the dangers of "romantic friendships" and the isolating qualities of communities of women, Arzner made a film that celebrates those very things. Although she eliminated the novel's most overtly lesbian character, Judith Mayne suggested it was less an attempt to maintain invisibility than an effort to depathologize Fabian's story.

Other films continued these themes. In *Christopher Strong* (1933) the feminist spirit of the aviatrix played by Katharine Hepburn empowers the film. She dresses like a man (or rather, like Arzner) throughout; career is as important to her as marriage. Her choice at the end to commit suicide is as much due to her conviction not to compromise her career as it is not to compromise her love.

In one of her more assertive interviews of the period, Arzner revealed more of her ideas of gender equality than she usually let on. "In the next war, women will be used on a great scale," she predicted. "They will be employed in the army, navy, marine corps, and in aviation. This talk about men refusing to fight women is wrong. Both sides shot down women and children during the last war. Why would they have any qualms killing women with guns? Women are writing the literary works of today; women are achieving wonders in science, in aviation, in every walk of life. They will next take over war as their business."

Yet to label her a feminist or early liberationist is tricky. In 1976, Deborah Derow, a student at Barnard College in New York, sent Arzner her senior thesis, which examined and analyzed the director's career. Dorothy wrote commentary in the margins, offering the historian a fascinating glimpse into her thoughts. When Derow expounded on the women's suffrage movement as a possible influence on the young Dorothy, the director scrawled: "I was completely unconscious of it." When Derow speculated that Arzner felt alienated from other women in the male-dominated director field, Arzner countered: "This is a lot of nonsense." But when Derow implied some of Arzner's pictures might be considered "women's weepies," Arzner took great umbrage. "I never had women weeping!" she responded (exclamation point hers).

Most telling is this: Derow quoted the critic Molly Haskell as saying Arzner's films could be considered "an expression of the discomfort of a woman who feels herself an artist in an alien land, but is nevertheless trying, always, to bridge the gap: between Hollywood and her artistic aspirations, between the romantic conventions and her own feminist sensibility."

To which Arzner replied, simply and profoundly: "True."

Yet although she would eventually embrace—if with some suspicion—the label "feminist," she refused to even entertain the word "lesbian."

"Ridiculous!" she scrawled on Derow's thesis when the student suggested a "covert lesbianism" between Stella and Helen in *The Wild Party*—so obvious to audiences today, and no doubt in 1929 as well. Arzner took offense, writing boldly in the margin: "Ridiculous—tag put onto friend-ship."

This, of course, after sharing her life and her home with another woman for some fifty years. Details of her relationship with Marion Morgan have never been presented at length before. Born in New Jersey, Morgan was sixteen years older than Arzner; she'd been married and had a son. Like Nazimova, she may have been taken with Dorothy's youthful tomboy persona. Morgan's admiration for strong, athletic young women was well known: she was the founder and director of the famed Marion Morgan Dancers, an all-woman troupe that had briefly been a vaudeville sensation. A physical education teacher at Manual Arts High School in Los Angeles, Morgan recruited first six, then twelve, and finally forty "graceful, beauti-fully made girls" for an Orpheum circuit dance tour. Barefoot and wearing revealing, gauzy gowns, the Marion Morgan Dancers caused a sensation, offering interpretive renditions of the classics. "Marion Morgan does more than give a marvelously perfect repertoire of Egyptian, Greek and Roman dances," wrote one critic. "She proves what the highest ideals in the art of dancing have accomplished." In one notorious publicity stunt, she had her girls dance barefoot in the ice and snow in New York's Central Park, caus-ing a crowd.

Marion's outspoken views on women's equality caused almost as much notice as her dancers. In 1918, at the height of the war, she said she didn't see why women shouldn't be in combat, as her dancers went through train-ing as vigorous as any soldier: "It matters little who handles a gun, man, woman or child, so long as the gun can be fired straight." Arzner's words nearly echo hers a decade later; it's clear they saw eye to eye.

They met in Hollywood while Marion was choreographing a dance rou-tine for Allen Holubar's film *Man Woman Marriage* (1921). It was a passion-ate coupling, according to friends and confirmed by letters in Arzner's personal collection. They also began a professional collaboration, with Morgan choreographing the fashion show for Arzner's first directorial ef-fort, *Fashions for Women*. She repeated the duty for the next several Arzner films; in *Manhattan Cocktail,* she choreographed a dance right out of her own troupe, the tale of Theseus and Ariadne.

In 1930 Arzner and Morgan moved into the home on Mountain Oak Drive they'd share for some twenty years before moving to Palm Springs. They christened it "Armor," the way Pickford and Fairbanks had called their home "Pickfair." If wags around town called William Haines and Jim-mie Shields "the happiest married couple in Hollywood," it was only be-cause Arzner and Morgan were more reclusive. Certainly their union lasted as long.

Marion's friend George Brendan Dowell would write to Dorothy: "You understood her, you loved her so dearly. What a monument to your own love was that princely house—Armor is marked in the cornerstone and you shared so much of its beauty with others."

Marion may have been more than a decade older than Dorothy, but she enjoyed playing the femme to her partner's butch. A photograph of the two of them on the set of *Manhattan Cocktail* shows Morgan in fashionable white suit, cloche hat, and stockings; Arzner is in trademark male hat and tie. Dowell, in letters to Arzner after Marion's death, would recall fondly Morgan's "black chiffon Princess gown—the one from Hattie Carnegie's she loved so much."

During the 1930s, Marion traveled frequently to New York and Europe. Arzner saved all of her postcards, each addressed to "Dearest" or "Darling" and signed with variations of "Love." Dorothy was never far from her thoughts: "We must spend next August here," Marion wrote from Germany. "Someday we must tour these towns together," she wrote from New England.

Even when Morgan went east to attend the Yale School of Drama (she would graduate in 1934, at age fifty-three!), the relationship continued. Dowell, a classmate of Marion's, would recall Dorothy's visits, particularly one night when they all went to see Billy Rose's "Jumbo" at the Hippodrome in New York. "You were in a lovely relaxed mood and Marion was so anxious that you see and do everything! I can hear you saying now, 'Dearie.'"

In Hollywood, they weren't part of the crowd at the Vendome or the Brown Derby, but correspondence reveals they did socialize with a chosen few: the actor David Manners and his (male) partner; George Cukor; the landscape gardener Florence Yoch. There were others, too, obviously lesbian: after Marion's death, one couple, Beth and Ann, wrote they could appreciate Dorothy's grief "knowing what anguish it would be if one of us were to lose the other."

Their commitment was real and solid. That didn't mean it couldn't be flexible, especially during Marion's prolonged absences. In 1936, *The Hollywood Reporter* noted that Arzner was staying with Billie Burke, one of her favorite and most frequently used actresses, while her own home was being remodeled. At fifty, Burke, the former wife of Florenz Ziegfeld, was still youthful and pretty; Glinda the Good Witch, her ticket to immortality, was still a few years in the future. Rumors of her preference for women had been rife for years. Andrew Stone, a fellow director at Paramount, said years later he was aware that Arzner and Burke were having an affair. In a fascinating *Screen Snapshots* short subject from that same year, the two women are seen arriving together at a movie premiere in Palm Springs. But when Burke spots the newsreel camera, she hastily retreats from Arzner's side.

Certainly it was no secret within the industry that Arzner was a lesbian; the press, as ever, could read the code, and so could some of the public. Arzner was nearly always described for her masculine traits: "Miss Arzner wears tailored clothes, low-heeled shoes. Her bob is mannish, her hair dark and frosted with silver. She is unmarried, probably because no man has been able to overcome the fascination of her work."

In June 1932 her contract expired at Paramount, and her option wasn't renewed. It was a time of Depression-era cutbacks at the studio, which was in bad financial condition, and Arzner had refused to accept a pay cut. Given her independent means, she could afford to go freelance, and for a few years it worked to her advantage: two of her best pictures, *Christopher Strong* and *Craig's Wife,* would come from outside the Paramount banner.

Yet had she really been "one of the boys"—as some have suggested—she might have been exempt from Paramount's request for sacrifice. The box-office success of her last picture, *Merrily We Go to Hell,* should have secured her position. But Hollywood was in a vise grip: financial panic on one side and increasing calls for censorship on the other. (For a fuller discussion of this period, see Chapter 5, "Wild Pansies.") A director whose image screamed "lesbian" in the press and whose pictures explored "the fragility of the heterosexual couple" wasn't in the strongest position to bargain. Even with no overt sexism or homophobia behind her break with Paramount, Dorothy Arzner stood apart from the establishment—and in trying times, it's always the outsiders who are first to go.

THE GIRL WITH GREEN SKIN: ZOE AKINS

Of course, Arzner wasn't alone in her exploration of subtly subversive themes. Her films at Paramount were almost all scripted by women: Doris Anderson, Hope Loring, Ethel Doherty, and most notably, Zoe Akins, who also wrote *Christopher Strong* when Dorothy moved over to RKO in 1933.

Zoe Akins was an eccentric figure in Hollywood. Small, fat, with an affected British accent, she lived with a female companion, the actress Jobyna Howland, at 6350 Franklin Avenue in Hollywood. Their home bustled with famous folk: in addition to Arzner, there was Ethel Barrymore, Judith Anderson, Gilmor Brown, Billie Burke, Peggy Wood, Somerset Maugham, and George Cukor. Writing about his first visit to the film colony in *Vogue* in 1931, Cecil Beaton singled out for distinction "the house shared by the Misses Zoe Akins and Jobyna Howland, full of the most exquisite objects, full of charming and literary personalities."

Zoe was distinctive all right. "She thought she was a grand lady," said El-liot Morgan, a friend and head of the research department at MGM. "She came from a prominent background and had prominent friends, but she was so silly, even a little dizzy. She gave wonderful parties—Norma Shearer and Fannie Brice, just *everybody*. I said to her once, 'Zoe, this is such a won-derful party.' She said, 'Oh, I don't know who's here. I've just shaken hands with a waiter.'"

She loved the good life but was forever just *this close* to the poorhouse. "She had a beautiful emerald ring," recalled another friend, the producer David Lewis. "When it was on her finger you knew she was in the chips, so beware. But when it was absent, you knew it was in the hock shop and she was desperate to get it out."

She was born in 1886 in Missouri, the daughter of wealthy parents. Her father was the postmaster of St. Louis and a Republican National Committee-man. At eighteen, with her disapproving father shaking his head in the wings, Zoe made her stage debut as a male page in a local production of "Romeo and Juliet." "There are those who disapprove of my decision," Zoe told a reporter at the time, "and certain old women, I fear, have ceased to love me for this reason. Why, do you know that everybody who loves me prays for me now? Isn't that most peculiar?"

Not really. Short, plump, with broad features, Zoe wasn't exactly leading-lady material, but she knew that. "I am not what you'd call pretty," she ad-mitted to a St. Louis reporter, "but I've been told by artists that I have a green skin and a pagan face, and I think that will offset the advantages of beauty."

Just in case it didn't, the little green-skinned girl turned to writing, both poetry and plays. Audaciously, she began rewriting "Camille," considering some of its lines "stilted." She wrote stories and essays for a local literary magazine and in 1909 moved to New York, determined to find her way to the stage. To pay her bills, she wrote for several magazines, becoming in the process a protégé of Willa Cather, then editor of *McClure's*. Cather helped Akins publish her first collection of verse, *Interpretations* (1911), and they remained lifelong friends. Akins took inspiration not only from her men-tor's brilliant career as a novelist, but also from her personal life: Cather lived openly in Greenwich Village with her female partner, Edith Lewis, for forty years.

Like Cather, Akins tended toward political conservatism; friends joked about her Anglophilia and fascination with aristocracy. Yet, again like her mentor, Akins' work, while undeniably romantic, has an unconventional appeal. Her first play, "Papa," produced in Los Angeles in 1916 and in New York in 1919, was billed as an "amorality play," with one reviewer calling its characters "unaware of the decencies of the real world." Fallen women, errant wives—success at heterosexual love and marriage was never part of Zoe Akins' *oeuvre*.

She refused to rewrite her plays to fit convention, even if that meant it took her a decade to hit the big time. "Miss Akins' rather lengthy lingering on the horizon probably can be attributed to the fact that she has stuck to her guns," opined the *New York Times*. "They were her plays, and she stuck to them." In this, she was following the explicit advice of Cather, who had counseled her in a letter written in 1909 to disregard what she thought the critics *wanted* to hear and to write what she *believed*.

Teaming up with Ethel Barrymore assured Akins' arrival. Zoe, the ugly duckling, would admit to having had a girlish crush on the comely, aristocratic actress. In 1920, at the height of their collaboration in "Declassée," Akins published an unabashed love poem to Barrymore in *Vanity Fair*. "The face is like a flower abloom in May/ The head is lifted for a wreath of bay/ The steady eyes—of what world are they?" and so on, concluding with, "O, in a world of sadness and despair/ 'Tis good to find a gracious thing and fair/ A face serene, nor restless with old fears/ Set calm and star-like toward the coming years!"

Barrymore, for her part, would recall seeing Zoe for the first time with Jobyna Howland, and asking Howland later who "the little Polish woman" was.

Certainly Zoe and Joby were a study in contrasts. One short, stubby, and dark; the other tall, Junoesque, and fair. At the turn of the nineteenth century, Jobyna Howland had been one of the original Gibson Girls, those legendary models for illustrator Charles Dana Gibson. She was six feet tall, perfect for statuesque roles like Princess Flavia in "Rupert of Hentzau" in 1899; but after that, towering over modern-dress leading men, her career stalled. Moving into burlesque and character roles, she toured for a time with Clay Clement, Jack Kerrigan's brother-in-law. She married Arthur Stringer, a writer, but rarely saw him. They'd divorce years later, after Joby was living with Zoe in Hollywood.

Zoe gave her friend's career a boost in 1922 when she wrote "The Texas Nightingale" especially for her. Joby scored terrific reviews playing the part of a temperamental opera diva. A few years later, when Zoe's health caused her to move to California, Joby followed. Letters from friends reveal the depth of devotion between them. One of their closest friends was the Austrian filmmaker and stage director Leontine Sagan, whose film *Madchen in Uniform* (1931) caused an international uproar for its frank, sympathetic depiction of a lesbian love story. Tellingly, Sagan would write to Akins of how much she admired her relationship with Joby.

In Hollywood, the now matronly Joby acted in such fluff pictures as *The Cohens and Kellys in Trouble,* while Zoe, embraced by the studios in the wake of sound, found greater acclaim. Akins' first films still crackle with sexy, feminist undertones, especially those she wrote for Dorothy Arzner. In *Working Girls,* Judith Wood's sassy line "I even know how to say no and yes at the same time" sums up the film's wily defiance of male authority. In *Christopher Strong,* after Hepburn is given a bracelet by Colin Clive, she reacts queerly: "I've never cared a button about jewels before," she says. "Now I'm shackled."

It was a brilliant collaboration. Arzner insisted that Zoe be on the set at all times, so great was her respect for the writer in the creative process. Their films together—which, significantly, also had female editors—are remarkably modern in spirit. The attention they paid to women's lives, loves, careers, and friendships was new and notable. In *Sarah and Son,* Ruth Chatterton is not just a noble, self-sacrificing mother, an early version of Stella Dallas, but rather a woman making choices about her own life and desires. In *Anybody's Woman,* as in many of Akins' plays, it is the woman of "questionable" virtue who turns out to be the most virtuous.

Of course, the prevailing patriarchy of the cinema cannot be denied; the studio era's sexist practices and presumptions restricted women both on- and offscreen. Yet there remained pockets of startling freshness and liberty, with the Arzner-Akins pictures ranking high among them. As Judith Mayne describes, these films offer "a perspective on women's relationship to the classical cinema that challenges any monolithic definition of man as subject, woman as object, from the vantage point of women who actually *did* contribute actively to the film medium."

Akins would write to her friend George Cukor: "I'm sure the secret mystery of all creation is a passionate will. What we will we can do. And the most frightening line in poetry is to me '. . . When the will has forgotten its life-long aim.' I'm always afraid of forgetting—or no longer caring. Please don't let me."

Akins' will was indeed passionate, and one of her greatest passions was her place in society. On March 12, 1932 she married Hugo Rumbold, a British painter and set designer. He was from an old British aristocratic family, the brother of the ambassador to Berlin, and about as effete as they come.

"Zoe just loved saying, 'You know, my sister-in-law is *Lady Rumbold,*'" said her friend Elliot Morgan. "Oh, yes, the marriage to Hugo was one of convenience—*Zoe's* convenience in becoming an aristocrat."

They were married at Zoe's home in Pasadena, with a reception hosted by Noël Coward, George Cukor, William Haines, and Tallulah Bankhead. There's no mention of Jobyna Howland among the guests, although that doesn't mean she wasn't present. After the marriage, of course, Joby and Zoe no longer lived together, with Joby taking a home in Beverly Hills.

There, she pointedly told an interviewer her only companion was a Pomeranian she'd named Zoe.

Billie Burke, around the time of her affair with Dorothy Arzner, wrote to the new bride urging her to find happiness with Hugo. He was someone, Burke said, who could appreciate and understand her. Burke lamented all the fun poked at marriage among their friends: When the right fit was found, as Zoe had so obviously found with Hugo, Burke was certain that wedlock could be sweet.

But happiness wasn't to be. As much as Zoe reveled in her status as Mrs. Rumbold, she spent very little time with Hugo. His letters to her over the first few months of their marriage are filled with complaints of never seeing her, of being fed up with delays and excuses. He was in Mexico, and she was busy working on *Christopher Strong* with Arzner, for whom Rumbold expressed a strong dislike in his letters. He wrote in frustration in November that he had expected an idyllic married life, but he'd discovered instead that his wife wrote better love scenes for the screen than she did for her own husband.

Just a few days after he sent this letter, poor Hugo was dead. Reports of the cause of death varied from a heart attack to lingering injuries he'd sustained in World War I. He and Zoe had been married just eight months; Zoe's brief excursion into heterosexual married life had been about as successful as those of her dramatic heroines.

Soon the papers were back to reporting that Zoe and Joby showed up "arm-in-arm" at Hollywood functions. In 1935, Joby starred in Zoe's play "O Evening Star," based on the life of Marie Dressler. It came close to being an all-gay production: Zoe, Joby, the director Leontine Sagan, scenic designer Stewart Chaney, and at least one actor in the cast, Zoe's good chum Anderson Lawler. When Joby died of a heart attack in 1936, Zoe was listed among her survivors as her "intimate friend," seated in a "place of honor" at the funeral. Leontine Sagan would write of being touched by Zoe's care for Joby at the end; by 1938 Sagan is asking after the nice Hungarian girl Zoe had with her in London, observing that it speaks highly of their relationship that they were still together.

HOLLYWOOD'S LESBIAN SOCIAL SET

The increasing recognition of lesbian life in Hollywood in the early 1930s was due to a fascinating gallery of high-profile women who pushed limits and defied definitions. Tallulah Bankhead was a star of the Broadway stage; in New York she flouted all rules of public behavior and convention, reveling in her status as iconoclastic rebel. Hollywood never knew quite what to do with her, either on-screen or off. In 1931, Joseph Breen at the Studio Relations Department wrote to Will Hays that "one very prominent lady star told a group of correspondents who were interviewing her that she is a lesbian." Most likely he was referring to the irrepressible Tallu, and although the declaration was never printed except as blind items, it did reflect an awareness of lesbian identity and culture in 1930s Hollywood.

Bankhead became the focus of fanciful, apochryphal legends and the punch line of endless jokes. Yet in the end, despite her dalliances in Tinseltown, she was never really at home there. The more freewheeling, less bourgeois milieu of New York suited her far better. But still she pushed the cinematic envelope and encouraged others in their own nonconformity.

Greta Garbo, unlike Bankhead, was a creature of the cinema, and yet still she remained apart. All of her press reflects her difference, her independence from traditional heterosexual love and marriage. For a time in the 1920s she lived openly with John Gilbert; later, she conducted her relationship with Mercedes de Acosta with similar directness and lack of pretense. There were stories of affairs with the actresses Lilyan Tashman and Fifi D'Orsay, although these may be apocryphal. The public sensed that Garbo was not quite like most women, with photos of her and Marlene Dietrich, both wearing pants, running under the banner "Members of the Same Club." Both stars cultivated supremely glamorous and yet sexually ambiguous personas. As part of their mystique and allure, such was encouraged by their studios and their directors. After all, what makes a star? What ineffable quality makes the public respond to a star's persona? Valentino's gender ambivalence had been copied by scores of other male stars; now writers and directors incorporated the enigma of Garbo's and Dietrich's sexuality into their films.

"I shall die a bachelor!" Garbo proclaims in *Queen Christina,* dressed as a man, moments after kissing Elizabeth Allan in a passionate, aggressive embrace. As critic Patricia White has observed, "The film mobilized everything about Garbo's already highly codified persona that connoted gender inversion." It's not surprising that the film was partially scripted by de Acosta, who was told by MGM's brilliant and enlightened Irving Thalberg to see Leontine Sagan's *Madchen in Uniform* as inspiration. De Acosta, although frequently not credited, was often a creative consultant on Garbo's films.

Dietrich was even more outspoken about her lesbian traditions. Having come of age in postwar Berlin, where a vital gay and lesbian culture thrived, her experiences were similar to those who came out of Greenwich Village in the 1920s. Lesbian life was not only familiar to her, but *part* of her: she came to the United States not fully grasping the more rigid lines drawn around sexuality by American culture. At the German premiere of

Der Blaue Engel, the film that catapulted her to international stardom in 1930, she walked out onto the stage with a bunch of violets pinned to the crotch of her gown. Violets, the symbol of lesbianism—sure to be understood by an audience of her friends in Berlin. As the writer W. K. Martin theorized, Dietrich "was linking lesbianism and glamour . . . it was a gesture for 'the girls,' as she fondly referred to the set of 'unstraight' women she counted as comrades . . . and a challenge to Hollywood—Marlene Dietrich, it was clear, was not going to be easy to classify."

Dietrich's relationships with women would continue throughout her time in Hollywood: she, too, would form a passionate partnership with de Acosta. She would also have affairs with men, including her director Von Sternberg. All along, she remained married to Rudolph Sieber. "I haven't a strong sense of possession toward a man," she told a reporter. "Maybe that's because I am not particularly feminine in my reactions. I never have been."

• • •

Neither was Marie Dressler, the beloved, blowsy matron of the movies, whose partner, actress Claire Dubrey, served as her secretary. Dubrey, who died at age one hundred in 1993, left behind a frank, unpublished memoir of her relationship with Dressler. Though she never mentions sex, she doesn't shy away from their intimacy, whether in shared hotel rooms or in quiet domestic evenings at home.

Few knew about Dressler. She was sixty-one in 1930, and American culture has long presumed older people asexual. Louis B. Mayer adored Dressler, and even acknowledged her special friendship with Dubrey, likely because Dressler's age prevented him from attaching a lesbian component to it. That Dressler, in her youth, had consorted with many in the lesbian subculture of New York—Elisabeth Marbury, Elsie de Wolfe, Anne Morgan—seems to have been forgotten by Hollywood in the 1930s. But when Dressler died in 1934 and all of Hollywood's elite crammed into the Wee Kirk o' the Heather Chapel at Forest Lawn for the funeral, it was Claire Dubrey who sat in the front pew.

By the early 1930s there was no mistaking a certain element among Hollywood's women. There were the traditional feminine types like Esther Ralston and Loretta Young, and then there were others: the independents, the iconoclasts, the free-thinkers; women like Mercedes de Acosta and Lilyan Tashman (see Chapter 4, "Sex Without Sin"), who played by their own rules and made little secret of their sexuality. Women like Ann Page (later the wife of Jack Warner) and Lili Damita and Jean Howard, actresses who partied with the "fey or gay boys" (Howard's words) and who were suspected of disregarding sexual lines themselves. Women like Hattie Mc-

Daniel, who despite several marriages, formed her closest and most sustained relationship with another woman, journalist Ruby Goodwin. McDaniel's story, in fact, is illustrative. Coming out of a tradition of African-American performers—Gladys Bentley, Bessie Smith, Ethel Waters—where bisexuality among women was common and accepted, McDaniel's letters to Goodwin reveal a deep, loving commitment. She may not have moved among Hollywood's white lesbian set—the racial lines in the film colony were far more rigid than the sexual ones—yet Marlene Dietrich did call McDaniel a friend to the press, fueling rumors among the subculture of an affair.

While there was no "sewing circle" of prominent lesbians meeting clandestinely for parties or sexual favors (a silly term appropriated by recent chroniclers), they *did* seem to find each other. In June 1935, Carole Lombard threw a party—a rather infamous one, as it turned out—at an amusement park in Venice Beach. The guest list as reported in the press was made up predominately of "sophisticated" types—especially the women. Lombard invited girls with spunk, irreverence, "imagination": Dietrich, Damita, Josephine Hutchinson (lover of Eva LeGallienne), Claudette Colbert. The Associated Press was there to take pictures, and noted that the gala, lasting into the wee hours of the morning, was deemed by Hollywood "the most unique in years."

Certainly the photos caused a stir, especially the one of Colbert nestled between Dietrich's legs as they slid down a chute together. Later, after Colbert's death, her companion, Helen O'Hagan, with whom she'd lived for more than twenty years, would tell reporters that Claudette barely knew Dietrich, despite the fact that they were Paramount stars on the lot at the same time. Friend Leonard Gershe insisted that Claudette told him "some photographer pushed her" onto the slide with Dietrich. And besides, Gershe insisted, "Marlene and Claudette didn't even like each other. Dietrich described her as 'that ugly Claudette Colbert, so shopgirl French.'"

Yet the photographs of Jerome Zerbe, taken roughly at the same time as Lombard's party, reveal these two supposed foes very close and friendly. Indeed, other friends recall the Dietrich-Colbert connection quite differently. "Maybe they became unfriendly later, but I'm quite sure they were lovers for a time before [Claudette] married [second husband] Jack Pressman," said the writer Robert Shaw, who became close with Colbert in the 1950s. "I know Claudette *adored* Dietrich. I used to kid Claudette about her all the time."

As for a photographer pushing Colbert between Dietrich's legs, the Associated Press reported it differently at the time: "Marlene Dietrich bobbed up in shorts . . . Claudette Colbert took refuge in coveralls, but she pulled them up to show a handsome black-and-blue mark on one knee. Where-upon she seized Miss Dietrich and the two went down the chute-the-chute together."

Colbert had come to Hollywood from the New York stage in 1929. In her first interviews with the fan magazines, she projected a "sophisticated" appeal, eschewing the idea of marriage altogether: "No man ought ever to marry an actress. A man can be ideally happy only if he is married to a woman who is completely interested in him. An actress never is."

Yet the actress was, in truth, *already* married, a fact not noticed at first by reporters. For their entire seven-year arrangement, Colbert and husband Norman Foster, an actor and later a director, never lived together. When reporters finally caught on, inquiring why Colbert still lived with her mother when she had a husband in the same town, Claudette told them it was because Mom needed her more than Hubby (yet again, Mother as explanation for a curious marital situation).

Pressed, however, Colbert admitted there was more to it than that. Although she might love Foster, she said, she wasn't sure she *liked* him. "We do not like the same people. My friends would be unbearable to him. I am not one bit domestic. I don't know anything about housekeeping and don't want to." Foster added that meanwhile no one should expect them to live like hermits. (Try to imagine such an attitude printed in the post-Code Hollywood press.) "We go where we please and with whom we please," Foster said.

To some, the facts were plain. When Robert Shaw first met Claudette in the late 1950s, she was very close with a painter, Verna Hull, with whom she'd have a nasty break a few years later. Helen O'Hagan then became her constant companion. "I don't know if she ever used the word [lesbian] or not," Shaw said, "and I know she cared about Jack Pressman a great deal. But after he was gone, she told all her friends they should treat Helen the way they had treated Jack—as her spouse."

Another friend requesting anonymity agreed. "She certainly moved with great ease in gay circles," he said. "I used to see her at George Cukor's, and there would be quite the carrying-on. She was never shocked. It was a world she was comfortable in. It was taken for granted that she was gay, or at least not conventionally straight."

"We used to call her 'Uncle Claude,'" said Don Bachardy, the lover of the writer Christopher Isherwood. "Actually, I think she's really a good example of a very closeted situation. Only well within her own circle did they know the truth."

But that was later: in the early 1930s, living separately from Foster, Colbert lived, as many did in the days before the Production Code, with relative freedom and impunity. Never as indiscreet as Lilyan Tashman or as obvious as Bankhead, Colbert was nevertheless known for marching to a different drummer. For women—among whom there existed a tradition of intense, even romantic, but ultimately platonic friendships (the idea of the "Boston marriage")—sexual definitions were often more fluid and different from men. William Haines, friends with Colbert for years, reportedly expressed surprise when Shaw told him in the 1960s that Colbert had had an affair with Dietrich. "I never knew she was a dyke," Haines said. (To which Shaw replied: "You know, Billy, you don't own a *patent* on it.")

The Colbert-Dietrich relationship was likely casual and brief, occurring in the months before Colbert's marriage to Dr. Joel Pressman in 1935. (Earlier that year she'd finally divorced Foster.) In such "sophisticated" circles, such an affair was not necessarily momentous, and certainly not cause on its own to redefine one's identity.

• • •

Such was also the case with Janet Gaynor, the gamine ingenue who won the first Academy Award for Best Actress in 1929 for *Street Angel, Seventh Heaven,* and *Sunrise* (that first year, awards were given for multiple films). She married three times, and all her husbands were apparently homosexual, and she herself was romantically linked to at least two actresses, Margaret Lindsay and Mary Martin. Reporter Ben Maddox, himself gay, wrote, "Janet doesn't have to pretend and play the Hollywood game. Naturally this annoys those who envy her for clicking without sacrificing her ideals." (For more on Gaynor, particularly her marriage to Adrian, see Chapter 7, "Queer Work.")

Yet Gaynor, like Colbert, may never have actually used the term "lesbian." Dorothy Arzner, who was far more overt than either of them, was herself offended by the word. Longtime acquaintances of both actresses have defensively pushed forward their relationships with men as somehow being "proof" that they were conventionally heterosexual; yet Garbo, Dietrich, and Bankhead also had relationships with men, and the complexity of their sexuality is now accepted as fact.

Kay Francis, queen of the Warner Brothers lot before being bumped by Bette Davis, was certainly more "in the life" than either Gaynor or Colbert. Costume designer Miles White recalled an "all-gay" pool party at Francis' house in the 1930s; that Francis was lesbian was something he and the others simply presumed. She had a checkered marital history, four husbands, no children, many lovers. Her name turned up in the gossip columns often linked to gay men, who were in truth merely pals and escorts. The notoriously homosexual Anderson Lawler (about whom much more is written in the next chapter) was one of her most frequent companions. He was reportedly paid ten thousand dollars by Warner Bros. to accompany her to

Europe in 1934. Lawler told the writer George Eells that while they were in London, Kay—roaring drunk and totally nude—walked into his hotel room and declared, "I'm not a star, I'm a woman, and I want to get *fucked*." Asked by Eells how he "handled the crisis," Lawler replied: "I earned my ten thousand dollars."

Eells, gay himself, went to some pains to deny any lesbianism or bisexuality on Francis' part, citing her personal diaries that reveal long-term, anguished feelings over her various husbands and (male) lovers. He quoted an unnamed friend as admitting, however, that there may have been some affairs with women: "But that wasn't where her head was. There was never the slightest doubt that she was man-oriented."

Such description, in truth, only makes Francis—like Colbert, Gaynor, and others—more interesting. (Joan Crawford, too, has been reported to have had affairs with women, despite being essentially heterosexual.) They experienced Hollywood at its most tolerant and sexually adventuresome; all were part of a vibrant lesbian subculture that thrived during the period George Cukor would recall fondly as "La Belle Epoque." No one could have predicted how beautiful, or how brief, it would turn out to be.

SEX WITHOUT SIN

THE GAY SUBCULTURE OF EARLY HOLLYWOOD

1922-1935

t started with a corpse: William Desmond Taylor, stretched out on the purple Axminster carpet of the living room, his arms stiff and straight at his sides. He was wearing the tan gabardine jacket his lover George James Hopkins had helped him pick out. He'd been shot in the head.

The battle between Hollywood's sophisticates and its middle-class guardians, always roiling under the surface, would erupt in the aftermath of that portentous Thursday morning, February 2, 1922, when police and studio executives vied for control of the crime scene. For many, Taylor's death was the last straw in Hollywood's downward spiral of immorality and vice. Less than a year had passed since the mysterious barbituate death of actress Olive Thomas, and the headlines of the notorious rape-and-murder trial of comedian Fatty Arbuckle were still in the papers even as Taylor's death would elbow them for space.

In his unpublished memoirs, Hopkins wrote that he arrived at Taylor's apartment only to be handed a basket of papers by Paramount executive Charles Eyton. He was told to take them to the studio and lock them up. Hopkins—always a loyal studio employee—obeyed orders. He left his lover's body, drove to Paramount, and secured the evidence. He became an accessory to the crime of removing evidence, though he—and no one else either—would ever be charged.

Adela Rogers St. Johns would forever shake her head over such studio manipulation of Taylor's murder, insisting their interference was the reason his killer was never found. Police came to talk to Hopkins only once, to corroborate some small piece of evidence against another suspect. No statements were taken; no interviews were conducted. Strange, because Hopkins had been a far more constant companion of the director than either Mabel Normand or Mary Miles Minter, who bore the brunt of suspicion.

In truth, as far as we can know, there was never any word breathed to investigators about Taylor's relationship with Hopkins. Even when the lurid accounts of the all-male love cults surfaced—tales perhaps corroborated in Hopkins' memoirs—the designer's name was never implicated. It's been suggested that Zukor, Lasky, and other studio executives played up Taylor's supposed womanizing to deflect any hint of a homosexual scandal, even if it had nothing to do with the actual crime. The media circus that blared all sorts of sex-related headlines after Taylor's death—accusing Minter and Normand and revealing the existence of a pink nightgown in the director's boudoir—was devastating, but ultimately preferable to stories of male brothels and bodybuilders for hire.

"You may look all the world over and I am sure you could not find a cleaner man than Mr. Taylor," said Cecil B. DeMille. "I never once heard a word of gossip reflecting unfavorably on him."

While it's true that Taylor was highly regarded, it's difficult to believe that DeMille could have escaped hearing rumors about him. But that was the system's response. It was a way of controlling the situation without appearing to control it at all. The studio's united front in the face of Taylor's death would be mirrored down through the decades, with each successive Hollywood scandal.

With a system now in place to produce films, there was also a system to manage the publicity when things got out of hand. There *had* to be: for just as one side was forever living too large and too free—encouraged by the extravagance of the Roaring Twenties—the other side was always ready to stand and accuse. For the next dozen years the battle lines would be tense, always at the brink of all-out war.

Yet was Hollywood really a snake pit of human decadence, as the moralists charged? It depended upon the viewpoint of the observer. Visiting the Movie Sodom to see for himself, evangelist John Brown returned to his congregation to proclaim that "what little they may have read of the degradation and vice existing in the motion picture colonies had but touched at the edges of things as they are. . . . Their fetes could not have been surpassed in wicked Sodom and Gomorrah of old." In May 1922, a few months after Taylor's death, a "Hollywood newspaperman" (later revealed to be Ed Roberts) published *The Sins of Hollywood: An Expose of Movie Vice,* in which he wrote (using no names) of drug use and easy sex. "The sins of Hollywood are facts—not fiction!" he exclaimed, charging the studio heads with tolerating such excess.

The Zukors and Laskys—striving so hard for middle-class acceptance—must have shuddered at such accusations. Writer-publisher Rob Wagner (*Rob Wagner's Script*) came to their defense, insisting that "Eastern newspapers are painting pictures of a movie colony that surpass anything our wildest directors ever put on the screen to show decadance and crime." He scoffed at the stories, saying, "Puzzled reader, these tales of 'love cults' and 'dope rings' are just good old newspaper hokum."

The truth, as ever, lay in the middle. There were, of course, the beefsteak dinners and pinochle games of the Director's Association, and everyone gathered for the yearly American Legion gala at Clune's Auditorium, just as they did in Peoria and Little Rock. But there existed in the film capital the same schism that had been there from the start, between the "straight shooters" and the "sophisticates." Much of Hollywood—the electricians and the cameramen, the carpenters and the painters, the draughtsmen and the sound technicians—punched their time clocks, did their jobs, and went home at night to their wives. One local told the *New York Herald:* "Hollywood at night is just like your New England village, a dormitory for the cops. . . . Oh, for a jolly old orgy to take the creak out of these joints."

But orgies there were. The poet Hart Crane, visiting Los Angeles, marveled at what he saw in Pershing Square. "The number of faggots cruising around here is legion," he wrote to friends back East. "Here are little fairies who can quote Rimbaud before they are eighteen." Crane hated everything else about the city, but the sex was divine. "Besides which," he wrote breathlessly to a friend, "I have met the Circe of them all—a movie actor who has them dancing naked, twenty at a time, around the banquet table."

Just who Crane's Circe was is unknown. It may have been actor William Haines, whose daisy-chain parties became legendary. It may have been Eugene O'Brien or Edmund Lowe, or some extra whose name has been lost to history. By the mid-1920s it could have been any number of Hollywood figures, for by then, as Crane documents, the homosexual subculture in the movie colony had exploded. Indeed, the moralists *did* have something to thump their Bibles about, and the thumping would only get louder as the decade progressed.

THE LUSTY, LIBIDINOUS EDMUND GOULDING

Every revelry has its master of ceremonies, and in Hollywood, it was a British director with a shock of silver-blond hair and a look of devil-may-care insouciance in his eyes: Edmund Goulding. "His name evokes a vision of sex without sin," recalled Louise Brooks, "which paralyzes the guilty mind of Hollywood."

Paralysis indeed. When historian Kevin Brownlow was compiling his landmark study of the silent era in the 1970s, he asked people about Edmund Goulding, one of the most successful and prolific of the early studio writers-directors. But he found few would talk about the man who made *Love* and *Grand Hotel*.

What Goulding represented—what he conjured up for those survivors of a lost era—was apparently too much for them to remember, at least out loud. The freedom of those days, the license—George Cukor would simply sigh and smile enigmatically when someone would mention Edmund Goulding's name. "La Belle Epoque," he'd whisper, and close his eyes.

It's not surprising that Goulding was an habitué of the Garden of Alla, Nazimova's converted home-into-hotel that continued its tradition of soirees for the sophisticated crowd. It's not surprising that he became an intimate of Garbo, of Noël Coward—of Cukor and William Haines and Cecil Beaton and Cole Porter and Louise Brooks. "Handsome and distinguished in appearance, he possesses further qualifications, too," observed no less a personage than Bosley Crowther. "His hair is iron-gray, like a first-class bank director's; his face ruddy and suavely composed, and his dress is impeccable. And, being an Englishman by origin, he speaks with precise inflection and with the same fine command of nice phrases as a character from a Noel Coward play."

He was, like his friend George James Hopkins, a Renaissance man: screenwriter, director, composer, playwright, novelist. He followed no prescribed route; he fit no model. Goulding was a man, really, like none before in the movie capital.

"Studio people think I'm a little crazy," he admitted. "Actually my trouble is that I'm a dilettante, a wandering minstrel at heart. I've never got settled, never married, never have any money and come to work only because I need the dough." Studio press releases quoted him as believing he had "gypsy blood," because he would never remain long in any one spot.

That may have been because he was always looking over his shoulder for somebody's husband—or wife. If Goulding came into work only because he needed the dough, he needed it to sustain a profligate lifestyle that was reproached by some ("dissolute" according to screenwriter Frederica Maas) and extolled by others (Cukor). His parties became legendary: a happy mix of men and women, straight and gay.

There were stories of outrageous bisexual galas, one of which allegedly landed two women in the hospital and prompted Irving Thalberg to send Goulding to Europe until the furor died down. In London he apparently got into still further trouble, for studio lawyer Mabel Willebrandt had to write to the State Department in December 1932 inquiring into Goulding's detainment on "an immorality charge of some kind." But like most legends, the details have become spotty, overlaid by decades of invention and myth-making. "All for love he directed his sexual events with the same attention he gave the directing of films," Louise Brooks tantalized. "His clients might be the British aristocracy, bankers or corporate executives. His call girls might be waitresses or movie stars."

Orgies, they've been called. Bacchanalias. Goulding served as "master of ceremonies," according to Maas, who, at age ninety-nine, remained as scandalized by his "seamy, lecherous world" as she had been in the 1920s. Goulding "initiated more women and men into more kinds of kinky sexual practices than one can possibly imagine," Maas said, using as bait the promise of a screen test or a bit part in a movie. Maas rebuffed his attempts to lure her in, but she didn't seem to mind the more vicarious thrill of serving as his "mother confessor, to ease his troubled conscience." According to Maas, Goulding claimed to be "an ardent Christian Scientist who read his Bible every morning when he got up."

Freddie Maas is the only one, however, who has recalled a "troubled conscience" for Goulding. In truth, he was a happy-go-lucky hedonist, never bothering to make much of a secret of his lifestyle. His preference for males at such events was widely known; the women tended to be corraled by fellow director (and rake) Mickey Neilan.

"Everyone from the grips to the executives knew what Goulding was up to," Maas said. "Sexual excesses were rampant everywhere but particularly at MGM. If anything went wrong, MGM managed to save itself from notoriety, all the while being permissive with dissolutes like Edmund Goulding."

That the studio with the most tyrannical moralizing chief, Louis B. Mayer, should also be filmdom's most licentious is both ironic and easily explained: as Maas points out, MGM, being the biggest, also had the greatest publicity machine and influence with the press and police. In the days before the Production Code clampdown, Goulding's entertainments were not only tolerated by the studio brass, but possibly even tacitly encouraged, with such studio heads as Hunt Stromberg rumored to take part. (However, producer David Lewis, who was gay, would recall never having seen anything more than "heavy drinking" on Goulding's part.)

Still, Goulding's galas must have been exceptional to elicit the wicked grin on Cukor's face that his friends describe, and the strong reaction even seventy years later from the aged Freddie Maas. That people clammed up when asked about Goulding suggests the director represented the deepest, darkest, and yet most precious secrets Hollywood held.

If Hollywood had not changed—had there been no enforcement of the Production Code in 1934 and no sweeping change in the political climate—Goulding might not have become such a mythical figure. But as it is, he represents A Time Before in a present so colored by What Came After.

Goulding arrived in Hollywood at a time of the greatest freedom the movies have ever known. The studio system was still new, and the young industry, suddenly swelled by theater people and so-called "sophisticates," proceeded in the tradition of the pioneers: a creative cohabitation of disparate peoples, a balance between values affected and values actually held.

In the aftermath of the war, a new generation of young people had claimed the front lines of popular culture, their energies devoted to dismantling the traditions of their Victorian parents. Women had won the vote in 1920; rapid advances in technology freed them from the home and men from mindless, repetitive labor in factories and warehouses. Old ways were questioned; old rules rejected; a new energy and optimism prevailed. Fitzgerald wrote that the Flaming Youth of the post-war era found "all gods dead, all wars fought, all faiths in man shaken." What was there left to do but kick up one's heels and dance?

In a nation officially sober (Prohibition was enacted in 1919) much of the populace pursued a course of rebellion. In the progressive cities, women and men smoked, drank, and had sex with each other without shame. In places like New York's Greenwich Village—and yes, Hollywood—men and women lived together unmarried; recreational drugs and alcohol were common; and homosexuality was fully integrated into the order of things. Hollywood was, in truth, a haven for same-sex lovers—not merely tolerating them but actually considering them *chic*. It was, as Nazimova's paramour Mercedes de Acosta would recall, "the era when many young women wanted to look masculine and many young men wanted to look feminine."

Throughout the 1920s, the image of the male hero on the screen became increasingly androgynous. Valentino, Ramon Novarro, Antonio Moreno, even John Barrymore and John Gilbert were far cries from the masculine cowboys and stolid hawk-nosed heroes of the Teens. The sexually free and ambiguous Twenties made men as much symbols of sex as women, similar to the phenomenon in the comparable 1970s. These prettier, more effeminate male stars represented a new era, when sexual ambiguity suggested culture, culture inspired success, and success was considered sexy.

"The Bill Harts and Tom Mixes aren't the screen heroes anymore," Goulding observed, a few years into the trend. "The he-men in beards and buckskins are only favorites with the very juvenile minds. Today, the suave, cultured, rich athletic boys with the brains are the heroes of the mob. You'll find a decided tendency among the movie heroes to combine culture and polish with a certain facility in *amour.*"

Valentino, prettified in silk tights and powdered wigs designed by his wife Natacha Rambova, was the new hero of the vogue. He seems to have been essentially heterosexual, yet he and Rambova (a lover of Nazimova) were surely cognizant of what they were playing with. In such a culture, homosexuality became less a taboo and more an exotic indulgence.

Such was the context of the times. Goulding's reputation, both on and off the screen, cannot be seen outside of that context. He was a man in easy lockstep with his era.

He was born in Feltham, southwest of London, on March 20, 1891, to "humble" parents, the fancifully named Goalding Goulding and Charlotte Hartshorn. Father disappears from the record fairly early, but Mother, a theatre devotee, had Eddie singing in London music halls by the time he was nine. Singing led to acting, and soon he was playing the Walrus in "Alice in Wonderland" and the Crier in Sir Herbert Beerbohm Tree's "Henry VIII." Goulding grew up on the stage, "steeped in the atmosphere of the theater, getting [my] experience on the run and behind the scenes."

The night Britain declared war on Germany in 1914, he wrote a one-act play, "God Save the King," which he cast the next afternoon and presented the following Monday at the Palladium Theater, all before marching off himself. He was twice wounded in action in France before being honorably discharged in 1915.

He crossed the pond soon after, departing from Liverpool on May 29, 1915, and arriving in New York on June 7. Once settled, he began performing in English grand opera at the Winter Garden. He also became a fan of the movies, finding the medium's potential fascinating. His friend Elsie Janis, the popular Broadway and vaudeville star, gave him a job writing her first Selznick picture, *A Regular Girl* (1919). Janis would remain a big booster, writing about the "something 'sympathique'" between her and Goulding. (Janis, according to some historians, was gay herself.)

After a brief reenlistment in the war in September 1917, Goulding took a sideline job as a cutter at Selznick's New York studios, making $40 a week. Like Arzner, he would learn the craft of movie directing from all sides. He kept churning out scenarios, selling them at $1,000 a pop. *The Perfect Lover* and *Sealed Hearts* both starred Eugene O'Brien, with whom Goulding also shared "something sympathique." They became close friends.

Goulding wrote *Madonnas and Men* for yet another New York–based gay actor, Edmund Lowe, in 1920. By this time his stock had grown considerably in the industry. James Young, one of the industry's top directors, came to New York from Hollywood with the express purpose of securing Goulding to adapt "The Devil" for George Arliss. This led to *Tol'able David,* directed by Henry King and starring Richard Barthelmess, which became one of the major hits of 1921.

The story of a young boy in the rural South, forced to grow up ahead of his years, *Tol'able David* is one of Goulding's earliest films to survive, and it holds up beautifully. Goulding could relate to the young hero of Joseph Hergesheimer's novel: a young, sensitive, *different* boy, yearning to do something meaningful, something *bigger* than the world into which he was born. In young David's case, it was to drive the mail, a position of great honor and trust. In young Eddie's case, of course, it was to write and act and *create.*

It was the perfect ticket to fame for Goulding. Unlike George James Hopkins or Dorothy Arzner, Goulding came from the working class. And the *British* working class—where social standing is an ingrained part of one's identity from birth. His class status had real influence on his life: unlike Arzner, who would admit her privilege in having family money to buffer her career, Goulding could spare no idle months between writing jobs, supplementing his income by cutting film. He would remain fiercely determined to prove himself at every opportunity, a not unfamiliar situation among those of the working classes moving among people they perceive as social superiors. He told the story, over and over, of dining with Hergesheimer while he was adapting *Tol'able David.* The author, full of himself, disparaged the movies and belittled the talent of movie writers. "I got so mad," Goulding would recall, "I went home that night and wrote two chapters of a novel on hotel stationery."

The novel, *Fury,* a seafaring adventure, took him six weeks to write. It was published by Dodd-Mead in 1922 and became a runaway bestseller, with nine printings. He later adapted it to the screen in a project that reunited Barthelmess as star and King as director.

He kept writing pictures, notably the Mae Murray films *Peacock Alley, Broadway Rose,* and *Jazzmania,* which helped crystallize Murray's extravagant stardom. He adored her: she was larger than life, outrageous—*campy* before the word was coined. By early 1923 Goulding was "one of the best known scenarists in the industry," and in March moved out to Hollywood as a contract writer for Warner Bros. Edmund Goulding had arrived; the brash and eager young movieland would never be the same.

GAY HOLLYWOOD IN THE ROARING TWENTIES

The Hollywood that Edmund Goulding found in 1923 was a town still sowing its wild oats. No matter that Fatty Arbuckle had been caught with his pants down and charged with a girl's death. No matter that Wallace Reid had died a hopeless addict. No matter the nasty rumors still swirling around concerning the murder of William Desmond Taylor. The party continued unabated.

Thoreau Cronyn, a Hollywood-based writer for the *New York Herald,* wrote a series over several months in the early 1920s reportedly telling "the truth" about the movie colony. According to his research, there was a greater percentage of unmarried couples living together in Hollywood than he had found anywhere else, "except possibly New York." But what made Hollywood "exceptional," he wrote, was that "apparently everybody in the picture fraternity knows who these couples are."

There it was: the crux of it all. Cronyn wrote: "Liberal may seem the social code of a community which regards the other fellow's private affairs as strictly his own business. . . . One wonders to what extent Hollywood realizes how strange its notions seem to the 'good church people,' or to small town people generally, who constitute most of the audience in motion picture theaters."

The moguls, chasing after their own middle-class aspirations, surely *did* think about those "good church people." They couldn't (as yet) control off-screen behavior very effectively, but they *could* at least make a nominal gesture toward cleaning up the movies themselves. Former Postmaster General Will H. Hays agreed to head up the newly organized Motion Picture Producers and Distributors of America (MPPDA), of which all the major studios were members. Hays' job was to play watchdog, to make sure the output of Hollywood met certain standards that—in the beginning at least—were very vague.

The establishment of censorship went hand-in-glove with the entrenchment of the studio system as the industry's driving structure. In 1924, the Hays Office, as the MPPDA came to be known, came up with "The Formula," a producers' credo to "maintain the highest possible moral and artistic standards of motion picture production." All scripts were to be submitted to Hays before production: his readers would "advise" the studios about questionable themes or storylines. Although the Formula carried no legal weight of enforcement, Hays insisted that members of the MP-

PDA, if they did not comply, would be violating not only their articles of incorporation but also their pledge to the public.

In 1927, with the structure of a Studio Relations Department headed by Col. Jason Joy in place, the Hays Office took another step in regulation: the "Don'ts and Be Carefuls." The "Be Carefuls" were slippery in definition, but the "Don'ts" were pretty specific—eleven circumstances expressly forbidden to *ever* be depicted on-screen: profanity, nudity, drug use, white slavery, miscegenation, veneral disease, childbirth, children's sex organs, ridicule of the clergy, willful offense to nation or creed, and "any inference of sex perversion"—*read:* homosexuality.

Of course, with no enforcement measures to back up the regulations, the "Don'ts" carried as little authority as the earlier Formula. Producers could—and *would*—blatantly disregard the strictures as their scripts (and box-office receipts) demanded. The 1920s, in fact, produced some of the most risqué films for another forty years: DeMille's pagan bacchanalias, the nearly soft-porn of Erich Von Stroheim, Betty Blyth naked as the queen of Sheba. The critics were hardly contented by Hays' efforts.

Besides, the Hays Office was chiefly concerned with what was allowed *on-screen*. At least as compelling to the public was the *offscreen* exploits of the film folk, something of which Will Hays was all too aware. Accordingly, one of his first acts as Movie Czar was to order a report on the film colony's drug situation. Prepared in March 1923, the study showed that "conditions in Los Angeles and environs have been magnified and that few of the sensational reports circulated throughout the East were based on fact." But at the same time the newspapers were filled with stories of Los Angeles police raiding a Hollywood party in which hypodermic needles were passed around on refreshment platters. And, reassuring reports by locals to the contrary, the legions of fairies quoting Rimbaud in Pershing Square would never have been found in a typical New England village.

Columnist Edward Doherty would acknowledge that the majority of those in the industry had no time for revelries and orgies. "But there is a minority that *does* find the time," he wrote. "We did not say the majority was rotten. We *do* say the minority is."

Again, that split. And of course, among that minority were the gays. Not much was explicitly said about the gay subculture in the press frenzy of the 1920s; cultural invisibility can have its advantages. But homosexuals were visible enough to those who knew what to look for.

In *The Sins of Hollywood,* Roberts included in his itemization the creation of "the male vamp—*nothing* has been too vile to exploit." George James Hopkins wrote of a gay underground in Los Angeles that offered boys for sale in which both he and William Desmond Taylor had taken part. Taylor may or may not have been part of an all-male opium "love cult," as was alleged after his death, but the description of one such place suggests there was *something* queer going on in the back rooms of Chinatown. The *Chicago American* wrote of a "British nobleman in exile" hosting gatherings of "men dressed as women" who engaged in "minor depravities," including the auctioning off of a boy, hidden in a coffin, to the highest bidder.

It's a description that seems to jibe with the libidinous gay underworld detailed by Hopkins and experienced by Hart Crane. Others, too, described it: "In the 1920s, Los Angeles was just beginning to come into its own as a gay town," wrote "Toto le Grand," a pseudonmyous essayist for the gay newspaper *Bay Area Reporter* who had been a young man in Los Angeles during the period. "There were probably hundreds of gay ones in the studios. But in the colony of artists, who cared?" As a teenager in screenland, Toto discovered the ins and outs of gay life, especially cruising along Main Street. "While Main Street had not then attained the dubious distinction of Skid Row, it was deteriorating fast. . . . It was where the big red cars came from and left for the harbor at San Pedro. Sixth and Main was often a delightful field of blue uniforms." With Prohibition in place, Toto wrote, "if you had a bottle and a room, you had it made."

This was the heart of gay Hollywood. Nazimova and Goulding may have entertained the elites and swapped sophisticated stories among the swells, but for those "hundreds of gay ones in the studios"—the writers and editors and designers and wardrobe people—Sixth and Main was where the party happened. There—and in Pershing Square and along Hollywood Boulevard—the men in the purple and red neckties could find sailors, sex, and each other.

So it was that, by the late 1920s, Edmund Goulding ruled over a new gay world in Hollywood. By then he had become a top name in the industry. With Edgar Selwyn, he'd written a play, "Dancing Mothers," which became a long-running Broadway hit in 1924–25. Signing up with the Tiffany of movie studios, Metro-Goldwyn-Mayer, Goulding announced he wanted to direct. *Sally, Irene and Mary* (1925), which he also scripted, is the tale of three showgirls and their fates. Sally (Constance Bennett) is brassy and self-assured, always on the prowl for a sugar daddy. Irene (Joan Crawford) is dreamy and easy to con. Mary (Sally O'Neil) is the film's heroine, who puts aside all the sordidness of the stage to settle down with an upstanding plumber, played by William Haines. Ostensibly, we're supposed to identify with good girl O'Neil, but it's the brassy Bennett who holds our attention. She makes up her own rules, just like Goulding.

"Bill Haines always had fond memories of that picture," said longtime Haines friend Robert Shaw. "It fit his sensibility, something he shared with Goulding."

The director took particular interest in Haines, who'd become a regular at Goulding's parties. By 1927, after smash hits in *Brown of Harvard* and *Tell It to the Marines,* he was MGM's biggest draw. His screen characterizations of punkish college pranksters and egotistical sports stars were fresh and original, a new screen type. Haines is dangerous on-screen: not just to the women he pursues, but to everyone around him, including the men. There's a flirtatious quality, a subtextual homoeroticism in many of his films—and sometimes not so subtextual. In *Brown of Harvard* he's clearly more passionate for Jack Pickford than Mary Brian: in *Tell It to the Marines* he swishes a lot, and when asked if he's ever been married, he laughs uproariously, responding (via title card): "Who, me? I'm America's Sweetheart!"

In an era when actors did not disguise their sexual orientation to directors and writers, it's very possible that Haines' on-screen queerness was a deliberate effort. After all, his unique screen characterization was merely an extension of his real-life personality: manic, witty, and irreverent. Haines' humor and values had been honed among the drag queens and gay sophisticates of New York's Greenwich Village: that's what comes through on-screen, and indeed, what made him so popular in the 1920s. Like Kerrigan's "sensitive" cowboys, Haines' campy city slickers were embraced by moviegoers precisely for their difference. His queerness, in effect, is what made him box-office gold. He'd often ad-lib on the set, with writers inserting his quips as intertitles. His campy asides and comments became part of his screen persona, a gay sensibility at work within the confines of the studio system.

His reputation offscreen was no less notorious. Toto le Grand would see him out at night, remembering him as "crude, brash, and rowdy." Protected by the invisibility of the gay world to the larger culture, Haines (and others) moved with relative ease and comfort in cruising areas and speakeasies. "He may have worked hard eight to ten hours a day," Toto wrote, "but he pursued young men—preferably sailors—for at least eight hours most nights."

• • •

Sex without sin. Well, sometimes.

Haines' colleague at MGM, Ramon Novarro, was also known to be gay throughout the industry. Novarro was Haines' polar opposite: quiet, reserved, a devout Roman Catholic, having been raised in a religious family in Mexico (three of his sisters became nuns). Yet at the same time, he was as much involved in the gay subculture as Billy Haines—although he usually prayed for absolution the next day.

Toto le Grand knew Novarro better than he knew Haines. "We'd cavort on Main Street and in nearby hotels on most Saturday nights," he said.

"Then we'd all meet for an early Mass at St. Vibiana's Cathedral, at Second and Main, after which we'd join an understanding priest for a glass of good wine. Prohibition, you remember."

Novarro was an exquisitely beautiful young man. In his early pictures, directors would often find excuses for him to take off his clothes. In *Where the Pavement Ends,* he's nearly naked, causing one reviewer to scoff that he was "almost too beautiful to be taken seriously." In the galley scenes of *Ben-Hur,* his muscles move sinuously as he rows; stills show a tantalizing glimpse of pubic hair. He'd started as a dancer, touring in 1918 with the Marion Morgan troupe in "Attilla in the Time of the Huns." When he auditioned for Rex Ingram for *The Prisoner of Zenda,* the director was impressed enough to give him a sexy supporting role. Novarro proved a sensation.

Like that of Haines, Novarro's homosexuality could be tapped by clever directors for good use when the opportunity arose. In *The Student Prince,* Ernst Lubitsch reportedly plucked a good-looking and obviously gay extra for Novarro to hug, sing, and laugh with in a crowd scene, playing up the charge between them. The story originated with King Vidor, who said Novarro was uncomfortable doing it, but that Lubitsch wanted the inevitable homoeroticism on-screen: he found American skittishness toward the subject absurd. The scene, unfortunately, was cut.

Novarro's megastar status is important to bear in mind when the stories are told about his nightly escapades in the gay subculture of Los Angeles. Except for the time he and Billy Haines were scolded by Louis B. Mayer for patronizing a male brothel on Wilshire Boulevard—a tale originating with Anita Loos—there were no reprimands or repercussions for their carousing.

"We had our Bill Haineses and Ramon Novarros," said Hal Elias, an MGM publicist. "Those are the people who were discussed. Not negatively exactly—their so-called transgressions were considered important, but not in a negative sense exactly. They weren't condemned for it, let me put it that way."

Novarro and Haines, two of the leading box-office stars of the 1920s, could partake in the revelry with relative impunity. And what revelry it was. As Hart Crane would exult: "O André Gide! No Paris ever yielded such as this!"

THE MOST POLISHED FORM OF WIT: THE PRESS AND HOLLYWOOD'S GAYS

From the start, Hollywood's gay subculture was shaped and sustained by the press that covered the movies' myths and make-believe. By the mid-1920s, Hollywood's great fan-magazine tradition had blossomed. The success of these publications was in great part due to the mutually beneficial cooperative relationship they enjoyed with the studios.

"My uncle literally created the fan-magazine format," said Lawrence Quirk about James Quirk, who headed *Photoplay* in its glory years. "Gossip columns, celebrity profiles, notes on movie productions. He knew America needed heroes, and he saw Hollywood as the dream capital, full of glamour, excitement, and adventure. His version of *Photoplay* reflected just that."

The fan magazines were in contrast to the daily newspapers, most of which also ran movie articles and were more independent of the studios (and often far nastier). Many out-of-town newspapers had correspondents living in Los Angeles, like the strident Edward Doherty of the tabloid *New York News*. They were the background chorus, the outsiders wagging their tongues at Hollywood excess, whom the studios tried to drown out with the more glamorous reporting of the fan magazines. Yet those newspaper writers who developed working relationships with the studios, like Louella Parsons, had the longest and most influential careers (often writing for the fan magazines as well).

The best writers understood how the game was played from both ends of the court. Herbert Howe, for example, was not only a journalist, but also worked as a press agent for the director Jerome Storm. Katherine Albert, who began her career as a studio publicist at MGM, would later become head writer at *Photoplay*. Lincoln Quarberg, who started as a journalist, became publicity chief for producer Howard Hughes. "I have often blushed to think that fate had cast me into a vocation which, as a one-time newspaperman, I regard as an illegitimate offspring of journalism," Quarberg wrote, calling public relations "the world's second oldest profession."

Certainly publicists had to know how to sell themselves and the product they were hawking. Crossing over from journalist to studio publicist (and back) was common. By the late 1920s MGM had over a hundred employees in its publicity department, each with their own assigned stars, directors, and films. "Our job at the studio level was to create the publicity, the stories," recalled Hubert Voight, who started in the MGM publicity department in 1925 under Pete Smith. "We had to have a good sense of what makes news, what makes good publicity."

And what makes bad. Studio officials had been rightfully concerned about keeping damaging stories about the Taylor murder to a minimum. Louis B. Mayer showed understandable pique at reports of Novarro and Haines at the male brothel. Yet if Hal Elias is to be believed, publicists generally shrugged over the "transgressions" of Haines and Novarro: gay extracurricular activities weren't considered any more outrageous than John Gilbert's womanizing, in part because such activities were still treated as if invisible by the press.

There was another reason as well. With so many of the press being gay themselves, the game could be played expertly. It's impossible to know how many of the Hollywood journalists were gay, but from the 1920s through the 1950s, the number that we do know is striking. John Ten Eyck certainly seemed "in the life" with his knowing interviews with Eugene O'Brien. As far back as 1914, Richard Willis, a close friend of J. Warren Kerrigan's, wrote in *Photoplay* that he knew the star "as he really is" and that all the talk about his "loving the girls" was "silly and foolish."

By 1930, there was also Marquis Busby, a bright-eyed, eager young re-porter who lived with his parents in Los Angeles. A recent graduate of the University of Southern California when he began writing for the *Los An-geles Times,* he moved over to the *Examiner* and finally to *Photoplay* and the Universal syndicate. Just in his early twenties when he began interviewing the stars, Busby was taken under the wing (and maybe the sheets, accord-ing to rumors) of Billy Haines and Eddie Goulding. Busby's articles are in-telligent and a bit sly, and he should have had a long and brilliant career. But he died in 1934 at age thirty-one of scarlet fever.

There was also Herbert Howe, Ben Maddox, Samuel Richard Mook, and Harriet Parsons, daughter of Louella, who began her distinguished ca-reer as a fan-magazine writer. That's probably just scratching the surface. Reading their work today, there is a sense of fun, of tweaking the more so-phisticated reader. They knew exactly what they were writing. If it reads like a double entendre, it probably is.

"The marrying age for a man is twenty to twenty-five," the twenty-nine-year-old Billy Haines told Marquis Busby. "After that he becomes a little more 'picky,' less inclined to compromise between sheets and blankets and take sheets." Samuel Richard Mook quipped enigmatically, "It's not likely Ramon Novarro needs help from his boyfriend Roy D'Arcy when calling upon Marcelline Day. Roy is quite sure his turn will come for the kiss." From Novarro, Herbert Howe coaxed some telling insight. "I was a dancer before I entered pictures," Novarro revealed in April 1923. "But I didn't take the work seriously. I was afraid of being thought a sis. But I'm not now. They don't like me to say it, but I *like* dancing."

• • •

Howe was the most famous of early Hollywood's gay journalists. His story provides an outstanding example of how the press both revealed and pro-tected the gay subculture. He tried to come off as a cynical Eastern news-paperman—but the romantic in him was exposed by the soft brown eyes of Ramon Novarro. "A brilliance in black and white," Howe wrote of the star as they sailed together to Europe, "those eyes illuminating a face of Span-ish pallor. . . . His eyes so mesmerize a mood that you forget to listen."

Not a good thing for a journalist. Howe had been sent by *Photoplay* to cover the story of Novarro's latest picture, *The Arab,* to be directed by Rex Ingram on location in North Africa. He'd briefly met the star before, and hadn't thought very much of him. "I didn't know him," he'd remember. "No one does out there. He keeps as aloof as Pola Negri." But on the deck, in the moonlight, their relationship began.

"Novarro seduced Herbert Howe," said Lawrence Quirk, who knew both men. "That's what I always understood, that he seduced Howe and they had quite the romance. Howe even became a Roman Catholic."

In 1927, writing the "life story" of Novarro for *Motion Picture* magazine, Howe would admit that "biography should be impersonal. This isn't." Howe couldn't manage objectivity when it came to Ramon: "Friend and advisor, I've known Novarro for four years and I still admire him." He did not shy away from the obviously romantic description of their shipboard friendship. "I must have touched a secret spring to his confidence," he wrote, "for that evening was one of charmed revelation."

The relationship between Ramon Novarro and Herbert Howe symbolizes the relationship between gay Hollywood and the fan-magazine press. Figuratively and sometimes literally, they were in bed together. That so many of the early fan writers were gay is not surprising. What *is* surprising is how unrecognized their role in promulgating the myths of Hollywood has been, not to mention the part they played in protecting and sustaining the gay subculture.

In the morning, after landing at Cherbourg, Howe and Novarro set forth on a three-month journey over three continents, far from the studio's watchful eye. Traveling with them was the director, Rex Ingram, and his wife, actress Alice Terry, both of whom were open-minded about sexual matters. According to Anthony Slide, Ingram—whose confidence in Harold Grieve's inate sensibility had given the designer his start—was "fascinated by all aspects of sexual behavior." Later Ingram would give publicist Herb Sterne a list of gay hot spots in Morocco, information likely, at least in part, gleaned from this African trip with Novarro and Howe.

Returning to Hollywood, Howe gushed to his readers about spending Christmas Eve with Ramon in a desert hotel. Early in the evening, Ramon entertained him by doing impressions of Minnie Madden Fiske; then he disappeared for Midnight Mass. "I've made a lot of prophecies in my time," Howe wrote, "but there's no one whom I could so readily stake my wealth upon as this young champ Novarro. If he ever visits the Vatican, the Apollo Belvedere is going to get down from his pedestal and apologize for having taken up so much time."

Howe was probably the best fan-magazine writer ever. Sharp, erudite, witty, he had a grasp of language that made reading his work sheer joy.

Adela Rogers St. Johns, a colleague at *Photoplay,* quoted a literary critic who told her: "I don't know if your readers appreciate the literary gems they get from him because his stuff is so entertaining. It's the most polished form of wit."

He was born in 1893 in Sioux Falls, South Dakota, the son of a New York–born civil engineer. While his father helped design the city's infrastructure, young Herb grew up in a wilderness of big country and sky, with Indians in buckskin and feathers still a common sight on downtown streets. As a teenager Herb would sit for hours in a nickelodeon operated by his uncle, mooning over such early stars as Florence Lawrence and Jack Kerrigan. After graduating from the State University, he found his way to New York, where he worked for various film companies as a publicist. He served in the World War in the Tank Corps "and looked very handsome in his officer's uniform," according to St. Johns. After the war he got a job with the *New York Telegraph,* which in 1920 sent him to Hollywood as a correspondent. He also began writing for *Picture Play* magazine, a position he resigned in the spring of 1921 to become the western representative for the Brewster publications (*Shadowland, Motion Picture, Motion Picture Classic*). In 1922 he began his long-running engagement with *Photoplay,* writing the column "Close-Ups and Long Shots: Witty Comments on Screen Personalities."

A familiar face at industry functions, Howe lived in the Hollywood hills with his brother Milton. He was Florence Vidor's escort to the Hollywood Bowl; he dined often with Pola Negri and took tea with Mrs. Charles Ray. His byline was prestigious; studios clamored for him to write about their up-and-comers. Along with Adela Rogers St. Johns, Herbert Howe represented the elite of the Hollywood press in the 1920s.

In his own words, he was—echoing George James Hopkins—a "New York sophisticate," and proud of it. He told colleagues at the *New York Telegraph* that he reversed the conventional wisdom of New Yorkers coming to California for their health; he needed regular trips back East to keep his sanity. The writer DeWitt Bodeen called Howe "frequently very cryptic"—and Bodeen knew from crypticism, being a master at it himself. Indeed, all of Hollywood's stories were well known to Howe, and he wrote in such a way as to maintain propriety without compromising his own integrity as a journalist. "The secret of Herbert Howe's success as an interviewer," St. Johns wrote, "is that he knows everybody worth knowing in pictures—and he doesn't care what he says about them." Except, of course, that he *did*—he cared that he not be taken along simply for the publicity ride.

The best of the Hollywood journalists—Howe, Mook, Maddox, Katherine Albert, both Louella and Harriet Parsons—weren't hacks: they were thoughtful writers who didn't merely regurgitate studio publicity. According to Lawrence Quirk, his uncle James knew which stars were gay, and encouraged his writers to find creative solutions when writing about them. Code words like "loner" or "independent" were used; with Billy Haines, it was "wisecracker." When the inevitable Marriage Question was posed, Haines made a joke of it, telling reporters he was waiting for Polly Moran—the gap-toothed comedienne twice his age. The writers went along with the gag; some readers got it, some didn't. Such was the way the publicity game was played.

Howe consistently offered the most fascinating insight. In 1923 he penned a piece for *Photoplay* commenting on the new effeminacy of screen heroes:

> From the moment Valentino hoofed that tango in *The Four Horse-men* and set the flappers cuckooing, the movie boys haven't been the same. They're all racing around wearing spit curls, bobbed hair and silk panties. . . . There seems to be no end to gallantry these days—gallantry, hair and ruffles. Ramon Novarro, who wore less than Gunga Din but with more chic in *Where the Pavement Ends,* is Scaramouching around Hollywood dressed up like Caesar's pet horse. This can't keep up. All the boys can't be Valentino knights. . . . The public can stand just so many ruffles and no more. Some of the boys had better walk up one flight and get some blue serge nifties. It's a cinch if they don't change their panties some of the producers are going to lose theirs.

It's not likely that Howe was personally offended by the ruffles and spit curls. Was he, rather, sending a warning signal as only someone on the inside could? Howe was a shrewd observer, and nothing if not prophetic; there would indeed be a public backlash to the swishiness of the boy stars, although not for several years.

Just how long Howe's affair with Novarro lasted is unclear. It seems to still have been going on in 1925 when Howe again accompanied the star to Europe for the filming of *Ben-Hur.* They arrived together to be presented to the king and queen of Italy; a photo of them dining with each other in Monte Carlo was printed in *Photoplay.* Howe had a lot of fun chronicling their escapades in his column, especially in detailing how they'd sneak off to avoid the crowds of women who were perpetually trying to get to Ramon. When an Italian princess made a nuisance of herself, Howe was Novarro's savior, whisking him away. "As a princess," Ramon told him, "I consider her badly miscast."

Gay Hollywood, in all its sly humor, was right there in the fan magazines for anyone who cared to look.

FREE LOVERS OF THE HOLLYWOOD TYPE

Howe and Novarro weren't the only same-sex couple visible within the industry but just below the radar screen for the general public. In 1928, a new arrival in Hollywood—the actor Anderson Lawler—landed an equally lofty prize: the It Boy, Gary Cooper.

In letters to his mother in Virginia, Lawler wrote of slipping away with Cooper to Catalina Island for the weekend—a break from the studio and Gary's volatile girlfriend, Lupe Velez. It would just be the two of them. Just the guys.

Yet Lawler sounded like a schoolgirl. Cooper was "a fine boy," he wrote, assuring his mother she'd like him. He described their idyll on the island, scaling a mountain, sitting shoulder to shoulder and looking down at "the sea as blue as the sky."

Andy Lawler was in love with Gary Cooper. That much is obvious from the letters and scrapbooks he left behind, as well as the memories of others. In one scrapbook Lawler pasted pictures of Cooper carefully cut from fan magazines. Beside them is mounted every clipping mentioning the two of them together, along with every photograph and every telegram Gary ever sent him, all carefully pasted and preserved.

And who *wouldn't* be in love with Gary Cooper? He was quite possibly the most beautiful male star of the era, back in 1928 when he was still soft and long-lashed and pouty lipped, before he became the solemn, taciturn cowboy of the Thirties and Forties.

A few months before their Catalina excursion, Andy had moved in with Gary at 7511 Franklin Avenue, just a few blocks down from Zoe Akins and Jobyna Howland. Andy and Zoe were tight: she would always be on the lookout for parts for him in her plays and films. There was no question Andy was dazzled by the warm embrace given him by Hollywood's trendiest circles. But most dazzling of all was his friendship with Cooper.

Some still tie themselves in knots over whether Cooper was homosexual. "Coop queer? Are you kidding?" was Jack Oakie's outraged response to biographer Larry Swindell. But the question seems extraneous, beside the point. The demarcations of sexuality were far more fluid in 1929 than they are today. Just as the 1970s would foster an era of sexual exploration, so did the Twenties offer more relaxed attitudes and tolerant experimentation. Columnists had taken to referring to those men and women in New York who moved easily and often between sexual and romantic partners, sometimes even crossing gender lines, as "free lovers of the Greenwich Village type." Many had found their way to Hollywood, too, and Cooper—a Montana native who'd come to California to pursue dreams and discover fame and freedom—had found such people a happy and exciting influence.

Michael Pearman, close with Cole Porter and George Cukor, recalled coming to Hollywood in 1929 for a party at William Haines' showplace home on North Stanley Drive and seeing Andy and Gary there together. Other friends corroborate, recalling the stories Haines would tell of the It Boy mixing with his crowd. Certainly Cooper wasn't blind to the impression he was creating by consorting with Lawler. "Andy Lawler was probably the best-known homosexual in Hollywood during that time," said Robert Wheaton, who knew Lawler through Cukor.

Andy was also indisputably Gary Cooper's closest friend, his favorite hunting and fishing buddy. "Gary gets more kick out of the periodic chicken-hawk hunts in which he and his chum, Andy Lawler, indulge, than he could ever get out of a Hollywood dinner dance," wrote Patsy DuBuis for *Photoplay*. "When he gets a day off, he and mother and pa and Andy go out to a friend's ranch near Riverside and ride horseback all day." Yes, there was Lupe, but only at the end of the article does DuBuis get around to mentioning her, and then what she writes is telling: "They do not intend to marry, because they believe that marriage is incompatible with career."

Lawler was a far more accommodating partner than Velez. "Andy knew how to fire a gun, having grown up in a small, rural town," said his cousin William Kizer, who has conducted considerable research into Andy's life. "But hunting for game didn't interest him. He agreed simply because Gary wanted to."

They met in mid-1929, soon after Andy's arrival on the Paramount lot. Andy was witty, erudite, and free with the bottle. With sandy hair that was thinning prematurely, he was cute rather than handsome, a freckle-faced puck with blue eyes. Cooper was then filming *Betrayal* with Emil Jannings. Andy, strolling by, evinced fascination with Cooper's charcoal drawings of Jannings and Esther Ralston, and asked the star if he could see his other work. That night Cooper took Lawler home to show him his etchings.

They became inseparable. For *The Virginian*, Gary needed to adopt a Southern accent, so he asked the Alabama-born Andy Lawler to coach him. "I am trying to pound some good ole nigger talk into his head," Andy wrote his mother. When Gary decided it was time to move out of his parents' home, Lupe Velez suggested they move in together. But instead he decided to get his own place, and Andy moved in with him.

After Cooper became an American icon, the facts of his relationship with Andy Lawler were denied, ignored, and then forgotten. What stories survived mutated into tales of an older, wealthy homosexual who "kept"

Cooper in the early days. In these accounts, Cooper was not the homosexual himself, but rather an ambitious boy consenting to reap the benefits of his patron's influence, as so many straight actors have done throughout Hollywood history.

But Andy Lawler was neither wealthy nor influential; if anything, it was Gary (the far bigger star) who gave the boost to Andy's career, not the other way around. When Andy took a part in the ironically named play "Let Us Be Gay," (William Haines wired him for the L.A. premiere, "Now that Duse is dead, you are supreme"), press items hyped the show by touting Andy's "leisure time hunting with Gary Cooper. . . . They have a joint collection of stuffed birds of prey." To the play's publicists, the Cooper connection was obviously manna from heaven.

The two friends had pet nicknames for each other: Andy called Gary "Jamey" and Gary called Andy "Nin." On nights Cooper wasn't out with Lupe Velez, he and Andy attended the theater and concerts at the Hollywood Bowl. For Gary, Andy offered a whole new world among the Zoe Akins-Billy Haines-George Cukor set—but Lawler could also play butch enough to mix easily with the Jack Oakie and Richard Arlen crowd, with whom they'd go drinking and fishing and skinny-dipping.

Yet if we can be fairly certain of Andy's feelings toward Gary, what was coming back from Cooper? His biographers seem to have missed a series of fascinating and enigmatic telegrams Gary sent to Andy, carefully preserved in the Lawler scrapbooks.

"Touched that you use your first moment of leisure to write me, thought I was forgotten," Gary wired to Andy on August 2, 1929. (Gary was in Hollywood, Andy on the East Coast for a play.) "It will be nice to see you again. So far I never approved of long-term contracts. Don't worry. G."

On September 4, an attempt at reassurance of some kind: "Thanks for the nice letter," Gary wrote to Andy at the Biltmore Hotel in Providence. "Sorry you think I turned out bad. Will write. Love, G."

A month later, it's Gary who's on the road, writing Andy on October 23, 1929, at the home they shared: "Flying to Tampa, arrive tomorrow. Let me know dope if any. Be home next week, old sock. Gary."

Then there's a curious telegram to Andy from an "Aunt Emma," which shows that whatever the two men's relationship, it was acknowledged in some fashion by others. "Come next week if possible," Aunt Emma writes. "Kathleen giving supper Sunday the 27th. Will ask her to include you and Gary. Want both to occupy one guest room? Answer soon as possible."

William Kizer said there was no "Aunt Emma" or "Kathleen" among

Lawler relatives. But their family *did* know about the relationship, he said, and at least some believed it to be sexual. "Andy's brother Ernest knew," Kaiser said. "Well, he knew what Andy told him. In his later years, he revealed a lot to me. I think he felt that he had an obligation to pass on certain bits of 'historical' data and I seemed to be the only one interested at the time."

Allowing for the possibility of a romantic, sexual relationship between Lawler and Cooper is not really such a radical idea. In the Twenties, a time of cultural provocation, flappers were raising their skirts and kicking over convention. Men dared to be soft. Mystery, enigma, even androgyny had a defiant appeal. For the industry, it was a trend to ride so long as it remained viable. Yet no doubt the studios feared all along that somehow, at some point, the line would be crossed and the deviance exposed—the illusion they'd worked so hard to create shattered.

William Desmond Taylor's murder had threatened to do just that. As the decade went on, there would be more threats, especially as a burgeoning bohemian population pushed the limits of homosocial relationships. Although Paramount was no MGM, ruled by the moralizing fist of Louis B. Mayer, front-office execs may have become concerned about the Lawler-Cooper friendship. A blind item, clearly placed by press agents, follows up interestingly on itself, saying Gary Cooper and Lupe Velez "are more 'that way' than ever," perhaps to reassure fans skeptical of the "chumming" with Andy. The item then immediately segues to Andy Lawler and Nils Asther sunbathing "stag" on the Hollywood Athletic Club roof. Yet again, perhaps, an in-joke from a scribe who knew more than he let on.

Another piece, in Dorothy Herzog's column, was also possibly planted, but it's difficult to understand why: Cooper and Lawler trudge into studio executives' offices and ask if they can go off for a weekend hunting together. "Can Andy go bear huntin' with me?" Gary asks, a little boy to his stern fathers. They say no: just as they eventually may have put the squash on the friendship.

Andy Lawler would remain embittered by his treatment by Paramount. Touted for a part in Nancy Carroll's *The Devil's Holiday,* he was inexplicably canned. By the middle of 1930 he was freelancing: his dreams of fortune and fame were not to be. He and Cooper would remain friendly, but Andy moved out of "Jamey's" and into George Cukor's. Soon after, Cooper quarreled with Velez and with his parents, then suffered a breakdown. His weight dropped from 180 to 148 pounds. Blaming it on overwork, the studio sent him to Europe to recover. There Cooper met the considerably older Countess Dorothy Di Frasso, one of Hollywood's most delicious hostesses. He'd return to screenland several months later on the countess' arm, her very pubic gigolo.

• • •

Anderson Lawler personifies, in his relationship with Gary Cooper, the free-love experience of the late 1920s and early 1930s. Through his career, too, he offers an unparalleled tour of the town's vibrant gay subculture. Andy Lawler knew everyone, and everyone loved Andy. While his screen career ended with a resounding thud, he's a brilliant example of how one could become successful even without success.

Born Sidney Anderson Lawler in 1902 in Russellville, Alabama, he was named after his maternal grandfather, a captain in the Confederate army. Andy was always distinctly Southern, with an accent sweet as sugarcane and a manner so charming that he endeared himself to types as diverse as Cooper and Cukor, Virginia Zanuck and Tallulah Bankhead. He attended both the University of Alabama and Washington and Lee University, where he was a member of the glee clubs. At Washington and Lee, he became friendly with Lydell Peck, director of the Dramatic Club, and later the first husband of Janet Gaynor. After graduation, Andy's theatrical aspirations led him to Fritz Leiber's company, with whom he toured in "Everyman." Settling in New York, he proved his gumption by walking right past the theater doorman and into actor Basil Sidney's dressing room. Sidney, so the story goes, was so impressed with the youth's pluck he made him his understudy.

Andy always had a knack for finding well-placed and often homosexual friends. He became close with the dancer Ted Shawn, who'd also boosted Mitchell Leisen's career. By the late Twenties, Andy was a member of George Cukor's stock company in Rochester, New York, playing the leads in several productions. There were also parts on Broadway.

Making the trip west in early 1929, Andy hooked up with old friend Lydell Peck, then an assistant director to Cecil B. DeMille. Peck helped him get a contract at Paramount. In his second film, *Half-Marriage* (1929), Andy's character jumps to his death from an apartment window in distress over losing Olive Borden. It took a great deal of persuasion to convince Andy's mother back home that her son was really all right.

That fall ironically proved the high point in Andy's film career. After being let go by Paramount, his friend George Cukor gave him a spritely part in *Girls About Town,* but all that led to were friendships with stars Lilyan Tashman and Kay Francis. By 1932 he was doing just walk-ons, but it didn't matter, for Andy had launched into a new career: *escort.* Tallulah Bankhead adored him, often showing up at parties with Andy on her arm. Over the years, Andy became Hollywood's most reliable "walker," escorting Kay Francis, Ina Claire, Zoe Akins, Ilka Chase, Hedda Hopper, Ruth Chatterton, Marlene Dietrich, Paulette Goddard, Constance Bennett—even the Countess Di Frasso, after Cooper dumped her. Studio heads entrusted their wives to him: "He was considered 'very safe,'" remembered Joseph Mankiewicz. One of Andy's most frequent dates, and a close friend, was Virginia Zanuck, wife of Darryl Zanuck of 20th Century-Fox. Mrs. B. P. Schulberg, also a fan, was delighted by Andy's backgammon game. In her column, Louella Parsons called Andy "the backgammon champion of Malibu Beach," but said he "denies he is thinking of giving lessons."

Thus Anderson Lawler performed as important a function in Hollywood as an escort as he might have as an actor. Liked by studio executives and stars alike, he was kept busy in small parts during the day and with social activities at night. As butterfly and gadabout, he turned up everywhere, and with nearly everyone. Flipping through his scrapbooks is a walk through gay Hollywood: he arrives with Zoe Akins and Kay Francis at a party thrown by Lilyan Tashman and Edmund Lowe, and at another with Francis, Billy Haines, and Eddie Goulding. He welcomes David Manners back to Hollywood with George Cukor. Zoe Akins telegrams from New York asking him to give George her love and to "kiss all the supervisors for me." Lilyan Tashman writes to George Cukor, asking if he's seen "Ilk and Zoo and Andy" and to give them all her love. The *Hollywood Reporter* notes that, after a luncheon at Mrs. B. P. Schulberg's, the "sophisticated" clique headed to Andy's for dinner: Ina Claire, Lilyan Tashman, Edmund Lowe, Ethel Barrymore, Billy Haines, Jobyna Howland, Tom Douglas. At a Countess Di Frasso gala, Andy arrives with Kay Francis, Marlene Dietrich, Cary Grant, and the Earl of Warwick (rumored lover of Edmund Goulding). He poses with Dietrich as part of her clique of "male admirers"; among the others gathered around her, Goulding and his handsome earl.

These were the names that were linked together over and over in the fan magazines and gossip columns. These were the "smart set," the hippest of the hip: and they were, by and large, queer. Even those heterosexual names who mixed with the crowd—Claire, Barrymore, Di Frasso, Ilka Chase— were clued into (and comfortable with) the life and the culture.

In one notable clip in Lawler's scrapbook, we get a near-panoramic snapshot of gay Hollywood, circa 1932: "Greta Garbo and Mercedes de Acosta, well-known New York authoress, attending a performance at the Filmarte Theater. Sitting in the same row on the same night: Ina Claire, Anderson Lawler, George Cukor, and Lilyan Tashman. Glimpsed at the same theater: Marlene Dietrich, her husband, her daughter, and Josef von Sternberg, all dressed in tailored white flannel suits."

The image of Garbo and de Acosta just a few rows down from Dietrich and her alternative family—husband, daughter, lover, all dressed alike in male attire—is positively irresistible. Andy Lawler provides a link into the lesbian demimonde of 1930s Hollywood, as he'd escort most of them at one time or another. In his scrapbook is this undated clip from the *Holly-wood Reporter:*

> Portrait of a cad: An executive of a major studio sent for a young actor the other morning. This actor is known to be a very dear friend of a certain actress recently arrived under contract to the company of this executive. The actor, thinking the call was for work, rushed over to see the executive, whom he had never met. First question the executive popped was, "You're a very good friend of Miss So and So's, aren't you?"
>
> "Yes," said the actor.
>
> "Tell me," said the executive, "is she a Lesbian?"
>
> Whereupon the actor punched the executive in the nose and walked out.

Given that the piece is pasted in Lawler's scrapbook, and knowing his friendships with many lesbian actresses, it's fairly safe to assume the actor in question is he. The most obvious candidate for the actress is, of course, Tallulah Bankhead. And the punched-out executive? Louis B. Mayer of MGM. The date of the clip is likely 1932: MGM had just hired Bankhead for a picture (*Faithless*). The hiring came on the heels of several interviews in which she was critical of the Hays Office and its attempts to censor films, and of Joseph Breen's letter to Hays that apparently references her as a lesbian. The ever-moralizing Mayer was understandably frightened of Tallu's outrageous, unpredictable personality. It's actually very believable that he might have called Lawler in to get the lowdown on her.

What's less believable is that Andy punched him. Surely that was a tag Andy placed onto the anecdote as a kind of wish fulfillment—who *didn't* dream of punching Louis B. Mayer in the nose? No doubt the item originates with Lawler. It tells us several things: that studio officials were not above inquiring into performers' sex lives; that such sex lives were becoming an increasing concern; that the gay subculture was visible enough to be directly referenced in the press; and that the subculture itself—personified by Lawler, in this case—recognized a threat to its existence.

Going to the press was both a way of shaming Mayer and galvanizing support among the progressive, "sophisticated" community. If *Tallulah* could be inquired after, who else was next? The symbolic punch wasn't so much tacked onto the anecdote to defend Tallulah's honor—for of course she *was* a lesbian, and everyone knew it—but to demonstrate that such inquiries would get producers nowhere.

The gay scene was also documented at this time by the photographer Jerome Zerbe, who spent "three gay months" (his words) in the movie colony. The most likely candidates for Zerbe's shutter were actors willing to take off their shirts or drop their pants; Zerbe snared a classic butt shot of Bruce Cabot. More fascinating, however, are his many photos of Cary Grant and Randolph Scott, attesting to their involvement in the gay scene: Scott arriving at a party at Zerbe's apartment, several lovely poses of Grant in a bathing suit.

Zerbe's photographs of the Countess Di Frasso's party in the summer of 1935, however, remain the most intriguing. The writer Brendan Gill would recount a tale as told to him by Zerbe, in which the countess, known for her malicious sense of humor, secured recording devices to the undersides of all her garden benches. On the day of her party, the wily countess nailed some pretty incriminating tales from her unsuspecting guests. Zerbe's photographs document the party, and reveal the guests to have all been part of the "sophisticated" clique. Although Cary Grant arrived with perennial date Betty Furness, he posed jauntily with William Haines, George Cukor, and Clifton Webb; Claudette Colbert mugged playfully next to Dietrich, refuting for posterity charges that they barely knew each other. In one shot, Zerbe captured Colbert taking home movies of Dietrich.

A few weeks later, the countess invited the same group back for another party. Gill reported: "She played back for them the indiscreet conversations they had carried on in the supposed privacy of the garden. The prank was not well received." Indeed, *Photoplay*'s pseudonymous "Cal York" (perhaps at this point the gay writer Jerry Asher) reported that Di Frasso received five *urgent* (York's emphasis) pleadings from unnamed persons to *not* play the recordings at her next party—or ever again. Whether she did or not is unknown; but the discovery of those wax disks, reported by York to be preserved for posterity, would certainly be a goldmine for historians today.

• • •

Anderson Lawler was just one of a tremendous influx of gay actors into Hollywood in the late 1920s and early 1930s. Among the others, who achieved varying degrees of fame: Nils Asther, Gavin Gordon, David Manners, Douglass Montgomery, Richard Cromwell, Louis Mason, David Rollins, Ross Alexander, Alexander Kirkland, Tom Douglas, John Darrow, and, of course, Charles Laughton. With the onset of sound, the studios enrolled a whole new class of actors from the stage; that a good number of them were homosexual shouldn't be surprising. Laughton was a giant, both physically and in terms of his talent. His orientation was never much of a secret within the industry, although he had a very public marriage to Elsa Lanchester. A number of the other gay actors were also married; others, the ones termed "bachelors," became regulars at George Cukor's poolside parties. Still others did a mix of both.

Nils Asther had been brought from Sweden by Joseph Schenck in 1926. The exquisitely handsome actor would move to MGM, where he was cast memorably opposite Joan Crawford in *Our Dancing Daughters* (1928) and Greta Garbo, in both *Wild Orchids* and *The Single Standard*. Along Hollywood Boulevard, his cruising was well known. Garbo, during a kissing scene in *The Single Standard,* pushed him away from her, saying, "I'm not one of your sailors." It wasn't hostile, just a point of reference: she felt he wasn't playing the scene with enough finesse.

The rest of the new gay class was a varied lot. Gavin Gordon, a veteran of the Morosco stock company in Los Angeles, was also a Garbo leading man, in *Romance* (1930). He'd later play the very effete Lord Byron in James Whale's *The Bride of Frankenstein*. Richard Cromwell got his start in the 1930 remake of *Tol'able David*. He became a good friend of Cukor and Billy Haines, but he also married Angela Lansbury in an attempt to "go straight." David Manners was an intense, serious actor born Rauff de Ryther Duan Acklom in Halifax, Nova Scotia, in 1901. He, too, was close with Cukor, acting for him on the New York stage before coming to Hollywood. In films, he got his start with James Whale in *Journey's End* (1930) and then became best known for his stalwart leading men in four classic horror films (*Dracula, The Mummy, The Black Cat,* and *The Mystery of Edwin Drood*).

In the hearts of many, Tom Douglas would hold a special place. George Cukor would remember "La Belle Epoque" as much for Douglas' ethereal beauty as Goulding's rowdy revelries. Douglas had actually made his first film in 1922, playing with Dorothy Gish in *The Country Flapper* for D. W. Griffith. But the Kentucky-born teenager found his niche on the London stage, wowing British audiences as the American boy in "Merton of the Movies." He followed that success with a string of hits in England, among them "Fata Morgana" and "Young Woodley," written expressly for him by the gay playwright John Van Druten, who fell hard for the pretty young actor. In his memoir, Emlyn Williams, too, would admit to being smitten with Douglas: "With his short nose and wide soft mouth that seemed not to know its potency, he cast a spell over his own sex, as often as not in unexpected quarters."

By the time Douglas returned to Hollywood—playing "The Boy" in the mystery *The Phantom of Crestwood* in 1932—his fabled beauty had started to fade, partly due to his fast-and-furious high living among the Cukor-Haines-Goulding circle. Stardom demanded not just ambition and talent but eternal youth: Douglas would wisely opt for interior decoration after a Monogram quickie, *West of Singapore,* in 1933. He'd remain a popular star in the gay subculture, however, frequently popping up in the letters and stories of many.

One of Douglas' compatriots at Cukor's gatherings was John Darrow, whose long career would take some interesting twists. Born Harry Simpson in 1907 in New Jersey, he went to Washington, DC, as a teenager, becoming known as "the handsomest page-boy in the Capitol." After selling insurance for a while, he came to Hollywood, where his brother, Allan Simpson, had already broken into pictures. Darrow was chosen to play the title character in Paramount's *High School Hero* in 1927, a knock-off of William Haines' success in the previous year's *Brown of Harvard*. For the next several years, "Johnnie" Darrow was a popular second-rank juvenile star, a precursor of later teen idols, through *The Racket, Prep and Pep,* and *Girls Gone Wild*.

By the early 1930s he was being groomed for more adult roles, supporting Ben Lyon in Howard Hughes' *Hell's Angels*. He never quite took off, however—playing leads in Poverty Row pictures and bits in quality ones. Like Tom Douglas, he took to the stage when film roles weren't plenty. He starred opposite Marian Marsh in "Young Sinners" in 1930—yet another flaming-youth melodrama, with "bad little boys waving flasks and cocktail glasses." For Darrow and many like him, La Belle Epoque had taken its toll: his friends say that, again like Douglas, his looks faded quickly. But whereas Douglas would leave the industry for interior decoration, Darrow would remain, reinventing himself as a successful agent, applying what he'd learned to a whole new generation of gay stars. (For his later career, see Chapter 9, "Pinkos, Commies, and Queers.")

THE INIMITABLE LILYAN TASHMAN

The quintessential star of La Belle Epoque, however, was not a man. Lilyan Tashman was a comet passing over Hollywood for a handful of years—ultimately vanishing, as comets do, leaving those behind still blinking from the glare.

Lil called the shots. "She goes where she wants to go, does what she wants to do, and in short, acts herself," wrote *Silver Screen* in 1931. "Tash" set the style, the vogue, the trends. She was dubbed the best-dressed, the most beautiful, the jewel in the crown. She was also the biggest dyke Tinseltown had ever seen.

"When Lilyan had some drinks, it was best not to go in the powder room with her," said Irene Mayer Selznick, daughter of Louis B. and wife of David O. "I did once and was never so startled in my life. I'd known Lil from way back, but nothing like that had ever happened to me in my life. So overt. I'd never seen anything like it—couldn't believe it was happening. Didn't know it *ever* happened."

What Lil wanted, she went after. According to columnist Jimmy Starr, she seduced actress Estelle Taylor, the vampy star who'd played Lucrezia Borgia in *Don Juan*. She tossed protocol out the window. "Ever since she was a girl," *Silver Screen* told its readers, "'Tash' has been lugging the 'different' label, but has never been bothered by it."

Never indeed: She *thrived* on that difference. Born October 23, 1896, in New York, the youngest child of orthodox Jewish immigrants Morris and Rosie Tashman, Lil was a hellion from the start. The family lived at 340 East 4th Street in Brooklyn, where Morris worked as a tailor. Born in Poland, he moved to Germany around 1877, where he married Rose Cook and had a daughter. He emigrated to the United States in 1879, with Rose and the baby following a couple of years later. Seven more children followed in rapid succession, ending with Lillie.

Her mother wanted her to be a teacher, but her father, bewitched by his youngest child's pluck and independence, told her she should be a lawyer. But that would require study and commitment, and Lilyan didn't have the patience for any of that. Like many whose lives turn out to be brief, she seemed always in a hurry. Studio biographies would report she attended Hunter College, but if so, it wasn't for long. To help support the family, young Lillie went on the stage at the age of seventeen. The next year she was touring with Eddie Cantor and Al Lee in vaudeville; on November 30, 1914, she married Lee (real name Cunningham) in Milwaukee.

Married or not, Lil would admit to reporter Gladys Hall that she played "pretty fresh" with Florenz Ziegfeld at a theater party soon after at the old Martin Restaurant. When he asked to see her knees, she willingly lifted her skirt. Next she knew, she was cast in Ziegield's 1916 "Follies." Her father was outraged, considering the Follies risqué. Lil had to agree, but that's precisely why she loved them: "Sables, Rollses, leases flood in and may be had for the choosing," she told Hall.

Lilyan Tashman's story is quite unlike that of other lesbians who made their mark in the movies. She didn't gravitate to lesbian communities as Nazimova or Mercedes de Acosta had; she was no ugly duckling worshipful of beautiful women like Zoe Akins; she didn't cultivate an androgynous image like Dietrich; and she certainly didn't reject male attention like Dorothy Arzner. Rather, Tashman played her looks and femininity for all they could get her—a "lipstick lesbian" years before the term was coined. A poor girl, daughter of a working-class Brooklyn tailor, Lil loved the feel of fur and satin, and thrilled at each new diamond bracelet. She made it the only way she knew how.

And—this is significant—she was far more honest and far less ambiguous about her desires than even Dietrich, whose style—violets aside—was certainly not about making passes in ladies' powder rooms. (Actress Lina Basquette is also on record as being cornered in a ladies' room by Lilyan Tashman.) Honesty was a hallmark of Lil's—whether it be about her Jewishness or her lesbianism. Once again, like Howard Greer compared to Adrian, it is the working-class "Tash" who lived far more overtly than her middle-class sisters Akins or Arzner. One suspects that, had Tashman lived, she would have been far more forthright in her twilight years about herself and her lifestyle than either of them were. Lil Tashman had no patience for pretense or semantics.

Yet she was married—happily and successfully, to her second husband Edmund Lowe—one more detail of Tashman's anomaly. She separated from Al Lee in 1920, after being linked in the press for several years with Lowe, the purple-tie-wearing actor who'd become a star on the West Coast stage before moving to Broadway. They'd met in 1918; Lil was appearing in her third edition of the "Follies" and Lowe was at his Broadway peak, having just come off a successful run with Maude Fulton in "The Brat."

Studio publicity later insisted breathlessly that Lowe saw the shapely Lil onstage, fell madly in love, and demanded to meet her. Not likely. It's more credible to assume they met through mutual acquaintances (they'd acknowledge comedian Walter Catlett as the first to introduce them) and struck up a friendship. Both were fond of the good life and liked the trappings of fame: splendid wardrobes, chauffeured limousines, first-class travel on cruise ships and trains. They also had raucous senses of humor and, even more importantly, a sophisticated, pansexual attitude toward sex.

"Free lovers of the Greenwich Village type" they certainly were. Lilyan received tremendous press in 1920 for winning first place in the lavish Chu Chin Chow costume ball, held at the Hotel des Artistes and hosted by the Greenwich Village "bohemian colony." Columnists gushed over Lil's slinky, spangled gown and her overall "daring and splendor" at the "all-night and all-morning revel." In such a world, Ed and Lil could be both friends and lovers; theirs was an easy, relaxed, nonexclusive relationship. Often separated by Lowe's jaunts to Hollywood to make pictures, they were certainly aware of the other's affairs with both men and women.

Lil would take her own chance on screenland in 1924. Her parts in *Manhandled, A Broadway Butterfly,* and the film adaptation of Zoe Akins' *Declassée* were extensions of the tough gold digger she'd popularized on the stage. She freelanced, appearing in *Pretty Ladies* at MGM, and with Eddie in his *Ports of Call* at Fox. They were frequently seen on the town together, and the fan magazines began linking their names.

"I don't believe in marriage for actors," Lowe told Marna Tully of *Photoplay,* in what began as a typical response to the Marriage Question for a gay actor. "In fact, I don't think I believe much in marriage under any circumstances. And yet—I'm going to get married, because I can't live without this woman. Lilyan Tashman is the one woman in the world who is tactful and understanding enough to be the wife of an actor."

Lil concurred: "Eddie and I have known each other for seven years. After this stretch of time I never have a qualm—never think for a minute that I am making a mistake. In fact, I feel sure that our marriage will be a great success. Knowing that my marriage will in no way interfere with the development of my career, I know it will be a great advantage."

Once they tied the knot—on September 1, 1925 in San Francisco—Ed and Lil became the sophisticated crowd's answer to Doug and Mary. Sparkling, witty, fun, they were the hosts of screenland's most fabulous soirees. Their guest lists were noticeable for the lack of stuffy, stodgy names. Instead, it was William Haines, George Cukor, Zoe Akins, Eddie Goulding, Andy Lawler, and Kay Francis who were invited to their swanky, modern, all-red-and-white Beverly Hills home, which they dubbed "Lilowe."

Marriage *was* an advantage for them—not so much for publicity purposes, as has been the assumption made by modern observers looking back, but rather for the greater social mobility marriage—as an *institution*—offered its members. Marriage provided a veneer of social respectability: it was far preferable to be invited to an industry function (and subsequently written up in the columns) as "the Edmund Lowes" rather than as the perennial "George Cukor and date," which only served as a reminder of one's outsider status. Having a "Mr. and Mrs." attached to one's name offered a far better chance for establishment in the social arena.

It's interesting to note that those who never married, like Cukor, tended to withdraw socially after a few years of playing solo. As survivors of the era have pointed out, the protocol was always "boy-girl, boy-girl"—for invitations, for table seating, for arrivals at premieres. (Remember Billie Burke's beeline away from Arzner when she spotted the newsreel camera at a premiere.) Gays didn't necessarily view this protocol as oppressive; it was simply the way things were arranged. They accommodated either by marrying or finding opposite-sex dates. Only William Haines, arriving with his lover Jimmie Shields at his side, dared to break the pattern; hosts knew he wouldn't attend without Jimmie. Yet even Haines was offended once when a well-meaning hostess actually placed their name cards *next to each other* and at *the same table*—instead of the usual boy-girl pattern.

Marriage was *the protocol of the times,* offering very real cachet to those who subscribed. In a community that prized middle-class tradition, marriage was a tool to accommodate the customs and expectations of community leaders. Had Lowe and Tashman stayed in New York, maybe they wouldn't have wed; New York theater circles didn't put as much stock in middle-class mores (although some historians have suggested such marriages as Katharine Cornell and Guthrie McClintic and Alfred Lunt and Lynn Fontanne were not dissimilar to the Lowe-Tashman union). But it was Hollywood where they decided to put down roots—to become not only community members, but also arbiters of community style and trends. Marriage, then, became their entrée into the kind of world they not only desired, but in fact helped to create.

None of this should suggest a cynical underpinning to their relationship. "Marriage of convenience" implies far more than it should, as if once the vows were taken, the couple never saw each other again except for the occasional publicity photo. Over and over, the stories of gay men and women in marriages—sometimes married to each other, sometimes not—reveal complex and always *individual* situations. These were not the "twilight tandems" (another silly term) that gossip writers like to imagine. For the most part, when these people married, there was affection, commitment, even devotion: Cole and Linda Porter, Adrian and Janet Gaynor, Charles Laughton and Elsa Lanchester, to name just a few.

From all accounts, Edmund Lowe and Lilyan Tashman loved each other very much. Fan magazines weren't just writing fluff when they noted Lil and Eddie were "supremely happy in a town where most marriages are just one long tug of war." Just because both were gay shouldn't discount their affection or commitment. How often they expressed that affection physically is unknown—but sex, after all, is only one part of a committed relationship, and not even an absolutely essential one at that.

In many ways, despite their "sophistication," their marriage was traditional. Their assests became common; they provided for the right of survivorship; they bought real estate together. They shared a home, despite being frequently apart, and even—if press reports are to be believed—contemplated having a child. "Sophistication is no reason to suppose that there are no normal feelings," Lil told Gladys Hall. "It should mean merely a knowledge of life, and that knowledge should include the fact that maternity is important."

They weren't the only "sophisticates" to marry. Zoe Akins married Hugo Rumbold; Kay Francis married Kenneth MacKenna; and on November 28, 1931, Edmund Goulding married British dancer Marjorie Moss—much to Hollywood's shock. "Eddie Goulding's journey to City Hall with Marjorie Moss gave Cinemaland the greatest surprise," wrote Florabel Muir. Another reporter described the community as "unhorsed" when they learned the news that "the soprano-voiced director intended to renounce bachelorhood. . . . Mr. Goulding has been a bachelor so long that everybody thought he preferred that state above any other."

But Marjorie Moss was an old friend. The marriage came about after her diagnosis with tuberculosis; the doctors gave her less than three years to live. According to Louise Brooks, Goulding married Moss because she was depressed and poor, and he wanted her to live her last years comfortably, surrounded by friends. Indeed, two years later, they would be forced to deny reports that they had separated; they had never, in fact, lived together. Marjorie spent most of her time in Palm Springs, where she died (outliving predictions) in 1935. Goulding flew in to be with her, but arrived a few minutes after her death.

No matter his reasons for marriage, Goulding did reap some additional benefits, a certain respectability he hadn't had before. When the papers reported "the Edmund Gouldings" were entertaining the visiting Cecil Beaton, there was no winking suggestion of outrageous goings-on. In fact, directly after their wedding ceremony, the new Mr. and Mrs. Goulding obliged the press, "going out of their way to entertain the fourth estate . . . the reception looked like a mass meeting of newspaper people." The resultant publicity could only have been appreciated by Goulding's boss, Louis B. Mayer.

None of the "sophisticated" pairings, however, were as successful as Lil and Eddie's. From the start it was a union blessed by honesty and flexibility. To George Cukor, Lilyan would write of her escapades with "Julie" and "Alice," while casually mentioning that Ed was starting a new picture. She'd refer, third-person, to "the Lowes having a large anniversary party"—as if "the Lowes" were a separate entity from "Ed" and "Lil."

In many ways, they were. Their marriage was a creation of their iconoclastic friendship. "Sex, oddly enough, does not always dominate," Lilyan admitted to one reporter, adding she'd never been jealous of Eddie. "I pride myself that I interest him more than any other woman."

That much was no doubt true. Eddie called her "Mom" and thoroughly approved of her career. "I am fortunate in loving a man who loves the thought of my career second only to myself," Lil said. "If I hadn't met him, I doubt if I would have ever married. So few men feel as he does about a woman's career." Lowe *did* appear refreshingly feminist: "Every woman would feel better, I think," he said, "and her life would be happier, if she were able to make her own living—if her own efforts made her independent."

Lowe is an interesting if neglected figure. By 1926 he had become one of the nation's top box-office stars with his astounding success in *What Price Glory.* Playing the tough-talking Sergeant Quirt, forever battling with Captain Flagg (Victor McLaglen), Lowe defied the odds—and the trend toward effeminate male screen images—by becoming a macho hero, with lip-readers delighting in picking up the very real profanity tossed back and forth in the silent picture. The *New York Times* observed, "Lowe's roles . . . made him popular with both the thrill-seeking element and every young man of the scrapping, two-fisted type holding down a 'he-man's' job."

The irony is delicious: Edmund Lowe, erudite, sartorial, homosexual, bucking the Beau Brummell trend and making Sergeant Quirk a household name. "Sez you!" became his catch phrase, which amused this well-read, articulate gentleman to no end. Interviewers loved to draw the comparison between real and reel life, remarking that offscreen, the actor never appeared without his yellow gloves.

Only once did scandal touch the Lowes. In May 1931, a female bit player, Alona Marlowe, sister of actress June Marlowe, alleged that Edmund Lowe invited her and another woman back to his bungalow on the Fox lot. He'd reportedly suggested they "get out of the sun" while they awaited their call to the set. Once there, he left them; moments later, Tashman arrived. According to a complaint filed by Marlowe, Tashman attacked—beating, kicking, and scratching her. The row made headlines; Lilyan denied the whole thing.

The implication most people read into the account was that Lil assumed the girls were there for a tryst with her husband. In the hindsight of sixty years, knowing now what we do about Lowe and Tashman, another possibility emerges: could Eddie have been arranging a tryst not for himself, but for his wife? He left the women alone, after all, and then Lilyan appeared; she was certainly known to aggressively pursue those she fancied. If Marlowe refused her advances—or even changed her mind once things began—Lilyan may have gotten belligerent. Marlowe claimed that after the assault, she was locked in the dressing room and Lil stormed off.

Although the publicity certainly wasn't welcome, the spin put onto it by the Fox lawyers made it seem, well, *understandable* to any decent married person. "Mr. Lowe was working on the set and did not see Miss Marlowe or anyone else in his dressing room," said attorney Milton Cohen. "Neither did he invite anyone to go there."

That took care of Eddie. Now for Lil: "Miss Tashman walked in and saw a strange woman. She asked her what she was doing there. The woman became angry. I don't know whether Miss Tashman tried to put her out, or whether Miss Marlowe tried to put Miss Tashman out—but there was an argument. There was no battle and no blows struck. There was not even any hair pulling."

Neither Tashman not Marlowe showed up at the city prosecutor's office, so the case was dropped. But Tashman cemented her fiery reputation. She had developed an almost cult-like following—not unlike Tallulah Bankhead's "gallery girls," young women who would appear in the balconies of

Tallu's performances, screaming in near hysteria every time she made an entrance. The Lilyan Tashman Fan Club was fervid by the early 1930s; reporters knew Lilyan made great copy and that thousands of readers hung on her pronouncements. Among Tashman's tips: the most unsexy garment a woman could wear was a bathing suit, because it exposed too much; black was definitely out for the new decade; dull food was as bad as dull clothes; jewelry, like liquor and cigarettes, should be used carefully and sparingly.

Lil knew her audience. Writing for *Collier's* in 1932, she acknowledged that Depression-weary girls couldn't afford all the latest styles, but that didn't mean they should give up. Well-styled hair, a clean complexion, and an optimistic outlook were just as important as high fashion. "If you have to go without an extra hat, an extra pair of gloves or even an extra dress, do pay more attention to *yourself.* It's the secret of poise and the very first step in smartness."

Stories about catfights with Constance Bennett, who dared rival her for the best-dressed crown, titillated readers. Then suddenly it was all over, almost without warning.

In late 1932 Lilyan was admitted to a New York hospital for what the press was told was an appendectomy. In truth, she had a tumor removed from her stomach—cancerous, although Lowe kept the truth from her. "It seems odd," he'd tell Gladys Hall. "Lilyan who could think around corners—perhaps she did know. Perhaps it was for my sake she never brought it up."

She seemed to rally, and resumed work, but in February 1934, while she was ironically back in New York to shoot a picture, she collapsed. In mid-March she was admitted to Doctor's Hospital, where surgeons performed palliative surgery. They told Lowe it would be merciful if she didn't get well. She didn't. On the afternoon of March 21, 1934, Lilyan Tashman died, aged 37, her husband holding her hand.

Crowds turned out for the Orthodox Jewish funeral at Temple Emmanu-El on Fifth Avenue, and police estimated that ten thousand people crushed into Washington Cemetery in Brooklyn. A riot broke out. The *New York Sun* reported: "Hysterical women rushed past the police, jumped over hedges, bumped into and in some cases knocked down gravemarkers in their eagerness to get a close-up of the scene." Several distraught female fans almost fell into the grave; two were injured and had to be carted away in ambulances. Mary Pickford stormed off, "disgusted" by the whole scene. The *Boston Post* headline:

10,000, MOSTLY WOMEN, IN WILD MELEE AT GRAVE.

Lil Tashman's status as a lesbian icon was assured. Edmund Lowe seemed to understand the outpouring. "People have said it was bad taste, irreverent," he said. "I don't think so. Lilyan didn't think so either. It was their way of showing they cared."

It's fitting that Lilyan Tashman should have died when she did. She was, in every way, a creature of pre-Code Hollywood. Her films, her outlook, her lifestyle: it's hard to imagine her existing in the era that was to come. Even as she lay dying, the finishing touches were being put on an agreement that would enforce the Production Code, changing Hollywood forever. Lilyan Tashman would have had difficulty adapting to Hollywood's new political climate. The town, the community, the industry, had once looked to her—as outrageous a lesbian who ever lived and worked among them—as its social arbiter. Now those same forces would increasingly turn in on themselves, forever altering the gay experience in the land of myth and make-believe.

WILD PANSIES

HOLLYWOOD'S SISSIES AND THE
PRODUCTION-CODE CLAMPDOWN
1930–1941

In his 1930 comedy *Way Out West,* William Haines played a ranch hand working for Leila Hyams. In one scene, Hyams mistakes him for her maid, calling him "Pansy." At this, Haines can't resist a knowing little smile. He waits a beat, looks quickly into the camera, and replies: "I'm the wildest pansy you ever picked."

No kidding. Named the number-one box office star that year, Haines had grown a little too cocky: *Way Out West* pushed the limits of his screen characterization, exaggerating his effeminacy and campiness beyond anything he'd done before. He swishes, dishes, flicks his wrist. He tells the cowboys they're "too rough" and calls an Indian chief "sweetheart." Seeing the film today, it's impossible to believe the campiness wasn't deliberate: as Haines had done on numerous pictures, he ad-libbed and improvised, and director Fred Niblo incorporated his queerness right into the film. The result was one of the gayest films to come out of Hollywood—and a resounding box-office flop.

Haines' swishy boots had been far better suited to silent pictures than they were to sound. The "talkers" only made everything far more real; in the silent days, Haines' characters were that much more removed from audiences. With the coming of sound, they were suddenly *too* outrageous—too recognizable, too much like the queer down the block.

Even the use of the word "pansy" in *Way Out West* wasn't coincidental: "pansy" was all over the lexicon of the 1930s, with the "pansy craze"—drag clubs with big-name entertainers—spreading from city to city (discussed below). When filmmakers used the word, there was no doubt as to their meaning. In *Palmy Days* (1931), for example, Edward Sutherland included a scene where a flaming swish orders a cake. He insists forcefully that the baker decorate it *not* with roses—but with *pansies.*

In the first years of the decade, a time of profound shifts in the American psyche, homosexuality was unavoidable in popular culture. With the onset of the Great Depression, the legacy of the Roaring Twenties was directly challenged and repudiated. With many men out of work, their sense of mastery over their lives and families was threatened, and traditional gender assignments took on a kind of sacredness. Men were supposed to be men and women were supposed to be women, with all that implied. The excesses of the Twenties were blamed for the hardships the country was enduring, and chief among the culprits were the hedonists and "sophisticates" and queers.

The historian George Chauncey has observed, "The revulsion against gay life in the early 1930s was part of a larger reaction to the perceived 'excesses' of the Prohibition years and the blurring of the boundaries between acceptable and unacceptable public sociability." In the 1930s, homosexuals took on greater menace because by their nature, they called into question such fundamental societal cornerstones as male supremacy, gender and social arrangements, and the sanctity of church and family.

It's not surprising, then, that homosexuality became specifically forbidden as movie content. With the startling onset of sound, the reformist critics of the film industry were galvanized into new life. Father Daniel Lord's famous intonation that "silent smut had been bad [but] vocal smut cried to the censors for vengeance" became a rallying cry. With boycotts threatened from Catholic pulpits every Sunday, Will Hays was faced with a serious situation. Turning to Martin Quigley, an ardent lay-Catholic and publisher of the industry trade paper *Exhibitors' Herald-World,* Hays appealed for help in preventing outside censorship. If the government were to step in to mollify the Catholics, Hays and the studio chiefs believed (no doubt accurately) that it would wreck the movies as both industry and art form.

After meeting with top Catholic leaders, Quigley returned with a monumental proposal. If the industry were to adopt a system of *self*-censorship, albeit one based on Catholic principles, the reformist clerics would drop their calls for boycotts. Hays and the moguls had little choice but to agree.

"What emerged," wrote historian Gregory Black, "was a fascinating combination of Catholic theology, conservative politics, and pop psychology—an amalgam that would control the content of Hollywood films for three decades."

The Production Code was adopted in early 1930, building upon Hays' list of "Don'ts and Be Carefuls." It codified the old rules: "Sex perversion or any inference to it is forbidden," the Code read. Yet the Code was more philosophy than checklist: "Producers recognize the high trust and confidence placed in them by the people of the world. Hence the sympathy of the audience shall never be thrown to the side of crime, wrong-doing, evil or sin. Correct standards of life . . . shall be presented. Law, natural or human, shall not be ridiculed, nor shall sympathy be created for its violation."

While producers nominally agreed to the Code, once again there were nor teeth to enforce it. Even as they shook hands with Lord and Quigley and Hays, the studio chiefs were planning their next productions: *Possessed*, where Joan Crawford lives with Clark Gable without being married; *Morocco*, where a tuxedoed Dietrich kisses another woman on the lips; and *Madam Satan*, which climaxes with an orgy on a dirigible. Openly flouted, the Code paid mere lip service to the small but very vocal minority that called for reform. To them, there had been no alleviation of Hollywood's immorality since the Arbuckle scandal and the Taylor murder, and they weren't going to go away quietly. Even the most jaded producer, ignoring the edicts of the Code, had to know appeasement of this segment of the public was inevitable.

THE WAR AGAINST THE PANSIES

William Haines' career didn't long survive the fiasco of *Way Out West*. Neither did the careers of most of the old male stars—John Gilbert, Norman Kerry, Rod LaRocque, to name only a few—whose images were too soft, too gender ambiguous, to withstand the sudden impact of Depression-era machismo. The Thirties ushered in a new breed of male stars: Clark Gable, who backhanded Norma Shearer in *A Free Soul;* James Cagney, who squashed a grapefruit in Mae Clarke's face in *The Public Enemy;* and Edward G. Robinson, a cop-killing gangster every young, impressionable boy idolized. Even Gary Cooper was transformed from the wide-eyed, long-lashed It Boy into a solemn man of stony gaze and few words.

The first rumblings of the shift had actually come in 1926, with the infamous *Chicago Tribune* editorial that labeled Valentino a "pink powder puff." The paper asked, "When will we be rid of these effeminate youths, pomaded, powdered, bejeweled and bedizened in the image of Rudy—

that painted pansy?" None other than Pope Pius XI joined the chorus of critics attacking the "vogue for effeminacy" among men, charging the morals of male youths were under assault from "feminizing influences in post-war Europe and the United States." (Ironically, Herbert Howe had predicted such a backlash three years earlier, and just as ironic, it was a gay actor, Edmund Lowe, who became the first post-Valentino macho star.)

Yet it took sound to finally kill off the "effeminate youth" among leading men: even among the new crop, the daintiest among them (Darrow, Douglas, Gordon) didn't last long. Effeminacy didn't entirely disappear, however: the old heroes simply transmuted into the character players. In a sense, William Haines evolved into Grady Sutton. The sissies of the Thirties were the direct descendants of the effeminate stars of the Twenties. But while Haines—and Valentino and Gilbert and Novarro—might have been "soft," they were nonetheless *sexual*. The new "sissies" were asexual buffoons.

In George Cukor's *Our Betters* (1933), Tyrell Davis played one of the swishiest of them all. He appears just in the last minutes of the film, waltzing into the drawing room of Constance Bennett, his wrists limp, his nose in the air, his painted lips pursed as if for a kiss. "You must *excuse* me for coming in my town clothes," he lisps, "but your chauffeur said there wasn't a *moment* to lose, so I came *just* as I am!"

Just as he was: in waistcoat and tails, a carnation in his lapel, and done up with eyebrow pencil and lipstick. He wore more make-up, in fact, then Bennett. *Our Betters* was based on a script by Cukor's good friend Somerset Maugham (who, not incidentally, was also gay), and was all about rewriting sexual mores. Of course, RKO press releases tried to present it as something else ("an exposé of snobbery"), but it's really just an exercise for characters to sleep together at will, break up, reconcile, and pair off with others. The picture ends with Tyrell Davis as Mr. Ernest teaching them all to dance—the queer teaching the straights how to have fun. When Bennett kisses her rival, Violet Kemble Cooper, on the lips, Mr. Ernest clasps his hands together and gushes: "*That's* what I like to see. Two ladies of title— *kissing.*" Fade out, the end—and the censors, apoplectic, ran for their telephones.

With the arrival of the pansies in the films of the 1930s, "sex perversion" came to mean not just the direct depiction of homosexual life that Taylor and Hopkins had once gotten away with in *The Soul of Youth*. Now *any* suggestion of a character's deviancy was suspect—and Tyrell Davis' swishy walk, mincing talk, and above all, his *make-up*, seemed *mighty* suspicious. "Surely one can be effeminate without underscoring it with *lipstick*," the Hays Office quoted one outraged reviewer.

Cukor knew Tyrell Davis. Like James Whale hiring his effeminate friend

Ernest Thesiger for *The Bride of Frankenstein,* Cukor chose Davis specifically for the swishy interpretation he knew he'd bring to the small but climactic part. In this way, gay directors made gay life visible on the screen. Straight directors used sissies, too, but usually as the butts of jokes or slapstick comedy relief. The sissies of Cukor and Whale, on the other hand, are shrewd, coy, and arrogant: comic, yes, but in positions to command some power. Thesiger's Dr. Pretorius actually holds the key to life itself: he has the power to lure Henry Frankenstein away from his bride and command him to do his bidding. Davis' Mr. Ernest is admired by the titled ladies who hire him; Constance Bennett calls him in to teach her pals some class. It's this exalted status—as much as the lipstick—that offended the censors.

For his part, Hays was being backed into a corner by the unceasing critics. Joseph Breen, then working for the Studio Relations Department, was in direct communcation with Catholic reform leaders. Writing Father Wilfrid Parsons, Breen said, "Nobody out here cares a damn for the Code or any of its provisions." Martin Quigley, calling Hays on his responsibility, pointed out one trend in particular: "It may be noted that the angle of perverted sex has crept so broadly into several items of recent product that it will be fortunate indeed if it escapes notice in the newspapers."

It didn't. "Effeminate boys crept occasionally into motion pictures before," *Variety* observed. "Winked at, they are now apparently the stock comedy business easiest at hand." The trend reflected the increased visibility of homosexuality in the culture in general: Jean Malin, Karyl Norman, Rae Bourbon, and a host of other obvious homosexuals starred in nightclubs and revues in New York and, starting in 1932, in Hollywood. Malin even headlined on Broadway. It shouldn't be surprising, then, to see a preponderance of pansies in the movies of the same period. *The Celluloid Closet,* book and film, documented dozens of sissies flitting and frolicking their way across the screen: Grady Sutton screeching atop a table when he spies a mouse in *Movie Crazy;* Franklin Pangborn "wooh-hooing" in *International House;* Edward Everett Horton as "Aunt" Egbert in *The Gay Divorcee.*

This invasion of "perverts" was blamed by some of the movies' critics specifically on gays themselves. "Sexual perversion is rampant," Joseph Breen wrote to the Catholic reformer Wilfrid Parsons in October 1932. "Any number of our directors and stars are perverts."

That would have placed Cukor square in the center of suspicion when *Our Betters* was released just a couple of months later. When James Wingate at the Studio Relations Department viewed the film, he was staggered by the "unfortunate lapse in good taste" in both the characterization and make-up of Mr. Ernest. "In the last script submitted," Wingate wrote in outrage to Merian C. Cooper, production chief at RKO, "Ernest was described as being dressed like a tailor's dummy, as being overwhelmingly gentlemanly, and speaking in mincing tones, but there was no indication that he would be portrayed as a pansy."

Cukor had insisted the scene remain as it was, Cooper had apparently backed him up, and *Our Betters* went into general release, at which point Wingate wrote frantically to Hays: "As you already are aware, we called the studio's attention to this, informing them that while there was admittedly no indication of active perversion, nevertheless, the man's make-up and gestures were so exaggerated and unpleasant, that we felt it violated the Code's clauses covering vulgarity and sexual perversion. We are still waiting to see what action will be taken."

In the end: none. *Our Betters* remained intact, and while the escapades of Constance Bennett and her aristocratic friends elicited mostly yawns from reviewers, most were struck by the deus ex machina of the pansy ending. Many wondered why Cukor had tacked it on to the film; Mr. Ernest has nothing to do with anything that comes before. "At the finish they ring in a pansy dancing teacher, played by Tyrell Davis with rouged lips and all," *Variety* commented. "It's the most broadly painted character of the kind yet attempted on the screen."

For the reformers, the timing couldn't have been more expedient. *Variety* headlined another article in that same edition: FILMS TOO 'WISE' FOR MEN; SOPHISTICATION EXPLAINS DROP. The article blamed "sophisticated pictures"—of which *Our Betters* was a classic example—as driving men (read, *straight* men) away from movies. Hand-in-hand with that piece ran still another article, headed: TSK, TSK, SUCH GOINGS ON. Laying it out plain, the paper reported: "Producers are going heavy on the panz stuff in current pix, despite the watchful eye of the Hays office, which is *attempting to keep the dual-sex boys and lesbos out of films*" (emphasis supplied).

After reading the article, Will Hays was quick to fire off a letter to James Wingate:

> There is a story in yesterday's *Variety* repeating an apparent rumor that some individuals seem to have an idea they can incorporate suggestions of sex perversion in pictures. I have in mind your own worry in connection with the effeminate character in *Our Betters*. To make certain there be no possible basis for such gossip, I know you will watch this very carefully. As you have indicated heretofore, a script may be entirely proper, yet the material may be handled in such a manner by the director and actor that the final result carries unlooked-for implications. I suggest you talk this over very earnestly with Mr. Breen. . . . Such a thing, of course, is unthinkable.

Such a thing . . . unthinkable. Clearly this was an accusation against Cukor: the "some individuals" Hays referred to included him, in conjunction with *Our Betters.* Cukor left no record of his reaction to the fuss made over the picture, except that he opposed any revision of it. But *Our Betters* was made during a period of great personal freedom for the director. His name often appeared in the gossip columns, out on the town with Andy Lawler or Billy Haines or Kay Francis. There's a terrific photo of Cukor and Haines camping it up at the Vendome with Lil Tashman and Eddie Lowe. His films were just as boisterous—remember *Girls About Town*—and so the inclusion of a pansy scene fits within his general *oeuvre.*

Increasingly, the suspicion and blame for subversive elements in pictures was laid directly at the perverts' doors, and Cukor wasn't the only culprit. Breen certainly must have had Edmund Goulding in mind when he wrote of "rampant" perversion in the industry. Father Daniel Lord wrote to Hays that merely seeing Goulding's *No Man of Her Own* (1932), which celebrated the free-loving worldview of a gambler played by Clark Gable, "was a sin." Mitchell Leisen was responsible for the lesbian seduction dance in De-Mille's *The Sign of the Cross,* which Lord insisted was unquestionably "sex perversion." Leisen was also behind the styling of Charles Laughton, as the depraved homosexual emperor Nero, and the casting of hunky Georges Bruggeman as his sex slave. As critic Mark Vieira has observed, "Their seminude propinquity brought new meaning to the line 'Delicious debauchery.'"

In the wake of all this "panz stuff," as *Variety* dubbed it, Hays' recommendation that Wingate "talk this over" with Joseph Breen is also significant. Breen's virulent and undisguised homophobia and anti-Semitism (as revealed in his letters to Catholic reformers) would play a large part in the political reaction of the censors. Hays' delegation of authority to him indicates still further that by 1933 the attitude toward homosexuals within the industry was in the midst of a sea change.

It's important to realize that this attitude came not just from the censors, but also from the studio chiefs, who had once tolerated and actually integrated the homosexuals into their midst. In March 1933, Fox executive Sidney Kent wrote to his boss, Winfield Sheehan, "I think the quicker we get away from degenerates and fairies in our stories, the better off we are going to be. I *do not want any of them* in Fox pictures" (emphasis supplied).

By 1933, there was a war against homosexuals in the movies, a war instigated by the reformers but carried out by the industry itself. Actually, the mood had been shifting for a number of years. Ever since the renewed calls for censorship had arisen and the Code drafted in 1930, producers had become more leery of gay players. In June 1930, *Variety* reported, "Only he-men are wanted by the studios for chorus boys" in musical pictures. The article continued:

> Each chorus boy is individually considered. If too pretty, dainty or over-marcelled, he is aired off the casting lists. It has been discovered the average American film fans resent effeminate men in operettas, musicals, etc. Often the fans don't get the Broadway angle but take an instinctive dislike. Even though a male chorus line might have only a couple of geraniums, the fans quickly spot 'em. Camera seems to intensify the effeminate mannerisms of the male crocheters, making them much more conspicuous than in stage musicals.

Once again is acknowledged the dichotomy between Broadway and Hollywood, and their differing attitudes toward gay visibility. Once again, it is the *camera*—the instrument by which the illusion of reality is created—that is singled out as the reason. In the image being projected to America, queers could not be present. They were the bad apples that soured the whole bunch; no matter how benign, no matter if there was no indication of "active perversion"—the very presence of gays on-screen was vulgar enough.

It's important, too, that this wasn't just directed at the *portrayal* of homosexuality, but against homosexuals themselves: analyzing chorus boys to weed out the obvious pansies, the subtle and not-so-subtle pressure the studios placed on stars like William Haines, Ramon Novarro, and Nils Asther to get married. Hays' campaign to "keep the dual-sex boys and lesbos out of films" is direct and unambiguous, aimed not just at the portrayals but also at the portray*ers*. Such active discrimination was a large part of the Production Code clampdown of the early 1930s; without that context, the story of gays in Hollywood cannot be understood.

It's interesting to note that the appearance of an articulated, official homophobia came about partly as a response to a parallel rise of anti-Semitism. In the same letter to Catholic reformers in which Joseph Breen railed against the "perverts," he also attacked the "lousy Jews" who ran the industry as "the scum of the earth." Breen wrote: "These Jews seem to think of nothing but money-making and sexual indulgence. The vilest kind of sin is a common indulgence hereabouts and the men and women who engage in this sort of business are the men and women who decide what the film fare of the nation is to be."

The moguls, canny enough to know that their own position was being challenged, would no longer be quite so indulgent with those dual-sex boys and lesbos.

EDWARD EVERETT HORTON AND COMPANY

By this time, however, there were so many of them on-screen that any co-ordinated attempt at keeping them out would have been preposterous. Rather, each case was individual and particular, although few escaped some degree of coercion or pressure.

The pansies were the most visible of the queers on-screen: gay men who played gay, hiding in plain sight. This made them both vulnerable—poor Tyrell Davis was forever regarded as suspect by the studios—but also, in a curious way, safe: no one *expected* Franklin Pangborn to be married in real life, or seriously dating some starlet, as they came to expect of Ramon Novarro.

Gay actors shunning gay parts is a relatively recent phenomena. In the 1930s, gay parts (the harried store clerk, the dressmaker, the hairdresser, the effete butler) were certainly understood to be *queer*—but stripped of all sexuality, they weren't decisively *homosexual*. Much later, when gay roles "came out of the closet," so to speak—with their homosexuality actually referenced within the script—a gay actor might fear that playing them would expose his own truth. But for Pangborn and Davis—and Edward Everett Horton, Grady Sutton, Johnny Arthur, Rex O'Malley, and numerous others—playing "fey" on-screen meant steady paychecks and a certain degree of fame.

During the movies' own pansy craze, no sissy was more famous than Edward Everett Horton. Extremely popular with audiences and within the industry, he was called by Frances Marion "one of the kindest men in the theatrical business." As manager and lead actor of Los Angeles' Majestic Theater, Horton was both part of and separate from the movie industry. He was not dependent upon the studios for his living, and in fact, wielded the kind of authority over his own players that the moguls held over their employees.

Born in Brooklyn on March 18, 1886, he was the son of Edward Everett Horton Sr., and Isabella Diack; Edward senior was the foreman in the proof room at the *New York Times*. Whereas many gay Hollywood narratives begin with stagestruck mothers and disapproving fathers, it was Horton *pere* who loved the theater and encouraged his son's ambition, and Isabella who voiced opposition. "Mother was a Scot and had no use for the theater," Horton would recall. Even after he'd become successful on the stage and screen and lorded over his own estate in the San Fernando Valley, she was still somewhat disparaging of his lifestyle. "Mother wanted me to settle down and amount to something in the community," her son remembered. "I would protest, 'But, Mother, I have twenty-two acres and relatives all about—all I need is a post office.' Her last word on the subject would be 'Then you really should go to church more.'" Still, Edward would remain devoted to her, as devoted as Jack Kerrigan was to his Dear One.

He dropped out of Columbia to pursue a career on the stage. "I was an ambitious lad, smitten with the smell of greasepaint and Minnie Maddern Fiske," he recalled. In 1908, he joined the troupe of noted actor Louis Mann, from whom he learned all the basics of the theater: props, sound effects, stage management, acting. Eddie wasn't handsome, but photographs from the period reveal he wasn't without appeal. Thick dark hair, deep round eyes, and that same crooked smile that would become so familiar to movie audiences. "I played all kinds of parts then," he remembered. But with *A Fool There Was*—the play Theda Bara would make famous on the screen—his overwrought, hysterical husband brought the house down. It was supposed to be a dramatic part, but Horton's theatrics changed all that. "That was when I realized I must be a comedian. The audience *made* me realize it."

In 1919, at the age of thirty-three, he joined the Thomas Wilkes company at the Majestic Theatre in Los Angeles. It was here that he caught up with fame; the Wilkes productions starring Horton were rated as the best in stock throughout the country. He also signed up for three films at Vitagraph, making his debut playing a harried salesman in *Too Much Business* in 1922. Overall, his moviemaking in the 1920s was spotty, as he remained busy at the Majestic. His biggest silent-screen success was Paramount's *Ruggles of Red Gap* (1923), playing the "veddy" proper English butler made more famous by Charles Laughton a decade later.

On the stage, he found more variety. Becoming a producer himself, he leased the Vine Street Theatre (later the Huntington Hartford) in February 1928. Perhaps the quintessential Horton play was "The Nervous Wreck," costarring Lois Wilson, which he'd performed first for Wilkes in 1923 and played again with his own company. Edward was the title character; in his words, a "sap." *Sap, fussbudget, hypochondriac, sissy, pansy*—no matter the label, they were all the same: fluttery, dithery, distinctly unmasculine. On film, the sissies had no sexuality; they were men posing as maiden aunties without the drag. But on the stage, Horton's "saps" often got the girl. As he explained to reporter Dorothy Spensley: "The audience figures that if a girl as sweet and charming as Lois Wilson can like the hypochondriac who plays the hero, then he can't be such a bad guy and maybe they'll like him a little too. When she falls in love with him, that puts him ace high with the audience. That takes the curse off of sap roles."

The curse, of course, was the specter of queerness. Once Horton brought his "saps" to film, however, the curse wasn't as easy to lift. The sissies of the movies were not leading men; no girls as sweet as Lois Wilson would fall in love with them, reassuring audiences of their heterosexuality. The realism that movies demanded wouldn't allow sissies the leeway they had onstage. (It's significant that when Horton's biggest stage hit, "Springtime for Henry," was made into a film in 1934, Otto Kruger replaced him as the flustered—but nevertheless *girl-winning*—hero.)

Horton, a superb actor, recognized early that the movies could offer him fame and fortune, but artistic challenge and diversity weren't going to be found in the film studios. Although he gave up stage-producer status in early 1930, he continued appearing in local productions, and his legacy as a producer was trumpeted by critics. That reputation gave him unusual clout in the movie industry. He became one of filmdom's most popular character actors without ever signing a long-term studio contract, allowing him the flexibility to move back and forth with the stage. But on the screen, he was, in his own words, a "mouse"—like "sap," just another euphemism for sissy or queer. "It pays to be a mouse," he said, "or at least it pays me. And as long as it pays, I'm going on with my mousing, just as long as the producers ask for it."

And ask they did: his dozens of bumbling, fluttering, stuttering characters guarantee him screen immortality. In *The Front Page* (1931) he's Bensinger, the pansy reporter who, by contrast, assures the heterosexual credentials of Adolphe Menjou and Pat O'Brien. ("All those New York reporters wear lipstick.") For Lubitsch, he played the cuckolded husband in *Deisgn for Living* (1933) and the harried ambassador in *The Merry Widow* (1934). In *The Gay Divorcee,* he's Fred Astaire's fairy friend "Aunt" Egbert, who plays with dolls and waxes nostalgic about his childhood pale pink pajamas. As Vito Russo observed, Egbert is "scrubbed on the surface but brimming with tantalizing sexual and psychological ambiguities."

Horton seemed to comprehend such ambiguity. Looking back on his career, he'd itemize the "thirty-five best friends, twenty-six timid clerks, and thirty-seven 'frustrated' men" he'd played with some humor. "I have often wondered," he mused, "what Dr. Sigmund Freud would have to say about my case. It was his contention that frustration warped the soul, and thereby caused certain disturbances in the psyche. Now, I make a living out of frustration. If I ever became brash in a film, the audiences would not believe it. While others have piled up complexes, I have used this business of being a mouse to get what I want out of life. I am both comfortable and contented—and I have my place in the valley."

That he did. Those of Hollywood's gays who knew how to adapt to the system, indeed how to *use* the system, could achieve the kind of mainstream success and acceptance they might never have found elsewhere. The moguls weren't the only ones pursuing middle-class dreams. Horton bought a twenty-one-acre tract of land in Encino, which he dubbed "Belly Acres." There he brought his mother and siblings, raising farm animals and cultivating fruit trees. "I am not a confirmed bachelor," he told the press. "It is merely that I've had experience only as a bachelor. But I do know that building a house for a man is the same sort of creation that having a child is for a woman." When reporter Patricia Keats set out to uncover Horton's "home and sex life," all she ended up with was a series of one-liners gleaned from her interview with him—"one of the gayest hours of my life," she wrote.

That was as far as it went exploring the love lives of the sissies. In the gay subculture, Horton was rumored to be romantically involved with Gavin Gordon, who had been an actor with his company. Yet among Horton's papers there is no letter to or from Gordon, or any mention of him in other correspondence.

In *The Celluloid Closet,* Vito Russo made a broad assumption that the movie sissies were "playing homosexual" with "little consciousness of that fact." Given that Russo's study confined itself to *on-screen* depictions of gayness and made no inquiry into the real-life experience of gays in the studios, such an assumption seems premature. In fact, given that nearly *all* of the movie sissies were gay in real life, it is likely that there *was* a consciousness of what they were doing. Directors had been using gays to play gay roles since Griffith tapped J. Jiquel Lanoe for *Judith of Bethulia* back in 1913. Just as the verisimilitude of talking pictures outdated blackface and demanded that real African Americans take on Negro parts, so, too, does it seem that actual homosexuals were frequently assigned the pansiest of pansy roles.

For Horton was hardly alone among them. Tyrell Davis swished not only through *Our Betters* but also *Mother's Boy, God's Gift to Women* (playing "Pompom"), and *Dinner at the Ritz* (1938). James Whale tapped Ernest Thesiger not only for *The Bride of Frankenstein* but also for *The Old Dark House*—classic camp portrayals both. Johnny Arthur had been playing his whiny, timid characters since 1923, most notably in *The Desert Song.* William Austin played effete butlers and Englishmen from the silents until the 1940s.

Then there was Grady Sutton, born in 1906 in Chattanooga, Tennessee. In college he began a relationship with Robert Seiter, the brother of film director William Seiter. In 1924, Bobby Seiter, having moved to California, secured Grady some extra work at Universal in his brother's pictures. Sutton would go on to larger parts, specializing in the daffy Southerner, befuddled and flustered around pretty women. His most famous roles came in four W. C. Fields pictures: *The Pharmacist* (1933), *The Man on the Flying Trapeze* (1935), *You Can't Cheat an Honest Man* (1939), and *The Bank Dick* (1940).

George Cukor's favorite sissy was London-born Rex O'Malley, an effeminate stage actor known for playing parts of "the suave, sophisticated Noel Coward type," according to one press account. Cukor hired him in 1936 for *Camille,* in which he essayed Gaston, Garbo's devoted (and, to many audiences, obviously gay) friend. Cukor used him again in *Zaza* (1939). That same year, Mitchell Leisen, who had moved from set design to directing, cast O'Malley somewhat against type in *Midnight.* "Rex was a wonderful comedian," Leisen remembered. "I made him play his part in *Midnight* as straight as he could; it's about the straightest part he ever did."

But his queerness came through nonetheless. When Leisen attempted to use O'Malley as a model for other players, one actor balked because "he didn't want to get established as that kind of faggoty character." It's clear that the line between gay roles and gay actors was thin indeed, and recognized as such. The pansies were pansies, on-screen and off.

"PANGIE" PANGBORN
AND THE "WHOLEHEARTED SUSPICION"

Next to Horton, the most famous of the movie sissies was Franklin Pangborn—or "Pangie," as he was known in the industry. In John M. Stahl's *Only Yesterday* (1933), he played an interior decorator who arrives at a party with a handsome escort (Barry Norton)—a rare suggestion that a sissy might actually have a sexuality. Stopping to gush over a shop window, Pangborn says: "Look! That heavenly blue against that mauve curtain. Doesn't it excite you? You know, blue like that *does* something to me!"

Even more than Horton's "mice," Pangborn's pansies are undeniably, blatantly *gay*. So was *he,* living—yet again—with Mother and the occasional boyfriend in a comfortable home in Laguna Beach. His story echoes those of many Hollywood gays: the "different" son who breaks away from home and convention only to make good and lavish his family with riches and luxury. Pangborn was born in 1888 in Newark, New Jersey, the son of an electrical engineer. Both his parents frowned on his stage aspirations: "To mention the stage to my mother was to bring a tragic look on her face and a sob to her voice," Pangborn recalled. Refusing to give him money even to buy a suitcase, Franklin's father forced his son to borrow a trunk for the trip to New York.

Eventually, the young actor landed a place in Mildred Holland's stock company, touring with her across the country. From there he hopped over to Nazimova's company in 1911, playing a major role in her play "The Marionettes." Like Horton, Pangborn wasn't confined to sissy parts during his stage years. In fact, he played Messala in Klaw and Erlanger's production of "Ben-Hur." For Jessie Bonstelle's stock company, his roles ranged from comedy to melodrama to tragedy.

Yet even in his most dramatic parts, there was always something a little queer about Pangie. During every performance of "The Professor's Love Story," he wore two kerchiefs tied around his neck, one red and the other yellow. He told the *Detroit Free Press* that the kerchiefs were his most treasured possessions, having been brought from India to England by his great-great-grandmother, and to America by his mother's aunt in 1839. His mother had presented the kerchiefs to him on his twenty-first birthday. Jessie Bonstelle and Nazimova had both tried to coax them from him, he said: "I was assailed on every side for one of my kerchiefs. It has now become an amusing occupation to display one of these scarfs, then to listen to the pleas from the fair sex."

No doubt he had to leave his kerchiefs home when he was drafted into the World War soon after. He attained the rank of corporal in the 312th Infantry, seeing battle in France in September 1918 and again in October in the famous Battle of the Argonne. He was wounded and gassed, but recovered in time to become part of the hospital's entertainment program, doing imitations of Sarah Bernhardt in a "negligee all ruffles and a big red wig." But one night, done up in the costume of a Follies chorus girl, he began stammering and couldn't finish his act. Suffering the delayed effects of shell shock, he was shipped back to the U.S. and discharged. It took weeks for the stuttering and delirium to disappear.

Heading to Hollywood, he signed a contract with the Majestic Theatre, where Edward Everett Horton was already regaling audiences. Later, he'd follow Horton again to the Vine Theatre, where he produced plays on his own, although not as successfully as Horton. If Pangborn had been trailing in Horton's footsteps ever since he arrived in Hollywood, he ultimately couldn't measure up to his enormous talent. Still, he followed Horton once more, from the stage into increased film work. He made a number of hilarious appearances in short subjects, most notably as the harried photographer-nemesis of little Spanky McFarland in the "Our Gang" entry, *Wild Poses* (1933). From there it was a quick leap into major character parts in features: competing with Horton for fluttery honors in *Design for Living* (1933), harassed by Carole Lombard in *My Man Godfrey* (1936), and dunked underwater in Shirley Temple's *Just around the Corner* (1938).

There was no end to the indignities suffered by the sissies of the 1930s.

"I've never quite understood why America considers a top hat something to be smashed," Pangborn said. "I know it does, because I've had to be under so many as they were being sacrificed to the tradition. No knockabout clown in patched pantaloons has had to take the punishment regularly meted out to the comedian unlucky enough to have become identified with dress clothes."

Why was that? Certainly it's funny to watch a well-dressed snob, regardless of any perceived sexuality, slip on a banana peel or take a pie in the face, and the "always faultlessly groomed" Pangborn, wrote one columnist, "has been a professional pie-target for so many seasons that the fans have become conditioned to squeal with glee as soon as he appears on the screen." But there was more to it than that: "The long-suffering Mr. Pangborn himself blames his uneasy career on the whole-hearted suspicion all America feels for a man who can carry a white tie."

Indeed, the "whole-hearted suspicion" America had of sissies is precisely what made the front office so nervous. The sissies and the pansies and the fairies might make moviegoers squeal with glee, but they had to be kept in their place: dunked underwater, hit with pies, smashed under their top hats. Except for the sissies of gay directors, the rest of the lot was kept with dignity perpetually overturned, lest any of the sex perversion within begin to show through.

TOMBOYS AND OLD MAIDS:
HOLLYWOOD'S LESBIAN CHARACTER ACTRESSES

The flip side of the sissy, on first glance, is the tomboy. Hardly as numerous, the tomboys were also not as identifiably queer. Joan Davis was a boyish, knockabout comedienne, but she chased men on-screen with rolling-eye abandon. Polly Moran may have been an expert at pratfalls, but her shtick about being hopelessly in love with William Haines was a tired industry in-joke. Tomboys weren't objects of scorn or ridicule the way their male sissy counterparts were either. Rather, they were the gum-snapping sidekicks to the leading lady or the hillbilly in love with the leading man. They might challenge some gender expectations but were nonetheless presented with a certain charm and wit. The prevailing misogyny of the culture has long regarded boyish traits in young girls far more kindly than girlish traits in boys.

Most of the tomboy players—Davis, Moran, Louise Fazenda—were, in fact, straight; Hollywood's lesbian character actresses tended to be older and more stage-established, like Marie Dressler and Judith Anderson. The oral traditions of the gay subculture have long claimed as lesbian a number of character players—Anderson, Hope Emerson, Agnes Moorehead, Marjorie

Main—who specialized in old maids or sexually deviant parts: the repressed schoolmarm, predatory prison guard, or uptight shrew. (Usually that claim has also included the pixieish Spring Byington, probably because she shared a house with Main in the Hollywood hills.) So it's not really surprising to discover that the true counterpart to the male sissy is not the tomboy but the old maid. Like the intertextual personas that embraced the actresses playing them, the screen's old maids projected a sexual deviancy that the tomboys, for all their gender play, did not.

Yet unlike the actors playing the sissies, the actresses playing the old maids lived decidedly outside the subculture, despite retroactive claims of "sewing circles." Of all of them, only Emerson turns up in the columns with any degree of homosociality: there are mentions of her at parties thrown by Cole Porter and the journalist Mike Connolly. While Main and Byington lived across the street from George Cukor, they don't appear to have mixed with his crowd. Neither were any of them regulars within the Dietrich or de Acosta lesbian circles. Few anecdotes turn up in their press in the way they do in the clippings of Horton or Pangborn or William Haines (or, as we shall see, Patsy Kelly or Margaret Lindsay). And despite the claims of some spurious but oft-repeated quotes that label Anderson, Main, Moorehead, and others as "dykes," in truth none of the gay survivors interviewed for this study recalled ever having met them or hearing any stories about them. (For more on the lives of these actresses, see notes.)

Still, as we have seen before, each of these actresses was embraced by an intertextual impression of queerness, and producers couldn't have been blind to it. As they would with the sissies, the studios both exploited and shaped the old maids' personas, both on- and offscreen, to reinforce the meanings latent in their film roles. Judith Anderson can't read any more lesbian than she does in *Rebecca;* Agnes Moorehead brings a definite queerness to the part of the madam in *The Revolt of Mamie Stover;* and Hope Emerson, all six-feet-two of her, was cast on purpose to give a lesbian read to both the prison warden in *Caged* and the circus strongwoman in *Adam's Rib.*

Yet this is moving away from the scope of this study. *Onscreen,* Moorehead and Anderson might be as queer as Horton and Pangborn, but *offscreen* they aren't nearly as comparable, for they left little record of their queer lives.

Not so Ona Munson. Her affair with Mercedes de Acosta was well documented by Mercedes herself and remembered by many in the subculture. Munson had been a Broadway headliner before coming to Hollywood in 1930, but her starring screen career never really took off. By the end of the decade she was playing character parts far more glamorous than the ones given to Emerson or Main—the penultimate of them being, of course,

Belle Watling in *Gone With the Wind*. Notably, Munson's press hinted at her lesbianism far more obviously than that of her less beautiful colleagues. Interviewers found her "difficult," and she was often cited as marching to her own drummer. In truth, she was conflicted about her lesbianism, marrying three times and engaging in affairs with men (including Ernst Lubitsch) to offset those with women. Her career in decline by the mid-Forties, Ona clearly hoped her last marriage, to stage designer and artist Eugene Berman, would offer her some renewed cachet in Hollywood. She sent several notes to Hedda Hopper gushing about how wonderful Eugene was, even though he was rarely with her, always in New York or Europe "on business." In 1955 Ona Munson took her own life, leaving a note that read: "This is the only way I know to be free again."

Not nearly so conflicted was Margaret Lindsay, as feminine and as glamorous as Munson and about as far from a tomboy or an old maid as one might get. The Dubuque, Iowa, native made a splash in *Cavalcade* (1933), bluffing her way into the all-British cast by pretending to be London-born. The analogy is too obvious to resist: she also pretended to be straight, and landed glamorous supporting parts in a string of Warner Bros. films, most notably as Bette Davis' rival in *Jezebel*.

Lindsay's offscreen activities may help explain why she never progressed to big-budget leads, however. She was friendly with some of the shady underworld that surrounded screen actress Thelma Todd; after Todd was found dead in 1935, Lindsay was called to testify before a grand jury about Todd's ex-husband (and reputed gangster) Pat DiCicco. Some columnists implied that Lindsay and DeCicco were involved romantically; more sophisticated wags, however, hinted her *real* lover was Janet Gaynor, with whom Lindsay took refuge after her grand-jury testimony. Many newspapers carried items about Maggie and Janet crisscrossing the country, ducking into hotels to escape reporters. In July 1936 they headed for a getaway in Hawaii.

Lindsay moved with the high-spirited crowd of Jean Howard and Ann Warner, and became something of a prototype feminist at the studio, refusing to "grin and bear it"—the customary response, she said, when a director got "fresh." She told Ben Maddox: "I don't care to be called by my first name and to be 'darling' to everyone on the lot." Early on she vetoed marriage outright, saying having both husband and career just didn't mix. In 1937, in the midst of the grapevine chatter linking her to Gaynor, she blasted rumormongers, saying she intended to go on living her own life "and letting others live theirs."

That she did, eventually buying a house in the Hollywood hills with her longtime partner, comedienne Mary McCarty. If she was seen with a man, it was often Liberace. She appeared in the occasional film through the 1960s, but Hollywood didn't quite know what to do with a glamorous lesbian who refused to play the game. At least Lilyan Tashman (and Ona Munson) had gotten married.

Patsy Kelly, on the other hand, was anything but glamorous. One of the few movie tomboys to actually be gay, she was a hard-drinking, rabble-rousing dyke, according to those who remember her. "Not only was she open about it," said one friend, a neighbor of hers in the 1950s, "she was *all over the place* with it." She made her debut in 1933, replacing Zasu Pitts in a series of Hal Roach short subjects costarring Thelma Todd. Todd was the lithe femme to Kelly's wisecracking butch, but both played slapstick with equal gusto, making the series extremely popular. Todd's death pushed Patsy to center stage, and she made a few starring vehicles (*Kelly the Second, Pigskin Parade*) before her career faded in the early 1940s.

Like Lindsay, Kelly led an offscreen life a bit too unpredictable for Hollywood. Just months after her arrival, she began cavorting with none other than Jean Malin, the notorious drag-queen entertainer then wowing Los Angeles nightclub patrons (discussed below). She was a passenger in Malin's car during his fatal accident backing off a pier at Venice Beach; although Roach downplayed her injuries, she was in a coma for several days. The association with Malin was not received well by the studio, but Patsy wasn't easily leashed. She would continue to play in the margins of "respectable" society, and seemed cavalier about its impact on her career.

Indeed, she lived openly with her lover, Wilma Cox, a bit player in Charley Chase shorts. Photographs reveal Cox as dark, delicate, very pretty with bee-stung lips—a far cry from Patsy's square, cosmetics-free face and masculine swagger. When Gladys Hall visited their home, Patsy was quick to credit Wilma with the house's decoration; she, Patsy, had no interest in such things. Asked about marriage, Kelly demurred: "I'm having too much fun as I am," she said. "Often Wilma and I have a few folks in for the evening, not picture folks very often. I like my life. I'm happy."

She had always been defiant. "If we'd had Women's Lib, I'd have been a fireman," she said, looking back on her life. Born in 1910 to Irish immigrant parents in Brooklyn, her father was a garage foreman and later a policeman. They were just this side of poor; in her usual deadpan style, Kelly would remember: "There was almost always enough to eat." It didn't take long for Sarah Veronica Rose Kelly to become Patsy. "I guess I was kind of a tomboy," she admitted. Playing baseball on the boys' team and hanging out at the firehouse, she was a "wild kid who preferred boys and their sports to the namby-pamby amusements of other girls."

Her parents found the cash to get their little hooligan off the streets and into dancing school. She didn't care for the frilly tutus, she said, but she enjoyed the dancing. She made friends with another young girl, Ruby Keeler; soon they'd both be hoofing around New York vaudeville stages. As a teenager, Patsy toured in a song-and-dance act with Frank Fay, and later played with Al Jolson and Clifton Webb on Broadway. By 1928 the *New York Times* was heralding her "merry, nonchalant personality," and in 1930 immortalized her in a sketch with Jack Benny for the latest edition of Earl Carroll's "Vanities."

Her working-class, New York stage roots led inevitably to a more overt lifestyle in Hollywood, a rarity among screen women. In an increasingly conservative climate, she nonetheless remained the maverick. She told writer Julia Gwin in *Silver Screen* that she'd refused any glamour treatment: "Even the plainest movie star couldn't be jealous of a pan like mine, and I've got sense enough to realize I didn't get where I am because of my beauty." Sidney Skolsky reported that clothes didn't interest her and that she preferred to wear slacks over dresses. "She seldom gets a manicure or goes to the beauty parlor," Skolsky revealed.

Such was clearly not the image of a Hollywood movie star. It's no wonder Kelly never made it to the kinds of leading parts landed by other comediennes like Carole Lombard or Lucille Ball, known as much for their glamour as their slapstick. Yet despite her offbeat ways, Patsy's press—unlike that of the pansies—did not mock her. Irene Thirer headed one article "Funny Patsy Kelly calls herself 'just a mug,'" but presented the "hoyden" actress as a delightful, smart, sassy, self-deprecating talent. By 1938 the *New York Post* called her "the most sought after feminine funster in Hollywood."

Indeed, her image, though unconventional, does not seem to have engendered the kind of "suspicion" that attached itself to Pangborn and his sissy brethren. Kelly likely would have continued playing showy supporting parts for decades if it hadn't been for her drinking, which eventually discouraged producers from hiring her. When Wilma Cox went back to New York, where she made a name for herself singing at the Rainbow Room in Rockefeller Center, Patsy followed, although they seem to have separated soon afterward. Patsy was near bankruptcy when Tallulah Bankhead gave her a job as her live-in secretary. Friends said it was more "housemaid"; Patsy told her pal, gay columnist Lee Graham, that her duties were to "fix madam a drink, hand her a Kleenex—you know, general slob."

It would appear to have been a sorry end to one of the screen's most original players, an independent lesbian who had defied the Hollywood game and won, yet lost her larger battle with life. But the resilient Patsy Kelly would have the last laugh.

THE CODE GAINS TEETH

In the summer of 1933, with the war on pansies still playing out in the trade papers, the battle over enforcement of the Production Code was reaching a crisis point. Responding to a fever pitch of criticism from Catholic and other religious leaders, once again threatening a massive boycott of the movies, the federal government announced it would consider regulating the film industry. In doing so, it would put into law many of the tenets of the Production Code.

No one except diehard reformers like Fathers Daniel Lord and Wilfrid Parsons wanted this: not Hays, not Quigley, certainly not the studio chiefs. And among them, the biggest opponent of government censorship was MGM's wunderkind Irving Thalberg, who despised the limitations the Code put on artists and who actively (if clandestinely) encouraged his directors to defy it. Thalberg had pushed through such Code-defiant pictures as *Letty Lynton, The Mask of Fu Manchu, Blondie of the Follies,* and *Queen Christina,* much to the indignation of studio head Mayer, who bore the brunt of the heat from Will Hays. Thalberg also propped up the careers of Edmund Goulding and William Haines at a time when Joseph Breen was crying "pervert." Thalberg had attempted to offer a counterproposal when the Code was drafted in 1930, arguing that the movies should not be subjected to any more restrictions than other art forms.

But Thalberg was out of commission when the Code battles were coming to a head. Always of frail constitution, he had suffered a heart attack in December 1932, and had gone to Europe to recover with his wife, Norma Shearer. Thus was one of the few voices of reason effectively silenced at a critical juncture.

Will Hays visited with studio chiefs in Hollywood before heading to Washington in August. He was making the rounds to urge an alternative to outside censorship: a rigid policy of *self*-enforcement. He argued, with some logic, that giving him veto power over finished pictures was the only way to stave off both economic disaster *and* government regulation. With studio finances badly shaken by the Depression, the boycott threat was taken very seriously. MGM's profits for 1933 were roughly half of what they had been in 1932; Universal and Warner Brothers posted losses; and Paramount was in reorganization. Of even more concern, the number of weekly moviegoers had dropped by some twenty million since 1930. The moguls really had no choice but to agree to Hays' proposal; even Thalberg, reporting back to the studio too late to do much else, had to agree it was the lesser of two evils.

The decision that came out of Washington in September 1933 was essentially Hays' self-censorship proposal. Agreed to by all of the major studios, it was put into strict effect as of July 1, 1934. None other than Joseph Breen was named head of the Production Code Administration (PCA), to which all scripts were submitted for clearance before production began, and all finished films were submitted for a final seal of approval. Any film denied an official MPPDA seal would be, under the agreement, also denied a release. Breen and his watchdogs would scour both scripts and final product for any reference, any inference, any suggestion no matter *how* vague, that violated the provisions of the Code.

That the movies were now subject to a distinctly conservative Christian perspective, based on the concept of *sin,* is documented by numerous letters in the PCA files and among the voluminous papers left by Will Hays. Breen wrote openly about Catholic theology; Hays himself admitted the necessity of following Christian principles. MPPDA secretary Carl Milliken put it succinctly in a letter to a prominent clergyman in 1934, soon after the Code was given teeth: "I was convinced of the great importance, from the Christian standpoint, of improving screen standards." The Jewish moguls had little recourse but to rubber-stamp the theology of Breen and Father Daniel Lord into studio policy.

The party was over. Sex came now only *with* sin. And *homo*-sex no longer existed at all.

Overnight, Hollywood films were sterilized. No more full-mouth kisses between Dietrich and other women. No more pagan revelries or boy prostitutes. And no more pansies.

At least, no more pansies as strident as Mr. Ernest. Breen's staff tooth-combed each script for any suggestion of male effeminacy. And in contrast to the contemptuous indifference Cukor had exhibited on *Our Betters,* now directors and producers routinely acquiesced to Breen's demands.

The few attempts over the next decade to use gay characters was met by blunt force from the Breen office. They were quite suspicious of the character of "Dr. Stall" in W. C. Fields' script for *The Bank Dick* (1940), writing to Universal that Stall's "fairly feminine voice" (as described in the text) "should not have about it any possible suggestion of a 'pansy.'" On the defensive, director Edward F. Cline responded obsequiously, "His 'fairly feminine voice' was never intended as 'pansy.' It possibly should have read that he is business-like with the patient and solicitious over the telephone."

What's striking is that the script, in typical Fieldsian humor, includes a father hitting his child over the head with a bottle and threatening her with an urn—but all Breen found to object to was the doctor's "fairly feminine voice." In the finished product, Dr. Stall, as played by Harlan Briggs, comes across as a pipe-smoking, gruff old man. Even Franklin Pangborn, playing the foppish J. Pinkerton Snoopington, underplayed his part, eschewing his trademark fluttery mannerisms despite his monocle and bowler hat. He even tells Fields, just in case there might be any question, "I'm a married man with a grown daughter eighteen years of age." It's Grady Sutton, in fact, playing the suitor of Fields' daughter, who's the nelliest of the bunch.

That same year, Pangborn was involved in a more controversial exchange with Breen. The original script of Hal Roach's *Turnabout* (1940) included a character named Mr. Pingboom, a throwback to the blatant pansies of the pre-Code period. Reading the script, Breen was appalled. "This characterization of Mr. Pingboom as a 'pansy' is absolutely unacceptable," he wrote, "and must be omitted from the finished picture. If there is any such flavor, either in casting, direction or dialogue, we will be unable to approve the picture."

Breen knew from experience—*Our Betters* had been a perfect example— of how a certain actor or director could inject "perversion" into a character or situation that, on paper, appeared harmless. In *The Bride of Frankenstein,* as another example, there had been no initial objection to the character of Dr. Pretorius as a pansy. Breen's chief concerns had been about the film's apparent blasphemy, although he seems to have suspected *something* queer in Pretorius' line "We are all three infidels, scoffers at all marriage ties." Whale agreed to change the word "infidels" to "skeptics," and "marriage" to "normal." Breen was placated, and filming was allowed to begin. Yet *Bride's* final cut is about as queer as can be, with Pretorius' arch effeminacy (and yes, quite obvious perversion) coming through without use of lipstick or specific dialogue. It was all done through Ernest Thesiger's eyes and the lilt of his voice, and Whale's subversive direction. (For further discussion, see Chapter 6, "Auteur Theories.") Thus Breen certainly had cause to be suspicious of any character that hinted at "pansyism," even if such a character appeared benign enough in the script.

That's why he took such an interest in *Turnabout.* It was a project he thoroughly disapproved of from the start, the story of a man and woman whose souls are switched, with all sorts of ensuing gender confusion. He was outraged by the ending—the man discovers he is pregnant—finding the entire proceedings "tasteless." But most of his ire was reserved for Mr. Pingboom, and when it was announced that Franklin Pangborn would play the part, Breen was convinced Roach was asking for trouble.

"As written, the scenes between Willows and Pingboom seem to us to have a questionable flavor, in view of the characterization of the two actors," Breen wrote. As this was before production began, it would appear that Breen's objection stemmed from Pangborn's reputation as a "pansy player," as some press accounts called him. (John Hubbard, who played

Willows, wasn't known for particularly effeminate mannerisms, but apparently playing opposite Pangborn was enough to give Breen pause.)

Specifically, Breen asked for several deletions: the reference to Pingboom as a "big petunia;" another character's observation that "The guys swishes, and I don't like swishers;" and Pingboom's own line to Willows, "Toodle-oo, Timsy," after Willows shows him his legs. It's clear Roach was going for broke here: subtlety was out the window. It makes sense: a film about gender reversal was inevitably going to touch on homosexuality.

Not if Breen had his way, however. Roach agreed to the cuts, bowdlerizing a film that could have been very funny, and instead turned out to be a flop. Even in its expurgated form, *Turnabout* received a "Partly Objectionable" rating from the Legion of Decency, the Catholic watchdog group that sprang up to rate films independently for the MPPDA after the enforcement of the Code. Roach was actually glad to settle for "Partly Objectionable" after being threatened with an outright "Condemned."

The *Turnabout* brouhaha came to be known as "the Pangborn incident," further stamping Pangborn—and by extension, all his sissy colleagues— with the mark of subversion. Indeed, Production Code Administration files reveal that Breen remained leery of Pangborn. Concerned over the way Pangborn might handle his role in W. C. Fields' *Never Give a Sucker an Even Break,* Breen threatened to refuse a seal of approval "if Pangborn plays his role in a way suggestive of a pansy." He didn't.

Benign and silly they might seem today, but in the Thirties and Forties, Hollywood's pansies had the studio executives and censors quaking in their shoes.

A GAY OLD TIME:
THE PANSY CLUBS AND THE POST-CODE METAMORPHOSIS

If Hollywood in the Thirties was obsessed with the pansy on-screen, it was in large part because their real-life counterparts were enjoying a renaissance. Historian George Chauncey has documented the "pansy craze" that spread through the nation's large urban areas in the early part of the decade. In New York, both Harlem and Greenwich Village in the mid-Twenties were the sites of enormously popular drag balls, attended by both gay and straight patrons. By the late Twenties and early part of the Thirties, the "pansy" had moved out from the margins of the city and into Times Square, where female impersonator Jean Malin became the toast of Broadway.

Unlike an earlier generation of female impersonators like Julian Eltinge, who attempted to project the notion of being a "normal" man engaged in an unusual art, the pansy entertainers of the 1930s flaunted their difference—their *queerness*. Chauncey observed: "Jean Malin and his imitators forced their audiences to contend with them directly in unequal verbal contests that left audiences alternately charmed, bewildered, dazzled, and outraged. At least some gay performers seized the opportunities Prohibition culture provided to expand the space available for gay self-representation and to challenge the conventions of ridicule and disdain that governed the straight world's response to them."

In some ways, the brazen integrity of the pansy performers mirrors the on-screen pansies of Cukor and Whale: daring to use their own voices, flaunting their outrageousness while asserting a kind of social and intellectual superiority over their heterosexual observers. The pansy craze became as popular as it did precisely *because of* its subversive challenge: it allowed audiences to affirm their own sense of "sophistication" while mocking the obtuseness of mainstream culture.

For a brief, wondrous moment drag queens ruled Hollywood's nightlife. Most of the big names from New York—Malin, Karyl Norman, Francis Renault—settled in Los Angeles once their vogue in the East had peaked. *Variety* noted in September 1932: "While the whoops idea is just getting a hold locally, it has passed out in most eastern cities. Several oo-la-la entertainers are figuring on opening spots here, believing the craze will build up, and hold at least over the winter." It's not surprising to note whom the *Hollywood Reporter* reported as the audience for the pansy clubs: Haines, Lowe, Cukor, Akins, Bankhead, Kay Francis, Tom Douglas, Lil Tashman, Ina Claire, Ethel Barrymore, Cary Grant—the same "sophisticated" gay and gay-friendly crowd that Andy Lawler chronicled in his scrapbooks and Jerome Zerbe documented with his camera.

In truth, gay bars had been part of the Hollywood scene since 1929, when Thomas Gannon opened Jimmy's Back Yard on Ivar Street on New Year's Eve. With Prohibition still in place, the establishments officially served no alcohol, but bootleggers and cocaine dealers kept patrons well supplied. Harry Hay would remember seeing Hollywood names among the crowd at such clubs, among them Haines and Edmund Lowe. "We called them 'temperamental' clubs then," he said, "because we were 'temperamental' people." Other such places included Freddy's and Allen's, both of which were raided for their bathtub gin. "You kept your ear cocked to hear about whoever's new place about every six weeks," Hay said.

David Hanna, a writer for the *Hollywood Reporter* during the 1930s, recalled they were referred to as "queer clubs." *Variety* labeled them "panze joints." Whatever they were called, by late 1932 their notoriety elevated Hollywood's gay nightlife to a new and far more visible level.

Jimmy's Back Yard hosted Rae Bourbon's "Boys Will Be Girls" extravaganza; Harry Hay worked there as a shill, drumming up crowds. Bourbon was a flamboyant, larger-than-life character, born in Texas to cattle-farming parents. He ran off to join a carnival and had been performing in drag ever since. He'd prove durable, remaining a fixture in Hollywood nightlife for many years. After Jimmy's Back Yard, he moved over to other clubs, notably Rendezvous and Chez Boheme. Of his act, *Variety* reported in the 1940s: "He has a wealth of Kinseyesque but cleverly written material. . . . He's excellent for late spots, where no family trade exists."

David Hanna recalled Bourbon fondly. "He used phrases like 'Get you, Nelly'—swish, campy expressions, chatter-and-patter songs such as 'I'm a Link in a Daisy Chain,' 'Sailor Boy,' and 'When I Said No to Joe.' He was a very bold queen. He used to have a great big touring car and thought nothing of driving up and down Hollywood Boulevard being as swishy as he wanted to be."

The insouciance of performers like Bourbon made the pansy clubs huge hits. *Variety* reported in September 1932 they were "paying off," every one of them operating at a profit. By early 1933 there were several flourishing. B.B.B.'s Cellar, run by Bobby Burns Berman, had a revue of ten boys dressed as girls. The *Hollywood Reporter* caught Tallulah Bankhead, William Haines, Ethel Barrymore, and Howard Hughes there one night, each guest with a hammer, instructed to pound the table every time a new guest arrived. It aroused much laughter, but also kept them on their toes abut any possible raid. Bruz Fletcher ran his eponymous establishment on Sunset Boulevard; later, he'd headline at Cafe Bali. There was also Karyl Norman, who performed in the guise of various Hollywood actresses at La Boheme, also on Sunset Boulevard. The *Hollywood Reporter* spotted William Haines and Joan Crawford in the audience to see Norman's takeoff on Crawford as Sadie Thompson in late 1932. *Variety* called Norman "a true artiste," and singled out his backup performer, La Verde, who did "a mean rumba and is plenty of 'hot cha' when it comes to appearance."

No pansy performer was more celebrated than Jean Malin, however, who arrived in Hollywood in late 1931, fresh from his Broadway laurels. Born in Brooklyn in 1908 to Polish-Lithuanian parents, he was only in his early teens when he won a drag contest at a Greenwich Village ball, taking the name Imogene Wilson, one of the most flamboyant of the Ziegfeld Follies showgirls. Six feet, two hundred pounds, Malin was a force to be reckoned with. Performing in the Village's gay bars, he'd later give "Broadway its first glimpse of pansy night life." Heckled by men in the audience, Malin's back would arch, his chin lift in defiance. "He had a lisp, and an attitude, but he also had a sharp tongue," one reporter observed. "The wisecracks of the men who hooted at his act found ready answer." The New York tabloid *Broadway Brevities* reported that the city's "pansies hailed La Malin as their queen."

It was with such a defiant, undisguised queerness that Malin arrived in the film colony—significantly, just as the battles over the Production Code and on-screen pansy life were escalating. Billy Haines immediately reached out and brought Malin into the Hollywood social scene, fixing him up with his pal, Polly Moran, as an escort, whenever Patsy Kelly was unavailable. The gossip columnists noted Malin's comings and goings as they did any movie star's, often mentioning his "close friend" Jimmy Forlenza. The elite audiences he brought into his club solidified his social standing among the town's sophisticates. *Variety* suggested that while the "local filmities" found Malin entertaining, some of the "local crowd" (read, "straight") felt as if the joke went over their heads: "Wisecracks and flip remarks, especially to noisy guests, had the home boys and girls wondering what it was all about."

Malin, like his sister queens, elicited as much loathing as he did admiration. "Polly Moran's companion at all the theaters and gay places was, of all things, Jean Malin," one item reported. To a certain segment in Hollywood, Malin was a "thing"—neither male nor female, not even human. Certainly anyone socializing with him also became suspect. Malin had pushed the limits of Hollywood's tolerance to the very edge: it's not surprising that he and his comrades did not last long in the post-Prohibition, post–Production Code era.

The pansy clubs were gone almost as soon as they appeared. It was part of a nationwide trend: in 1931 the RKO vaudeville circuit management banned the use of the words "pansy" and "fairy" by any of their performers, and in January 1933 Atlantic City banned all pansy acts from its stages. San Francisco was soon to follow. John Loughery has written, "The fears for the future unleashed by the Depression were singularly powerful motivations in accelerating an ugly process." Nowhere was it uglier than in Los Angeles, where police began clamping down in the fall of 1932. On October 1, they raided B.B.B.'s Cellar, arresting nine men. Next they swooped down on Jimmy's Back Yard, cuffing five men and hauling them down to the station. *Variety* reported it was "a drive on the Nance and Lesbian amusement places in town." The pansy clubs' days were numbered.

Over the next several months each was raided in turn. The owners were charged with violating the Prohibition act; patrons were nailed on being drunk or in possession of liquor. Bail was set high, usually around $1,500. Then, in the midst of the police clampdown, Prohibition was lifted; seeking a new rationale for its campaign against the pansy clubs, police discovered an ordinance prohibiting the appearance of anyone in drag unless employed in the establishment. "That killed the lavender spots," *Variety* reported in November 1933.

The caveat of the ordinance suggests that many club patrons had *them-*

selves been in drag. By 1940, when the famous Julian Eltinge was booked to appear at the Rendezvous, a club on North Cahuenga Boulevard, a new law had been enacted forbidding even entertainers from wearing the clothing of the opposite gender. Eltinge, given his reputation, asked for a waiver but was refused; police called the Rendezvous a place of "questionable morals." The star was reduced to wearing a tuxedo, displaying his gowns on a rack and giving the glorious history of each.

Those performers who survived the demise of the pansy clubs didn't have it easy. David Hanna recalled a distinct change in Rae Bourbon's act. Gone were the feathers and boas and wigs, but the biting wit and campy repartee remained. "For some reason," Hanna said, "the LAPD had it in for Bourbon. Time and again he was hauled off to jail by the police and charged with giving a 'lewd, indecent performance.'" Indeed, tragic fates awaited most of the great pansy performers of the Thirties. Jean Malin died in a car accident in 1933; Bruz Fletcher committed suicide in 1941. Even Bourbon, who went on to perform with Mae West on Broadway, was later implicated in murder and died in prison, begging for help from his friends, in 1971.

It's vital to see all this in the context of the period. At the *exact same time* the reformers had achieved enforcement of the Production Code, the police were enacting a concurrent clampdown on the pansy clubs. Hollywood's gay subculture had come under direct assault by 1933. Visibility was not to be permitted; gay establishments, like gay film roles, had to be expurgated of any overt distinguishing characteristics.

Suddenly, those places identified by the subculture as "gay" were officially *not*. The Montmartre, once the hippest of the hip in the Twenties, catered primarily to homosexuals as the Thirties went on, but never self-named itself as a pansy club or queer bar. The Crown Jewel, on South Hill Street, was "discreet and elegant," according to Fred Frisbie, an early gay activist who lived in Hollywood at the time. A driver's license was needed to enter. "There was a code of conduct in such bars that normally prohibited any same-sex touching," Frisbie remembered, "making it difficult at times to tell a gay bar from a straight one."

That's as apt a description if ever there was one of Cafe Gala, perhaps the most famous of the post-Code gay nightspots in Hollywood. "Not that it advertised itself as a gay bar or even had an exclusively gay patronage," said David Hanna, "but a gay bar it essentially was."

The fashion critic Mr. Blackwell, then a young designer just getting his start, also recalled the place fondly: "The elegant nightclub held a sentimental affection for us—romantic, glamorous, brimming with café society and lacquered luxury." Judy Garland or Lena Horne might be called up onto the stage for an impromptu number. Cole Porter and Elsa Maxwell might be spotted holding court at a table next to Igor Stravinsky or Lady Mendl (Elsie de Wolfe). Located on Sunset Boulevard on the site later occupied by Spago, Cafe Gala was opened in 1939 by the Baroness Catherine d'Erlanger. "Poor old thing, she was kind of in her dotage then, with her hair dyed red and white roots," recalled Frank Lysinger, then in the music department at MGM and a frequent patron. "But a sweet old gal. She'd wander around and make all of us feel at home."

Born in France to a titled family in 1875, Catherine de Robert d'Aqueria de Rochegard had been a famous beauty, hosting salons in Paris and Venice in the years between the wars. She married Baron Emile d'Erlanger, a French banker; their son was chairman of British Overseas Airways. After her husband's death and the outbreak of war, the baroness came to America with her fortune sewed into her clothing. She had met the flamboyant singer Johnny Walsh in London; devoted to him, she opened Cafe Gala as a showcase for his talents.

"Johnny never failed to sing 'It's a Long Long Time from May to December,' with more handerkchief action than Hildegarde," remembered one patron. Walsh was "America's version of Noël Coward," added Mr. Blackwell, who "loved watching a tuxedoed Walsh perform in his scintillatingly chic way. . . . Impeccable phrasing, superb arrangements, and a fabulous sense of humor made Walsh legendary in the Los Angeles nightclub world."

Like the pansy clubs, Cafe Gala attracted Hollywood's smart set regardless of sexuality. At the tables, studio executives could often be spotted with rising young starlets and their agents, but around the bar, as costume designer Walter Plunkett remembered, "there tended to be a lot more gaiety." David Hanna recalled the reason Cafe Gala could enjoy long-running success in the new, more conservative atmosphere in Hollywood:

> Johnny [Walsh] was at once manager, doorman, and performer at the Gala. He was also gay, and this contributed very much to the success of the club. Night after night, Hollywood's gay population turned out. . . . It felt safe. Johnny saw to it that no undesirables entered. Patrons had to meet a dress code, and Johnny enforced standards of behavior inside. At the bar, which was often crowded with men two or three deep, Johnny would tell someone to sit facing forward. The inference was obvious: no groping on the premises, which in effect meant, "Don't provoke the Vice."

Without the fear of raids, "The Gala was a special gift for gay men and women in the film industry," Hanna said. "It meant for the first time they could spend an evening with other gay men or lesbians at a Hollywood nightspot without fear. . . . The gossip columnists treated it no differently than they did other clubs. All this gave the place a measure of respectability."

Cafe Gala epitomizes both the social scene and the status of homosexuals within the industry in immediate post-Code Hollywood. With a veneer of "respectability"—a façade that could not be overtly identified as "queer" or "deviant"—both the Gala and the gays within the studio structure could thrive. "The "undesirables"—which meant essentially the nonindustry, working-class gays of Los Angeles, the kind who worried less about "image"—were kept out, so the party was protected and insulated. But as delightful as it all might be, such rapture was never essentially reliable. There was always the sense of danger, a fear that the illusion would be discovered. "Who knew how long it could last?" one man remembered. "In those days, you never knew when you might be struck down."

THE NEW HOLLYWOOD PRESS

The new, more conservative climate was manifested not only by the police and the censors, but also by the press. In the Twenties, the vitriol had been left to such "yellow journalists" as Edward Doherty and Ed Roberts, with the fan magazines and daily columnists largely working in cooperation with the studios to produce glowing portraits of the stars and directors. Certainly innuendo had crept in smartly between the lines, but rarely was there anything damning, judgmental, or assaultive.

In the post-Code era, however, even the fan magazines took on a certain edge. To be sure, most coverage was still cooperative, a balanced relationship between journalist, studio publicist, and star. Yet given the mandate of the reformers, there was hay to be made and newspapers to be sold from writing about transgressions that a decade ago would have been studiously avoided. Anita Loos recalled Louella Parsons badgering the mother of Constance Talmadge for the full story of Constance being caught in a raid with William Haines at a Hollywood speakeasy. "Peg [Talmadge] broke into a cold sweat and waited for the dread item to appear," Loos wrote.

In the old days, it had been rare indeed for anybody to break into cold sweats, unless they were part of a scandal that had been just too big to contain, like the Arbuckle trial or the Taylor murder. Indeed, columnists like Parsons were tame compared to the underground press that appeared in the early 1930s, rags like *The Coast Reporter,* which printed outrageous half-truths about Clara Bow. The It Girl might have been sexually adventurous, but the scandal sheet had her so busy she would never have found time to act. Its publisher, Frederic Girnau, was arrested for obscenity and misuse of the mails. So salacious was this underground press that federal prosecutors promised a war on scandal sheets: "We are watching not only Girnau's publication," said U.S. District Attorney Samuel W. McNabb, "but others leaning toward the printing of obscene and insinuating articles."

Careful not to cross or even get too close to that line, the mainstream press nonetheless pushed the envelope farther than it had before. With people like Girnau now defining the fringe, the center could dare to be more extreme. Reading the fan magazines, issue after issue, year after year, a clear picture emerges of the progression of this stridency—a trend historian Alexander Walker called the "latent sadism" of the press of the early sound era. In the mid-1920s, J. Warren Kerrigan and Eugene O'Brien could wax poetic when the Marriage Question was posed; a decade later, newer stars were jabbed one, two, three, or more times until they gave a satisfactory answer. Faith Service, writing for *Motion Picture* in August 1932, pressed Claudette Colbert repeatedly for the "real reason" she and husband Norman Foster lived apart. Several writers, weary of William Haines' wisecracking about his "romance" with Polly Moran, openly bemoaned his lack of respect for the Marriage Question. "He just won't be serious on the question of matrimony," wrote a fed-up Alice Tildesley. Valmond Maurice Guest called Haines a "funny bachelor" in *Film Weekly,* and a juicy, suggestive account of his friendship with Prince Charles of Belgium was played up in none other than *The Los Angeles Times.* So many anecdotes and descriptions, increasingly nasty, were written about Haines in the 1931–1933 period that they couldn't help but impact his career—an example, once again, of an "intertextual" understanding of a star's persona, which surely could not have escaped the notice of the studio front office.

One of the clearest displays of this new, more aggressive press concerns Ramon Novarro. May Allison, former actress and widow of *Photoplay* editor James Quirk, positioned her entire April 1933 telephone interview with Novarro around the question of why he wasn't married. Allison, who clearly *knew* the answer, nonetheless pushed him over and over to be more specific:

> ALLISON: Any idea of marrying soon, Ramon?
> NOVARRO: I've always had ideas. Still have the old ones. You remember what I told you once before about that.
> ALLISON: Are you in love with anyone?
> NOVARRO: Oh, I love a great many people.

When she pushed for names, he hung up on her. The intrepid Allison called him right back, reminding him of how she and Doris Kenyon used to try to fix him up with girls. This was *the entire point* of her piece: his failure to play the Hollywood game. "Are you afraid of marriage?" she asked finally. When she received yet another evasive answer, Allison concluded that when Novarro *did* marry (not *if*), he'd have to find an older woman: "The average flapper wouldn't know what to do with him," she wrote.

Having been a star for over a decade, Novarro and his bachelorhood were ripe for journalists' nitpicking. In the new climate, readers were given peeks through the veil of studio-manufactured publicity that they'd been expected to buy as "truth" for so long. Writing for *Modern Screen* in the mid-1930s, Katherine Albert, who'd been an MGM publicist herself, told her readers not to believe everything they read, that the majority of the romances in the fan magazines were spun out of publicists' concoctions. Then, however, she went on to spin one of her own: that Novarro and Myrna Loy were engaged in a "genuine" love affair.

Notably, such disingenuous reporting was not often penned by gay journalists. Scribes like Ben Maddox continued, for the most part, to write about the stars in the old style: telling the truth without spilling the beans or sounding the alarm. Maddox's famous (some would say infamous) 1933 *Modern Screen* profile of Cary Grant and Randolph Scott, with pictures of them at the home they shared, said all it needed to: "Cary is the gay, impetuous one. Randy is serious, cautious. Cary is temperamental . . . Randy is calm and quiet." Both *gay* and *tempermental,* used within the homosexual subculture, were enough to signal Maddox's meaning.

An extraordinary piece ran in the December 1939 issue of *Modern Screen,* titled "Vincent's Priceless Hat—Being the Revelations of a Very Gay Fedora on His Even Gayer Boss." Vincent Price was a young actor who, early on, had moved fairly openly within the gay subculture. But—as many did in the post-Code era—he married and "settled down," prompting this gimmicky piece allegedly "written" by his fedora, remembering the gay days in Vienna when it and Vincent were inseparable. "Somebody must have planted a suggestion that I be retired," the hat lamented.

Such an early form of "outing" would not have occurred in the days before the Code. The Price article is nasty and mean-spirited, not coy or clever. The innuendo of the piece is not so much between the lines as splashed ungainly on top of them: a silly device masking cruel intent.

Depending on their mood and what favors were needed at the moment, the fan magazines might either run verbatim a fluff piece generated by the studio publicity department or tear it to shreds. A telling memo survives in the *Photoplay* archives from Maude Lathem, secretary to James Quirk, showing the independence of the fan magazines. "Before Mr. Quirk came out he okayed a story on Eddie Goulding which was the result of Eddie's personal appeal to him," Lathem wrote. Although Quirk assigned Harriet

Parsons to write up the piece to placate Goulding, Lathem didn't think Quirk intended "to use it at all."

The newfound independence of the press corps was unnerving to the studios. According to the trade journal *Cinema Digest,* as early as 1932 there was talk of establishing an in-house censor board "to pass on all interviews before writers submit them to their publishers," deleting "all items they consider in bad taste or detrimental to the studios, regardless of their truth or interest." Writing in the *Kansas City Star,* reporter John Moffitt expressed outrage at such a notion. "The history of American journalism does not indicate that the public has much interest in an industry's attempt to tell its own story," he said. "The public will not be interested in faked smoke-screens and there will be no reason for their publication."

Such a system was not officially put in place, for journalists eager for access and exclusives were always willing to cooperate with the studios. Drafts of interviews in various collections at the Academy of Motion Picture Arts and Sciences reveal the blue pencil of a studio publicist's first look, making suggestions for cuts or revisions. But for the most part, the post-Code press was an independent and often unruly bunch, led by a couple of moralizing, middle-class matrons forever at war with each other, still recognizable today by just their first names: Hedda and Louella.

FROM UNDER THEIR HATS: PARSONS AND HOPPER

Walter Winchell, the East Coast's gossip counterpart to Hedda and Louella, didn't have a lot of respect for the Hollywood press. After visiting screenland, he said he could never work there. Hollywood columnists, he explained, were required to turn over major stories of divorce or romance to the city desks for coverage as "news." The columnist might still write the story, but forfeit a byline—or at least lose the impact such an item would have had as the lead of his or her column. "I would rather perish first," Winchell sniffed, heading back to New York.

In Hollywood, the news wasn't pothole ordinances or votes at City Hall: it was divorce and romance among the stars. This was what gave Hedda Hopper and Louella Parsons, as well as such second-rank columnists as Edith Gwynne, Jimmie Fidler, Jimmy Starr, Florabel Muir, and many others—such power. They weren't "merely" gossip columnists; they were the arbiters of the news, of community standards, of who was in and who was out.

Louella had been writing her column for the Hearst syndicate since the early silent days and pretty much ruled the roost pre-Code. But when the exponential growth of movie audiences precipitated a parallel growth in the movie press, she was forced to share some of her power. She remained embittered about losing her forty-eight hours' preferential treatment from the studios, and resented having to elbow her way to the front with people she considered hacks. She retaliated by setting up special deals with actors' agents, who slipped her material ahead of the studio publicity department.

It became an often chaotic, all-out war—especially in 1938, when Hedda Hopper was set up by the *Los Angeles Times* as competitor to Louella, whose column ran in the *Los Angeles Examiner.* Hopper had been an actress and "mother confessor" at various studios for the past two decades: she knew as many of Hollywood's secrets as Parsons did, if not more. Both women were feared, courted, loathed, and lavished with gifts on birthdays and Christmas. Both were conservative, moralizing, and, in the end, lonely women who used their powers to fill the aching emptiness of their personal lives.

Both also had a curious, even *schizophrenic,* relationship with Holly-wood's gay culture. Maybe it's not so curious, after all, given that their attitudes merely reflected Hollywood's own schizophrenia on the subject. Both Hedda and Louella had gay assistants, and pretty overt ones at that. King Kennedy was a young actor when he signed on as a "legman" to Parsons: in 1939 he married her daughter Harriet. Both King and Harriet were gay; how much Louella knew at the time is unknown, but historian Anthony Slide was convinced that she had to eventually know the truth about Harriet, who lived with a series of female lovers after divorcing Kennedy. Later, Parsons employed Leo Castillo, who was part of Christopher Isherwood's circle.

Hopper was even more enmeshed in gay culture. From the very beginning, she was tight with William Haines; he remained a friend for life, even serving as one of her honorary pallbearers. She was close with Travis Banton, who was always designing new dresses and hats for her, and with Orry-Kelly, the costume designer at Warner Brothers and one of the most outrageous queens in Hollywood. As her right-hand woman, Hedda employed Dema Harshbarger, described by Anthony Slide as "a well-known Hollywood lesbian . . . a massive barrel of a woman who sported short, masculine haircuts [and] dark spartan-like suits." Hedda depended on Harshbarger for everything: personal management, deadlines, protection from libel.

In fact, it was Harshbarger who had given Hedda her start. In 1936, sensing her acting career was at its end, Hedda had turned to Dema, founder of the NBC Artists Bureau (an actors' agency). "I want to get on the air," Hedda told her.

"In half an hour," Harshbarger recalled, "she told me more about Holly-wood than I could learn in two years of constant study." Signing on as Hedda's manager, Dema secured her a twenty-six-week radio show that eventually led to her column with the *Times.* From that point on, Hedda deferred to Harshbarger in all business matters, calling her "The Brain."

Hedda's letters, carefully preserved and cataloged, are frank and sympathetic describing Harshbarger's life, telling friends all about Dema's new love affair with a much younger woman. Hedda placed no more emphasis or judgment on Dema's personal life than she did her own son's marriage and divorce. She remained fiercely devoted to Harshbarger until the latter's death.

Hopper had other gay help as well. After leaving Louella, King Kennedy signed on with her, and later, the television writer Robert Shaw also played informant. Shaw revealed that many other gay men performed legwork for Hedda over the years. Gays—perhaps better than anyone else—knew how to find the gossip, uncover the rumors, and separate falsehoods from truth.

Yet both Parsons and Hopper weren't above gay-bashing when the situation arose. Louella seemed to be implying that Nelson Eddy was gay in 1936 when she said "the big laugh in Hollywood these days is Nelson Eddy's feminine pursuers. . . . Come on, Mr. Eddy, even the hinterlands are wise to you." Whether or not Eddy was in fact gay is unclear; but Louella wasn't above making the insinuation—perhaps gossip passed on by one of her gay assistants.

The lesser lights followed Parsons' lead. Edith Gwynne also played the gay card writing for *The Hollywood Reporter,* which prided itself on its independence from the studios. Gwynne was particularly nasty about housemates Cary Grant and Randolph Scott, at one point remarking about a "long-haired town for males" populated by Grant, Scott, Gary Cooper, and (improbably) James Cagney. Likewise, after seeing the Maddox article with photographs of Grant and Scott in matching aprons, Jimmie Fidler sniped in his column that the two were "carrying the buddy business a bit too far."

But it was Hedda, as ever, who was by far the most vitriolic. As her personal correspondence reveals, she frequently indulged in gay-baiting and gay-bashing, despite her many gay friends. When *Look* magazine profiled Cary Grant, extolling his manly virtues and appeal to women, Hedda dashed off a letter to publisher Mike Cowles. "Whom does he think he is fooling?" she wrote about Grant. "He started with the boys and now he's gone back to them."

With a network of informants keeping her posted on any queer shenanigans, Hedda carefully preserved and cross-referenced all the information. One spy wrote to her that the real reason Ray Milland had walked off the set of *The Bride of Vengeance* was because director Mitchell Leisen wanted too many bare-chested shots of the actor. Another wrote to smear Howard Greer. The anonymous informant had found Greer's fashion show in San Francisco too outrageous—especially the antics of one Bruce MacIntosh, "mincing minion of Dressmaker Greer," whose runway command to "milk it, honey, milk it!" lost the informant as a customer "right then and there period."

Still, through it all, Hedda would arrive at parties escorted by Billy Haines or Orry-Kelly, and spend Christmas Eve with Travis Banton or Robert Shaw. "She was very lonely," said Shaw. "Gay men could afford to spend a lot of time with her because we had no wives, no children."

"She seemed to shy away from any real love," another assistant, Spec McClure, told author George Eells. "I think that's why she had a strange attraction to fags. They were good dancers. A lot of them were witty, talented people. They didn't paw her. The only problem she had when she got home was to keep them from coming in and drinking her liquor."

OUT WITH THE DUAL-SEX BOYS AND LESBOS

Just as the Code wiped out any overt evidence of gayness on the screen, and just as Vice shut down the pansy clubs, so, too, did the careers of the gay (and gay-perceived) stars of the Twenties and early Thirties come to an end. There is a vast world of difference between the earlier era's cast of leading men—even the apparently straight ones like Charles Farrell, Antonio Moreno, and John Gilbert—and the new breed that came in with the early days of sound, almost entirely macho: Gable, Tracy, Robert Montgomery, John Wayne, Edward G. Robinson, Humphrey Bogart, even James Stewart. Those who survived, like Gary Cooper and Cary Grant, had to transition from their soft, subtle androgyny to harder, unquestionable masculinity.

Of course, there were many reasons, as articulated earlier, for such a cultural shift, and the end of film careers for Haines, Novarro, and the rest can be attributed to a variety of factors. Yet even *these* are part of the Depression-era *Zeitgeist*—what George Chauncey called the public's "revulsion against gay life in the early 1930s." What was acceptable a decade before was no longer, by the middle part of the decade, even palatable.

The studio chiefs, long accustomed to tolerance of the gays in their ranks, were certainly aware of such a climate change. In early 1933, William Haines was terminated by Louis B. Mayer. According to Haines' contracts, recently released by Turner Entertainment, which holds the MGM archive, he had been kept on a short leash since 1931, when his three-year contract expired. After publicly floating the idea of letting him go entirely, the studio renewed his employment (at reduced salary) on a year-to-year basis. Although Haines' contract file does not reveal a smoking gun, it's clear from the stories he told friends that such treatment was a result of studio concern over his after-hours activities. Tales of arrests in Pershing Square and being present at raids on pansy clubs were numerous.

Since the mid-Twenties, the studios had attempted to control the off-screen behavior of its stars through "morals clauses." Before the Code was enforced, these were little more than boilerplate reassurances to Will Hays that they'd play the game like good boys and girls. Big stars could, and often did, refuse to honor such clauses. Warner Baxter crossed out a paragraph in his 1928 contract with Fox that imposed immediate termination should the star "offend against decency, morality, or social proprieties." The big X is initialed by both Baxter and Fox chief Winfield Sheehan. Clara Bow, too, rejected any morals clause, but Paramount, unnerved by the image of an untethered It Girl, made her annual bonus contingent upon her behavior.

The screenwriter Frances Marion, a close friend of Billy Haines, had insisted that Haines at his peak had similarly eighty-sixed his morals clause. Yet such wasn't the case: in his 1928 contract, it's stated quite plainly: "The artist agrees to conduct himself with due regard to public conventions and morals, and agrees that he will not do or commit any act or thing that will tend to degrade him in society or bring him into public hatred, contempt, scorn, or ridicule, or that will tend to shock, insult, or offend the community or ridicule public morals or decency, or prejudice the producer or the motion picture industry in general."

There's no sanction indicated, however—no threat of termination. (Interestingly, in the margin beside the clause, someone in the MGM front office—at some point or another—made a check mark in ink.) The clause remained in Haines' 1931 contract, and by implication in each of the one-year option agreements the studio made with him after that.

By that time, given the impetus of the struggle over the Code, the morals clause had taken on far greater authority. It was likely invoked during that fateful final encounter between Haines and Mayer, sometime in early 1933. Mayer, according to several accounts, urged the star to get married for the sake of appearance. When Haines refused, he was, in effect, terminated. Although a new one-year agreement had been reached in late 1932, he made no further pictures at the studio. On September 11, 1933, there's just this terse note in his file: "Contract terminates, option not exercised."

Mayer, always homophobic, surely had had his fill of Haines' innuendo-ridden press, especially in the increasingly intolerant atmosphere of Hollywood in early 1933. Haines had been perhaps their most difficult star to restrain, but in the era of "La Belle Epoque" few were goody-two-shoes. Nils Asther was moody and belligerent to reporters; even after a much-ballyhooed marriage to Vivian Duncan, he was given to wandering off. Reports of a live-in male friend cashing bad checks in his name reached the papers. Soon after he split from Duncan, MGM terminated Asther as well.

A romance was—at long last—cooked up for Ramon Novarro, but sputtered out when the targeted love interest, the spunky Myrna Loy, refused to play along. With Novarro dreaming about singing opera in his last fan-magazine articles, he, too, was dropped from the MGM roster.

Unlike Haines and Asther, however, Novarro's pictures had remained moneymakers, and so he was indulged as long as his box office held up. With the financial stress the Depression had placed on the studios, they could afford indulgence only for those who brought in the cash. When Novarro's popularity, too, was felled by the changing times and tastes, he left the studio where he had been a star for twelve years and found sporadic work elsewhere.

That wasn't the case for Haines, who despite his best efforts could land only two pictures at Mascot, a Poverty Row studio. What's significant about Haines' termination with MGM was the dearth of opportunities he found outside its gates. Although he'd eventually discover success as a tony interior decorator, in 1933 he wanted desperately to remain in movies. For the rest of his life, he'd insist that Mayer blackballed him at other studios, an assertion that's not difficult to believe, given Mayer's temperament and the fact that *nothing*—not even second leads or character parts—were made available to Haines, with the exception of the Mascot quickies. Meanwhile, however, other more pliant and less obviously gay leading men moved comfortably into supporting roles: Edmund Lowe, Richard Cromwell, even Novarro.

If evidence is still needed that such actions in 1933 were a part of a campaign that was—at least in part—conscious and deliberate, one need only recall *Variety*'s report in February about the Hays Office's "attempt to keep the dual-sex boys and lesbos out of films" and Sidney Kent's assertion in March that he didn't want "degenerates and fairies" in Fox pictures. The campaign against the pansies in 1932 and 1933, so specifically and vociferously articulated in the press and in private correspondence, was bound to be felt by the gay actors, and even gays behind the scenes. The repercussions are seen in sudden, striking examples of conformity: the toppling of gay leading men, the "straight" veneer of gay nightclubs, the reluctance of gay directors to tackle queer themes (discussed in the next chapter), and the marriages of even costume designers and set decorators, up until now presumably "safe" in their gayness (discussed in Chapter 7, "Queer Work").

The sea change is also manifested in the experiences of gay actors who came in after 1933. Cesar Romero participated in a kind of press that was nonexistent in the heyday of Billy Haines, Eddie Lowe and Lil Tashman. In 1941, he obligingly posed in a room in his house, which he called his "empty bridal suite," lamenting the fact that he had yet to find a wife. He "confided" to *Photoplay* writer Gladys Hall just how lonely he was: "If I can't find her, I wish she would find me." In April of that same year, he was profiled in *Silver Screen* by Jerry Asher, as gay as Cesar and one more journalist who'd make the jump to publicist. In Asher's piece, "Bachelor Behavior in Hollywood," Romero once again rambled on about how he was fed up with bachelorhood. He was weary of his houseboy, he said, "who doesn't know his fanny from his forehead."

It was a far cry from the kind of press of just a few years before, when Ramon Novarro hung up on May Allison when she pressed the Marriage Question a little too hard. Romero, on the other hand, was an active participant in framing the newly required answer.

But Romero lived in a far different Hollywood. *Motion Picture* stressed that he was that rare Latin lover who was also a "he-man"—more like Gary Cooper, the magazine insisted significantly, than Valentino. Cooper was now a paragon of masculinity, while Valentino had been forever tarnished as a pink powder puff. Always photographed with a woman on his arm, Romero was touted as a "ladies' man"—although his "dates" with Joan Crawford, Barbara Stanwyck, or Betty Furness were nothing more than a couple of pals out on the town. Asher wrote, clearly knowing the score, "Cesar has dated more of the leading Hollywood glamour gals than any other bachelor. And there isn't one who doesn't speak enthusiastically about him. But somehow Cesar had never become engaged."

Whereas Romero was paraded before the public as a ladykiller to disguise his queerness, an indisputable heterosexual like Clark Gable could, at the same time, tell the press: "I'm no ladies' man. I'm more at home with men than with women. But I think most men are." Most *straight* men, anyway. Such a statement from a gay actor would never have been permitted. With Gable it only added to his image and appeal.

Yet despite all the women photographed with him, Romero remained suspect, probably the reason his publicists engineered the "empty bridal suite" photographs. No matter how hard they tried—or in some cases, *didn't* try—fan-magazine writers just couldn't sound persuasive in describing Cesar's "dates" as genuine. There were too many markers: dapper dresser, killer dance partner, a gentleman who always brought the lady home on time and shook her hand platonically. In 1939 he and Joan Crawford lent their names to a *Photoplay* article on dance. As if Clark Gable would ever do *that*.

As usual, the truth was known within the industry, even if by the end of the decade there was a greater premium placed on its silence. Romero, a former ballroom dancer, was the grandson of the Cuban patriot José Martí, a fact curiously missing from much of his early publicity and only heralded later, starting in the 1940s. Many survivors of the era speak of the long relationship between Cesar and fellow Fox actor Tyrone Power. Romero, however, insisted that Power "loved the ladies . . . he couldn't help it, every place he went, boy, those women were there." True enough—Power's affairs with women are well documented—but the star was also, as documented by his biographer Hector Arce, involved with a number of men. The designer Mr. Blackwell, then a young actor known as Dick Ellis and, in his own words, a popular "boy toy," was another of Power's romances. They met for "romantic moments in his dressing room [and] took long rides, speeding down Sunset to Malibu."

Power is a classic example of that "second era" of gay star who played the game, and played it quite well. He was talked about among the crowd at the gay parties given by Cukor or Cole Porter or Christopher Isherwood, but he was known only tangentially. "Tyrone would never have come to a gathering where there were mostly gays," said Robert Wheaton, close with both Cukor and Porter. Another Cukor associate, Charles Williamson, recalled a friend of his who was procured by Cesar Romero as a trick for Power, who, unlike other stars, preferred middle-class boys over street kids. "He felt it was safer, that they were less likely to cause a scandal," said Williamson. "They understood the need for discretion."

• • •

Notable, too, is the classic case of Cary Grant. In 1934, just as the Code was put solidly into place and the campaign against the pansies both on- and off-screen had reached its peak, Grant left the home he shared with Randolph Scott and married actress Virginia Cherrill. From the start, their marriage was a disaster: the once-carefree Grant, as light and bubbly as his on-screen portrayals, attempted suicide after only a few months. In March 1935 Cherrill divorced him, describing him as sullen and drunk, claiming in court that he'd told her "a number of times" that he didn't want to live with her. Freed by his divorce, he'd go back to living with Randy.

At roughly the same period, Jerome Zerbe painted a far more complimentary portrait of Grant. During his "three-gay-month" sojourn in the movie colony, Zerbe often stayed with Grant and Scott, finding them both warm, charming, and happy. He'd later confide to several friends that he had affairs with both of them. Likewise, Mr. Blackwell, still as Dick Ellis, spent a few months living with Grant and Scott, considering them "deeply, madly in love, their devotion complete . . . Behind closed doors they were warm, kind, loving and caring, and unembarrassed about showing it."

In the beginning, perhaps, Grant and Scott had assumed they might live as their predecessors had. William Haines had, after all, shared his home quite openly with Jimmie Shields since 1926, hosting everyone from Irving Thalberg to members of the press. But 1934 was eight years and a lifetime away. The Grant-Scott cohabitation would finally be severed permanently by new marriages for both of them, although they remained friends for the rest of their lives. Grant's biographer, Roy Moseley, interviewed the maître d' at the Beverly Hillcrest Hotel who recalled seeing the two of them in the 1970s, now old and white-haired, sitting in the back of the restaurant, late at night, after all the other diners had left. They were holding hands.

The choice for stars post-Code was to either conform or get out. For character actors, it was a different story, and ironically the Hortons and Pangborns—whose sissy images had started the brouhaha—actually *thrived* in post-Code Hollywood. Still, it's striking to witness the change that came over both their screen portrayals and their personal press. The sissies after 1934 are as much the butt of jokes as ever, but gone are the lipstick and mincing walks. They no longer suggest active deviance: they read "British" or "upper-class" as much as "gay."

The actors who played these parts weren't immune to the forces that had exiled their star brethren. In 1938 Franklin Pangborn was reported to agree to a part in *Topper Takes a Trip* only on the condition he not have to faint in the film. "In three previous pictures," the article said, "he's had to faint, and he says he's tired of being typed as a 'fainter.'" Pangborn (or his publicists) had apparently decided his image needed a little tweaking: in one of the studio press releases around the same time, the point was made that if you called Pangborn a "sissy" offstage, he'd "implant five hard knuckles on your proboscis." Such was hardly likely from an actor friends remembered as not much different from the parts he played on-screen.

The post-Code imposition of gender conventionality also dictated changes in the press of Margaret Lindsay. No longer adamantly opposed to marriage, she was romantically linked to the clean-cut Dick Powell and quoted as saying she often dreamed of falling in love and becoming a wife. But her favorite Hollywood date? Cesar Romero, she said, still winking at those who knew the score, because when Cesar brought her home, he never asked for a good-night kiss.

That same year, the *New York Times* headlined its piece on Edward Everett Horton "Hailing a New Horton." The actor, the *Times* observed, had "developed a certain muliebrity of manner which has caused certain of the more captious among filmgoers to accuse him of effeminacy. . . . That's why it's all the more remarkable to find Edward Everett Horton, of all people, playing a straight college professor [in the film *Holiday*, ironically directed by George Cukor]. Suddenly a new Horton is hatched, a Horton without a double-take-em to his name, without grimaces or mock shudders, a Horton with authentic dignity and—crowning wonder—a Horton married to a wife who respects his manly feelings."

Horton with *manly feelings*. Hollywood's pansies—not to mention Hollywood itself—would never be the same.

AUTEUR THEORIES

THE GAY DIRECTORS AND PRODUCERS
OF HOLLYWOOD'S GOLDEN AGE
1935–1955

The auteur theory, so popular in the 1950s and 1960s, posited the director as author of a film, giving him or her full credit for its distinctive qualities. The theory offered scant attention to the essential collaborative nature of cinema, disregarding or trivializing the contributions of screenwriter, cameraman, art director, costume designer, set decorator, and editor. As such, the auteur theory canceled out gay authorship far more often than it affirmed it, given the mere handful of gay directors in the studio era.

It is a school of thought that has been largely discredited in the ensuing three decades, as studies have documented the contributions of film's other creators. Yet despite the overreaching of auteur theorists, it is undeniable that a large part of a film's creative imprimatur does indeed rest with the director. What has come more and more to light, however, is the role of the creative *producer* in the studio era, who often preceded the director on a project and was responsible for setting the tone, the style, and the approach the director would follow. Not just money men, the best of Hollywood's producers (also sometimes called supervisors) were also part of the forma-tive process, to the point where some—like David O. Selznick, Val Lewton, Roger Edens, and Ross Hunter—left a greater imprint on the final product than even the director. Selznick argued that "great films, successful films, are made in their every detail according to the vision of one man, and through supporting that one man."

Indeed, no other figure was as intimately involved in all aspects of film-making. "It was the producer who saw the script budgeted, cast the film, helped choose the director, and greatly influenced the filming itself," ob-served James Curtis, the editor of producer David Lewis' memoirs. "Once shooting was complete, it was the producer who stayed with the project through editing and previews." Lewis' particular strength, Curtis said, "was in his ability to influence the writing of his films, the best of which bore his imprint as clearly as that of any auteur."

With this in mind, considering the work of classic Hollywood's gay directors and gay producers—a small but vital subset of the studio system—suggests "queer cinema" might not be such a modern postulate. Occasion-ally, a convergence of director, producer, writer, and star came together, such as happened with *Camille* (1937). The gay writer DeWitt Bodeen said that *Camille* "represents a meeting of talents that were perfect for its inter-pretation." In fact, wags like to call the picture a rare "all-gay" studio pro-duction, and in some ways it comes close: producer David Lewis, director George Cukor, screenwriter Zoe Akins. Garbo, too, and Mercedes de Acosta had a hand in an early draft of the script before Akins took over. Robert Taylor, who played a stunningly beautiful Armand, was rumored to be having an affair with the film's set decorator, Jack Moore. There was also Adrian on costumes and Sydney Guilaroff doing hair. Rex O'Malley in-fused his Gaston with a natural feyness, a quality perhaps intended by Cukor and Akins, and another gay actor, Rex Evans, played several bit parts. ("Who is that big man and what part is he playing?" Garbo asked Cukor. "That man is Rex Evans," the director replied, "and he's playing the part of a friend who needs a job.")

Cukor also maneuvered the hiring of another friend—and another gay man—as the picture's true art director, supplanting the ubiquitous Cedric Gibbons, whose contract nonetheless decreed screen credit. This was Oliver Messel, esteemed scenic and costume designer from the London stage, whose outsider status evoked suspicion in the competitive world of the Hollywood studios. It wasn't Messel's first encounter with the studio bureaucracy; in 1935, during the filming of *Romeo and Juliet*, Cukor had caused a near war by insisting Messel design the costumes instead of Adrian—whom Cukor, according to several friends, viewed as pompous and pretentious. They weren't exactly sure why he held such antipathy for

Adrian, but Cukor, as discreet as he was, never tried to obfuscate either his Jewishness *or* his gayness in the way Adrian did.

"I get annoyed with statements that call George 'closeted,'" said his longtime friend and *Los Angeles Times* film critic Kevin Thomas. "George was never closeted. He never pretended to be anything he wasn't. He lived according to the rules of his time, that's all."

In fact, few of the gay directors of Hollywood's golden age played straight. They could be prickly, they could be coy, and they were always, in the parlance of the day, *circumspect*. But Hollywood's queer studio septet— Cukor, James Whale, Edmund Goulding, Mitchell Leisen, Irving Rapper, Arthur Lubin, and (later) Charles Walters—lived quite forthright gay lives, and although individually they've received varying degrees of scrutiny, they've never been considered together. Until now.

• • •

They knew who each other was: some were friends and some were rivals. Cukor had been in awe of Edmund Goulding since he first arrived in Hollywood in 1930, and the two retained an affection until Goulding's death in 1959. Irving Rapper was an occasional guest at Cukor's poolside parties; they shared several mutual friends. Cukor was close with Charles Walters' lover, the actor-turned-agent John Darrow; among Cukor's letters there's a note from Walters campily signed "Madeleine Carroll."

On the other hand, there was a certain animosity between Cukor and James Whale. They had likely first met through Whale's lover, David Lewis, and occasionally found themselves in each other's company at the salons of Salka Viertel in the 1930s. But Cukor found Whale indiscreet, and Whale found Cukor pompous. In a note to David Lewis, Whale wrote he didn't care for Alexander Pantages because he was "too much like George Cukor."

Mitchell Leisen also received a level of scorn from Cukor. Friends say Cukor considered Leisen crass; when David Chierichetti showed Cukor his book on Leisen, the director's only comment was "Very nice pictures." Of the seven, only Arthur Lubin seemed separate from the bunch, probably because he was a B-picture director among very status-conscious A's.

"For the most part," observed screenwriter Gavin Lambert, "the gay directors didn't mix [together] very much, at least not like straight directors did. Maybe there was a certain caution, a sense of not wanting to be identified with each other."

Still, there was an understood connection among them. As one friend said, "They knew who each other were—the ones who didn't get married or play any of that old game. I always kind of thought of them as the Magnificent Seven."

Actually, two of them *did* marry: Goulding and Leisen, but in both cases the marriages were personal and individual, not really attempts at obfuscation. That there were other directors who did "play that old game" is undeniable: Vincente Minnelli, Nicholas Ray, and later, near the end of the studio era, Tony Richardson. It must be pointed out, however, that these three arrived on the scene well after the Code had become entrenched and the heterosexual standard compulsory. (The directors of this later period were far more likely to be deeply circumspect or personally conflicted about their homosexuality. As Gavin Lambert wrote about his friend Richardson, "Coming of professional age when homosexuality was a criminal offense, exposure a threat to the careers of so many people, and police harassment at its peak, he placed his female lovers center stage and relegated his male lovers to the wings.")

For the "Magnificent Seven," however, flourishing in an earlier time, it was different: Goulding had been around since the silent days; Cukor and Whale were imported with the arrival of sound; Leisen turned to directing in 1933 after a decade in set design; and Arthur Lubin helmed his first picture in 1934. Homosexuality carried the same criminal penalties and social sanctions it would for Richardson some decades later, but in pre-Code Hollywood it prompted little of the same cultural paranoia or aggressive persecution. It's significant that in the decade following enforcement of the Code, only one gay director would emerge (Irving Rapper), suggesting at least that doors had become more difficult to budge. (Charles Walters didn't step up from choreography to direction until 1947.)

Yet it's also true that each of the five who arrived before the Code *thrived* following its imposition; indeed, their best work lay beyond 1934. This suggests something else: they learned to adapt. Having had the good fortune to enter the industry at a time when their services were in greatest need—the transition to sound—they quickly mastered not only the techniques of moviemaking but of studio politics as well.

It was politics of a different sort than that faced by outsiders: when, at the tail end of the silent era, Mauritz Stiller and F. W. Murnau were imported to Hollywood, their homosexuality was a known commodity. Like the designer Erté, they enjoyed as Europeans greater latitude in their personal freedom, perhaps because their "foreignness" already set them apart. (It should be remembered that contemporary with Goulding, Cukor, Whale, and other American gay directors, Anthony Asquith was directing pictures in Britain with far greater leeway permitted in his personal life. Certainly Asquith—a bachelor known as "Puffin"—benefited from his connections to the British aristocracy, but his homosexuality was nonetheless extraordinarily obvious and uncensored.) Various reports have indicated that Stiller, at MGM, faced a hostile Louis B. Mayer, but this was as much due to Stiller's independence and quick temper as it was to Mayer's homo-phobia. Murnau had an easier time. After a series of magnificent German films (*Nosferatu* and *The Last Laugh* prime among them), Murnau's first film for William Fox, *Sunrise*, was a tremendous critical success, and he was pretty much able to write his own ticket after that. Charmed by the young actor David Rollins, Murnau asked him to pose for nude photographs around his swimming pool. Rollins complied, and when he asked the stu-dio later if this was usual procedure, he was told simply that he "should be nice to the director."

GEORGE CUKOR:
FIRST AMONG "THE MAGNIFICENT SEVEN"

No such accommodation for Cukor, however, who toed the line carefully in a career that spanned some fifty years. Yet for all his reverence of the sta-tus quo, it's notable how often Cukor empowered gay friends and col-leagues. Messel is a good example; so is George Hoyningen-Heune, whose work as artistic consultant on many of Cukor's films actually overruled de-cisions by the cameraman or art director. At least a dozen gay actors would benefit from Cukor's early mentorship, and his stable of favorite writers was, if not always gay, then at least comfortable within his *oeuvre*. One of his closest friends, who'd serve as his dialogue director on *Romeo and Juliet* and others, was James Vincent, who'd been stage manager for Katharine Cor-nell. He was also, possibly, the same James Vincent who had been lovers with J. Warren Kerrigan; if so, it's an intriguing link between silent gay Hollywood and the gay circles of Cukor's era (see notes).

Arriving in Hollywood in 1930 after a run of several hit plays on Broad-way, Cukor quickly became a part of Hollywood's gay scene. His poolside parties at his stylish house in the Hollywood hills became legendary, both the ones for the high and mighty (Vivien Leigh, Laurence Olivier, Ethel Barrymore) and the ones for the "boys": his group of gay friends and their tricks. He also quickly established himself as a director of note, launching his film career with such sophisticated fare as Tallulah Bankhead's *Tarnished Lady* and the biting parody *What Price Hollywood?*—the original *A Star is Born*.

As *Our Betters* demonstrated, the early Cukor had a sly impulse to tweak the prevailing culture. That's part of the reason he so adored Zoe Akins, turning to her story, "Girls About Town," for that freewheeling knockout of a picture starring Kay Francis and Lilyan Tashman in 1931. When Fran-cis strips down to reveal skimpy lingerie, it's a declaration that sex and sex-uality are defined here not by moralists and tradition, but by people who break rules and make up their own. One review called *Girls About Town* "very gay—*very* gay," adding, "Naughty, but nice enough to get by Papa Hays and the censors."

Cukor would say of the "tarts" played by Francis and Tashman: "They had lovely clothes and lots of money and a succession of rich men [even though] they always said 'Good night' at the door. Of course, the audience smelled something. They thought, 'Well, they may say good night, but where the hell do they get all those clothes?'"

It was the whiff of subversion that the audiences smelled. And with *Sylvia Scarlett*, Cukor made the most subversive film of his entire career—indeed, one of the most subversive films of the post-Code studio era. Filmed in the summer and fall of 1935, *Sylvia Scarlett* was the story of a girl (Katharine Hepburn) disguised as a boy who teams up with a con man (Cary Grant) and falls in love. Gender confusion and the fluidity of desire are rampant: Dennie Moore as a housemaid gets the hots for Sylvia/Sylvester; so does Brian Aherne as a bohemian artist, who labels it a "queer feeling." Cary Grant, meanwhile, struggles with his own feelings, and although the truth is eventually revealed and conventional mores apparently upheld, he seems to have already concluded that whoever—*whatever*—Hepburn is, he *loves* her—or him.

It was Hepburn's idea. She brought the story to Cukor; he liked its naughty challenge to traditional male-female relationships. He took it to Pandro Berman, for whom he owed one last film on his RKO contract before settling in at MGM. Later, Berman would snarl that *Sylvia Scarlett* had been "a private promotional deal of Hepburn and Cukor; they conned me into it and had a script written. I tried to stop them, but they were hell-bent, claiming this was the greatest thing they had ever found."

For screenwriter, they engaged John Collier, a British novelist recently brought to Hollywood. It was a *sympatico* collaboration, despite the fact that Collier was straight. "He was fascinated, just *fascinated*, by the queer world," said Don Bachardy, who, with his lover Christopher Isherwood, often hosted Collier at their Santa Monica home. "He wasn't the least bit gay, but he'd pump Chris for information about parties or dates he'd gone on."

It's a timely reminder that the divide in Hollywood was never a simple break between gay and straight, that it was always more between progressive and repressive, imaginative and conventional. On the side of the Cukors and the Akinses there were always the Thalbergs and the Colliers; a "gay sensibility" or "alternative worldview" wasn't always the sole product of homosexuals.

Of course, Joseph Breen could be expected to object, and he did. In August, after having read the latest script, he dashed off a five-page letter to

RKO president B. B. Kahane, citing nearly fifty objections to "sex confusion." In many of the scenes, Breen wrote, clearly exasperated, "It is difficult to make any specific criticism or suggestion, as it is the general flavor . . . which is open to objection."

Most troublesome was the scene between Hepburn and Dennie Moore. "We suggest that thought be given to the danger of overemphasizing or playing upon any possible relationship between Sylvia and another woman based upon the fact that she is masquerading as a boy," Breen wrote. "In any case, here and elsewhere in the script, there should be no physical contact, and such matters should not be treated for light comedy, and nothing suggestively emphasized by any horrified reaction on the part of Sylvia."

The irony was that by denying the suggestion of same-sex attraction, Breen was actually spotlighting it. The Code's own restrictions against acknowledging even the *possibility* of homosexuality actually made *Sylvia Scarlett* even gayer: without a "horrified reaction," Sylvia seems rather nonchalant about Dennie Moore's overtures. Breen suggested the elimination of her line "Don't! I don't like it!"—which, of course, left open the possibility that she *did*. Today the scene draws startled cheers from gay audiences: certainly audiences in 1935 must have been just as startled, and the homosexuals among them secretly delighted.

But like Nazimova's more outrageous productions and William Haines' *Way Out West*—other films that pushed the queer envelope just a bit too far—*Sylvia Scarlett* wasn't exactly made for the mainstream. After the film's preview in December, Cukor wired Hepburn at her parents' home in Connecticut: "Previewed our little love child last night. Audience interested if a bit confused." The criticis were confused, too, but not at all interested: "The film skirts the border of absurdity," wrote *Variety*, with the *New York Times* calling it "a sprawling and ineffective essay in dramatic chaos." Within weeks it was clear the picture was a resounding flop. Stung, Cukor wrote Hepburn: "We all did our best and I think none of us have been done in by it at all."

Yet they *were*. It took Hepburn three years to recover, plummeting into "box-office poison" territory. Cukor, although his career proceeded on a rapid clip, never again touched such obviously radical material.

That's not to say that a gay sensibility can't be discerned in the director's later films. It's just that never again would it be as overt as in *Sylvia Scarlett*—or, for that matter, as irreverent as in *Girls About Town* or *Our Betters*.

His take on filmmaking was different enough, recognizing and honoring its essential collaborative nature while insisting that the director's touch remain "invisible." The "problem" with studying Cukor's work, according to critic Scott F. Stoddart, "is its subtlety—a quality that continues to baffle those critics who pay more attention to camera movement as a plot contribution than to Cukor's whole reason for making films: to tell stories of people." The director himself insisted: "You should never move the camera unless you have to. If you do a lot of fancy footwork, maybe they notice you as a director, but I think it hurts the story."

He was distrustful of film theory. "The whole auteur theory disconcerts me," he said. "To begin with, damn few directors can write. I have too much respect for good writers to think of taking over that job. . . . I suppose I influence a great deal in many ways. I have ideas about a script, I influence the performances very much, and visually I go on a great deal about sets and clothes."

For Cukor, it was story, performance, sets, and clothes—areas in which, as we have seen (and developed further in the next chapter), gays had the most involvement in the studios. Indeed, technical details seemed to bore Cukor, and he often left them to others. Perhaps this partly explains why some critics and theorists have treated him rather condescendingly, dismissing him as a "woman's director." If he wasn't concerned with the "manly" aspects of filmmaking, then he wasn't a "real" filmmaker worthy of study.

Certainly Cukor's habit of eschewing the kind of attention a Hawks or a Hitchcock would give to a film's "formal details"—while concentrating instead on text and performance—*is* a rather queer primer on how to make a film. But Cukor's way wasn't most directors' way, and assessments of his work as "failing to use the medium" seem not unlike an English-speaking critic reviewing a Chinese-language film without understanding Chinese. For in many ways, Cukor *was* using another language to make his films, one that rejected much of the traditional way studio films were conceived and constructed. Camera, lighting, sound recording, even art direction (i.e., the architectural design of sets)—with all the heterosexual tradition they carried—had little interest to him. To impart his visual style, he'd often sidestep the studio architects and cinematographers and go with a Messel or Hoyningen-Huene. That both were gay is significant, yet it's important not to claim too much: it's highly doubtful that any of this was a conscious attempt on the director's part to subvert heterosexual domination and empower a gay sensibility. Cukor's abiding interest was always the film's text and performances, and his aim was to enhance these aspects of his work.

Yet it's interesting that, regardless of his conscious motives, Cukor's "invisible" approach did often allow for an idiosyncratic, alternative (read, *queer*) worldview to come through. If he was working from a text by a writer whose perspective dovetailed with his own, Cukor would consciously "disappear," shepherding the story almost as proxy for the author. In *The Actress* (1953), the sheer notion of heterosexual coupling is brushed off by Jean Simmons; her suitor, Anthony Perkins, exists not for romantic interest but as a symbol of the life she, as an aspiring actress, is rejecting. Cukor wouldn't have made the film any other way, wouldn't have tolerated any conventional Hollywood meddling with his friend Ruth Gordon's autobiographical narrative.

Yet the disaster he faced with *Sylvia Scarlett* convinced him that the Code had indeed altered the landscape, and to survive he had to adapt to new rules. When he tried a little naughtiness in *Two-Faced Woman* (1942), Joseph Breen had a fit, and Cukor this time had to agree to reshoot parts of it, completely undercutting the film's premise. It was a new era, and Cukor developed a cautious approach both professionally and personally. The story in the gay subculture always held that when Cukor moved over to MGM, Louis B. Mayer called him into his office and asked him point-blank whether he was a homosexual. (It's plausible: recall the Andy Lawler anecdote of a mogul, apparently Mayer, inquiring whether an actress, apparently Tallulah Bankhead, was a lesbian. Karen Morley also remembered Mayer calling her in around the same time and asking if she was a lesbian.)

Under this new paradigm, Cukor had reason to be cautious. Whether he knew it at the time or not, he would be nixed as director of the film adaptation of Tennessee Williams' *Cat on a Hot Tin Roof* by producer Pandro Berman, who—still apparently smarting over *Sylvia Scarlett*—feared he'd turn it into "a homosexual piece." Indeed, there are instances in his later work where Cukor actually appeared to *squash* any gay inferences: the relationship between Pickering and Higgins, seen as homoerotic in the stage musical of *My Fair Lady*, is "flattened" in Cukor's film, "much of the affection and comedy between them stepped on."

In his personal life, too, he became less outgoing and social, his nightclubbing with "Ilk and Zoo and Andy" a thing of the past. Soon after *Sylvia Scarlett* was released and just prior to starting work on *Camille*, the legend goes that Cukor was arrested on a morals charge. No record remains of such an incident. Most likely, it was a close call rather than an actual arrest, and it appears to have occurred in May 1936, at the Manhattan Beach summer house of William Haines and Jimmie Shields. On the night of May 31, a mob attacked Haines and several of his friends, later accusing Shields of molesting a six-year-old boy. Haines was off the screen by this time, but the incident still prompted headlines across the country. A gay-bashing it certainly was, but in the days before hate-crimes laws, all the victims wanted was for it to go away. The hastiness with which the case was dropped by officials suggests somebody more important was involved than merely a former movie star who had no publicity machine left to protect him. This was likely Cukor's legendary "arrest": given the drama Haines endured, any other sex episode involving Cukor seems unlikely.

Despite the stilling of his more radical impulses, Cukor retained a fondness for the youth he once had been. When *Sylvia Scarlett* was rereleased in the 1970s and received cult acclaim, he felt some vindication. "It took a mere thirty-five years before we came into our own with *Sylvia Scarlett*," he wrote to John Collier. "You see, John, we were right all the time—it was just 'before its day.' "

WOMEN'S DIRECTORS:
EDMUND GOULDING AND MITCHELL LEISEN

It was code, and most knew it: "women's picture" equalled "queer." So-called "real" men weren't going to sit through *Dark Victory* or *Now, Voyager*, those were *women's* pictures, and any man who enjoyed them was suspect. Even without sissies or pansies or any obvious "perversion," they were *queer films*.

"The important thing to remember about 'gay influence' in movies," observed Gavin Lambert, "is that it was obviously never direct. It was all subliminal. It couldn't be direct because the mass audience would say, Hey, no way. Yet I think if you look at the work of the gay directors, you do see it. It's there. There's a sense of involvement with their characters that seems very personal. But their personalities as filmmakers were all very different. For every general thing I can think of that links them, I can think of an exception. Like, they were all wonderful with actresses, which they *were*. But so were many straight directors. Max Ophuls, who was very straight, was just as good with actresses as George Cukor."

Nonetheless, it remains significant that of the "Magnificent Seven," *five*—Cukor, Goulding, Leisen, Rapper, and, later, Charles Walters—were often labeled in the press (and by their studio bosses) as "women's directors." They were singled out as being *different* from the rest, an outsider status that, no matter how successful they became, couldn't help but have an impact.

"If you view Hollywood as a colony of immigrants," said critic and historian Michael Bronski, "there is a way of seeing its [gay filmmakers] from an immigrant experience, even if they were born in America. Remember, Hollywood was made up of people who were considered 'outside' of what a real American citizen was supposed to be. They were Jews, they were homosexuals, they were independent women, they were actual immigrants. So in many ways, all of Hollywood was familiar with having to 'pass.'

"Now, there are two ways of being an immigrant," Bronski continued. "One is to try to assimilate, to totally be like the mainstream. And the other way—whether you call it subversive or not—is actually remaining who you are and 'sneaking' your way in. It seems to me that what occurred—whether those in charge knew it or not—was that gay directors were actually putting their own dreams and wishes and alternative visions up there."

Those visions were, in fact, recognized as different by the critics. Cukor, easily offended, chafed against the label "woman's director." But Edmund Goulding actually embraced it, telling columnist Ezra Goodman that he was proud to craft screen tear jerkers. "Why, the tear jerker is an art in itself," he exclaimed. "There is a certain psychiatric technique to it. You see, no one will cry about anyone who cries about himself. In *Dark Victory*, for instance, I wrote into the picture a character in the person of Geraldine Fitzgerald who did all the crying for Miss Davis. If Miss Davis had wept, no one would have wept with her, but Miss Fitzgerald was in the position of the audience, weeping behind Miss Davis' back, and that gave Miss Davis a clear course of martyrdom."

Goulding, having risen from the ranks of screenwriters and having had success as a playwright, was less reticent than Cukor in revising and tweaking the script to fit his needs as director. And, as the example of *Dark Victory* illustrates, his insights were usually on target. That classic tale of a terminally ill woman (Bette Davis) holds up remarkably well. Even when it's obvious that Goulding is craftily manipulating our emotions, it still works.

Goulding was not the artist that Cukor was, and yet his films are superb examples of studio craftsmanship. By the late 1930s, his nearly fifteen years' experience had made him one of the most polished and capable filmmakers in America. Unlike Cukor, he took great interest in such things as camera work, being particularly fond of the dolly shot. Observed the *Los Angeles Times*, "He probably walked more actors more miles than any other in film history, to take the curse off talk, talk, talk."

Like Cukor, however, his skill seemed to work best with actresses, an affinity he ascribed to "chemistry, or a natural fusion of temperament." He elaborated to Ezra Goodman, "I adore women, and they have faith in me. An actress' career is at stake with every picture she makes, more so than with a man, and it is important for her to rely on someone's sympathy and judgment." Goulding empathized with his actress, sharing Cukor's habit of acting out scenes with them from the sidelines. Sometimes he'd actually play the scene himself first, costumes and all: "The sight of him tripping into a room with a frilly party frock lashed to his middle is said to be something that verges on the terrific," said one reporter. At the time of *The Constant Nymph* (1943), photographs of Goulding with a dress tied to his middle were circulated by studio press agents. (What *were* they thinking?) Several papers ran the picture, with this caption typical: "Director Goulding pretending he's Joan Fontaine entering a room a-bubble with gaiety."

Goulding never worried too much about hiding such gaiety. In *Blondie of the Follies* (1932) he inserted a "very funny routine" for the Rocky Twins, drag queens he'd seen at a gay bar in Venice Beach. In *The Razor's Edge*, he encouraged the very gay Clifton Webb to play his character the same way. In *Dark Victory*, he gave similar advice to Ronald Reagan, essaying the part of Davis' devoted pal Alec. But the straitlaced Reagan balked: "Mr. Goulding wanted me to play my character as if he were the kind of guy who wouldn't care if a young lady were undressing in front of him." Despite Reagan's discomfort, Alec can still be read as gay in the final film (like Rex O'Malley in Cukor's *Camille*).

In his personal life Goulding had settled down, living with his mother and sister, less inclined toward the old bacchanalias. In 1956 he made an attempt to regain some currency, both writing (with his friend Charles Brackett) and directing a comeback vehicle for Ginger Rogers called *Teenage Rebel*. But hot rods and rock and roll were hardly Goulding's forté; when he died a few years later, it would be *Grand Hotel* and *Dark Victory* with which his obituaries would lead.

• • •

In 1944, Hedda Hopper observed that "Mitchell Leisen is outranking George Cukor as Hollywood's Number One lion tamer—pardon, please!—lioness tamer.

"Mitchell has a way with the ladies," the columnist continued, ticking off Leisen's list: Colbert, Dietrich, Barbara Stanwyck, Joan Fontaine, Jean Arthur, Olivia de Havilland, Paulette Goddard, Ginger Rogers. "He is supersensitive to moods. That's great woman bait. So few men are. When one of his leading ladies is emotionally upset, he knows it and keeps his gay and noisy sets quiet as a church until it passes."

Leisen had started in costumes and moved to set design, but by the early 1930s had shifted his energies again. He had become enamored of the idea of directing, having filled in for DeMille on several scenes in *The Sign of the Cross*. To avoid being returned to sets, Leisen convinced Paramount to allow him to assist Stuart Walker on *Tonight Is Ours*, based on Noël Coward's play "The Queen Was in the Parlor."

Like Goulding (and unlike Cukor), Leisen was fascinated by all aspects of filmmaking, including the technical. "I learned photography as we went along," he recalled. "I'd tell the cameraman, Karl Struss, 'Let's go in, I want to get closer,' and he'd say, 'Let's just change the lens.'" In Leisen's classic *Death Takes a Holiday*, the director had cinematographer Charles Lang pull his camera farther back than he ever had before, in one of the most elaborate crane shots in film history.

Leisen's stamp is, in fact, all over his pictures. Whereas Cukor's "author-ship" of his films emerged from his allegiance to the text and the infusion of his own sensibility in the final product, it's with Leisen that an auteur theory seems most applicable. He was intimately connected to *all* aspects of filmmaking—not only costumes and set design, where his experience was bound to have influence, but also in cinematography, an area not often the province of gay artists. In the writing, too—in what would have been anathema to Cukor—Leisen often changed so much that the script became more his than the screenwriter's.

"I don't consider myself infallible," Leisen told Thomas Pryor of the *New York Times*, "but that doesn't mean I don't have set ideas. Sometimes I'll insist upon a scene being done a certain way, no matter who argues to the contrary. When you're directing, you have to hold the reins, and let everybody know you're in full command."

Such absolutism often put him at loggerheads with his writers: his leg-endary feuds with Preston Sturges and Billy Wilder led to their demands that they be allowed to direct their own scripts. As writer Dennis Drabelle has pointed out, today the reputations of Sturges and Wilder "tower over that of the man who galvanized them," yet the films Leisen made of their scripts (notably Sturges' *Easy Living* and Wilder's *Midnight*) hold up well against the "all-Sturges and all-Wilder productions." Drabelle wrote: "[Lei-sen] was a shape-giver who knew where to cut flab out of a script and where to let a movie collect itself and breathe."

He certainly had his ways of getting what he wanted. "Sometimes when things go wrong," Leisen said, "I just lie down on the floor and go to sleep for five minutes. I really sleep and wake up refreshed, and the sight of me sprawled out always seems to make everybody else forget their troubles."

He was known for an outlandish eccentricity, which was probably why the decorum-minded Cukor didn't like him. "I think Leisen was a bit too outrageous for Cukor," mused David Chierichetti, despite the fact that it was Leisen, not Cukor, who had married (his wife, an opera singer, lived in Paris until World War II) and who actually had genuine affairs with women. In the mid-1930s, too, according to his (lesbian) secretary Eleanor Broder, Leisen began taking hormone shots in the hopes they might "cure" his homosexuality. (That this occurred as the Code dramatically shifted the political climate of the industry can't be ignored.) He also began living with a woman, Natalie Visart, a costume designer who later miscarried his child.

Yet while he and Visart would remain lifelong close friends, no amount of cohabitation or hormone shots could alter his basic orientation. Soon Eddie Anderson, a pilot who had taught Leisen to fly, had taken Visart's place in Leisen's home. Leisen secured Anderson a job on the set of *The Big Broadcast of 1938*, where the handsome pilot had an affair with the actress Shirley Ross. Brokenhearted by this betrayal, Leisen suffered a nearly fatal heart attack. It was a long recovery, but the Mitchell Leisen who emerged was very different from the one before, as if the brush with death had emboldened him to throw caution to the wind. "He got so audacious in the 1940s that he really seemed not to care," said David Chierichetti. "He'd do very outrageous things, like making passes at his leading men."

It's a charge confirmed in the files of Hedda Hopper, where an informant recounted how Ray Milland, fed up with Leisen's interest during the making of *The Bride of Vengeance* (1949), told him to "leave his sex life out of his work" and walked off the picture. (He was replaced by John Lund.) Leisen's outrageousness didn't end there: the same writer told Hedda that the director had insisted male extras for *Frenchman's Creek* be interviewed in the nude.

Chierichetti expressed doubt about the Milland report; after all, the actor had made several pictures with Leisen by that time, and was actually "pretty sophisticated about that kind of thing." Stories about the discomfort of another frequent leading man, however, have more the ring of truth. "I know Leisen's passes troubled Fred MacMurray a good deal," Chierichetti said. MacMurray, a rather stolid, conventional actor, appeared in eight of Leisen's films, several among the director's best, but remained uncomfortable with the director's flirtations.

During this period, Leisen became involved in a new romance with the dancer Billy Daniels, who moved in with him. "Part of Leisen's change in personality was to make his relationship with Billy Daniels known to everybody whether they were interested or not," said Chierichetti. It was a relationship that would last several years: Leisen was instrumental in getting Daniels choreography work at Paramount. Such an undisguised liaison harked back to the pre-Code days of William Haines and Jimmie Shields.

In fact, Leisen seemed determined to ignore the political shift of the post-Code years. "There were lots of studio pressures at the time—budget cuts, the war, and then the post-war flux," said Chierichetti. "But his response, rather than to become more accommodating, was to become more outrageous."

Finally, during the making of *Bedevilled* in 1955, Leisen went too far. "He was coming on to every handsome man who crossed his path," remembered his leading lady, Anne Baxter, "including an actor in the picture we all knew was not interested. The actor complained and Mitch was behind schedule, so MGM took him off the picture."

Such behavior was thoroughly abhorrent to Cukor. Coming on to any actor, let alone an obviously heterosexual one, was beyond obscene to him.

Yet Leisen, for all his indiscretion—or perhaps *because* of it—was able to insert a far more overt gay sensibility into his work than any other gay director, except James Whale. In *No Time For Love* (1943), he constantly offers a back-and-forth comparison between the men of Claudette Colbert's social circle (gay) and the "brawling mudhogs" of Fred MacMurray's world (straight). Richard Haydn makes no objection to being called a "pantywaist;" MacMurray, meanwhile, is tagged with "ape," "gorilla," and "King Kong." It's clear which side Leisen feels is superior (like Cukor and Whale, he imbued his sissies with power and authority), even if, according to custom, Colbert ultimately chooses MacMurray over the more effete Paul McGrath.

Yet it's significant that *she* chooses *him*: throughout the picture, MacMurray is the object, Colbert the subject, reversing traditional gender roles and, in fact, presenting desire from a gay male perspective. "You look at Leisen's movies," Gavin Lambert observed, "and Fred MacMurray is very sexy. He's not sexy in anybody else's movies. Obviously Leisen was attracted to him and brought [that sexiness] out." It was a recurrent theme in Leisen's pictures, with MacMurray often the awkward center of attention: Carole Lombard ogles him in *Hands Across the Table*; Rosalind Russell hires him as her "trophy secretary" (Dennis Drabelle's words) in *Take a Letter, Darling*. Classic is the scene in the backseat of the limousine, where, just as the sexual tension builds, MacMurray's top hat springs up in his lap.

Leisen got away with stuff nobody else did. Bodybuilders and gymnasts preen and pose; pretty boys are at least as common as pretty girls. Mischa Auer, playing a photographer in *Lady in the Dark*, gushes over Jon Hall: "I've taken pictures of beautiful men before, but this one is the end—the absolute end." That Leisen's offscreen obsessions would be given on-screen manifestation is perhaps not surprising; what *is* surprising is the degree to which he was able to flout the Code and get away with it. After reading the script for *No Time For Love*, Joseph Breen, referring to Haydn's character, wrote that "this half-pint priss" must not be suggestive of a pansy in the final product. He was, of course, and somehow the film received a seal of approval and was released.

It was a matter of degree: Haydn, for all his half-pint prissiness, was no lipsticked-and-rouged Mr. Ernest. Leisen was clever enough to insert such characters and such scenes in ways that proved ultimately satisfactory to the censors. Colbert might call MacMurray an "ape," but she marries him in the end. Gay men in the audience might ogle the shirtless torsos of bodybuilders along with Colbert and Lombard, but so long as the focus of identification remained women, Leisen could, in a sense, pull the wool over Breen's eyes and maintain the illusion that homosexual desire and identity did not exist. In this, he was the most subversive of all gay directors.

"MELODRAMAS AND STAR ACTRESSES":
THE CAREER OF IRVING RAPPER

If Cukor, Goulding, and Leisen—and their gayness—have all received some biographical analysis, their final "woman's director" comrade, Irving Rapper, has lacked much study. He survived them all, dying in 1999 at the age of 101, part of the reason few have written about his personal life up to now, and how it impacted his work.

"Irving Rapper seems to fit best the stereotype of the gay director," said Gavin Lambert, "with all his melodramas and star actresses. I know Bette Davis liked him because she was able to tell him what to do. And he didn't mind very much."

Irving Rapper directed four Davis films, including that quintessential "woman's picture" *Now, Voyager*. Rapper was easy to work with, usually deferring to the temperamental star: "Bette Davis had a marvellously probing intelligence," he said, "which gave great strength to the director working with her." Yet it's hard to imagine Cukor—or, in fact, any of them—letting the star actress call the shots. Rapper was in awe of Davis, and of others he viewed as greater artists than he. "I'd sometimes begin with fully detailed plans and sketches," he'd admit, "but then Bette or someone would yell out, 'Why did you do that?' And I'd throw them all away."

Rapper had talent—*Now, Voyager* and *Voice of the Turtle* demonstrate that—yet he seemed always unsure of himself, masquerading his insecurity with indifference. Recalling the shoot of *Deception* (1946), again with Davis, he said he liked the script (by *Sylvia Scarlett*'s John Collier). "It was supposed to have a gay, light, natural, 'so what?' ending," Rapper remembered, with the three principals walking off together as friends. But La Davis insisted on melodrama, with her character shooting Claude Rains and being hauled off to prison: "Bette wanted a dramatic conclusion; she insisted on it; and I didn't care very much either way, so I gave in."

Occasionally Rapper stiffened his backbone. He was suspended by Warners *ten times*, in fact, for refusing assignments he felt were either unworthy or beyond his scope. "I would refuse, say, a crime picture I wouldn't even know how to begin, or some Nazi picture when I thought people were tired of them," he said. The truth is plain: criminals and Nazis were not Rapper's element. He much preferred long-suffering women and their noble pursuits of love.

He was born on January 16, 1898 in London, the only boy among five sisters. The family emigrated to the United States, settling first in Boston, when Irving was ten. "If I'd stayed in England and received an English ed-

ucation," he said, "I probably never would have been interested in the theater—but I would have been more satisfied with myself."

There it is again: that discontent, that lack of self-satisfaction. His father
had wanted him to go into business, but he died when Irving was still very
young. Uncertain of his future, Irving studied law at NYU and, concurrently, journalism at Columbia. But, like Edward Everett Horton, he found
greater fascination with the varsity shows. He might credit coming to
America with spurring his love for theater, but his story fits with the pattern established with other homosexual figures in this study. It was his sense
of being different that ultimately pushed him toward a culture that actually
embraced and celebrated that difference. One of his earliest memories was
of gazing up at a New York theater, too young to read all the print on the
posters and too short to reach the box-office window. He knew then and
there what he wanted to do with his life.

Had he not been gay, Irving Rapper—like so many others—might have
blithely continued along the path set out for him by his family, and not
been unhappy at that. Even *he* thought he might have been "more satisfied"
with himself had he chosen that route. But something inside him pushed
him along another path, even if he remained ambivalent about making the
choice.

Such ambivalence would remain with him all his life. Two of Rapper's
friends recalled his nervousness at being seen in public with them. "We
were the boys then," said one. "If he went out with a group of gay boys,
Irving would never dine close to town. He'd insist on going to a place far
out on La Cienega, near the airport. That's just how he was."

Nonetheless, his early connections (again like so many others) came
through a homosexual network. With pal Moss Hart, he went out in search
of acting jobs; Guthrie McClintic allowed the inexperienced undergradu-
ate to watch him direct. Rapper's limited resumé at that time would hardly
have been sufficient cause to secure the acquaintance of McClintic, who
was then coming into his own as a Broadway director and who had recently
married Katharine Cornell. But McClintic was also gay, just five years older
than Rapper. Then as now, there were ways of making connections other
than by resumé alone.

For Irving was a handsome youth, with dark hair and eyebrows, sharp
eyes, and a high forehead. He had retained "just a little" of his British accent, and spoke in clipped, careful sentences. In every manner he projected
an image of sophistication and culture. Broadway theatrical circles embraced him warmly, and his ascent was rapid. British producer Gilbert
Miller, who would later direct the lesbian-sympathetic play "The Captive"
on Broadway, hired Rapper to direct "The Animal Kingdom" and "The
Late Christopher Bean" in both London and New York. Later Irving ac-

cepted an invitation from the Soviet government to direct a Moscow production of Louis Weitzenkorn's "Five Star Final." But at the last minute,
he apparently decided to go to London instead, where Miller was producing "Grand Hotel." It was a fortuitous decision, for some twenty years later
such an association with the Soviets would have made him suspect in
McCarthy-era Hollywood.

In 1936, he was hired as a dialogue director by Warner Bros., charged
with sharpening dialogue and polishing up the work of both actors and directors. His success at dialogue prompted his promotion to director in 1940,
a singular achievement for a gay man in those immediate post–Code years.
His friendship with Bette Davis must have helped, as well as his deferential
apprenticeships with such directors as Michael Curtiz, whom he called his
mentor. That his direct superior at the studio was Henry Blanke, "the most
sympathetic, versatile and intelligent producer at Warners," in Rapper's
words, must have enabled his career climb as well.

But for all their success together, Bette Davis didn't seem to retain much
affection for Rapper, unlike her glowing reminiscences of Goulding. She
dismissed any directorial input he might have had, claiming—in some cases
accurately—her own creative stamp on their films together. Rapper took
umbrage at her dismissals at least once, when Davis insisted that she and
Paul Henreid had invented the famous cigarette scene at the end of *Now,
Voyager.* "She's a very mercurial personality," Rapper said, "but I never
thought she'd turn on me."

Although Bette had once appreciated Rapper for his subservient direction, that very attribute may have ultimately earned her disrespect. Rapper's
late-blooming combativeness on the set of *The Corn is Green* may have also
left her brooding. Accustomed to his acquiescence, Davis was stunned
when Rapper finally exploded after she attempted to tell the grips what to
do. They worked together one last time, in *Another Man's Poison* (1951), shot
in England. Again they fought, with Rapper unable to control either script
or performance. Their relationship never recovered after the film took a
beating at the box office as severe as Rapper took on the seat.

His true skill was not as auteur, but as arranger. "I have a rule that I must
have the greatest cameramen in the world," he said. "I always try to get
the best composers as well." It was by assembling a top-notch team that
Rapper could orchestrate his best pictures. Yet something of himself came
through as well, for all of his most highly regarded films have gay appeal.
The Voice of the Turtle (1947) written by gay playwright John van Druten and
starring Eleanor Parker and Ronald Reagan, offers a rather unorthodox
take on sex, with an implicit refusal to condemn promiscuity. *The Brave One*
(1956), Rapper's favorite, was a simple story of a sensitive boy and his love

for a bull destined to die in the arena. "My agent begged me not to do it," Rapper recalled, "but the script was so beautiful that I decided I had to." His tender treatment of the young boy, different from the others, made the film a gigantic hit.

But his gayest film—and his masterpiece—remains *Now, Voyager*. Few gay men fail to relate to Charlotte Vale, the sheltered, browbeaten ugly duckling who blossoms triumphantly when she discovers her true, beautiful inner self. The gay playwright and actor Harvey Fierstein has acknowledged the special bond many gay men have with the film, "deciding whether they are Bette Davis or Paul Henreid." But lesbians, too, see resonance in the film: as Patricia White has written, Charlotte refuses heterosexual "fulfillment" and makes for herself a largely female world.

Rapper, however, sought the kind of fulfillment his heroine rejected. "He was a lonely man," said one friend, "always looking for love." The sensibility Rapper brought to his pictures was the worldview of a gay man living circumspectly and yet actively enough to know *what might be*. He knew Billy Haines and Jimmie Shields; he was certainly aware of the defiant cohabitation of James Whale and David Lewis. But—like Cukor—he lived very much alone, relying on flings here and there to assuage the loneliness.

Robert Wheaton, a young, handsome serviceman when he arrived in Hollywood in 1943, recalled being picked up while hitchhiking one day on Sunset Boulevard. Wheaton didn't know the driver, who took him up to a house in the Hollywood hills. "It was Irving Rapper's house," Wheaton said. "He was in the midst of making *Rhapsody in Blue*, I remember. He asked me if I wanted to hear the sound recording from the film. I said yes— and then I looked around. My ride had taken off." With a wartime gasoline shortage, Rapper protested he couldn't make a special trip into town. He asked slyly if Wheaton would be willing to spend the night. "So I did," Wheaton said. "That was my introduction to Hollywood directors."

Wheaton remembered Rapper as warm and friendly, but the director had a sharper side as well, especially as he got older. "He was bitter, an old loudmouth," remembered another friend. "He used to tell some nasty untruths about John Dall [whom Rapper had made a star with *The Corn is Green*]. He'd go on about Dall being involved in all sorts of affairs, fooling around with boys on the set. These things weren't true. I think he was just envious. It was quite sad."

The actor John Gilmore recalled a sloppy seduction attempt by Rapper in the early 1950s. Arranging a nighttime "interview" with the good-looking teenager, Rapper proceeded to get drunk. "People must fall in love with you all the time," he gushed. "What if *I* was in love with you?" The director dropped to his knees in front of Gilmore, his hands on the youth's legs. When Gilmore declined his offer to spend the night, Rapper lost all interest in him for whatever picture he'd had in mind.

Rapper on his knees, drunk, begging a teenaged boy for sex, is a picture even more undignified than Mitchell Leisen at his most salacious. It was behavior that would have chilled George Cukor to the bone. That's probably why Cukor kept Rapper at arm's length, only occasionally allowing his presence poolside. "Rapper very much wanted to be good friends with George," said Robert Wheaton. "But Cukor was always a little cool to him. A difference in temperaments, I guess."

An understatement. Cukor had what Rapper wanted: *respect*. But Cukor had managed to walk the line between circumspection and authenticity with ironic grace. Irving Rapper, lacking Cukor's fundamental fortitude, ultimately managed neither.

OPPOSITE ENDS: ARTHUR LUBIN AND JAMES WHALE

Despite the fact that both were gay, few filmmakers could be as different from each other as Arthur Lubin and James Whale. The latter was the brilliant, sly, transgressive iconoclast who made *The Old Dark House* and *The Bride of Frankenstein*; the former the prosaic, unassuming, obedient studio lackey who made *Francis the Talking Mule* and Abbott and Costello pictures. Yet among the "Magnificent Seven" they were the only ones not typed as "women's directors," and their careers, while wildly different, inform each other's as well as those of their colleagues.

Richard Schickel has called Arthur Lubin "kindly, efficient, untroubled and untroubling . . . the kind of craftsman, competent but uninspired, who flourished when studios, functioning along industrial lines, needed to grind out product." *Untroubled and untroubling*—a rare combination in gay Hollywood. "I think working at a studio depends upon the relationship that you have with your producer," Lubin once said. "My assignments were, have always been, very pleasant. The studio liked me very much because they knew I came in on budget, I came in on schedule, which has always been my reputation. If you enjoy your work, you enjoy everything around it."

There would be no firings of Arthur Lubin for inappropriate behavior on the set as there were for Mitchell Leisen; no stories of sloppy seductions of teenagers as there were for Irving Rapper; no tales of wild debauchery of the kind that surrounded Edmund Goulding. There would also be no clashes with studio brass or censors as there were for George Cukor, and no great pictures either—no Hollywood classics or narratives reverberating with a foxy gay sensibility. Lubin was an ordinary workhorse, turning out sixty films in thirty years. He came to work, did his job, collected his pay, and went home to his house on Seattle Drive—and was perfectly happy and content with his lot, even considering himself fortunate.

And why wouldn't he? At his death he left an estate worth millions. In 1963, the *Los Angeles Herald-Express* ran a pictorial spread on his lovely home filled with priceless antiques: a teapot that belonged to the Empress Josephine, porcelain made for Queen Victoria, 150-year-old Japanese dolls. And he shared that home with another man, Frank Burford, for many years.

Lubin's career suggests that for every John Collier—straight but not narrow, as they say, helping to craft films of markedly unorthodox worldviews—there were also men (and women) like Arthur Lubin, gay but not transgressive, outsiders who nonetheless felt in many ways already *in*, who harbored no need to challenge, to provoke, to do anything other than live out their lives quietly and amenably, with a balance of conformity and integrity.

Lubin's story, however, still begins as most of the others have. He was the dreamer, the different boy, looking for a way and a life divergent from the path laid down by his family. He was born on July 25, 1898, in Los Angeles, the son of Polish-born itinerent peddler William Lubovsky. Coming to the United States in 1889, William first settled in the little town of Willsborough, Pennsylvania, where he took the "Lubin" from pioneering filmmaker Siegmund Lubin in nearby Philadelphia. But William Lubin was never in one place long. From Willsborough he and his wife, Helen, trekked out to Los Angeles, where they established a regular route up the coast to Oakland selling trousers and overcoats.

Soon after Arthur was born, they put down roots in Jerome, Arizona (later a well-known ghost town), where William invested in copper mines. There Helen Lubin helped organize amateur theatrics. "Whatever ability I have," Arthur remembered, "I think I inherited from my mother." Early on he decided he wasn't going to sell overcoats door-to-door like his father. In high school in San Diego, he was head of the dramatic and debating societies, and hooked up with a local stock company as both actor and set dresser. After a stint in the navy during World War I, he was accepted to the Carnegie Institute in Pittsburgh. There "the urge toward the dramatic" continued. He played the leads in all of the school plays, graduating in 1922 with the firm conviction he would become a great actor.

Sharing that view was Gilmor Brown at the Pasadena Playhouse, who gave Arthur his acting start, as he would dozens of gay actors through the years, including Randolph Scott, Tyrone Power, and Laird Cregar. From there Arthur got other stage work; in 1925 he was part of a production of Eugene O'Neill's "Desire Under the Elms," which was closed by the L.A.

police for being "obscene." He also got work in movies: he played Louis XIII in *Bardelys the Magnificent* (1926) and had a sizable part in Paramount's *Afraid to Love* (1927), secured by his friend, the producer Paul Bern.

But the acting bug was wearing off, and he became fascinated by the mechanics behind the scenes. Moving to New York, Lubin was hired by Edgar Selwyn as a director. He helmed "This One Man" with Paul Muni and "When the Bow Breaks" with Pauline Frederick, among others, before returning to the movies as an assistant to Paramount producer William LeBaron. His first assignments were Mae West's *Night After Night* and *She Done Him Wrong*.

For the next thirty-some years, Arthur Lubin was never out of work in the Hollywood studios. He directed his first picture, a quickie called *A Successful Failure*, for Monogram in 1934, following it up with a string of low-budget features with second-rank stars: William Collier, Sidney Blackmer, Ben Lyon, Phillips Holmes. They were a grabbag of comedies, thrillers, and mysteries, and Arthur Lubin was having a ball.

"I've never considered myself a great director," he'd admit frankly. "I consider myself a good director, a director that produces because I am not temperamental. I do not have fits of anger and tear my hair. I get along well with the actors and the production department."

In the latter part of the Thirties, he worked primarily at Universal, churning out mysteries and potboilers. He directed the delightful *Beloved Brat* (1938) with spritely Bonita Granville for Warner Bros., but in November 1940 signed a seven-year contract with Universal, where he was given the plum assignment of directing Bud Abbott and Lou Costello. "I loved the boys so much and enjoyed working with them so much," Lubin said. His first outing with them grossed a phenomenal $10 million. The boys, however, pretty much directed themselves, although Lubin kept the pace going: he helmed their next three pictures, the best being *Hold That Ghost* (1941).

His heady success with Abbott and Costello convinced Universal to let Lubin try his hands at a bigger-budget picture, *Ali Baba and the Forty Thieves*. If it is possible to discern any gay sensibility in Lubin's films—an idea most observers greet with a bemused little smile—it is *Ali Baba* that offers the best evidence. If not *gay*, then certainly *camp*: Jon Hall struts about as the hunky prince, Andy Devine hams it up with purple dialogue lifted directly from "The Arabian Knights," and Maria Montez, well—despite the fact that she couldn't act, dance, or sing, she skyrocketed into cult celebrity after this film. Lubin claimed credit for discovering her and molding her extravagantly costumed, camel-riding, over-the-top cinema persona.

On the strength of *Ali Baba*, Universal assigned Lubin the remake of *The Phantom of the Opera* in 1943, which ended up being released first. "I tried to get the best out of [the actors] because the picture meant a great deal to me," he remembered. "It was my first really big picture." His efforts paid off: finally, after a decade grinding out so many sausages, as D. W. Griffith used to say, Arthur Lubin had directed a prestigious big-budget picture, and one that stands as his masterpiece. Not a great work of art, it is nonetheless crisply, efficiently, and even somewhat stylishly made. There's a softer quality to Claude Rains' phantom than Lon Chaney's more menacing figure in the 1925 original, and the film isn't so much a horror film as a musical mystery. Lubin would say he didn't want the audience thinking about Chaney; he wanted them to relate to the Phantom as a romantic figure, a perspective followed in more recent stage and screen adaptations of the story. If nothing else, Arthur Lubin was prescient.

Yet in 1947, after the box-office flop of *A Night in Paradise* starring Turhan Bey, Lubin's contract with Universal was not renewed. Adrift in the flux of post-war Hollywood, he became a "packager," developing scripts to sell off, with himself as director, to the highest bidder. The idea he pitched to Universal went directly counter to the trend of dark, psychological, *noir* studies that predominated in the late 1940s (see Chapter 8, "War Spirit"). It was Lubin's contention that moviegoers wanted a break from all that; what better, he suggested, than a talking mule?

Universal decided to take a gamble on it, and *Francis the Talking Mule* was made in 1949 for just $125,000. It ended up turning a $2 million profit for the studio. Donald O'Connor played the loyal but dim G.I. who, thanks to his talking mule, becomes a national hero. The picture was so successful it was launched into a series, averaging one a year until 1956, although Lubin quit after the first six. Talking mules led to other oddities: a cat who inherits a baseball team in *Rhubarb* (1951) and a naked but carefully concealed Maureen O'Hara as *Lady Godiva* (1955). It was camp for the masses—although gay audiences probably got a special laugh from George Nader in fur-trimmed tunic, who spots Godiva and exclaims, hand on hip: "In heaven's name, who *is* this she-wolf?"

Lubin was reportedly quite taken with the good-looking Nader; the director had a definite weakness for handsome, well-built young men. He served as mentor to the twenty-something actor-turned-producer Ross Hunter, and a few years later turned his attention to a breathtakingly beautiful young gas-station attendant named Clint Eastwood. "Clint was working in a gasoline station on Sunset," Lubin remembered. "Somebody told me he had possibilities." The director agreed: friends recall he became smitten with the young man. Arranging a screen test for Eastwood at Universal, Arthur insisted that Clint wear only a pair of trunks. "He had great sexual appeal," he observed. "As you will notice, I used him as much as possible in every one of my pictures."

Eastwood remained under personal contract to Lubin for a number of years; Arthur would claim he supported the young actor financially before his rise to prominence on TV's "Rawhide." Eastwood himself has rarely acknowledged the connection to Lubin, although biographer Richard Schickel reported that after his nomination for an Oscar in 1992 for *Unforgiven*, Clint did call Arthur to say he remembered with gratitude the director's early support.

Though Lubin played star maker with Eastwood, his skill always had more to do with story than personality. "The story's the thing," he said. "If you don't have a solid story, you'll have no picture—no matter how many stars or how much money you put into it." Words that could have been uttered by Cukor, that devoted servant to the text. Yet Cukor, although never above making entertainment, imparted his own personal art by imprinting himself onto the narrative. Lubin, on the other hand, used the story to simply serve the goods and get the audience hooked for an hour or so in the theater. "I have done such a great variety [of pictures] that there is no definite style that I could trace or, I don't think, anyone else could trace," he said. "I tried *not* to make a style, so that each picture would have its own."

In the final analysis, Arthur Lubin had fun and gave fun. And who's to say that's not just as good as making art sometimes?

• • •

If style was in fact *erased* by Lubin, it's what *defined* James Whale. So much has been written about Whale's style that it needs only be referenced here, and *too* much, perhaps, has been suggested for his obviously gay sensibility, particularly his quartet of horror films made for Universal: *Frankenstein, The Old Dark House, The Invisible Man*, and *The Bride of Frankenstein*. Yet his biographer, James Curtis, seemed reluctant to acknowledge even a *hint* of deliberation on Whale's part in imparting his queerness through celluloid. "Most likely, Whale would have been appalled by the inference of a gay agenda in his films," Curtis wrote, pointing out that Whale's longtime lover, David Lewis, had rejected the notion.

But it is not a gay *agenda*—with that word's implication of politics and modern identity—that is so apparent in Whale's films. Rather, it is a consciousness inspired by Whale's idiosyncrasy, which continues to resonate with gay audiences. Despite Curtis' viewpoint that Whale's gay sensibility is "[tough] to discern," manifesting itself mostly through "frills and fripperies [and] outlandish props," Whale was in fact the most striking auteur of an alternative, queer worldview ever to work in the studio system. Monika Morgan called *The Bride of Frankenstein* "a homosexual joke on the heterosexual communities Whale—a gay man—served: his 'masters' at Universal and the mass audience to whom he could present unconventional images and ideas and see them unknowingly endorsed and approved in the most direct way possible—by ticket sales."

Morgan's extravagance is matched by Curtis' reticence, and the truth lies somewhere between. Whale knew what he was doing with his films. His celluloid indulgence was felt by some to mirror his personal life. "Cukor didn't approve of James Whale," Gavin Lambert said. "He thought Whale asked for it by flaunting it."

"Flaunting it," to Cukor, meant living openly with David Lewis and showing up with him (or other men) at industry functions, a major rupture of the boy-girl protocol Cukor so prized. When Nazimova appeared in Ibsen's "Ghosts" at the Biltmore, Whale took a male friend, Jack Latham, then an MGM office boy, to opening night. "Everybody in Hollywood was in attendance, and I was Jimmy's date," Latham told James Curtis. "He didn't call up a woman, and he was going to be surrounded by the top people in his profession. It strikes me it was not a problem for him."

Whale and Lewis were an obvious couple. They rented a Mediterranean-style house at 4565 Dundee Drive, in the Los Feliz area of Los Angeles. Such an undisguised "way of life" (David Lewis' phrase) could not have been missed by Hollywood, and wasn't: at one point Lewis' agent, Phil Berg, asked him if he "had" to live with Jimmy Whale. (Lewis' response: "I don't *have* to. I want to.") If others were cognizant of Whale's outsider status, then certainly he was aware of it himself. Arthur Lubin might share his home with a man, but he didn't bring an MGM office boy as his date to Nazimova's premiere. He wasn't known as "the Queen of Hollywood" the way Whale was—an epithet deserved not for any effeminacy or stereotypical mannerisms, but for Whale's challenge to the system and his eccentric yet nonetheless dignified persona.

It follows, then, that Whale would carry such sedition to his films as well. When he was assigned, in the wake of Universal's success with *Dracula*, to make a film of Mary Shelley's *Frankenstein*, he "became absorbed in its possibilities. . . . I decided I'd try to do something with it to sort of top all thrillers." With its male-male procreation, *Frankenstein* was perfect fodder for Whale's sensibilities, and his hand is felt in every aspect of the film. A number of screenwriters had made attempts to adapt Shelley's classic, but none had proven satisfactory. Whale was given the key to the film's heart from David Lewis, who, after reading the novel, told his lover: "I was sorry for the goddamn monster." And so *Frankenstein* became not the tale of a demon, as *Dracula* had been, but rather the story of a frightened, misunderstood, ostracized, *different* child.

Whale's influence on the script was considerable. He had screenwriter

Francis Edward Faragoh model the shrill, neurotic characterization of Henry Frankenstein on his friend Colin Clive. Surely, too, he would have appreciated the irony of much of the dialogue, such as the old Baron's observation that Henry's lab was "a queer sort of place for a son of mine to be in." In fact, Whale consciously created Henry's world as queer, a world apart from the values and goals of "normal" society.

Modern gay audiences often see in *Frankenstein* an allegory of the gay experience, a tale of scapegoating, isolation, and persecution. There is, as well, the classic underpinning of the tale: father rejects son when son turns out to be not what he expected—different—*queer*. The famous ending, of the Monster being pursued to the windmill by the crazed villagers and then set on fire, has echoes of gay bashings everywhere, and anticipates the demise of Sebastian Venable in Tennessee Williams' "Suddenly Last Summer."

Once again, how conscious Whale was in imprinting this paradigm remains, of course, debatable. Yet given his lifestyle and general *oeuvre*, it seems likely that he had to be aware of at least *some* parallels, *some* relationship between story and life. Certainly we see recurring motifs in his other work: critic Harry Benshoff has called *The Old Dark House* (1932) "flamboyantly gay," and posited that Whale signaled his queer intent for the film by casting Elspeth Dudgeon, a woman, to play the aged patriarch of the family, Roderick Femm. Indeed, *The Old Dark House* shimmers throughout with a twisted sensibility, from Eva Moore's lascivious leering at pretty Gloria Stuart to the interplay between the "normal" heterosexual couple and the queer-seeming characters surrounding them (all played grandly by such charismatic actors as Moore, Boris Karloff, Melvyn Douglas, Lilian Bond, and, notably, two gay actors, Ernest Thesiger and Charles Laughton.) Queerest of all is the "family secret"—brother Saul, played by Brember Wills with a creepy feyness anticipant of Anthony Perkins in *Psycho*—who tells Douglas the biblical story of Jonathan and David before announcing he loves him and attempting to stab him with a knife.

It is finally, however, *The Bride of Frankenstein* (1935) that stands as Whale's masterpiece and the film most cited as the queerest in his canon—indeed, in the entire studio era. Already referenced several times here, *Bride* is monumental and deserving of every accolade it has received. Once again, Whale was actively involved in all aspects of the film, even enjoying a freer hand this time; studio head Carl Laemmle Jr. was in Europe for most of the filming, leaving Whale to function essentially as his own producer. Even more than the original, then, the sequel is Whale's baby from start to finish—from the heavy input he gave scriptwriter John L. Balderston to the final editing of the Bride's creation sequence, with its crazy forced perspectives and tilted angles defining its odd beauty. Different yet again from Cukor in his fascination with cinematography, Whale worked with cameraman John Mescall to achieve a "Rembrandt" look to the film: hard light with dark shadows and brilliant highlights.

But it's Ernest Thesiger as Dr. Pretorius who brings the film's queerness into sharpest relief, and once again, he was there at Whale's express wish. Thesiger was an actor on the London stage when he first met the young James Whale, who was playing a nonspeaking role in a Christmastide production of "The Merry Wives of Windsor." Whale was twenty-nine, but looked much younger, with the shock of his experience in World War I still in his eyes; Thesiger would remember Jimmy as "a frail ex-prisoner of war with a faun-like charm." They became good friends, with Whale modeling his manners after the cultured older man. There was another influence, too: Thesiger, although married, made little secret of his homosexuality. "He was camp and feminine and proud of it," observed historian Anthony Slide, "long before such attributes became fashionable in certain quarters of the gay community."

When Whale achieved prominence at Universal, he brought Thesiger over from London to work under personal contract to him. Whale knew what Thesiger could bring to a role. Already his reputation in Hollywood was notable: stories swirled of his entering one party and loudly asking, "Anyone fancy a spot of buggery?" Thesiger's portrayals in both *The Bride of Frankenstein* and *The Old Dark House* are standouts; Whale would remain grateful to him for the rest of his life.

In her analysis of *Bride*, Monika Morgan saw Pretorius as the linchpin of both the film's artistic success and its queer resonance. It is the "forced marriage" of Pretorius and Frankenstein that gives birth to the Monster's Mate in the creation sequence. "Whale's magical rendering of this scene not only validates the power of Pretorius-Henry's homosexual creativity," Morgan wrote, "but also of his own tremendous abilities as a gay artist. The intense dynamism of this scene serves as Whale's emphatic reminder . . . of the majesty and power of the homosexual creator."

Whale's career did not survive long in post-Code Hollywood. Despite a move away from horror films and a moderating of his more outrageous impulses, Whale's last film for Universal, *The Road Back*, was taken from him and severely edited by other directors. This despite a successful version of *Show Boat* in 1936, which should have made Whale untouchable. Although industry folklore long held that Whale's homosexuality was to blame for the end of his movie career, in truth it was the power shift at Universal that worked against him. (Laemmle, his champion, had been booted out.) The disastrous shooting of *The Road Back* only furthered his new bosses' resolve that he be let go.

Yet, as ever, the folklore contains a grain of truth. Like Dorothy Arzner, Whale was too much the iconoclast to last in an industry suddenly seized with a fetish for conformity. George Cukor always felt that Whale's exile after 1940 was simply his comeuppance for being too much the maverick. "That kind of flamboyance," he told Gavin Lambert, "was no help to any of us." Even with no conscious homophobia at work, James Whale's gayness *did* play a role in his banishment from post-Code Hollywood. A company man like Arthur Lubin could go on and on; so could Cukor and Irving Rapper, who understood the rules (even if subtly subverting them from time to time). But a James Whale: not likely. He'd retire to the house he shared with David Lewis, increasingly reclusive, finding solace through painting.

THE PRODUCERS: DAVID LEWIS AND HARRIET PARSONS

Whale couldn't have expected to continue untethered in the studios forever. For in truth, the Hollywood front offices were still ruled by men from the other side of the divide: the heirs to the traditions of the founders, for whom convention and middle-class canon were both the rule and the goal. An Irving Thalberg was exceedingly rare, a producer who defied assumptions and pushed limits, who mentored artists and encouraged individuality. And by 1937, Thalberg was dead.

There had been others: notably Paul Bern, also at MGM, whose suicide in 1932 ignited a scandal not matched since the William Desmond Taylor case. Bern was possibly homosexual, although that did not preclude deep, passionate attachments to beautiful women like Barbara La Marr and Jean Harlow, the latter of whom he married. An account by MGM story editor Samuel Marx of an emergency meeting called among producers and executives in the wake of Bern's death offers a glimpse into what it was like being homosexual in the front office. Louis B. Mayer, enraged at post-mortem rumors reaching his ears that Bern had been gay, demanded to know if they were true. None present knew for sure: Hunt Stromberg reportedly called Bern a "fairy." Although Marx's stories, on reflection, often seem to contain a degree of hyperbole, there is a glimpse of an underlying truth here. Unlike other areas of the industry—where one's homosexuality was frequently a known, accepted, commonplace *fact*—among the old-boy world of producers it was strictly *unmentionable*.

That's what makes the case of David Lewis so extraordinary. He managed to live quite openly with James Whale while his career, both pre- and post-Code, remained in ascent. Although they worked at separate studios, there was a collaboration on projects over the dinner table and in bed at night. Lewis had offered pertinent advice on the *Frankenstein* script; his strength in writing and seeing into the story bolstered many of his lover's films. Junior Laemmle, aware of Lewis' influence, explained the reason he never attempted to hire him: "When I hire Whale, I always get you for free."

That keen understanding of story is what made Lewis so good at what he did. At MGM, he was actually an associate producer, working under Irving Thalberg, whose own influence on all of his productions was, of course, undeniable. But Thalberg left to his associates many of the fine details, one of which, for *Camille*, demonstrates the formative role producers like Lewis could play. Not only did Lewis suggest Zoe Akins for the script, but he provided the necessary direction to make the story relevant to modern audiences (just as he'd given Whale the key to understanding the character of the Monster in *Frankenstein*). As Lewis recalled in his memoirs, Thalberg was worried about audience reaction to Alexandre Dumas' rather antiquated tale of the doomed prostitute and her ill-fated love for an aristocrat. Thalberg observed, "Men marry whores in our present society, and they very often make marvelous wives. In this town you find them all over the place." Armand's fear that his life would be ruined by marrying a hooker seemed archaic and quaint by 1935. "We have to live within the mores of the day," Thalberg told Lewis. "[Audiences] will think Armand is an awful little prig if his life can be ruined by marriage to Marguerite."

Lewis supplied the solution. "It isn't a question of his life being ruined by her past," he said, after giving the matter some thought. "It's a question of his *jealousy* ruining his life." Thalberg loved it. Lewis had provided, in his own words, the "one magic thing that would bring [the script] into the twentieth century."

A modern man was David Lewis. No judgments on Marguerite, no moralizing, no preaching. Not from a man who, when confronted about living with Whale, had arched his back and dug in his heels. He didn't *have* to, remember; he *wanted* to.

David Lewis was born David Levy in 1903 in Trinidad, Colorado, the second son of Russian Jewish immigrants. His father, Phan Levy, was a real-estate and insurance salesman, arriving in the U.S. in 1892 and crisscrossing the country from Utah to Colorado and finally to Seattle, where the family settled when David was about five. They were middle class but on the edge: in Seattle they lived in a neighborhood of civil engineers, business managers, and laborers. In addition, the Levys, like the Greenbergs in Connecticut, were the only Jews, and Phan Levy's fierce determination to succeed should be understood within this context. He lived with a desire to prove his family as successful as any of those around them.

"My father was a very difficult man," Lewis recalled. "Everything that belonged to anyone in the family was his, including all my money, which I gave him since it was easier to give him my money than to give him my love."

It was older son Melvin on whom Phan Levy lavished his attention and affection, while despairing of David's "different" ways. "I was a very difficult child," Lewis would admit. "I had my own way of doing things." Starstruck by the movies, he worshiped the early Vitagraph star Anita Stewart. Determined to become an actor himself, he (like so many before and since) risked his father's wrath by opting out of the ready-made future Phan had planned for him. Being a salesman for the rest of his life, David said, "was a frightening thought. . . . I surely didn't want to get caught in that."

He didn't. After graduation from the University of Washington he headed to New York and enrolled in the American Laboratory Theater on 57th Street, presided over by Richard Boleslawsky. One of Lewis' acting teachers was the great Maria Ouspenskaya. If success on the stage was measured by looks alone, David should have become a big star. Every account of Lewis' life remarks on his appearance. Tall and blond, he had a kind of golden-boy charm about him.

Yet as good-looking as he was, David Lewis wasn't destined to be an actor. In 1928, after a few parts onstage, he came down with a severe bronchial affection that impaired his voice. California beckoned as a place to recover; that it was the seat of his earliest fantasies only made it more appealing. Lewis managed to get a job as an assistant to producer Bud Lighton at Paramount. It wasn't long before story editor Eddie Montagne nabbed him for other duties.

"[Montagne] said I had done the best synopses he had ever seen and had the best story mind that you could ever imagine," Lewis remembered. Promoted to script supervisor, he developed an expertise on "how stories were formed and what the essence of story was."

He met James Whale soon afterward, during the director's brief tenure at Paramount. Lewis, just twenty-five, enjoyed playing tour guide to the older man, then forty, who was dazzled by California and the film colony. Whale was even more smitten with Lewis himself, although their romance seems not to have started immediately. After Whale left Paramount for Universal, they stayed in touch, and quite soon had fallen in love. By 1931 they were living together in Los Feliz, and in 1937 bought a house on Amalfi Drive. Whale and Lewis held on to the tradition of same-sex cohabitation that had been fairly common in the 1920s and early 1930s but largely abandoned by the middle part of the decade.

Lewis' talent and ability are the best explanation for how he—almost singularly in the studio era—managed to live an undisguised homosexual life while maintaining a career as a studio producer. That he was Jewish in a club dominated by Jews certainly helped; while he'd changed the Levy to

Lewis when he was in New York, there was no attempt to obscure his Jewishness, at least from his studio peers. He was also known as an insightful observer, someone who could, after only a short perusal of the material, refashion it into something better—and more profitable. So long as he didn't rattle protocol too much—and there must have been times some felt he did, given agent Phil Berg's remark—he was allowed to live as he pleased.

Studio brass liked him, too, because he was, in some ways, their ally in wresting creative authority away from directors. "I feel that the writer and producer should do the creative work, perhaps eighty percent of the picture," he insisted, defiant of conventional wisdom, "and the director and actors the interpretation, perhaps twenty percent." In other words, keep films the product of the studio, and not of auteurs.

Yet he was never merely a studio hack. He was passionate about movies, pouring his heart and soul into them. "I like tragedy," he said. "I think I understand it. It all started with *Camille*, the one with Greta Garbo. Since then I've always tried to make emotional dramas."

"Mr. Lewis is a producer who frankly is never satisfied with any of his productions," opined reporter Eileen Creelman. "He can, and does, pick apart any of his pictures, no matter what the public or critics may think of it. A perfectionist, he blames himself always for any flaws."

Working with Irving Thalberg had obviously left a lasting influence on his view of filmmaking. When he worked with directors and writers he admired, a harmony would occur, resulting in films of lasting impact that transcended mere studio product. *Camille*, of course, but others, too, after he'd left Metro and moved over to Warner Bros.: *Each Dawn I Die* (1939) and *King's Row* (1942). It's interesting to note that three of his most successful films—*Camille, Dark Victory,* and *Frenchman's Creek*—were made with gay directors. On *Dark Victory*, Edmund Goulding was appreciative of Lewis' input, one more queer confluence on a film that has become an enduring part of the gay canon. But he clashed with Leisen on *Frenchman's Creek* (1944). In his memoirs, Lewis wrote he went into the picture disliking both Leisen and his work. He wasn't clear why, although as they began working together, he became resentful of Leisen's clout with Paramount brass. Lewis wrote: "A former art director, [Leisen] was much more interested in the costuming and decor and spent days in the wardrobe department sewing chain mail on the costumes." Such seems a gross exaggeration (perhaps even a bit homophobic) given Leisen's reputation as an autocrat on his sets.

Lewis' distaste for Leisen may actually offer a clue to explain his ability to survive as a relatively undisguised gay man among the studio hierarchy. By 1944, Leisen was well known as someone who was definitely *not* circumspect. Despite the fact that David Lewis lived openly with James Whale—or perhaps, *because* of it—he could not be seen as too friendly with the likes of Leisen. The grapevine stories of the director's brazen behavior would naturally offend Lewis, who—to preserve his own lifestyle—had managed to become an expert at walking the tightrope between convention and independence.

In the 1940s one of his friends was the young screenwriter Arthur Laurents, who, like Lewis, shared his home with another man (the actor Farley Granger). "I became friendly with Lewis," Laurents recalled, "and I was surprised at how scared he was. He lived in mortal terror of someone finding out that he was gay when of course, everyone knew. It was fear of not doing the right thing or messing up the image, I suppose."

There are other suggestions that Lewis may have felt this way: his arched-back reaction to Whale being called a "queen"—("He wasn't a fairy," he insisted, "he was a *man*")—and his subtle disdain for the Cukor crowd. Although friendly during *Camille* and an occasional dinner guest of Cukor's, Lewis "did not particularly like the atmosphere" at Cukor's house. "There was a lot of gossip and chitchat, and I hate that," he said. "I probably said something to George, because he always said thereafter that I was a square." (Interesting, because at the same time Cukor considered Whale, Lewis' partner, too flamboyant.)

There's also Lewis' claim to have nearly married Norma Shearer after the death of Irving Thalberg. He wrote that they had an affair (curiously, a number of Hollywood homosexuals would claim affairs with Shearer, including Eugene O'Brien and William Haines) and that Whale worried he was going to lose him. But it didn't happen: as Lewis would write to a friend, "It had become completely impossible to untangle the web that life had spun around Jimmy and me."

Like many couples, straight and gay, the glow had begun to fade from their relationship after the first several years, although they remained committed and indeed bought a house together. As Whale's career declined, Lewis assumed more and more responsibility for him, calling his daily worries about Jimmy "monumental." By the late 1940s, however, Lewis was having his own career problems, facing a massive depression following the failure of *Arch of Triumph* (1948). It was a precarious time in Hollywood, adjusting to post-war realities and the arrival of television (see Chapters 9, "Pinkos, Commies, and Queers," and 10, "The Bold Ones"). Lewis didn't work for seven years. When Whale suddenly indulged a midlife attraction to a much younger man, Lewis moved out of their Amalfi Drive home.

Still, their bond was never really broken. Lewis continued to visit, and when Whale committed suicide in 1957 by jumping headfirst into his swimming pool, it was Lewis who was called and Lewis who took charge of arrangements. He hid Whale's suicide note for many years, not wanting his lover's memory shamed. It would be David Lewis who kept the legacy of James Whale alive.

• • •

There was one other notable nonheterosexual producer in the studio era, and it was a woman. And not just any woman, but the daughter of one of the most powerful figures in the industry. From an early age Harriet Parsons had all eyes on her. Her mother, columnist queen Louella Parsons, engineered Harriet's star turn as "Baby Parsons" in a series of Essanay films in 1913. Later, as "first daughter of the press," Harriet wrote for *Photoplay* and the Hearst syndicate.

But she was always more than just Louella's daughter. Bright and perceptive, Harriet learned the Hollywood playbook from all sides of the game: journalist, publicist, scenario writer. She had pluck, courage, and determination. "If you believe in something," she once said, "stick to your guns and fight it through."

In her own words, she was a "tomboy" as a child. Wanting to forge her own image apart from Louella's domineering shadow, she went off to college at Wellesley. Although after graduation in 1928 she worked briefly as an MGM scenario writer, she soon was settled in New York, far from Louella's dominance. As a writer for the fan magazines there, her bosses were less beholden to Mother than studio chieftains had been.

A case of pneumonia in 1934, however, landed her back in California for her health, where she succumbed to pressure from her mother to take a job at Columbia. "For someone as independent as I was," Harriet recalled, "it didn't massage the ego to be forced to come to Hollywood. I disliked it greatly. I never intended to stay."

But stay she did, taking over as a producer of the Screen Snapshots series. It engendered a fascination with the whole craft of filmmaking, and Harriet determined to make it as a producer. It was certainly a heady goal for a woman. "I could always get my foot in the door through Mother, but then I had to work twice as hard," Harriet remembered. "I had two strikes against me: I was the woman behind the camera at a time when there were none, and I was Louella's daughter."

Unlike Dorothy Arzner some fifteen years earlier, Harriet Parsons wasn't reluctant to put a name to Hollywood's sexism. The front offices were predominantly male, although a few women *had* broken through: in January 1945 the *New York Times* ran a piece on the increasing number of women in producing positions, including Virginia Van Upp at Columbia and Joan Harrison at Universal. Most notable, however, was Harriet, who then had *three* pictures in production at RKO. Her first stop had been at Republic, where the struggle she faced was driven home for her. Watching in outrage as picture after picture was reassigned away from her, Harriet grew so furious that she quit. "The studio didn't trust me," she said plainly, "because I was a woman."

At RKO, the battle only continued. She began development of Arthur Wing Pinero's fantasy "The Enchanted Cottage," only to have it wrested from her and given to Dudley Nichols. Ironically, it was Mother's rival, Hedda Hopper, who came to Harriet's defense, charging RKO in her column with a "dirty deal." The picture was summarily returned to Harriet, and her career shifted into high gear.

The Enchanted Cottage (1945) is a moving, tender fable of a homely woman and a disfigured man who, within the magic walls of the cottage, find themselves transformed. It's interesting to speculate on Harriet's initial attraction to the project, based on a play she'd admit to considering "banal." Yet somehow the story had resonated with her. That it should be her ticket to fame is perhaps appropriate: no great beauty herself, a misfit in many ways—not least of which was her lesbianism—she could bring a particular understanding and sensitivity to the premise.

Like David Lewis, she never saw her role as merely a money handler or administrator, but rather as a creative influence on what she envisioned the final product should be. "The first thing a producer does," she wrote, "is find a property—a story—which he thinks will make a good movie." (Even Harriet wasn't immune to the sexist boilerplate standard for the day.) "Then he must get the writer best for that particular story. The writer turns his work over to the producer a sequence or two at a time. Sometimes the producer asks for changes as the script goes along; sometimes he waits until the writer's first draft."

Parson's collaboration with her hand-chosen writer was significant. She'd known the brilliant, sensitive, homosexual DeWitt Bodeen for years; she knew he'd be perfect for *The Enchanted Cottage*. Together, as Bodeen recalled, they recrafted the play in their own fashion. "What I had to rebuild," he wrote, "was a modern romance that would be credible, omit all the sentimentality and rely upon the plausibility of love between a plain and unwanted spinster and a bitter crippled soldier, each of whom sought to hide away from a world that had rejected them."

The Enchanted Cottage is an excellent example of homosexual expression as enacted through heterosexual guise. Harriet clearly wanted DeWitt because they shared "something sympathique," as Elsie Janis had once said about Edmund Goulding. Although Bodeen acknowledged that the film's director, John Cromwell, made his own contributions to the final picture, no part of the film was incongruous with the vision Bodeen and Parsons had already established. Seen today, the film does echo with a sense of longing to fit in, yet also celebrates the joy of difference and of finding others who share a particular worldview—the way, indeed, that Parsons and Bodeen had found each other.

"They were very good, lifelong friends, extraordinarily devoted to each other," remembered the writer Charles Higham, who knew Bodeen. With DeWitt, Harriet felt a trust and camaraderie neither found in many other areas of Hollywood. Friends of both recall a sense of alienation shared by the two friends, despite their success within the system. Harriet would admit, "Even when I was at the top of the ladder at RKO, I had to fight for every film."

Being a woman in a man's job, of course, necessitated that fight, and being a lesbian could only have added to her defensive posture. At just four-feet-eleven, she'd often sit on telephone books behind her desk to make herself seem more imposing. Her marriage to King Kennedy (orchestrated, she'd later admit, by her mother) was a classic "cover," and they hardly ever lived together. They divorced in 1946, and by the 1950s she was living with publicist Lynn Bowers. Later, Harriet was involved with a well-known actress-singer; they were viewed as a couple by many within the industry. By this time Louella had to have been sharp enough to know the truth, but Harriet was also finally independent enough to live as she chose.

She had other important successes, notably *I Remember Mama* (1948), also written by Bodeen, and *Clash by Night* (1952), one of the most powerful of Barbara Stanwyck's later films. On the latter, she fought with director Fritz Lang over the ending, saying it was "too defeatist" and threatening to rewrite it herself. Her heavy-handedness worked, although the film suffers from the change. "I suppose there are those," she admitted, naming especially the film's screenwriter Clifford Odets, "who would say I should have kept the ending. But I had no qualms . . . I believe in happy endings."

Maybe that's because she wanted one in her own life, which she managed, finally, settling down in Palm Springs with a companion, Evelyn Farney, a former dancer whom she also legally adopted. She left RKO in 1956, tried her hand at Broadway (she produced one play, "The Rape of the Belt," which flopped), and then got involved in real estate. "I had become disenchanted with Hollywood," she said, looking back. Elsewhere, she explained, "Despite the male charge that this country has disintegrated to a state of matriarchy and 'momism,' this is still a man's world. And if there is anything men are less enthusiastic about than women drivers it is women executives. The more efficient she becomes in her field, the deeper the resentment."

Her memoirs were written with a "feminist, career-oriented slant," she said in 1982, some months before her death. They were never published; one friend recalled that they were quite "explosive" and that her former lover, the singer, had begged her not to go ahead with it. She had toyed with various titles: *I Didn't Tell Mother; On My Own; Twice in My Life.* All would have been appropriate, summing up as best as possible in just a few words an extraordinary life. Harriet Parsons died on January 2, 1983. Her singularly feminist outlook during her short but acclaimed career in the studio system makes her overdue for rediscovery.

QUEER WORK

THE "BEHIND-THE-SCENES QUEENS"
OF THE HOLLYWOOD STUDIOS
1935-1955

Frank Lysinger was a messenger boy at Metro-Goldwyn-Mayer in the late 1930s. "I got to see everybody and everything," he remembered, and that included the various studio departments. Each had its own traditions and atmosphere, Lysinger remembered: in the prop department, there was always "lots of gaiety," with set decorators Henry Grace, Jack Moore, Richard Pefferle, Keogh Gleason, and research chief Elliot Morgan camping it up and carrying on. "Oh, my, yes, camp humor certainly did bounce off the walls," Morgan concurred.

Meanwhile, over in wardrobe, Lysinger found the men more effete and standoffish, and in the technical departments, there was always lots of "guy talk" about baseball and broads.

In the studios, the "queer quotient" varied dramatically from field to field. An employee in the writers' department at Warner Bros. remembered, "You'd think the conversation there would be about books and plays. But it wasn't. It was about the World Series and Joe DiMaggio's scores. There were lots of 'behind-the-scenes' queens who felt left out of all that."

Lysinger, who'd move from messenger boy to assistant in the music department, agreed. "The departments were all very different from each other," he said. "Some were more gay than others. Some weren't gay at all."

The studio system had created units that together functioned like clockwork, maintaining a regular production of shorts, newsreels, serials, and features—"like so many Model-T's off the assembly line," in the words of historian Thomas Schatz. Yet each of these interdependent departments was also highly unique, holding specific traditions, customs, and mores. The bar of "circumspection" was therefore correspondingly relative: in the property department, Elliot Morgan recalled sometimes paging Henry Grace with a campy "Calling Grace Moore"—but every Friday night, gay screenwriter George Oppenheimer dutifully attended the prizefights at the American Legion with his heterosexual coworkers.

From the hegemony in wardrobe to the de facto prohibition in the technical fields, the placement of gays within the studios is telling. It offers an example of "queer work"—labor associated with one gender but assumed by the other. Not only is queer work *viewed* as predominantly homosexual, but actually *is,* offering gays and lesbians a rare opportunity to be both overt *and* successful in their chosen professions.

As economist Julia Matthaei has explained, "The sexual division of labor, present in all previously known societies, has assigned the biological sexes (male and female) to different and complementary work activities, 'men's work' and 'women's work'. . . . Preparation for and involvement in [such] activities makes the sexes into different and complementary genders, 'masculine men' and 'feminine women.'" Work within the home or family unit, Matthaei observed, was assigned to women; work outside the home (or market-oriented) was given to men.

Therefore, a man working in costume design or interior decoration—both "home"-centered occupations—is automatically considered "feminine," while a woman at the loading dock is considered masculine. In the Depression-era 1930s, the prevailing conservative *Zeitgeist* made such irregularities undesirable, with social and cultural leaders actively discouraging them. Professional women were often portrayed in the press and movies as "un-womanly"; not surprisingly, then, their numbers dropped by over 50,000 between 1930 and 1940, despite the growth of the overall female labor force by more than half a million in that same period.

Such a social imperative against gender transgression meant that queer work would carry some stigma. Writing of the pre-Stonewall gay world, Alan Helms observed that, "save for a few artists and hairdressers and decorators and dancers," everyone else went through "the workaday world passing for straight." It was more than just a social convention: homosexual activity remained outside the law, and to be associated with work that read as queer suggested not only deviancy but illegality.

Such deviance, then, implied courage as well as stigma: it was Helms and his convention-bound counterparts who spent their days in terror of discovery, not the more obvious artists, hairdressers, and costume designers. "[Some homosexuals] openly admit and practice homosexuality," observed Maurice Leznoff and William Westley in their groundbreaking study of homosexual communities, first published in 1956. "They usually work in occupations where the homosexual is tolerated, withdraw from uncompromising heterosexual groups, and confine most of their social life to homosexual circles."

Studying both "overt" and "secret" homosexuals, Leznoff and Westley found a telling breakdown of occupations. Of fifteen "overts," three were artists, six were in the service industries, and five were in clerical or sales; none were in professional or managerial occupations. Among twenty-five "secret" homosexuals, however, thirteen were classified as professional or managerial, and none as artists or in service industries. In such an arrangement, a picture of "queer work" emerges, and it's striking how closely the Hollywood studios bear it out.

"You couldn't be a cameraman or a sound person," screenwriter Faith Hubley said, referring to an unwritten rule against women in those fields, a rule that by extension also excluded overt gays. Hubley described an incredibly macho-defined environment: "They would say, 'We're not relaxed with you, you don't swear.' Then we would practice saying 'fuck' and 'shit,' walking through the studio saying 'Fuck shit fuck shit,' and then they would say, 'That's no way for a girl to talk.'"

An undisguised gay man would have been just as unwelcome. "A gay cameraman in those days, if one existed, would have had to be in the closet—*way* in the closet," said publicist Alan Cahan. "There wasn't a single one that I knew."

Statistics bear this impression out. In Leo Rosten's famous late 1930s–early 1940s sociological study of Hollywood, he found that a full *90 percent* of studio cameramen were married, as compared to about 70 percent of assistant directors and about 80 percent of film editors. Perhaps even more telling, cameramen were far more likely to be married only once, to the same wife, than other groups.

Such data, of course, can't be taken simply at face value. Since the first film pioneers cut the path to the West, there were undoubtedly gay men and women in all areas of the industry. But in certain fields there was an image to maintain, and if one were gay, it would be a secret best kept. Marriage was often a choice in such cases, and if a particular individual was homosexual, the historian today will likely not suspect it from the existing record. Among the thousands of *Variety* obituaries perused for this study, only a few of those for cameramen, sound editors, and electricians contained the flag-raising phrases of "no immediate survivors" or "lifelong bachelor." Yet even the names of these few elicited no spark of recollection from gay-subculture survivors. "I don't think I ever knew any cameramen," said Charles Williamson, echoing Cahan. Don Bachardy said, "There weren't very many from the technical fields that I knew."

A few names *have* filtered down. Robert Seiter, the college boyfriend of Grady Sutton and brother of film director William Seiter, briefly worked as a cameraman in the 1930s, thanks to his brother's connections. Charles Aufderheide, a good friend of Christopher Isherwood, worked in the Technicolor labs. Among other nonstereotypical fields, Mike Steen was a stunt man before compiling several interview books, many conducted with figures he knew from the gay social scene. Donald Vining worked as an extra at Paramount after he was discharged from World War II; in his diary, he also mentioned a gay studio security guard.

Surely there were dozens—hundreds?—of gays in the ranks of extras. *Bachelor* magazine, that not-so-surreptitious chronicle of the gay subculture, recounted in February 1938 the story of the many "sensitive" men who were discouraged and depressed, never having made it beyond bit parts and walk-ons. "If he's phlegmatic, he won't be hurt much," the magazine opined, "but if he has *imagination,* a sense of the finer things in life, you can't conceive of the indignities he endures, of the snubbing and snobbery." To escape, *Bachelor* reported, groups of male extras hung around Cahuenga and Vine, gossiping about the studios.

The magazine also revealed that female extras held their male counterparts in contempt: "Women will often do things, unashamed, which they despise in a man." Extra work, then, had a tinge of queerness to it, too. Often it was precisely this shared, shoulder-to-shoulder experience with women that made an occupation "suspect," while the *absence* of women from such fields as cinematography and sound technology made those fields indisputably straight.

Of course, the queerness of studio work existed along a spectrum: the opposite extremes of wardrobe and cinematography were not the norm. Editing, for example, was hardly considered "queer work," and yet there were some notable gay editors of the studio era. Beginning as predominately "women's work" in the Teens (recall Dorothy Arzner's experience as an editor), the field of editing by the Thirties and Forties still included many women, several of whom had trained the men who worked under them.

This less rigid gender construction allowed gays to carve out careers that embraced some degree of authentic expression in their work lives. Such observation is supported by Rosten, who reported that, as a group, film editors had the second-highest percentage (almost 20 percent) of never-married employees in the study. (Wardrobe and art department staff were not surveyed).

Robert Seiter moved into editing after his brief stint as a cameraman, helped this time not so much by his brother but by his status as a favored "trick" of George Cukor and his friends. He had a career that lasted into the television era. Jerry Rogers was an editor at 20th Century-Fox with another long career; he died of AIDS in 1990. The obituaries of at least ten other film editors of the studio era make one suspect they may have been gay, with the telltale "lifelong bachelor" description giving pause to the researcher.

The most notable gay figure in editing was William Reynolds, named by *Film Comment* as one of the top three film editors of all time. Born in 1910 in Elmira, New York, to an affluent family, he graduated from Princeton with a degree in English, but in 1935 joined a "swing gang"—prop movers—at Fox, so determined was he to get into the movie business. "I very quickly zeroed in on the cutting department, and just by sort of making a nuisance of myself, I managed to get in as an apprentice," he recalled. He quickly mastered the craft. "Keep it simple" became his guiding philosophy: "Keep the storyline clean so the audience understands what's happening."

Director Robert Wise would say of Reynolds, "I valued Bill's judgment more than I did anybody's. It's part of the editor's job to evaluate what he has—and sometimes not use all of it. Bill had very good taste." *The Los Angeles Times* called Reynolds "one of the quiet legends of Hollywood, a gentle man with impeccable timing and an innate sense of what an audience wanted to see." His films included *Algiers, 52nd Street, Carousel, South Pacific, The Day the Earth Stood Still,* and *Bus Stop.* He won an Oscar for *The Sound of Music,* and was still editing into the 1980s. His opening sequence for *The Godfather* was hailed as an editing masterpiece. "He had an extraordinarily successful Hollywood career," said a longtime friend, speaking on condition of anonymity. "He certainly would not have felt [his homosexuality] ever inhibited his career. He kept his life very private, very separate from his career."

Part of that separation was the requisite female date to industry functions like the Academy Awards. But Reynolds' friend insisted that the editor was never attempting to obfuscate his homosexuality: "People knew. It didn't make a whit of difference to anyone."

That's true as far as it goes: to some, of course, it would have made an *enormous* difference had Reynolds shown up with a man the way Jimmy

Whale and David Lewis showed up together. It could be argued, in fact, that Reynolds had less to lose than Whale, that—as an editor—he was in a much less visible position than a director or an actor; to arrive at an industry function with a male partner would not have attracted public notice in the same way. But it *would* have drawn the eyes of his bosses, and a breach of protocol—any breach—was not good form when one is interested in advancing one's career.

In many ways, William Reynolds spent his life in deference to others. His job as an editor was to subjugate his own vision to that of another. "The editor's object," he recalled, "is not to make his own wonderful version out of this material that the director has given him [but rather] to make the film the director had in mind." Reynolds followed social etiquette with as much precision. He made it to the very top of his chosen profession by keeping his own image low, and was rewarded at the end of his career with the respect of his peers and the reverence of a younger generation of editors. Yet his success was based not only on his undeniable talent, but also on his ability to play studio politics.

That's not a criticism of him, merely an observation. He played the game and won, surviving the Darryl Zanucks and Louis B. Mayers to emerge into the post-studio, post-Stonewall world with aplomb—editing, in fact, Hollywood's very first openly gay romance, *Making Love*, in 1982.

GAY WRITERS IN STRAIGHT HOLLYWOOD

The experience of gay writers is particularly fascinating. Just as it had in the art department, the coming of sound resulted in an overhaul of the old scenario department. Though some survived (Frances Marion and Anita Loos chief among them), the number of women writing pictures dropped significantly as the studios retooled themselves for sound. Imported now were playwrights and journalists, professions both dominated by men. The playwrights came and went, but many journalists settled into the studio structure: John Balderston, William Slavens McNutt, Herbert Clyde Lewis, John Howard Lawson, Samson Raphaelson, Ring Lardner Jr., Charles Brackett. Journalism, like architecture, was not a field known for overt homosexuals. The image of the hard-boiled journalist as popularized by the play (and later film) *The Front Page* became the dominant stereotype of the movie writer: cigar-chomping, shirtsleeved, banging away at his typewriter, the air as thick with profanity as smoke—and beware any "dame" who ventured into the lion's den.

Leo Rosten observed several characteristics of the "tough-skinned" and "pragmatic" screenwriters. They were younger, on the whole, than directors or producers, and they tended to be native-born. They were also likely to be married: almost 90 percent had spouses. And of those who were single, the survey found *all* had been divorced at least once.

Rosten's numbers seem to have missed at least two bachelors: Rowland Leigh and George Oppenheimer. Leigh had written *The Charge of the Light Brigade* (1936) and *Vigil in the Night* (1940), but he never quite fit into the screenwriting world of Hollywood. He preferred his duties writing the book for Cole Porter's Broadway musical "You Never Know," starring Clifton Webb and Rex O'Malley in 1938. "I always got the sense he didn't feel very comfortable in the studios," said a friend. "He preferred the theater." He was better known as one of the regular wits gossiping around George Cukor's swimming pool.

Oppenheimer, on the other hand, was a proper, precise fellow who wrote *Roman Scandals* (1933), *Libeled Lady* (1936), *A Day at the Races* (1937) with the Marx Brothers, and *A Yank at Oxford* (1938), among others. From an affluent family, he had studied at Harvard with George Pierce Baker and founded Viking Press in New York with Harold Gunsberg in 1925. With such impeccable credentials, he was immediately embraced by Hollywood society, but his memoirs, carefully worded, suggest he was never quite "in." Although he enjoyed the film colony at first, he found it "inbred and insular, small town and small-minded." He attended practically every party to which he was invited, but never felt at home among Hollywood types, preferring to spend time with fellow writer Charlie Lederer and his aunt Marion Davies, who was regularly surrounded by gay men.

Oppenheimer found other breaks from society and parties. Harry Hay recalled being picked up by Oppenheimer on the corner of Hollywood and Vine around 1935; they saw each other on and off after that. Hay claimed he helped Oppenheimer revise movie scripts: "For these ghost-writing tussles he would give me fifteen to twenty-five dollars a hit." But when Hay begged to be taken to an industry gala, Oppenheimer refused, telling him he was "too obvious."

Oppenheimer knew the line that had to be toed. For the most part, Hollywood's writers were tolerant, open-minded people. They weren't like the status-seeking moguls or the cameramen with their homes in the valley. They were veterans of the Algonquin Round Table, playwrights and novelists, F. Scott Fitzgerald and John Collier. Despite their wives and cigar smoke, most nonetheless moved in a sophisticated, cosmopolitan world. They tended to be better educated than anyone else in the studios; nearly 70 percent had college degrees, compared to 35 percent of cameramen. In a poll they ranked peers like Dudley Nichols, Robert Riskin, Donald Ogden Stewart, and Lillian Hellman as the writers they most admired. These weren't small-minded people.

That a number of them were Eastern Jews is significant. "Poor, young, educated Jews growing up in New York in the Twenties and the Thirties, which described so many of the writers in Hollywood, could scarcely escape [having a political conscience]," Neal Gabler wrote. Screenwriter Milton Sperling described his father as belonging to a union and reading the Jewish Socialist newspaper. Philip Dunne estimated 70 percent of Hollywood's writers were solid liberals. "Politics and aesthetics merged," Gabler said. "Young Jews with a gift for writing wanted to use it to right wrongs, expose injustices, redress grievances, and create new worlds."

Still, liberal though it was, the world of screenwriting remained an old-boys' club, with that particular fraternity that often develops among liberal old boys, evidenced by Oppenheimer's obligatory Friday night prizefights. Writer Julius Epstein recalled, "Going to a [Writers'] Guild meeting was like going to the Elks."

Hollywood has always been a small town, and appearances were important. That many writers harbored secrets is undeniable. George Oppenheimer thought Harry Hay might reveal his and put an end to their relationship. Others had no choice. Wilfred H. Petitt, screenwriter of such spectacles as *A Thousand and One Nights* (1945) and *The Bandit of Sherwood Forest* (1946), hanged himself aboard his yacht on December 8, 1948, wearing his wife's clothes. *The Los Angeles Times* reported all the salacious details, and Hedda Hopper dutifully clipped it out and saved it in her files—just in case it might ever come in handy.

• • •

The juiciest secret of all involved one of screenwriting's leading lights, the eminent and august Charles Brackett. Scion of a New York banking family, Harvard law graduate, married to a prominent heiress, Brackett was the quintessential Eastern aristocrat. "If I were casting a picture and I needed a Supreme Court judge, it would be Charlie Brackett," said his longtime writing partner, Billy Wilder, with whom he collaborated on *Ninotchka, The Lost Weekend,* and *Sunset Boulevard,* among others. "He was a right-wing Republican conservative, a formal man, always impeccably dressed, who made entries in his diary every evening."

Brackett was the epitome of the establishment. As vice-president of the Screen Writers Guild in the 1930s, his reputation helped keep the group from being officially tarred as Communist, despite the socialist leanings of many of its members. From 1949 to 1955 he served as president of the Academy of Motion Picture Arts and Sciences. One couldn't get much more Establishment than that.

"I think it likely that the Bracketts posed for the words 'lady' and 'gentlemen,'" George Oppenheimer wrote. "Certainly they were two of the most civilized people in Hollywood. . . . They surrounded themselves with many of the more intelligent members of the movie colony, a meeting place of natives and outlanders, a crucible of Western and Eastern culture with excellent Bloody Marys."

But as time went on, Elizabeth Brackett grew a bit too fond of those Bloody Marys, and increasingly became a recluse. There was something dark behind Charlie Brackett's glory, and Oppenheimer surely knew what it was. Most in the subculture did.

"It was a very weird, dark, Hollywood drama," said Gavin Lambert, who, as a young writer in Hollywood, was embraced by Brackett and his crowd. "Charlie was one of the first people I met when I came out here. I'd go to the Sunday lunches at his house. They were all very Hollywood establishment. I got to know Charlie fairly well. There was a certain subtext between us. We didn't have to discuss it. He knew I was gay, I knew he was."

What Lambert didn't know for certain, however, was the exact nature of the relationship between Charlie and the young man who acted as his assistant on several pictures—the young man Charlie had arranged to marry his daughter Alexandra, or "Zan," as everyone called her. The young man who had fathered his own grandson.

His name was James Larmore. Photographs reveal a strikingly handsome youth with deep-set eyes and full lips. He'd appeared in the play "Russet Mantle" and come to Hollywood as part of the "Winged Victory" company after World War II, whereupon he acted in several pictures before becoming Brackett's assistant. And son-in-law. And most likely lover.

Lambert stated he believed the stories of a lover relationship between Brackett and Larmore to be true. Christopher Isherwood believed them as well. "It was an accepted fact among everyone," said Isherwood's lover, Don Bachardy, who was often both guest and host of Brackett. The playwright John Van Druten, a mutual friend, reportedly knew the affair as a fact, having been a confidant of both Brackett and Larmore. "One just *knew*," said Bachardy. "They'd be together and one just knew. It's not as if we could have asked him. It was out of the question to be intimate in that way with Charlie."

In 1948, Elizabeth Brackett died; soon after, Charlie married her sister, Buff, with whom he continued the tradition of Sunday lunches for the elite of the industry.

In his pre-Hollywood days, Brackett had written a novel, *American Colony*, in which one of the characters, Sydney, is a gay man living among upper-crust straight friends. Sydney despairs of the "malice and crowding intimacy" he'd known in the gay world, wanting desperately to fit in with his "normal" friends. When a straight pal assures him that "nobody cares nowadays" about homosexuality, Sydney laughs, admitting that while his gayness might be a "fashionable vice," it remained so only as "long as it isn't found out. . . . Just let me get clapped in the Black Maria, and how many of you do you think will jump up on the step to wish me a good journey? There's the time when your hand-washing will begin."

Sydney may well offer an insight into Brackett himself. "Charlie is an example of someone who was just totally, totally in the closet, totally circumspect," said Gavin Lambert. "And I think ultimately it affected his work. I think in some sense that's why he and Billy Wilder split up. Charlie did not want to go too far. He thought *Sunset Boulevard* was too ghastly. He won an Oscar for it, but he wanted nothing to do with it. He felt Wilder had become just too unconventional."

Indeed, much of Brackett's post-Wilder career is little more than fluff: *Titanic* (1953), *The Girl in the Red Velvet Swing* (1955), Edmund Goulding's *Teenage Rebel* (1956). Critic Richard Corliss has assessed that such films merely enforce "the belief that [Brackett's] role [with Wilder] had been that of the resourceful private secretary to an immigrant never completely confident in his grasp of English."

The irony is obvious, of course: that it was the homosexual partner (Brackett) who was the voice of restraint and convention and the heterosexual (Wilder) who was the maverick, imaginative thinker, and that alone the homosexual would wither up creatively and die. But a lifetime spent in constraint and self-censorship takes a toll.

"I don't think one can be fully creative and not be at peace with one's sexuality," observed the screenwriter Arthur Laurents. "It all springs from there."

Gavin Lambert mused, "I suppose there must have been some terrible guilt for Charlie, and that can be very bad creatively. I think just as he was uptight about being gay, so was he uptight creatively. He didn't want to overstep any line, push any envelope. It might have made people think, 'Oh, there's more to Charlie Brackett than I thought.'"

Like William Reynolds, Brackett played the game, but unlike Reynolds, he didn't win. It's difficult to judge him, given his background and his employment in a field dominated by old-boy traditions and rules—where even his partner, Wilder, occasionally made "faggot" remarks on the set. Yet Brackett's life, despite the achievements, despite the oh-so-fashionable-and-cultured reputation, seemed enveloped in misery. So much drinking: Larmore, too, and daughter Zan, who died from a drunken fall down the stairs. Brackett himself died a lonely and confused man, haggling over his memoirs, in 1969.

• • •

There were, of course, writers who lived far more authentically than Charles Brackett. Once again, those who first achieved prominence in the theater and then came to Hollywood as a result of that fame were far more likely to be undisguised about their homosexuality. John Colton, author of "Rain," had been in Hollywood since the early 1920s, where he became a close friend of Irving Thalberg. A vital part of the Hollywood gay scene, Colton shared a home with Mercedes de Acosta and often turned up in the gossip columns "out on the town" with Cukor or Orry-Kelly. Under the heading "So We're the Same, Are We?" (reflecting the post-Code admonition that the stars were just plain folks), Lloyd Pantages recounted in *Photoplay* a drag act Colton performed at Orry-Kelly's, done up in a flowered robe and roses in his hair, imitating Sarah Bernhardt and Mrs. Leslie Carter. There was also Edgar Allan Woolf, whom MGM story editor Samuel Marx described as "a wild red-headed homosexual." Woolf was a playwright before coming to Hollywood, where he wrote such films as *The Mask of Fu Manchu* and *Freaks* (both 1932), as well as serving as one of three credited writers on *The Wizard of Oz*.

Both John Van Druten and John Patrick began as screenwriters in the 1930s, but found greater fame on the stage, returning to Hollywood with greater glory in the 1940s. Van Druten wrote *Gaslight* for George Cukor in 1944, a brilliant study of paranoid terror, and then adapted his own stage success, *The Voice of the Turtle,* for Irving Rapper. John Patrick's greatest Hollywood success came after he'd scripted the hit plays "Curious Savage" and the Pulitzer-winning "Teahouse of the August Moon." He then wrote *Les Girls* for Cukor, as well as *Three Coins in the Fountain* (1954) and *Love Is a Many Splendored Thing* (1955).

Yet while both would become parts of the Hollywood social scene, neither was really part of the studio structure. The same was true for Christopher Isherwood, renowned author of "The Berlin Stories," who wrote a few screenplays in the 1940s but was more significant as a Hollywood host and, later, as a social agitator. The same pattern was again followed by William Inge, who arrived in Hollywood in the 1950s after his Broadway success with "Come Back Little Sheba," "Picnic," and "Bus Stop," all of which were made into films (adapted by others). Inge's first screenplay wasn't until *Splendor in the Grass* in 1961, for which he won an Academy Award.

For these men, their work in Hollywood was pretty much on their terms. Their sexuality was simply not an issue—although Don Bachardy stated he felt Isherwood might have gotten more film assignments if he hadn't been "so queer."

In some ways, the experience of the gay playwrights in Hollywood in the 1940s and 1950s mirrors that of the gay European directors in Hollywood in the 1920s and 1930s: although engaged in moviemaking, they remained outside, a status that gave them a certain freedom their studio counterparts lacked. John Patrick lived quite openly with a male partner for close to fifty years. Patrick, Van Druten, and Inge were all part of the Christopher Isherwood circle, where they were far more open about themselves than Charlie Brackett ever was.

Stage writers had more opportunity than movie writers to infuse their stories with a gay sensibility: witness just about anything written by Tennessee Williams. Gavin Lambert, a gay screenwriter who was first hired at Fox as assistant to director Nicholas Ray in the mid 1950s, said it would have taken extraordinary effort to consciously inject gay subtext into a studio film: "Remember, a [film] writer was always writing about a straight subject. Anything else would be noticed, even something subliminal, and it would be taken out."

Gore Vidal has gone on record as deliberately injecting a gay subtext into his script for *Ben-Hur* (1959). Like John Van Druten and William Inge, Vidal was another outsider, a well-known novelist. With director William Wyler's assent, he concocted as back story a homosexual love affair between Ben-Hur and Messala, played by Charlton Heston and Stephen Boyd. Vidal clued Boyd in to the idea, but kept the homophobic Heston in the dark. The result was a certain shine in Boyd's eyes during the scene where the two old friends link arms to toast one another, and a certain inflection in his words of devotion.

Vidal, who is famous for rejecting a strict gay-straight dichotomy, nonetheless admitted the possibility of a gay sensibility, perhaps unconsciously, coming through in a writer's work: "Someone who feels excluded from the life of the world because of prejudice—sex, race, religion, nationality," he said, "might indeed come up with Frankenstein's monster."

THE CHALLENGER: DEWITT BODEEN

Vidal might have also said "a woman who turns into a panther when aroused"—referencing DeWitt Bodeen's classic *Cat People.* Of the handful of gay writers working in the studios with no stage reputation to bolster them, it is Bodeen—Harriet Parsons' collaborator—who stands apart. In his own quiet, distinctive way, Bodeen challenged the prevailing orthodoxy of movie content.

Even more than his lovely *Enchanted Cottage,* his films for producer Val Lewton at RKO are stunning visualizations of queer desire and alienation. In *Cat People* (1942), Irena Dubrovna (Simone Simon) is a Serbian woman in middle-class America. She hides out, painfully aware of her difference from the mainstream. She has no friends; she lives as an observer of the culture rather than as a participant. When we first see her, she is sketching a panther: the object of both her fear and her desire, and the thing that ultimately prevents her from engaging with the world at large. Some critics have read the panther as a metaphor for homosexuality: when Irena's desire is kindled, she *becomes* that panther, the incarnation of her secret self—a self that is both wondrous but ultimately fatal, to herself and those she loves.

While producer Lewton and director Jacques Tourneur were involved in story conferences to develop the film's themes, it is Bodeen's script on which everything is based. Lewton came up with the basic idea, but left it to Bodeen to devise the plot and characters. "It permitted me to develop several themes," Bodeen remembered, "keeping in mind all the story points we had discussed and feeling free to invent new sequences if they came to me."

No matter how much Lewton and Tourneur later reshaped her, Irena Dubrovna remains a creation of DeWitt Bodeen. The dialogue he gave to her is significant: she fears if she were "to fall in love and if a lover were to kiss her, take her into her embrace, she would be driven by her own evil to kill him." Bodeen acknowledged that the film was intended to turn on Irena's repressed desire; he also wrote that nothing in the film "just happened," that everything—from Irena's characterization to the tiger lilies in the window—was there deliberately. Irena's desire is obviously different, abnormal, queer: if *everything* is deliberate, then it is not too far-fetched to suggest a degree of consciousness of Bodeen's *own* queer desire as he wrote of Irena's struggle with the demons within. As the critic J. P. Telotte has written, "Indeed, [Irena] seems to long for that sexuality, for absence to assume a masculine and authoritative shape. . . . If she could only embrace it, Irena might vanquish the fears which beset her."

Knowing some of Bodeen's life suggests that, consciously or not, he *did* bring a sympathetic perspective to Irena, and one that seems to fit a queer interpretation. "DeWitt had a certain poetic quality," said the writer Charles Higham, "a sensitivity that couldn't survive long in Hollywood. He became very bitter toward the industry. His favorite phrase was 'They eat their young.' He said one word dominated everything in Hollywood, and that word was 'fear.' He saw fear as the predominating emotion behind everything in Hollywood." At the end of his life, living in New York and writing to his friend, the historian Anthony Slide, DeWitt would remember Los Angeles as always "weary, dreary, and teary"—a place he'd once seen, however, as "the wonderful city of Oz."

Indeed, in the beginning, he was considerably more affectionate toward Hollywood. Born Homer DeWitt Bodeen in 1909 in Fresno, California, his father, Gustaf, was the son of Swedish immigrants and the manager of the Fresno Savings Bank. As a boy, he was fascinated with swimming movie star Annette Kellermann. His friend, the writer and publicist Herb Sterne, would write humorously that for several weeks after seeing Kellermann in

Neptune's Daughter, "the boy could be espied within the irrigation ditches without Fresno, seeking to emulate the star's more astounding aquatic stunts."

Fired with the desire to act, DeWitt headed down to the Pasadena Playhouse as a teenager—one more young actor taken under Gilmor Brown's wing—appearing as Orsino in "Twelfth Night." Later, as a student at UCLA, he wrote a play on the life of Keats, and Brown produced the work at the Playhouse. This led to another play, "Embers of Haworth," on the Brontës, which in turn led to a screenwriting contract at Warner Bros. When his script for an unnamed picture was completely rewritten, he angrily left the studio, his first disillusionment with the movies he had once so worshiped. Working for David O. Selznick, he fared better, serving as research adviser on *Jane Eyre.* RKO hired him then as a writer, assigning him to Val Lewton.

It was a good match, for Bodeen never fit in among the old-boy network of screenwriters. Lewton, with his quirky tastes and unique vision, welcomed Bodeen's eccentric appreciation of both high and popular culture. Herb Sterne described him: "He leads his bachelor life in a single apartment crowded with a mammoth radio-phonograph, some ten thousand records, half as many books, and complete files of *Theater, Stage,* and *Theater Arts* magazines." On one wall hung a shadow box containing an autographed slipper from silent star Marguerite Clark; each day Bodeen would reverentially fill it with fresh forget-me-nots. On another wall—his "Wall of Genius"—hung portraits of Gish, Garbo, and Duse.

It was perhaps inevitable that such character would come through in his work. Critic Michael Bronski has written that few classical Hollywood films can be charged with "deconstructing widely accepted moral absolutes or narrative conventions"—but of those that *can,* two of them are Val Lewton's *The Seventh Victim* and *The Curse of the Cat People.* DeWitt Bodeen was the writer of both. As much as Lewton should receive credit, Bodeen's contributions to the pictures were formative, and have been underrated—a judgment he may have agreed with. "Of all the arts and crafts that contribute to the creation of a movie," he wrote, "screenwriting has been the least appreciated. [Screenwriters'] contributions to particular films are usually underestimated, and their importance to film history has been almost totally suppressed."

Bodeen's talent sprang from his peculiar outlook on the world. When the facts weren't just as he might like them, he'd embellish them, or invent new stories altogether, just to keep life fresh and interesting. "If there was an opportunity to look at life through rose-colored glasses, DeWitt would do so," his friend, the author James Robert Parish, remembered, "because it would [allow him to] avoid being more aggressive in the world. That just wasn't his style. He was cultured, gentlemanly. It was the image he wished [the world] could be."

In *Curse of the Cat People* (1944), his best film, that image is central: the triumph of youthful innocence and belief over the harsh, adult, supposedly "real" world. Once again given the bare bones from Lewton—little girl conjures up imaginary friend—Bodeen set to work on what he called a "tender, haunting" story. They were stuck with the unfortunate title: RKO had demanded it to capitalize on the success of the original. But *Curse* is far from a horror picture. Rather, it is the tale of a lonely, imaginative girl who lives in a world of her own dreams and wonder, teased by her classmates and despaired of by her father—as close to himself as anything Bodeen ever wrote.

In the film, the girl focuses her dreams on a photograph she discovers of Irena Dubrovna, her father's first wife—much as the young dreamer De-Witt had mooned over Annette Kellermann back in Fresno. Irena appears to her and becomes her only friend; the film's message is based on this supernatural premise, that the reality of the world of order and tradition—as represented by the girl's father and teacher—is *not* the only course to truth. Such was a radical thesis for a Hollywood picture to take; indeed, there is a startling scene where the father spanks the little girl, fed up with her difference, that makes us despise him, even though he is the ostensible hero of the piece. Our sympathy is always with the queer little child and the otherworldly ghost she befriends.

Bodeen would insist the entire film, including dialogue, was exactly as he wrote it, except for the ending. Lewton changed the film's climax from an ethereal scene wherein the girl discovers Irena is a ghost to a scene more focused on the corporeal characters. Writer and producer clashed: Lewton kept trying to tinker with Bodeen's characterizations, with the notable exception of the old actress played by Julia Dean. "Leave the old actress alone," Lewton said with a mixture of humor and contempt. "She's De-Witt's. He *likes* old actresses."

Indeed he did, and in his later years he'd seek out and befriend lots of them—May Allison, Dorothy Davenport, Theda Bara—writing their stories in the pages of *Films in Review* and *Focus on Film*. Writing *about* film became more frequent than writing *for* film. Although after his break with Lewton, he had some success with his pal Harriet Parsons, adapting both *The Enchanted Cottage* and *I Remember Mama,* he found adaptation not nearly as fulfilling as writing original stories. "Writing an original screenplay is certainly less confining and always more creative," he said. "There are no boundaries; imagination can do with you as it will; one is free."

He didn't give up hope that he might once again find the kind of creative niche he'd known with Lewton. "DeWitt told me that the reason he began writing the career articles in *Films in Review* was in order to get his name back into print and into public view," recalled Anthony Slide. "He had hopes—unrealized—that it might lead to a screenwriting contract."

It would be eleven years before Bodeen worked on another film. "He had felt comfortable in the rather cottage atmosphere of RKO," said Charles Higham. "But once that was gone and he was out in the field, there was no room for his brand of somewhat whimsical, charming, old-fashioned, old-world, delicate writing. It got to the point where he couldn't get work of any kind."

DeWitt told columnist Frank Eng that "doors open and doors close at an unpredictable rate." He continued writing about a vanished Hollywood, helping to shape how a new generation would come to see Hollywood's history, documenting its myths and preserving the make-believe. He preferred that world of shadows and glamour, of illusion and innocence, to the harsh reality of what the industry had become.

THE DEFENDER: LEONARD SPIGELGASS

Leonard Spigelgass had no time for such nonsense. He was a studio man, one of the big guys at MGM, at least after Dore Schary came in—a card-carrying member of the old boys' club. Like David Lewis he carved out a place for himself in the studio hierarchy by craftily walking the line between circumspection and authenticity. He might be homosexual, but he was also a Jew and a New Yorker, bonds that mattered among many writers. Along with Schary, Ralph Rainger, Allen Rivkin, and William Fadiman, he was a member of the informal "Five Guys Club," a group of writers who'd known each other on the East Coast. Spigelgass was genuinely liked by his peers. "Just by being in his presence," said Ernest Lehman, "we all felt impelled to play over our heads, and actually did so, thanks to Lennie's inspiration."

Spigelgass was no DeWitt Bodeen, lingering on the sidelines, consumed by fear. He lived in the midst of power, and everyone knew the truth. "He lived for a while with a boyfriend on the beach in Malibu," remembered costume designer Miles White, who had a house nearby and occasionally attended parties at Spigelgass' house. "He was very well connected, very influential and very respected—and everyone knew he was gay. It was hard to hide. After a few drinks, he'd get very outrageous, very melodramatic. He was a character."

Christopher Isherwood and Don Bachardy would sometimes socialize with Spigelgass and his boyfriend, the actor Brandon Toomey, who played a few small parts in a handful of films. Spigelgass made no secret to his friends that he'd appreciate any help they could give Toomey's career. "I wouldn't say Spigelgass was open about being gay," Bachardy said. "He could be very cagey. But it was generally known."

Again like David Lewis, the sheer force of his personality protected him. But whereas Lewis was cultured and diplomatic, Spigelgass was bombastic, authoritative, aggressive. He could lock horns with any straight man and hold his own, and usually emerged the victor. Moving easily in the macho world of other writers, he collaborated with none other than Damon Runyon on a couple of films in the 1940s. "Damon showed me his world," Lennie remembered, "the prizefighters and the crap games." Gangster Mickey Cohen told Spigelgass if he ever needed anything, just to call. Well-placed friends in fact ensured his success: when Dore Schary replaced Louis B. Mayer as MGM chief, Spigelgass' clout only increased.

He'd always believed he was destined for greatness. Born on November 26, 1908 in Brooklyn, his father, Abram, was the son of a poor Russian immigrant tailor, but had scrimped and saved and studied hard to become a lawyer, representing mostly his poor and working-class neighborhood. Lennie Spigelgass grew up believing he, too, could make it—and he grew up among his own kind. Unlike Adrian Greenberg, he was surrounded by other Jews in his St. Johns Place neighborhood in Brooklyn. It was an experience that grounded him: he never tried to obscure his Jewishness, often sprinkling Yiddish phrases into interviews and serving—at the height of his career—as a director of the Hebrew Education Society.

Tall, thin, with a "tweedy" voice, Lennie was never shy about expressing an opinion. He graduated from New York University in 1929 and became a literary and drama critic for *The Brooklyn Eagle*. His sights, however, were set on Hollywood. He'd admit, "Anyone who tells you he came out here for any other reason than money is a liar." At RKO, he learned the necessary skills as a continuity writer. Significantly, he was brought into the club by two women, holdovers from the old days: Doris Molloy ("who knew more about the creation of a motion picture than anybody I ever knew") and Sonya Levien, who was good friends with Zoe Akins. Spigelgass recalled Levien was an "enormous influence" on his life. About the time he met her, she was in the news as being the reason Germany had banned the film *The Country Doctor;* Hitler had objected to the "non-Aryan" name of the screenwriter.

Spigelgass occasionally served as an associate producer at Universal but by the end of the Thirties was established as a competent, reliable company writer. He'd admit to some creative frustration: "The real problems were that you were writing for hire. You were [never] trying to please the ultimate consumer—[but rather asking] 'Will Eddie Knopf like it? Will Junior Laemmle like it? Will the director like it?'"

But like it they did, and Spigelgass enjoyed a steady rise in the studio system. He wasn't a prickly, eccentric artist like Bodeen; he knew how the game was played and played it. But neither was he as circumspect as Charlie Brackett or George Oppenheimer. His work may have been less prestigious and weighty than much of theirs, but that very buoyancy reflects his more independent spirit. He penned the lighthearted *Million Dollar Baby* and in 1942 was nominated for an Academy Award for the farce *Butch Minds the Baby*. The next year, he shared writing credit with Oppenheimer on *The Youngest Profession*—two gay men writing about starstruck adolescent girls mooning over Robert Taylor.

During World War II, he attained the rank of lieutenant colonel in the Special Services Division, serving from August 1942 to July 1945. Specifically, he wrote propaganda films for the U.S. Armed Services, 175 half-hour newsreels called *The Army-Navy Screen Magazine*. He also worked on *Why We Fight,* directed by Frank Capra, the official U.S. government film series defining the enemies of the Allies and why they needed to be vanquished.

It was after the war that he reached his heights. At Fox he wrote the script for *I Was a Male War Bride* (1949)—light, crisp, and more than a little campy. Cary Grant in drag, trying to accompany WAC wife Ann Sheridan back to the U.S., is a hoot. In 1950 Spigelgass settled in at MGM, where his buddy Dore Schary was soon running the show.

Spigelgass' scripts were never radical, never subversive, but in many of them, there's *something*—a perspective that seems a little different from most, a filtering of the world through the eyes of a gay Jew. *Mystery Street* (1950) is a taut little thriller in which the hero-detective, played by Ricardo Montalban, can be read as gay: the obligatory romance is missing, and he evinces complete disinterest when his assistant slobbers over the picture of a pretty girl. The only glimpse of his private life, in fact, is handball with male friends. Being Portuguese, he's clearly the outsider. The Wasp villain snarls: "My family has been around these parts since before there was a USA. From the sound of you, your family hasn't been around long." It's not difficult to observe Spigelgass' personal history behind the character.

In *Scandal at Scourie* (1953), Lennie again sided with the outsiders: Catholics, in this case, in a tale of a Protestant couple (Greer Garson and Walter Pidgeon) who adopt a Catholic child and agree to raise her as such. "I had a collaborator [Karl Tunberg] and a producer [Edwin Knopf] who thought that was just disgusting," Spigelgass revealed. "'How dare the Catholics do that, and we must take a stand against it in the picture.' I said, 'I understand it perfectly.' We had terrible arguments. I was called a reactionary and a turncoat."

What he was—despite his success, despite his skill at playing the game, despite making a place for himself at the old boys' table—was an outsider, just like the Catholics in the film, just like Ricardo Montalban's Portuguese detective. He was a homosexual and a Jew in an industry and a town that was committed to making sure America saw neither. He stood apart from the status quo, yet Leonard Spigelgass would go to his grave defending it. He had worked hard to get inside: as we will see, he would guard his membership in the system with the passion of a zealot.

"JUST A BUNCH OF CURTAIN-HANGERS": THE SET DECORATORS

If it was the rare Lennie Spigelgass who elbowed himself into the ranks of screenwriters, over in the set-decoration department there was no need for such effort. There gays actually called the shots, often taking all the plums and leaving the mundane assignments to straights.

The studio set decorators have received almost no study, yet their contributions were vital, providing the flair and ornamentation necessary for the bare sets constructed by the architect–art directors. "I'm sure you've seen barren sets on empty sound stages come to life under the set decorator's touch," said longtime MGM decorator Henry Grace. "Compare it to the architect who has completed a house, but it is the interior decorator who breathes life into the rooms."

The lowly "set dressers" of the early sound era had become, by the late Thirties, creative contributors with considerable authority. "At first," said Elliot Morgan, MGM research chief, "they were seen as just a bunch of curtain-hangers. But they were the ones who gave a picture its reality. They decided how a room would look, what kinds of furniture fit the story, everything."

Arthur Krams, who worked as a decorator at both MGM and Paramount, explained his role: "The set decorator starts with a bare set, three walls and a floor, provided by the art director. The actual decoration of this bare set is gathered from the screenplay, which tells the action involved, the time, contemporary or period. There has to be a close working relationship with the wardrobe people to coordinate the costumes of the star so that the colors of the set and the colors she wears complement each other. It would be a dreadful thing, for instance, for a star in a blue gown to suddenly find herself sitting on a blue sofa."

Dreadful indeed. Henry Grace would recall movie sets circa 1931 as "pretty sad affairs." But the rise of the set decorator reestablished a gay presence in set design. "There were a few men of vision in the industry who realized that sets required more than a conglomeration of furniture and props," Grace said. "It required trained people who knew how to combine things to reflect the character, period, or even to create a new style."

In his unpublished memoirs, Grace elaborated: "Set decorators [were] drawn mostly from the ranks of property men . . . [but] occasionally a decorator would be brought in from the decoration profession." Such a move was necessary, he wrote, because while the property men "showed some talent in arranging furniture combined with speed of execution," they had "little or no knowledge of period design and decoration." What he left unstated was nevertheless obvious: the new "men of vision" who were changing the screen were in fact homosexual. "Half a dozen young interior designers from New York and southern California were absorbed into the motion picture industry . . . so that today a high standard of design is maintained."

Both Arthur Krams and Henry Grace were gay; decorator Hal Gausman, who wasn't, estimated that during the studio era about a third of his colleagues were homosexual, and admitted that might be a conservative guess. "You didn't pay attention to it because they were just there," he said. "I don't know why it was [that so many were homosexual]. I guess one guy gets a job and then gets another in."

That's precisely how it happened. As head of the MGM property department, Edwin Willis, gay himself, was the direct supervisor of the set decorators. From the recollections of others, it's clear that he had a preference for hiring homosexuals, or for at least making sure they were the ones given the most influence. Yet like Cukor's employment of gay associates, Willis' hiring practices weren't intended to achieve any kind of "gay power" or clout. It was simply the fact that these were the men Willis felt "the most artistic and insightful," according to Frank Lysinger, the companion of decorator Richard Pefferle and the same man who had been a messenger boy at the studio.

In 1933, assembling his team, Willis first hired Henry Grace, an interior designer from the firm of Cannell and Chaffin, and Jack Moore, a window dresser from the H. T. Lockwood shop. Later hirees included Pefferle, a Sorbonne art student doing windows for Lord & Taylor, and Arthur Krams, who'd been the interior decorator of Pickfair. All were gay.

On the other hand, straight decorators like Gausman usually started as prop movers. Hugh Hunt, MGM's lone straight decorator, got his start unloading trucks for the property department. At RKO, Darrell Silvera was building props at age seventeen and was eventually made head of the prop department with oversight over set decoration. "That's how you started," Gausman explained. "You're carrying the stuff as lead man for somebody

else, a decorator, and then hopefully you get good enough and you yourself can be promoted."

Although "lead men" were technically assistants to the decorator, the
studios and unions often did not distinguish between them when counting
the number of decorators on staff. Understanding this breakdown enables
us to estimate the number of homosexuals working in set decoration. In the
decorators' 1942 contract with MGM, the ratio between "interior decorators" and "assistants" was stipulated as "no more than one to two." At the
time of the labor strikes of 1945, it was reported that there were seventy-
seven set decorators working in the industry. If the one-to-two ratio is applied, that means roughly twenty-five of the seventy-seven were actual
decorators and about fifty were lead men. Simply listing the names of
known homosexual set decorators at the time supplies more than half of
the twenty-five. Gausman's estimate of "a third" thus suggests a majority
of the actual decorators were gay, while a majority of their lead men were
straight.

The gay set decorators, by and large, *were* a different breed. Few started
by moving props or unloading trucks; they came instead from backgrounds
in interior decoration or the fine arts. Of course, for every generalization
there are exceptions: Joseph Kish, who was straight, had a background in
art, and Samuel Comer, who was gay, began as a prop mover at Paramount
in 1919. (He was later named head set decorator at the studio.) But the
record bears out the truth: most gay decorators came from a certain background and most straights from another.

It was a trend observed at all of the studios. The most prominent decorators were usually gay: Comer and Ross Dowd at Paramount; Paul Fox at
20th Century-Fox; Howard Bristol for Samuel Goldwyn. The trend was
most obvious at MGM, where homosexuals were considerably higher in
the pecking order. According to Frank Lysinger, the more prestigious assignments were doled out by Ed Willis to Pefferle, Grace, Moore, and
Keogh Gleason, while Hugh Hunt would be given "the character sets—
cowboy pictures and the like." (Indeed, Hunt's filmography indicates he
handled more Western pictures than the others, but he also worked on such
films as *Libeled Lady* and *The Picture of Dorian Gray*.) Hunt didn't resent his
assignments, rather liking Westerns, and in fact enjoyed good relationships
with his gay colleagues.

"Knowing these men," said Lysinger, "I'd have to say there was something very inherent about their style and skill. That's why Willis chose
them. He knew they had the most flair. I don't know if that's a gay sensibility at work or what. But Dick [Pefferle] was the only one with formal
art-school training. The others just seemed to come by it naturally."

• • •

With the rise of the set decorator, one old veteran returned to the industry: George James Hopkins. Hired by Warner Bros. in 1941, he went on to dress the sets for many unqualified classics: *Casablanca, Mildred Pierce,* Irving Rapper's *Deception, Life with Father, A Streetcar Named Desire, Auntie Mame* (for which his understanding of camp worked overtime), Cukor's *A Star Is Born,* and three for Hitchcock: *Strangers on a Train, I Confess,* and *Dial M for Murder.*

In his memoirs, Hopkins left a detailed description of the creative input of the set decorator. Working closely with director Michael Curtiz, Hopkins proceeded to secure the right look for *Casablanca.* "I discarded the studio's research and created a completely imaginary Casablanca," Hopkins remembered. "Mike agreed with me. He said, 'To hell with realism. Let's make our own exciting place.'" Accordingly, Hopkins allowed his "imagination to run riot in the street scenes," where he placed vendors presiding over brass ornaments and rugs, exotic birds, fruits, and flowers. To enhance the "evil pomposity" of the Sidney Greenstreet character, he tacked up nude pictures of "brown boys and white-limbed chorus girls" and piled his desk with "aged paperback editions of risqué French novels and trays filled with the butts of Turkish cigarettes."

For *A Streetcar Named Desire,* he concocted similar verisimilitude with an almost fanatical attention to detail:

> Many people who saw the apartment set on the stage while [director Elia] Kazan was shooting in it spoke to me of details they had noticed but had not seen later on the screen. They mentioned such things as the faded watercolor of Belle Rive, which Blanche had brought from her trunk, the inside lid of which was decorated with valentines and various souvenirs of her happy youth; the miniatures of herself and Stella on the ledge behind her shawl-draped couch. These details may not have been seen by many people seeing the picture, but I'm sure they were sensed! In any case, they were sensed and appreciated by the actors, who derived from such things the greatest possible sense of reality.

Hopkins was a true original, and a remarkable survivor. To start with Theda Bara and William Desmond Taylor and then go on to create the look of so many great Forties and Fifties films would have been extraordinary enough. But Hopkins thrived even into the post-studio era, winning Academy Awards for *My Fair Lady* (1964) and *Who's Afraid of Virginia Woolf?* (1966). Among his last films were *1776* in 1972 and *Day of the Locust* in 1975. Then he slipped into obscurity and, despite his incredible career, died pretty much forgotten in 1985.

• • •

If not as lengthy, the careers of other gay set decorators were just as notable. At MGM, Jack Moore did the poppy field for *The Wizard of Oz,* combining three soundstages to give the illusion of poppies stretching for miles. For *Conquest,* with Garbo and Charles Boyer, he decorated the set of the château where Napoleon's troops come charging through the great hall and leap over a grand piano. Rather than damage the authentic Aubuisson carpet he'd installed, Moore sewed together dozens of cocomats for that one scene, painting the finished product with the exact design of the carpet. "Cocomats are relatively skid-proof, thank God," he said, "and the real carpet was safe in the prop department."

Henry Grace would credit two MGM films—*Dinner at Eight* (1933) and *When Ladies Meet* (1934)—as being responsible for increased attention to set decoration. "Movies had great influence on interior design [across the country]," he said. *When Ladies Meet* generated interest in early Americana; chintz and ruffled organdy curtains "swept the nation," Grace said. "A flood of fan mail demanding blueprints, sketches, photographs, and information regarding the smallest decorative details awakened the studio heads to the fact that interiors well done could be a tremendous attraction."

Set decoration became a highly specialized craft. "If the dressing of a set were merely a question of furnishing a given room properly, the matter would be comparatively simple," Grace wrote. Instead, the decorator drew up one-quarter-inch-scale blueprints and plotted everything from furniture groupings to color schemes, always mindful of other contributions to the film. For *The Women* (1939), Grace designed the interior of the ranch house in plaid. "Then Norma Shearer turns up in a plaid dress," he remembered. "You may think it would be easier to use another dress, but it's not. We re-did the interior."

The legendary MGM prop department was itself largely the creation of gay hands. The standing joke around Hollywood was that whenever anyone would ask where to get the best antiques in Los Angeles, they were told the MGM prop department. Most of the studio's antiques, chandeliers, china, crystal, and *objets d'art* had been assembled by the discerning taste of Ed Willis, Dick Pefferle, Henry Grace, Jack Moore, or Keogh Gleason.

"I was fascinated the first time I went into that prop building," remembered Frank Lysinger. "Four floors with some of the most beautiful furniture and antiques. Ed Willis used to go to Europe and buy masses of French, English, and German antiques and chandeliers. But you know, they treated it all rather badly. I remember there was a pink satin sofa where a cat had her litter. But they figured if they damaged something they had all the experts on hand to fix it."

Property chief Edwin Willis was viewed as somewhat arrogant and aloof by his staff, even a bit sadistic, canceling vacations cavalierly at the last minute. His homosexuality was known, but there was little fraternization. Among the rest of them, however, there was a very real brotherhood. "Henry Grace, Jack Moore, Dick Pefferle, and Keogh Gleason shared an office, each with their own desk," Lysinger recalled. "There was always a lot of carrying on. Jack and Henry also shared a house down in Manhattan Beach where they'd have some pretty wild weekends."

The MGM decorators shared more than an office and a beach house in common. All were roughly the same age: Pefferle was born in 1905, Moore and Gleason in 1906, and Grace in 1907. With the exception of Moore, they were all from the working class, once again suggesting the correlation between class and "overtness." Pefferle's father, the son of German immigrants, managed an iron foundry in Sidney, Ohio; he got Dick a job there and expected him to make a career of it. But Dick wanted desperately to be an artist, a secret he confided to his mother. When Mike Pefferle died, his wife took the insurance money and sent her only child to France to study at the Sorbonne.

Henry Grace's experience was similar. The son of a railroad worker, the young Henry was born in Bakersfield, California, but lived in several desert towns, notably Needles and Bagdad. Originally hailing from Kentucky, the Grace family was part of a strong Southern Democrat tradition; Henry's mother was the cousin of Alben Barkley, Vice President under Harry S Truman. From early in life, Henry had an artistic inclination, recalling in his memoirs a "fascination" for period design. His father being a chronic alcoholic, Henry's future was largely dependent on the efforts of his strong and determined mother, Elsie, who, despite their limited means, supported Henry's initial desire to become a classical pianist. Moving to Glendale, Elsie would eventually divorce her husband and concentrate on raising Henry and his brother, Saunders.

The suicide of an uncle when he was just a boy left enough of an impression on the young Henry for him to include it seventy years later as one of the important landmarks in the chronology of his life. According to Henry's nephew Michael Grace, this uncle was also gay; what impact that knowledge may have had on the young Henry is unknown. But he seems to have accepted his difference fairly early on, disappearing from family picnics to hunker down in the library with piles of history books.

In 1925, upon graduation from high school, he won a scholarship to the Chouinard Art Institute in Los Angeles. There he was enrolled in architecture classes, but a course with the prominent interior decorator George

Townsend changed his mind. Henry became fascinated with the field's potential, which encompassed art history, architecture, lighting, painting, and fabric. Even before he was finished with his schooling, he secured work with the top Los Angeles interior design firm, Cannel and Chaffin, and with them decorated the homes of film stars Harold Lloyd and Corinne Griffith. In 1931, he set up his own shop in Westwood Village. Ed Willis became a regular customer, eventually offering Henry a job at the studio. "The Depression was at its lowest," Grace remembered. "I took his offer."

Willis knew talent when he saw it. In New York in 1935, he was impressed with a window at Lord & Taylor which had used Garbo's *Queen Christina* as motif, even borrowing some props from MGM. Inquiring after the designer, Willis was introduced to a young Sorbonne graduate, Dick Pefferle. He hired Pefferle on the spot at $75 a week.

A store window also brought Jack Moore to Willis' attention. But Moore was content with his job at H. T. Lockwood in Los Angeles, and at first turned down Willis' offer of employment. He only agreed after the persistent property chief doubled the salary. Like Pefferle, Moore was an Ohio boy, but from an upper-middle-class Toledo family. He was an artist and a dreamer whose father despaired of him, calling him a sissy. Having had enough of Toledo and his father's hostility, Jack made his way west, hoping to find his fortune. He got his wish when Ed Willis spotted that store window.

"Jack Moore truly enjoyed his success," Frank Lysinger remembered. "His apartment was very stylish. He always insisted on having a houseman. Dick and Keogh used to tease him about it." His lavish parties, thrown with Jacque Mapes, a fellow decorator who worked briefly at MGM (he did *Singin' in the Rain*), became well known.

Among the first to be hired in the industry, Pefferle, Grace, Moore, and Gleason established the role of the movie set decorator. The other studios adopted the MGM model, with Paramount creating a set decoration unit under Sam Comer in 1938. Unlike other fields, there was an interstudio friendship among the gay decorators; Lysinger remembered Paul Fox often socializing with Pefferle and Moore.

Of the MGM group, Keogh Gleason was the only one to marry. Lysinger said the marriage was one of convenience: Gleason's wife, Jean Pettibone, an account executive for Ralston and Purina, was a lesbian who wanted to adopt a child. But when she discovered Keogh's involvement with an Italian actor several years later, she started divorce proceedings; Louella Parsons reported she was "very sorry" to hear of the break-up of the Gleasons' seventeen-year marriage.

The others, however, never took the marriage route. Colleagues knew Pefferle shared his home with another man. Henry Grace—tall, handsome, and perennially suntanned—was remembered by many as always having attractive boyfriends in tow. The set decorators lived and worked in an extraordinary environment of not just tolerance, but integration. And, just as it was in costume design, being homosexual might actually (if implicitly) have been a career *advantage.* Ed Willis' hiring and mentoring of gay decorators seems to support such an idea, a de facto policy continued by Henry Grace when he took over after Willis' retirement in 1957. One of Grace's first hires was Jerry Wunderlich, a talented decorator well remembered within the gay subculture.

"There really wasn't any fear that you couldn't live the way you wanted," Lysinger said, "not unless you were doing it in the streets."

And they weren't, certainly: even if the bar for circumspection was lower among set decorators than it was for most other fields, the individuals involved were still conscious of their image. As late as 1968, Dick Pefferle snuck out of a theater while watching *The Killing of Sister George* when he realized it had a lesbian theme. "I thought how silly that was," Lysinger said. "He was actually afraid someone would see him watching this film and make some kind of connection. Even after such a long and successful career."

Michael Grace would remember two sides of his uncle Henry. While he recalled his mother once expressing surprise at discovering a pair of women's high-heeled shoes in Henry's closet, he also insisted that his uncle was very straight-acting and professional among colleagues. "I don't think he had a boy in tow except at gay functions," Grace said. Henry was often photographed escorting Dorothy Manners or department-store heiress Virginia Robinson, and had a running marriage gag with columnist Ruth Waterbury, a good friend. Citing his bachelorhood, one publicity release suggested enigmatically that the war had "ruined" any chance of marriage for Grace, adding that he chose not to elaborate further.

Although the decorators might not have needed to be as discreet as actors, they still knew what was at stake. In 1953, Howard Bristol, nominated for Academy Awards for *The Little Foxes* and *Pride of the Yankees,* was gay-bashed in a Santa Monica park. Police found him in the rest room in a pool of blood, his hands tied with his belt and his trousers knotted around his legs. Neighbors reported hearing "rhythmic incantations" and "sounds like preaching" ("You will burn in hell," perhaps?) during the assault. The wife of one of the men charged in the crime would admit to police that her husband had "lured" Bristol from a bar to the park, where he and an accomplice stabbed the decorator "until the knife broke," robbing him of his wallet and wristwatch.

The incident was covered widely in the Los Angeles papers; the industry certainly was savvy enough to read between the lines and understand the nature of the assault. Bristol's wounds appear to have healed considerably faster than his career: a freelancer, he moved from prestige films before the attack (*Rope* and *Hans Christian Andersen*) to B pictures immediately afterward (*China Venture* and the Vincent price horror flick *The Mad Magician*). Not until *Kiss Me Deadly* and *Guys and Dolls* in 1955 was he again working on big-budget films, and then, notably, his most frequent employer was the gay producer Ross Hunter.

• • •

Most decorators, however, had nothing but good fortune working in the industry. The liberty they enjoyed spilled over into their sister department—research—where Elliot Morgan was chief for some thirty years. Morgan had studied library science and graduated from Oxford. In 1933, when F. Scott Fitzgerald was writing scenarios at MGM, he asked for an assistant, someone who could speak "English English." A friend in the research department suggested Elliot, who quickly rose through the ranks to top dog.

Morgan was still a camp at the age of ninety-two. "Whenever anyone wanted to know what kind of jewelry was popular in the Twenties—or whatever—they'd come to me," he said proudly. "I had all the answers. We had an enormous library. There wasn't any particular place for us so they put us in the art department with the set decorators." There they developed a simpatico rapport, inspiring the fond memories of Lysinger and others.

"Everybody in research [at MGM] was gay except for the two women secretaries," said George Schoenbrunn, who started in the department in the 1950s, when it had five employees. That would include James Earie, who earlier had been a researcher at Fox and who would take over as chief when Morgan retired in the 1960s. "Of course people knew. How could they not?"

Whether the studio was engaging in conscious ghettoization is impossible to know, but the two largely gay departments worked closely. The job of the researchers was to counsel and give advice; whether it was always taken by the decorators was another matter. "Oh, those decorators with all their high tastes," Schoenbrunn remembered. "I'd tell them over and over that if they have a rich person's house, for it to be *real* the furniture must be old and look as if it had been there for generations and generations. They never listened. They'd always pick out everything shiny and new. But that's Hollywood."

It certainly is. And at least in the research and decoration of movie sets, it was a place of extraordinary gay influence and freedom.

THE BEAUTY PARLOR:
MAKE-UP, HAIR, AND SYDNEY GUILAROFF

Given prevailing stereotypes, one might actually predict the gayness of the set-decoration department. Yet the same stereotype does not hold for the make-up department of the studio era, where most practitioners worried less about an actress' eyeshadow than about the application of yak-hair whiskers to a character actor's face.

The studio make-up artists came out of the tradition of the traveling stock-company actor, who hauled around his own make-up box filled with pancake and rouge but also with putty noses and fake beards. "Many of the early make-up artists came from the ranks of actors," said William Tuttle, who headed the MGM make-up department, "actors who were not too good at acting but quite adept at changing their appearance, since they got more work that way."

Make-up men Bert Hadley and Bert Such were both silent-screen cowboys; Jack Dawn, Tuttle's predecessor and former boss at MGM, had played bits at Biograph. Like art direction and cinematography—other largely straight fields—make-up skills were often passed down through generations. F. B. Phillips learned how to apply make-up as an actor for D. W. Griffith at Biograph, later training his son, Fred, in the craft. Fred, in turn, taught his daughter, Janna, who worked with him on *Star Trek: The Motion Picture* before branching out on her own.

Like Universal's genius Jack Pierce and the much-married Westmore brothers, make-up artists were celebrated more for their special effects than for any subtle shading. Jack Dawn convinced Irving Thalberg to create a make-up lab in 1935 after disguising himself as an eighty-year-old Chinaman, fooling everyone on the lot. Dawn was a bluff, swaggering fellow whose macho credentials allowed him to suggest beauty tips for women without suspicion, although in magazine layouts with famous actresses he was often pictured with his wife. He had the reputation of an autocrat, running the make-up department as his own personal fief, his cigar clenched firmly between his teeth. "Dawn was a very tough taskmaster," William Tuttle recalled. "He was almost Prussian in his manner. You almost snapped to attention when he walked in the room."

Tuttle's wife was one of the studio hairdressers; indeed, if women were found at all in the early make-up departments, it was in this role. "All the make-up artists were men and all the hairstylists were women," recalled Paramount stylist Nellie Manley, who was one of the organizers of the union that covered both fields. Perhaps, then, it's not surprising that when

celebrated hairstylist Sydney Guilaroff walked into this midst—female colleagues on one side and macho make-up men on the other—he tried as
hard as he could to draw a veil of secrecy over his private life. A gauzy,
translucent, see-through veil, as it turned out, but a veil nonetheless.

Guilaroff was both one of the most effete of all the studio homosexuals
and one of the most determined to deny it. Even in the 1990s, writing his
memoirs, he was still trying to pass as straight, flatly declaring himself not
homosexual and claiming sexual affairs with Garbo and Ava Gardner. Most
reviewers and historians greeted such audacious stories with amusement. "I
think even Sydney was a little embarrassed reading all that when it came
out," said his longtime companion, Michael Logothetis. "He knew no one
believed it."

Guilaroff was a very private man. Few photographs exist; he reportedly
refused to pose with his devoted star clientele—which included Garbo,
Gardner, Joan Crawford, Katharine Hepburn, Judy Garland, Marilyn Monroe, and Elizabeth Taylor—for fear of exploiting them. He was also fiercely
self-conscious of his own image. In 1939 he had made headlines as the first
never-married man in the country to adopt a child—a son he named "Jon,"
after good pal Joan Crawford. In his memoirs, he wrote he desired father-
hood but didn't want "the complications and commitments of matrimony."
He later adopted a second boy he named Eugene.

What caused Guilaroff to be so self-conscious, so driven in his desire to
not be perceived as gay? Born in Winnipeg, Manitoba, Canada, he was the
son of a Russian Jewish immigrant who was not above strapping his son for
minor offenses. Teased ruthlessly by his classmates for being "different,"
Sydney was told by teachers he was the "least likely to succeed." He left
school after eighth grade—and home, too, running off to Montreal and
then to New York. At sixteen he was working as a hairstylist at the McAlpin
Hotel, where he claimed he met the actress Louise Brooks, creating her
trademark shingle hairstyle. From there he found work at the fashionable
Antoine's salon, located at Saks Fifth Avenue, where he said he first cut
Claudette Colbert's hair, creating the bangs and bob she'd keep all her life.
Soon "Mr. Sydney" had his own salon at Bonwit-Teller.

It was Joan Crawford who, becoming a fan on her trips East, brought
him to MGM. There he created some classic Hollywood looks: Hepburn's
sophisticated coif in *The Philadelphia Story* and Norma Shearer's twenty-
pound bejeweled wigs in *Marie Antoinette*. He claimed he was the one who
convinced a brunette Lucille Ball to dye her hair red. But for several years,
he refused to join the make-up and hairstylists union, fearing it would put
him out with his bosses. His refusal may have placated Louis B. Mayer, but
it incurred the wrath of department head (and loyal union man) Jack
Dawn.

Guilaroff's heterosexual charade, no matter how unconvincing, can perhaps be better understood in the context of Dawn's straight-male-dominated make-up department. The hostility with Dawn likely went beyond union conflicts. "He hated me from the start," Sydney would say, claiming Dawn was jealous of his close friendships with movie queens. That seems unlikely, but Sydney nonetheless found Dawn "thoroughly disagreeable," and they clashed repeatedly.

Possibly because of this, Guilaroff avoided the spotlight; even his mannerisms, although effete, were controlled. When a newsreel director once asked him "to make with the hands, like a hairdresser was supposed to do," Sydney refused. "What kind of character is this Guilaroff," lamented the director, "if he doesn't set a head of hair with his little finger sticking out?"

Whether Guilaroff kept his low profile out of fear of anti-gay bias from Dawn or his crew is unknown, but he *did* acknowledge that, given his profession, people were likely to view him negatively. During the adoption proceedings for his first son, he worried that authorities might suspect, "as a man engaged in a profession in which most of its practitioners were either female or homosexual, I must be the latter."

He *was,* of course—no matter what he said in his memoirs. Michael Logothetis, who lived with Guilaroff for many years, acknowledged that Sydney did his best to hide his "secret." A student at UCLA when he moved into Guilaroff's Beverly Hills home in the late 1940s, Logothetis said he and Sydney were close friends but never lovers. "I knew Sydney was 'that way' [homosexual]," Logothetis said. "If I came home and there was a young man with him on the couch, I'd ask that it not be done when I was around."

Sydney doted on Logothetis; at one point, he signed over his property to him. "We were all the time together, except we separated to go to sleep," Logothetis told the Los Angeles Superior Court when a property dispute erupted between them in their later years. "Many times [Sydney] was sick, so every time something is wrong, we go to the hospital or the doctor. Sidney would cook. He is a wonderful cook. We would eat together. We watched the news until eleven, eleven-thirty every night, sometimes twelve o'clock."

It was a lifestyle Guilaroff tried desperately to shield from the rest of the world. Passionate about privacy, he granted a rare interview to the writer John Kobal in the 1950s but refused to be tape-recorded. Unwilling to reveal much about himself, Sydney did prove to be a "fascinating gossip" about *other* people, calling Cecil Beaton "a swishy little boy" and Oliver Messel "small-minded and nasty." His sons had proven headaches, he revealed to Kobal, with Eugene serving time in jail. "At first I used to cry about it at night," he said, "but now I'm used to it."

Yet perhaps his low-profile strategy worked, for Guilaroff continued dressing star actresses's hair into the 1980s, boasting—at 857 pictures—one of the longest screen credits in history. "Guilaroff has always been so proper," wrote one observer, "as to appear to be almost ashamed of being in the movie business." Not ashamed—but cautious. Cautious to the point where he may actually have believed he had succeeded in fooling people.

Shortly before Guilaroff's death, he would reconcile with Logothetis. "We were friends for a long time," Logothetis said, "and his last years were very sad." Previous to this, Sydney had lived with a much younger man he called his "adopted grandson," who, after posing for Sydney's memoirs, reportedly took off. The memoirs, meanwhile, were rejected by all the top publishing houses, despite a drumroll of support from gossip columnist Liz Smith; they were eventually published by a small press. Reviewers chuckled over Sydney's reports of movie-star affairs, but he kept his chin high, even as his health rapidly declined. Nearly blind, he was moved into a rest home, where he died on May 28, 1997. His story is important for the way he tried to obscure it, and the insight it offers into a very particular side to the gay experience in the Hollywood studios.

THE DRESSMAKERS: WALTER PLUNKETT AND ORRY-KELLY

As gay as set decoration was, the most obvious and undisguised gay ghetto in Hollywood remained wardrobe. By the mid-1930s, every studio had its prima donna designer backed up by two or three junior designers and dozens of sketch artists, fitters, and seamstresses. While nearly all of the major players were homosexual, few were as comfortable in their skins as Walter Plunkett, forever remembered as the man who designed the costumes for *Gone With the Wind*.

"I'd say Walter Plunkett was very at ease with who he was," said Don Bachardy. In this, he resembled not so much Adrian or Travis Banton, but Howard Greer, with whom he was friends. "They were very much alike, Walter and Howard," said their mutual friend Satch LaValley. "They never pretended—not for one minute."

In fact, it was Howard Greer who suggested that Plunkett, then a stage designer, try Hollywood. Greer was, at the time, still happily ensconced at Paramount, carefree and gay, in all meanings of the term. Plunkett was understandably dazzled by the older designer's good fortune, both in terms of money and personal liberty. It was everything he had dreamed of, ever since he was a tyke acting out little play dramas in his backyard in Oakland, California.

Born on June 5, 1902, the son of James Plunkett, a dentist, and his wife,

Frances, Walter had studied law at the University of California at Berkeley. But he couldn't stay awake during the lectures, reserving all his energy for the campus theater group. Shortly before graduation, his father—far more indulgent than Dick Pefferle's or Jack Moore's (or many others in this chronicle)—bought him a ticket to New York and told him to give the stage a try. In the fall of 1923, Walter snagged a small part in "Out of the Seven Seas," a "crude melodrama," according to the *New York Times,* staged at the Frazee Theatre. In both this and his next play, "The Man Who Ate the Popomack," he played Chinamen; the latter ran at the Cherry Lane Playhouse in Greenwich Village in March 1924—a time we've already seen was a hotbed of visible gay culture in the Village.

It's probable this is where he met Greer, who was then designing costumes for the *Greenwich Village Follies.* Friends have said there was a romance between them, or at least an infatuation on Greer's part with the much younger Plunkett. In any event, Greer extended an invitation to follow him out to Hollywood, and Walter, discouraged with his "inability to act," accepted. There he found work as an extra, collecting fifteen dollars a week. He can be spotted in Von Stroheim's *The Merry Widow* waltzing with Irene Lentz, who'd find her own fame as a designer. Greer then helped him land a job working in wardrobe at the old FBO studios. Plunkett's first duty: painting roses on the breasts of chorus girls. "No one with any pride would have taken the job," he'd recall, "but I did." At forty dollars a week, he couldn't say no.

FBO became RKO, and in the interim Plunkett created an efficient, functioning wardrobe department based on Greer's model at Paramount. By the early 1930s RKO had moved away from the serials and Westerns for which FBO had been known, and Plunkett found himself designing gowns for leading ladies like Ginger Rogers in *Flying Down to Rio* and Katharine Hepburn in *Little Women.* "He was completely self-taught," said Satch La-Valley. "He had no formal training. He just had an eye and a talent."

Being in the right place at the right time offered Plunkett the extraordinary opportunity to suddenly play in the same league as such monumental talents as Adrian and Banton. He was never known for their artistry, but he became a superb craftsman of period style. Research was important to him; his designs were often lifted exactly from photographs or illustrations from encyclopedias and history texts. Unlike George James Hopkins twenty years earlier—who'd eschewed authenticity in favor of his own imagination—Plunkett was working in an era that demanded realism. His adherence to authenticity quite possibly had the added benefit of disguising any deficiencies when his work was compared to the unique creations of Adrian and Banton at competing studios.

Yet Plunkett's work contains its own flights of fancy. Take the watermelon-pink dress trimmed in turquoise and rhinestones that Bebe Daniels wears in the early Technicolor film *Rio Rita* (1929). Decades later, he saw a print of the film and shuddered. "It was hysterical," he said, "but at the time, we thought it was beautiful." Or consider the outrageous "leg-o-mutton" sleeves Irene Dunne wears in *Cimarron* (1931). Authentic to the period, yes, but certainly whimsical. Or—best of all—the magnificent silver metallic moth costume Hepburn wears in Dorothy Arzner's *Christopher Strong.* A few minutes under the hot lights and Kate was frying like bacon. Plunkett had to design a last-minute fitted lining.

Overworked and underpaid (just $75 a week), Plunkett quit RKO in a huff in 1935 and went back to New York, where he worked as a designer for a shop on Seventh Avenue. But Hepburn brought him back for *Mary of Scotland,* and he stayed on as a freelancer. Of course, the picture he'll forever be associated with is *Gone With the Wind.* His famous contributions to that classic have been documented many times, especially his *pièce de résistance,* the green velvet dress Scarlett fashions from her mother's draperies. As ever, he was a stickler for authenticity, traveling to Atlanta to meet with Margaret Mitchell and research Civil War fashions. Yet he never felt it was his best work, considering the costumes he created for Lana Turner in *Diane* (1956) his apex.

In 1945, Plunkett settled in at MGM, accepting an offer from head designer Irene—his dance partner from *The Merry Widow*—to handle all of the studio's period pictures. "Everything at MGM was grander and bigger than anywhere else," Plunkett said. "I was always in a bit of awe there. The wardrobe department was just enormous. There were ten or more head cutters and fitters and each had their own staff under them."

Admitting to his awe was part of Plunkett's essential nature: easygoing, modest, compassionate. His kindness is legendary, especially tales of how he'd often go down to the courthouse and put up bail for gay men arrested for cruising Pershing Square or Griffith Park. "That's true," insisted his friend Satch LaValley. "He'd often post bail for boys who were arrested. He didn't even have to know them. That was just part of his nature. He'd hear of some boy's story and go down and try to help."

He lived in West Los Angeles on Goshen Avenue with his devoted and much younger partner, Lee. Christopher Isherwood and Don Bachardy would visit them occasionally. "They were both into knitting," Bachardy remembered. "They knitted covers for their toilet seats. They knitted things all over the place."

Plunkett retired in 1966. He was disillusioned by post-studio Hollywood, when there was "nothing to design but T-shirts and discolored blue jeans." He spent his last years painting, and officially adopted Lee, to whom he left his entire estate. Walter Plunkett died on March 8, 1982.

• • •

Plunkett won an Oscar for his contributions to *An American in Paris* (1951), a prize he shared with Irene Sharaff and Orry-Kelly, who also worked on the picture. Satch LaValley would remember Walter uncharacteristically grumbling, "I can't believe I have to share one-third of this damn Oscar with that son-of-a-bitch Orry-Kelly."

Orry brought that kind of response out in people, even the nice ones like Plunkett. People either loved Orry-Kelly or *despised* him. As edgy as Plunkett was easygoing, Orry was an opinionated, headstrong alcoholic who could dissolve his friends into laughter and shoot down his foes with one well-timed barb. "Orry-Kelly was completely unpredictable," said his friend Robert Shaw. "One minute he was sweet and kind, making you laugh. The next he was sharpening his claws against you."

Born George Kelly in Kiama, Australia, on December 31, 1897, he was originally known as Jack. His father, William Kelly, said he added the "Orry" in homage to the kings of his native Isle of Man. His mother, however, insisted it was taken from the Orry carnations she grew in her garden. Wherever it came from, this much is clear: the hyphen didn't arrive until much later, slipped in by a Warner Bros. publicist.

William Kelly was a tailor, and the young Jack would hand-paint ties and shawls for his father's customers. Acting in a local theater in Kiama and assisting with costumes, he decided at an early age that the theater was his calling. His parents insisted he take a bank job after he finished school, but that lasted just eight months. Sailing first for London and then for New York, he pursued his dream, landing bit parts and work as a chorus boy. When his father fell ill, he returned to Australia, where he opened a clothes shop in Sydney. After his father's death, he returned to New York.

Jack Kelly was a good-looking, stocky, doe-eyed young man whose hair, by the time he was in his late twenties, had turned prematurely gray. By 1921 he was working as a tailor's assistant in the garment district, selling hand-painted neckties as a sideline. It was about this time that he met a seventeen-year-old vaudeville acrobat by the name of Archie Leach. Within a few months they were sharing a Greenwich Village loft, just behind the present site of the Cherry Lane Theater. Their third roommate was Charlie Phelps, who, as Charlie Spangles, played in drag at the Metropole Club.

Archie Leach, of course, would later become Cary Grant. They lived together, on and off, for the next nine years, until Archie left for Hollywood in January 1932. Orry would tell friends that they were lovers for some of that time. Orry's press of the Thirties and Forties rarely mentions his friendship with Grant, and never (as far as has been discovered) revealed

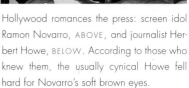

Hollywood romances the press: screen idol Ramon Novarro, ABOVE, and journalist Herbert Howe, BELOW. According to those who knew them, the usually cynical Howe fell hard for Novarro's soft brown eyes.

he now-forgotten J. Warren errigan was the screen's ery first male superstar— part because he had a ofter, more sensitive appeal than most movie cowoys.

One of the men who helped create Hollywood style: George James Hopkins, whose career stretched from Theda Bara to Elizabeth Taylor.

Director Dorothy Arzner, FAR RIGHT, was the obvious butch to choreographer Marion Morgan's femme, CENTER. They were lovers for some fifty years, occasionally collaborating on projects such as *Manhattan Cocktail* (1928), with Georges Bruggeman.

"Sex without sin." That was the motto for the Hollywood of director Edmund Goulding, the force behind *Grand Hotel* and *Dark Victory.*

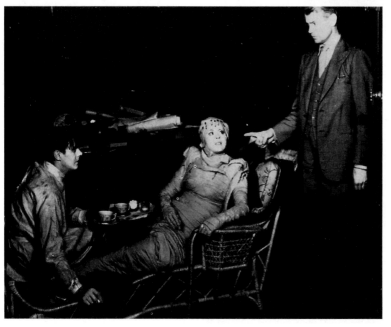

The sly, subversive, brilliant James Whale here RIGHT, with Colin Clive and Elsa Lanchester. Few studio era films were more queer than his *The Bride of Frankenstein* (1935).

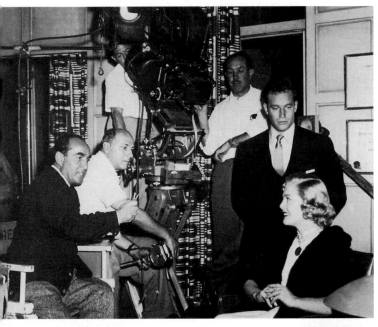

Bette Davis both loved and hated Irving Rapper, IN DIRECTOR'S CHAIR, as a director because she could boss him around. Lizabeth Scott, pictured here on the set of *Bad for Each Other* (1954), was more congenial. Within months she'd be broadsided by the scandal rag *Confidential*.

The great George Cukor. Actresses (like Norma Shearer, pictured here) adored him because he cared more profoundly about performance than any other aspect of filmmaking.

Mitchell Leisen knew how to pull the wool over the censors' eyes. His films are both sexy and charming, a rarity in Hollywood.

The ethereal beauty of actor Tom Douglas inspired George Cukor to remember the early 1930s as "La Belle Epoque."

The critics called Cukor's *Girls About Town* "gay—very gay." Certainly its stars were: that popular man-about-town Anderson Lawler and his gal pals, Lil Tashman and Kay Francis.

"Don't worry—I w... ...ou any trouble"

She published a love poem to Ethel Barrymore in *Vanity Fair*, then the eccentric Zoe Akins won the Pulitzer Prize and wrote a series of proto-feminist scripts directed by Dorothy Arzner.

Lilyan Tashman was just about the brashest, most glamorous, and least apologetic lesbian Hollywood has ever known. She enjoyed a happy marriage with the equally gay leading man, Edmund Lowe. (The inscription on Lil's photo is to Andy Lawler.)

Opposite in style but sisters in substance: Neither the boyish Patsy Kelly, ABOVE (here with Thelma Todd), nor the very feminine Margaret Lindsay, RIGHT, made much of a secret of why they never married.

Franklin Pangborn's sissy portrayals were so well-known that even his name alone on a script made the Hays Office wary.

The face that put the censors up in arms: Tyrell Davis, sans the lipstick that would so offend Will Hays in *Our Betters* (1933).

A marvelous actor, Edward Everett Horton once calculated that he'd played thirty-five best friends, twenty-seven timid clerks, and thirty-seven "frustrated" men.

GB-56

Howard Greer—pioneer in establishing both film costume design and the brazen overtness of the wardrobe department—discussing fittings with Sylvia Sidney.

Transcendent Travis Banton. Probably the greatest film costume designer of all time. Here he is in the midst of turning Carole Lombard from "tootsie" into a glamorous star.

The brilliant Adrian lived an undisguised gay life in his early years at MGM. Later, marrying Janet Gaynor, he cultivated a very different image.

In wardrobe, the men were all gay and the women often let folks think they were: FROM LEFT TO RIGHT, unknown, Milo Anderson, Miles White, Leah Rhodes, Edward Stevenson, Edith Head, Irene, and Walter Plunkett.

When flamboyant costume designer Howard Shoup showed up in his Army uniform on the set of *DuBarry Was a Lady*, Lucille Ball burst into laughter and said, "Now I've seen everything."

Orry-Kelly: as outrageous as he was talented. Jack Warner said he "did the things he wanted to do, said the things he wanted to say."

The MGM set decorators enjoyed a camaraderie both at the studio and at home. Jack Moore, Richard Pefferle, Keogh Gleason, ABOVE, are pictured together; their colleague Henry Grace, RIGHT, pictured with Vincent Price, won an Academy Award for *Gigi*. His resemblance to Eisenhower also landed him a cameo in *The Longest Day*.

David Lewis, longtime partner of director James Whale, enjoyed a distinguished career as a producer, one of the few undisguised gay men to do so.

Defender of the faith: Leonard Spigelgass, who worshipped the system that had given him so much.

Friends and collaborators: the trailblazing producer Harriet Parsons and the eccentric writer DeWitt Bodeen.

Without producer and musical arranger Roger Edens, there would be no Judy Garland. Along the way, he also modernized the American musical as the real leader of MGM's Freed Unit.

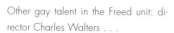

Other gay talent in the Freed unit: director Charles Walters . . .

. . . director Vincente Minnelli, here with baby Liza . . .

. . . and innovative choreographer Jack Cole, to whom Marilyn Monroe turned for advice not only about musical numbers but about life in general.

Laird Cregar said he had an "inner thin man," and his quest to set him free resulted in his death.

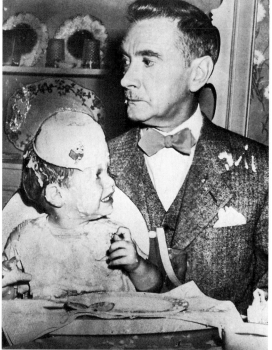

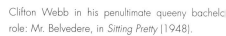

Clifton Webb in his penultimate queeny bachelor role: Mr. Belvedere, in *Sitting Pretty* (1948).

Webb, here with his protege Robert Wagner, was the unlikeliest of movie stars, one of the most unique screen characters of all time.

Frank McCarthy, RIGHT, started his Hollywood career as a lively military advisor on *Brother Rat* (1938). He went on to become both a Brigadier General and Hollywood producer, but not before being dismissed from the State Department under mysterious circumstances.

●
●
●

Ross Hunter was a popular teen idol before becoming producer of some of Hollywood's most memorable tearjerkers in the 1950s. He had more in common with Cary Grant, pictured with him here, RIGHT, than just the glasses.

A second-rank Rock Hudson, George Nader was able to live far less cir
cumspectly than Rock, enjoying a committed relationship with publicist Mar
Miller that endures today.

that they'd lived together in New York. Only in the Sixties did Orry allow himself to admit the connection. At a showing of his paintings in New York, Orry included in his artist biography the fact that the young Archie Leach once helped him paint "lecherous frogs" on murals in Greenwich Village speakeasies.

During their heydays, however, there was a distance between the two old friends that some found unsettling. While filming *Arsenic and Old Lace* in 1944, the only film of Cary's for which Orry did the costumes, costar Priscilla Lane observed the two as decidedly unfriendly. George James Hopkins, who knew Orry well, recalled in his memoirs a possible reason for that unfriendliness. "Although Orry hadn't seen Grant in years," Hopkins wrote, "he still considered him his friend." But that first day on the set, a radio game show had brought one of its winners for a tour. On the show's limousine was painted the title: QUEEN FOR A DAY. Spotting it, Grant turned to Orry and quipped: "Your limousine is waiting outside."

Orry, who could apparently dish it out better than he could take it, was infuriated. Hopkins wrote, "He resented the insinuation from a man many considered a deadbeat."

Surely this tension between Orry-Kelly and Cary Grant reflects the basic conflict between the overt and the circumspect. Whether they had been lovers or not (and most of Orry's friends believe they were), Orry and Grant were just too far at opposite ends of the spectrum to ever coexist with much harmony in Hollywood.

Still, Orry owed Grant his break, for Cary had put him in touch with the agent Minna Wallis, who showed to Warner Bros. sketches of gowns he'd designed for Ethel Barrymore on Broadway. The studio liked his designs enough to hire Orry for Ruth Chatterton's *The Rich Are Always With Us* (1932). Within a year, he was head of the wardrobe department.

He'd have a long love-hate relationship with studio chief Jack Warner. "I used to tell Kelly he should have been a prizefighter," Warner said. "He could be trouble, loved the spotlight, and was stubborn as hell. When he had too many drinks he'd get mean, start swearing and throwing punches. But he could be a damn nice guy when he wanted to be. His costumes had the one thing I always insisted on in everything—*quality*."

With Adrian and Banton, Orry-Kelly formed the fashion triumvirate of the Thirties and early Forties. But whereas the other two were known for extravagance and high style, Orry designed far more simply, as befit the more workaday, down-to-earth Warner Bros. "The general tone of the studio was set by Kelly," observed fashion historian David Chierichetti, "utter simplicity and high fashion without theatricality." Orry stuck to middle grays to contrast his look from Adrian's stark black-and-white designs.

His no-frills approach worked perfectly for the queen of the lot, Bette Davis, on whom the more elaborate designs of an Adrian or Banton would have looked absurd. Her neck was long, which Orry often had to disguise with high collars. Yet to emphasize her ugly-duckling-into-a-swan role in *Now, Voyager,* he created gowns with low-cut V-necklines to actually highlight and enhance her neck.

The difference in style among designers can be best seen in *An American in Paris.* Irene Sharaff's costumes in the long ballet sequence are loud, vibrant, in many shapes and colors. Walter Plunkett's designs for the Beaux Art ball are over the top, with capes and diamond shapes everywhere. But the rest of the film, designed by Orry-Kelly, is a marvel of simple, elegant lines. Nina Foch's one-shoulder-bared, strapless white gown is stunning. "That's some dress you're almost wearing," Gene Kelly asks her. "What's holding it up?" Foch replies, "Modesty."

Ironic that the more modest Plunkett should design more boldly and the irreverent Orry-Kelly should be known for understatement. For in life, Orry pulled no punches: When a director once told him that his wife didn't care for Orry's clothes, the designer quipped, "I don't like your wife's taste either."

He was drafted into the war in 1943, not a happy experience for a hard-drinking, flamboyant gay man in his mid-40s. He'd remember being accosted by a sergeant, who said, "So your name's Kelly, and you come from Hollywood, and you have something to do with women's clothes. Well, Kelly, pick up a shovel and start on the trench—because now you're going to have something to do with work!" It was an experience that rankled. "I'd like to meet that sergeant again," Orry said, "now that I'm out of the Army and back in Hollywood. I'd like to have met him twelve years ago, when I was designing clothes in New York. Maybe I could show him what work really is!"

He was discharged from the army for drinking, which was also the reason Warner Bros. eventually let him go, giving more responsibility to the younger and less temperamental Milo Anderson. Still, Orry would remain close with Ann Warner, Jack's wife, and through her graces would return to the studio on a freelance basis. But his drinking only got worse: the story of his leaving a party and flagging down a police car, thinking it was a cab, may be apocryphal, yet it sums up his reputation. His good pals Louella Parsons and Hedda Hopper often went to bat for him, trying to reassure jittery studio chiefs of Orry's reliability. But although he'd win Oscars for *An American in Paris, Les Girls,* and *Some Like It Hot*—in which he had a ball dressing Jack Lemmon and Tony Curtis in drag—his influence as a designer had waned.

He didn't go gracefully. He continued to needle those he felt needling, and often they were other homosexuals. In one of Hedda's columns, he sniped at Don Loper, designer and choreographer: "And M'Lord Don Loper—Guess what my fish came wrapped in the other day? Your article on fashion decor, ancestry, freak outfits, good manners and taste." In 1961, he pounced on Noël Coward when the famed wit suggested America still suffered from "war guilt." In an open letter to *The Hollywood Reporter,* Orry boasted of wearing a private's uniform in the U.S. Army and suggested it was time America began resenting Coward's "dated behavior."

Like Plunkett, Orry turned to painting when film jobs dried up, but unlike Plunkett's dogs and cats, Kelly's landscapes and city blocks were judged very highly by critics. Friends recall that for several years in the Forties and Fifties he had a boyfriend named "Bob"—possibly Robert Roberts, who would serve as an honorary pallbearer at Orry's funeral. In his will, Orry referenced an earlier document, where the bulk of his estate was left to "my partner R. E. Roberts, who is now most successful and is no longer my partner." The relationship with Bob did not endure: Orry was very much alone at the end, with only Ann Warner at his bedside.

All those years of drinking had taken their toll: he suffered for months with liver cancer. He lapsed into a semi-coma, coming out of it now and again to mouth off at an invisible director or dish with the long-dead Fannie Brice. Orry-Kelly died, still talking, on February 26, 1964.

"He did the things that he wanted to do," Jack Warner eulogized. "He said the things he wanted to say. And nobody can ask any more out of life than that."

THE CAPITULATION OF ADRIAN AND BANTON

If Orry-Kelly did the things he wanted to do and said the things he wanted to say—in essence, living life on his terms and everyone else's be damned—he did so within a field that accommodated such individuality, such difference—such *queerness,* in effect. Why, then, at the same time, did his two most notable peers—Adrian and Travis Banton—do exactly the opposite, falling instead into lockstep with the prevailing status quo?

They hadn't started out that way, but in post-Code Hollywood these two giants of design found it desirable for a variety of reasons to alter their images. In 1938 Adrian married Janet Gaynor, whose sheer all-American wholesomeness offset his enigmatic foreignness. In 1942, Banton also married, assuring Hedda Hopper that he was "settling down" for good.

For Adrian, perhaps the "kidding" of his effeminacy by the men on the lot had reached a breaking point. Perhaps the allusions to "daintiness" and "lace handkerchiefs" in his press had gotten under his skin. Yet his decision to marry was not really so incongruous with the way he'd always presented himself: carefully, discreetly, self-consciously. If his press gave no hint of his Jewishness, so, too, would it no longer suggest any queerness.

Hollywood was clearly stunned by the marriage, however. "Adrian has gone and fallen for lovely little Janet Gaynor, giving jaded Hollywood something to talk about," quipped a columnist for the *Los Angeles Daily News.* Ruth Waterbury wrote up the marriage for *Photoplay.* "Adrian has never been in love before," she confided to her readers. She also offered a curious assessment: "the little Gaynor" was not what she seemed, but Adrian was "*exactly* what he looks: sensitive, intelligent, artistic, worldly and utterly charming."

Waterbury, a keen observer who Anthony Slide remembered as "having no illusions about the Hollywood she covered," was surely aware of the meaning of her words. For they are certainly telling: Gaynor, whose demure, feminine on-screen image was anything but lesbian, *was* in fact "not what she seems"—especially given all the press she'd shared with Margaret Lindsay over the past two years. But Adrian, on the other hand, whose image *screamed* gay, *was* indeed "exactly what he looks."

Yet to dismiss the Gaynor-Adrian marriage as merely a sham is to forget the example set by Edmund Lowe and Lilyan Tashman. "One day Adrian came to me, into my dressing room," remembered the actress Luise Rainer, "and he said, as though he was questioning himself in front of me, 'You know, I've fallen in love.' I said, 'Well, that's wonderful. Who?' He said, 'I fell in love with a woman.' He was flabbergasted himself."

Adrian and Gaynor in fact enjoyed a committed, devoted partnership until his death some twenty years later. In July 1940, they had a son, Robin, and the press was filled with stories of Adrian designing chic maternity dresses for Janet. (It's probably apocryphal that, during labor, doctors feared Gaynor might lose the baby, prompting Adrian to remark, "Oh, no, I'll have to go through *that* again.")

In truth, from all accounts, they were a happy, contented family. But one should not see the union outside the context of the post-Code climate, nor discount the other benefits Adrian's marriage had on his career. Already he had a sense that he was moving beyond the confines of the wardrobe department at MGM. He had set his sights on a bigger prize: independent couture. In 1940, he was voted the number-one American designer in a poll of fashion buyers for U.S. companies; he placed third among all designers worldwide (topped only by Schiaparelli and Hattie Carnegie, and beating out Chanel, Lelong, and Valentina, not to mention Travis Banton and Howard Greer).

The next year he bid good-bye to the studio where he'd once reigned like a prince, after a furious row over Garbo's pedestrian costumes in *Two-*

Faced Woman. ("When the glamour ends for Garbo," Adrian huffed, "it ends for me.") He opened a *moderne* salon on Beverly Drive and continued designing clothes. He received tremendous coverage, often photographed with wife and son, and Adrian Greenberg seemed finally to have achieved the life he always wanted. He retired after a heart attack in 1952 and moved to Brazil, where he built a house in the jungle and lost himself in painting. To keep Janet company, her best friend, Mary Martin, built a house on an adjoining lot with her husband, Richard Halliday. Adrian, for his part, was planning a comeback, designing the costumes for a Broadway show, when a cerebral hemorrhage took his life on September 13, 1959.

• • •

Travis Banton would have given anything for Adrian's post-studio life, but he had neither Adrian's fortitude nor determination. He seems to have been as touchy as Adrian when it came to teasing on the lot, insisting as early as 1934 that he had "no lace handkerchief in his cuff." But not so touchy that he stopped his carousing: by the end of the decade, his drinking, like that of Howard Greer, led Paramount to drop him, replacing him with Edith Head.

Within the industry, his image was a mess, and to reclaim his career, he went on a massive public relations quest, enlisting the help of Hedda Hopper. His letters to her are revealing and pathetic, painting the picture of a man trying desperately to overcome his homosexuality and alcoholism. In 1941 he wrote to Hopper that he had few Hollywood contacts left, but he wanted her to know that he'd been doing "none of the night spots—or any of the gay life." Whatever he needed to do to get back on top, he'd *do* it, he assured her. Accordingly, in July 1942 he married an old college friend, Biddy Kleitz, which Hedda announced with great fanfare in her column, along with a reminder to the industry of just how talented Banton was.

Soon after the wedding, Banton's mother wrote to Hedda. "You might like to know what Travis' mother feels about this marriage of his," Margaret Banton confided. "I am delighted over it! I have never in my life seen such a change in any human being as the one that has taken place in Travis. The things that hurt have disappeared, and once again he is the son in whom I can take such pride."

Whether Mom convinced Hedda of the marriage's authenticity is unknown, but the columnist continued on as an ally. Others, too, took up the cause. Virginia Wright of the *Los Angeles Daily News,* in a lengthy profile, divulged that when it was suggested to the teenaged Travis that he might someday make a good costume designer, the idea had "horrified" the boy. "He could think of no worse profession for a man," Wright said. Such a tale flies directly in the face of Banton's earlier press, in which he was portrayed as eagerly seeking a career in fashion. But in a new era, trying to prove himself a "changed man," his very choice of career needed to somehow be explained away.

Banton's negative reputation had, of course, been much more the result of his alcoholism than his homosexuality, for surely Walter Plunkett and Orry-Kelly and dozens of other overt gays remained profitably employed in the studios. But in the minds of many, the two things were conflated; just as Kerrigan's perceived cowardice in World War I had been linked to his homosexuality, so, too, were Banton's indiscretions tied into his being gay. Clearly Banton was attempting to use his marriage as a reflection of a new image, as a means to "prove" he was now ready to play by the rules. His alcoholism—perhaps to him even more than the studio chiefs—was enmeshed with his homosexuality, and so both had to be proven vanquished.

Was that why so many of the costume designers drank? Banton, Greer, Orry-Kelly, Howard Shoup, Edward Stevenson—all were drunks at various points in their careers. They were also among the most overt homosexuals in the film colony. Adrian, more discreet than most, wasn't known to have a drinking problem, yet the correlation is not exact: neither was Walter Plunkett known to drink to excess, and Plunkett was perhaps the most grounded and open with his gayness of any of them.

In any event, Banton's marriage didn't work; letters between Biddy Banton and Hedda Hopper reveal that, although they never divorced, they soon separated. Neither did his movie comeback prove successful. Banton would work on a number of pictures (*Scarlet Street, A Double Life, Mourning Becomes Electra, Auntie Mame*) but always as a freelancer; his days of great influence were decidedly over. Travis Banton died in 1958, reportedly still hitting the bottle and cruising the parks for tricks.

The irony to the stories of both Adrian and Banton is that they worked in the queerest of all fields in the industry. The designers who replaced them—Orry-Kelly, Walter Plunkett, Milo Anderson, Howard Shoup, and numerous others—never attempted a similar obfuscation, living quite plainly with male partners and not being penalized for it. Even the sketch artists and assistants in wardrobe were frequently gay, like Richard Hopper and Waldo Angelo, who both worked for a time for Edith Head. Hopper, who according to his friend Don Bachardy was a talented, "unsung" designer, would later open his own shop. Angelo, stymied in the studios by having to forfeit all credit to Head, moved to Broadway, where he was a longtime collaborator with noted designer Raoul Pene du Bois.

So closely identified with gayness did the wardrobe department remain that (as it was with Head) even those few who *weren't* gay were often rumored to be. Irene Lentz, who, as simply Irene, took over as head of the MGM costume department from Adrian, was gossiped about as a lesbian, but friends insist she was not. Perhaps she was confused with Broadway designer Irene Sharaff, who worked on several notable films and was indeed a lesbian. By the mid-1940s the "queerness" of wardrobe had allowed for a number of women to rise to prominence within the field, and some of the gay male hegemony began to break down. There were even some straight men who became top designers, although once again, figures like William Travilla (who may have had an affair with Marilyn Monroe) and Jean-Louis (who married Loretta Young) were gossiped about as being at least sexually ambiguous.

They were still the exceptions, however: by far the majority of designers remained undisguisedly homosexual. Charles LeMaire, Adrian's old Broadway nemesis, took over as head of the Fox wardrobe department in 1943. "If a woman plays a chimney sweep in one film and a princess in the next one, who does the most to transform her?" LeMaire asked. "Not the script writer, not the sound man, not the director, not the musician—the costume designer does!"

The sheer number of gay costume designers—Edward Stevenson, who started at MGM in 1925 and had a career that lasted into television; Gile Steel, who did many of the MGM male fashions, while Adrian handled the women; Kalloch, who had taught both Adrian and Banton and then signed on as Columbia's first contract designer, before moving to MGM and RKO—makes it impossible to discuss them all. But suffice it to say that their numbers alone prove how wardrobe was an obvious bastion of queer work in the Hollywood studios, a place of gay influence and opportunity unmatched in any other industry anywhere else at the time.

WAR SPIRIT

THE GAY AWAKENING DURING WORLD WAR II

AND THE POST-WAR YEARS

1941-1955

ostume designer Howard Shoup had come to bid farewell to cast
and crew of *DuBarry Was a Lady*. It was the height of World War II,
and he was being shipped off to basic training. Arriving on the lot
resplendent in his air force uniform, his pants were sharply creased and his
gold buttons gleaming. But when Lucille Ball took one look at him, she
burst out laughing. "Now," she managed to say, "I've seen everything."

Howard Shoup wasn't exactly the traditional image of a war hero. "Howard was a screamer," said one man who knew him well. "You know how
some guys are just so obvious? That was Howard. Open his mouth and a
purse fell out."

Slight and delicate, Shoup had never made any pretense about being gay.
Following in the tradition of Walter Plunkett and Orry-Kelly, he was
blithely unconcerned with image, and so fully appreciated the laughter of
Ball and the crew. He well understood the irony.

Of the new generation of film-industry workers who blossomed during
and after World War II, Howard Shoup is perhaps the best example. Not

only did he make no bones about his homosexuality, but he took the overt-ness of Plunkett and Orry-Kelly a step further: he lived quite openly with an artist of equal stature, the sculptor Sascha Brastoff, for some forty years. Their names were linked in press accounts; they often arrived together for social functions, sometimes with female dates, sometimes not.

Shoup is the perfect transition figure: both committed to the style, glam-our, and ways of old Hollywood while also independent and contemporary enough to survive in the changing postwar era. He was part of a generation who hadn't lived through the Code upheavals a decade earlier and who ex-pected to live with a degree of authenticity his predecessors had largely abandoned after 1934. The war, with its inevitable challenge to social con-vention, only furthered their resolve.

For Hollywood, the Second World War would prove different from the First. From the start, there was near-universal support, with few "beautiful slackers" among the big names. Robert Montgomery and Douglas Fair-banks Jr. had enlisted even before the United States officially entered the war in 1941. By the next year nearly every major star and director had ei-ther been drafted or enlisted on his own: Gable, Flynn, Robert Taylor. Even the unlikely served: George Cukor made war films; William Haines worked in camouflage. Henry Grace saw action in the Philippines and was awarded the Bronze Star. The few who stayed out, like John Garfield and Lew Ayres, were ostracized both personally and professionally.

Yet both world wars had similar impacts on social mores and conven-tions. World War I had broken down Victorian rigidity for a generation who then plunged headfirst into the Roaring Twenties. World War II shat-tered the carefully constructed decorum that arose out of the Depression-era cultural backlash. Once again, the rules of gender were challenged. With their husbands and fathers at war, women were forced to go to work, supporting not only their families but the very war effort itself. "Rosie the Riveter" welding the hull of a battleship became a common patriotic im-age. The strong, independent, even *masculine* woman—so disparaged in the Thirties—was suddenly *celebrated*.

Meanwhile, the corollary was also true: images of effeminate men as women were common wartime entertainments. Howard Shoup, in fact, met Sascha Brastoff while in drag. Commissioned by Moss Hart to do the costumes for his war-themed Broadway morale booster, "Winged Victory," Shoup created for Brastoff an outrageous Carmen Miranda costume, done up in a mix of cartridge belts and bananas. Hart called it "the greatest sight gag in show business." At some point during the production, Shoup and Brastoff fell in love. Brastoff became, in the words of Shoup's nephew, "Howard's truest and closest family."

"G.I. drag" was a tradition within the armed forces as well. To entertain the troops, all-male productions of "The Women" and revues featuring female impersonators as Mae West and the Andrews Sisters became standard fare. "Winged Victory" showcased this tradition both in its stage production and later in the subsequent film (directed by George Cukor), preserving for all generations Brastoff's campy Carmen Miranda. After the war, Brastoff would continue his act on the Los Angeles social scene, turning up in 1952 in the pages of *Harper's Bazaar* dolled up in bananas and hootchee-kootchee costume—designed by Howard, of course. "I don't like zis boy," Miranda reportedly said. "He looks more like me zan me."

Although obviously not all of the G.I.s in drag were homosexual, a good many were—giving them, in the words of historian Charles Kaiser, "a secret opportunity to communicate with one another—and their comrades-in-arms in the audience." The army set up a special school at Fort Meade to teach theater arts for soldier shows, such as Irving Berlin's "This Is the Army." As Allan Berubé has documented, countless gay men signed up for these shows, and were often assigned permanently to Special Services if they had necessary skills (costume design, set experience, musical talent).

For all its tragedy, inhumanity, and loss of life, the war gave to homosexuals a rare gift: a way to connect, a touching place, a meeting ground. Having found a community of others like them while serving in the war, many gays and lesbians weren't about to abandon that when they returned to civilian life. Hundreds, even thousands, arrived in Los Angeles with a greater sense of themselves and a decreased tolerance for disguising their lives. An observer wrote at the time that the war had made homosexuality a "conventional thing. . . . One gay youngster remarked to me, 'Give us another war and the world is ours.'"

It was a nationwide phenomenon. Starting in the summer of 1942—the first after the start of the war—thousands of servicemen and women began flooding into American cities. Young, cocky, emboldened by the war or by the prospect of being sent overseas, these soldiers and sailors filled every nightclub and bar. Anti-vice campaigns weren't far behind. In many places, military police were stationed at the doors of gay or female-impersonator clubs to prevent any serviceman from entering.

Yet that couldn't stop the inevitable: gays were finding each other and building communities. "Why in hell can't they let us have at least a few places where we can be free?" wrote early activist Jim Kepner to a friend in 1943. Such a sentiment came out of a new, more defiant spirit, mirrored by many. "People sort of did with their gay behavior what they did with everything else," one man told historian Charles Kaiser, "which was take chances and risks and try to enjoy things because who knows where you might be sent tomorrow." Another observed, "This war spirit was starting to invade everything."

Certainly it brought Howard Shoup and Sascha Brastoff together, and their devotion to each other inspired them to live freely and openly. But in truth, Howard had *always* lived a life of happy freedom, dating back to a very young age. Born in Dallas, Texas, on August 29, 1903, Howard was a feminine little boy, an attribute that unnerved his father, Francis, an engineer for the telephone company. In 1910, Howard was sent to Sewanee, Tennessee, to spend a summer with his grandaunt, the novelist Sarah Barnwell Elliott.

In a moving letter that could serve as a manifesto for the new generation of gays, "Aunt Sada" wrote to Howard's mother:

> I hear that Francis does not approve of the turn that Howard's talents take. Tell him that he's behind the times. If he tries to warp or deflect that child's gifts I'll never forgive him. In all life there is nothing so cruel as to put Pegasus to the plough. The love of the beautiful—the artistic sense—is wonderfully visible in the child, and to twist it or quench it would be brutal cruelty. You've hatched a duck egg—let the small bird swim. [Just] because you and Francis do not swim and prefer dry land is no reason why Howard should be compelled to walk in the dusty roads. Make him happily free—don't make him struggle for it.

Thanks to Aunt Sada, Shoup's family appears to have come around, and Howard remained close and affectionate with them all his life. Such early grounding set the stage. He began college at the University of Washington in St. Louis but soon transferred to the Pratt Institute in New York to study design. In 1924 he got a job at Hattie Carnegie; in 1929 he moved over to the noted fashion house Bonwit-Teller. Hollywood agent Minna Wallis met him at a party and encouraged him to give movies a try. Hired by Warner Bros., Shoup's presence was resented by Orry-Kelly; consequently, Howard worked mostly on lower-budget pictures. He would come into his own after moving to MGM in the Forties, and then returned to Warner Bros. in the early Fifties, creating the costumes for *Calamity Jane* (very butch cowhide for Doris Day), *The Helen Morgan Story, Marjorie Morningstar,* and *The Young Philadelphians,* among many others.

His undisguised lifestyle—including his lover's very public female impersonation—did not prevent Shoup from becoming president in 1953 of the newly formed Costume Designers Guild and serving four terms. They had a gay old time for themselves, Howard and Sascha: Howard designing outrageous costumes and Sascha wearing them every year to the famous Artists and Models Ball in Los Angeles. They bought a home together on Military Avenue, and Brastoff ran a ceramic business, designing lamps, china, and jewelry. They shared their lives until Howard's death in 1987. Although Brastoff wasn't mentioned in Shoup's obituary, by the time of Brastoff's death in 1993, Shoup *was* retrospectively acknowledged, so markedly had the times changed.

It's not surprising that Shoup was close friends with Milo Anderson, whom he'd met at Warner Bros. and who would step up to prominence after the departure of Orry-Kelly. Anderson was just as overt and undisguised as Shoup. "Very gay," said David Chierichetti, who knew him well, "and absolutely unapologetic about it. In fact, I'd say, looking at his designs, they were the farthest 'out there' of any in the 1940s."

Anderson designed broadly and daringly, with frills and outlandish touches, but is probably best remembered for the tight angora sweater he slipped onto Lana Turner in *They Won't Forget,* the picture that skyrocketed her to stardom. Milo knew what worked, what caught the eye, and from his youth had never been afraid to say so. The only boy in his Fairfax High School class in fashion design, he had a steady boyfriend by the age of seventeen—a young man, as he would confide to Chierichetti, who was also fancied by Adrian. Showing the veteran designer his sketches, the teenaged Milo received little encouragement, but was then surprised to discover Adrian had actually recommended him, apparently as a joke, to Samuel Goldwyn. The joke was on Adrian: Anderson got the job on *The Greeks Had a Word For It* (1932) and went on to become the boy wonder of costume design, with a career lasting into the 1960s.

"A WONDERFUL PLACE TO BE GAY IN": HOLLYWOOD DURING AND AFTER THE WAR

Despite the MPs stationed at the doors of their clubs and the continued insistence at such places as Cafe Gala to "sit facing forward," gays in Hollywood enjoyed an empowering invigoration after 1942. "Economic times were better," recalled publicist David Hanna, "and gays were learning how to demand what they wanted, not just accept what the powers that be would allow. The most important factor was the war itself. The war produced a heavy concentration of gay people in the big cities. For many, it was a new experience to see how many others like themselves there were. Gay men and women started to see themselves in a new way—as part of a community."

That shouldn't imply that gay life had completely disappeared during the more oppressive Thirties. That would be patently absurd: despite trials, gay men and lesbians are no less resilient than any other group. In fact, in 1937 an undercover reporter wrote a detailed piece for the *Los Angeles Evening News* called "Night Court: The Homosexuals," in which he observed, "They are a tribe, with incantations and grapevines of their own. They know each other by secret signs even when their tragedy is hidden from the multitude." Gay life endured, if underground.

The war, however, made it increasingly visible once again. The crush of servicemen created a sexual binge reminiscent of Hart Crane's revelries in the 1920s. Donald Vining, working as a janitor at Paramount, recounted in his diary his nightly cruising of Pershing Square and the ease with which gay soldiers, sailors, and marines found each other. David Hanna said Los Angeles during the war years was "open season, a wonderful place to be gay in. . . . Snap your fingers and there were soldiers all over the place. You could bring them home for dinner, give them baths, whatever. It was heavenly, and heavenly for the soldiers too, because there was a great gay population ready and eager to take care of them."

Hollywood, perhaps not surprisingly, also became the birthplace of the modern gay pornography industry. In 1945 Bob Mizer founded the Athletic Model Guild, and soon had a 5,000-name mailing list for his pictorial spreads of young buff men (barely) dressed as gladiators, football players, and the like. With so many willing models streaming into Los Angeles on a daily basis, Mizer built up quite the business and inspired a long line of physique imitators.

"Things were looser during the war," Hanna continued. "Civilian police activity diminished because they lost their manpower to the war. I would say the war marked a big change in the lives of many gay people. There were so many of us."

At Los Angeles hot spots, there was a renewed spirit of gaiety both despite and because of the body bags. Gays became more obvious in their presence at such nightspots as the Mocambo (designed by regular patron William Haines) and Ciro's, where gay men were frequently in attendance to watch choreographer Jack Cole's incredibly homoerotic shows. Cafe Gala also continued to be popular until the latter part of the decade.

For the film colony during and post-wartime, there was a certain allure to being entertained by homosexuals. One of the town's leading private hosts was the self-styled "celebrity warlock" Samson deBrier, an intimate of André Gide and Gertrude Stein, who threw parties for the Hollywood elite wearing emeralds and Oriental robes, burning incense and seated among velvet pillows. For important visitors, the homes of George Cukor and Cole Porter were the first stops elite visitors to Hollywood always made, with Laurence Olivier, Ethel Barrymore, Noël Coward, Jean Cocteau, and

Lady Mendl regularly paying homage to those rival queens and lifelong friends.

Leonard Spigelgass rather famously observed, as only he could: "Homosexuality in that period had two levels. One, it was held in major contempt, and the other, it was the most exclusive club. That's terribly important to realize—that it was a club into which [heterosexual Hollywood] couldn't get. I mean, no ordinary certified public accountant could get into the Cole Porter-Larry Hart-George Cukor world. That was their world. That was Somerset Maugham. That was Noël Coward. . . .On the one hand, if you said, 'They're homosexual,' 'Oh, my, isn't that terrible' was the reaction. On the other hand, if you said, 'My God, the other night I was at dinner with Cole Porter,' the immediate reaction was, 'What did he have on? What did he say? Were you at the party? Were you at one of those Sunday brunches?' So you had this awful ambivalence."

An ambivalence Spigelgass struggled with himself, walking the tightrope between inclusion in both worlds. For many in the subculture, it was a dichotomy that occasionally reared its head in unexpected moments. Costume designer Miles White remembered having lunch at Romanoff's in 1944 with Elsa Maxwell and Lauren Bacall, as well as with a reporter he described as "very straight and very prim." The reporter brought up the headline-grabbing Wayne Lonergan case, in which Lonergan had killed his wife after he had an affair with her father. Everyone was talking about the case.

"I'll never forget what Elsa said," recalled White, then a young designer recently arrived from New York. "She said, 'Oh, it's simply horrible what these homosexuals do! It's so perverse!' Well, I'm sitting right next to her, thinking, 'You big old *dyke*.' Betty Bacall and I just looked at each other; I think we were both thinking the same thing. Then Elsa realized she might be offending me, so she quickly added, 'Of course, it's different for *talented* homosexuals—people like Cole Porter.' It was a way of saying, 'I don't mean you, Miles.' And the reporter, as I remember, was very surprised to learn Cole Porter was gay. Some people were so naive."

For Maxwell, a lesbian whose closest friends were gay men (including Porter and columnist Lucius Beebe), there was no contradiction in making such a distinction. The lower-class "perverts" *were* in fact different creatures from Porter and Beebe. Maxwell was part of the old generation, a generation for whom sexuality was not intrinsic to public identity, whose community—even if predominated with homosexuals—was defined more by class and privilege than anything else. Scandal-sheet columnist Lee Mortimer also zeroed in on this dichotomy, positing that while "the exceptional ones drift to Broadway and Hollywood," the "dull, dumb deviates" of small towns were simply "obvious and odious."

For White, it was an antiquated way of seeing things. Increasingly there would be a clash in Hollywood, not only the decades-old battle between the forces of convention and the forces of progression, but now also between old-school homosexuals and the post-war class of gays.

Born in San Francisco in 1914, Miles White knew he was gay at age five. "At least I knew I was different," he said. "There's a photo of my brother and me. I'm about five. He's dressed as a soldier, and I'm done up as a Red Cross army nurse."

He always knew he wanted to be a designer. "Fashion attracted me. At a very young age I was reading *Vogue* to see what the latest fashions were." After graduating with a degree in art from the University of California at Berkeley, White recalled, "I defied my family's wishes and went to Hollywood. I was convinced this was where I wanted a career." He was surprised and disappointed by the lack of welcome and support he got from the industry's older homosexuals. Even Walter Plunkett, a fellow Berkeley alumnus, didn't help him, "either professionally or personally."

It was the late 1930s. The industry was still in a vise grip between the Code and the Depression. White would have to go to Broadway to prove himself. Making a huge splash with "George White's Scandals" in 1942 and the "Ziegfeld Follies" of 1943, he was hired by Samuel Goldwyn on a three-picture contract working on Danny Kaye films. As part of the deal, White also secured a contract for his close friend, scenic designer Stewart Chaney. "I wanted someone I could work with," he said. "Scenic designers for the stage tended to be gay far more often than art directors in Hollywood and I knew I could work with Stewart. The others I wasn't so sure."

Although White would always be, once again, "circumspect and discreet," his gayness was hardly a secret, not to Goldwyn nor later, when he went to work for producer Mike Todd. He recounted one story when Todd gathered his crew together so he could give them his vision for *Around the World in Eighty Days*. "Todd said, 'I want it camp, but not campy,'" White recalled. "He looked around the room, and stopped at me. I was the only gay person there. He said, 'There's only one person here who knows what I mean.' And of course, I *did*. There's a fine line but a big difference between something that is *camp* and something that is *campy*."

The story reaffirms the idea that within given fields, one's gayness might actually be seen as an advantage. For, in fact, White understood Todd's point perfectly: *Around the World* had to be taken seriously enough as an adventure not to lose its audience, but also quirky enough to permit a surreality to the situations and characters. (Cantinflas, anyone?)

Todd would later ask White's opinions of various actresses in the cast. "Are they camp?" he'd inquire. Most of them White dismissed with a wave of his hand. "They were real dogs," he said. "But then he asked me about Shirley MacLaine. 'Is she camp?' he asked me." White smiled broadly. "'Most *definitely,*' I said."

• • •

Like Miles White, the writer Arthur Laurents arrived in Hollywood expecting to be guided along by the industry's established gay community. As a Broadway playwright, he had known a network of gay friends and acquaintances in New York. Arriving in Hollywood in 1947, he said, he looked for a similar "gay friend" to show him the way: "I knew nothing about the attitudes toward homosexuality in the city of Los Physically Desirable."

Although the handsome writer was quickly welcomed into Hollywood's gay circles, making the acquaintanceships of Leonard Spigelgass, George Cukor, and David Lewis, Laurents was disappointed by their deep commitment to circumspection. "The first time I met Lennie Spigelgass," he remembered, "he chased me around the room. It misled me. I thought it meant he was going to be more open than he was." Laurents found Spigelgass "very conservative," very guarded about his image and place in the Hollywood social structure. Not to Laurents did he seem less circumspect than others; to him, in fact, the George Oppenheimers and Charlie Bracketts were completely below the radar screen.

It's not that Laurents and his contemporaries were looking to be "openly gay" in the modern sense. It's just that they expected to live private lives of greater authenticity and veracity than what they saw among the immediate post-Code Hollywood homosexuals. In a way, they harkened back to an earlier, freer era. Within a short time of his arrival in the film colony, Laurents had become lovers with the actor Farley Granger, and they moved in together—an arrangement William Haines and Jimmie Shields had blithely undertaken in 1926 and which Cary Grant and Randolph Scott had hastily abandoned a decade later. "People still say to me, 'Oh, you were so brave, living openly with your lover,'" he recalled. "But I really didn't think of it that way. It wasn't intended as a political statement. I just felt I had to live my life the way that was right for me. There's no way I could have lived that pretense the way these other guys did."

Over time, Laurents figured out the system and how it worked. "Look, Hollywood only cares about image. If you projected the right image, they didn't care what the truth was. They were very practical. They'd encourage their serfs to find the right image. So long as they could use you, all they cared about was appearance. But everyone knew what the truth was. You could be gay and still be a big success if you kept up the right image. Peo-

248 • BEHIND THE SCREEN

ple in the industry just saw this as part of the business—you got married, or you had a lady on your arm at studio functions. It's funny, because after some guy had left with his escort, there'd be all this smirking behind his back. The remarks were made to show they knew the score. It's like they didn't want anyone to think they were fooled."

In the immediate post-war years, homosexuality was increasingly difficult to avoid. The artificial walls of invisibility erected by the Code and the clampdowns on the pansy clubs in the 1930s were effectively smashed by the war. Gayness was once more apparent, in both positive and negative associations. In 1946 Gore Vidal published his groundbreaking novel *The City and the Pillar*, which explored the gay subculture without condemnation or apology. The next year, tennis star Bill Tilden was arrested for having sex with a fourteen-year-old boy. "You have been the idol of youngsters all over the world," scolded the sentencing judge. "It has been a great shock to sports fans to read about your troubles."

And then came Kinsey: in 1948, *Sexual Behavior in the Human Male*, an 804-page treatise on Alfred Kinsey's landmark scientific study, suggested that homosexuality was a naturally occurring and not uncommon part of Americans' sexual lives. A full *10 percent* of the population was estimated to have experienced same-sex activity—a stunning documentation of a lifestyle hitherto consigned to the murky fringe. The actor George Nader remembered being fascinated by Kinsey; both he and his pal Rock Hudson pored over the text. The historian John D'Emilio observed: "By revealing that millions of Americans exhibited a strong erotic interest in their own sex, [Kinsey offered] an added push at a crucial time to the emergence of an urban gay subculture."

Although such subcultures weren't exactly new, the difference is that post-war gay communities were far more likely to self-consciously identify as gay. They were also far more ubiquitous, emerging not only in large metropolises like New York, San Francisco, and Los Angeles but also in smaller provincial cities like Cleveland and Seattle and Hartford.

It was a phenomenon directly in contrast to the tide of mainstream America, which in the years after the war was becoming decidedly *anti-urban*, with returning G.I.s marrying and taking their families into the newly built suburbs. As Robert Corber has argued, this "domestication of masculinity" became the dominant paradigm for the next several decades. Male homosexuality, then, offered the same kind of challenge to society that it had during the early days of the Depression. It offered a choice outside the prevailing model, a choice that would increasingly be seen (as we shall see) as not only anti-male and anti-social but also as anti-*American*.

Still, in the mid-Forties there was a gaiety to it all, a certain headiness that did indeed summon the spirit of a long-gone era. Arthur Laurents described the Hollywood he first encountered after the war as extraordinarily sexual. "It didn't matter if you were straight or gay or bisexual," he said. "If a new attractive person came to town, the others felt free to call up and say, 'Come on over and let's fuck.' And they did."

It's an outdated notion that post-war gays were unable to accept their homosexuality, basing their relationships with other homosexuals only on sex and not some sense of solidarity. Robert Corber has argued that the World War II generation was in fact quite conscious of a unifying gay identity and their own place in a social movement. They were championed in some ways by the works of such writers as Tennessee Williams, Gore Vidal, and James Baldwin, all of whom wrote explicitly of gay life and gay themes in the years after the war. "These writers," Corber argued, "conceived of sexuality as an emancipatory force that had the potential to disrupt postwar relations of power. In their work, gay male identity is defined less by sexual preference than by resistance to the dominant political and social order."

It is a view that appears to hold in considering the Hollywood gays of the late 1940s and early 1950s. Arthur Laurents, Howard Shoup, Milo Anderson, Miles White, Farley Granger, William Eythe, Clifton Webb, the "Freed Fairies" at MGM—all were a different breed from most who came before. There was an articulated consciousness of their place as gay men within both the studio structure and Hollywood society. While the protocol remained in place and circumspection still prevailed, there was increasingly an unavoidable awareness of *difference*—not only to those within the industry, but, significantly, to the public as well.

CLIFTON WEBB AS CLIFTON WEBB

In 1949, John Bainbridge wrote in *Life:* "Mr. Belevdere of the films is Clifton Webb of Beverly Hills. Nature has seldom come closer to imitating art."

Fifty years later, in retrospect, the identification has become even more obvious. "Onscreen and off," critic Leonard Leff observed, "[Webb's] performances called attention to themselves as performances. Webb lacked the range of several of his peers, like George Sanders, who played comparable roles. He nonetheless played Clifton Webb exceptionally well."

It's impossible to separate Webb's offscreen star persona—urbane, caustic, arch, and decidedly homosexual—from his screen roles: Waldo Lydecker in *Laura* (1944), Hardy Cathcart in *The Dark Corner* (1946), Elliott Templeton in *The Razor's Edge* (1946), Lynn Belvedere in *Sitting Pretty* (1948). Clifton was always playing himself. "His characters were straight enough for the censor," Leff observed, "and gay enough to lend color to the narrative and offer pleasure to homosexuals in the audience."

Clifton Webb was the William Haines of the 1940s. His gayness was undisguised within the industry and easily decipherable in his press; moreover, he created a unique screen persona very similar to his own, informed by the traditions and customs of the gay subculture. Such a character would not have been permitted in the Code-strangled years that had intervened between Haines' heyday and the relative liberation of the postwar years. Indeed, an earlier attempt by Webb to infiltrate the movies in the mid-1930s had gone nowhere.

In fact, even by the time director Otto Preminger wanted him for *Laura,* there was still a sense that the longtime Broadway headliner was too hot for Hollywood to handle. The response of Fox casting director Rufus LeMaire to Preminger has become legendary: "You can't have Clifton Webb play this part," he said. "He *flies.*"

But that was precisely why Preminger *wanted* him. He knew Webb was "a little effeminate," having seen him in Noël Coward's "Blithe Spirit" at Los Angeles' Biltmore Theatre. The director decided then and there that Webb was right for the conniving, clever, dandified villain of *Laura.* Webb, of course, got the part and scored a huge critical triumph, with Bosley Crowther famously writing in the *New York Times* that his performance "fits like a fine suede glove."

Waldo Lydecker is, on the surface, a jealous heterosexual lover spurned by Gene Tierney's Laura; yet, as any viewing of the film reveals, he reads conspicuously as gay. Hedda Hopper said Waldo was "a combination of Cholly Knickerbocker [aka Maury Paul] and Alex Woolcott"—both well-known homosexuals. *The New Republic* commented on Webb's "perfumed literary style" and "auntyish effeminacy." Indeed: Waldo composes on his typewriter while sitting in his bathtub, carries a cane and wears natty clothes, and offers acerbic commentary to anyone who'll listen. Preminger had fought for Webb precisely for what he'd bring to the role—his *gayness*—especially as compared to the studio's choice, the lumbering Laird Cregar (ironically, also gay). Although ostensibly a heterosexual, Waldo was *intended* by Preminger to be read as gay, and perhaps he wasn't adverse to other queer twists as well: critic James Naremore has suggested that "any movie that puts Clifton Webb, Judith Anderson and Vincent Price in the same drawing room is inviting a mood of fey theatricality."

Webb came to Hollywood with his persona well known. The queer markers were all there: he was unmarried, prissy, concerned with clothes and social etiquette. Most notably, in an arrangement harking back to J. Warren Kerrigan, his mother was his closest and most constant companion. Mabelle Webb—actually, Mabelle Parmelee Hollenbeck Raum—was a feisty, high-kicking, devoted presence throughout her son's life. Their relationship as reported in the press bordered on the incestuous: Clifton going "demented" if his mother couldn't be at his side, mother and son holding hands as they posed for photographers, "the Webbs" invited for tea along with "the Rathbones" and "the Zanucks." Mabelle was accorded the place normally reserved for spouses. "So thoroughly [was Mabelle] the gay companion of my life and travels," Clifton told Hedda Hopper, that any autobiography on his part would have to be a joint project—"the story of two people and their adventure with life."

Mabelle knew she had a good thing going. "Not all mothers are afraid that their sons will grow up to be homosexuals," observed Merle Miller, a gay movie writer, in a piece that could certainly have been inspired by the well-known Clifton-Mabelle relationship. "Everywhere among us are those dominant ladies who welcome homosexuality in their sons. That way the mothers know they won't lose them to another woman."

In fact, so thoroughly had the two of them collaborated in erasing Clifton's father from the picture that they could, in fact, be seen as husband and wife. They refused to speak of Webb *pere* when asked, except to say (in some early interviews) that he'd been a lawyer. Friends would laugh that Clifton must have been a virgin birth, and Mabelle smiled along. So conspicuous by his absence was Mr. Webb—or Mr. Hollenbeck, as Clifton grudgingly admitted had been his original name—that Sidney Skolsky headlined one of his columns about Clifton in the 1950s: "Nobody Mentions Father." Skolsky wrote: "The legend is that Father said he wasn't interested in show business, and Mother and her three-year-old son were so horrified and ashamed that they marched out of the house, never to return or see him again."

The true story of Clifton Webb's family has never before been told. In truth, Jacob Hollenbeck was no lawyer, nor did he come from a long line of lawyers and generals, as Clifton once asserted. Rather, he was a ticket clerk for the Indianapolis-St. Louis Railroad, the son of a grocer from an old Indiana farming family. It was this working-class existence as much as any stage ambition that inspired Mabelle's rebellion. Although she'd claim she, too, was the daughter of a lawyer and the granddaughter of a Yale university president (claims she never repeated after her son had reached a certain level of fame), she was in fact working class herself. Her father, Dave Parmelee, was a railroad conductor, likely the connection through which she met Jacob Hollenbeck. But life along the rails had no place in the dreams of Mabelle Parmelee. She was an aspiring actress who wanted "lace tablecloths and fine dresses," who saw her ambitions thwarted first by an unsympathetic father and then by a "Puritanical" husband.

Their son, born Webb Parmelee Hollenbeck on November 19, 1889, became Mabelle's ticket out of the dreary little flat they rented at 305 N. Mississippi Street in Indianapolis. The boy had star quality from the start. A photo of baby Webb taken when he couldn't have been more than a year old shows him standing with an air of imperious dignity in a ribbed undershirt, holding on to the back of a chair as if to say, "I rule here. No one can tell me otherwise." Another photo, when he was probably seven or eight, shows the child actor he'd already become: dressed in velvet waistcoat and satin bow tie, with a mop of curls and a dreamy gaze, his chin lifted haughtily to the camera.

There's no reason to disbelieve the stories that Mabelle left her husband and took Webb to New York when the boy was just three. Clifton would tell Lucius Beebe, "I loathe the accent of the Middle West as I loathe the Middle West itself. Fortunately I was dragged away from my birthplace at the tender age of three." In official early versions, obviously trying to downplay the stigma of a broken marriage, the narrative was adjusted to have the whole family move to New York. But the record clearly shows Jacob Hollenbeck still in Indianapolis working for the railroad in 1895, a time when we know Clifton was already on the stage.

His father would be tarred with the role of villain in accounts Clifton gave of his career. "If you stick to this crazy business, young man," Jacob supposedly admonished, "you'll be shining shoes when you're twenty-one and on the road to the poorhouse a few years later." Jacob may have given such advice, but not to a three-year-old, the age Clifton was when Mabelle whisked him off to New York. Some reports say Clifton never again saw his father after that, and the complete disregard with which he is treated in Clifton's press suggests Mabelle held a long-standing grudge. Although it was never mentioned, there was, in fact, a divorce, for in 1898 Jacob remarried Ethel Brown in St. Louis, where he set up a new life, still working the rails, dying in 1939 at the age of seventy-two. What he thought of his son's stardom can only be guessed at; one report said he never once saw Clifton perform onstage.

Mabelle remarried as well, to a man with the odd name of Green Raum Jr. It was during this time that Webb began his stage career, using the name Webb Raum. So completely had they erased Jacob that Mabelle lied to a census enumerator in 1900, saying she and Raum had been married for eleven years, giving the impression he was her son's father. But Green Raum proved ultimately as unsatisfactory a husband as Jacob. He may have provided a New York address (101 West 77th Street) from which to base Webb's career, but he himself labored in a copper factory. Much later, Hedda Hopper would write that at the age of seventeen, Webb "threw his stepfather out of the house." After that it was just mother and son, Mabelle and Webb.

"The mainspring of Clifton's life was Mabelle," Hopper wrote, and indeed, he owed his career to her single-minded determination. By age five he was taking dancing lessons; at seven he made his official debut with the

Children's Theatre in Palmer Cox's "The Brownies" at Carnegie Hall. This was followed by a tour in vaudeville with "The Master of Charlton Hall" and then "Oliver Twist." Later he played Tom Sawyer in "Huckleberry Finn." When Webb was still a young teenager, Mabelle arranged for him to study painting with Robert Henri and music with Victor Maurel. This led to Webb's debut in light opera in 1906, with the Boston-based Aborn Opera Company's production of "Mignon."

A 1911 autograph book found among his papers dates from his time with Aborn. Fellow members of the company warmly record their affection for Webb: "Charles F." wrote, "Pleasant memories of our first party"; Alexius Maddern inscribed, "Next in bathing suits"; Walter Sampson, in the wee hours of the morning on September 12, 1911, wrote: "Ain't it awful, Mabel?" Although he writes his name in the date book as "Webb Parm," he had become "Clifton Webb" by this point (a "George S." remarks on his first music lesson from "Mr. Webb"). Legend has it that Mabelle, traveling through Clifton, New Jersey, liked the cadence of the name and rechristened her son, further removing any remnant of Jacob from their lives.

Back in New York, he teamed with Mae Murray in a ballroom dance act, touring the Keith circuit and performing in Manhattan restaurants, riding the same wave of interest in dance that propelled Marion Morgan and her troupe to fame. He was also studying voice again with Victor Maurel, but there was a falling out. (It may be worth remembering that Maurel's wife was the overt lesbian Fred de Gresac.) In October 1914 Maurel had Webb arrested for lack of payment; Webb claimed that Mabelle, now operating a theater called the Folies Marigny, "took all he earned." According to the account, Webb "begged to be allowed to secure bail," insisting "a night or so in Ludlow Street Jail was abhorrent to him." He was allowed to put up $200, borrowed from a friend at the Jardin de Danse; whether or not he ever settled with Maurel is unknown, but he'd proudly point to their association for the rest of his life.

It would thereafter be dancing rather than music that Webb would pursue. "He is known for his dancing," wrote one press report. "It is seldom remembered that he can sing at all." By 1917 he was the sinewy, sensuous dancing star of "Love O'Mike," a musical comedy produced by Elisabeth Marbury and Lee Shubert. During the show's run, Dr. Karl Reiland, rector of St. George's Episcopal Church in New York, publicly objected to Webb's dancing, calling modern dance nothing more than "jungle antics." Clifton went on the counterattack, issuing a statement that was published in several papers:

> Dr. Reiland says patronizingly that while he does not dance, he is musician and psychologist enough to know that the "music ac-

companying some of the modern dances has a real effect on the moral substance of those habitually swayed by it." Now I can state just as appropriately that while I am not a preacher I am philosopher and psychologist enough to appreciate that the noises and antics accompanying the pulpit outpourings of Billy Sunday have a real effect on the moral substance of those habitually swayed by them. I claim that they are injurious to the artistic sensibilities of people who attend the meetings of the wealthy revivalist. If Dr. Reiland's artistic nature is marred by the so-called "jungle antics" of a few isolated dancers, let him avoid them as I am sure the artistic dancers will avoid Billy Sunday.

It's as direct an attack as one could imagine, of a kind that could never be launched in Hollywood, where the powers that be always sided with the moralists. Here, however, Marbury and Shubert no doubt encouraged Clifton in (and perhaps helped him prepare) his response.

By the mid-Twenties, Webb was one of Broadway's highest-paid stars, reaching his apex with "Three's a Crowd" in 1930 (performing a crowd-pleasing snake-hips dance with Libby Holman) and "As Thousands Cheer" in 1933 (impersonating Mahatma Gandhi, Douglas Fairbanks Jr., and Noël Coward's butler mimicking Coward's effete mannerisms). It was only a matter of time before Hollywood beckoned.

In fact, he had made several silent films in New York, but it wasn't until 1935 that Hollywood offered him star billing, in an MGM picture opposite Joan Crawford. Positioned as a dancing star in the Fred Astaire mode, Clifton went west for a round of high-profile social appearances. He arrived white-gloved and top-hatted, with Mabelle on his arm and trailing his fancy-cut French poodle on a leash. The picture, meanwhile, kept being delayed. Lloyd Pantages observed, "Clifton Webb's debut into pictures is a little tougher than one might suspect." The pseudonymous "Cal York" in *Photoplay* wondered if Crawford—recalling the biting parody of her divorce from Fairbanks that Webb had played in "As Thousands Cheer"—had nixed the idea. More likely it was a studio dilemma with Clifton *himself:* in a period when many were still shell-shocked by the Code clampdown, a white-gloved Broadway star with a parrot named Goo Goo wasn't exactly the sort most producers wanted to embrace.

His contract torn up, Webb gave an interview back at the Lombardy Hotel in New York, Goo Goo perched haughtily upon his wrist like a falcon. Asked about his sojourn in Hollywood, Webb referenced the current scandal *du jour:* the shocking Mary Astor diaries, revealed in divorce court. "It's stupid," he said, "to write down intimate things and doubly stupid to keep the writings. In other words, I don't believe in diaries."

For all his obviousness, Clifton Webb understood the value of circumspection. The prohibition against public acknowledgment of homosexuality protected him, giving him the freedom to exhibit all the markers of queerness: the effete mannerisms, the dandy wardrobe, the devotion to Mabelle, the precious pets. (In addition to Goo Goo, his poodle was named Ernest, after Oscar Wilde's "The Importance of Being Earnest.")

"Everyone knew about Clifton," remembered one of the actors who played with Webb in the Chicago company of "The Man Who Came to Dinner," "but he would have been mortally offended if anyone said, 'You silly fag.' Nobody did that. One's private life was private."

By the time of *Laura* in 1944, however, Hollywood had sufficiently recovered from its Code-induced post-traumatic stress, and decided to take another gamble on Webb. In the process, it discovered one of its most unexpected and unique stars.

He was certainly an unlikely leading man. At fifty-five in 1944, he was still handsome but undeniably gray, with a perpetually arrogant tilt to his eyebrows and chin. Thin and just under six feet, he appeared taller and broader by holding himself "stiff and erect, like a British drillmaster." A snapshot from his personal collection shows him during the making of *The Man Who Never Was* (1956), in wide-brimmed hat, floral-print shirt, dark sport jacket, hands on hips with a cigarette between his fingers. On the back, someone—Clifton himself?—has written: "Pose so typical."

After his memorable villains, he was offered a change of pace: the urbane, acerbic baby-sitter Mr. Belvedere in Walter Lang's comedy *Sitting Pretty* (1948). Webb stole the picture from its nominal stars, Robert Young and Maureen O'Hara, and was promptly launched on a series of starring vehicles showcasing his "fliply arrogant" personality. He played Belvedere again in two sequels, as well as an ironic angel in *For Heaven's Sake* and an eccentric professor in *Dreamboat*. The fathers he essayed in *Cheaper by the Dozen* and *Elopement* are ostensibly heterosexual married men, but are in fact prickly, haughty, exacting old queens.

"I've destroyed their formula completely," Webb said. "I'm not young, I don't get the girl in the end and I don't swallow her tonsils, but I have become a national figure."

Louella Parsons agreed: "This violated all the rules, for Clifton isn't young or particularly handsome, and he never gets the girl. He is an intellectual and a sophisticate."

The "sophisticate" was clearly taking some delight in turning the tables on "their" formula. Like J. Warren Kerrigan and William Haines, it was Webb's very queerness that made him box-office gold, but ultimately he transcends even them in his subversive appeal—for Kerrigan and Haines, after all, *did* end up getting the girl. Webb was the one Hollywood leading man who seemed bored by the very idea of leading ladies.

He is best in *Sitting Pretty*, which contains the classic movie moment of Belvedere/Webb dumping a bowl of spaghetti on a child's head. "There was novelty in having me play the babysitter," he admitted. "Me, of all people." Belvedere's apparent disdain for children and their antics masks a heart of gold, however, which prompted a flood of letters to the studio from parents who wanted advice from Webb on how to raise their own brood. The queer as child-rearing sage: the irony is delicious, as far removed from the myth of queer as child molester as possible. Webb would go on to play fathers often throughout the decade, shrugging off critics who pointed out his own bachelorhood. "I may not be a family man," he said, "but I am an actor. I didn't have to kill to play the murderer in *Laura*. I think I'm good enough an actor to pretend I'm a father."

In the end, Webb created an image that, no matter its queerness, was embraced by the larger culture. "Mr. Belvedere is a piece of pure Americana," John Bainbridge wrote in *Life* magazine, "an elegant addition to U.S. folklore."

His offscreen image was no less gay. Like descriptions of Dorothy Arzner's "mannish" clothes and hairstyles, Webb's queerness was referenced in nearly every article written about him, and this intertextual understanding of his stardom informed both *reel* and *real*-life personas. He was forever described as a "perennial" or "confirmed" bachelor; he was a "sophisticate," a "cosmopolite," "the only man in Hollywood who knows how to hold a fish fork properly."

For his part, Webb made no attempt to restrain himself. In an interview with Sidney Skolsky, Webb calls the columnist "honey" and "darling" throughout. He was happy to chat about his poodles and their "chi-chi tastes." He told Hedda Hopper that Ernest was "a very snooty fellow who doesn't go in for proletarian backgrounds." The markers of his queerness were not only acknowledged but actually highlighted in a way not seen since Kerrigan or Eugene O'Brien. He could get away with it because, as Arthur Laurents pointed out, "When it's that apparent, people don't *think* it's apparent."

That didn't mean the studio was blithely unconcerned with how their new star was being perceived by the public. When fan-magazine reporter Gladys Hall submitted a draft of an upcoming interview with Clifton to the publicity department at Fox, objections were raised. Several of Webb's comments ("I *love* myself on the screen") made him sound, in the studio's words, "too-too." But it was Hall's emphasis on Webb's bachelorhood that was their prime concern. A Fox publicist wrote to Hall: "Don't you think you can find another ending and leave the married status out? Sorry to be such a nuisance, but as you can understand a piece of this kind has to be gone over very carefully or we will destroy the very thing we are all building in advertising and publicizing an unusual personality like Clifton Webb."

Unusual was an understatement: marketing Clifton Webb was very different from marketing a Tab Hunter or Rock Hudson, whose public images were anything but swishy and for whom photo-op dates seemed plausible. Only once was the suggestion made in Webb's press that he might be "available." It occurred early, only a few months after *Laura,* in one of the fan magazines, where reporter Leslie Traine wrote that although Webb didn't expect to go to the altar after so many years of bachelorhood, "his eyes laugh when he says this." Traine editorialized: "Why can't some lucky lassie do something about it?"

The answer, even to much of the public, was obvious. When he starred in *Titanic* (1953), the jokes were inevitable. Among the mementos he left, now archived at Boston University, there is this: a plaque bestowing the "Sybil and Richard Burton Award to Clifton Webb for the excellence of his going down (on the Titanic, of course)."

For all his undisguised gayness, however, Clifton seemed to have no great love other than Mabelle. "I don't remember him ever having a lover," said Charles Williamson, who knew him through George Cukor. He did, however, enjoy the company of young men, who often gathered poolside at his pink stucco house on Rexford Drive in Beverly Hills. "I remember Clifton would disappear with them into the poolhouse, telling his mother they were off to check the garden," said Robert Wheaton. "Mabelle would keep quiet for about a half hour and then she'd call out, 'Clifton, where are you?' And he'd say, 'Coming, Mother.'"

There was also a close mentorship of the young Robert Wagner, mirroring Arthur Lubin's of Clint Eastwood: both relationships have been described as "infatuations" by observers. Webb and Wagner had worked together in *Stars and Stripes Forever* and *Titanic,* and the older actor took the younger one under his wing. "Webb simply adored Bob Wagner, who was then just about the best-looking actor in Hollywood," said Wheaton. Wagner himself recalled Webb as "very kind and very generous . . . part of the family, in fact." Indeed, Webb remained in the actor's life even after Wagner's marriage in 1957 to Natalie Wood; a snapshot in Webb's private collection shows him in a simple cardigan sweater, beaming like a proud grandfather, surrounded by Wagner and his daughters.

Webb was a good person to know. He counted among his friends anyone who was anybody, and his social life was as apt to include European aristocrats as industry types. After a private showing in Paris of *Mr. Belvedere*

Goes to College for the Duke and Duchess of Windsor, Webb wrote to Hedda Hopper: "As you might surmise I am moving in the correct circles—match!"

Still, he wasn't unfamiliar with the gay circles in the film colony. Hopper wrote that he socialized with Monty Woolley and Laird Cregar. He was often a guest (with Mabelle) at Cukor's, and even more frequently at Cole Porter's. He was very close to William Haines and Jimmie Shields. The television actor Richard Deacon became a good friend, and at one point threw a party for Clifton, trying to set him up with a young man. The actor Ray Stricklyn, who played Clifton's son in *The Remarkable Mr. Pennypacker,* remembered the potential date arrived wearing very short denim cutoffs, "his enormous cock practically poking out from below." Stricklyn said Clifton was "appalled, thinking him quite crude, and refused to have anything to do with him."

Despite his overtness, like many gay men of his era, Webb may have struggled at some point with his sexuality. Some have recalled he had sessions with the notoriously anti-gay analyst Lawrence Kubie. Yet like another Kubie patient, Tennessee Williams, Webb couldn't have put up with the counsel for very long: he was simply too self-aware and too self-confident to give such ideas very much credence.

For—as much as he was a stickler for a certain etiquette—Webb was not one to suffer gladly any obvious anti-homosexual bias. Ray Stricklyn remembered an incident during the making of *The Remarkable Mr. Pennypacker.* Webb had obtained tickets for him and another young actor from the cast, Ron Ely (later TV's Tarzan), to see Noël Coward in "Nude With Violin." When Clifton inquired later how they liked the play, Ely remarked, "Oh, it was okay, but that Coward guy was kinda—" He made a gesture that indicated "swishy."

"I thought Clifton was going to explode," Stricklyn said. "He quickly exited the set. He later told me that he'd gone to Buddy Adler's office to demand that Ron be fired—'I don't want anybody that stupid working in my picture!'" It was too late to recast Ely's part, however, so Webb simply cold-shouldered him for the rest of the shoot.

Despite his anathema to diaries, he told reporters many times that he was writing his memoirs. But by 1952 he said he had gotten "bogged down" in the process; a few years later, he jettisoned the whole idea, saying it would be impossible for him to write the truth without offending someone. "Truth is a desirable quality in an autobiography," he explained, "though obviously not indispensable, and candor, I have found, compels me to put certain persons and events in a revealing rather than a flattering light." There would be no Webb autobiography.

He spent the 1950s, not an easy time for many homosexuals, as Hollywood's *"arbiter elegantium,"* according to Sebastian Flyte of the *Los Angeles Examiner.* Proving Lennie Spigelgass' assessment of the "two levels of homosexuality," everyone from Debbie Reynolds and Darryl Zanuck to Lady Mendl and Lord Snowdon flocked to Webb's elite parties and delighted in his campy humor. Flyte even reported a saucy little anecdote of Clifton disguising himself as "Lady Mary Gordon" when he called his friends.

"'People just don't talk that way,' you say," Flyte wrote. "But Clifton Webb on the screen plays the same Clifton Webb in Beverly Hills, using every bit of the flip arrogance for which he is famous. The others may fool you with their quiet evenings at home, their hamburgers and ice-cream cones. But it's all true about Clifton Webb, all true."

THE POST-WAR GAY STARS

The post-war years were comparable to the early 1930s, when the arrival of sound brought in a new class of actors to Hollywood, a large percentage gay. The end of the war did the same: importing from the stage or elevating from the ranks new faces who better suited the changing times. With the war's relaxation of rigid gender conformity, actors didn't necessarily have to be as roguish as Gable or Cagney. Of the gay stars who blossomed in the 1940s, most harked back to the softer, somewhat ambiguous sexual image of the Twenties and early Thirties: Webb obviously, but also (all in their own way) William Eythe, Hurd Hatfield, Vincent Price, John Dall, Farley Granger, Roddy McDowall, Laird Cregar, and of course, Montgomery Clift. (As ever, there were exceptions, such as the rough-edged, heavy-set character actor Thomas Gomez.)

That several gay stars—Webb, Cregar, Eythe, and briefly Granger and Dall—were based at Twentieth Century-Fox is perhaps not surprising: Darryl Zanuck was among the most tolerant of studio chiefs. The Fox actors tended to be far less disguised than their counterparts at other studios, especially MGM, where Louis B. Mayer still reigned. One of Metro's top stars of the war years was gay—a boyish actor who skyrocketed to fame in a series of lighthearted comedies and musicals, becoming an idol to the bobby-soxer crowd. He married and divorced, playing the game Mayer so dearly prized. At the time of this writing he was still alive, unreceptive to requests for interviews.

Still, his story was fairly common knowledge within the industry, even if his marriage helped deflect the kind of press innuendo some of the other stars faced. By the Forties, marriage had become expected, with fan magazines often running charts of who was (and who had previously been) married to who. Those who remained unattached (and it's noteworthy that in the post-war era, most of the new gay stars did) were considered suspect. Despite Monty Clift's publicity-generated "romance" with Terry Moore, Hedda Hopper knew the truth: she had a report of a morals charge to prove it. She never used the information, but Clift reportedly lived in anguish. McDowall avoided being targeted until much later because he started as a child star and "grew up" in the industry, becoming in the process a good friend and confidant to many. But William Eythe had a much harder time: never one to play games easily, he chafed against the studio rules and was early branded a "rebel." Hedda Hopper called him the "Brash Brat."

The press liked to call him "the man from Mars," for he was born in Mars, Pennsylvania, a little town outside Pittsburgh, on April 7, 1918, the youngest child of Carl and Kathleen Eyth. (The final "e" was added when he went on the stage.) As a boy, Bill lived in the shadow of his older brother, a jock everybody called "Dutch." Both brothers attended Carnegie Tech, where the lion's share of attention again went to Dutch, who became an All-American halfback on the football field. Bill meanwhile was a drama major, with much of his interest directed at set design and costume. He put together several fashion shows for local department stores.

His parents seem to have been supportive of his interests, and Eythe would go on to join several stock companies after graduation. Appearing with Ruth Chatterton in Cohasset, Massachusetts, he was spotted by Broadway producer Oscar Serlin, who gave him a part in *The Moon Is Down,* which opened at the Martin Beck Theatre in April 1942. A war drama set in occupied Norway, the play was a smash hit, with Bill's performance as a sympathetic German soldier a standout. On the strength of this, he was brought to Hollywood and given a long-term contract with Fox. His "discoverer" may well have been Anderson Lawler, the well-known Hollywood "walker" who was then working as a talent scout for Fox.

The William Eythe who arrived in Hollywood was twenty-four years old, dark-haired and dark-eyed, handsome in an ordinary kind of way. He was not a transcendent beauty like the studio's top star Tyrone Power, but had down-to-earth, approachable good looks. His eardrum having been punctured in a stage accident, he stayed out of the war due to hearing loss. With Power and so many others off the screen, Eythe had few rivals, and received good notices for his first film, *The Ox-Bow Incident* with Henry Fonda. After playing the noble young French boy who gives up his love for Jennifer Jones in *The Song of Bernadette,* he was named a "Star of Tomorrow" by film exhibitors. *Variety* predicted he had "a bright future."

Fox publicity promptly shifted into high gear. Already by March 1944 there's evidence the studio felt the need to dodge potential image problems, putting out the word that the only reason Bill wasn't a college football hero like his brother was his ear problem—an injury that, in fact, hadn't occurred until he was an adult. A *Photoplay* blurb stressed that Eythe was "a wonderful catch" for any girl, though it cautioned, "But girls, you have to like bowling and no kidding about it." By November of that same year Eythe was obliged to take part in an article headlined "Why I'm Still Single." He was quoted: "I'm going to wait until after the war before I even look seriously for a girl, because I want to see what the war does to women—I want neither a military disciplinarian nor a frilly doll."

Using the war's own upheaval of gender roles to mask his homosexuality was a novel approach. By the time of his first starring part in *A Royal Scandal,* as the reluctant amour of Tallulah Bankhead's Catherine the Great, there was clearly some sense that his maverick image would have to be "explained" to the public. Hedda Hopper took up the challenge. "He's a fresh, original personality," she stated honestly. "I think his deepest instinct is to be himself." His penchant for wearing blue jeans and T-shirts to places like the Brown Derby was spun into an asset: "Bill's got the courage of his convictions. Lives to suit himself, not Hollywood."

The studio's attempt at fictionalizing Eythe's life and personality didn't fool everyone. Journalist Paul Benedict found Eythe "intense and serious" despite Fox's insistence that he was a "screwball, fun guy." Then there was the issue of girls. Eythe told both Benedict and Hopper that stories of a romance with Anne Baxter were dreamed up by the publicity department. But he did resort to the old "unnamed girl back home" myth, telling Benedict "she isn't in pictures, doesn't want to be, nobody knows her, which suits us both fine."

Nobody knew her because, in all likelihood, she didn't exist. For Eythe was in a relationship with someone much closer at hand, and most reporters knew it. Like Farley Granger, Eythe defied Code-era tradition by living openly with another man, Lon McCallister, a fellow "Star of Tomorrow." Although McCallister declined to be interviewed for this book, press accounts at the time did note their friendship as well as the fact that McCallister—who'd achieved some wartime popularity playing young soldiers in *Stage Door Canteen* and the filmed version of *Winged Victory*—traveled to London in the summer of 1946 to be with Eythe during the filming of *Meet Me at Dawn*.

It would be Eythe's last major film. Poised on the brink of stardom, Eythe was suddenly yanked back. Studio chief Darryl Zanuck, despite his geniality, "wasn't too happy" about the Eythe-McCallister friendship, according to actor Ray Stricklyn. The Hollywood gay subculture has always held that Zanuck insisted the pair not be seen in public, and when they defied him, he released Eythe from his contract. Suddenly adrift, Eythe soon married the eighteen-year-old Buff Cobb, an actress and granddaughter of the author Irvin S. Cobb (and later the wife of television newsman Mike Wallace). The marriage was brief and unhappy: after only a few months, Cobb filed for a divorce in January 1949, claiming Eythe had "struck her with great violence." Ordered to pay her a $2,500 settlement, Eythe refused and spent a night in jail.

The Brash Brat was self-destructing. Unlike William Haines, who had also been bumped from the studios for being too indiscreet, Eythe was unable to rebound in a new profession. He made some minor pictures at Paramount and Columbia and did some early television work. He also returned to the theater, although during the run of "Lend an Ear" in Los Angeles, he frequently forgot his lines and had to leave the stage. A series of arrests for drunken driving made headlines; in 1952 he spent another night in the county jail after "getting loaded" (his words) in Malibu.

Eythe's decline can't be blamed entirely on Zanuck and Hollywood's homophobia; others were living fairly authentic lifestyles at the time and managed to keep their careers afloat. Yet the promise of stardom had been *so* close, so within his grasp, that such a loss must have been traumatic. Still, his release from the studios did allow him to resume his relationship with Mc-Callister. They traveled extensively and made some films for the Hilton hotel chain. When asked why both had left acting, McCallister joked: "Bill's too fat and I'm too old." They lived together in Malibu for a number of years, with McCallister helping to care for Eythe when he fell ill with hepatitis and liver disease. William Eythe died on January 17, 1957, aged only thirty-eight.

• • •

Farley Granger's story was far less tragic. Though he lived with Arthur Laurents as openly as Eythe lived with McCallister, Granger was never as "brash" or pugnacious as Eythe. At just nineteen, he made his debut playing a Russian youth in Samuel Goldwin's wartime *The North Star* (1943). In the strikingly good-looking actor, Goldwyn saw major star potential. He tried to discourage Granger's relationship with Laurents, whose gayness and left-wing politics made the producer uncomfortable. That didn't stop Granger and Laurents from setting up house together, however, although they were clearly cautious. Laurents would remember that they actually had few gay friends, tending to mix more with tolerant straights.

As Fox had done with Eythe, Goldwyn attempted to mold an image for Farley in the press. In a September 1944 *Photoplay* article depicting Granger in uniform, there's a quote from his mother insisting (apropos of nothing) that her son was "a normal boy" who had lots of girlfriends. The reporter coyly points out that while that might be true, it was Roddy McDowall who was his "busom pal."

A similar press treatment was given to John Dall, Granger's costar in *Rope,* a film written by Laurents in which they both played (subtextually) gay men (see discussion below). Dall had been married and divorced by the time his Hollywood career shifted into high gear. "It didn't last," he told reporter Gladys Hall. "Just one of those things. Just didn't work out, that's all. Once bitten, twice shy." But he added quickly: "Believe me, I think girls are here to stay. I'm extremely susceptible."

It was a standard line in the press for all of the gay stars of the Forties, most of whom, like Eythe, Granger, and Dall, declined to follow the lifestyle pattern of post-Code Hollywood. Few of them married. Granger recalled being tempted to walk down the aisle with Janice Rule, with whom he lived for a time. "But something was saying, 'Don't do this,'" he remembered in 1996. "I'm glad I didn't."

Although they lived more freely than their counterparts a decade earlier, there was still a protocol to be followed. "We knew who was gay," Granger said, "but there was no big deal made about it. You didn't get together with friends and say, 'Did you hear about so-an-so?' You kept it to yourself."

In other words, they knew the rules. Hurd Hatfield told *Silver Screen* he was dating a female dancer he'd met in the MGM commissary, but in truth the star of *The Picture of Dorian Gray* was well known within the industry as homosexual—perhaps the reason he was both chosen for the Oscar Wilde adaptation and then pretty much abandoned after that classic picture. Although there would always be those who lived with utter discretion—Vincent Price comes to mind—most of the World War II–era gay actors were defiant in some way. Perhaps that partly explains why, like Eythe and Hatfield, few of these actors enjoyed film careers of much duration. Granger hit his peak with Hitchcock's *Strangers on a Train* (1951); after that, he floundered about, finding his best films in Europe. After *The Man Who Cheated Himself* (1951), John Dall wasn't back on the screen until *Spartacus* (1960). The thrice-married Price, however, whose own daughter acknowledged how carefully he hid his homosexuality, enjoyed a career renaissance as a horror star in the Fifties and Sixties.

Laird Cregar, too, had a brief career. Like Clifton Webb, he was an unlikely Hollywood star: a honey-voiced, shifty-eyed, six-foot-three, three-hundred-pound villain in trenchcoat and fedora. Historian Gregory Mank called him "an anguished homosexual"—yet those few who remember him don't consider his sexuality the only, or even the chief, cause of his anguish. "He was very ambitious," said one friend, "and it was the *weight* that he blamed for keeping him from becoming a star." Gay activist Harry Hay recalled Cregar living quite happily with a boyfriend in the late 1930s: "There was no attempt to hide it. He wasn't troubled by being gay."

Not about being gay, perhaps, but Laird Cregar *was* troubled—troubled in the way any obese person might be in a society obsessed with appearance. And Hollywood was the hub of that obsession: the ambitious Cregar, who'd dreamed of being a movie star from his "first day of consciousness," spent his short life raging against the image he saw reflected in his own mirror.

He was born Samuel Laird Cregar (pronounced Cre-*gar*, as in "cigar") on July 28, 1913, in Philadelphia, and was always known to family and friends as Sammy. His family was affluent, his father a woolen importer and well-known local cricket player. He had five older brothers, and Sammy Cregar became the spoiled baby. "Sam was different from his brothers," his niece remembered later. "He was moody and tempered with a quiet innocence. He broke rules, talked back, and made up outrageous stories that he believed as gospel truths."

He himself admitted childhood eccentricities: "I used to spend hours making faces into the mirror," Cregar said. "They thought I was mad."

It's no wonder that Edward Cregar shipped Sammy off to England when he was eight, enrolling the youth at the disciplinarian Winchester Academy. During his school breaks, he signed on with the Stratford-on-Avon players, taking the role of a page boy in several productions. The experience convinced him acting would be his life.

He returned to Philadelphia when his father died, and was sent to a series of private schools before the 1929 stock market crash wiped out the Cregar fortune. His mother was forced to take a job in a department store to continue paying for her sons' educations. Sammy meanwhile hopped a ship and fled by steerage to Miami, where he worked as a dishwasher in a restaurant. His salary included meals, but he was fired after his boss discovered just how much the rapidly growing teenager ate.

"Pleasingly plump as a child," he remembered, "it developed into the frighteningly fat between the ages of sixteen and eighteen. It gave me terrific inferiority and I suffered. It was my lack of appeal for girls that troubled me."

He may not have appealed to girls, but he *did* have a boyfriend within a few years, if Harry Hay is to be believed. They worked together in a Los Angeles stock company; Laird had gone west with the desire to break into movies. At one point he worked as a bouncer at a nightclub, sleeping in his car at night, for which he was arrested on a charge of vagrancy and spent some time in jail. Once free, he went back to Philadelphia, where a friend of the family gave him $400 to fulfill a dream: to study at the Pasadena Playhouse and emerge a professional actor.

At Pasadena, he met DeWitt Bodeen. "I knew Laird Cregar quite well," Bodeen recalled. "He always had a weight problem. Sometimes he'd actually starve himself for a week until he looked like a leading man."

After scoring a hit playing none other than Oscar Wilde at Hollywood's El Capitan Theater in 1940, Cregar was signed to a seven-year contract at Fox. Right away he was put into "fat" parts: buffoon sidekick to Paul Muni in *Hudson's Bay,* smarmy foil to Tyrone Power in *Blood and Sand,* psychopathic detective in *I Wake Up Screaming.* The villains eventually overtook the comics, because Cregar brought a certain edgy style to them: like Webb in his pre-Belvedere roles, Cregar imbued his characters with a sly, menacing sexuality. Of his most famous part, Jack the Ripper in *The Lodger* (1944), critic Joel Greenburg later observed: "Laird Cregar—plump, soft-spoken, suggesting reserves of violence and rage held barely in check—found in the role of the Ripper an almost therapeutic alleviation of his private angst, the misogyny of a tormented homosexual."

Although once again there is the misguided equation of homosexuality with misogyny and torment, Greenburg was indeed picking up on something. Cregar's villains are both dangerous and effeminate, and this same edge could be detected in the actor's offscreen behavior. The actor Henry Brandon recalled when, at the height of his career, Laird went onstage at a Los Angeles theater in place of his chorus-boy lover, an incongruous fat man among a line of well-built boys. "Zanuck found out about it," Brandon said, "and put his foot down with a bang."

Such is not the image of a self-loathing homosexual. His fame apparently trumped his girth in allowing him to find boyfriends. By 1943, he was romantically involved with the actor David Bacon, who'd played a few small parts at Universal and Republic, notably in *The Masked Marvel.* In September of that year, Bacon was found dead with a knife in his back; the headlines suggested he'd met his fate at a gay bathhouse in Venice Beach. Several accounts also ran pictures of Laird, noting he was "such a good friend."

For such an accommodating mogul, Darryl Zanuck certainly had his patience tried by such stars as Cregar and Bill Eythe. The publicity department did its best to repair Laird's image. The whole point of a *Silver Screen* article—obviously arranged shortly after the Bacon scandal—was that despite his weight, Cregar did indeed have sex appeal for women. Many female fans, according to the studio, wrote to plead with Laird that he drop some weight and play the hero for a change. The piece played up supposed romances with Dorothy McGuire and Robert Stack's sister-in-law, yet admitted that "on this subject Laird has nothing to say."

It's clear that by early 1944 Cregar's publicists were actively trying to change his image. It was as much his own desire as the studio's, friends insisted. "He wanted to be considered attractive," said one acquaintance. "He always wanted to be a handsome leading man." Remembered DeWitt Bodeen, "He was like a big Saint Bernard who couldn't understand why you didn't want him in your lap."

Bodeen would tell author Gregory Mank that what Cregar wanted was to "attract a young girl to become his lover." Although Bodeen was ever eager to maintain the Hollywood closet, there may be some truth to his statement. Laird Cregar wanted to be a Movie Star—capital M, capital S—and that meant losing not only the weight but the homosexual image. "Some actors who are homosexual are quite content," remembered Laird's *Hangover Square* costar Alan Napier, "[but] Cregar was not content—he wanted to be Clark Gable." He began taking weight-loss drugs and underwent plastic surgery on his face. During the course of filming, he dropped eighty pounds. The once charming and easygoing actor became surly and temperamental.

Yet it would be worth all the pain and struggle if he could become a new man. On December 4, 1944, he entered Good Samaritan Hospital for an abdominal operation that was intended to shrink his stomach and curtail his food intake. Five days after the procedure, he suffered a massive heart attack. The stress of the rapid weight loss, drugs, and plastic surgeries had taken its toll. Laird Cregar died on the afternoon of December 9, 1944. He was just thirty-one years old.

He once told Gladys Hall that dishonesty had been his "ever-present friend." As a young boy, he'd learned how to lie his way into the theater and onto Pullman trains. He implied that it was a talent that came in handy in Hollywood, too. Indeed, he told Theodore Strauss of the *New York Times:* "Dishonesty is a quality, which sometimes, especially for actors, is extremely useful." The Laird Cregar who first came to Hollywood in 1940 was as forthright and authentic as his contemporaries Eythe and Webb; hadn't he gladly chosen Oscar Wilde, of all parts, to bring himself to industry attention? Yet a few years into his career he realized that to get what he really wanted—to be Clark Gable—he'd need to *lie*. The inner "thin man" he told Strauss he cultivated was also, in truth, a *straight* man, but the dishonesty he so prized ultimately cost him his life. "What a sad, sad tale it was," recalled one friend. "Laird wanted the Hollywood dream so bad, but—fat or thin—it could never have been his. If only he could have seen that. Such a promising actor. So sad."

DANGEROUS SISSIES:
THE FILMS OF POST-WAR HOLLYWOOD

In *This Gun For Hire* (1942) Laird Cregar played a prissy, arrogant, effeminate villain with the habit of popping peppermints as he reposed in silk pajamas. In *Blood and Sand,* his venomous bullfight critic was likened by one writer to "a fat, effeminate iguana lounging in the ringside sun." Meanwhile, Clifton Webb was archly essaying Waldo Lydecker in *Laura* and Hardy Cathcart in *The Dark Corner*. By the early 1940s, the screen's sissies were no longer the comic flatterers made popular by Edward Everett Horton and Franklin Pangborn. Conniving, manipulative, and dangerous, the sissy had suddenly turned *lethal*.

Film critic Richard Dyer has observed that film noir—that amorphous genre of dark, cynical, fatalistic films that emerged in the post-war years, and to which *This Gun For Hire, Laura,* and *The Dark Corner* belong—expressed "a certain anxiety over the existence and definition of masculinity and normality." Often the villains of noir were women or effeminate men, and the disillusioned heroes were, in critic Frank Krutnick's words, "traumatized or castrated males." The war had, as we have seen, put traditional masculinity in a state of crisis; noir reflected this sudden American preoccupation. Characters who are intended to be read as gay often turn up in villainous or antagonistic roles: not only Cregar and Webb, but Peter Lorre in *The Maltese Falcon,* Robert Walker in *Strangers on a Train,* George Macready in *Gilda*.

Noir's superficial homophobia belies its true nature, however. Critic James Naremore posited that the genre actually challenged existing social and gender assumptions by raising "a modernist ambiguity . . . [soliciting a] potentially deconstructive critical discourse" of the status quo. Indeed, the old definitions of "man" and "woman" are not so much *defended* by film noir as they are *mocked:* despite their villainy, it's the femme fatales and homosexuals who hold the real power. One well-known noir, *Crossfire* (1947), actually had its origins in a direct attack on homophobia, being based on a novel about an anti-gay murder. With the Code prohibition on "sex perversion" still in place, it was changed to an anti-Semitic killing for the film. Still, the message was one of tolerance and compassion in a post-war world that had become dark and uncaring.

The pendulum was swinging in Hollywood. The dramatic shift to the right of the mid-Thirties was reversing itself, with liberals winning key battles. In 1945 *The Nation* applauded the decline in film stereotypes of minority groups (homosexuals were, of course, not mentioned): "The people who work in Hollywood have, through their war experience, gained immeasurably in social awareness. Hollywood may in time assume the progressive leadership of the nation." There was reason for such optimism. A study taken after the release of *Gentleman's Agreement* (1947), a stinging indictment of anti-Semitism, showed both a rise in tolerance of Jews and a willingness on the part of the public to see more films dealing with the treatment of minorities.

Industry leadership was changing, too: in 1950, after a stunning outburst of anti-Jewish and anti-liberal invective, Cecil B. DeMille was forced to resign from the board of the Screen Directors Guild, and most of his right-wing, old-time cronies went with him. They were replaced by liberals William Wyler, John Huston, Billy Wilder, and others. The next year, the reactionary Louis B. Mayer was toppled from his throne at MGM, with the progressive Dore Schary taking over. A note found among George Cukor's papers, in which he and Schary, now studio head, banter back and forth about "the fat content of Mazola," is a telling detail of the change in climate: one cannot imagine such lighthearted gaiety from Mayer.

The new regime in Hollywood gave the green light to a number of progressive, thoughtful pictures that broke the old mold. Defying the Code had become increasingly frequent ever since Howard Hughes released *The Outlaw* in 1941 without official sanction. Thus challenged, Joseph Breen was forced to give his stamp of approval on projects that ten years before would never have even made it to his desk: *The Postman Always Rings Twice, Double Indemnity, Duel in the Sun*. Recognizing the loosening of moral absolutes engendered by the war, Breen was also persuaded to bend the rules by an awareness of the studios' financial realities. The war had cut off important overseas markets, and by war's end the industry was faced with the rise of television. As early as 1939 the *New York World-Telegram* observed, "It's understood that an extra degree of latitude is to be granted moviemakers now that the war-hobbled industry needs more customers. Of course, the Hays Office itself never would make such an admission."

Whether they admitted it or not, the censors were obviously relaxing their policies. Films dealing with racial bigotry, abortion, mental illness, and sexual promiscuity began appearing, albeit in sometimes coded language. Foreign films like *The Bicycle Thief*—a forerunner in the move toward a cinema of "realism"—suddenly commanded American screens, and the studios felt the pressure to keep up. Breen held his nose ("When these people talk of realism," he complained, "they usually talk about *filth*"), but he went along. As historian Leonard Leff has observed, "With Hollywood's audience vanishing, studio executives hungry, and exhibitors willing to screen *The Bicycle Thief* even without the Seal [of Approval from the Code], Breen was forced to see the virtue of pliancy."

Homosexuality remained unmentionable, but, as ever, directors found a way to play with it when they needed. There were no complaints specifically about homosexuality from the Breen office over the script for *Laura;* once again, it was performer and director who brought out the queer nuances in an ostensibly "straight" story. In fact, Breen's only concern had been about Waldo's lines "I made her" and "She was mine," insinuating a sexual relationship between Waldo and Laura. Ironically, by eliminating any direct mention of *hetero*sexuality—in a sense, neutering Waldo, just as the earlier sissies had been asexual—his *homo*sexuality is made more apparent, especially given that Webb's sissiness was confrontational and aggressive, impossible to ignore.

It's significant to point out that these sophisticated, intelligent films challenging both Code and convention were not being made by Hollywood's gays. Although Naremore credits Cukor and Vincente Minnelli with being drawn to "noir themes or motifs," in truth neither director ventured very often into such provocative territory. Cukor's *A Life of Her Own* has been called noir, but is really not much different from any other of his melodramas. Likewise Minnelli's *The Bad and the Beautiful:* an excellent film, but hardly noir. Gay directors seemed determined to keep as far away as possible from the kind of challenges some of their heterosexual colleagues were daring to make. Mitchell Leisen was turning out such traditional fare as *To Each His Own* and *Suddenly It's Spring;* Irving Rapper, *The Corn is Green* and *Rhapsody in Blue;* and Arthur Lubin went so far as to disparage "serious, psychological films" when he proposed *Francis the Talking Mule* to Universal.

Indeed, unlike a decade previous—when most of the screen's pansies were also gay offscreen—the "dangerous sissies" of the Forties and Fifties were mostly played by heterosexuals (with the notable exceptions of Webb and Cregar). Such gay reticence to join in with the progressive challenge to Hollywood tradition is perhaps understandable: the purge of the Code years had not yet been forgotten, and after 1947 the inquisitions of the House Un-American Activities Committee (HUAC) would naturally have kept industry homosexuals skittish and cautious. (For a detailed discussion of this period, see the next chapter.)

While the homosexual subtext of much of film noir and other post-war film genres is fascinating, it is, in truth, beyond the scope of this study, except where gay actors, writers, or directors may have had influence on the outcome. Such was the rare case with Alfred Hitchcock's *Rope* (1948), based on the British play by Patrick Hamilton about homosexual lovers who commit a twisted murder. Here there was no sneaking around or obfuscation: nearly everyone involved in the project knew they were making a film about homosexuality—and that homosexuals were a big part of the making.

Much has been written already about the gay subtext of *Rope,* a subtext so apparent it is practically a misnomer. Suffice it to say here that for screenwriter Arthur Laurents, it was the defining characteristic of all three major roles in the film, and served as the tension underlying all the action. He didn't shy away from the subject matter, and neither did the film's stars, Farley Granger and John Dall. Neither, for that matter, did Hitchcock. "The actual word *homosexuality* was never said aloud in conferences on *Rope* or on the set," Laurents remembered, "but [Hitchcock] alluded to the subject so often—slyly and naughtily, never nastily—that he seemed fixated if not obsessed."

The Breen office picked up on some of it, insisting certain phrases they termed "homosexual dialogue" (basically "my dear boy" and fey expressions of the like) be deleted. But *Rope* went out pretty much as the homosexual writer had written it and the homosexual actors had played it and the heterosexual-but-fascinated director had directed it. Of course, Laurents had wanted Cary Grant to play the James Stewart part ("There was no gay energy coming from Jimmy Stewart at all") and thought Montgomery Clift should've done the Dall part. But both stars, perhaps not surprisingly, said no.

"Plain and simple," Laurents said, "*Rope* is a gay film. That, along with Hitchcock, is what attracted me to the project. Hitch might not have said the word, but he knew. We all knew."

What Hollywood *didn't* know was that this sudden burst of gay energy, this stunning turn to the left, was set to once again transform the screen and the industry—and set off yet another backlash, this one even more obdurate and ruinous than the last.

FREED'S FAIRIES: THE ARTHUR FREED UNIT AT MGM

If gays weren't making the film noirs and dark, psychological dramas, they *were* largely responsible for another genre of the period: the movie musical. Some were light and frothy; others transcended convention to push at the edges of form and style.

With the exception of wardrobe, nowhere in the studio system was gay input more concentrated than in the Arthur Freed production unit at MGM. Producer, directors, composers, arrangers, choreographers, dancers: the gay presence in nearly every one of the forty-plus films of the Freed unit (many of which have become classics) was remarkable. And *obvious:* in the industry, they were known as "Freed's Fairies."

The Arthur Freed unit was considered throughout the industry as the pacesetter in the production of musicals. Freed had worked as a songwriter at MGM since the late 1920s. By the mid-1930s he had helped assemble a music department par excellence: musical director George Stoll, composer Nacio Herb Brown, lyricist Yip Harburg, and especially arranger Roger Edens, whom Freed had known in New York. It was *The Wizard of Oz* that resulted in Freed being elevated to full producer status with a regular department established under him for the production of big-budget musicals.

The gayness of the Freed unit took a little longer to coalesce. Freed himself wasn't gay, but neither was he the true creative heart of the unit. The real maestro was Roger Edens—arranger, songwriter, and eventually associate producer. Edens was genial, cultured, and brilliant—and a gay man who brought in other brilliant gay men as collaborators; hence, "Freed's Fairies." Like George Cukor and Edwin Willis, Edens wasn't assembling his team based on sexuality, but it remains true that those he considered the best also often happened to be gay.

To be sure, many of the key players of the Freed unit who lent their inimitable stamp to its output were heterosexual: Stanley Donen, Gene Kelly, Lennie Hayton, André Previn, Betty Comden, Adolph Green, Michael Kidd, Alan Jay Lerner. But there was a special camaraderie among the gay members of the team, one or more of whom was credited in nearly every film of the unit: director Charles Walters, orchestral arranger Conrad Salinger, choreographers Robert Alton and Jack Cole, dancer and Freed assistant Don Loper, frequent composers Cole Porter and Frederick Loewe, as well as others, including—although he wasn't identified as such except in whispers—director Vincente Minnelli. That's not taking into account gay involvement in these films from other departments: Richard Pefferle and Keogh Gleason were frequent set decorators, and Kalloch, Gile Steel, Walter Plunkett, Howard Shoup, Irene Sharaff, and Orry-Kelly were among the costume designers.

Prime among all of them was Edens, whose touch was pervasive, whether it be creating the musical vamp ("doodlee doo doodlee doo") that opens Gene Kelly's number in *Singin' in the Rain* or gathering Bobby Tucker, Kay Thompson, and Connie Salinger around the grand piano he kept in his office and helping them pull together arrangements. As associate producer, he was the one to decide what scenes needed to be reshot, what footage needed to be cut, what song needed to be rearranged, and what director needed to be hired or fired.

"Roger *was* the Freed unit," insisted Lela Simone, one of the team's production assistants. "Roger was so tactful and knew Freed so well that he never blundered in with 'We must do this and we must do that.' It was always, 'Let's see what happens.'. . . Freed did not occupy himself with details, because he had Roger and he knew that Roger was going to do the best job there is."

Edens was responsible for some of the best musicals of all time: *The Harvey Girls, Cabin in the Sky, Easter Parade, Good News, The Barkleys of Broadway, Take Me Out to the Ball Game, Pagan Love Song, Words and Music, Annie Get Your Gun, The Band Wagon, Show Boat, An American in Paris,* and *Singin' in the Rain.* That's not even including the films for which he provided musical adaptation or original songs: *The Wizard of Oz, Babes in Arms, Babes on Broadway, Strike Up the Band, Meet Me in St. Louis, Lady be Good, DuBarry Was a Lady, Ziegfeld Follies, For Me and My Gal, Girl Crazy, The Pirate,* and *On the Town.*

Edens has been credited with "modernizing" the musical, of creating a new genre distinct from the old Busby Berkeley extravaganzas, where the music was separate from the narrative. "You have to be careful about music in films," Edens told an interviewer. "So many musicals have been made in which the plot and the songs have nothing to do with each other. I believe songs in film musicals should be part of the script itself." As an example, he pointed to *Funny Face* (which he produced independently after leaving the Freed unit). "When Astaire begins singing 'Bonjour Paris,' he gets out of the cab, hesitates for a minute, and then just *bursts* into that wonderful walk of his. You couldn't make this live away from the movie itself—you have to see the action."

But it's another creation for which Edens is best remembered: Judy Garland. "Professionally, Roger 'created' Judy Garland," said her daughter Lorna Luft. "He recognized not only my mother's extraordinary musical gifts, but also her emotional sensitivity. It was Roger who gave Mama the courage to let the softness, the vulnerability that was part of her, into her singing. Without Roger, we might never have had 'Over the Rainbow,' at least not the way we all remember it."

Gay man as molder of gay icon: it had happened before (William Haines and Joan Crawford, New York drag queens and Mae West) and would happen again (Jack Cole and Marilyn Monroe), but nowhere is it as striking as with Edens and Garland. Judy viewed him as a father figure, filling the void left by her real father. As a young performer, it was Edens she looked to for support and encouragement. He knew she had something special. Assigned as vocal coach to the gangly, awkward teenager soon after she arrived at MGM, Edens would later say hearing her sing was like discovering gold where none had been expected. He became her indefatigable champion after that, training her in the morning and promoting her name to the studio in the afternoon. Arranging for her to sing "Dear Mr. Gable" at a birthday party for Clark Gable, Edens assured Judy's stardom. She was soon cast in *Broadway Melody of 1938* and then, pivotally, in the Andy Hardy pictures and *The Wizard of Oz*, for which Edens arranged the music and continued to coach his protégé.

They would remain close for the rest of their lives. "I loved Roger Edens when I was a girl," Lorna Luft recalled. "I loved his deep voice and Southern accent, and I'd go running to meet him when he came through the door. He'd always pick me up and throw me in the air and carry me around."

His colleagues in the Freed unit felt similarly. "He was a darling man," said Kay Thompson, who worked as a vocal arranger. "Absolute peaches and cream." Lela Simone remembered him as "very civilized . . . I don't think Roger ever screamed in his life. Let's not forget, Roger was a gentleman from the South and that played a great deal in his character."

Yet the South from which Edens hailed was not quite the magnolia-shaded, aristocratic place he may have wished his colleagues to imagine. "That was a pretty rough and tough family back there," said his nephew, J. C. Edens. "All of Roger's brothers were pretty rowdy. He was never the roughnecks they were."

He was born Rollins Edens on November 9, 1905, in Hillsboro, Texas, the eighth and youngest son of Edward Edens, a cotton salesman, and his wife, Grace, who was forty-four when the baby—called "Buster" by the family—was born. His brothers were railroad brakemen or wagon drivers; his uncles were sheriffs in the western boomtown. "He admired all of them," said J. C. Edens, "but he always had a more artistic bent. He had a yearning. He loved his family, but Hills County wasn't where Buster wanted to stay."

His parents supported their youngest son's ambition, scrimping and saving to send him to the University of Texas, the only Edens to receive a college education. After graduation he landed a job as a pianist on a cruise ship, where a chance meeting with a New York manager led to a stint with a jazz band after the ship docked. Taking a house on Long Island with other band members, he persuaded his mother, now a widow, to move up and keep house for the boys. (He'd remain close with his family, later helping some of them find work in Hollywood. A nephew, Alric Edens, served as cameraman on the television series "The Virginian" and "Dragnet.")

It was on Long Island that Rollins Edens—the baby, the artistic son, the one with the "yearning"—became Roger Edens. The reasons for the name change are unclear, but it was peculiar, given the fact that one of his brothers already had the name, albeit spelled *Rodger*. "He asked permission of his brother to do it," said J. C. Edens, "so long as he dropped the 'd'." Wanting to be more like his rough-and-tumble brothers, it's possible he considered "Rollins" just too precious, too dandy, for the hard-drinking, woman-chasing world of orchestras and musicians. At some point, the new Roger Edens also got married, to a college sweetheart, "a tall, striking, beautiful blonde, impeccably dressed," according to his nephew. Martha LaPrelle Edens was in fact a very modern woman. A buyer for a fashion house, she traveled a great deal on her own, creating long separations for her and her husband.

Meanwhile, Roger's own career took off. By 1930 he was playing in the pit of the Alvin Theater on Broadway with the Red Nichols Orchestra, which included Tommy Dorsey, Gene Krupa, and Glenn Miller. Ethel Merman had just made a socko opening in the Gershwins' "Girl Crazy," and in one of those classic show-biz moments, her personal pianist had a heart attack on the second night of the show. She called Edens up from the pit to fill in. Once again, the Merm brought down the house, and as the curtain dropped, she turned to Roger and said, "Baby, let's stick together."

True to her word, when Paramount brought her out to Hollywood, Ethel took Roger with her. Too big a presence to ever be adequately captured on film, Merman's movie career never took off. But Eden's abilities were quickly recognized by the studios: in 1935, Arthur Freed snapped him up for MGM.

At first, Martha accompanied him to Hollywood. "Mr. and Mrs. Roger Edens" were reported among the guests at Ginger Rogers' wedding to Lew Ayres in 1934. But by the time of the great Freed musicals, Martha had moved back East. Like Linda Porter, who found husband Cole's Hollywood lifestyle too much to handle, Martha Edens "never cared much for Hollywood," said J. C. Edens. Kay Thompson, who would become one of Roger's closest friends and frequent escort, saw her only once. "She was not around," Thompson said.

Roger Edens was never as apparent in his homosexuality as, say, David Lewis, his fellow MGM producer. Even after their separation and eventual divorce, Edens kept a large photograph of Martha on his desk. Yet working within the nearly autonomous fiefdom of the Freed unit, some of the necessity for absolute discretion vanished. Roy Yoneda, whose parents worked for Edens in the 1940s and 1950s, residing on his estate, recalled Roger living with a man early on—probably the same who friends said was so outrageous he was called "Pansie Schmanzie" behind his back. Michael Morrison, business partner in William Haines' decorating business and a good friend of Edens, also remembered a boyfriend. "Roger was a very handsome guy, very personable, charming," Morrison said. "All sorts of people were drawn to him."

Former studio messenger boy Frank Lysinger agreed. He had taken a job in the music department in 1939, and one night, working late on the score of a picture, he and Edens caught each other's eye. With a recording of Tommy Dorsey's orchestra playing in the background, Edens approached him and asked him to dinner. "It was really quite lovely," Lysinger remembered. They became good friends, seeing each other frequently until Lysinger went off to the war. Often their dinner companions were Lena Horne and musical director Lennie Hayton, who had been officially forbidden to date by Louis B. Mayer, concerned about publicity over an interracial romance.

"Roger would arrange for them to get together," Lysinger recalled. "It would be Lennie and Lena and Roger and me. I remember once Lena singing, and Lennie and Roger on the piano. Here was little me, fresh out of Iowa. The fact that Lennie and Lena weren't supposed to see each other, and here I was, with them, with Roger—I really felt 'in' with it."

It's a lovely image: two officially unsanctioned pairings taking pleasure and solace in each other's company. Lela Simone remembered Edens acting as Horne's "protector," defending her to studio bigwigs who worried that she "looked too Negro." Said Simone: "Lena surrounded herself instinctively with people who she knew adored her no matter what, who didn't have a drop of anti-Negro in themselves." That many of those folks were homosexual is likely not coincidental.

• • •

Certainly the core team of the Freed unit saw themselves as modern thinkers, trendsetters, ahead of the curve. "Old school" composers like Georgie Stoll were "fading out," according to Lela Simone, treated as "more or less a laugh" by the younger, cocksure, new talent. Yet a reputation as one of "Freed's Fairies" in the culturally conservative Fifties was both industry affirmation and potential liability. At least one Freed unit member, the young, up-and-coming writer Leonard Gershe, was reportedly uncomfortable with the association. "Lennie's work was almost on the sidelines," said Lela Simone. "I have a feeling that was probably Lennie's wish. He did not want to, under any circumstances, be the protégé of a man who was more or less known as a homosexual. . . . He did not want to be known as Roger's protégé."

Nevertheless, Gershe did collaborate memorably with Edens on a number of projects, notably on *Funny Face* and the "Born in a Trunk" number for Cukor's *A Star is Born*. They would remain close until Edens' death in 1970, with Gershe designated in Edens' will to coordinate the distribution of all his music, scores, and records.

Gershe's reticence isn't entirely difficult to understand given the context of the times. Yet within the Freed unit it *was* a minority attitude—shared perhaps only with Minnelli. Edens lived openly with another man, as did choreographer Jack Cole. Salinger was famously indiscreet, and Charles Walters's long relationship with the agent and former actor John Darrow was known throughout the industry.

In truth, the Freed unit *was* on the cultural vanguard, and that independent spirit comes through in the films. The work of these artists fundamentally reshaped the musical genre, moving away from, in the words of writer Stephen Silverman, "clunky backstage musicals [and] syrupy, snail-paced concoctions, fancifully dressed yet hollow at their core" and toward a naturalistic integration of song, dance, and plot.

"Naturalistic" is, of course, relative: Fred Astaire bounding out of a taxi and into song is hardly the stuff of real life, and neither is Judy Garland launching into "The Trolley Song" aboard a car in downtown St. Louis. If anything, in fact, the new movie musical was a fun-house mirror effect on what life was like—or perhaps, what it *could* be like. Writer Matthew Tinkcom has argued that a distinct camp sensibility exists in the films produced by the Freed unit, the result of "the labor of gay subjects." In fact, he argued that what made these movies so popular was their very "differentiated style" from other films (not unlike what set Kerrigan, Haines, and Webb apart as actors). The Freed-produced pictures, especially the early ones, tended to prioritize "dazzling sets, costumes, use of color and choreography" over storyline—elements more associated with gay workers than straight ones, and not traditionally used as the essential building blocks on which a film was structured.

But content, too, had a certain camp appeal. Tinkcom pointed to the "Great Lady" sequence in *Ziegfeld Follies* (1946) in which Garland, parodying a star, enters with an entourage of obviously gay male admirers who dance with themselves as much as with her. Since the film had already broken the convention of narrative—it has no plot—it could concentrate on dancing and sets and color and style. "Liberated from the constraints of cause/effect relations, even from the idea of events themselves," Tinkcom wrote, "*Follies* plunges into the camp pleasures of texture, masquerade and performance."

Ziegfeld Follies was directed by Vincente Minnelli. Indeed, there is a definite "queer read" to much of the director's work. Take *Meet Me in St. Louis,* his masterpiece: little plot, but there *is* plenty to listen to and look at—the orchestrations, the beautiful sets, the stunning costumes, the dancing, the raw emotion of Garland and little Margaret O'Brien. It is made up, once again, of elements ordinarily used as background to plot, but which here become the focus.

Yet George Cukor had nothing but disdain for Minnelli's work. "Take away his cranes and you've got nothing there," Cukor would say to Gavin Lambert. Cukor was often dismissive of the work of deeply closeted artists. Minnelli's homosexuality was not treated by the industry as the same kind of "open secret" that Cukor's was. This despite the fact that Minnelli, a former Broadway costume and set designer, was far more effeminate in manner and style than either Cukor or his Freed colleague Charles Walters. Minnelli's absolute circumspection had to do with his own idiosyncrasies, and only recently has the full story of his sexuality begun to be documented. There were rumors, of course, of his days in New York, but once Minnelli came to Hollywood he was determined to leave that life behind. He and Judy Garland, starting out as antagonists on *Meet Me in St. Louis,* were brought together by matchmaker Don Loper, Freed's assistant and a (gay) friend of Minnelli's. Garland and Minnelli soon put aside their differences and were married.

A full-scale biographical study of Minnelli is needed, taking his sexuality into account and fully integrating it into his life and work. As Lela Simone would say: "Minnelli was a man of a completely different style [from other directors]. He tried to [direct] in a soft and nice way. He worked in, let's say—I don't know whether you will understand what I say—he worked like a homosexual. I don't mean that nastily. I have nothing against homosexuals."

In other words, Minnelli made films in a manner profoundly *different* from others, and the same could, in truth, be said to describe the entire Freed unit, gay and straight: *They worked like homosexuals.* Tinkcom wrote that "the very anonymity of production, in addition to the anonymity for sexuality" allowed "the corporate structure of MGM [to] inadvertently provide the gay makers of camp Freed musicals with a venue in which to work." It is true that very few in the audience paid attention to the names rolling past them in the credits; to most, a film was the work of its stars and occasionally its director. Who paid attention to the names Roger Edens, Conrad Salinger, Robert Alton, Jack Cole?

Yet those "anonymous" gay laborers were the backbone of the unit. Edens' closest collaborator was his orchestrator, Salinger. Always sharply dressed, erudite, fluent in French, Connie Salinger was, in the words of one historian, "the antithesis of what musicians presumably are like." Born in Boston in 1901, he was a Harvard boy, refined and educated. After graduation he headed to Paris, where he studied harmony and orchestration with Nadja Boulanger and Ravel. He came to New York as an orchestrator on Broadway, where he met Edens. When Edens began assembling a team for Arthur Freed, Salinger was one of his first recruits.

"Connie was very talented," remembered Frank Lysinger. "Roger would write a single line of melody and hand it to Connie and Connie would fill in all the harmony as well as what instruments would be playing at the time." Critic Hugh Fordin has called Salinger's orchestration of *Meet Me in St. Louis* masterful: "It conveyed all the color, the motion, the excitement that eventually was going to be seen on the screen. Salinger always maintained sonority and texture in his writing, which made his a very special sound and style that has never been equaled in the American movie musical."

For all his style, however, Salinger was a lonely, unhappy man: physically unattractive, he was forever trying to snare a handsome boyfriend, often getting very drunk in the process. "He was so brilliant in so many ways," said one friend, "but he just couldn't see what he was doing to himself."

Hotheaded, he'd frequently get angry at friends over dinner and storm off, leaving them with the bill. He'd throw lavish parties with set decorators Jack Moore and Henry Grace, where everyone would drink to excess—Salinger's ultimate undoing.

"A great talent in everything but knowing how to drink," observed another friend. Still, he managed to orchestrate the music on nearly every Freed unit picture, from *For Me and My Gal* to *Gigi.* "One of the great orchestrators of all time," Lela Simone declared. After the Freed unit dissolved in the late 1950s, Salinger turned to television, composing for the series "Bachelor Father." In 1961 a wildfire in Bel-Air destroyed his home; in June 1962, still despondent, he committed suicide by taking an overdose of sleeping pills.

"So tragic," said a friend. "But every time I see *Meet Me in St. Louis,* I think of him. That's his legacy. That will never fade."

• • •

Tinkcom's phrase, "the labor of gay subjects" offers a perspective from which to view the work of Salinger and other gays within the Freed unit. Significant among them was Charles Walters, who, after Minnelli and Stanley Donen, was the unit's most important director, helming four of its best pictures, including *Easter Parade,* as well as shooting retakes on *Gigi.* Earlier, he'd also been choreographer on several pictures, including *Meet Me in St. Louis* and *Ziegfeld Follies.*

Choreography was queer work, no doubt about it. An earlier, largely heterosexual generation—Busby Berkeley, Hermes Pan, Seymour Felix—had called themselves simply "dance directors." Walters explained, "Choreography, a much grander term, was only for the ballet." Yet while Berkeley had learned his moves staging marching maneuvers in World War I, most of the new names in the field had had formal training—including ballet—and most were, in fact, gay: Walters, Jack Cole, Robert Alton, Richard Barstow, Lester Horton, Don Loper, Jerome Robbins. In the movie musical of the Forties and Fifties, pioneered by the Freed unit, the dancing is a vital, integrated, narrative element—far removed from Fred and Ginger's ballroom moves or Berkeley's tap-dancing chorus girls. In "Choreography," a musical number in *White Christmas,* Danny Kaye actually seems to mock the queer roots of the new dance directors, done up quite fey (he actually resembles Jack Cole), mincing and prancing about the stage.

Dance—and in particular, this new "choreography"—had the tendency to make the sexuality of its practitioners questionable. So many male dancers were gay that Arthur Laurents attributed Gene Kelly's occasional homophobic diatribes to the fact that he was "in dance, and that made him suspect." Remarkable, then, was Charles Walters' overtness when he arrived in Hollywood in 1942, when the shock of the Code clampdown had still not fully worn off. But like David Lewis' talent for refocusing a script, Walters' knack for salvaging musical numbers made him valuable. He was able to build a house with Darrow in Malibu and continue living pretty much as they had in New York.

A California boy from the beginning, Walters was born in Anaheim on November 17, 1911. "I've danced as long as I can remember," he said. "That's all I can remember, is dancing. That's all I wanted to do. Oh, we tried art, [and] the family wanted me to be a lawyer, [but] all I wanted to do is dance. . . . And I'd never had a dancing lesson. Who had heard of Fred Astaire and Clifton Webb in Anaheim? Nobody. So I was a freak more or less—a man just didn't dance in those days. At least in Anaheim."

That "freak" was itching to get out of there, to head to New York, but his family insisted he attend the University of Southern California. He lasted only a year before running off with the musical road show of Fanchon and Marco, and finally made it to New York in 1933. There he landed a dancing gig in the Broadway revue "New Faces," twirling Imogene Coca across the stage. He put together a nightclub dance act with Dorothy Fox, and was noticed by Robert Alton, then a top Broadway choreographer. Alton was influential in securing Walters the part of the prince in Cole Porter's "Jubilee," as well as offering the inspiration for Walters' own dancing style. "I learned so much from that man," Chuck would say. "Style and fluidity, and so amenable."

Alton was indeed a trendsetter—in some ways the herald of the new movement in dance. Among the first to style himself a "choreographer," he revolutionized choral dancing by breaking up the old chorus line into smaller groups, filling the stage with fluid movement and color. A decade older than Walters, Alton had been born Robert Alton Hart in Vermont, a high-strung child who ran away from home to join the circus. Later, he found his way into drama and ballet school in New York. In 1926 he married his dance partner, Marjorie Fielding; they had a son, Robert Jr., before divorcing in 1929.

That Bob Alton was gay has been affirmed by several who knew him, including Broadway designer Miles White. That he took a particular shine to the young, tall, blue-eyed, handsome Chuck Walters (who Dorothy Kilgallen said looked like "a brunette Duke of Windsor") has been merely guessed at. But the two would remain lifelong friends, and their career paths would continue to intersect.

Walters' success in "Jubilee" led to a wide range of shows, including being directed by George Balanchine in "I Married an Angel" in 1938. His popularity surged: Kilgallen noted that despite sharing the stage with such "glamour girls" as June Knight, Mitzi Mayfair, and Vilma Ebsen, he'd "managed to hold up his end of the fan mail." Yet already most of New York had his number: Kilgallen coyly wrote that Chuck "looks gay on a stage, and he is." *The New York World Telegram* headlined an article about him, "Glamour Girls' Partner Prefers to Dance Alone," explaining that he didn't like sharing the spotlight. In several instances his press toys with this ambiguity between headline and content: "Girls Are All Right in Certain Places, But Not in Others" top-lined a piece in the *Herald Tribune* in January 1938, with the body of the article going on to again recount Chuck's disinclination to share the spotlight. A subhead proclaiming he's "No Woman Hater" suggests, of course, that some might have felt he was.

By this time, Chuck had met and fallen in love with John Darrow, the same man who had been briefly a juvenile movie star in the late 1920s and then a regular at George Cukor's Sunday gatherings. Darrow had moved to New York after the flush of youth had faded and become a radio agent; he and Walters lived together in a fashionable duplex in Murray Hill. Lucius Beebe laid it on the line in a July 1938 "Stage Asides" column for the *Herald Tribune*. Describing their "bachelor" quarters as "finished with chocolate walls, plum-colored carpets, white woolly string rugs and zebra-striped sofa pillows," Beebe revealed that Walters and Darrow had dinner together "almost every evening," rejecting the "round of perpetual gayety [sic] . . . of the town's professional celebrities." It was a cozy domestic arrangement that in New York was greeted with little more than a raised eyebrow, if that; in Hollywood, Beebe would have been guilty of career homicide.

Walters was as independent-minded about his art as he was about his lifestyle. "I have watched stage dancing now for some few years," he said, "and have come to the conclusion that a clever synthesis of the various forms—tap, specialty, ballet—would prove a striking novelty. This may sound odd at first, but consider . . . a dancer versed in all of these forms could work out routines combining them all in a startling and pleasing manner. That is the essence of what I should like to do."

Two 1941 revues, "Let's Face it" and "Banjo Eyes," brought him considerable notice. Darrow, who had expanded his agency to Hollywood, landed him a four-week choreography gig at MGM on *DuBarry Was a Lady*. Walters hadn't planned on turning to movies, but that's what happened. "The studio liked the number and they gave me another," he remembered. "They liked that and gave me another number. And finally I did the whole picture. They liked the picture and gave me a contract, and I was there twenty-two years. From a four-week contract. Yes, I'm kind of proud of that."

Thus it was that Charles Walters became a member of the Freed unit. Little has been written about Walters as a director, overshadowed as he has been by Minnelli and Donen. Yet his films are lively, well crafted, and almost always entertaining; if his filmography has none of the superlative highs of his Freed peers—or his gay colleagues like Cukor, Whale, or Leisen—there are none of the lows either. "If the word 'nice' could be defined with any precision," opined *Film Culture,* "it would apply to most of his films."

In 1947, Walters was given the assignment to direct his first picture, *Good News,* after proclaiming to Freed that he'd directed and choreographed it in high school. Still, the soundstages of MGM were a bit more intimidating than the auditorium of Anaheim High, and Walters was nervous about the straight-dialogue scenes. "I begged Arthur to let me start with a number so that I could get acclimated," he said. "It was the only thing I was familiar with."

Despite his qualms, he brought *Good News* in on time and under budget. It ended up grossing nearly three million dollars for the studio. Wisely, Walters had concentrated his energies on the nonmusical parts of the film, learning the job of director, while turning over the picture's two big production numbers—the now-famous "Pass That Peace Pipe" and "The Varsity Drag"—to his old friend and mentor, Robert Alton. Alton fulfilled Walters' hopes: the numbers are energetic, creative, and beautifully staged. Together they crafted one of the top MGM musicals, assuring Walters' future as a director.

Alton had been choreographing for Freed since 1945, and made his own step up to full direction with *Pagan Love Song* in 1950, starring Esther Williams and filmed partly in Hawaii. Alton was even more a nervous wreck than Walters had been. "He was panic-stricken," Simone recalled. "He didn't do very well. When he went into a series of shots that was just unmakable, I stopped him. I explained to him it was impossible . . . Alton didn't know anything about filming. He was a dancer."

After seven months of shooting, Alton knew he'd never direct another picture. Although a financial success, *Pagan Love Song* was generally panned by the critics. The experience shouldn't detract from Alton's talent, however: he was a choreographer, after all, not a director, and his dance numbers are among the best in any Freed film. Still, his old protégé Walters had made the transition smoothly—in fact, after *Good News,* Walters was signed to direct *Easter Parade,* one of the quintessential Freed musicals. That picture's enormous success cemented Walters as a top director in the unit.

Rivalry with Minnelli was inevitable. Several times Walters was called in to help on a Minnelli film, most notably for the "The Night They Invented Champagne" number in *Gigi.* "Walters' thing was done because it had to be done," said Lela Simone. "I mean, they were in a panic. Absolute panic. And dragged Chuck in. And first of all, Chuck can't stand Minnelli, and I'm not so sure that Minnelli likes Chuck. But as I said, it was necessary that somebody save that one number."

What was the animosity between them? "Two types of people," Simone said. "It was nothing really tragic between [them, just] in not being of one cloth. That's what it was. Chuck usually made fun of what Vincente did, you know."

Walters, like Cukor, found overly circumspect types pretentious. Hosting gay friends at their Malibu home, Walters and Darrow were anything but disguised, and friends remember the ribaldry bouncing off the walls. Darrow, especially, was outrageous, often focusing his cutting humor on his partner. "Darrow always wanted to be the center of attention over Chuck," said Alan Cahan. "I'd have dinner with them, and Chuck would say something, and Darrow would say, 'Oh, what do you know, you faggot?' I don't know how Chuck put up with it."

Still, they were together some thirty years, although late in life there was a separation. In his sixties, Chuck met a younger man and brought him in to live with him; he referred to him as his "adopted son." But Darrow, despite the nastiness, would remain close to his heart; a few months after Darrow's death in 1980, Walters told an interviewer he'd lost his "dearest friend."

Walters was well liked in Hollywood. Joe Pasternak secured him to direct Judy Garland in *Summer Stock* in 1950, his first film outside the Freed unit. One critic has called it "a relaxed, discreet exhibition of both [Garland's] and Walters' total mastery of visual and vocal effect." Indeed, his early jitters had long ago been soothed, and throughout the rest of his career, Walters perfected an easy, naturalistic style. Critics commented on his particular gift for directing women, just as they had for Cukor, Leisen, Goulding, and Rapper: Leslie Caron in the enchanting *Lili* (1953), Grace Kelly in *High Society* (1956), Doris Day in *Please Don't Eat the Daisies* (1960, in which he also found small parts for Patsy Kelly and Margaret Lindsay), and Debbie Reynolds in *The Unsinkable Molly Brown* (1964). When Joan Crawford, not having made a musical in nearly twenty years, proved anxious during *Torch Song* (1953), he agreed to dance on-screen with her, playing a clumsy, bumbling nitwit: exactly the antithesis of Charles Walters, the most suave, graceful, and elegant of all gay directors.

QUEER MOVES: THE CHOREOGRAPHY OF JACK COLE

If Walters and Alton had been among the first of a new breed of choreographer, then Jack Cole took the art one bold leap further—to the sound of East Indian drums. "Jack changed musical theater," said Gwen Verdon, who worked both as his assistant and as one of his dancers. "He is responsible for what we call jazz today. He introduced ethnic dance. He influenced all the choreographers who followed, from Jerome Robbins, Michael Kidd, Bob Fosse down to Michael Bennett and Ron Field."

Cole made just one picture for the Freed unit: *Kismet* in 1955. He'd been set to choreograph for *Ziegfeld Follies* but had offended Freed when he'd started denouncing studio politics at Metro, griping about all the "queen bees" like Cedric Gibbons and Roger Edens. Cole was never one to mince words or suffer fools gladly. "He was an absolute dictator," said Lela Simone. "'Either do it the way I think it should be done or don't do it all.'"

"If you were willing to work like an animal, he wasn't difficult," Verdon said. "He could get very angry. He hated when things went wrong." For their legendary fistfight, however, she blamed herself. "When I told him I was leaving the show ['Can-Can'], he said something that I felt crossed a line, so I took a punch at him. He shoved me. But I threw a punch at him first."

Jack Cole did not fit easily into the Hollywood studio structure. He was more at home staging numbers on Broadway or in nightclubs, where his word was law. "He didn't like Hollywood," said Verdon, "but that's where he could make his money, where he could fill his coffers, as he used to say." Off the lot, he found the climate more to his liking, living in a fabulous mansion on Kew Drive in Los Angeles with his lover, David Gray, where they hosted "very naughty and very gay" poolside parties, according to Miles White. "I have this image in my mind," said White, "of David Gray up on the diving board, getting ready to jump off, and he's wearing high heels."

Early on, Cole had married and had a son, but like Minnelli, he tried to pretend his early life had never happened—except that Minnelli was trying to forget the *gay* part and Cole the *straight*. "Jack never tried to hide the fact that he was gay," said Verdon. "Oh, no, never. There would have been no reason to. Only his mother had no idea. I remember once, she was visiting just before we all went onstage, and Jack was in his costume, with all his jewels, and she looked at him, very innocently, and said, 'You look like something right out of a storybook. You look like a real fairy!' Of course, we all laughed so hard at that, especially Jack, but his mother didn't realize what she had said."

By the early 1950s Cole had become the most influential of the new generation of dance directors, and nowhere is the gayness of choreography more explicit. In New York, he slunk across the stage in his trademark pure-gold mesh pants and bejeweled Indian armbands, gyrating and con-torting in traditional Hindu dance to modern American jazz. This combi-nation of the ancient and the new created a stir, but not as much as his rapid-fire striptease down to a small pair of shorts, from which he pulled a bouquet of flowers and tossed them into the audience. His eyebrows were tweezed and drawn upward, his lashes coated with spiky mascara. Combined with a sharp nose and angular face, he had the look of an erotic cat.

Hollywood, he complained, was afraid of too much stylization in dance. Working on *The Merry Widow* (1952), he "tried to capture the soft, gay atmosphere of another century," but was stymied when the studio insisted on bright lights for all the dance numbers. "I begged for pink color filters, for shadows," he said. "Shadows on Lana Turner? They thought I was insane!"

He found ways to get what he wanted. There are few moments as simple and erotic as Rita Hayworth removing her gloves in her sinewy rendition of "Put the Blame on Mame" in *Gilda*. "Provocative, if not downright *hot*," said *Motion Picture Herald*. In *Kismet*, his one Freed film, directed by Minnelli, critic Arthur Knight said Cole's "energetic, angular, pseudo-Oriental routines possess a wit and urbane sureness, a cleanness and precision visible nowhere else in this handsome, heavy and stupendously dull production."

On the stage, Cole was famous for employing barely clothed athletic male dancers, and it's a penchant he followed in his films as well. Like Mitchell Leisen, he was a rare studio-era artist to consciously celebrate, even exploit, the aesthetics of the male body. In *The I Don't Care Girl*, slinky cat men in black tights steal much of the erotic impact from Mitzi Gaynor's entrance. At least one of the male dancers in that film, Marc Wilder (he catches Mitzi after a back somersault), was gay; he appeared in a number of Cole's shows and also in several films (*Meet Me in St. Louis, Can-Can*.) Presumably, he was far from being the only one.

For gay audiences, the classic Cole number remains "Is There Anyone Here For Love?" featuring Jane Russell and a gymnasium full of bodybuilders in *Gentlemen Prefer Blondes* (1953). Cole didn't so much teach the bodybuilders to dance as coordinate their already-established exercise routines to music. The resulting images could have come straight out of the then-popular gay-subculture magazine *Physique Pictorial*, with muscle men posing, stretching, and kicking; every now and then a gymnast leaps through the frame. It is male-only space, with the women secured in a roped-off area. Russell is the lone intruder, and the men pay no attention to her as she looks in vain for love. At one point—in a scene that would never have passed the more vigilant censors of the 1930s and early 1940s— the bodybuilders bend over and begin pumping their buttocks up and down in rhythm, an outrageous simulation of gay sex. Knowing a gay man choreographed this routine—and an overt gay man *notorious* for challenging convention—makes seeing it in *The Celluloid Closet* that much more relevant.

Cole's other numbers in *Gentlemen Prefer Blondes* push the envelope as well. Marilyn Monroe's "Diamonds Are a Girl's Best Friend" is set up like an orgy, with a vivid red background and women forming a human chandelier. Monroe slaps the faces of the male dancers with a black fan, saying "no, no, no," but her body language is saying "yes." When she grabs the diamonds she is orgasmic, breathing "Tiffany's" and "Cartier" as if in post-climactic bliss.

Cole was close with Monroe, who came to rely on him not only as dance director but as personal guru. Anxious about the musical numbers in *There's No Business Like Show Business,* she requested that Cole handle her solos instead of Robert Alton, the film's official choreographer. While critics panned her "Heat Wave" number as vulgar, it's appropriately so, since we're made to understand Ethel Merman's outrage over Monroe's character. And once again, Cole has near-naked muscle men surrounding her, with lots of drums and grinding of hips.

Monroe became increasingly dependent on him, insisting on Cole's input even when he wasn't credited (*Some Like It Hot*) and conferring with him more frequently than with director George Cukor on *Let's Make Love*. With Cole, Monroe felt a rare sense of confidence, something few of her directors could inspire. There was no sexual tension, and besides, Cole had no loyalty to the studios in the way her directors might: he loathed them and all they stood for, and so could afford to be fully present and attentive to Monroe's insecurities.

"He understood how to give her things to do which could work and were right for her screen personality," said fellow choreographer Donald Saddler. "She never really danced on the screen. But what she did, she did in her way better than anyone else could have done it. Jack Cole preserved that 'it' quality she had."

Jack Cole offered one of the most visible gay presences in Hollywood and created some of the most overt gay images on the screen since the days before the Code. He stands as both a singular artist and as a symbol of that brief period after the war when Hollywood once again took a chance on brilliance, originality, and nonconformity.

PINKOS, COMMIES, QUEERS

HOLLYWOOD'S GAYS AND THE COLD-WAR INQUISITIONS

1945-1960

t was the set decorators who started it: the most unlikely group of social agitators one might imagine. "Here we were, with our hair messed and practically in housecoats," remembered Elliot Morgan. "They'd wake us up in the middle of the night to go walk the picket lines. I'd say to Grace Moore [Henry Grace], 'What have you gotten us into?'"

The motion-picture strikes of 1945 fundamentally changed the industry, and not only in terms of labor relations. They also led directly to the House Un-American Activities Committee's investigations of Hollywood and the swing of the pendulum back to the right. The gay connection to the strikes, never before documented, is both fascinating and illuminating, given the prevailing and blatant homophobia that would descend over Hollywood during the 1950s.

For many, sexual perversion and political subversion became interchangeable. The Right linked homosexuality with sedition, equating it with moral weakness and conflating it with Communism. For the first time, gayness was named: it became an articulated bogeyman rather than the vague, unnamed suspicion it had been in the past. That gays were part of the driving force behind the labor insurrection that ignited the ideological wars could not have gone unnoticed, and likely helped crystallize the connection between "queers" and "pinkos" to many observers.

It had begun innocently enough. By 1940 Henry Grace was fed up with the lack of recognition for the industry's set decorators. Not represented by any of the Hollywood unions, the decorators' lot depended upon the whims of producers and art directors. Grace helped found the Society of Motion Picture Interior Decorators (SMPID), with himself as president, and in May 1940 the guild kicked off a national campaign to bring their case directly to the public. "The SMPID has long felt that its profession has been slighted and its importance minimized, both within and without the industry," noted *The Hollywood Reporter.* "Negotiations for a new agreement, calling for an increase in wages, are, at the present time, stymied with the producers having turned down previous demands." A contract was finally hammered out in April 1942, dictating a pay rate of $130 a week for set decorators and $75 for their assistants (lead men). Decorators were also to be given screen credit, vacation time and sick leave, and a five-year contract.

Henry Grace would remain justifiably proud of those achievements for the remainder of his life. Grace is a singular figure in gay Hollywood: the rare activist, a political person in a largely apolitical culture. Coming from a strong Southern Democrat tradition explains part of his motivation, yet he became even further politicized after serving as a captain in the army during World War II. "It's interesting that Henry went back to union issues directly after coming home from the war," reflected his nephew Michael Grace. "He had just left the Pacific where he saw friends die and injured. Everyone loathed studio bosses who sat the war out and then put the screws on employees, many returning from the war, who wanted to organize a union."

Grace realized his work was not yet done. Decorators might have screen credit, but without official union representation, their contracts were often ignored. The International Alliance of Theatrical Stage Employees (IATSE) had attempted to include the decorators in a new Local 44 that also covered carpenters and painters. But Henry Grace and the board of the SMPID wanted no part of that: the IATSE was then riddled with corruption and mob control under the leadership of Willie Bioff and George Browne.

"Grace knew about the corruption, and he wanted to keep things clean," Elliot Morgan remembered. Instead, Grace approached Herbert Sorrell, who had built up an anti-IATSE coalition of nine unions called the Conference of Studio Unions (CSU). Like the IATSE, the ten-thousand-member CSU was affiliated with the American Federation of Labor, but was, in the words of Otto Friedrich, "everything that IATSE was not: militant, leftist, and honest." Sorrell was a former boxer who liked to call himself "just a dumb painter," but in fact he was an intelligent socialist with grand dreams of challenging American capitalism. He represented a threat both to the IATSE's hegemony over Hollywood workers *and* to the studio producers, who widely regarded him as a Communist.

That Henry Grace and the set decorators' guild should fraternize with such a man was prejudicial in the minds of many: Hal Gausman recalled that decorators were often jeered on the set as "Commies" and "pinkos." No matter: guild membership voted to affiliate with Local 1421 of Sorrell's painters' union, an organization that also covered designers, illustrators, and model-builders. It was left to Sorrell to then call for new contracts to cover the seventy-seven decorators and lead men working in the industry—a call the IATSE immediately labeled invalid, claiming only *they* had the right to represent the decorators. The studios, secretly delighted by this internecine labor war, simply shrugged and said they were powerless to do anything, trapped between two rival unions. Both sides, despite labor's wartime no-strike pledge, threatened walkouts, though it was the IATSE's promise to strike their projectionists all across the country that most unnerved the industry. "As far as the producers were concerned," wrote historian Nancy Lynn Schwartz, "they had their choice of a bunch of unhappy communist set decorators or dark screens."

On March 11, 1945, a rally of some two thousand cheering unionists was held at Hollywood Legion Stadium in support of the decorators. Frank Drdlik, the rough-and-tumble president of the painters' union, spoke for the decorators in asking for the support of all labor in the anticipated strike. Edward Mussa, a lead man at MGM and business representative for Local 1421, declared, "This is not a strike against the motion picture industry. We believe that it is a strike of the motion picture industry against the government of the United States!"

The next day Sorrell called the strike to start at 6 o'clock in the morning. Picket lines were thrown around all the major studios. The set decorators and their lead men were joined by the painters, film technicians, machinists, and carpenters, as well as by the Hollywood local of the International Brotherhood of Electrical Workers, a member of the CSU. Without the electricians to set their generators, Fox and RKO couldn't operate. Universal and Warner Bros. called off all shooting because too few workers showed up. MGM managed some limited operations, but there was no one in the famed property department to haul out any props.

In a matter of days, the strike grew, with sympathetic unions walking out in support of the decorators. When forty property men walked out at Warner Bros., refusing to take over the carpenters' jobs, they were met with a thunderous ovation from the picket line. At MGM, unit art director

George Gibson walked off the job, writing a letter stating that the current labor dispute made it impossible for him to fulfill his duties.

At first, the atmosphere on the picket lines was peaceful and upbeat. "Save for a few clashes between individuals," the *Nation* reported, "there has been no violence; the picket lines have been gay and good-humored, pretty girls in the white-collar unions marching with young men from the crafts."

Henry Grace rallied his fellow decorators. The sense of camaraderie that arose in the initial weeks of the strike was apparent to everyone; what remained unspoken was the surprise and gratitude felt by many gay strikers. Since the strike had been called on account of a group of workers who were widely perceived as gay, it was inevitable that many would see the action as solidarity among labor transcending even the seemingly insurmountable divide of sexual orientation.

Of course, as the *Nation* pointed out, what was at stake was a crucial issue: "the right of employees to belong to unions of their own choice." Yet the decorators seemed to inspire extraordinary loyalty from other unions, and much of that can be credited to Henry Grace, who forged a wide and diverse set of friendships throughout the industry. Grace had charisma to spare: while he could be disarmingly outrageous with his gay colleagues, he could also be gracious and masculine enough to win friends among his straight peers. (That he bore an uncanny resemblance to Dwight Eisenhower could only have helped.) "He might have been campy with other gays," recalled his nephew Michael Grace, "but I believe he kept that side separate from a lot of his social life. He was a very political man."

His politics achieved results. As a result of Grace's encouragement, even people who could never imagine themselves on a picket line took up their positions in front of the studio by day and outside local theaters at night.

"We were all out there," Elliot Morgan recalled. "Everybody seemed to support it in the beginning. Who knew it would last so long?"

Production was "slowed to a walk" all that spring, with interior decorators, painters, and carpenters being imported from New York and Florida. Striking employees were officially dismissed by the major film studios after three weeks' absence; on April 18, *Variety* reported just twenty-five pictures in production.

Support for the strike began to wane after the first few weeks, however. A number of unions—story analysts, publicists, and office employees—voted for their members to return to work. When in July *The Peoples' Daily World* reversed position to support the strike— "It is obvious the strike must be supported and must be won"—it appeared to some as if the CSU and the decorators were merely agents of Stalin. The socialist writer Salka Viertel recalled a discussion with studio secretaries who had been sympathetic to the strikers but later turned against them, considering them "just a bunch of Communists that a decent person had to be against." Even among the decorators, there's evidence of a split: when the National Labor Relations Board finally ruled that the CSU had jurisdiction over the decorators, it was based on a razor-thin victory (three votes) by Local 1421 supporters. Almost half had cast their ballots to align with the IATSE.

Although the initial labor dispute had been led by Henry Grace, the close vote suggests there was no unanimity among the gay decorators in their feelings about the strike. It's also significant to note the only decorators mentioned in the press by name were heterosexual lead men like Mussa. The absence of the names of actual set decorators suggests that once hostilities began, men like Henry Grace stepped back from leadership positions. To be sure, since the majority of the actual decorators was gay, there may have been some reluctance to draw attention to themselves, especially with the increasing association between the strike and communism. Yet one gay man, costume designer Miles White, chose to take a quite public stand, refusing to cross the picket line even though his union wasn't striking, losing his job with Samuel Goldwyn in the process.

White was an exception. Even before the strike, the officers of the Society of Motion Picture Interior Decorators were mostly heterosexual, with Grace (as president) and Howard Bristol (as a member of the board) the only gays in the mix. Indeed, the agitators during the strike described as "decorators" were in fact all straight lead men, like the group that beat up a grip on March 26 outside the front gates at Columbia. The violence that erupted was beyond anything Grace and his colleagues had anticipated when they first called for reform. In October, in response to the studios' implacability in the face of the NLRB ruling, Sorrell targeted Warner Bros. for a massive demonstration, a day remembered as "Bloody Friday." A riot broke out and several people were brutally beaten. The violence continued for nearly a week.

"That wasn't anything we wanted," Elliot Morgan said. "It had gone too far. I can say we [gays] were not a part of that. That was between painters and the strike-breakers."

The names of those injured and arrested in the October riots do not include any known homosexuals, but rather, once again, heterosexual "decorators" (lead men) like Joseph Daniels and Macklyn Hall. Indeed, some gay decorators were actively subverting the strike. That old veteran George James Hopkins, who had been "appalled when told I had to walk a picket line," conspired with Warner Bros. to sneak back in "under cover of night" to scab for striking decorators.

It was not in the nature of most of Hollywood's gays to be overtly political, and certainly not politically Left. The experience of the strike of 1945 no doubt only further convinced them of the supposed wisdom of complicity with the power structure. Although the strike finally ended by late October, few of the larger ideological and jurisdictional issues that had arisen between the IATSE and the CSU were settled. A series of new strikes would break out in 1946 before Sorrell and his leftist coalition were finally crushed by an alliance between the studios and the IATSE. (Significantly, of the MGM set decorators, only the lone heterosexual, Hugh Hunt, walked out during this second round of strikes, according to studio records.)

Meanwhile, the lot of the decorators had barely improved. With jurisdiction still up in the air, they were signed to one-year contracts in April 1946, only to have the contracts terminated the following January. The decorators were then employed on a week-to-week basis until new representatives under the IATSE could negotiate replacement contracts.

Because of the strike, they would also now face a lingering perception of sedition. As actress Karen Morley observed, "What the strike really managed to do was make it clear who was who." In differing conflations, the industry saw the decorators as both gay *and* Communists; *ergo,* gays were Communists. While admittedly this accounts for only part of the reason homosexuality became associated with subversion in Hollywood during the 1950s, it cannot be discounted as an early influence. Certainly it was a lesson not lost on the industry's gays: not for another forty years would they again put themselves on the political front lines in Hollywood.

HUAC AND THE STATE DEPARTMENT: A CLIMATE OF FEAR

The strike also had the direct result of bringing about HUAC, which cast its own long shadow over gay Hollywood. In the fall of 1947, prompted by the political leanings of the strike leaders as well as a long-simmering suspicion of Hollywood leftists, the House Committee on Un-American Activities (incorrectly, and some said prejudicially, acronymed HUAC) sent out subpoenas to both friendly and unfriendly witnesses to appear at hearings in Washington. Among the first group, Jack Warner was glad to name names and be rid of any "termites"—Communists or Communist sympathizers—at his studio. Walt Disney claimed the Communists had tried to seize control of the cartoonists' guild. The outrageous Lela Rogers, Ginger's mother, said her daughter had refused the Commies' demand in *Tender Comrade* that she utter the line "Share and share alike—that's democracy."

With the end of World War II and the beginning of the Cold War with the Soviet Union, the hunt was on to root out any and all subversives who would destroy the American way of life. In the beginning, many in Hollywood failed to take HUAC seriously. Even when the famous "Hollywood

Ten"—a defiant group of screenwriters and directors charged with having ties to the Communist Party—were summoned before the panel, many failed to see the long-term dangers. "The committee members seemed only stupid," said the screenwriter Walter Bernstein. "I understood their bigotry but not their power. Who, really, could be on their side?"

Within a few years, however, Bernstein would be blacklisted and out of work; a number of the Hollywood Ten would be in jail. It would have been hard to imagine such an outcome in the fall of 1947, with democracy and freedom seeming to have triumphed over fascism. On the screen, issues of social justice and tolerance were finally being explored; in the nightclubs gay men and lesbians were enjoying newfound visibility and community. Yet in truth the old competing forces in Hollywood were once more battling for supremacy. Hollywood's traditionalists were outraged by the social changes that had encouraged the new filmmaking and permitted the greater gay expression. The progressives, meanwhile, were convinced that the war was over and that they had won.

The progressives were wrong. There was a reaction going on—not only in Hollywood, but all across the country—a backlash against the left-wing intelligensia that had held power throughout the long Roosevelt and Truman years. Gunning for subversives would become common sport for the next ten years, and the hunt ultimately mattered more than the kill. "The real function of the Great Inquisition of the 1950s," wrote historian Richard Hofstadter, "was not anything so simply rational as to turn up spies or prevent espionage, but to discharge resentments and frustrations, to punish, to satisfy enmities whose roots lay elsewhere than in the Communist issue itself. . . . Communism was not the target but the weapon."

Whereas in the Twenties reformers had criticized Hollywood for a lack of moral and social conformity, now it was the charge of political subversion that brought out the critics. Yet ultimately it was the same instinct: to protect the status quo, to safeguard traditional values, to quell new ideas and stifle social change. "What actors didn't realize at that period," observed the actor Will Geer, himself blacklisted, "[was that] we were simply window-dressing for a major drive on the part of Congressmen and people in power who wanted to stop all sorts of thinking on many scores. They were really after the scientists, the teachers, and others."

And, once again, gender was a core area of conflict. With the war having exposed the constructs of "male" and "female" in sharp relief, the Right mounted a rabid defense of traditional definitions. What the writer Robert Corber has called "the post-war crisis of masculinity" led to a paradigm of stark male-female behavior in the 1950s that emphasized domestic commitment and capitalist dedication. Life as a consumer-driven, breadwinning suburban husband and father replaced the independent entrepreneur as the American male ideal—a model permanently stamped on the psyche of a generation by such newly popular television programs as "Father Knows Best," "The Adventures of Ozzie & Harriet," "Make Room for Daddy" and "Leave It to Beaver."

Homosexuality, as its representations in film noir had shown, presented a direct and uncompromising alternative to this paradigm. It wasn't the only alternative, of course: the rise of the "swinger" lifestyle, popularized with the debut of *Playboy* in 1953, and the beat culture—not to mention motorcycle gangs and rock and roll—were all part of "the contested terrain" of masculinity during the 1950s. The choices were fewer for women, who could either be happy homemakers or dried-up old maids—or the evil, twisted dykes of *Caged*.

In the conservative backlash to the progressive forces unleashed by the war, homosexuality, like Communism, became as much weapon as target. As Corber argued, "The politicization of homosexuality was crucial to the consolidation of the Cold War consensus." The queers needed to be rooted out if the American idea of manhood—the underpinning on which postwar society was based—was to be maintained. In the infamous homosexual purge of the State Department, the "security risk" charge was merely justification to ferret out "degenerates." Many saw it as only the beginning: eradication of queers from all walks of life was the next logical step.

It was a situation that couldn't have gone unnoticed in Hollywood. Hedda Hopper's columns were filled with tirades juxtaposing the twin dangers of "moral degeneracy" and "political subversion." In fact, within a few years, the link between homosexuality and political sedition would be specifically spelled out by the *Los Angeles Mirror*. Columnist Paul Coates revealed that the Mattachine Society, the first-in-the-nation gay-rights group cofounded by Harry Hay in Los Angeles in 1950, had used a lawyer who had also represented unfriendly witnesses for HUAC. Coates warned that Mattachine heralded a day when homosexuals might band together and "swing tremendous political power," vulnerable to "a well-trained subversive [who] could move in and forge that power into a dangerous political weapon." A year later, the scandal magazine *Confidential* told America to be "on guard," explaining that the gays were organizing and they had links to the Commies. "Don't sell the twisted twerps short!" the magazine warned.

By 1950, there was no longer any denying of what was happening. The Hollywood Ten had gone to jail and the blacklist had been established: even after they finished their year in prison, few of the Ten could find work. Desperate to reclaim his career, Edward Dmytryk, the director of *Crossfire*, would agree to name names in a new round of hearings set for the following year. This was not a passing fad: the political climate had shifted even further to the right than in the immediate post-Code years.

Hollywood gays couldn't have escaped the impact of the escalating gay-baiting out of Washington. In April 1950, Republican National Chairman Guy George Gabrielson charged that "sexual perverts who have infiltrated our government in recent years [were] perhaps as dangerous as the actual Communists." In the *New York Daily News,* John O'Donnell wrote that the State Department was "dominated by an all-powerful, super-secret inner circle of highly educated, socially highly-placed sexual misfits, all easy to blackmail, all susceptible to blandishments by homosexuals in foreign nations." Republicans made an issue of it during the campaign that fall, claiming there were "3,500 deviates" in the executive branch and charging the Truman Administration with "harboring sexual perverts." Republican Senator Everett Dirksen of Illinois promised if reelected he'd kick out all "the lavender lads" from the State Department.

To counter these charges, the State Department would claim that in the years since the end of the war, it had uncovered and fired ninety-one homosexuals in its midst. But the charges only intensified, especially with the publication of *Washington Confidential,* a scandal-ridden so-called "exposé" of government corruption. Included was a chapter on "the twilight sex," the great "lavender menace" that was easy prey for Russian homosexual spies. Republican Senator Kenneth Wherry of Nebraska made a renewed call for action: "There should be no people of that type working in any position in the government." Wherry asserted that Hitler had had a list of homosexuals worldwide, a list that had now fallen into the hands of Stalin. "You can't separate homosexuals from subversives," Wherry insisted. "Mind you, I don't say every homosexual is a subversive, and I don't say every subversive is a homosexual. But a man of low morality is a menace in the government, whatever he is, and they are all tied up together."

John Loughery has written: "Three decades of thought about Reds and three decades of thought about sexual dissidents had at last dovetailed. . . . Both groups were antifamily, antireligious, scornful of bourgeois morality, devious, manipulative, cynical, loyal only to one another and their cause, abhorrent to God, eager to convert the young and remake America." It was right there on the screen in *My Son John* (1951), in which Helen Hayes discovers that her son (Robert Walker) is a Communist—or gay. Certainly he reads queer as much as Red.

At the same time the HUAC hearings were weeding out political undesirables in Hollywood, the State Department publicly dismissed 425 employees due to "homosexual proclivities." The State Department purge sent chills through gay Hollywood. "Of course, it was frightening," said Don

Bachardy. "It seemed no one was safe." His lover, Christopher Isherwood, received a visit from the FBI, although nothing came of it.

Harry Hay recalled, "I knew gays in the motion-picture industry who thought they'd be next. Look at what was happening at the State Department. Why wouldn't they think it?"

The connection was clear and ominous, and for some in the film colony, it was highly personal—for the State Department inquisition had ramifications for one of their own.

THE GAY GENERAL: FRANK McCARTHY

"It's hilarious when you think about it," said Gavin Lambert about Frank McCarthy. "All the trouble he went through to pretend. So much work. It must have been very tiring."

When Lambert arrived as a young writer on the Fox lot in 1956, Frank McCarthy was a *presence*. He had achieved the rank of colonel during his wartime service in the army; within months of Lambert's arrival, McCarthy would be named a brigadier general in the army reserves. He wasn't a big man—no more than five-ten and always slender—but he carried himself with all the precision of a military officer: even in civilian clothes, people swore they could see medals gleaming against his chest.

He was personal friends with Presidents Truman and Eisenhower and had been right-hand man to General George C. Marshall. He had the respect of Fox president Darryl Zanuck and the ear of Eric Johnston, Will Hays' successor at the MPPDA (now rechristened the Motion Picture Association of America, or MPAA). No question about it: Frank McCarthy was *important*. He was influential. He was powerful. And, added Lambert, "He was an uptight closet queen."

Indeed, Frank McCarthy's story has never been fully told, and it's worth going into here for its significance to not only the story of gays in Hollywood but also to the broader experience of homosexuals during the Cold War. For in his pre-movie career, McCarthy had risen high in the army and the State Department, so high he was nearly cabinet level. Then, just as the political tides changed after the war, he beat a hasty retreat to Hollywood under somewhat mysterious circumstances. But he'd discover that his new home was as much in the grip of paranoia as the Washington he'd fled.

"I used to watch him," Lambert recalled, "he and his lover, Rupert Allan, who was a publicist and really very nice, an adorable man. They would always arrive separately at parties with separate girlfriends, and they'd act surprised to see each other. 'Oh, how are you?' and all that. It was hilarious because everyone knew what was going on. But that's the way things were."

Such was indeed the climate of the period—although people like Roger Edens and Harriet Parsons, producers contemporary with McCarthy, managed somewhat greater degrees of personal authenticity. But discretion had always been a watchword for McCarthy, ever since his days as a young, ambitious, disciplined student at the Virginia Military Institute. From a comfortable middle-class Virginia family, Frank was born on June 8, 1912, and had grown up with black servants in an upscale neighborhood of Richmond. His father, for whom he was named, was a well-respected agent for the Home Life Insurance Company and a member of the exclusive Commonwealth Club. His mother was the former Lillian Binford, of an old and equally prominent Virginia clan.

When Frank McCarthy Sr. died in 1927, it made the front page of the local paper. Young Frank had just turned fifteen. It had been his father's dream that he attend the Virginia Military Institute in Lexington—"the West Point of the Confederacy," the younger Frank called it. Enrolling upon his high school graduation in 1929, he was as good a student as he was a son, eager to please his parents and make them proud. During his time as a Brother Rat (cadet) at VMI, Frank was a captain in the Corps of Cadets, editor of the yearbook, and a reporter for the school newspaper. Upon graduation in 1933, he was awarded the Cincinnati Medal, given to the cadet who had most distinguished himself by efficiency of service and excellence of character. He was also commissioned as a captain in the army reserves.

Unlike most of the others in this account, Frank McCarthy hadn't given in to the lure of wanderlust; he'd stuck with tradition, to the course his family had laid down for him. To an outside observer, he'd been very successful: both his civilian and military superiors looked upon him with great admiration and expectation. But Frank McCarthy had grown tired of Virginia and classrooms and military uniforms. After a short period teaching at VMI, he went to work as a police reporter for the *Richmond News-Leader*. But what he really wanted to do was go to Broadway.

He'd watched with some envy as his former fellow cadets, Fred Finklehoffe and John Monks, had gone on to theatrical success with their play "Brother Rat," based on their experiences at VMI. Through them, Frank managed to get hired as a press agent for producer George Abbott. "I looked very young then," he called, " and I can testify that most press agents didn't look a bit like me." When "Brother Rat" was made into a movie by Warner Bros. in 1938, McCarthy was sent out to Hollywood to serve as technical adviser. He stayed at the Hollywood Athletic Club with Eddie Albert, one of the stars of the film, and even did a cameo himself, showing Priscilla Lane how to use a saber.

"Bill Keighley [the director] was a great one for practical jokes," McCarthy remembered. "One day I went to the set and I couldn't believe what

I saw. The cadets had their hats on the back of their heads, their blouses were open, they were pitching pennies into Stonewall Jackson's cannon. Keighley said, 'Roll 'em,' the camera started rolling, and it lasted about twenty minutes before I realized it had been a joke."

There had been no such hijinks at the real VMI. "That experience sort of whetted my appetite for a movie career," he'd later admit. "I made a mental note to try to get back to it someday." But after working again for Abbott, on the road promoting the play "What a Life," McCarthy made the rather surprising decision to instead go back to school for a graduate degree. "I decided against the movies," he said. "I'm not sure why."

What pulled him back? His fellow publicists all agreed that he could have had a successful career in show business; in fact, in May 1939 he had been named Abbott's chief rep. But just a few weeks later, he abruptly resigned from Abbott's employ and returned to the South—the first of the mysterious about-turns in McCarthy's career.

Or maybe not so mysterious. War clouds had spread dark and thick over Europe, and with the invasion of Poland in September 1939 it was only a matter of time, most predicted, before the United States would get involved. Frank McCarthy was still in the army reserves; he had to be more aware than most of what was going on. He'd recall a former commandant of his telling him at the time, "Things are very serious here, and you're going to have to go to active duty soon." By enrolling in a graduate program at the University of Virginia, he was heeding his friend's advice "to get smart and come into the army now—with your degree, you have a good chance at promotion."

Better to come into the war as a grad student than as a Broadway press agent. He signed up for active duty in July 1940 with the intelligence division, studying reports received from Germany and disseminating them to officers. Whether he maneuvered it that way or not, he thus avoided combat duty. Although he'd later claim to have seen action in France, there is no record of it in his military files.

Fellow VMI graduate General George C. Marshall snatched him up as his secretary. They became close; perhaps not coincidentally, it was Marshall who in 1942 was instrumental in suspending the military's practice of court-martialing homosexuals, calling it a costly drain on time and manpower. In 1941 Marshall supported McCarthy's elevation to captain; less than a year later, with the onset of American involvement in the war, the young secretary was appointed major. By 1943 he was a colonel—the army's wunderkind, just thirty years old.

As Marshall's right-hand man, McCarthy traveled to all the major Allied conferences, from the Roosevelt-Churchill meeting at Casablanca to the final conference of the Big Three at Potsdam. When the war was over in 1945, he was awarded the Distinguished Service Medal, the army's highest award for achievement, for his efficiency and devotion to duty.

The best, however, was supposed to be still to come for Frank McCarthy. On August 21, 1945, President Truman announced his appointment as assistant secretary of state in charge of administration, where he would be entrusted with reorganizing (of all things) the State Department. The *New York Times,* noting McCarthy's "rapid ascension," reported that the recess appointment would be sent to the Senate for official confirmation the following month.

There was much hoopla over the appointment. McCarthy's young age and boyish good looks prompted a glowing profile in *The New York Times Magazine* in early September. "He is of modest stature," wrote Cabell Phillips, sounding like a fan-magazine scribe. "He is unmarried. He put away his schoolbooks for the last time but five years ago. He has the ruddy, gleaming cheek of youth and a shy and charming deference toward his elders." Interestingly, a new spin was given to his brief flirtation with Broadway and Hollywood: "Show business could not long hold the interest of an essentially serious young man such as Frank McCarthy."

Yet neither, apparently, could government. On October 8, just three weeks after Truman sent his name to the Senate for confirmation, McCarthy resigned "due to ill health." The president accepted his resignation "with regret." The bright and promising young secretary seemed to disappear from public view.

What had happened? Two years later, when his old mentor George C. Marshall was named secretary of state, McCarthy's name was again floated to the press as a possible appointee. To explain away his resignation in 1945, the "ill health" was described as "bursitis in his shoulder"—a painful condition, to be sure, but one most wouldn't consider grievous enough to forfeit a promising career. Much later, having apparently forgotten all about the bursitis, McCarthy offered a more candid explanation, telling an interviewer he'd been "miserable" at the State Department. "I didn't stay there very long because I really didn't like it. I'd been in official Washington for so long that I really wanted to get out."

But he *hadn't* been in official Washington long—just a matter of weeks, in fact. Long enough, however, to meet Rupert Allan, the young Oxford-educated Rhodes scholar working as a political affairs officer at the State Department. Friends recall this is where the longtime lovers first met, either during or after the war.

So why was he miserable? McCarthy and Allan were living in the midst of a gay renaissance in Washington, DC. Whether they partook of the freedom and merriment is unknown, but the testimony of countless other gay men depicts the nation's capital during World War II and immediately afterward as "the ideal place to be." One War Department employee told the historian John Loughery, "I made more new friends, had more sex, and thought less about the stigma of being queer between Pearl Harbor and V-J Day than at any time of my life."

There is no record that McCarthy's resignation from the State Department had anything to do with his homosexuality or his relationship with Allan. But one cannot ignore the homosexual purge that would happen at State just a few years later. Nor can we fail to consider what was already a growing reputation for the department. *Washington Confidential* reported in early 1951 that for several years "the gag around Washington [was] you had to speak with a British accent, wear a homburg hat, or have a queer quirk" if you wanted to get into State. Most knew about Undersecretary of State Sumner Welles, caught in a homosexual encounter with a porter on the funeral train to bury House Speaker William Bankhead, Tallulah's father. Roosevelt hushed up the scandal, but under pressure from FBI director J. Edgar Hoover, Welles was eventually forced to resign.

Even more sensational had been the case of Senator David I. Walsh, a Democrat from Massachusetts and Chairman of the Naval Affairs Committee, arrested in May 1942 at a male brothel in Brooklyn. Although charges were eventually dropped, with the brothel manager telling reporters he had misidentified Walsh, a precedent had been set. "For the first time," John Loughery wrote, "the wayward sexual practices of a bachelor member of Congress had been the focus of widespread discussion." McCarthy could not have been blind to this lesson.

The political climate of persecution that had descended over Washington, along with an ever-present fear of discovery, could well explain McCarthy's "misery" in the nation's capital. But there was clearly more to the problem with his nomination process than even that. According to Senate records, the Foreign Relations Committee had reported his name favorably to the full Senate on September 19; the clerk had even set the date for a final vote. But McCarthy would resign a week before that vote was to be held. The record contains no controversy about McCarthy, but does reveal a problem with his *fellow* nominee, Spruille Braden. Braden's nomination was held for three weeks, opposed by none other than the fiercely partisan Kenneth Wherry, who thought Braden too liberal. Wherry's name in the record raises a lavender flag: in just a few years' time, he would be the one to lead the charge against homosexuals in the State Department. It raises the very real possibility that McCarthy may have taken the fall in a backroom deal that traded him for Braden.

Wherry and others likely knew McCarthy was gay: he was investigated by the FBI that summer of 1945. His file starts with an apparently benign letter of congratulations from J. Edgar Hoover upon McCarthy's appointment to State. But at the same time, the FBI director was having a dossier prepared on the golden-boy appointee. Dated August 23, 1945, it quoted an army official as saying he "doubted if Colonel McCarthy had sufficient background for the position which he is presently assuming," but that ultimately he felt he'd live up to the job. Beyond that, the report is positive, with only an ominous handwritten note at the bottom giving pause: "Additional background information being obtained."

That "additional background" is not found in McCarthy's file; in fact, nothing pertaining to his subsequent resignation is included. Odd, given Hoover's obsessive stockpiling. It's likely that evidence was uncovered on McCarthy's homosexuality and either never placed in his file—he did, after all, have friends in high places—or removed later when he became an important contact for the government in Hollywood. But surely it was known to Wherry and the Republicans at the time of his nomination. It seems clear that an ultimatum was made to the Truman Administration: if they wanted Braden, they'd have to drop the queer. If David Walsh's private life had made the paper, what might be written about McCarthy?

Braden was confirmed; Wherry even voted for him, but went on record as saying he still disagreed with his politics. McCarthy, meanwhile, his bursitis apparently getting the best of him, moved to California. The official purge of homosexuals from the State Department would not begin for another few years, but Frank McCarthy may have been one of its first victims.

Trading Washington for Hollywood enabled McCarthy to secure the kind of power and influence he'd lost at the State Department. Having sacrificed him on the altar of politics, Democratic politicians and military leaders owed a debt to McCarthy, and he didn't take long to cash in his chips. Eric Johnston at the MPAA was persuaded to create a position expressly for him, as a diplomat, representing the film industry to both government and corporate America. Rupert Allan, too, was hired, and in 1948 both Allan and McCarthy were sent to Paris to help reinvigorate European markets for American films. Few homosexuals of the period could have imagined a cozier or more privileged assignment.

McCarthy did indeed have impressive connections. He'd attend President Eisenhower's inauguration as personal guest of Ike and Mamie. He even became friendly through his duties at MPAA with Hoover. When he was investigated again by the FBI in August 1951, as part of his work with the Voice of America, it was during the height of the State Department purges; yet there is again no mention of homosexuality in the report, and even his resignation from State is barely referenced. Frank McCarthy had become too useful to both Washington and Hollywood for anyone to want to threaten his position.

As much as he might have loved Paris, however, Frank remained the starstruck kid who'd so briefly tasted showbiz as George Abbott's press agent. He convinced Darryl Zanuck, for whom he had helped secure wartime assignments during the movie mogul's tour of duty, to create a position for him. Once more, extraordinary access and privilege: McCarthy arrived on the Fox lot with little more to do than soak up the mechanics of moviemaking and collect his paycheck. Eventually he produced two pictures at Fox, the war dramas *Decision Before Dawn* (1951) and *Sailor of the King* (1953), and in 1962 served as military adviser on *The Longest Day* (in which MGM set decorator Henry Grace was cast as Eisenhower, given his striking resemblance to the general).

McCarthy found his greatest influence, however, in the newly formed position of studio public relations director. As liaison with the MPAA, he was the in-house censor who watchdogged films before they were passed on for Production Code approval. "When Brigadier General Frank McCarthy was serving in military intelligence during World War II," wrote columnist Lee Belser, "he never dreamed he'd one day be using that training to ferret out highly questionable situations in motion picture scripts. When a star's neckline is daringly low [or] when a line of dialogue is overly suggestive, it's McCarthy who gets the SOS to straighten out the situation."

Today the irony is apparent: a gay man—at a time when gay men were being "ferreted" out of government and looked upon with suspicion in Hollywood—was in charge of policing the morals of Fox films. And it may have been apparent then, too: McCarthy recalled for Belser that his position had become "a standing joke around the lot. . . . They 'stage' love scenes for me now. One day I walked on the set of *From the Terrace* and found Paul Newman and Joanne Woodward in a clinch so hot it sizzled the paper off the walls. I gasped and then everybody cracked up. They had heard I was on the way over!"

In *Let's Make Love,* he objected to love scenes between Yves Montand and Marilyn Monroe, telling director George Cukor there was no use shooting them, as the MPAA would certainly insist on cuts. Cukor held out (friends recall Cukor, predictably, didn't care for McCarthy, although they were cordial), and so Geoffrey Shurlock from the MPAA came out personally. He sided, of course, with McCarthy. "There were lots of that type of incident where we argued with the censor," McCarthy said. "Sometimes we won, sometimes we didn't."

In his role as moral guardian, McCarthy won the favor of Hedda Hopper, and he often escorted her to industry functions. But many of the town's gays, less rigidly circumspect than he, viewed McCarthy with some distrust—and he them. "Frank was rather cool to me at first," Gavin Lambert recalled. "I think because he felt if he got friendly with me, since people knew I was gay, they'd think something was up. But when he discovered that I had friends he felt he should know, like Tennessee Williams, that changed."

Such discretion was followed even in his home on Seabright Place, high in the Hollywood hills. On the former tennis courts of the King Vidor estate, he and Rupert Allan actually built *two* structures, linked by a covered gallery lined with art by Toulouse-Lautrec. They shared a living room with a stunning view of Los Angeles and a courtyard complete with swimming pool, but their two separate kitchens and bedrooms gave at least the nominal appearance of living separately.

"It was typical that I got to know them separately and, as they lived in separate houses, was at first unaware of their relationship," recalled Gavin Lambert. "It was also typical that I learned about it from Rupert. He had come to terms with his sexuality and enjoyed letting down his guard with friends. Unlike McCarthy, who was conflicted and devious, and had no real friends."

"They tried so hard," said one man, whose lover worked with Allan. "They really did care about keeping up the appearance. I wonder why on some level, for everyone in the industry knew, and the public—well, they didn't care about producers or publicists. But it was just the way things were done then, even if it was very transparent."

Transparent indeed. When a reporter from the *Los Angeles Herald-Examiner* arrived to do a profile of the house, he found McCarthy listening to Broadway scores. "I listen systemically," McCarthy explained. "I started with the A's and here we are up to 'Wonderful Town.' When I finish the Broadway shows, I'll start the operas—with 'Aida,' of course."

Frank McCarthy enjoyed a life of privilege, a life many of his class often took for granted: access to the corridors of power during wartime that kept him largely free from danger; connections that enabled appointments, recommendations, and favors; the cooperation of superiors in both his careers that permitted him a lifestyle for which others were being persecuted. True to the pattern, the affluent middle-class achiever McCarthy lived a life rigidly contained, a life built on a model of discretion and circumspection—one that, as Lambert suggested, must have been both hilarious to observe and exhausting to live. He remains one of filmdom's most fascinating ironies, a gay man who served not only as Hollywood's censor but as its adviser and liaison on military affairs during the most oppressive period the industry ever knew. It simply points up again the hypocrisy of the era, as if further evidence is really needed. The persecution of homosexuals—indeed the entire atmosphere of inquisition during the Fifties—was never as much about anything as it was about power and influence and access and control.

GAYS AND THE BLACKLIST

From all sides, it was getting worse. In 1950, the Right began distribution of a booklet called *Red Channels,* purporting to list all those in the industry whose loyalty to the United States was questionable. It was, in effect, a list of Hollywood's liberals, anyone who had ever signed a petition, offered an opinion, or, in some cases, married someone who had. (Jean Porter was listed because she was Edward Dmytryk's wife.) Soon *Red Channels* was on every producer's desk. Those who dared speak out—people like Humphrey Bogart, Lauren Bacall, Gene Kelly, Danny Kaye, Marsha Hunt—were immediately pounced upon, with Hedda Hopper leading the charge. "[She] took it upon herself to badger all of us who had protested the hearings in Washington and to make *our* loyalty suspect," Hunt recalled. "It was appalling! The very people who had defended the industry were now being made suspect in the industry. It was an unbelievable turnabout." Although industry leaders denied there was a blacklist, any look at the careers of those tagged with the label "subversive" offers evidence to the contrary.

As with its capitulation under the strong arm of Production Code enforcement in 1934, Hollywood's surrender to the forces of reaction in the early 1950s was also market-driven. With the forced divestiture of their theater chains and the rise of television (see next chapter), the studios were faced with their biggest financial losses since the Depression. Between 1950 and 1953, three thousand theaters closed across the nation, and box-office revenues plummeted.

"The motion picture business was really running very, very scared," said director Michael Gordon, one of those blacklisted. "It was in the throes of a severe financial pinch, and the studio heads felt they were at the mercy of any kind of adverse publicity which could have a deleterious impact on their destiny."

In early 1951 the HUAC hearings resumed. Some witnesses called before the panel, like director Elia Kazan, named names and kept working; others, like actor Howard DaSilva, remained uncooperative and watched their careers disintegrate. By this time the mood in the nation was unbearably tense: the Korean War had broken out, the Alger Hiss spy case was in full swing, the Rosenbergs had been tried for nuclear espionage, and the State Department was being extermined of queers. A demagogic senator from Wisconsin, Joseph McCarthy, had risen to prominence in part with an attack on General George Marshall (mentor of that other McCarthy, Frank), charging him with being soft on Communism. Senator McCarthy claimed to possess a list of Communists in all walks of American life, and he bullied the Senate into holding hearings to flush them all out.

The fear was greatest for those outside the white, Christian, suburban, nuclear-family, organization-man model. Arthur Laurents recalled that of those who had explored Communism in 1930s, many were "Jews and blacks who felt understandably persecuted and who were looking for an alternative." The racism and anti-Semitism of both Hollywood's blacklist and the government's inquiries are obvious; just being black or Jewish was reason enough to be suspect. The number of Jews among those blacklisted speaks for itself, as does the particular intensity with which black actors Paul Robeson and Canada Lee were persecuted.

The suspicion of homosexuals fits this pattern, yet the situation is not exactly analogous. Certainly the purge at the State Department put many homosexuals on edge throughout the country; further fears were raised by Joseph McCarthy's hearings into army subversion in 1953, during which more allegations of homosexual security risks were made. Yet, in truth, among all the hundreds of Hollywood names given to HUAC as being Communists or Communist-sympathizers, virtually none are known to be gay. The set decorators who started the 1945 strikes were largely ignored, except for the lead-men agitators, who we have seen were largely straight.

Why the glaring omission of gays from Hollywood's blacklist? One reason, ironically, is the discrimination gays faced at the hands of the Communist Party itself. Unlike blacks and Jews, who were actively recruited to join in the 1930s, Party rules forbade homosexuality. "I knew a number of black and white men from the performing arts in the Communist Party who were gay," said Harry Hay, "but the Party didn't seem to suspect. I realized that since they weren't that noticeable, certain Party people saw the necessity of tolerating and covering for them."

No doubt, there *were* homosexual names on the blacklist, but it is only the more "overt" ones that we can identify, and overt gays weren't going to be members of the Communist Party. And not only because they weren't allowed, either. "I can't think of any homosexual who was involved in the Red Scare," said Don Bachardy. "Queerness and communism seemed instinctively incompatible. There was a squareness to Communism, many [gays] thought. It lacked color and excitement and fun."

Bachardy and others in the gay subculture may have seen gayness and Communism as "instinctively incompatible," but certainly that wasn't the conventional wisdom. Everywhere else the connection between deviance and subversion seemed obvious: the investigations at State and in the army, the allegations being made of homosexual subversion in the comic book and publishing industries, the increasing gay baiting of the scandal sheets. There must have been fear among Hollywood's gays that sooner or later, somehow or other, the witch-hunts would turn toward them. Already, the rumor that Broadway choreographer Jerome Robbins had named names under threat of homosexual blackmail had spread throughout the subculture. Said Harry Hay, "It was obvious McCarthy was setting up the pattern for a new scapegoat, and it was going to be us—gays."

That may be hyperbole, yet Robert Wheaton, who had worked at the State Department before returning to Los Angeles and Cukor's Sunday parties, said that no one was "ever really far away from it. . . . It was always there, all of what was going on [in Washington], somewhere in the back of your mind."

The one gay name that *does* stand out on the blacklist is that of actor Will Geer. A militant leftist and former lover of Harry Hay, Geer was not very well known in the largely apolitical gay subculture of Hollywood. Alan Cahan, who worked as a publicist on Geer's later television series, "The Waltons," said it was "the biggest shock" to learn after Geer's death that the actor had been gay. "It had never entered my mind," said Cahan. But in the 1930s, Geer moved within gay leftist worker circles, involved in labor causes with Hay. Subsequently he married a woman prominent in the Communist Party and had a family.

Still, even in his early press there's a hint of camp. Recalling his barnstorming days, Geer would tell one reporter that he'd played "the ingenue" in the company of Minnie Maddern Fiske until, "after a few children, I lost my figure." Later, in old age, he'd talk of enjoying drag queens and learning from Gay Lib, and spoke of his wife overlooking his more "radical eccentric qualities"—among which, recalled one neighboring gay couple, was occasionally crawling through their window and into bed with them.

Geer made a career playing in social protest plays, most notably as Jeeter Lester in "Tobacco Road" in 1939. His film work was sporadic but notable (he played in Irving Rapper's *Anna Lucasta*) and was on the rise when called to testify before HUAC in April 1951. Emblazoned in a purple shirt, he refused to say whether he had ever been a member of the Communist Party, observing that "the word Communist is an emotional word—like the word 'witch' in Salem." The resultant blacklisting of Geer in Hollywood was due to such recalcitrance, not to the fact of his occasional gay encounters, of which studio heads were likely unaware.

Still, there are a couple of intriguing scenes in Otto Preminger's *Advise & Consent* (1962). Preminger, the first director to defy the blacklist, cast Geer in a supporting part in his morality play on the McCarthy era. Right after a young U.S. senator (Don Murray) receives a blackmail call threatening to reveal a past homosexual affair, Preminger cuts sharply to Geer, as the Senate minority leader, addressing his colleagues. Even more glaring is the pan the camera makes to focus in on Geer immediately following Walter Pidgeon's impassioned denunciation of the blacklisting of Murray. While the film does play up the old chestnut of gays as security risks, it nonetheless condemns the excesses of the period.

At first glance, then, the long-held presumption of gay persecution in Hollywood during the McCarthy era seems inaccurate. Arthur Laurents was blacklisted, to be sure—but he insisted that his being gay had nothing to do with it, that in fact he felt "no added fear in a fearful time" over the fact of his homosexuality. That few gays were actually Communist Party members helped, but there's another consideration as well. Gays in Hollywood benefited from the old double standard Elsa Maxwell had expressed to Miles White: the difference between the low-class, "perverse" homosexuals and the upper-class, "talented" ones—"people like Cole Porter," Maxwell had said. It was the same dichotomy Hedda Hopper apparently rationalized for herself; attacking "perverts" in her column by day and having dinner with Billy Haines and Jimmie Shields by night. *Washington Confidential* would make a similar distinction between the "exceptional" gays of Broadway and Hollywood and the "dull, dumb deviates" of the State Department. Certainly Hollywood's gays didn't consider State Department lackeys in their league, and judging from the experiences of not only Frank McCarthy but also George Cukor, Roger Edens, Charles Walters, Harriet Parsons, Vincente Minnelli, Arthur Lubin, and Charles Brackett—all of whom remained productive and influential throughout the era—neither did the powers that be.

Yet such an observation demands closer scrutiny. Of those named, McCarthy, Minnelli, and Brackett were *extremely* circumspect, and compared to the previous decade, the number of homosexuals in positions of power actually declined dramatically. David Lewis produced only two films in the Fifties, both nearing the end of the blacklist era. Directors like Mitchell Leisen, Edmund Goulding, and Irving Rapper had declined in both prestige and prolificacy by this time, and, more significantly, *there was no new gay blood to replace them.* (Only Ross Hunter, and he didn't really get going until the blacklist era was nearing its end.) Among writers, Laurents was blacklisted, DeWitt Bodeen left Hollywood in disillusion, and Leonard Spigelgass was tarred with being "too liberal" by Hedda Hopper (who certainly made the connection to both his Jewishness and his homosexuality).

Each of these examples is, of course, individual within its own unique experience. But one cannot dismiss the overall picture, which by the early 1950s was striking in its decline of gay creative control (the significant exception being the Freed unit—and even here, some critics consider the later films as less identifiably "gay" than those of the 1940s). Gay hegemony remained in wardrobe and set decoration, although it's notable that during this period straight women began to rival gay men in both fields. The trend seems obvious: in the 1950s, gays—no matter what field or class they occupied—were definitely on the wrong side of the *Zeitgeist*.

Of all of them, only Spigelgass spoke out against what was happening. It made sense: he viewed the inquisitions as attacks on the system he so prized, and himself as coming to its defense. In a speech to exhibitors in 1949 he condemned "the people who persist in spreading the gross and shameful lie that Hollywood is a mass of swimming pools and Communists, of dope fiends and Fascists." It's actually pretty tame language, even complicit in a way, but enough to earn the enmity of Hedda Hopper, especially in his observation about why the attacks persisted: "Because so great a medium of information persists in refusing to favor one religion above another, one section of the country above another, one man above another." Such unabashed liberalism was like blood in the water to right-wing sharks. Spigelgass, like everyone else, fell generally silent as the inquisitions only intensified.

That many gays of the period actually felt more comfortable among conservatives has long been an apparent conundrum for many contemporary historians. Yet it had its own logic: Hollywood's conservatives were not the ones who had to defend themselves against charges of subversion, and thus could mix far more openly with homosexuals. William Haines became the designer and confidant to a long line of Republican women and their husbands, from the Mays to the Bloomingdales to the Annenbergs to the Reagans. Ross Hunter hobnobbed with industry leaders and politicians. Few of Hollywood's gays were ardent leftists like Will Geer or even assimilationist liberals like Spigelgass. Arthur Laurents observed that most of his left-wing acquaintances were, in fact, straight. The Left, fearful of association, often kept gays at arm's length. In 1955, for example, after the *Los Angeles Mirror* exposé, one prominent liberal lawyer refused to represent Harry Hay at an appearance before HUAC, saying he didn't want to give the impression his other clients condoned queers.

For gays in Hollywood, the strategy was simple: remain as apolitical and discreet as possible. It was the only path for an era in which the gloves were off, when all the old rules were being rewritten, and the fate of their entire worlds, so wrapped up in the studios, was being called into question.

HOMOS IN THE HEADLINES: THE NEW SCANDAL PRESS

"Montgomery Clift's Odd Sex Secret." "When Johnnie Ray Was Noël Coward's Houseguest." "The Night Dan Dailey Was Dolly Dawn." "Sexcapades of Tallulah."

In 1951, the year the second round of HUAC hearings began in Hollywood, another kind of persecution began in screenland. Just as the introduction of the Production Code had emboldened a more aggressive reporting in the 1930s, so did the political climate of the Fifties generate a press that was far more combative and vituperative than ever before. It began with *The Hollywood Life Newsweekly of the West,* a subscription-only trade publication put out by renegade publicist Jimmy Tarantino, promising "the real inside truth, behind the news." *The Hollywood Life* made its way to the desks of studio chiefs and producers, who could now read about singer Johnnie Ray's 1951 Detroit arrest for homosexual solicitation. What was once merely background whispering was now in stark black and white.

By the next year, two magazines of similar temper had appeared on newsstands, bringing Hollywood's dirty laundry directly to the consumer. The first was *Top Secret,* which would enjoy a thirteen-year run; the second was the legendary *Confidential,* the most influential and powerful of the thirty-some scandal magazines that would flourish throughout the decade. In its heyday, *Confidential* sold four million copies a month and kept Los Angeles–area private detectives working overtime. The son of its editor recalled that the magazine was "dedicated to flipping over the rock of the sleepytime Eisenhower '50s and showing the creepy stuff underneath." It did even more than that: it forever changed how gay Hollywood was seen—by the industry, the public, and itself—creating, for the first time, an articulated, visible threat out of homosexuality.

It's not surprising that Howard Rushmore, *Confidential's* first editor, was a rabid anti-Communist who had testified as a friendly witness at HUAC and later served as an investigator for Joseph McCarthy. It's actually telling of *Confidential's* politics that Rushmore left McCarthy because he considered the Senator *not tough enough* on Commies. Rushmore was especially critical of McCarthy's gay henchman, Roy Cohn, and extraordinarily tight with the racist, homophobic gossip columnist Walter Winchell, whose enthusiastic promotion of *Confidential* gave the magazine considerable sway. Rushmore developed a circus of shady sources: madams, prostitutes, double-dealing private investigators, cops on the take, drug dealers, junkies.

So long as circulation stayed high, such sloppy journalism wasn't a problem for publisher Robert Harrison, described by Harold Conrad as "a weird-looking bird with eyes like a hooded falcon." Harrison had started out working for Martin Quigley at the *Motion Picture Herald*. But Quigley, the lay Catholic instrumental behind the Production Code, fired him after finding out about Harrison's side job, publishing soft-porn "girlie" magazines like *Titter, Wink,* and *Flirt.* So Harrison went into porn full-time, specializing in fetishism: girls in spiked heels, girls in chains, girls whipping men in spiked heels and chains. From there it was a short and even logical jump to *Confidential*.

Exposing Hollywood's gays was "a curious preoccupation" of Harrison's, recalled *Confidential's* second editor, A. P. Govoni. The publisher would "spend thousands of dollars, if necessary, to check facts and line up witnesses." He certainly had "the goods" on all of the Fifties' biggest stars, but just like Hedda and Louella, he was willing to play ball when he could score a hit. His deal with Universal in 1955 to kill a proposed piece identifying Rock Hudson as homosexual, in exchange for a piece on Rory Calhoun's prison record, has become legendary. (As journalist David Ehrenstein has noted, however, such supposed quid pro quo was hardly an even trade-off, and a blackmail payment is a far more believable explanation for the recall of the Hudson story.) Harrison also certainly knew the truth about Montgomery Clift, but Clift's gayness never made the pages of *Confidential,* nor did George Nader's nor Anthony Perkins'.

Others weren't so lucky. By this time, *Confidential* had a couple dozen competitors, and all played the gay card. Not surprisingly, the "sapphic" exploits of Tallulah Bankhead and Marlene Dietrich turned up in *Uncensored* and *Whisper.* Noël Coward was called "Las Vegas' queerest hit" by *Rave,* and *Top Secret* suggested an affair between the playwright and Johnnie Ray. Sometimes editors signaled they knew more than they were telling through the use of suggestive headlines over relatively innocuous stories: *Private Lives* asked, "Is James Dean a Dandy?" and *Blast* offered "The Very Gay Life of Gary Cooper and Cary Grant."

If the scandal magazines seemed careless and cocky about the threat of libel, in fact they made sure to cover themselves by rarely offering specifics, sometimes even allowing opposing testimony as a way of pretending balance. But when they had an actual public record—police files, especially— they could go all-out. In its September 1955 issue, *Confidential* offered a queer double whammy: Tab Hunter's five-year-old lewd conduct arrest (with a bevy of other "limp-wristed lads") and Lizabeth Scott's inclusion in a list of clients' names discovered in a raid on a swanky Los Angeles house of prostitution. A few issues later came the revelation of an embezzlement charge against Charles Laughton's producer, Paul Gregory, who had allegedly fleeced an elderly Los Angeles matron of several thousand dollars in 1944, while bringing home "a steady parade of soldiers and sailors . . . for

Heavens only knew what capers?" (Gregory would go on to become husband number three for Janet Gaynor, after the death of Adrian.)

Such reporting was staggeringly unprecedented, yet in character not much different from the kind of revelations and exposés coming out of Washington's investigations or the purges at the State Department. A generation before, William Haines' arrests were not only covered up and expunged from the record through studio influence, but were considered off-limits by the press. Now, in a far more ferocious time, Tab Hunter's indiscretions were read by four million readers.

Just hitting his stride as Warner Bros.' golden-boy hero, Hunter would, however, survive the broadside by *Confidential*. The star of *Battle Cry* and *Damn Yankees* was always willing to play the publicity game. In the wake of the *Confidential* piece, Hunter would pose with Debbie Reynolds, Dorothy Malone, Mary Ann Mobley, and others for a flurry of photos distributed to the mainstream press. Such aggressive posturing deflected any gay talk; besides, no journalist worth his or her reputation would dare acknowledge what they'd surely read in the scandal sheets.

Although the industry was undoubtedly aware of the Hunter story, it counted on the fact that most of America was not: four million readers did not come close to the hundreds of millions reached by Hedda and Louella and magazines such as *Photoplay*. Early on, the industry adopted a policy of *no response* to the kind of press *Confidential* represented. To fight, they reasoned, would only have given the scandals more publicity. As Gavin Lambert has pointed out, the Hunter story only really became famous *years* after it first appeared. In 1955, "it wasn't seen as breaking on a national level," Lambert told David Ehrenstein. "Warner Bros. probably said the story was unfortunate, but it's not *The New York Times* or a Hearst paper. Say nothing and let it cool off." And that it did: Hunter would enjoy a career into the 1960s, despite his clandestine relationship with Anthony Perkins.

That shouldn't minimize the power of the scandal rags, however. Lizabeth Scott didn't escape her *Confidential* assault as unscathed as Hunter. But then Scott had never cultivated such a squeaky-clean image as Tab had. A former model, she was husky-voiced and given to wearing dungarees, hyped as the new Veronica Lake and rumored to be the mistress of producer Hal Wallis. With strong impressions in such noirs as *Pitfall* and *The Racket,* she pointedly refused to play up the glamour, sounding suspiciously unfeminine: "I hate frilly, fussy females," she told *Silver Screen,* complaining of the dresses and hairstyles Paramount had made her wear for screen tests. In 1951 Hedda Hopper reported that Scott "bypasses romance for career," quoting the actress as saying she loved her freedom and "wouldn't give it up for anything."

So when *Confidential* revealed that Scott's name was among those found in a book of clients at a high-class Los Angeles brothel, a reserve of suspicion was already in place. That the names of George Jessel and George Raft were also in the book seemed of little consequence, but Lizabeth's name stopped the vice squad cold, *Confidential* reported: "Could that name be that of the honey-blonde star they'd seen in a dozen top movies? If so, what was it doing rubbing elbows with a zesty collection of customers for a trio of cuddle-for-cash cuties?" The piece went on to, by the way, divulge Liz's penchants for men's pajamas, for calling herself "Scotty," and for friendships with "strange Parisians" like Frede, the "notorious Lesbian queen" of the Left Bank.

Scott chose not to ignore but *sue*. Joining with Robert Mitchum and tobacco heiress Doris Duke, subjects of their own attacks by *Confidential,* she filed a $2.5 million lawsuit against the magazine only days after the story's publication. While perhaps understandable, the action merely proved the studios' fears: it kept the allegations in the headlines. Even though mainstream newspapers generally did not repeat the details—saying only that *Confidential* had implied Scott was guilty of "highly offensive, illegal and indecent acts in her private life"—this very ambiguity left readers eager to find out more. Plus, Scott's combativeness seemed to goad other scandal rags into the fracas: *Uncensored* wrote the following March that Scott's "private life [was] no *open book*"—a clear reference to the scandal. "There's no point in *Uncensored* repeating what was said about Lizzy that brought on her tizzy, but the blunt truth is that she's been the subject of speculation among Hollywood's whisperers [for some time]. . . . When it comes to being a lively source of rumors, well, they just don't build 'em like Liz anymore."

Scott lost her suit on a technicality: *Confidential* was based in New York, and she'd sued them in California. But even a win wouldn't have reversed the damage: unlike Tab Hunter, who had pointedly declined to participate in the lawsuit, Lizabeth's career faltered and never recovered. She made no films during the scandal years of 1955 and 1956, and her appearance with Elvis Presley in *Loving You* (1957) was her last until an offbeat British film in 1972.

"I'm puzzled," she admitted in a rare interview long after her Hollywood career was over. (She didn't respond for an interview for this book.) "Why are there so many people in the world who are against everything? Let's be *for* things. There are too many who are *against* things."

What made the stories about Tab Hunter and Lizabeth Scott so significantly different from those concerning Cary Grant or Janet Gaynor in the 1930s was that the gayness was made explicit: the bogeyman was given a name. More and more, this became routine, and not just in the scandal sheets. A study of *Time* and *Newsweek* revealed a jump from two articles on homosexuals in the 1940s to *twenty-one* in the 1950s. According to a sampling of gossip columns by *The Nation* in the summer of 1956, homosexuality was twice a topic in columns by Dorothy Kilgallen and Lee Mortimer, the latter of whom, with Jack Lait, published *Washington Confidential, New York Confidential,* and *Chicago Confidential,* books that each included detailed sections on the gay underworld. In March 1957, Los Angeles entertainment critic Dick Williams condemned the homosexual references in the film *Crime in the Streets* as well as "an emphasis on homosexuality" in the local nightclub acts of the Aristocrats and Jack Carter. Walter Winchell, who'd publicly gay-baited rival columnist Danton Walker in the past, now made the link (both in print and on the air) between sexual deviance and Communism.

There's really not much distance between the naming of figures as Communist and naming them as gay, between publicly revealing the details of one's political involvements and revealing the peccadilloes of one's personal life. The exposé of public figures became common sport. Liberace was hunted for being a flamboyant homosexual nearly as vociferously as any political subversive. Called, among other things, a "quivering, giggling, fruit-flavored, mincing, ice-cream–covered heap of mother love," the outrageously effeminate pianist would sue for damages a number of times and—since calling someone a fruit in the 1950s was indisputably damaging—he usually won.

The case of Raymond Burr is also illustrative. Burr had risen to prominence as the villain in *Rear Window* and then shot to stardom on television with "Perry Mason" in 1957. Although he lived with his partner, Robert Benevides, on an island near Fiji that required two airplanes and two boats to reach, most reporters knew he was gay, according to the Associated Press' Bob Thomas. In April 1961, *Confidential* ran a splashy article about Burr's apparent mistaking of a drag queen, Libby Reynolds, for an actual woman at a Greenwich Village bar. Fooled and smitten, Burr (according to the account) accompanied Libby back to her place for a "nightcap," but fell asleep on her couch before he learned the truth. As written, the article gets Burr "off the hook": if he'd known Libby was a man, the article implied, he'd never have gone home with her.

Burr could hardly have been so naive. Hedda Hopper, whose son William costarred on "Perry Mason" as Paul Drake, would receive other incriminating evidence on the TV lawyer. Shortly after the *Confidential* article, she sent Burr a note with an enclosed letter (a copy of which does not survive in her files) from one of her informants. "Dear Ray," Hedda wrote. "What the hell did you do in Phoenix? If the enclosed letter is correct, this is the first intimation I have had of it." To reassure him, however, that his secret was safe with her, she promised all he had to do was "call on the mother of Paul Drake and I will stand up and swear anything for you."

The hypocrisy continued; the victims weren't random. Tab Hunter, with his studio's deep investment and an eager willingness to play the game, was protected. Lizabeth Scott, with a churlish disregard for Hollywood convention, was sacrificed. Raymond Burr, with Hedda Hopper on his side, became one of the most enduring and beloved stars on television. Dan Dailey—well, his was perhaps too bizarre a case for *anyone* to do much.

The singing-dancing star of *When My Baby Smiles at Me, The Pride of St. Louis,* and *There's No Business Like Show Business* was married with a son when the scandal rag *Inside* exposed him as a transvestite. "After every binge he shows up around the film colony, decked from head to toe in outlandish female attire," the magazine wrote. "It doesn't turn many heads any more—just a few pitying glances. After a couple of highballs, Dailey sincerely believes he is a woman. He talks in a high falsetto and struts like Miss America." Fox studio officials, *Inside* reported, were getting tired of covering up his "flights of feminine fantasy."

Dan Dailey's cross-dressing has become part of Hollywood legend. But was it true? André Previn, a musical director for the Freed unit, would later recount a tale of Dailey showing up in drag for a press screening of *It's Always Fair Weather,* a charge director Stanley Donen found absurd: "He'd never do such a thing. That would have ended his career. Now, he was drunk a lot, but he never showed up in a dress." In September 1955, *Uncensored* ran a piece ostensibly to dispel "those Dan Dailey rumors," explaining that the only time he'd done drag was for a comedy skit in which he played Juliet. Folks spotted him afterward at a pub and drew the wrong conclusion. Yet *Uncensored* was having it both ways, just as *Confidential* would with the Raymond Burr–Libby Reynolds story: simply by repeating the allegations and running a sensational headline, they pulled readers in—without getting Dailey's lawyers on their back.

It was a story that wouldn't die, however: in 1957 *Confidential* ran "The Night Dan Dailey was Dolly Dawn," recounting an unusually specific tale of the star, on the night of March 11, at an "offbeat Manhattan nightspot where boys will be girls," dressing up in a pink tulle dress and performing an impromptu number. "He did the inimitable Dan Dailey soft-shoe manner, despite his French-heeled dancing slippers, and the only bit that smacked of feminine grace was the curtsy at the end," the magazine disclosed.

It seems odd that Dailey, dogged by cross-dressing rumors for a number of years, would have actually performed in pink tulle in public, but it's possible that the supposed anonymity and collegial fraternity of a gay bar—not to mention a few drinks—might have given him a false sense of security. Whether true or not, Dailey was understandably upset by the *Confidential* article. He called the writer Harold Conrad, whom he knew had ghosted *Confidential* pieces in the past, and asked if he was the author this time. "How the hell would I know if you're dressing up in your girlfriend's clothes?" Conrad responded. "And if I did, you know me well enough to know that I wouldn't write that crap."

Of course, Dan Dailey may have been a heterosexual cross-dresser; his numerous wives may, in fact, be evidence of that. Few of Hollywood's gay survivors knew him; some remembered that he was close with Johnnie Ray, his costar in *There's No Business Like Show Business,* and so assumed he, like Ray, was homosexual. In a way, it doesn't matter whether Dailey was gay or not: certainly in the eyes of the press and some of the public, he was *queer,* and he would be treated the same. He certainly didn't want to testify against *Confidential* in a libel trial, where he'd be asked directly if the stories were true. So desperate was he to avoid a subpoena that he leaped over the footlights after emceeing a gig at the Hollywood Bowl and led the summons-bearing detective on a mad chase through the aisles, careening off in a friend's car.

During the ordeal, Dailey would admit he wanted to "quit living" and checked into the Menninger Clinic, telling columnist Aline Mosby that "his basic problem was too involved and personal to go into now." After 1957 Dan Dailey's career was essentially over, save for Las Vegas nightclubs and a brief television stint on "The Governor & J. J."

The end came for *Confidential* not long after, and was due to celebrities either braver or more innocent than Dailey. Dorothy Dandridge, winning a $10,000 out-of-court settlement over an article that alleged to reveal what she and several men "did in the woods," testified before a grand-jury panel investigating obscenity charges against scandal magazines. She was joined by Maureen O'Hara and Liberace, who all swore the stories printed about them were false. On May 15, 1957, Robert Harrison and A. P. Govoni were indicted for conspiracy to publish criminally libelous and obscene articles. In the trial that followed, former editor Rushmore (fired by Harrison) was called to testify. Asked if he'd meant to hurt the people about whom he published stories, Rushmore replied: "I certainly did."

The *Confidential* trial produced headlines for weeks, but in the end the jury proved deadlocked, and the judge declared a mistrial. Harrison knew it was time to quit, however, and pled guilty to a single charge of obscenity, promising the court to change editorial direction at *Confidential.* No more libelous exposés, which caused the magazine's circulation to plum-met. Although *Confidential* would continue for several years, it was but a shadow of what it once was.

But its legacy remained. Homosexuality was a genie out of the bottle. No longer unmentionable, it was in fact now part of the national discourse, from the corridors of Washington right down to the smutty scandal rags. *Confidential's* modus operandi was copied by weekly tabloids across the country, notably *The New York Inquirer,* which, after *Confidential's* fade-out, positioned itself as its successor, going nationwide as *The National Inquirer.*

Time correspondent and Hollywood observer Ezra Goodman reflected on the etiology of *Confidential* and, by extension, the whole scandal-magazine era. "What *Confidential* proved," Goodman wrote, "was that there was too much pallid, punches-pulled reporting elsewhere and that the average, un-tutored reader was probably wise to it and instinctively knew he was being hornswoggled. He undoubtedly realized that *Confidential,* in its own way, was giving him a glimmer of truth."

MEN'S MEN: THE GAY STARS OF THE FIFTIES

In *Tea and Sympathy,* both play and film, the shy, delicate, sensitive boy learns the hard way what had become a prevailing credo of the 1950s: if you looked like a fag and walked like a fag, you were a fag. Unlike their predecessors, the male stars of the decade had to ward off a very specific homosexual demon, which suddenly loomed as large and omnipresent a threat over them as it did any schoolboy taunted on the playground. Fears of being "too girly"—less than the rigidly codified post-war definition of masculine—became paramount. While confrontations with masculinity had occurred in the industry before, now they carried with them the po-tential for explicit public connotation of homosexuality.

By the middle part of the decade, nearly all of the "softer" stars of the Forties were off the screen or made irregular appearances: Farley Granger, John Dall, William Eythe, Hurd Hatfield. Even Clifton Webb, whose ad-vanced age permitted him some leeway in image, began playing more tra-ditionally masculine, grandfatherly parts. Montgomery Clift disappeared from the screen between 1953 and 1957, and when he returned he was craggy and hard, the result of both his heavy drinking and a disfiguring car accident.

The new crop of stars followed a pattern familiar to those who remem-bered the coming of the Code and the Great Depression. Men were again manly and women ultra-feminine, almost caricatures of gender: Marlon Brando in a sweaty T-shirt and Jayne Mansfield puckering up for the camera. No wonder Lizabeth Scott didn't last long. What lesbians remained tended to play character parts, where their butchness could be put to work: Agnes Moorehead, Hope Emerson, Judith Anderson. That's not to imply, of course, that all lesbians are butch—but the Fifties don't appear to have had their version of Lilyan Tashman or Margaret Lindsay. The corollary is also true for the men: with the exception of Webb and Anthony Perkins, none of the top gay male stars of the era were very feminine, and if they *had* any tendencies for camp or flamboyance, they learned very quickly to keep them tightly under wraps.

The model was Brando. And Rory Calhoun, Paul Newman, Tony Curtis, Anthony Quinn. And, of course, George Nader, James Dean, and Rock Hudson: three sexual "deviants" who helped set the tone and style of masculinity for a generation.

Nader is an interesting character, one who's been overshadowed by his more famous friend Hudson. Yet Nader survived the Fifties without ever surrendering much personal integrity. The star of such Universal costume epics as *The Sins of Jezebel* and *Lady Godiva,* the handsome, athletic star lived with his partner, publicist Mark Miller, throughout his film career; at the time of this writing, they were still together, living in Palm Springs. "Both of us were brought up to believe you fall in love and stay in love for life," Nader said. "The relationship had to be for the long run."

Born in Pasadena in 1921, the son of an oil broker, Nader's education at Occidental College was interrupted by a stint in the navy during World War II. When he returned, he decided to pursue an acting career. He met Mark Miller in 1947, when both were performing at (once again) the Pasadena Playhouse. Mark soon gave up his own ambitions to concentrate on boosting George's career. During the day he worked as Nader's manager, agent, and publicist; at night he slung hash as a carhop at Jack's Drive-In.

In 1951, they met another young, struggling actor named Rock Hudson, and the three became tight friends. Nader said their three-way friendship—never romantic or sexual—perfectly served the climate of the times. They could go out to restaurants as a trio and not attract attention; two men alone would have looked suspicious, and four men would have given the impression of two couples. Such calculations determined their social activities. Sometimes they'd have a few friends to their house in Laurel Canyon—Hudson, the agent Dick Clayton, the actor Tom Tryon, a few others—and they'd get an idea to go out to eat. But Nader would look around, shake his head, and rule: "Too many boys. Let's order in."

Early on in his film career—which took off after *Six Bridges to Cross* (1955), the story of the famous Brink's heist—Nader realized he'd have to fulfill his obligation to the publicity machine. Joan Crawford took him under her wing and used him as a frequent escort. But there was no mention of a love interest: he told Sidney Skolsky that he lived alone and liked it, that he'd only been in love once, with a girl who'd sent him a "Dear John" letter during the war. It wasn't so much betraying Mark as simply cooperating with him: Miller had, after all, set up the interview with Skolsky.

Yet anyone could have predicted that the old "I-haven't-found-her-yet" ploy was not going to work in the inquisitional Fifties. Accordingly, Universal kept Nader busy being seen on the town with a bevy of beauties including Martha Hyer, Barbara Rush, Piper Laurie, Julia Adams, and, most notably, Dani Crayne, his date to the 1955 Oscars. *Filmland* ran their photo with the caption "Dani Crayne and George Nader are proving their dates are not strictly publicity. This could be the real thing. But then . . ."

In fan-magazine profiles of Nader, it's easy to spot the publicist's talking points. "Like Gregory Peck and Clark Gable, George is not a pretty man," Don Allen wrote obediently in *Photoplay*. "Rather, his features are rugged and lively and interesting—the kind of looks that attract and hold a faithful fan following."

Linking Nader to Peck and Gable was a publicist's dream. Nader was All Man, the studio was blaring, and to prove it, featured his chiseled physique in dozens of beefcake shots. The star would recall that one shot in a pair of tight swimming trunks caused considerable stir. Apparently George showed too much bulge, and the studio balked at releasing it to the press. "Would you want your daughter looking at that?" the publicity chief asked him.

"Not having a daughter—or for that matter, a son," Nader remembered, he was at a loss for words. The photo was discarded.

But despite the beefcake, despite the starlets on his arm and his dutiful smile into the photographer's lens, Nader wasn't cooperating quite as fully as the studio would have liked. He remembered his publicist telling him: "You're losing parts because you're thirty-five and not married." Nader talked about the idea with Mark; a female secretary even agreed to an arranged marriage. But in the end George just couldn't go through with it. Mark would joke: "Besides, where would *I* sleep?"

In a fascinating, transcribed interview in Hedda Hopper's papers (which may or may not have actually been published), Nader makes some interesting observations about fan-magazine protocol. He comes across as refreshingly honest in his response to the age-old Marriage Question:

> I could give you the stock answer—when I find the right girl—
> and of course it's sort of true. . . . [But] I'm having a wonderful
> time. For fan magazines, one must have to want to get married
> desperately. In that medium, there are no extracurricular activi-
> ties—either one is married or wants to be. It's difficult to explain

that one is happy being a bachelor—in Southern California, it's very nice. You have to dream up something like "I just can't wait to get married."

Nader was actually pointing out a fundamental construct of Hollywood identity: *either one is married or wants to be.* There were no gays, only unattached heterosexuals waiting for the right girl. But Nader was insisting on a different space in which to live, on a different set of options from which to choose. This was radical, almost subversive—especially in an era in which, in the world outside the movies, there now existed a public creature called "homosexual." Demanding space for an identity beyond the Hollywood paradigm had been done before, but never in a time so potentially dangerous as this.

After *Movieland* reported in July 1956 that Nader's "engagement" to Crayne had changed to "friendship," Universal mounted a clever, aggressive campaign to bolster his hetero credentials. The studio hoped to deflect any growing suspicion about his bachelorhood not by obscuring it but rather by calling attention to it. In an obvious studio-arranged gimmick, *The American Weekly* named Nader "Hollywood's most eligible bachelor," quoting George as saying, "I like ladies," and insisting that "Ladies like George." *Photoplay* ran an article in October 1956 allegedly written by Nader himself, outlining the qualities a girl needed to win his heart. In May 1957, *Screen Parade* featured him in a "Wanted" poster, saying, "This man is dangerous! He may make a clever get-away!" In language as old as Hollywood itself, writer Chris Williams opined, "Perhaps there'll be a girl he hasn't as yet met who will knock down his defenses and have him running to the altar—or again maybe some moonlit night he'll look at Martha or Dani or one of the other lovelies he dates and think—this is it! And forthwith head to the preacher."

The Marriage Question was nothing new—but in the Fifties, an incorrect answer suggested a far more ominous and graphic reality than ever before. Soon after the *Screen Parade* article, it was obvious to Universal that their campaign had gone nowhere, and they failed to renew Nader's option. "The studio let it drop quietly," Sidney Skolsky reported.

Ray Stricklyn, a supporting actor in several films of the 1950s, would also see his film career sputter to a close soon after Nader's. "Do I think my sexual orientation hurt my career?" he asked in his memoirs. "Probably. I wasn't aware of it being a detriment in my early years, but I'm sure in some quarters it was a negative factor. The 1950s and 1960s were homophobic decades."

Of course, neither Stricklyn nor Nader were passed over solely because they were homosexual. Neither was pulling in the box office in the way, say, Rock Hudson was—and certainly the studio knew Hudson was gay. But George Nader had never played the game like Rock Hudson: he never married, and increasingly his ambivalence on the subject—like that of William Haines a generation before—made him suspect in a highly suspicious time. It was an intertextual perception of a gay star that dated back to Kerrigan and O'Brien. From the studio's point of view, why was someone like this worth keeping? As with Haines, to dismiss Nader's gayness as having *any* connection to the end of his movie career would be as simplistic as calling it the *only* factor. Had he been a big financial draw, he'd likely have been kept; had he been a cooperative *hetero*sexual B-picture player instead of an *un*cooperative *homo*sexual one, he also would likely have been kept.

Nader would achieve success outside American films, scoring a hit as an FBI agent in a number of German thrillers. He also starred in a few television series, notably "The Adventures of Ellery Queen," but by the mid Sixties had pretty much retired from acting. He wrote a sci-fi novel, *Chrome,* with explicit homoeroticism; free of the studios, he would talk increasingly openly about being gay and his long, successful relationship with Mark Miller.

• • •

Nader's story contrasts remarkably with that of Anthony Perkins, who seemed to have become *more* paranoid about his public image as he got older rather than less. Yet Perkins had never been like Nader, living comfortably (and, for the Fifties, conspicuously) with a male partner at the height of his fame. Instead, Perkins maintained a stressfully secret relationship with Tab Hunter, something even many close friends within the industry knew nothing about.

While Rock Hudson and Montgomery Clift would permit themselves a degree of veracity among their colleagues while maintaining a heterosexual image in public, Perkins allowed himself no such leeway. The writer Alan Helms described an affair with Perkins that was conducted with "obsessive privacy" in a rented New York studio apartment—clearly, Helms said, "a fuck pad." As time went on, Perkins would grow uneasy encountering gay acquaintances at industry functions or even private parties, especially if they were a couple. "He was so strange like that," said Tucker Fleming, who'd observe Tony "peaking around corners" at him and his partner, Charles Williamson. Once, spotting Don Bachardy and Christopher Isherwood at a party, Perkins grabbed his children and moved across the room—"for fear we'd pinch his ass or something," Bachardy said, "as if we were the high priests of queerdom."

Perkins' paranoia may have been extreme, yet in the Fifties one either had to conform or rebel. Most gay stars of the era found a middle ground: one that had its occasional hardships and complications, but that ultimately offered more peace of mind than Perkins seems ever to have achieved. George Nader was never a star of Perkins' rank, and has not achieved the kind of pop-culture immortality that Perkins won with *Psycho;* yet it can be argued that Nader was the far happier man. Yet even those two icons of the era—Rock Hudson and James Dean—never went to the obsessive lengths Perkins did to maintain an image. It simply proves again that while the context of one's time is vital to understand, eventually it is one's own psyche that determines choices and behavior.

For even in the midst of the most repressive cultural era of the twentieth century, there were those who did rebel. Nader's rebellion was to maintain an ongoing primary relationship with Mark Miller, yet James Dean rebelled even against that. Dean's disinclination to name himself gay was different from Perkins' internalized homophobia. Rather, Dean, like many young people—he was, after all, just twenty-four when he died—chose to defer categorization and identify only as "exploring." Dean's friend, the actor Jonathan Gilmore, remembered that Dean "had no conclusions about anything. For Jimmy, a conclusion would've conflicted with an almost uncontrollable need he had to try to go beyond the limitations set by others"—which would have included, for him, those set by other gay men.

Had Dean lived, he may well have (or not) eventually self-identified as gay in the way Hudson did. Certainly there is a queerness to his film work, a quality of misfit beauty that makes him one of the few male stars to become a gay icon on the level of a Garland, Davis, or West. That his director on *Rebel Without a Cause,* Nicholas Ray, was a deeply hidden homosexual (though, according to Gore Vidal, indiscreet enough to carry on an affair with the film's sixteen-year-old costar, Sal Mineo) perhaps added to that picture's particular queer poetry.

Gavin Lambert has written of his own youthful affair with Ray. Although the director would seek him out voraciously in the middle of the night for sex, he nonetheless insisted he wasn't homosexual, "as he'd been to bed with a great many women in his life, but only two or three men." Later Ray would counsel Lambert, hired as his assistant, on the importance of not being perceived as gay. "A butch handshake, he said, is very important," Lambert recalled, "then demonstrated a bone-crushing one, and gave his startling smile."

Hollywood, as ever, was about perception. It's a fascinating irony that the three most enduring iconographic stars of this most repressive of times were, in fact, sexually deviant: Dean; Brando, who'd acknowledge his own sexual experiences with men; and Hudson. Their on-screen alchemy is infused with such deviance. Hudson's carefully manufactured persona was almost an ode to masculinity, so perfect and so compelling that it—like everything else about Hollywood—seemed a charade. But it was real: Hudson was masculine on-screen the way he was off, a traditional "guy's guy" without the meanness. "Rock was about as one-hundred-percent masculine a man as you could ever meet in your life," said Kevin Thomas. "When I met him, it really shook up the stereotypes one internalizes."

Rock *was* masculine, but his was not the roguish masculinity of a Gable or even a Bogart; he was more like Cary Grant without the affectation. In *Magnificent Obsession* (1954), the film that catapulted Hudson to the top, he is far more beautiful to look at than Jane Wyman, but it's not an effeminate beauty like that of Tyrone Power or Robert Taylor. In *Written on the Wind,* he is sensitive and compassionate, but not delicate or ambiguous in the way Farley Granger or Monty Clift were. Rock Hudson projected an on-screen gayness different from any who came before. He is comfortable with the camp of *Pillow Talk* and yet never campy. Friends insist that was Hudson in real life as well.

As Warner Bros. had done with Tab Hunter, Universal would protect Hudson from scandal at all cost—and scandal was something that, given government inquisitions and *Confidential* exposés, seemed ready to happen at any time in Hollywood. So it's not surprising that by the Fifties, publicity had become perhaps a more important component of the studio system than ever before—nor should it surprise anyone to discover that the nexus of publicists, agents, and journalists that emerged was, to a considerable degree, gay.

THE IMAGE HANDLERS: HOLLYWOOD'S GAY PUBLICISTS, JOURNALISTS, AND AGENTS

"I don't wonder that so many of Hollywood's publicists were gay," said Kevin Thomas, longtime film critic for *The Los Angeles Times.* "After all, we grow up as gay men learning how to cope with a lot of things that never even occur to straight people. We know how to get around problems. We meet challenges by using whatever creative and artistic impulses we have. Certainly this can give us great empathy in dealing with other people's situations."

That the myth and magic of Hollywood—so dear and influential to gay culture—was in fact molded to a large extent by homosexuals themselves had been true for decades. From Herbert Howe to Jerry Asher, gay reporters and publicists had helped shape the public image of the stars and the industry. By the Fifties, however, the phenomenon had multiplied, with the emergence of a new breed of publicist or "press agent": the independent public-relations firm, working not for the studios but for individual stars, directors, or producers. It's not surprising that such a development should occur during the decade—for what period of time ever demanded more spin control?

That once again gays occupied significant positions in this new generation of publicity is also fitting. Many gays and lesbians had grown up learning how to be creative in telling their own stories: what to tell, what not to tell, how to tell the truth without revealing too much.

"The job was really custom-made for gay people," Thomas said. "I know I'm indulging in some generalization here, but the reality was there were and are many, many gay people in publicity positions. From time immemorial, an aspect of publicity has been *hand-holding*—above and beyond all the snappy copy and items passed to columnists and arranged screenings and all that. I have certainly known straight hand-holders, but so often it's been a gay man who's had the personality—and the *time*—to deal with stars with images to maintain. Especially female stars—what to wear, where to go, whether she should get a face-lift, what premiere to attend, who she should be seen with. Maybe that's confirming stereotypes, but it was the reality."

Former publicist Alan Cahan concurred. "Yes, there sure were many gays in publicity," he said. "I'm not sure why. But there were always three or four in every job I was at. We all knew who each other were, and sometimes we'd get together, but we were still pretty circumspect. You didn't take your partner to functions. You always had a beard. I had a marvelous girl and everybody loved her. She was gay, but no one would have known—the lipstick and the hair.

"Sometimes it was ironic," Cahan continued. "You'd hear about some magazine wanting to do a story on one of your clients who was gay. This was well before the word 'outing' existed, but that's what it was. And you had to deflect them, knowing full well they had the goods. You had to make up a story, but you tried to do so that it wasn't really lying. You had pictures taken [of the star and a woman] and let them speak for themselves. Things like that."

Cahan had begun working as a publicist in television during the early part of the decade. He'd later move over to work for Universal and for the public-relations firm of Rupert Allan, Frank McCarthy's lover. It was while working for Allan that Cahan remembered the most significant episode of homosexual cover-up. Even forty years later, still the committed publicist, he declined to give the actor's name, but he recalled the panic that gripped Allan's office: "Rupert had to pull in all sort of tickets and finally the editor [of the magazine] agreed to meet with Rupert and the star in question for a luncheon. They all talked and the story was killed. And everybody breathed a deep sigh of relief."

While Frank McCarthy was busy censoring films at Fox, his lover, Allan, was providing masks for gay actors to pass as straight. Yet to judge them would be unfair and also inaccurate. Kevin Thomas recalled them both as "wonderful people" who encouraged and supported him and others in their careers. "Rupert Allan was actually providing a service," Thomas insisted. "He was helping people, not hurting them."

In fact, it can be argued that publicists like Allan were keeping gays employed in the industry in the face of the assaults against them. Rupert Allan was one of the most influential publicists in Hollywood, "a very aristocratic man, very socially connected," Thomas remembered. Among his clients was the Principality of Monaco, an assignment owed to his close friendship with Princess Grace. It was Allan who, at Grace's marriage to Prince Rainier in 1956, managed the sixteen hundred reporters who showed up to cover the event. (They'd been expecting forty.) As a reward, he was named the consul general of Monaco in Los Angeles, and would later be named by Rainier a Chevalier de l'Ordre des Grimaldi, one of the country's highest honors.

Allan was a "hand-holder" par excellence, often counseling Grace during both her Hollywood career and her royal duties. He'd learned the skill early—and *literally*—in his first Hollywood job as West Coast editor of *Look* magazine. Interviewing Ava Gardner bedside at an abortion clinic, he'd held her hand as she poured out her tale of woe to him. Then he went back to his typewriter and banged out a fluff piece on how happy she was being married to Frank Sinatra.

He was also tight with Marilyn Monroe, whom he'd jokingly credit with turning him into a "flack"—his name for publicity agents. They had clicked during an interview he was doing for *Look,* and she begged him to sign on as her personal publicist. He worked with her for several years before heading off to Monaco.

"On the face of it," wrote historian Neal Gabler, "press agents were a strange, colorful breed who prided themselves as being characters in the Damon Runyan mold. But just beneath the surface of the image, one found an unsavory and largely forlorn group of men." He quoted veteran publicist Lee Meyers as saying, "Being a press agent was like a girl being a model. When a guy was arrested and they asked him what he did, he'd say 'publicity.' Everyone was in publicity."

The aristocratic Allan was an exception among the post-war rise of publicists, but he shared with them a common trait: Gabler called them "lapsed journalists" trying to find a new way to make a buck. Publicity's "unsavory" reputation—dating back at least to the 1930s when Lincoln Quarberg had shuddered at the idea of crossing over from journalism—was still strong enough in the early Sixties for Dale Olson, a *Variety* reviewer hired as a publicist for the Mirisch Company, to ask Kevin Thomas, "Will you still be friends with me?"

But it was an established practice: many gay publicists had gotten their starts writing about film for newspapers and magazines. Jerry Asher had moved from writing for *Silver Screen* to Warner Bros. studio publicist. Carl Combs, too, had joined Warners in 1945 after serving as drama critic for the *Hollywood Citizen-News*. Herb Sterne, starting out with *Rob Wagner's Script* and *The Hollywood Reporter,* became a top publicist for Columbia and later on his own. In 1954, *Newsweek* estimated there were 480 press agents working in Hollywood, with independents slightly outnumbering studio publicists, a reversal from four years previous. "Their influence is incalculable, although they seldom get public credit for it," *Newsweek* observed. "Out of their fertile minds come most of the Hollywood legends."

The number of gays working in the field is impossible to discern, yet just listing those known is a significant number. In addition to Allan, Asher, Cahan, Combs, Olson, and Sterne, there was Harry Mines, a Warner Bros. and, later, freelance publicist who founded the Publicists Guild Local 88; Stanley Musgrove, who worked for Guy Madison, Cole Porter, Mae West, and others; George Eells, who would go on to coauthor with Musgrove a book on West's life; Stafford Clark, who handled George Burns' publicity and created "Vampira" for television; and Charlie Earle, who labored at Paramount and ABC Television before starting his own company in 1960. There was also David Hanna, the former *Hollywood Reporter* columnist who became personal publicist for Ava Gardner. "I lived in the closet with the door open," he recalled, expertly summing up the experience of many of his colleagues. "It was never any secret what I was."

Publicity was also one field that seemed to offer a balance of opportunities for both gay men and lesbians. After Rupert Allan left for Monaco, Marilyn replaced him with Pat Newcomb, whose lesbianism had earlier been a matter of some concern to the star; eventually Newcomb's connections with Peter Lawford and the Kennedys secured her the job. There were also Rock Hudson's friends Pat Fitzgerald and Lynn Bowers. Fitzgerald had worked for several P.R. firms before forming her own agency, where her client roster included Hudson, Ross Hunter, and Troy Donahue. Lynn Bowers had begun her career in the 1930s as a publicist for the House of Westmore cosmetics firm. She'd later work as a ghost writer for Louella Parsons and then as executive assistant to daughter Harriet at RKO before moving into independent publicity. According to friends, Lynn and Harriet were also lovers for a period of time.

Louella paid press agents a rare tribute in *Newsweek,* calling them "helpful." In fact, the relationship between the publicist and the press was a vital connection, and as ever, it's also significant to note the number of gays writing about the movies. Homosexuals had continued to be a large part of the movie press, carrying on the traditions of Herbert Howe and Marquis Busby. Thus a gay publicist like Herb Sterne working for a gay client like George Cukor might work out a deal with a gay columnist like Mike Connolly—not *because* they were gay, necessarily, but with a facilitation that could prove surprisingly easy.

"I'd see Connolly at a party, for example," said one publicist who asked not to be identified. "We both liked to drink. We'd be eyeing some pretty young boy, and then I'd mention he was a client of mine. Or else I'd call him the next day and we'd still be laughing about whatever it was from the night before and he'd say, 'Sure, I'll get [the item] in [the column] for you.' You didn't get that with Hedda or Louella—though you might with some of their gay legmen."

In fact, *Newsweek* identified Connolly as "the most important 'plant' in town . . . probably the most influential columnist inside the movie colony itself." Connolly was the hard-drinking lead columnist for *The Hollywood Reporter,* which no respectable Hollywood breakfast table was ever without. Even more than the columnists from the higher-circulation dailies, Connolly had the ear and eye of the studio bigwigs, a fact that drove Hedda Hopper batty with jealousy. Every chance she got she denounced Connolly as a "drunken faggot." For his part, Connolly just went blithely along: "It is the forty-year-old, sleepy-eyed Connolly who gets the pick of the trade items, the industry rumors, the policy and casting switches," *Newsweek* reported in 1954. "He has been described as Hollywood's unofficial arbiter, prosecutor, jury talent scout, trend spotter and social register."

That's yet another remarkable position of power for a gay man in the 1950s. It's interesting to note how often gay figures crop up in Connolly's column, even those whose heyday had long since passed, like Billy Haines and Edmund Lowe. Connolly was very social, knowing everyone in Hollywood and the gay subculture. The female impersonator Charles Pierce would recall a party at Connolly's in the late 1950s notable for its gay guest list: Franklin Pangborn, Harriet Parsons, Mary McCarty, Margaret Lindsay, and Hope Emerson.

Connolly was hardly alone in the field. In the fan magazines, Lawrence Quirk was a favorite writer for many stars; Joan Crawford would often call him at two in the morning to ask his advice about something. Lee Graham started as a legman for Cobyna Wright at the *Herald-Examiner* and later wrote his own syndicated column for local papers. Gossip columnist Liz

Smith got her start at *Modern Screen* in the 1940s, and was later taken under the wing of Lynn Bowers. By the Sixties, Smith was touted as the successor to Hedda and Louella, with her syndicated column read by millions. Only recently has she acknowledged that her relationship with another woman was well known throughout Hollywood.

"Entertainment reporting has always been congenial for gay people," said Kevin Thomas, who started writing for the *Los Angeles Times* in 1961. "A lot of gay people who went to the movies as kids to escape from a hostile world grew up to write about the movies. Certainly in 1961 I wasn't coming into work wearing any pink triangle. There may have been times I faced a glass ceiling because I was as open as I was. Let's say it never worked in my favor, but I don't think it worked against me either."

• • •

The rise of independent publicists in the postwar era was parallel with the rise of independent agents. While stars, directors, and even producers often had agents as far back as the 1930s—recall Phil Berg advising David Lewis—by the Fifties there had emerged a kind of "superagent," a high-profile manager who coordinated nearly every aspect of a star's career. These agents not only discovered stars but promoted them, represented them to the studio, and acted as their publicist all in one. And once again, a significant cadre of gay agents wielded extraordinary power during the era.

The most famous—or infamous—was Henry Willson, star maker and agent to Rock Hudson, Tab Hunter, Guy Madison, and a dozen others. In the Fifties he was known as the king of monosyllabic masculinity. Describing his first meeting with the then-unknown Roy Fitzgerald, the *New York Times Magazine* wrote:

> Willson stared up at the massive natural phenomenon, walked around it, bruised his knuckles tapping its chest, then stepped back a few paces for a better view. 'He makes me think of something. What?' he asked himself. The critter just stood there, as impressive, expressionless, as the Rock of Gibraltar. 'Rock!' Willson shouted. 'Rock . . . Hudson!"

Of course, that's a bunch of far-fetched apocrypha, but if there's a glint of homoeroticism to the story, that much certainly is true. Today Henry Willson is remembered as the lecherous svengali of a generation of attractive male stars, some of whom were gay—Hudson, Hunter—and some who were not—Madison, Rory Calhoun—but all of whom were willing in some way to accommodate their powerful, high-profile agent. "He had a notorious reputation," recalled Ray Stricklyn, "especially among young actors whom he'd try to seduce—frequently succeeding. He destroyed more than one young man, believe me."

But he also made a few into huge stars, indeed, the absolute *biggest*—which was why, boy after boy, they kept flocking to Willson, even if they were straight and he was a beastly looking man, bald and fat. "Henry looked like a kind of Mafia guy," said the actor Jonathan Gilmore. "He tried real hard to get me to go to bed with him. I know a lot of guys did, but everything about him was simply repellent to me."

Gilmore was then a struggling young actor, very handsome, who'd already had experience fighting off the unwanted attentions of Irving Rapper. "I knew what Henry wanted, a payback in the form of a relationship. He made a lot of promises to people. I'd see him sitting in a restaurant on the Strip with a telephone at his table and always surrounded by young, attractive guys. He was a flustering, blustering kind of guy, but he had power. The studios always took his calls after he'd made Rock Hudson a star."

"Henry was a chameleon," wrote his secretary, Phyllis Gates, who'd also marry Rock Hudson. "He could be like a stern father to his young clients. He could be crisp and businesslike with studio bosses. He had a finely honed sense of humor, and he could charm a roomful of celebrities. He could play whatever role was needed to swing a deal or ingratiate himself."

Henry's father had been president of Columbia Records, and as a young man he'd secured a job as a talent scout for David O. Selznick. There he boosted the careers of Guy Madison and Rhonda Fleming, and convinced himself he could make it on his own. But it was a rocky road until his big breakthrough with Hudson: after that, he could write his own ticket. His power stemmed not only from his star making but, according to Gates, from the pimping service he offered producers. He supplied women to Howard Hughes and studs to moguls' wives—and "if a producer or director preferred boys, he could manage that too."

Ray Stricklyn remembered the "gang bangs" set up in Willson's house—"not an infrequent happening"—and that Rock Hudson was often the guest of honor. "There were dozens of the most attractive young men in Hollywood in attendance," he said, "including, to my surprise, several well-known, supposedly 'straight' movie actors." Gilmore once visited Willson's house in Bel-Air and saw Rory Calhoun lounging about; Willson showed him private photographs of Guy Madison in the nude. "There was no line between gay and straight in Hollywood," Gilmore insisted. "Not for ambitious young men."

Gilmore himself didn't end up on Willson's roster, but he did have a sexual relationship with his own agent, none other than John Darrow. Willson has attracted the lion's share of notoriety for his manipulation of young

men, but in fact, there was a network of gay agents in the Fifties who employed similar methods. In addition to Darrow, there was Warner Toub,
Robert Raison, and Dick Clayton. "They passed people along like fucking
postcards," Gilmore said. "It was really kind of sad. Toub would meet some
young guy just off the bus from Des Moines and tell him he'd help make
him a star. He'd sleep with him, then call Dick Clayton and tell the kid Clayton might have a job for him. So the kid would go meet with Clayton and
sleep with him too. Then Clayton would call Bob Raison and Bob Raison
would call Henry Willson. They were doing each other favors; they weren't
really looking for talent. They got to sleep with a bunch of good-looking
young men and the kids ended up nowhere, except maybe on the street."

Gilmore was reluctant to include Darrow in that list, retaining a fondness
for the man others described as nasty and cruel in his relationship with
Chuck Walters. "Darrow was very good to me, very influential in my life,"
Gilmore said. Interestingly, although Gilmore would spend nearly every
Friday night at Darrow's Westwood apartment and accompany him on Sat-
urdays to the Malibu beach house, he doesn't remember ever meeting Walters, nor any mention of him by Darrow. The only meanness Gilmore ever
saw from Darrow was directed toward other agents: "He could be very sar-
castic about the others and how they conducted themselves."

But Willson at least cared little about what others thought. "Henry
didn't give a shit if people were laughing behind his back, because he was
making so much money with his big stars," Gilmore recalled.

That such a homosexual cabal existed behind the scenes—making stars,
making money, wielding enormous power—would have, if known, confirmed many of the suspicions of the right-wing critics of Hollywood. The
descriptions of Gilmore, Stricklyn, and others of gang bangs and the boy
trade suggest that *Confidential* exposés were indeed onto something, and
that the studios had real reasons to be fearful. Yet contemporary finger-
wagging over the activities of Willson and the rest still seems puritanical,
especially given the fact that such sexual shenanigans had always been part
of Hollywood, gay *and* straight. Gilmore pointed out that Willson's stable
of boys was really not much different from a heterosexual agent's bevy of
girls, and that the latter model was the far more common. Willson has taken
a bad rap from writers ever since the stories of Hudson's homosexuality
came to light, with Hudson's partner, Tom Clark, branding him "diabolical" and George Nader and Mark Miller painting him with broad, movie-
villainous strokes in Hudson's so-called autobiography. That Willson and
agents like him could be unscrupulous or insensitive is not at issue: what
needs some finessing is their role in maintaining gay stars in a precarious time.

Willson may or may not have specifically arranged for Phyllis Gates to
marry Hudson, but he certainly facilitated the publicity surrounding it. The

true story of that union has been debated back and forth, but what matters here is what it did for Rock's career. Gates would recall how much Hudson enjoyed walking into parties with her on his arm. "Whether it was because he was becoming a major star or because he now had a wife to bring, Rock had started getting invitations to the most exclusive parties," she wrote. "He had been on the fringe before; now it was fashionable to invite Rock Hudson and his bride to join the cream of Hollywood society."

Willson had been instrumental in separating Hudson and a male lover shortly before the marriage, a move another box-office king, William Haines, had refused some twenty years earlier. But this was a different time, and Hudson wasn't as willing as Haines to walk away from the spotlight if push came to shove. By handling Rock's marriage—and subsequent divorce—Willson had ensured Hudson's immortality among the screen giants. Had there been no marriage, no quelling of the background noise about Hudson's sexuality, who's to say how long Rock's career might have lasted, or if he would have reached the same heights?

Hollywood's gay agents knew the score. True, they could be petty and manipulative, but such traits weren't unique to their sexual orientation. What set Willson and Darrow and the others apart was the fact that they were successful at a time when the tightrope was thinnest.

Henry Willson would end up on the skids once Hudson dropped him, and the many who'd felt used and manipulated by him were only too glad to see him go. No one raised a hand to help him, and he descended deeper into alcoholism, dying in 1978 at the Motion Picture Country Home of cirrhosis of the liver. That he may at times have indeed been diabolical should remain as only one part of his legacy; the rest should focus on the extraordinary power he was able to gather, both for himself and his clients, without ever disguising who or what he was—indeed, by being "notorious" for it. Gay survival during the blacklist and inquisition era can—at least in part—be credited to this colorful nexus of gay publicists, journalists, and agents who, sometimes by whatever means necessary, kept themselves in power and gay stars on the screen.

THE BOLD ONES

THE STONEWALL GENERATION
AND THE END OF THE STUDIO ERA
1953-1969

When Jack Larson arrived in New York, he couldn't ever have imagined going back to his native Los Angeles. New York was where he'd *dreamed* of coming: he wanted to write poetry and act off-Broadway in cutting-edge experimental plays. This would be his life, he thought, living among the Beats, in a little corner of the world where freedom and individuality thrived despite an era of repression and conformity. Here, he befriended the poet Frank O'Hara and other writers and artists; he presented his verse plays in loft-apartment readings. Like many of his crowd, he did some work in live television, at the time centered in New York. Then, in the first months of 1953, came the call: he would need to return to Hollywood, to play Jimmy Olsen in "The Adventures of Superman"—the latest entry in an innovative new trend: *television on film*.

Larson was distraught. He had made the "Superman" pilot before he'd left Los Angeles a year ago purely for the cash, never dreaming it would find a sponsor. The prospect of leaving New York and returning to Hollywood seemed disastrous. "I thought I would be typecast as an actor," he said, "and ruined forever as a writer."

Many felt this way, but there was no denying the reality. Television had not only arrived to stay, but now it was heading west across the country like the old movie pioneers some forty years earlier. *Time* noted the comparison: "Where the old-time film director sported puttees and riding crops, the TV director wears blue jeans and sneakers—and gets impressive results under tight schedules and pressures that [would] frighten veteran moviemakers."

Their craft had been honed in television's "Golden Age"—live, New York–based programming in such variety shows as Ed Sullivan's "Toast of the Town" and dramatic anthologies such as "Studio One." But by the mid-1950s, New York television production had declined dramatically, accounting for 50 percent of all TV programming in 1955 and just 31 percent in 1956. Meanwhile, there was a corresponding jump in network prime-time programming produced in Hollywood, from 40 to 71 percent. When "Studio One" moved to Hollywood's Television City in 1957, joining other CBS dramas like "Playhouse 90" and "Climax," the end of New York live dramatic television was assured.

"Almost overnight, production shifted from New York to Hollywood," said Robert Shaw, then a young television writer for NBC. "Those of us making a living in TV had only one choice: Go west." Shaw emigrated in 1959.

The statistics speak for themselves. A single TV studio, Desi Arnaz's and Lucille Ball's Desilu, employed one thousand workers and produced more film footage than all five major movie studios combined. The two largest talent agencies, William Morris and MCA, took in nine dollars in fees from TV deals to every one dollar they earned from films. One Hollywood-produced television show, NBC's daily "Matinee Theater," hired 2,400 actors a year for speaking parts—a 50 percent jump over the total used by Warner Bros. and Paramount *combined*. "Matinee Theater" also used as many scripts—250 a year— as all five of the major movie studios put together.

There were jobs in them thar Hollywood hills—and so once again, as had happened with the coming of sound and in the years after World War II, new blood was pumped into the film colony. "It's like a New York convention," Hotel Montecito manager Walter Smith told *Newsweek* of his TV transplants. "There has never been anything like this," said another "bedazzled" observer. "This is the gold strike. There are more actors working here now than at any time in history."

Old movie lots that had been gathering cobwebs since the silent days were polished up and fitted with television lights. "The Adventures of Ozzie and Harriet" filmed at the same studios where George James Hopkins had built sets for Theda Bara. CBS' vast Television City was erected on the field once used for location shooting of Valentino's *Four Horsemen of the Apocalypse.*

In the onslaught, Hollywood's tribal customs were shaken up, its social construction forever shattered. The Brown Derby buzzed with TV talk; its maître d' doled out the best tables to Lucy and Desi and Milton Berle. Hedda Hopper paid more attention in her column to Hugh (Wyatt Earp) O'Brian than she did many movie stars. Even the annual Academy Awards came to be regarded more as a sponsored TV event than an official film-industry function. With the exception of those in the running for an Oscar, few movie folk even bothered to attend.

"The rise of the TV era in Hollywood," noted *Time,* "has placed the movie people, themselves long cast as parvenus, in the odd role of the social old guard." In fact, that well-known mountebank "Prince" Mike Romanoff, Hollywood's leading restaurateur, was quoted as saying, "The TV actors can afford to eat here, but they haven't progressed beyond the drugstore counter. They think differently, behave differently, live differently."

Yet these were the folks who would transform Hollywood, both as town and industry. "What they lacked in glamour," observed historian Garth Jowett, "they made up in the youth and vitality they brought to the dying film capital." Rebellious types all: writers like Rod Serling and Paddy Chayefsky, directors like Delbert Mann and John Frankenheimer, actors like Jack Nicholson and Steve McQueen and Dennis Hopper—many of whom went on to become leaders in the film industry. These people didn't quake in fear before the Mayers and Warners and Zanucks. They hadn't lived under the thumb of the Production Code, nor had most of them known, except second-hand, the inquisitions of the early Fifties. And their arrival couldn't have come at a more momentously opportune time: the old system was irretrievably breaking down. Staggered by the twin onslaught of the HUAC hearings and the rise of television, the film industry was, by the late 1950s, in serious decline. The new guard—bold and brash in their bluejeans and New York attitudes—were poised and ready to build something new.

GAYS ON THE SMALL SCREEN

As ever, a significant amount of this new blood was gay—young, ambitious, mostly progressive-thinking and inspired by the independence they'd known in New York.

Jack Larson, Robert Shaw, Tony Perkins, James Dean—all came out to Hollywood in the television invasion. There was also Tom Tryon, who'd appeared on live TV in New York before coming to Hollywood and star-ring in several films, notably *The Longest Day* and *The Cardinal*. Among other gay pioneers: Richard Deacon, who alternated between bits in sci-fi films (*Invasion of the Body Snatchers, Them!*) and TV spots before reaching fame with "Leave it to Beaver" and "The Dick Van Dyke Show"; Paul Lynde, who first came out for "The Red Buttons Show" in 1955 and re-turned in the Sixties for "Bewitched"; Val Dufour, a frequent guest star on "Gunsmoke" and other Westerns before achieving soap-opera fame as Wal-ter Curtin on "Another World" (he'd also live with DeWitt Bodeen); Tedi Thurman, "Miss Monitor" on "The Tonight Show" and lover of former Ziegfeld girl Peggy Fears; Mary McCarty, a panelist on "Celebrity Time" and lover of Margaret Lindsay; and Robert Reed, then a young, off-Broadway actor who headed to Hollywood for bits on "Father Knows Best" and "Bronco" before achieving pop-culture immortality as the father of "The Brady Bunch."

Most of these actors looked upon their treks west far more enthusiasti-cally than Larson. Ray Stricklyn remembered his red-eye flight to Los An-geles on October 1, 1955, as "a new adventure and a new career." Starting out in New York with small parts on Ed Sullivan's "Toast of the Town" and "The Faye Emerson Show," Stricklyn had been convinced by his agent, Alec Alexander, that Hollywood was the place to be. So much production was leaving New York, Alexander explained, that he was closing down op-erations and moving westward. One of his other clients, Sal Mineo, had in fact just broken out of TV and into films with *Rebel Without a Cause*.

Hundreds—thousands—more gay men and lesbians flooded into Holly-wood, many of whom never made it as big as Dean or Mineo or even Lynde or Reed. Many of these, like Charles Williamson, stayed anyway, finding satisfying and prosperous careers outside film or television. No mat-ter their occupation, by their sheer numbers and presence, these new trans-plants once more changed the tenor and character of Hollywood.

"That whole freer, more theatrical sense from New York was brought out here," said Williamson. "Every time I'd go to the market, I'd run into someone else from New York. 'Oh, you've moved out here, too?' Every week you'd find this influx of new people."

A large percentage of them settled in West Hollywood. "It was not a very pretty place back then," said Williamson's partner, Tucker Fleming. "Santa Monica Boulevard was nothing but hardware stores and sawmills. But the little houses were cheap and people just moving here bought them up." Many houses were refurbished and decorated by a pair of set design-ers, Reg Allen and Jack Stephens, who had also arrived as part of the mid-Fifties emigration.

It wasn't just gay, of course: the West Hollywood mix also consisted of such sophisticates as Dorothy Parker and Alan Campbell. But the gay element was notable, first in the west end of West Hollywood and finally throughout the town itself, gradually becoming the separate, largely homosexual city it is today.

• • •

"Television opened doors that the movie studios had locked," said Robert Shaw. "I could never have had the wide variety of writing assignments in movies that I had in TV."

Shaw had started as a writer of radio serials in New York, creating "Front Page Farrell" and contributing to "Ma Perkins," "The Guiding Light," "Search for Tomorrow," and others. For television, he wrote original weekly dramas as part of "Robert Montgomery Presents," showcasing Rock Hudson, Rosalind Russell, and Claudette Colbert in their TV debuts. With Colbert, who became his houseguest in Connecticut, Shaw formed a lifelong friendship. With Montgomery himself, however, there was a safe distance. Known for being arch-conservative and homophobic, Montgomery was not well liked by his staff, many of whom were gay. "Most of us were for Adlai Stevenson and we wore little Stevenson buttons on our lapels," Shaw remembered. "Montgomery, of course, was for Eisenhower, so whenever we saw him we'd turn the buttons over."

Moving to Hollywood, Shaw found his new boss at Fox, Richard Zanuck, more tolerant. Zanuck, like many of the movie chiefs, had inaugurated a television production unit at the studio, coming "to the sensible conclusion that if they couldn't defeat us, they'd better join us," according to Shaw. Columbia had been the first to enter the field, with its Screen Gems division in 1951. The success of Disney's television programming persuaded the other studios to get into the act, with Fox, Warner Bros., and MGM all grinding out TV shows by 1955. One of Shaw's first assignments for Fox was to develop a TV series based on the film *Peyton Place;* accordingly, he created the nighttime serial that launched the careers of Mia Farrow and Ryan O'Neal.

That a number of gay men were writing for early television is salient, given the scarcity of gay screenwriters employed in the movies. In addition to Shaw, there was Jack Lloyd, who wrote for Red Skelton for thirteen years and later scripted "The Brady Bunch," "77 Sunset Strip," and "Love American Style," and Bernard Drew, who churned out episodes of "Dobie Gillis" and "My Favorite Husband." Like the early movies, television was an unclaimed wilderness, and the opportunity it provided was strikingly egalitarian. With so many positions in need of new talent, old barriers and traditions became irrelevant.

Not just in writing either: television offered inclusion in other areas not traditionally welcoming of gays. In cinema, gay men had been consigned to set decoration after the coming of sound, but in early television many were once again in charge of overall production design. Paul Barnes won the first Emmy given for art direction in 1956 for "Your Hit Parade"; consequently he was nominated nine more times for his work on "The Carol Burnett Show." John Pickette worked in the CBS design department for more than thirty years, overseeing the look of "Sergeant Bilko," "You Are There," "The $64,000 Question," "The Ed Sullivan Show" and several Hallmark Hall of Fame specials. Glen Holse was Steve Allen's art director before moving on to design Liberace's Las Vegas act. Jim Hassinger worked on "Ozzie and Harriet" and the Judy Garland specials. Jerry Maston designed a number of shows, including "The Courtship of Eddie's Father."

"There seemed to be more gay people in the TV networks as opposed to the film studios," recalled Joe Armetta, who worked as a set decorator under John Pickette at CBS. "The film studios were much more 'good old boys' and [there] the fag jokes were many."

Not unexpectedly, the gay presence in costume design and wardrobe carried over into TV: Robert Campbel, Noel Taylor, and Burton J. Miller were among notable early television designers. Movie veteran Edward Stevenson, with a career dating back to the 1930s, found even greater acclaim as chief designer at Desilu: Lucille Ball's classic fashions on "I Love Lucy," as well as her more wacky outfits, were mostly the work of Stevenson.

The most surprising breakthrough came in the technical fields, which had been implicitly off-limits to gays in the movie studios. Nelson Tetreault was a cameraman at both ABC and CBS beginning in the early 1960s; he died of AIDS in 1989. Mexican-born Alex Quiroga was manager of technical operations at NBC and an expert on color broadcasting, pioneering its use on "Bonanza." He was also an early lover of Don Bachardy's, occasionally socializing with him and Isherwood. There was also cameraman James Crabe, who began his career shooting TV inserts (more on Crabe below).

For actors, too, television offered new benefits. Movie players recognized the decreasing number of film roles and, contrary to popular wisdom, leaped at the opportunity presented by the new medium. "[Movie] producers are keeping the top eight or nine stars busy and to hell with the rest of us," Rory Calhoun told the press, just before he moved over to star in TV's "The Texan." Several gay film actors also found new life on the small screen. Ray Stricklyn said that his gayness was not nearly the issue in television that it was in the movies, citing his myriad "straight" roles: doctor, senator, sheriff, villain. Even Franklin Pangborn was given the chance to play more than fussy store managers and effete hairdressers on TV; in regu-

lar appearances on the series *Personal Appearance,* he often came across positively *butch.*

• • •

To those close to the industry, gay involvement in the new medium was
strikingly apparent; sooner or later, it was bound to attract comment. In
1962, television director James Yarborough was found bludgeoned to
death; Robert Richards, a bit-part TV actor ("Maverick") and described in
the papers as Yarborough's "former roommate," was arrested for the crime.
It might not have been as splashy as the William Desmond Taylor case, but
the scandal sheets jumped on it soon enough. Naming no names—a legacy
of the *Confidential* trials—*Inside Story* wrote that although the police "never
publicly labeled it a pervert killing, the motive was no secret to the lavender lads who talked about it for a long time at the 'gay' bars."

A new generation of scandal sheets was ready to pounce on the nation's
newest pasttime, in language more viciously homophobic than ever before.
"How the Homos Are Ruining TV" blared a cover headline of *Inside Story.*

> Nobody knows for sure how many pansies there are in TV. But
> things have gotten so out of hand in this new Sodom on the
> Coaxial Circuit that you can't tell the he-men from the she-men
> without a score card. . . . Right now the twisted twerps not only
> are in a position to tell you what you can see as entertainment,
> they are recruiting others of the lavender set to give it to you!
> Their numbers are legion. The shocking fact about homosexual-
> ity in TV is this: the queers make no effort to hide their twisted
> tendencies.

Several articles alleged a "homosexual Mafia" existed among television producers, keeping the "fairies and limp-wristed lads" entrenched. *Whisper*
charged that "the gay guys and dolls have become the real rulers of this
make-believe empire." The charge of "queers in control" was not new; recall Joseph Breen's allegation in 1932 that "any number" of Hollywood's
leaders were "perverts." It was and remains a recurring theme of the moral-
ist critics of popular entertainment.

While hardly as pervasive as the scandal rags made out, there *were* in fact
a number of gays in high places in television. Hunt Stromberg Jr., son of
the former MGM producer and remembered as an "obvious" homosexual
by many in the subculture, was the longtime program vice president at
CBS, supervising, among others, "The Beverly Hillbillies," "Green Acres"
and "Lost in Space." Agent Warner Toub served as a producer for Ida

Lupino's sitcom, "Mr. Adams and Eve." At one gay party arranged by Toub, actor Jonathan Gilmore recalled running into none other than a very well-known, prestigious, married-with-children producer of acclaimed dramatic anthology series.

"There's worry over the stranglehold queers possess," *Inside Story* reported, breathlessly detailing alleged "top-level" conferences and the work of private investigators to root out "the problem." How much of that was true is questionable, but certainly Sheila James Kuehl, a lesbian actress on "The Many Lives of Dobie Gillis," would remember her spin-off getting the ax because "the president of CBS thought I was a little butch." Executives had to be aware of the numerous blind-item attacks on Raymond Burr; recalling Hedda Hopper's letter to him about "what happened in Phoenix," Burr may have barely sidestepped a scandal in the early Sixties.

Television may have been a new medium and one that offered a broader range of opportunities for gays, but some things weren't all that much different from the movies. Dick Sargent, who acted in "Playhouse 90" and "Gunsmoke" before landing his star-marking turn on "Bewitched," would recall the painful necessity of having to deny the reality of his twenty-year relationship with a television scriptwriter, gamely smiling through a publicity romance with Connie Stevens. The more things changed, the more they stayed the same.

THE QUIET REVOLUTION OF GAYS IN HOLLYWOOD

"I think it's interesting," said one man, employed as a publicist at Warner Bros. in the early 1960s, "that just as the studios were declining, the gays were becoming more bold. Maybe it was the lessening of authority. Maybe it was television. Maybe it was just that they were fed up."

For decades, the studios had offered a haven to homosexuals, a place to thrive and, within parameters, live and work with a degree of personal authenticity. Yet since the end of the war there had been an increasing sense among many of the industry's homosexuals that it wasn't enough. It's impossible to separate the experience of gays in Hollywood from the times they lived in: the Sixties were a time of cultural challenge and, even if the phrase has been overworked, a loss of innocence. Both the war in Vietnam and the protests against it grew exponentially; the Kennedy and Martin Luther King assassinations further scarred the nation's psyche. Civil-rights movements for blacks and women soon swelled to embrace homosexuals and other minorities, and the sexual revolution was not far behind. If the 1920s had rewritten the rules of the old order, the 1960s decreed that there were no rules at all.

For many gays, it was simply *time*. The fear and repression of the past decade had left many exhausted and resentful. The author Merle Miller, an occasional movie screenwriter—*The Rains of Ranchipur* (1955) and *Kings Go Forth* (1958)—would reflect in a famous *New York Times Magazine* piece on the oppression homosexuals faced in the era. Citing Otto Kahn's famous statement that "a kike is a Jewish gentleman who has just left the room," Miller asked: "Is a fag a homosexual gentleman who has just stepped out? Me? I can never be sure, of course. I know it shouldn't bother me. That's what everybody says, but it does bother me . . . every time I enter a room in which there is anyone else. Friend or foe? Is there a difference?"

But Miller's radical new way of seeing the situation didn't end there: he pointed out the complicity of homosexuals themselves in their own oppression. Chastising the American Civil Liberties Union for its silence when gay people were being hunted down and expelled from "all kinds of government posts," he added that "the most silent of all was a closet queen who was a member of the board of directors, myself."

Miller didn't write that piece until 1971, after the Stonewall riots had upped the ante and the public discourse on homosexuality had changed considerably. Yet it's clear that these were emotions that had been brewing for a while. They arose from a larger shift in perspective that occurred in the post-inquisition years: a repugnance for McCarthyism, a repudiation of the politics of fear, a rejection of pretense. By the early 1960s, such directors as Otto Preminger were openly defying the blacklist, effectively ending its power, but the reaction against it had been building for a number of years. When Joseph Welch, chief counsel for the army, stood up to Joe McCarthy in 1954 and asked, "At long last, have you no sense of decency?" many Americans agreed. And, of course, Welch's rebuke was broadcast live on national television.

The rise of television globalized provincial attitudes. Entertainment, too, became far more democratic: the old monopoly on power enjoyed by the movies as shaper of American culture and thought was dealt a fatal blow. It would be the filmmakers themselves, in fact, weary of the shackles placed for too long on their creativity, who would expedite the collapse of studio control. Fighting both front offices and the Production Code, directors like Preminger, Elia Kazan, Stanley Kubrick, and Mike Nichols (note no gay directors among them) turned out increasingly provocative films: *The Man With the Golden Arm* (1955), *Baby Doll* (1956), *Lolita* (1962), and *Who's Afraid of Virginia Woolf?* (1966). Even with "Condemned" ratings from the Legion of Decency, many of these pictures were financial blockbusters for their studios—which, desperate for cash by the end of the Fifties, began giving the green light to other controversial projects.

The last nut to crack was the "sex perversion" clause, but it, too, finally shattered. The hero's queerness is barely disguised in *Cat on a Hot Tin Roof* (1958); another Tennessee Williams project, *Suddenly Last Summer,* went even farther the following year. In 1961, *Victim,* a British film by director Basil Dearborn, dared to treat homosexuality both explicitly *and* sympathetically. By the next year, gayness was integral in three American films: *Advise & Consent, The Children's Hour,* and *The Best Man.* No matter that its explicitness was as a pathological condition; good or bad, homosexuality was finally *spoken* on the American screen. The Code's prohibition—indeed, its entire power—was at long last destroyed.

It is interesting to speculate on how these developments—explicitly gay films, Merle Miller's article—were received by the old guard of Hollywood's gays, none of whom participated in the cultural revolution: George Cukor, Charles Walters, Roger Edens, Leonard Spigelgass, Frank McCarthy. Most of their acquaintances remember discomfort. When Isherwood and Bachardy took Cukor to see a gay play by Charles Ludlum—a parody, in fact, of "Camille"—the veteran director left after the first act. "His idea of style and humor was on another level," Bachardy remembered. "It was just fundamentally a generational difference."

But among the younger set just breaking in, there was solidarity with the changes being brought by the new decade. Writer Mart Crowley, who sold an unproduced lesbian-themed screenplay to Fox in 1962, would go on to write the groundbreaking play (and later film) "The Boys in the Band," first presented in 1968. Art director Paul Barnes would later try his hand at writing himself, penning an unproduced teleplay on the life of assassinated gay San Francisco Supervisor Harvey Milk. More and more of Hollywood's gays bucked the marriage route of the past two decades and returned to an earlier tradition of living with their same-sex partners: Dick Sargent and his scriptwriter boyfriend; Jack Larson and producer James Bridges; Raymond Burr and Robert Benevides; Victor Buono and a series of young men. "As far as coming out," said composer Jerry Herman, "I just went along with the time. At every opening night, I just quietly brought a boyfriend on my arm."

What had been radical behavior on the part of James Whale and David Lewis was no longer so anomalous. The revolution that erupted in 1969 at Stonewall didn't simply spontaneously combust: it was painstakingly prepared for by years of countless quiet personal rebellions like Herman's. In 1952, for the first time, a gay man, Dale Jennings, triumphed against the long arm of the Los Angeles Police Department, being found not guilty of lewd conduct by a jury in a case that was clearly about police entrapment. The pioneering studies of Dr. Evelyn Hooker, published in 1956, stunned the medical community by revealing no discernible psychological differences between gay and straight men, as well as by asserting that "overt" homosexuals could lead healthy, productive, well-adjusted lives. Hooker's work—conducted in Los Angeles and facilitated by her friendship with Christopher Isherwood—helped shape a new idea of gays as an oppressed minority.

It's notable how much of this activity took place in Los Angeles, in the very shadow of the movie studios. There, too, had the Mattachine Society been formed; in addition to Harry Hay, at least two of its early leaders— Konrad Stevens and Rudi Gernreich, who'd later become a notable name in fashion—had worked in the industry in various minor positions. Isherwood met with Mattachine in 1952, bringing Evelyn Hooker with him. Harry Hay would recall that Isherwood was rather dismissive of the group's socialist politics, suggesting that if they wanted real power, they should pursue prominent names in the film industry. Hay's memory may have been influenced with his pique at Isherwood, who declined to join the group himself.

Despite the split between the industry gays and the Mattachine "homophiles," as they called themselves, their influence on each other was inevitable. With homosexuality now a specific public threat, a corresponding and more positive construct also emerged: the self-identified, unapologetic gay man or lesbian. Cukor, Spigelgass, and the rest may have been undisguised within the industry, but to name oneself *publicly* as gay—"coming out," it came to be called—was a new and radical concept. Some were terrified by the idea; others found it liberating.

The historian John Loughery has written about this dichotomy, pointing out that for gay men of earlier generations, the term "coming out" held a satiric connotation of a "debutante's rite of passage." Before the late 1960s, a gay man did not "come out" to the world at large but rather "*to the life,* meaning he went to bed with a man and so became progressively more experienced as a homosexual." There is an enormous difference between the two variations of the same term: as Loughery wrote, "A need to tell heterosexuals who might be unsympathetic, especially relatives, would have struck most gay men of an earlier day as a bit odd."

That was the mind-set from which the Cukors and Spigelgasses sprang, but for people like Gavin Lambert and Arthur Laurents, the new paradigm seemed liberating. As part of the more liberal, independent, post-war influx, they viewed the changes and challenges of the Sixties with enthusiasm. Encouraged by the increasing license for gay themes in movies, Lambert's original screenplay for *Inside Daisy Clover* (1965) contained several intelligent scenes that shed light on the secret gay life of the character played by Robert Redford. But they were cut, leaving the conflict between

342 • BEHIND THE SCREEN

Redford and Natalie Wood frustratingly ambiguous. "Which was a pity," Lambert said, "because there were all these kinds of things that would have made the film more adventurous than it turned out to be."

Despite the disappointment, the very fact that Lambert could even *write* such scenes and hold out hope for a more "adventurous" film signaled a new era. Arthur Laurents also pushed the sexual limits of the Code in *Bonjour Tristesse* (1958) but did not return to Hollywood for over a decade. When he did, it was to take on the blacklist in *The Way We Were* (1973).

The changes of the early Sixties would reverberate for gays all throughout the industry. Director Tony Richardson, who won the Oscar for Best Director for *Tom Jones* in 1963, would, despite his marriage to Vanessa Redgrave and affair with Jeanne Moreau, increasingly live a gay life, "an open secret to his friends," according to Gavin Lambert. Montgomery Clift, his stardom having peaked, lived quite openly with a male lover. Sal Mineo, too, would discard most attempts to appear heterosexual. Curtis Harrington, an assistant to Jerry Wald at Columbia and later at Fox, would branch out on his own with *Night Tide* (1963), starring Dennis Hopper. This and his later films—*Who Slew Auntie Roo?, What's the Matter With Helen?*—contain a stylish and ironic sexual ambiguity cherished by gay audiences.

Most colorful was second-unit supervisor Maurice "Zubie" Zuberano, who friends recall as becoming increasingly more overt as the decade went on, throwing outrageous psychedelic parties in his home in the Hollywood hills. Whereas Richardson, Harrington, and even Clift might be associated with the youthful counterculture, Zuberano was *fifty-four* at the time he worked on *The Sound of Music* (1965). He was simply inspired by the permissive changes he saw around him, and his overtness didn't seem to hurt his career: he'd be promoted to production associate on *The Sand Pebbles, Star!,* and *Portnoy's Complaint.* "Zubie was a real character," remembered Robert Wheaton. "He got away with it, too. Everybody knew he was gay. I guess by then it didn't matter nearly so much. Every day, the times seemed to change a little bit more."

JAMES CRABE AND THE GAY GIRLS RIDING CLUB

In the early 1960s, veteran cameraman Arthur Miller watched with contempt as his profession—that final bastion of traditional masculinity—was gradually taken over by new blood. "The spics are coming in," he told Charles Higham, who was interviewing him for a book on Hollywood cinematographers. "Next we're going to have red Indians taking over the union. They're pushing out wonderful old men."

Wonderful old *white heterosexual* men, he meant. Miller was right: there *were* new faces—Mexican-born Alex Quiroga among them—coming into cinematography. In the late 1960s, cameraman Gordon Willis saw the change more positively: "The older generation of cameramen were never willing to teach," he said. "They were dying with their secrets. It's really only in the last five years or so that there's been any air in this town."

Air that let in—in addition to the "spics and red Indians"—a number of women and homosexuals. With the studios holding less and less sway over American moviemaking, new avenues of filmmaking opportunities opened up, and for the first time, a number of gay cinematographers emerged. Many of these were self-taught. Spanish-born Nestor Almendros made his first films in the early 1960s in Cuba and France after being called in by the director Eric Rohmer to replace a cameraman who'd walked off the job. He'd later make films in the United States, and died of AIDS in 1992. Likewise, Steven Katz learned on the job shooting exploitation films in the mid-to-late 1960s. Originally a fashion photographer, Katz would go on to acclaim with *'Night, Mother* and *Gods and Monsters,* the story of James Whale.

"Cinematography is all about the eye," said Katz. "You can have all the training you want, but if you don't have the eye, forget it."

Most would agree that award-winning cameraman James Crabe had "the eye." He, too, began his career on the fringes of the industry, teaching himself the basics of camera work while making such low-budget independent quickies as *The Slime People* in 1962. Meanwhile, in his off-hours, Crabe practiced his craft with a series of 16mm silent films he made with his friends in the legendary Gay Girls Riding Club: *Always on Sunday* (1961), *A Roman Springs at Mrs. Stone* (1962), and *What Really Happened to Baby Jane* (1963). Crabe offers the best example of the new breed of homosexual who emerged in the waning days of the studios. Not only naming himself as gay, he was actively involved in creating, celebrating, and documenting the gay subculture.

In fact, no name evoked such broad smiles and happy memories from survivors as Jimmy Crabe and GGRC. "Those were the golden years of fagdom," remembered Ron Anderegg, who attended every Halloween costume bash thrown by the GGRC during the 1960s. "Oh, my, yes, the GGRC," beamed the director Curtis Harrington. "Such fun we'd have going to their parties." Several interviewees, reluctant to talk about their days working in the movie studios, suddenly gushed endlessly about their exploits at a GGRC party. Billy Williams said simply, "Those were the days, and we thought they'd never end."

Jimmy Crabe was the heart and soul of the outrageous group, many of whom, like himself, were also employed in the film or television industries. At the time of his involvement with GGRC, Crabe was shooting commercials and working with independent director Tom Laughlin (later to achieve success with the *Billy Jack* movies) on such films as *Like Father Like Son* (1961) and *The Young Sinner* (1965). Among other GGRC members, Ray Harrison worked as an assistant on Spike Jones' TV show, and Jim Randall toiled as an assistant light man in both TV and film. Crabe shot the GGRC films with equipment he'd borrow from his current projects; Harrison wrote the scripts; Randall provided lighting; and the rest, adopting drag names like Clod Hopper, Roz Berri, and Patti Pope, played the parts.

According to Marshall Kendzy, one of the founders with Crabe of GGRC, the moviemaking began as kind of a lark. The group had come together for social outings, horse riding on Sunday morning along the beach in Santa Monica. "That's where the name came from," Kendzy explained. "We gave ourselves camp female names. Jimmy's was Connie—Connie Crabe. The first name had to start with the first letter of your last name. This way, we could be at work, or Jimmy at home with his parents, and anybody listening to us would think we were talking about a girl. 'Oh, I was with Connie last night.' Things like that."

Originally, there were about twelve members who, after their ride, would head over to the bars on Crystal Beach. "On the weekends there'd be two to three thousand queens along there," Kendzy remembered. In those queens, Crabe saw an audience—and, as "Connie B. DeMille," he set about producing films for them. The first vignettes he made, in 1959 and 1960, have been lost, but the others, all parodies of popular movies, retain a cult following.

Originally, the GGRC movies were shown in gay bars in Los Angeles and Long Beach. It was with the 1962 premiere of *A Roman Springs at Mrs. Stone* that the group's fame as party organizers began. Introducing the film with an elaborate production number, the Gay Girls sang and danced in drag, many for the first time. The show was a huge success; even Gavin Lambert, who'd written the original film, *The Roman Spring of Mrs. Stone,* adapted from Tennessee Williams' novella, remembered attending the gala and enjoying himself tremendously.

From there evolved the famous GGRC Halloween costume balls, organized by Ray Harrison and held at various places before finally settling at the International Hotel near the airport. Ron Anderegg would sometimes spend a full year designing his costumes. "Each year Ray would announce the theme for the next ball so we could have an entire year to design and make our costumes," he said. "The GGRC ball was the biggest costume ball in L.A., attended by many 'with-it' straights."

At the balls, the GGRC pictures would be screened, and by far the most requested was *What Really Happened to Baby Jane,* a brilliant slice of pre-Stonewall gay sensibility, filled with an irony and outrageousness that predicts the work of John Waters a few years later. The Bette Davis–Joan

Crawford film on which Crabe's parody is based was already a gay favorite, with the Long Beach drag queen Frieda giving a knockout impersonation of Davis as Baby Jane. In the scene where Jane kicks Blanche (played by Roz Berri) across the floor, Crabe stopped the camera to insert a dummy, allowing Jane to swing her sister around over her head as if she were Tarzan and Blanche a cheetah. Little queer moments abound throughout the film: Jane kills the maid using Blanche's bedpan, and the role of Edwin, played effeminately by Victor Buono in the original, is even more obviously gay here. The plot stays fairly close to the original film, except for the ending, which offers a gay-culture nod to Davis' failure to get an Oscar for the part.

Crabe's love for movies comes through clearly. "A true child of the movie industry," he called himself, having been born in Los Angeles in 1931, the son of Lyall Crabe, an animator at Disney. "I was always fascinated by the movies," he said. "As a youngster I would go to theaters and try to figure how the movies were made." It's not surprising that as a teenager he became a magician, with a regular spot on the TV show "You Asked For It." In fact, the doves that fly out of Blanche's dinner in *Baby Jane* were from his magic act. "He was quite the skilled magician," remembered Kendzy. "He would perform his act in gay bars and clubs. He was very popular."

But Crabe wanted a magic different than simply pulling rabbits out of hats. He began working with Laughlin in 1961 and was soon shooting television commercials for Marlboro and Max Factor; eventually, he'd win Clio awards for his work. By 1966 he was shooting *Agent for H.A.R.M.* at Universal, a spy drama originally intended for TV but released to theaters.

About this time, Kendzy remembered, Crabe stepped back from GGRC filmmaking. The later pictures associated with the group were made by someone else. "Jimmy was really getting started in the industry and needed to cover his tracks," said Kendzy. That doesn't mean he stopped attending GGRC galas or dropped out from his group of friends. "Oh, no, not at all," Kendzy insisted. "He was very comfortable with who he was, never tried to hide." Even while still living with his parents in Santa Monica, Jimmy started dating Bill Holland, with whom he'd remain for more than a decade.

Witty, talented, extraordinarily handsome, and with an incredible physique, Crabe was very popular among the gay subculture of Hollywood. As he grew within the industry, he made friends with a wide swath of people, from Isherwood and Bachardy to Curtis Harrington. He and his friends in the GGRC are transitional figures, linking old gay Hollywood with the post-Stonewall generation. In fact, they *are* that generation: it was their contemporaries who fought back in New York and organized the first gay pride parade in Los Angeles the following year. They were a bunch of high-spirited, ambitious young men in their twenties; it did not occur to them (at least in the beginning) that extracurricular activities like GGRC parties and camp films might hinder their careers. As such, they break radically from their predecessors; it's impossible to imagine Irving Rapper or Leonard Spigelgass—as undisguised as they might have been in their day—participating in such unambiguously queer shenanigans.

But Los Angeles in the years after the inquisitions was a city breaking wide open, as were many cities around the nation. There was a new sense of—if not freedom, then certainly the *possibility* of freedom. Many of the members of the Mattachine Society mixed regularly with partygoers at GGRC galas. "There was a real brotherhood," explained Marshall Kendzy. "There was a sense that things were happening, and that we were part of it."

That was certainly evidenced in the sudden rebirth of gay nightlife in the city, a phenomenon immeasurably aided by the revelries of the GGRC. By the late 1950s, despite the continuing hostility and harassment of the LAPD, a number of gay establishments had sprung up: the House of Ivy, the Cherokee House, Maxwell's, the Black Cat, the "356" bar downtown. Most gay bars had existed outside Los Angeles city limits, where county sheriffs were traditionally far more tolerant. Those few that now dared open their doors within the jurisdiction of the notoriously homophobic L.A. Police Chief William Parker did so with the conviction that if they had to fight, they'd fight. Most eventually went under: raids in the early 1960s killed such clubs as ChiChi's and Geri's, and the House of Ivy, after waging a valiant court battle to stay open with the help of a local musicians' union, was eventually forced to shut down.

But David Hanna recalled that the fear of Vice was changing. "A visit to the Cherokee House would have revealed a bolder crowd," he said. "The old uniform of white shirt and tie was gone, as patrons felt less of a need to appear 'respectable.' The young men acted tougher and less amenable to being pushed around. Inside the bar there was less talk of the Vice." He recalled an episode where an undercover cop was discovered among the crowd and severely beaten by patrons—"an isolated incident," he admitted, but a "small salvo in the cataclysmic changes" still to come. After a raid on the Black Cat in 1967, more than 200 people gathered in protest—nearly two years before the Stonewall rebellion in New York.

By the mid-Sixties, even such industry stalwarts as Henry Willson could be found in the Gallery Room, one of the most famous of the era's gay clubs, located at the corner of Crescent Heights and Santa Monica Boulevard. Frieda, from *What Really Happened to Baby Jane,* worked there for a time. "It was the focus of everything," remembered writer Charles Higham, who once took Irving Rapper there for a drink, watching as young gay actors swarmed around Willson in the hopes of being noticed. It was an interesting cross-generational mix coming together on the eve of Stonewall: old Hollywood (Rapper), who probably couldn't believe his eyes; 1950s Hollywood (Willson), who would soon be as passé as Rapper; and new Hollywood (the starstruck boys), some of whom would soon be marching in the Christopher Street West parade.

OLD VERSUS NEW

Leonard Spigelgass could get prickly in his defense of Old Hollywood. In an op-ed for *The New York Times* he excoriated the arrogance of cinema's new proprietors, chiefly the New York critics. "Let Vincent Canby and Penelope Gilliatt and Pauline Kael and Judith Crist, et. al., debate the merits of *A Clockwork Orange* and *Carnal Knowledge,* and we will simply accept their judgment," he wrote sarcastically. "What a relief!"

It was in response to Canby's complaint that Hollywood's "old guard" continued to vote at Oscar time for movies like *Airport, Fiddler on the Roof,* and *Nicholas and Alexandra* over edgier fare from newer directors. Spigelgass had had enough. Suggesting that perhaps members over the age of thirty-five be stripped of their votes, he needled: "We dum-dums vote for the *Airports* and the *Fiddlers* and the *Nicholases* because we just hate modern, relevant, avant-garde, impressionistic, soul-searching, violent, explicit films about rape, homosexuality, heroin, sadism, urinalysis, prostitution, and masturbation. And the reason we ignore these views of our society is that we are geriatric and conservative. We are Spiro Agnew; *you* are the free, untrammeled future."

Spigelgass intended his words as ironic and tongue-in-cheek, yet—whether he fully realized it at the time or not—they aren't far from the truth. Despite his old-time liberalism, he was, in fact, closer to Agnew's politics than he was to those of Hollywood's new generation. He did, in fact, despise "modern, relevant, avant-garde" films, and his grouping of homosexuality among rape, heroin, and sadism speaks volumes. Spigelgass—and many of his generation—had spent lives of carefully constructed order; the new actors, directors, and writers—and their films—were dismantling that order. Their depiction of homosexuality on the screen was unnerving to men like Spigelgass, who was not the only one to speak out against it. Cukor said he couldn't imagine making a film about homosexuality; he would "shudder like Aunt Pittypat," Don Bachardy remembered, whenever anything too sexual appeared on the screen.

Like Spigelgass and Cukor, Henry Grace was another liberal who nonetheless decried the changes to the old order. His nephew would recall this old Southern Democrat and union activist becoming a Republican in his later years. In his unpublished memoirs, Grace would actually blame part of Hollywood's decline on "union demands for more and more of the pie." Even more, he deplored the "degenerating morals" of the screen, with its "nude and lewd exhibitionism."

Even some younger gay actors defended the old value system as preferable to the new. Victor Buono positioned himself as a "conscientious objector" in the midst of the "morality revolution" of the early and mid-Sixties. Walking off the set of *The Strangler* (1964), he complained about the film's nudity. "I'm not a prude," Buono said—a fact seconded by many who knew him—"and I think the proof is in the picture. I'm still a sex maniac in it, you know. But it always depends on how you do a thing like that. I've lost several good parts outright because the producers couldn't see things my way. With pictures going wild, it's a serious situation for me, and I don't mind telling you I'm worried."

Yet Buono seems to have had no worries over playing the psychopathic title character as an effeminate, mother-dominated homosexual—not unsimilar to his part in *Whatever Happened to Baby Jane?* But then, this wasn't *gayness* he was playing, at least not any gayness he recognized; it was *perversion*. It was the same schizoid view of homosexuality that had long existed in Hollywood: the cultured elite ("people like Cole Porter") versus the low-class (and often criminal) "perverts." Buono's queer murderers and villains, not unlike those of Laird Cregar and Clifton Webb a decade earlier, may have been homosexual in conception and expression, but it was a homosexuality created by heterosexual writers and directors. As such, it resembled nothing in the lives of Spigelgass or Buono or any of them. In a way, this dichotomy actually provides a defense of Spigelgass' inclusion of homosexuality in his list of on-screen vices: the increasingly frequent depiction of gayness was rarely accurate or sympathetic. No wonder on-screen homosexuality should be offensive to Hollywood's gays: it was a fabrication of lies and fear.

But no amount of protests from Spigelgass or Buono could turn back the clock. The psychedelic Sixties saw the end to the old studio system. The process had begun as far back as 1948, when the Supreme Court ordered the studios to divest themselves of their theater chains, severely weakening their power by ending their vertical monopoly over exhibition. At the same time, television began draining audiences and dollars: movie attendance dropped from 90,000 in 1948 to 46,000 by 1953. Republic sold its backlog of old films to television and closed in 1958; that same year, RKO was sold to Desilu. Gimmicks like wide-screen and 3-D projection could sustain interest only so long. By 1958, a full 65 percent of Hollywood's movies were being made by independent producers, with stars and directors moving from one company to another. The once-busy soundstages of MGM, Fox, Warner Bros., and Universal were increasingly rented out for TV production.

The decline of the studios was also due to something less tangible than television or profits. Hollywood had never really recovered from the blow it took in the early 1950s from the blacklist, with progressive filmmakers banished and the screen awash in safe, unthreatening images and themes. As the historian Ronald Davis has pointed out, "Hollywood had become cautious and flabby at the very time it needed its strength." By the time some of the edge returned to Hollywood filmmaking, the studios had to contend with powerful rivals they'd never had before—not only television, but independent and foreign pictures, all of which had a better grip on the pulse of the times. The studios simply couldn't get back up to speed.

THE RESISTANCE OF ROSS HUNTER

Some felt that the answer lay not in the future but in the past. "I would like to bring back glamour, bring back the fantasy world, to live a dream again," a young, starry-eyed producer named Ross Hunter declared to his bosses at Universal in 1952. "I would like to do movies about the beautiful people."

Ross Hunter's films are part of the legendary magic of Hollywood, and deservedly so: tearjerkers colored in pastel hues, studded with glittery, overwrought stars. There is no winking at the audience, no self-conscious camp in Hunter's films: these were sincere, sumptuous epics of life, loss, and love, all designed according to Hunter's motto "Entertainment Through Beauty." At the tail end of the studio era came this one last gasp of old-style Hollywood glamour, led by one fiercely determined producer who just couldn't bear to see it all slip away. And it's probably not surprising to anyone that Ross Hunter was gay.

"His films are certainly filled with a gay sensibility," said film critic Kevin Thomas, "no question about that."

None whatsoever: Rock Hudson breathtakingly backlit in *Magnificent Obsession* (1954); Jane Wyman's defiance of society in *All That Heaven Allows* (1956); spunky Debbie Reynolds in *Tammy and the Bachelor* (1957); the catharsis of mother love and the theme of self-truth (not to mention Lana Turner's gowns) in *Imitation of Life* (1959); the double entendres between Hudson and Doris Day in *Pillow Talk* (1959); Hayley Mills as a girl not unlike a gay boy in *The Chalk Garden* (1964).

Hunter's moviemaking philosophy was simple. "If you want the girl next door," he'd say, "*go* next door." He yearned for that old-time glamour: "Gloria Swanson was absolutely right to go around with a leopard on a chain," he said. "So what that the leopard was on dope. The image *worked*." Gripping to Hedda Hopper that he was "sick nigh until death of dirty beatniks," he decried the trend toward "realism" in Hollywood. "You might just as well have a murder take place on an Oriental rug as on someone's dirty linoleum," he snapped.

Yet he had his own standards for authenticity. Insisting on real jewelry (over a million dollars' worth on *Imitation of Life*), he admitted audiences couldn't tell the difference, "but Lana knew they were real—that's why she radiated on the screen."

Critics said he was to movies what Liberace was to music: overblown, artificial, playing to sentiment. Hunter didn't necessarily disagree. He made no pretense that he was creating *art*. He shrugged off the barbs of the New York critics because *his pictures made money*—*big* money, the kind the studios had despaired of ever seeing again. "You guys give me no competition," he chided his colleagues at the Screen Producers Guild in 1961. "You are all so busy trying to impress Bosley Crowther that you've left me this shmaltz bonanza all to myself."

For a brief, shining moment, Hunter brought back old Hollywood in all its glory, tapping into a cultural reserve of nostalgia and a longing for a simpler and yet more glamorous era. "A producer has to have a handshake with the public," he said, "to find out what will tear them away from their homes. I went out there saying, 'You're going to see a picture with real stars looking glamorous in beautiful gowns on beautiful sets. No kitchen sinks. No violence. No pores. No messages.' And it *worked*."

To the *New York Times,* whose critics were among the most savaging to his films, he said, *"Hiroshima, Mon Amour* is great, but I wouldn't have produced it if I'd had the chance. It's for art houses, and the money is in the small towns. I want to get people back into the theaters."

Ross Hunter was the dying studios' last great hope. His heroes were Thalberg and Mayer; to anyone who'd listen, he'd insist the real problem besetting the movie industry wasn't television or the blacklist or anything else—it was a lapsed commitment to the ideals of the founders. "It's the oldest formula in the world," he said. "Louis B. Mayer and Irving Thalberg had it—*entertainment.*"

But entertainment wasn't the only thing the old movie moguls had had in mind. They'd wanted to establish the cinema as both shaper and guardian of the nation's middle-class values and ideals, a burden Ross Hunter now assumed as his own. His heroes are manly, moral, and noble; his heroines beautiful, virginal, and self-sacrificing. To a nation besieged by *Rebel Without a Cause, The Man With the Golden Arm, Lolita,* and the films of Tennessee Williams, Ross Hunter offered an antidote. "I'll leave all that to Tennessee," he'd say, scrunching up his face at the idea of "T-shirts and psychology" in the movies.

• • •

Ross Hunter was about as far from Tennessee Williams as one could get. That both were homosexual meant little. Hunter lived with his male partner but lied about it, telling one writer that it was his "stepbrother" who shared the house with him. Not even Frank McCarthy and Rupert Allan had gone so far; at least they acknowledged that they both lived on the same estate, if in separate quarters. But Ross Hunter wanted to go *back,* not forward. For him, the promise of the new generation held no appeal. He might be homosexual, but he was after the American dream as much as the founding fathers of Hollywood had been—and despite the war, despite the social movements and civil unrest, that dream still meant (for him) wealth, power, and *image.* His movies reflected his own aspirations. He'd admit, "The kind of life I put on the screen is the way I want life to be."

The critic Hollis Alpert knew the score. "When I met Ross Hunter," he said, "I discovered that he had a propensity for viewing his own career in much the same way that he viewed the tales he put up on the screen." Ross was, in some ways, as much a star as Rock Hudson or John Gavin. No background producer, he was photographed nearly as often as his actors; the "RH Factor" became industry shorthand for glamour and glitz. Accordingly, he actively promulgated the view that he was a ladies' man, making sure the cameras caught him each time he stepped out with a lovely actress on his arm.

He started as an actor, and could've been a movie star in his own right if stardom was based solely on looks. Standing over six feet, he was outrageously handsome in a boyish, devilish kind of way, his face lit up often and easily by a great smile of even, pearly-white teeth. Later, like Cary Grant, came the imposing eyeglasses that gave him a more serious, adult veneer, but all he had to do was smile and he was, once again, as beautiful as a matinee-idol heartthrob.

He was born Martin Fuss (pronounced Fooz) on May 6, 1920, in Cleveland, Ohio, the third child and only son of Austrian-Jewish immigrants, Eizik and Anna Fuss. Eizik, also known as Isadore, had emigrated in 1903, working as a tailor and presser in Cleveland's largely Jewish neighborhood of Glenville. As the years passed, the city's Austrian Jews, mostly adherents of Reform Judaism, assumed more middle-class status, while a new influx of Eastern European, mostly orthodox Jews replaced them as laborers and peddlers. Indeed, by the time Martin was born, the Fusses lived in a more well-to-do neighborhood of photo engravers, accountants, and bookkeepers. In 1921, with three partners and a capital of $40,000, Eizik founded the Mutual Cloak and Suit Company at 1220 West 6th Street. He would remain as vice-president of the company until it closed during the Depression. Eizik then returned to his own tailor shop.

Like many parents in this chronicle, particularly immigrants, Eizik and his wife instilled in their offspring the desire to *achieve*. In particular, the Fusses resembled the Spiegelgasses: first-generation Jews who obtained a degree of middle-class success and who prodded succeeding generations to even greater achievement, all the while never obscuring their ethnic roots. Eizik and Anna would be involved in their synagogue and remain in Jewish neighborhoods all their lives; daughter Freida would teach and later serve as principal at largely Jewish schools.

It was not, however, a cultural association their son would embrace with as much enthusiasm. He always wanted to break out, to find a place in the world outside of his own. "I come from a warm, schmaltzy, togetherness family that was mostly interested in education," he said. Little Martin, however, wanted to sing and dance. At a young age, he learned the banjo, sax, and harmonica. At age nine he was touring the RKO-Orpheum circuit in a vaudeville act with six other children. But Eizik eventually put an end to such nonsense, and his son returned to school and his parents' plan that he become a teacher.

He proved a deft student. His aptitude for languages won him a scholarship to Western Reserve University, but Martin nonetheless pleaded with his parents to be allowed to pursue a show-business career. The closest he came were campus productions and Cleveland's summer theater, where his performances drew the attention of local critics. Upon graduation, he took a variety of jobs, writing for the local newspaper, teaching in the city's high schools, and (his favorite) working as an usher at a local movie theater. There he was known as "the Movie Encyclopedia," with audiences attempting to stump him with Hollywood trivia questions.

Later accounts of his career would make much of his work as a reporter (for the sports section no less) and as a teacher, with glossy movie-star stories of girls taping "Dear Teacher" love notes to his door. But neither the local papers nor the high schools have any record of him in these positions, and the city directories only report his occupation as "usher," suggesting these other jobs were part-time or substitute. *The Cleveland Plain-Dealer,* writing of his move to Hollywood, acknowledged that he'd taught school, but quoted him as saying, "He would rather dramatize a 'Mr. Chips' role on the screen than play it in real life."

He was drafted into the army in 1942, where his knowledge of German came in handy in interpretative work. But his most memorable wartime service came with his direction of an all-male cast of "The Women," touring with the show for the Army Emergency Relief Fund throughout the Midwest.

Discharged for an undescribed medical condition, he moved to New York, where he worked in radio and did some modeling before being noticed by Columbia talent scout Max Arnow. He was signed to a seven-year contract in early 1944. The *Cleveland Plain-Dealer* reported, "The studio, which feels the [wartime] shortage of male leads acutely, wired him yesterday to report for film work immediately."

In a revealing interview, the young actor confided to a *Movieland* writer how upon his arrival at the studio he was teased relentlessly in the wardrobe department and slapped with the moniker "Bruce Foos." Apparently the more overt queens in the department couldn't resist teasing the pretty young newcomer, and the name stuck, even after Arnow came up with "Ross Hunter" to replace it.

"Bruce Foos" would quickly become a popular draw in B pictures like *Louisiana Hayride* (1944), *A Girl, a Guy and a Pal* (1945), and *Sweetheart of Sigma Chi* (1946). But studio chief Harry Cohn didn't like him; in later interviews, as part of the myth, Ross would claim it was because he was dating all the starlets on the lot. Cohn would reveal a different reason for his dislike to reporter Bill Davidson, a few years after Ross had become a bigwig producer. As an actor in army pictures, Cohn growled, Hunter "couldn't even carry a machine gun without falling over a twig [and] in love scenes, he was like Mickey Mouse."

Cohn let him go in 1947, in another vague transition episode in Hunter's winding career. When he made his comeback a few years later as a producer, the end of his acting career was blamed on a long recovery from an allergic reaction to penicillin. The reason he was on penicillin in the first place was just as vague. One report said he'd taken a shot in anticipation of spending time in the water during the filming of *The Duchess of Idaho,* for which he was replaced by Van Johnson. But *Duchess* was actually an MGM picture made *after* his exit from Columbia. In the early 1990s, looking back, Hunter made no mention of penicillin, saying only that his dismissal by Cohn was a "terrible, terrible shock. . . . The minute you're out, every door slams in your face."

He also claimed to have been married briefly during this period, but offered no details. We know he did go back to teaching school in the L.A. suburb of Downey. Nights and weekends, however, he worked at the Motion Picture Center, an independent studio where young, hopeful filmmakers could learn their craft. He studied editing, budgeting, and publicity, and by 1951 had convinced producer Leonard Goldstein at Universal to hire him as an assistant.

Goldstein, best known for the "Ma and Pa Kettle" series, was a maverick producer famous for juggling three or four projects at a time. He was impressed with Hunter's skill at trimming the fat from production budgets, but was perhaps even more enchanted with the young man's willingness to get up out of bed and attend one of Goldstein's impromptu midnight parties. It was a curious detail of their relationship that Hunter revealed to Hollis Alpert. Goldstein was then forty-eight and unmarried; he would die of a cerebral hemorrhage in 1954.

Goldstein's mentorship left Ross in a solid place at the studio. By 1953 he was producing B pictures on his own, although he despised the Westerns he was assigned. For the Audie Murphy oater *Tumbleweed,* he told Hollis Alpert he tried to sneak in a love angle, "to make a more glamorous Western than usual." He instructed his set decorators to design "the most ornate tepee ever to be seen on a screen," and decked leading lady Lori Nelson out in clothes hardly typical of Western ingenues. "She looked like she had been dressed by Givenchy," Hunter admitted.

His ticket to fame and fortune came courtesy of Barbara Stanwyck, who agreed to appear in *All I Desire,* a melodrama Hunter was itching to produce. As director, he hired Douglas Sirk, an artist in tune with his own glossy vision. In the final count, *All I Desire* returned *six times* its cost. "At Universal, [Ross Hunter] was thought to be someone who had his finger on a certain pulse in America," recalled Sirk, "and maybe they were right."

During his peak, journalists often wrote about Hunter as if he were the actual director of his films. Sheilah Graham, in a syndicated 1960 interview, even referred to him as such—and not just *any* kind of director, but as a "*women's* director," linking him to the tradition of Cukor, Leisen, and Goulding. From *All I Desire* on, every Ross Hunter production was a personal project; he took the role of "creative producer" to levels that only a handful had ever before achieved. Sirk's memoirs are filled with examples of Hunter's influence on his direction. "He was always coming to me and saying, 'Doug, Doug, make them weep! Please make them weep!' And every scene where I was trying to do something, he'd say, 'I want 500 handkerchiefs to come out at this point.'" Sirk complied: even today, it's only the most jaded who can sit through the ending of *Imitation of Life* dry-eyed.

Sirk directed some of Hunter's best pictures, their visions fusing to create stylish masterpieces of audacious melodrama. There is no better example of the "RH Factor" than the scene in *All That Heaven Allows* where Jane Wyman walks into the old barn Rock Hudson has converted into a house for her, and discovers the barn is now more opulent than the Taj Mahal. In *Imitation of Life,* Juanita Moore's funeral is bigger than Roosevelt's, with Mahalia Jackson singing "Trouble of the World."

Imitation of Life is Hunter's gayest film, not only in its sets, costumes, and sincere pathos—camp but not campy—but in its story: the rejection of

Moore, who is black, by her light-skinned daughter (Susan Kohner). It's the story of a girl who pretends to be something other than what she is, and the price she pays for it. It is, at its heart, a story of identity, of origins, of remaking oneself to fit within socially proscribed norms. It is about honesty, and integrity, and unconditional love. One cannot help but think of Ross Hunter's own story when viewing the film.

While Ross Hunter may never have forsaken Martin Fuss quite as dramatically as Susan Kohner turns her back on her Negro past, he couldn't have failed to see the parallels. If *Imitation of Life* is a morality lesson, it's one Hunter himself only partially and reluctantly took to heart. For there had never been any mention in the press about just what *kind* of name *Fuss* was. "I hate poor people because I was poor myself," he once told Sheilah Graham, mincing no words about his shame over who he was and where he came from. Exchange "poor" for "Jewish" (or, in fact, "gay") and perhaps a kernel of truth remains. Like Adrian before him, Ross Hunter had cultivated an image of affluent, debonair, heterosexual Waspdom.

In February 1962, his mother's death in Cleveland went unheralded in the Hollywood press. Even in her local obituary her son Martin was not identified as the famous movie producer Ross Hunter. Perhaps Anna Fuss' death changed him, for six months later, he finally acknowledged in an interview that his family was "German-Austrian-Jewish." When his father died the following year, Ross placed a notice in *Variety* and listed *both* his names—Hunter and Fuss—in Eizik's obituaries.

No such acknowledgment, however, not even tacitly, for that *other* part of his identity: his gayness. This despite the fact that by the late 1950s, he was living with a lover, a former set decorator who would also work as a producer—and who, approached for this book, politely refused an interview. ("I'm working on my own book," he said, "although not about what you're writing about.") Yet they were known as a couple throughout the industry, and while Ross often had Nancy Sinatra Sr. on his arm for industry functions, he and his male partner also socialized frequently and unambiguously together. "When they'd arrive," Alan Cahan remembered, "people would say, 'Oh, the Hunters are here.' That's how they were known."

"Ross could be rather uncouth at times," said Tucker Fleming, who, with his partner, Charles Williamson, occasionally mixed with the Hunters. "At one point, we hadn't seen them for a while, and I ran into Ross, who said to me, 'Oh, we've been *meaning* to have you both over, but we've just been so busy *entertaining*.' I don't think he even realized what he'd said."

Entertaining, most likely, *straight* Hollywood, which obligingly saw but didn't officially acknowledge his relationship with his lover. No Billy Haines

or Jimmy Whale, Ross didn't *want* such acknowledgment: such an arrangement, broadcast too far, would have interfered with the golden image he
wanted so desperately to recapture. The point was *this:* despite Haines, despite Whale, despite Ramon Novarro and George Cukor and La Belle
Epoque and the pansy clubs and Goulding and Arzner and Nazimova and
Dietrich and Webb—*there were no homosexuals in old Hollywood.* Homosexuals
were an invention of *new* Hollywood—ill-bred murderers and perverts who
sullied the screen, denounced by Lennie Spigelgass in the *New York Times.*

It's not surprising that, given this mind-set, Ross Hunter expected new
Hollywood to play by the old rules when it came to him, and largely it did.
His press, like his film work, is an anachronism. Even as Ingrid Bergman
was excoriated as an adulteress, even as *Confidential* pried into the bedrooms
of both gay and straight Hollywood, Ross Hunter's press reads like old *Pho-
toplays* circa 1926. He was given such consideration in part because he was
seen as Hollywood's savior, the lone producer bringing in the box office
during the Age of Television—and who wanted to upset the apple cart?
But he also kept himself as insulated as he kept his stars. In a letter to Hedda
Hopper, he wrote:

> The European producers all want to know why my pictures make
> so much money in their countries and I sincerely believe it is be-
> cause I give them (their peoples) what the European producers
> don't . . . My women and men look like they care about the way
> they look and they wrap themselves in glamour and therefore are
> so-called Untouchables—they live in glass cages and the audi-
> ences can look in—but never touch.

In an era when celebrities were becoming far more "touchable," Ross
Hunter was at the opposite extreme, promoting a fundamentally different
model. He told one interviewer he wanted to "put stars in cellophane
wrappings"—wrap them up, in other words, hide their true selves. What he
sold was not real, and to his credit he didn't claim that it was. Glamour, to
Hunter, was not something "that exists in a natural state . . . [it] must be
created or manufactured." He explained: "I don't want to hold up a mirror
to life as it is. I just want to show the part which is attractive."

This artificiality was the basis for not only Ross Hunter's films but for
himself as well. It was the way he believed it had been done in Hollywood's
Golden Age, and so, to him, it was the *only* way. At the premiere of *Magnificent Obsession,* Hunter squired Jane Wyman while arranging for Rock
Hudson to escort Betty Abbott. Nothing unusual there, but Rock's current
boyfriend, Jack Navaar, who was escorting actress Claudia Boyer, had at
least expected to sit in the same row. Once, forty years before at another

Hollywood premiere, George James Hopkins had sat defiantly beside William Desmond Taylor. Later, David Lewis had often sat with or at least near James Whale. Even more recently, John Darrow and Charles Walters had sat with only their dates between them, and Mark Miller had never been too far away from George Nader. But that wasn't the *official* history; that wasn't the record Ross Hunter was following or the image he had in his mind. At the last minute, in a move that rankled Navaar and surprised Hudson, Ross switched the seating, consigning both Navaar and his own lover to seats far in the back of the theater.

Hunter had to know of the examples set by the more overt gays in the industry. But he steered as far from their practice as possible. He was as influential as Henry Willson in shaping Rock Hudson's view on how to be gay in Hollywood; it was a secret to be guarded with your life. (If Douglas Sirk is to be believed, there may have even been an early affair between Hudson and Hunter. But Hunter's interest in Rock soon turned strictly professional, as he helped turn him into Hollywood's biggest star.)

Hunter also couldn't have been unaware of his gay audience. He would stress that he made films for women: "The woman is the one to work on. She's the one who decides what she and her husband are going to see. He'd rather stay home and watch the fights on TV." But most gay men would choose *Imitation of Life* over the fights any day, and they flocked to Hunter's movies as much as the straight women they were ostensibly made for. When Ross said that "the job of the movies is to give the average person a chance to escape and dream," the "average person" of his imagination was not the guy watching the fights, but someone like himself, one who *thought* the way he did: in truth, women and gay men. "Many people," he said, "have enough trouble in their own lives and they escape through glamorous settings, jewels and fairy stories." For a generation of gay men, Ross Hunter's films offered the perfect locus from which to dream.

On November 10, 1964, bucking the trend toward independent production, Ross Hunter signed an unprecedented $75 million, seven-year contract with Universal. By 1966, he had produced thirty-six pictures that had grossed $150 million, a staggering sum. He built an elegant home with a marble hall and fountains in the pool, and a projection room equipped as extensively as Grauman's Chinese. "This house is not a status symbol," Hunter insisted, "but a place I can enjoy. I'm at the studio at 5 or 6 in the morning and I don't leave until 8 or 9 in the evening. Why *shouldn't* I have a comfortable place to come home to?"

Why not indeed. Musing, he'd say: "I often wonder how a little guy from Cleveland could do all this." Like his predecessors—like Rapper and Spigelgass and the set decorators and the costume designers and all the actors from Kerrigan to Hudson—he was a homosexual who'd achieved not only fame and fortune, but *respect* and *power* in a world where the odds were decidedly stacked against any such thing. Why *shouldn't* he want to hold on to it—*all* of it—as tightly as he could?

"Abe, it's absolutely true," he told columnist Abe Greenberg in 1967. "I asked Nancy to marry me. You know what a wonderful person she is, and we've been seeing a lot of each other now for a quite a while and we're good for each other."

It was a statement that left many in the gay subculture shaking their heads. "I wonder how [Ross's partner] felt about that," said Robert Wheaton. "I remember all that talk about Ross and Nancy Sinatra Sr. They were always together, but no one really thought they were serious." Their impending marriage never took place, but always seemed just *on the verge* of happening. At least, that's the image Hunter wanted to project.

But 1967 wasn't 1947: acquaintances reveal that Hunter knew people were laughing at his talk of marriage to Sinatra, and that he didn't care. "He had his own way of seeing the world," said Tucker Fleming. Even at the time, Hollis Alpert observed: "He is not interested in creating an illusion so much as in substantiating a delusion." And Alpert wasn't just talking about Hunter's movies.

Despite the protests against police raids outside Los Angeles gay bars, despite the counterculture embrace of "gay power," Hunter soldiered on. In 1968, the year of some of the greatest social unrest the country had ever seen, he stood before a conservative audience at the Center of American Living in New York and, like Spigelgass, denounced the new Hollywood. "Fringe producers," he charged, "aided by the permissive laws that protect their right to exploit sex and violence, keep screaming, 'Don't tamper with honesty on the screen!' *Honesty!* What is honesty? Is honesty a long and lascivious camera close-up of some sexual aberration? Is honesty the glorification of the anti-hero? Doesn't honesty also embrace man's fine qualities—the good things that enrich our lives?"

Many of those applauding in that audience, had they known the truth, would have considered *Ross Hunter* a sexual aberration. It's apt that he would question the meaning of honesty, as his definition of it in his own life certainly did *not* include sexual close-ups or anti-heroes. Honesty, for him, *was* about "man's fine qualities"—qualities like style, success, glamour, about which he made movies and spun the myth of his own life. Qualities that were in direct opposition to his ever-lurking villain: *reality.*

In the old days, such a carefully constructed existence could endure, and often did. But Ross Hunter was not George Cukor, or even Charles Brackett: the world had moved on. "Perhaps I sound like a square but I am not," he wrote defensively in *Variety,* decrying the nudity in some new picture, trying to sound hip by using the new lingo. But he *was* a square, and an industry suddenly galvanized by the success of *Easy Rider* and films like it *knew* he was a square. He could grow his hair longer and drop all the "groovys" and "far outs" into his speech that he liked, but in the end, as hard as he fought to turn them back, the times passed Ross Hunter by.

In 1970 he bought out his contract with Universal, saying it had ceased being a "creative studio" and had become a "business." His race against change had been lost, though for a time, to give him his due, it *had* been neck and neck. But ultimately Hunter couldn't keep pace with the times. When Rock Hudson, shortly before his death from AIDS, agreed to have his story told—including the truth of his gayness—Hunter was suddenly back in the headlines, refusing to believe that his former protégé would ever allow the old rules to be so transgressed. "Not true!" he told anyone who was listening, but few were. Ross Hunter had become a relic. He died in 1996.

ROLL THE CREDITS: THE END

For all of Ross Hunter's idolizing of the old studio moguls, even during his heyday they were disappearing one by one. Darryl Zanuck deserted Fox for independent production in 1956; although he'd return in 1962 with his son Richard in charge of production, both were gone for good by 1971. Harry Cohn died of a heart attack in 1958, with Columbia staggering along under far less charismatic leadership until its reorganization ten years later. In 1982 the studio was sold to Coca-Cola, which in turn sold it to Sony of Japan. Jack Warner sold Warner Bros. to the Canadian-based Seven Arts in 1967; two years later, the studio passed to Kinney National Service, a former parking garage and funeral-parlor chain. The new Warner Communications had music, television, and publishing branches, and was acquired by Time, Inc. in 1989. Paramount, too, was sold in 1967—to Gulf and Western, a huge conglomerate where the once-mighty studio of Zukor and Lasky represented no more than 5 percent. In 1962, Universal was bought (along with Decca Records) by MCA; its new "movie mogul" was MCA chief Lew Wasserman.

The saddest demise was that of MGM. Dore Schary, who'd replaced Louis B. Mayer, was himself fired in 1956. Empty soundstages and massive reductions in personnel followed. "My last few years at Metro were like working amid the ruins," Lana Turner remembered. "The wardrobe and the prop departments began to thin out, and publicity people I'd known for so long were dismissed. It was all doom and gloom." Close to bankruptcy, the once-mighty studio was sold to Las Vegas entrepreneur Kirk Kerkorian in 1970, and fifty years of costumes and props went on the auction block. The legacies of Adrian, Shoup, Sharaff, and Edwin Willis' set decorators brought in $12 million for Kerkorian. Still, MGM never recovered, and in 1986 was bought by Turner Communications.

"I never thought I'd live to see the end of the Soviet Union or the end of MGM," reflected Elliot Morgan, research chief for the studio since 1933. "But I lived to see both. And I think the end of MGM still surprised me more."

Like its beginnings, the end of the studio era is amorphous and imprecise. Already in the mid-1950s there was a sense of decline; actress Carolyn Jones, hired by MGM in 1956, would recall that even then the studio reminded her of "an ancient dowager divesting herself of her jewels." By 1960 even films shot on studio lots had to bring in temporary workers to build sets and sew costumes. Some say the studio era ended in 1962 with the death of Marilyn Monroe, the last big studio-manufactured star. Others date it to the financial ruin at Fox after the disaster of *Cleopatra* (1963), with the studio forced to sell off its back lot, which became Century City. But there can be no greater symbol of the end of one era and the beginning of another than that day in 1967, when Jack Warner's last day at the studio he had founded coincided with the first day of a then-unknown twenty-two-year-old filmmaker named George Lucas.

The gay experience in Hollywood breaks conveniently here, too: the end of the studio era and the beginning of the modern gay political movement, touched off by the riots at the Stonewall Inn in New York in June 1969. Few of the gays of the old era survived into the new. Ross Hunter had his last success, *Airport,* in 1970, and while Frank McCarthy won an Academy Award for producing *Patton* that same year, he'd soon retire to his Hollywood hills home, Rupert Allan at his side. David Lewis had made one splashy return to Hollywood, the opulent *Raintree County* in 1957, but with the studio system dying, he found himself "helpless in a power crunch," and knew his days were numbered. He spent a restless retirement in West Hollywood. The Freed unit disintegrated when Roger Edens left to produce on his own; he had only a few more hits, starting with *Funny Face* (1957) and ending with *Hello, Dolly!* (1969). He produced John F. Kennedy's inaugural gala and spent his last years with Leonard Gershe as part of the Peter Lawford–Pat Kennedy crowd.

Leonard Spigelgass found the new Hollywood so abhorrent he turned to Broadway, where he found new success with his play "A Majority of One." DeWitt Bodeen scripted one last picture, the homoerotic *Billy Budd* (1961) in England, then moved to New York. Later, suffering a stroke, DeWitt returned to Hollywood, where George Cukor was instrumental in getting him into the Motion Picture Country Home. He died in 1988.

Among the directors, it was company man Arthur Lubin who fared best. When the studios dissolved, he simply moved into the new structure of television and directed several successful TV series: "Maverick," "The Addams Family," and "Mr. Ed," a reworking of his old *Francis* pictures. He'd also direct *The Incredible Mr. Limpet* (1964) with Don Knotts. Charles Walters also worked in television, coming out of retirement to direct a couple of programs for Lucille Ball, but his career essentially ended with *The Unsinkable Molly Brown* in 1964.

Without the matrix of the studio, many of the old-time directors felt adrift. Mitchell Leisen had thrived under the old system; lacking the "swarm of able technicians to carry out orders and a crew of writers to play pass-catch with each other's inspirations," as critic Dennis Drabelle described it, Leisen was at a loss on how to proceed. Cukor, more resourceful, would direct occasionally in the Seventies and once in the Eighties (*Rich and Famous* in 1981), but he, too, had been a creature of the studio system, and in his later productions there's a distinct sense of trying to "prove" himself to the new critics. Generally, they weren't very kind to him. Yet "he was never bitter," Gavin Lambert recalled, "never jealous of the younger generation. In a ruthlessly competitive world, he had never been corroded by ambition." Cukor died in 1983.

In the new era, even those qualities that had once been propitious for gay directors had become quaint, and in some cases, even liabilities. As early as 1958, when Irving Rapper feuded with Carroll Baker on the set of *The Miracle,* she told the press: "I'm quite a strong woman and he's more or less a woman-hater. In my first three pictures I had Elia Kazan, George Stevens, and William Wyler as directors and I would do things I felt wrong for them just because they are the kind of men they are"—read, *straight.* The label of "woman's director" had fallen into disrepute and disrespect, a condition only magnified by the growth of the women's movement. Rapper would finish up his career directing such oddities as *The Christine Jorgensen Story* (1970), an account of the famed transsexual, and *Born Again* (1978), the story of the spiritual awakening of Richard Nixon's special counsel, Charles Colson.

Actors faced new scrutiny in their personal lives. Rock Hudson had to deal with outrageous stories of a "marriage" to Jim Nabors, TV's "Gomer Pyle." Cary Grant was called a "homo" on national TV by Chevy Chase, and sued. The supermarket tabloids increasingly weren't shy to gay-bait popular players, targeting the television actors Tommy Kirk and George Maharis, among others. The gay card remains a staple of *The National Enquirer* and *The Star.*

Clifton Webb was spared any of that. Having become a recluse after Mabelle's death, he died in 1966. Ramon Novarro never made it past

Stonewall either. Bludgeoned to death by a pair of hustlers in 1967, his death symbolized a brutal end to old Hollywood. Anthony Perkins' death from AIDS, like Rock Hudson's before him, was also the sign of a new era.

The one who made out best in many ways was Patsy Kelly. On the skids for much of the 1950s, she was arrested in 1963 along with two female companions after a drunken brawl in La Jolla. But in the new Hollywood such misbehavior was no longer career suicide: in fact, the resulting publicity reminded producers Patsy was still around. Subsequently, she played one of Satan's followers in *Rosemary's Baby* (1968) and won a Tony in 1971 for her triumphant return to Broadway in "No, No, Nanette."

Mostly, however, the old made way for the new: people like cameraman James Crabe, who moved from the Gay Girls Riding Club to such important Hollywood films as *Save the Tiger, The China Syndrome,* and *The Formula,* for which he was nominated for an Academy Award. Crabe was also behind the lens for important TV films like "The Autobiography of Miss Jane Pittman" and "The Letter," which won him an Emmy. For gay audiences, his most memorable picture might be *Sextette* (1978), Mae West's bizarre last film, in which he struggled to keep the legendary actress looking (at best) a few years younger than her true eighty-six years. Crabe's career was cut short in 1989, when he, too, died of AIDS, at the age of fifty-seven.

In the Hollywood that supplanted the studio system, a new breed of gay directors emerged, people like Colin Higgins, John Schlesinger, James Bridges, and Robert Moore, who lived openly and even sometimes dealt with homosexual themes in their work. The underground films of Kenneth Anger, Andy Warhol, and John Waters were even more explicit. Meanwhile, a "queer cinema" was evolving from the work of such openly gay European directors as Rainer Werner Fassbinder and Pedro Almodovar—a paradigm impossible to imagine before Stonewall. In the post-studio era, all the models became different. Identity was reconfigured, with old definitions of "overt" or "circumspect" becoming obsolete. By the early Seventies, figures like Merle Miller would "come out" as gay; those who chose not to declare themselves publicly were considered "in the closet."

It was a world far different from that known by the homosexuals of the studio era, and they reacted to it with a mixture of disdain, confusion, and grudging respect. "For those of us who are a little older, we can understand how tough it is to change that way of thinking," said Kevin Thomas. "You really are conditioned not to be open about being gay if you're of a certain age." In such a context, it's perhaps easier to understand set decorator Richard Pefferle's unease at finding himself in the audience of *The Killing of Sister George.* For someone whose life had been constructed around a concept of imperceptibility, such overt displays of identity—an identity once unimaginable as public—must have been both disorienting and unsettling.

But some found in "Gay Lib" an opportunity for personal emancipation. Arthur Laurents, Miles White, George Nader, Jack Larson, Ray Stricklyn, and Farley Granger all would eventually (and in their own way) publicly declare their gayness. The majority, however, even in the face of monumental change, would maintain a studio-era philosophy of evasion: Ross Hunter, Roddy McDowall, Vincent Price, and Irving Rapper would all go to their graves in the Bill Clinton 1990s without ever stating for the record that they were gay. For some survivors of the studio era, it's an attitude that continues to prevail.

Others, had they chance, may have moved further. "I think if Cukor had maybe lived another five years," Kevin Thomas said, "it's conceivable he might have sat down for some kind of interview with *The Advocate*. It's possible, anyway." It's interesting to speculate what Dorothy Arzner might have shared had she lived into the Eighties or Nineties. Armistead Maupin remembered Rock Hudson considering the idea of "coming out" long before AIDS was an issue. What if he *hadn't* contracted the disease? What might he have discussed if he were alive today?

Gavin Lambert once asked Cukor if he'd ever felt limited by the old system, if he'd ever suffered from not being able to have "a complete, out-in-the-open love affair." Cukor had paused to think the question over. "Many of us suffered," he finally answered. But when "there's no choice," he added, "you either make the best of it or suffer even more."

The studio system had enabled homosexuals to carve out places where they could prosper and thrive, little islands of security and authenticity in a hostile society. That they made compromises and occasionally suffered oppression is undeniable, but the record of the studio era was actually far more favorable than the immediate decades to follow. With the studios gone, certain fields like cinematography, which had previously been inaccessible to gays (at least overt gays), were now opened up to new blood—yet the reverse was also true. Old gay enclaves like costume design and set decoration lost their homosexual hegemony. Labor historian and gaffer Michael Everett observed of the 1960s and 1970s: "My own experience of gays in [the various Hollywood unions] is [that] I recall no sense of a gay presence on the set—even in Wardrobe and Hair/Make-Up, but maybe they were so underground that I never would have known."

In the old days, there was nothing "underground" about a gay presence in Wardrobe. But with the mass production of motion pictures having ceased, it was now no longer practical to keep large numbers of personnel under long-term contract. Tailor-making pictures by independent producers made more economic sense. "Set decorating is a dying art," lamented Henry Grace to the *Los Angeles Times*. "They just can't afford to build whole sets the way they used to and they're more inclined to use existing facilities to save time and money. I remember the good old days, standing with director and friend George Cukor on the set I did for *Adam's Rib,* watching Hepburn and Tracy. But those moments are behind us now."

Without the regular departments of the old studios, there was less a chance for people like Howard Greer or Edwin Willis to assemble nearly all-gay teams of craft workers. Consequently, each new film would have a different cast of characters working behind the scenes. That many were likely gay is a matter of logic, but gone was the sense of identification that once had come from the old MGM prop department or the Paramount wardrobe crew.

There was another consideration as well. In a world where the new paradigm was either "openly gay" or "in the closet," the overtness of a Greer or Orry-Kelly or Jack Cole or Mitchell Leisen would have been viewed as tremendously suspect. While it is true that the Sixties ushered in among some circles a greater sense of tolerance, allowing people like Curtis Harrington or Maurice Zuberano to live more openly, that very cultural acknowledgment of homosexuality could make others more careful in how they were perceived. The "open secret" of the past had taken on a new and obvious specificity. "You learned not to say anything when the fag jokes started," Robert Shaw explained. "If you complained, people might think you doth protest too much." Set decorator Joe Armetta recalled, "Sometimes the toads would slip out of their mouths. I learned the hard way, being young and having a temper. I stood my ground [but] it still wasn't easy."

Queer jokes had, of course, been around since J. Warren Kerrigan was held underwater for the laughter of the crew. But as the Hollywood closet became institutionalized, homophobia was permitted greater license. Without the obvious gay presence that had once existed in the studios, films could be made in what one survivor, an assistant director, called "a straight vacuum—there were no obvious gays, so people just figured we didn't exist." Homosexuality had become an increasingly frequent theme of movie plots—with gays portrayed on-screen as murderers, suicides, villains, or victims who deserved what they got—while on the set there was no visible presence to counterbalance such portrayals. Insisting on anonymity, the assistant director admitted taking part in films that he personally found offensive. "That's how you made a living. So what if you had to work on a scene where the hero beats up a gay guy? You either did those scenes," he said, "or you didn't work.

"It might have been different," he mused, "if there were gay people around, you know, like the old-time gay queens who used to work in wardrobe or some fussy, obvious set designer. Maybe [the producers] would have thought, 'Gee, are we offending them?' But it was like there were no gays. We were all really, really deep in the closet." Films like *Cruising* and *Partners* and *Windows,* with scenes offensive to gays, could be made because there was no sense on the producers' parts that they might be personally offending members of their crew. "We were complicit in our silence," the assistant director said, recalling Merle Miller's self-indictment in his famous *New York Times* piece.

Certainly gay assistant directors, costume designers, and set decorators had worked on the films of the 1930s in which Franklin Pangborn or Edward Everett Horton had their dignities squashed—but the difference is that there were also gay directors like Cukor and Whale and Leisen who concurrently used the sissy character in far more empowering ways. In the post-studio era, it would not be until the late 1980s that gay directors would emerge who would directly challenge the prevailing homophobia and change the depiction of homosexuality on the screen. And there remains a large chasm of difference between Pangborn's pansies and the murderous queers of *Cruising.*

The Hollywood closet has not always existed. It is a relatively recent phenomenon, in many ways a post-Stonewall creation. But for the new Hollywood it quickly become as entrenched as if it had been in place for decades. Michael Kearns, a young gay actor fresh from his studies at the Goodman Theatre School in Chicago, arrived in Hollywood in 1971. He found himself a gay agent (Stan Kamen of the William Morris agency) who fixed him up with a lesbian casting director (Monique James at Universal), but he soon learned the old gay network that had once helped so many might no longer carry the same clout it once did.

"Universal was the only studio that still maintained remnants of the old studio system, including contract players," Kearns recalled. "This would have been the best possible scenario for a green actor from the Midwest. [But] there were all kinds of euphemisms employed to disqualify me—'theatrical' is one that stands out. I auditioned three times for James, and every time I felt like the audition was to prove my masculinity, not to prove I could act. Instead of getting better, I probably got worse with each callback, knowing, subconsciously at least, that I was being judged on my ability to play straight, not on my ability to act."

Kearns heard other words tossed around about him, too, like "soft." He remembered, "I never, thank God, heard 'light in the loafers,' although God knows what they said out of my earshot."

Yet more than once in the past, Hollywood had warmly embraced actors who were "soft"—importing whole *classes* of them, in fact, in the Twenties, Thirties, and (after the war) in the Forties. But more than ever before, by the early Seventies, such softness implied queerness. Even Universal's lesbian casting director apparently believed that Kearns, soft as he was, could never play straight—although ironically he'd play "superhetero" (his words) as John-Boy's roommate on "The Waltons." Later, he'd go on to become one of the most noted and outspoken names in gay theater.

"In retrospect," Kearns said, "this is all amusing and nothing else. At the time, it was probably forming the seed that would blossom into my eventual activism role. Some part of me knew that the discrimination had begun. Being a queer and being in Hollywood was a potentially toxic mix."

It was a world far, far different from what once had been. Many would indeed look back on the studio era with a sense of nostalgia. "It may not have been what the younger people today feel it should have been," said one man, a wise old survivor. "But it was ours. And we did all right. We had our time. We had our impact."

IN MEMORIUM

•

Zoe Akins	J. Warren Kerrigan
Milo Anderson	Arthur Krams
Dorothy Arzner	Anderson Lawler
Edwin August	Mitchell Leisen
Tallulah Bankhead	David Lewis
DeWitt Bodeen	Margaret Lindsay
Howard Bristol	Edmund Lowe
Montgomery Clift	Arthur Lubin
Jack Cole	Elliot Morgan
Mike Connolly	Jack Moore
James Crabe	Alla Nazimova
Laird Cregar	Ramon Novarro
George Cukor	Eugene O'Brien
John Darrow	Franklin Pangborn
Tyrell Davis	Harriet Parsons
Fred deGresac	Richard Pefferle
Marlene Dietrich	Walter Plunkett
Tom Douglas	Irving Rapper
Marie Dressler	Conrad Salinger
Roger Edens	Robert Shaw
Keogh Gleason	Howard Shoup
Edmund Goulding	Leonard Spigelgass
Henry Grace	Grady Sutton
Howard Greer	Lilyan Tashman
William Haines	William Desmond Taylor
David Hanna	Ernest Thesiger
George James Hopkins	Charles Walters
Edward Everett Horton	Clifton Webb
Herbert Howe	James Whale
Orry-Kelly	Miles White
Patsy Kelly	Edwin Willis

ACKNOWLEDGMENTS

•

No work such as this is ever entirely the author's own. I am indebted to many people who shared their insights and knowledge and sometimes their own archives.

Among my colleagues, I am particularly grateful to Allan Berubé, Michael Bronski, David Chierichetti, and Anthony Slide for helping shape my vision, challenging my conclusions, and offering all-important context. I thank also Cari Beauchamp, Aaron Betsky, Katherine Bucknell, Bill Condon, Victor D'Lugin, Raymond Dragon, Michael Everett, Charles Higham, Val Holley, Charles Kaiser, Matthew Kennedy, Robert Klepper, Leonard Leff, Glenn Loney, Patrick McGilligan, Ethan Mordden, Stephen O'Brien, James Robert Parish, Robrt Pela, Lawrence Quirk, Robert Schanke, Sylvia Shorris, Ed Sikov, Andre Soares, David Stenn, and Stacy Wolf.

Film historians are blessed to have men and women in place at the various archives and libraries who are both knowledgeable and devoted; they give self-lessly of their time and expertise. In particular I want to acknowledge Barbara Hall and Kristine Krueger at the Margaret Herrick Library of the Academy of Motion Picture Arts and Sciences; Lauren Buisson of the Arts Special Collections at UCLA; Charles Silver of the Museum of Modern Art; the staff (particularly Jeremy Morgan) of the New York Public Library for the Performing Arts; Kay Bost at the DeGolyer Library of Southern Methodist University;

Sean Noel of Boston University Special Collections, for the Clifton Webb papers; Rebecca Tuttle at the Huntington Library, for the Zoe Atkins letters; Carol Bowers at the University of Wyoming, for the Edward Everett Horton letters; Jean Geist at Bowling Green University, for the DeWitt Bodeen letters; Mary Wolfskill of the Library of Congress; Alan Betrock of Shake Books, who was generous in sharing his archive of scandal magazines from the 1950s and 60s; the staff at the Cinema-Television Library, University of Southern California; William Luebke at the Library of Virginia; Loran Fletcher at the Indianapolis Public Library; Rhonda Green at the Cleveland Public Library; Roger Mayer at Turner Entertainment; John O'Brien at the International Gay and Lesbian Archives, One Institute; Matthew Jaquith at the Amherst College Library; the staff of the Wisconsin Center for Film and Theater Research; and all those seemingly nameless clerks at the National Archives; the National Personnel Records Center in St. Louis (military records); the Boston Public Library; the Federal Bureau of Investigation; the New York Public Library; the Los Angeles Public Library; the Probate Division of the Los Angeles Superior Court; the California State Department of Health, Vital Records; the Probate Office of the New York County Court; Olin Library, Wesleyan University; and W.E.B. Dubois Library, University of Massachusetts.

At the heart of this book are the dozens of individuals who shared their memories and reflections of the era in interviews, correspondence, and background information. I was honored by their trust and fascinated by their stories. My profound gratitude to Robert Wheaton, who again graciously opened the door for me to many who otherwise would not have been found; Frank Lysinger; Charles Williamson; Tucker Fleming; Don Bachardy; Alan Cahan; Ron Anderegg; Joe Armetta; Frank D'Amico; Bill Dawson; J. C. Edens; Chatty Eliason; Douglas Fairbanks Jr.; Hal Gausman; John Gilmore; Michael Grace; Curtis Harrington; Gean Harwood; Harry Hay; Steven Katz; Michael Kearns; Marshall Kendzy; Gavin Lambert; Arthur Laurents; Satch LaValley; Al Lehman; Michael Logothetis; Armistead Maupin; Ian McKellan; Mark Miller; Elliot Morgan; Michael Morrison; George Nader; Michael Pearman; Robert Riley; George Schoenbrunn; Robert Shaw; Gloria Stuart; Kevin Thomas; Gwen Verdon; Gore Vidal; Robert Wagner; Edith Whalley; Miles White; Billy Williams; Roy Yoneda Jr.; and several who asked for anonymity.

For putting me in touch with contacts and material, I thank Richard Allynwood; Tom Barnes; Jay Blotcher; Rosemary Brandenburg of the Set Decorators Society; Claire Brandt; Rudolph Garcia of the costumers' union; Bruce Long; Tim Miller; Mike Nielsen; Charlene Patterson; Richard M. Pope; Gail Shoup of the Pasadena Playhouse; Joseph Yranski; and especially William Kizer, whose fascinating research into the life of Andy Lawler deserves a book of its own.

My original editor on this project, Ed Iwanicki, offered invaluable guidance in helping define its structure; his imprint remains. My second editor, Ray Roberts, brought much wisdom and insight to the final product. My debt and gratitude to both of them. As ever, I thank my agent, Malaga Baldi, and my partner, Tim Huber, who not only provided his usual love, support, and inspiration, but this time also proved a remarkably astute and resourceful researcher.

NOTES

•

ABBREVIATIONS:

AMPAS = Margaret Herrick Library, Academy of Motion Picture Arts
and Sciences, Beverly Hills
MoMA = Film Studies Department, Museum of Modern Art, New York
NYPL = New York Public Library for the Performing Arts, New York
PCA = Production Code Administration files
UCLA = Arts Special Collection, University of California, Los Angeles

MAIN COLLECTIONS CITED IN NOTES:

Zoe Akins Collection, Huntington Library, San Marino, California
Dorothy Arzner Collection, UCLA
George Cukor Collection, AMPAS
Hedda Hopper Collection, AMPAS
Edward Everett Horton Collection, University of Wyoming, Laramie
Anthony Slide Collection, Bowling Green State University, Bowling Green, Ohio
Clifton Webb Collection, Boston University, Boston
Production Code Administration files, AMPAS

NOTE: In some instances, in order to make reading easier, I have eliminated brackets and
ellipses from quotations from oral histories or previously published material. I have retained
them when I felt their removal might in some way interfere with accuracy or change the
thrust or intent of the quotation.

INTRODUCTION

x "Tell me anywhere . . .": This and other unidentified quotes throughout come from several interviews with Hollywood survivors who asked that their names not be used.

x "They didn't care . . .": Robert Shaw, interview with the author.

xi "It could be . . .": Alan Cahan, interview with the author.

xi "It was the . . .": Miles White, interview with the author.

xii "sexuality permeates . . .": Schanke and Marra, *Passing Performances,* pp. 3–4.

xii "Cinema is public . . .": Patricia White, *Uninvited,* p. xv.

xii Lambert on Anderson and Ray: Lambert, *Mainly About Lindsay Anderson,* p. 28, 87-89.

xv "shifting social constructions . . .": Schanke and Marra, p. 176.

xv "a concept . . .": Loughery, *The Other Side of Silence,* p. xii.

xv "People just knew . . .": Arthur Laurents, interview with the author.

xv "open secret": Sedgwick, *The Epistomology of the Closet.*

xvi "dirty kike": Friedrich, *City of Nets,* p. 340.

xviii "To insist on . . .": Neil Miller, *Out of the Past.*

xviii Novarro and Howe: Ellenberger, *Ramon Novarro,* p. 35.

xix "The invocation . . .": For a thorough discussion of the problems of identity, see Judith Butler, *Gender Trouble* (New York: Routledge, 1999).

xix "Women who love . . .": See Nancy F. Cott, et al. (eds.), *A Heritage of Their Own: Toward a New Social History of American Women.* New York: Simon & Schuster, 1979, p. 416.

xx Hattie McDaniel: See Carlton Jackson, *Hattie: The Life of Hattie McDaniel.* See also my own article, "High Hat Hattie," *Frontiers,* April 2000.

xx "those men who live . . .": Bucknell (ed.) Isherwood *Diaries.*

xx *"sexuality consists of . . .":* Martin Duberman, et al. (eds.), *Hidden from History: Reclaiming the Gay and Lesbian Past* (New York: Penguin, 1989).

xxi "Rumor and gossip . . .": Schanke and Marra, pp. 198–99.

xxi "If oral history . . .": Corey K. Creekmur and Alexander Doty (eds.), *Out in Culture: Gay, Lesbian and Queer Essays on Popular Culture.* Durham, NC: Duke University, 1995.

xxi "spoken in the . . .": Schmidgall, *Walt Whitman: A Gay Life.*

xxii "My being gay . . .": Frank Lysinger, interview with the author.

xxii Chauncey: See Chauncey, *Gay New York.*

xxii "predate the political . . .": Matthew Tinkcom, "Working Like a Homosexual: Camp Visual Codes and the Labor of Gay Subjects in the MGM Freed Unit," *Cinema Journal,* Winter 1996.

xxiii "My uncle . . .": Michael Grace, interview with author.

xxiv "the degree and . . .": Nietzsche, *Beyond Good and Evil,* 1886.

GREAT GODS

1 Kerrigan facedown in the water: Interview with Allan Dwan by Anthony Slide, courtesy Slide.

2 Dwan: Brownlow, *Hollywood: The Pioneers,* p. 55.

2 "pretty fond . . .": Bogdanovich, *Who the Devil Made It?,* p. 62.

2 Loiz Huyck: Lawton, *Santa Barbara's Flying A,* p. 99.

2 "when they leave me alone": *Blue Book,* May 1914.

2 Kerrigan and Vincent: U.S. Census, 1920, Los Angeles County, CA; Robert Wheaton, interview with the author.

3 Dwan quotes: Bogdanovich, p. 62-63.

3 "port of safety": Bronski, *Culture Clash,* p. 110-111. See also Bronski, *The Pleasure Principle,* p. 30-31.

4 American Film Company: See Lyons, *The Silent Partner;* Slide, *The American Film Industry; Moving Picture World,* October 15, 1910.

4 "Came the dawn . . .": unsourced clipping, 1915, Robinson Locke Collection, NYPL.

4 Sexual harassment: *Variety,* February 21, 1913; March 13, 1914; December 29, 1915.

5 "Los Angeles is . . .": Banham, *Los Angeles: The Architecture of Four Ecologies*. NY: Harper & Row, 1971.

5 "His stockings . . .": *Photoplay*, April 1914.

6 Kerrigan family: U.S. Census, 1880, Floyd County, Indiana.

6 "For a year . . .": *Photoplay*, January 1920.

6 "I often went . . .": *The Universal Weekly*, undated, New York Public Library.

6 "If there was . . .": *Photoplay*, February 1916.

6 "dens and tunnels . . .": *The Universal Weekly*.

6 Kathleen Kerrigan: *New York Evening Journal*, October 30, 1906; *New York Telegraph*, January 29, 1911.

6 "unlimited ambition . . .": Kerrigan, *How I Became . . .* , p. 20.

7 "Brown of Harvard" in Louisville: *Louisville Post*, December 19, 1908; December 29, 1908.

7 "Somehow I thought . . .": *The Universal Weekly*.

7 Sarah and Jack in Chicago: U.S. Census, 1910, Cooks County, Illinois.

7 Flying A studios and Kerrigan: *Moving Picture World*, December 7, 1912.

7 "The Great God": *Photoplay*, February 1916.

7 Fan magazines: Jowett, *Film: The Democratic Art*, p. 56.

8 "It has come . . .": *Motion Picture*, November 1912.

8 "effeminate": Albert Smith papers, UCLA, quoted in Slide, *The Big V*, p. 115.

8 Kerrigan poll: *Photoplay*, July 1913.

8 Pansy Motion Picture Club: *Meeting Picture World*, January 3, 1914.

9 Kumfy Kerrigan interview: *Motion Picture Supplement*, September 1915.

9 "where my best . . .": *Toledo Daily Blade*, March 10, 1916.

9 *Moving Picture Weekly* poll: May 27, 1916; *New York Telegraph* poll: March 19, 1916.

10 "Does Warren Kerrigan's . . .": *Columbus Dispatch*, November 26, 1916.

11 "homo": Blanche Sweet to Anthony Slide, see "The Silent Closet," *Film Quarterly*, Summer 1999.

11 pimento haricots: *Photoplay*, March 1915.

11 "Few people know": *Motion Picture*, July 1914.

11 "quite as wooden . . .": *New York Times*, February 24, 1910.

11 Biograph gays: See Arvidson, *When the Movies . . .* , and Slide, "The Silent Closet."

11 Mack Sennett, Ralph Graves: Slide, "The Silent Closet."

11 Lanoe and Hyde: 1920 Los Angeles city directory; *New York Times Index to the Theater*.

12 August career moves: Los Angeles city directory 1914, 1915.

12 August presidential campaign: *New York Star*, May 31, 1916; *New York Telegraph*, May 22, 1916.

12 "Have you not . . .": *New York Star*, June 21, 1916.

13 August as Santa: *Los Angeles Times*, December 16, 1944.

13 *A Stolen Identity:* see Eileen Bowser, *History of American Cinema, Vol. 2.*, pp. 246–48.

14 May 1916 poll: *Moving Picture Weekly*, May 27, 1916.

14 Kerrigan tour: *Columbus Dispatch*, April 8, 1917.

14 "I am not . . .": *Denver Times*, May 11, 1917.

15 "What is amazing . . .": Gabler, p. 6-7.

15 "the ideal . . .": Jowett, p. 65.

15 Peet quote: *Esquire*, September 1936, p. 109.

15 "The villains and . . .": *Photoplay*, August 1917.

16 Kerrigan breaks leg: *New York Telegraph*, September 9, 1917.

16 Universal wins: *Photoplay*, February 1918.

16 "soldier boys . . .": *Motion Picture*, May 1918.

17 "Ain't he . . .": Unsourced clip, 1918, MoMA.

17 "Exit J. Warren . . .": *Wisconsin News*, February 12, 1919.

17 Stephen Myronoff: *Cleveland News Leader*, October 21, 1919; *Detroit Journal*, October 30, 1919.

18 Kerrigan marriage proposals: *Columbus Dispatch*, April 8, 1920, various unsourced clips, Robinson Locke Collection, NYPL.

18 "Kerrigan's publicity man . . .": Unsourced clip, January 25, 1920, Robinson Locke Collection, NYPL.
18 Hughes military service: clippings, Robinson Locke Collection, NYPL.
19 "can touch . . .": *New York Times,* February, 28, 1916.
19 "the charm boy . . .": *The American Weekly,* February, 3, 1952.
19 "The young actor . . .": *Shadowland,* January 1921.
19 Viola Dana: see Slide, "The Silent Closet."
20 purple ties, sailor, and Lowe: *Los Angeles Examiner,* October 9, 1916.
21 Schenck's preference for gay costars: This was first written about in a profile of Eugene O'Brien by Larry Lee Holland in *Films in Review,* October 1986. The claim appears to have come from O'Brien himself, through screenwriter DeWitt Bodeen, who knew O'Brien well. See also Slide, "The Silent Closet."
21 Schenck, O'Brien friendship: *Motion Picture,* June 1925.
21 O'Brien and Talmadge: Holland, *Films in Review,* October 1986. Anthony Slide has expressed doubt about the veracity of this anecdote, wondering if it wasn't an exaggeration by DeWitt Bodeen.
22 O'Brien family background: U.S. Census, 1880, Boulder County, CO.
22 O'Brien early career: *Blue Book of the Screen.*
22 "plutocratic . . . sort of place . . .": *Motion Picture Classic,* July 1919.
23 "as enthusiastic as . . .": *Motion Picture Classic,* February 1922.
23 "I'm having . . .": *Motion Picture Classic,* July 1922.
23 Ten Eyck interview: *Photoplay,* November 1918.
24 "frame of reference": For more on intertextual perception, see Chon Noriega, "Something's Missing Here: Homosexuality and Film Reviews During the Production Code Era," *Cinema Journal,* Fall 1990. See also Patricia White, *Uninvited.*
25 "Do you like . . .": *Motion Picture Classic,* July 1922.
25 "Eugene O'Brien says . . .": *Hollywood Press Post,* August 5, 1927.
25 "I know it's . . .": unsourced clipping, circa 1927, AMPAS.
25 "passé . . .": *Motion Picture,* October 1923.
25 "Warren Kerrigan . . .": *Photoplay,* July 1923.
26 "too effeminate": Smith papers, UCLA, quoted in Slide, *The Big V,* p. 115.
26 "listless": *Variety,* September 10, 1924.
26 "From the time . . .": *Motion Picture,* September 1925.
26 "I never did . . .": *Photoplay,* undated clipping, 1930.

DESIGNING MEN

27 "At the time . . .": *Production Design,* September 1952.
27 "glorified carpenters": Frank H. Webster, "The Art of the Art Director," *The Blue Book of the Screen,* circa 1920.
28 Hopkins at Realart and Fox: Unpublished memoir manuscript by George James Hopkins, in possession of Charles Higham, quoted courtesy of Higham, hereafter referred to as Hopkins manuscript.
28 Gest office: Hopkins manuscript.
28 Gabler, *An Empire of Their Own,* p. 105.
29 "isn't this really . . .": Ethan Mordden, interview with the author.
29 Hopkins background: Hopkins manuscript.
30 "the most powerful . . .": Lambert, *Nazimova,* p. 113.
30 Frohman: See Schanke and Marra, *Passing Performances.*
31 Hopkins, Frohman, Gest, Ellis: Hopkins manuscript.
31 Ordynski career: *Variety* obituary, August 19, 1953.
31 Hopkins and Bara: Hopkins manuscript.
32 "Neje": "The Story of a Designing Man," *Picture Play,* October 1919.
32 "Aside from the . . .": *Production Design,* September 1952.
32 "He has twinkling . . .": *Picture Play,* October 1919.
32 "artistic executive": *Photoplay,* August 1916.

33 Frank Webster quote: *The Blue Book of the Screen,* circa 1920.

33 Taylor and Hopkins: Hopkins manuscript.

34 "tell each other . . .": *New York Telegraph,* July 9, 1916.

34 Background on Universal and studios: See Schatz, *The Genius of the System.*

34 "Taylor was . . .": *Los Angeles Express,* February 2, 1922.

34 "He made . . .": *New York News,* February 7, 1922.

34 Doherty and Taylor: For a detailed account of the press accusations of Taylor after his death, see the exceptional newsletter and Web site, *Taylorology,* created by Bruce Long, at www.silent-movies.com/Taylorology.

34 Taylor-Hopkins in public, and Taylor's murder: Hopkins manuscript.

35 sexual slavery scene: Some historians have expressed doubt such a scene existed. Hopkins did tend to sometimes embellish his memoirs, but an unsourced review of the film in the Robinson Locke Collection, NYPL, does mention a "bordello scene with young men," without giving more details. The film, sadly, has not survived.

35 "love cult": *New York News,* February 9, 1922.

36 "He has a weird . . .": *Honolulu Star Bulletin,* October 3, 1922.

37 Leisen architectural career: Sheilah Graham, "Nothing But the Best for Director Leisen," *The Sun* (Baltimore), December 2, 1945.

37 Leisen early film career: See Chierichetti, *Hollywood Director.*

37 Dwan on Leisen: Chierichetti, *Hollywood Director,* pp. 25–27.

38 Harold Grieve: Although he never discussed being homosexual, friends who knew Grieve in his old age strongly believed him to be. Anthony Slide often visited him and escorted him to various events and said, in his opinion, it was "unstated" but "obvious."

38 Grieve and Ingram: Oral history with Harold Grieve, conducted by Anthony Slide, AMPAS.

38 *Ben-Hur:* Grieve's notes on his set and costume designs are in the Harold Grieve Collection, AMPAS.

39 "All of the . . .": Miles White, interview with the author.

40 Greer early life: *Designing Male.*

40 Sam Greer work: U.S. Census, 1900, Johnson County, Nebraska.

41 Greer with Lucile and in New York: Greer, *Designing Male.*

41 "Howard was always . . .": Satch LaValley, interview with the author.

41 Cecile Sorel: *Theatre Magazine,* September 1920.

41 "This was the . . .": *Town and Country,* November 1950.

42 "On the basis . . .": Erté, *My Life, My Art,* p. 79.

43 "He is very . . .": Letter from Valerie Belletti to Irina Prina in New York, April 1926, AMPAS, courtesy Anthony Slide.

43 "Edith liked to . . .": David Chierichetti, interview with the author.

43 "I studied . . .": Head, *The Dress Doctor,* pp. 43–44.

44 Joab Banton: *Photoplay,* June 1936.

44 Banton physical description: World War I U.S. Navy records, dated January 3, 1918.

44 Banton early life: LaVine, *In a Glamorous Fashion;* Paramount studio press releases.

44 Banton military service: World War I U.S. Navy records.

45 "Clothes are used . . .": Rimoldi, Oscar, "The Great Hollywood Designers," *Hollywood Studio Magazine,* December 1982.

45 "The rest of us . . .": Chierichetti, *Hollywood Costume Design,* p. 158.

45 "Slowly but surely . . .": *New York Evening Journal,* May 17, 1935.

46 Banton, Joy Negri, short skirts: *Photoplay,* April 1936.

46 "He finds it . . .": *Photoplay,* May 1936.

46 "Banton never got . . .": *Women's Wear Daily,* November 29, 1963.

47 "To design for . . .": *Hollywood Studio Magazine,* December 1982.

47 "Carole Lombard was . . .": Chierichetti, *Hollywood Costume Design,* p. 50.

48 Greenberg family: U.S. Census, 1900, New Haven County, CT.

48 "His parents were . . .": undated (circa 1939) Hedda Hopper "Cosmopolite of the Month" column, AMPAS.

48 Gilbert and Helena Greenberg: Robert Riley, in Lee, *American Fashion,* p. 9.
49 Greenberg family: U.S. Census, 1920, New Haven County, CT.
49 "rather weird . . .": *New York Times,* May 27, 1945.
49 Adrian and *Oz: MGM Studio News,* August 14, 1939.
49 Adrian early career: Riley, in Lee, *American Fashion;* Joseph Simms, "Adrian—American Artist and Designer," *Journal of the Costume Society,* Volume 8 (1974).
49 "that his son . . .": Riley, in Lee, *American Fashion,* p. 14.
50 Adrian in Paris: Riley, in Lee, *American Fashion,* p. 21.
50 Adrian's note to Erté: Erté, *Things I Remember,* p. 87.
50 Adrian and Charles LeMaire: Riley, in Lee, *American Fashion.*
50 Erté on Adrian: Erté, *Things I Remember,* p. 87.
51 "just out of . . .": Chierichetti, *Hollywood Director,* p. 36.
51 "Leisen told me . . .": Chierichetti, *Hollywood Director,* p. 7.
51 Adrian contracts: Gilbert Adrian and Loew's Inc., July 27, 1928, June 28, 1935; July 16, 1938; MGM Art Department Records, AMPAS.
53 "Certainly, in the . . .": Laura Jacobs, "Glamor by Adrian," *Vanity Fair,* June 2000.
53 "This [had been] . . .": *Production Design,* September 1952.
54 Lonergan: Shorris and Bundy, *Talking Pictures,* p. 248.
54 "Hardly any . . .": Michael Grace, interview with the author.
54 "When I was . . .": Oral history with Harold Grieve, conducted by Anthony Slide, AMPAS.
55 Statistic of married employees in art department: "Manning Table and Replacement Schedule," January 27, 1943, MGM Art Department Records, AMPAS.
55 Townsend, Wiley: *Variety* obituaries, 1935.
55 Lonergan on Gibbons: Shorris and Bundy, *Talking Pictures,* p. 251.
55 "Gibbons' influence . . .": Hambley, *The Art of Hollywood,* p. 53.
56 Gibbons and Gibson: Scarfone, *The Wizardry of Oz,* p. 111.
56 Gibbons' secretary: Elliot Morgan, interview with the author.
56 Bodeen on Gibbons: Bodeen, *From Hollywood,* p. 285.
56 Del Rio breakdown: Bodeen, *From Hollywood,* p.285.
57 Gibbons and the press: *New York Times,* February 6, 1938.
57 Gibbons and set dressers: Frank Lysinger, interview with the author.
57 Willis marriage, family: U.S. Census, 1920, Los Angeles, CA; Edwin B. Willis, Last Will and Testament, filed November 27, 1963, Los Angeles County Probate Court.
57 "I always found . . .": Frank Lysinger, interview with the author.
57 miniature silver locomotive: MGM Art Department Records, Property Department, memo from Cedric Gibbons to Edwin Willis, September 4, 1931, AMPAS.

GIRLS WITH IMAGINATION

59 "With the nerve . . .": *Motion Picture Classic,* September 1929.
59 "separated falsehood . . .": Lambert, pp. 224–25.
60 "I knew this . . .": Hopkins manuscript.
60 Zanuck quote: Mosley, *Zanuck.*
60 "Her vogue . . .": Morris, *Madam Valentino,* p. 66.
61 LeGallienne: Schanke and Marra, p. 139.
61 Nazimova and Rambova: See Lambert, p. 235.
61 "There's nothing . . .": Lambert, p. 257.
61 "There is no . . .": Thoreau Cronyn, "The Truth About Hollywood," *New York Herald,* March 19–April 2, 1922.
62 "usually of a . . .": Nazimova Collection, Library of Congress, quoted in Schanke and Marra, p. 138.
62 Arzner birth and family background: U.S. Census, 1900, San Francisco, CA.
62 Arzner mother, grandmother: Arzner Collection, UCLA; also U.S. Census, 1910, Los Angeles County, CA.
62 "loving father": *Los Angeles Times,* January 24, 1975.

62 "It smelled of . . .": *Photoplay,* March 1927.
63 "Not true!": Arzner Collection.
63 Garth: Arzner Collection.
63 Arzner report cards: Arzner Collection.
64 "My dear young . . .": *Motion Picture Classic,* September 1929.
64 "The script is . . . " *Woman's Journal,* February 1929; also *The Hollywood Reporter,* May 16, 1932.
64 "In no line . . .": *Motion Picture Supplement,* September 1915, quoted in Martin F. Norden, "Women in the Early Film Industry," Staiger, *The Studio System.*
65 Bronski on gay transgressions: Michael Bronski, interview with the author. See also Bronski, *The Pleasure Principle,* pp. 29–32.
65 Maas and de Gresac: Maas, *The Shocking Miss Pilgrim,* p. 64.
65 Fred de Gresac career: *Variety* obituary, March 3, 1943; New York Times Theatrical Reviews.
66 Mike Leahy: Arzner Collection; *Variety* obituary, Agnes Brand Leahy, April 3, 1934.
66 "I felt a . . .": *The Hollywood Reporter,* May 16, 1932.
66 "I watched her . . .": Brownlow, *The Parade's Gone By,* p. 286.
67 "the different scenes . . .": *Moving Picture World,* December 20, 1913.
67 "I learned . . .": *Silver Screen,* December 1933.
68 Arzner on set of *Old Ironsides: Woman's Journal,* February 1929.
68 "I'd rather do . . .": Karyn Kay and Gerald Peary, "Interview with Dorothy Arzner," in Johnston, *The Work of Dorothy Arzner: Toward a Feminist Cinema,* p. 23.
68 "If I could . . .": *Photoplay,* March 1927.
69 "resented [Dorothy] . . .": DeWitt Bodeen to Anthony Slide, March 16, 1976, Anthony Slide Collection, Bowling Green University.
69 "neither aided nor . . .": *Motion Picture Classic,* September 1929.
69 "women with . . .": *New York Sun,* September 23, 1930.
69 "Women are too . . .": *Los Angeles Examiner,* November 4, 1932.
69 "A woman's . . .": *The Hollywood Reporter,* May 16, 1932.
69 Ralston on Arzner: Ralston, *Some Day We'll Laugh,* pp. 106–107.
70 Slide quote: Slide, *The Silent Feminists,* p. 110.
70 Arzner and technicians' slang: *New York Telegraph,* January 5, 1933.
70 "In the studios . . .": *Movie Classic,* December 1936.
70 "preoccupations with . . . " : Mayne, p. 32.
70 "Arzner deplores . . .": *Los Angeles Reader,* May 9, 1980.
71 "In the next . . .": unsourced clip, circa 1930, NYPL.
71 Derow senior thesis and Arzner's comments: Derow, Deborah, "What Is This We Hear—A Broad Is Going to Direct," senior thesis, May 1976, Barnard College, Columbia University, in Arzner Collection.
72 "Marion Morgan does . . .": *Buffalo News,* July 7, 1915.
72 ice and snow: *New York Times,* March 8, 1916.
72 "It matters little . . .": *Calvary Record,* March 1918.
73 "You understood . . .": George Brendan Dowell to Dorothy Arzner, November 11, 1971, Arzner Collection.
73 "her black chiffon . . .": George Brendan Dowell to Dorothy Arzner, circa 1971, Arzner Collection.
73 Morgan postcards: Arzner Collection.
73 "You were in . . .": George Brendan Dowell to Dorothy Arzner, circa 1971, Arzner Collection.
73 "knowing what . . .": Beth to Dorothy Arzner, circa 1971, Arzner Collection.
73 Arzner and Burke: Andrew Stone to Anthony Slide, "The Silent Closet," *Film Quarterly,* Summer 1999.
73 *Screen Snapshots:* Slide, "The Silent Closet."
74 "Miss Arzner wears . . .": unsourced clip, October 15, 1940, NYPL.
74 "the house shared . . ." *Vogue,* June 15, 1931.
75 "She thought she . . .": Elliot Morgan, interview with the author.

75 "She had a . . .": Lewis, *The Creative Producer,* p. 84.

75 "There are those . . .": Unsourced clipping, circa 1904, Zoe Akins file, NYPL.

75 "I am not . . .": Unsourced clipping, circa 1904, Zoe Akins file, NYPL.

75 Akins early career: *Dramatic Mirror,* July 29, 1919; *Town and Country,* November 10, 1919; *Vanity Fair,* December 1919; *New York Clipper,* October 6, 1920; *New York Times,* September 25, 1921.

75 Willa Cather: For a discussion of her lesbianism and her friendship with Akins, see Sharon O'Brien, *Will Cather: The Emerging Voice* (NY: Oxford University Press, 1987) and *Lives of Notable Gay Men and Lesbians: Will Cather,* general editor Martin Duberman, (NY: Chelsea House, 1995).

75 "unaware of . . .": *Town and Country,* December 1, 1916.

76 "Miss Akins' . . .": *New York Times,* October 12, 1919.

76 Cather advice to Akins: Willa Cather to Zoe Akins, letter dated January 27, 1909, Akins Collection, Huntington Library, San Marino, CA. A restriction on the collection prevents the direct quotation of any of the letters.

76 Akins' poem to Barrymore: *Vanity Fair,* June 1920.

76 little Polish woman: Barrymore, *Memories.*

76 Howland early career: *Green Book,* February 1912; *Moving Picture World,* July 10, 1918; *New York Herald Tribune,* June 9, 1936; *New York Daily News,* June 12, 1936.

76 Leontine Sagan to Akins: Letter dated June 29, 1936, Akins Collection.

77 "a perspective on . . .": Mayne, p. 45.

77 "I'm sure the . . .": Zoe Akins to George Cukor, October 22, 1954, Cukor Collection.

78 Burke letter: Billie Burke to Zoe Akins, two letters, undated 1932, Akins Collection.

78 Rumbold letters: Hugo Rumbold to Zoe Akins, March 29, 1938, Akins Collection.

78 Sagan letter: Leontine Sagan to Zoe Akins, March 29, 1938, Akins Collection.

79 "one very prominent . . .": Joseph Breen to Will Hays, August 29, 1931, Will H. Hays papers.

79 Garbo: See Paris, *Garbo;* Swenson, *Greta Garbo: A Life Apart;* de Acosta: *Here Lies the Heart.*

79 "The film mobilized . . .": Patricia White, *Uninvited,* p. 10.

80 Dietrich and the violets: Martin, *Marlene Dietrich,* pp. 53–55.

80 Dietrich: See Riva, *Marlene Dietrich;* Spoto, *The Blue Angel;* Higham, *Marlene.*

80 Dressler, Dubrey: See Kennedy, *Marie Dressler;* Lee, *Marie Dressler; The Unlikeliest Star.*

80 "fey or gay": Jean Stein, "West of Eden," *The New Yorker,* February 23, 1998.

80 McDaniel: See Jackson, *Hattie,* which denies any homosexuality but does document the closeness with Goodwin through their letters.

81 Gershe quote on Colbert-Dietrich: *Vanity Fair,* January 1998.

81 "Maybe they became . . .": Robert Shaw interview with the author.

81 "Marlene Dietrich bobbed . . .": Associated Press wire story, dated June 17, 1935, Colbert file, NYPL.

82 "No man ought . . .": *Silver Screen,* June 1931.

82 "We do not . . .": *Motion Picture,* August 1932.

82 "I don't know . . .": Robert Shaw, interview with the author.

82 "Uncle Claude": Don Bachardy, interview with the author

83 Haines, Shaw and Colbert: Robert Shaw, interview with the author.

83 Gaynor-Martin: See Stacy Wolf, "Mary Martin," Schanke and Marra, *Passing Performances.*

83 "Janet doesn't have . . .": *Silver Screen,* December 1934.

83 Francis pool party: Miles White, interview with the author.

83 Eells, Lawler and Francis: Eells, *Ginger, Loretta and Irene Who?*

SEX WITHOUT SIN

85 Taylor murder: Hopkins manuscript, *Taylorology,* extensive website and online newsletter for material relating to the career of William Desmond Taylor, his life and times: www.silent-movies.com/Taylorology.

86 DeMille quote: *New York Times,* February 4, 1922.

86 John Brown: *Chattanooga Times,* March 12, 1922.

87 *The Sins of Hollywood:* published in 1922 by the Hollywood Publishing Company, reprinted online at *Taylorology* website.

87 "Eastern newspapers . . .": *Oakland Tribune,* February 25, 1922.

87 American Legion gala: *Los Angeles Express,* February 21, 1920.

87 "Hollywood at night . . .": "The Truth about Hollywood," *New York Herald,* March 19–April 2, 1922.

87 "The number of . . .": Hart Crane to Wilbur Underwood, April 27, 1928; "Besides which . . .": Hart Crane to William Slater Brown, February 22, 1928, reprinted in Hammer, *O My Land, My Friend.*

88 "His name evokes . . .": *Focus on Film,* March 1978.

88 Cukor on Goulding: letter to Alex Tiers, 1968, Cukor Collection, AMPAS; Robert Wheaton, interview with the author.

88 "Handsome and distinguished . . .": *New York Times,* May 28, 1939.

88 "Studio people . . .": *Los Angeles Times,* May 18, 1947.

88 "dissolute": Maas, *The Shocking Miss Pilgrim,* p. 74.

89 Goulding morality charge: Mabel Willebrandt to the State Department, December 19, 1932. MGM was requesting his return to the U.S. as he was still under contract and his "services are needed in this country." The State Department wrote to the American Consul in London on January 4, 1933, inquiring into Goulding's case. On January 6, the Consul replied that "British authorities state no charge against Edmund Goulding." By then, he had left with wife Marjorie Moss for St. Moritz, Switzerland. He attended the Berlin premiere of *Grand Hotel* in early February, and was back in Hollywood by March. See correspondence in the Charles Higham Collection, Occidental College, Los Angeles. I am grateful to Matthew Kennedy for sharing this information.

89 "All for love . . .": *Focus on Film,* March 1978.

89 Maas on Goulding: Maas, *The Shocking Miss Pilgrim,* pp. 74–75.

89 David Lewis: Lewis, *The Creative Producer,* p. 151.

90 "the era when . . .": De Acosta, *Here Lies the Heart,* p. 162.

90 1920s Hollywood: See Mann, *Wisecracker,* pp. 57–58.

91 "The Bill Harts . . .": *New York Telegraph,* December 26, 1930.

91 Goulding birth: Feltham, not listed in standard biographies, comes from Goulding's ship passenger arrival record, *S.S. St. Louis,* arriving June 7, 1915. Parents names from death certificate.

91 Goulding early life and career: *New York Times,* August 17, 1924; *New York American,* December 21, 1930; studio press release biographies.

91 Goulding immigration: ship manifests, *S.S. St. Louis,* arriving June 7, 1915; *S.S. New York,* arriving July 18, 1915. For unknown reasons, he returned to England just weeks after his arrival, only to set sail again on July 10. He arrived for the second time on July 18.

92 "something 'sympathique' . . .": Janis, *So Far So Good,* p. 250.

92 Elsie Janis' lesbianism: See Lee Alan Morrow, "Elsie Janis: A Comfortable Goofiness," *Passing Performances* (eds. Schanke and Marra).

92 "The Devil": unsourced clip, August 28, 1920, Robinson Locke Collection, NYPL.

92 "I got so mad . . .": MGM studio biography.

92 "one of the . . .": *New York Telegraph,* March 11, 1923.

93 Cronyn: "The Truth About Hollywood," *New York Herald,* March 19–April 2, 1922.

93 Hays office: See Jowett, p. 236, 466.

94 Hays drug report: Will H. Hays papers, March 1923.

94 drug party: *New York Evening World,* February 13, 1922.

94 "But there is . . .": *Chicago Tribune,* March 6, 1922.

94 "British nobleman . . .": *Chicago American,* February 9, 1922.

94 "In the 1920s . . .": *Bay Area Reporter,* October 1974.

96 "crude, brash . . .": *Bay Area Reporter,* October 1974.

96 "We'd cavort . . .": *Bay Area Reporter,* October 1974.

97 Marion Morgan: clippings, Robinson Locke Collection, NYPL; *Picture Play,* June 1922.

97 Lubitsch and Novarro: Quirk, *Norma,* p. 95.

97 "We had our . . .": Hal Elias Oral History, AMPAS.

98 "My uncle . . .": *Vanity Fair,* April 1998.

98 Jerome Storm: *New York Telegraph,* February 13, 1921.

98 Quarberg: "Movie Press Agents are Pikers," circa 1933, Lincoln Quarberg Collection, AMPAS.

98 "Our job at . . .": Shorris and Bundy, *Talking Pictures,* p. 348.

99 Marquis Busby: Los Angeles City directories, 1925–1933; *Variety,* obituary March 13, 1934; interview with Lawrence Quirk by the author.

99 "The marrying age . . .": *Photoplay,* September 1929.

99 "It's not likely . . .": unsourced clip, probably *Photoplay,* 1927, Robinson Locke Collection, NYPL.

99 "I was a dancer . . .": *Photoplay,* April 1923.

99 "A brilliance . . .": *Motion Picture,* February 1927.

100 "I didn't know . . .": *Photoplay,* May 1924.

100 "Novarro seduced . . .": Lawrence Quirk, interview with the author.

100 Ingram: See Slide, "The Silent Closet."

100 "I've made . . .": *Photoplay,* May 1924.

101 "I don't know . . .": *Photoplay,* November 1923.

101 Howe childhood: U.S. Census, 1900, Minnehaha County, SD.

101 Howe background and career: *New York Telegraph,* July 10, 1921; *Photoplay,* November 1923.

101 Bodeen quote: Bodeen, *From Hollywood,* p. 79.

101 "The secret . . .": *Photoplay,* November 1923.

102 "From the moment . . .": *Photoplay,* July 1923.

102 "As a princess . . .": *Photoplay,* April 1925.

103 Lawler-Cooper to Catalina: Letter from Lawler to his mother, Mrs. Ernest Lawler, Lynchburg, Virginia, 1929, Lawler family collection.

103 "Coop queer?": Swindell, *The Last Hero,* p. 104.

104 Haines party: Michael Pearman, interview with the author.

104 "Andy Lawler was . . .": Bob Wheaton, interview with the author.

104 "Gary gets more . . .": *Photoplay,* 1929, Anderson Lawler scrapbook, NYPL.

104 Cooper-Lawler friendship: Anderson Lawler scrapbook, NYPL; Swindell, *The Last Hero.*

104 "I am trying . . .": Andy Lawler to Mother, 1929, Lawler family collection.

105 Haines telegram: January 5, 1930, Anderson Lawler scrapbook, NYPL.

105 "leisure time . . .": *Los Angeles Times,* March 18, 1930; *Los Angeles Illustrated News,* March 21, 1930.

105 Jamey and Nin: Swindell, p. 105–106.

105 Telegrams from Cooper to Lawler: Anderson Lawler scrapbook. NYPL. I have added punctuation to make them more readable.

105 "Andy's brother . . .": Letter from William Kizer to the author, June 11, 1999.

106 Cooper-Velez-Lawler-Asther: "Screenalities" column, undated, Anderson Lawler scrapbook. NYPL.

106 Dorothy Herzog: unsourced clip, June 18, 1929, NYPL.

107 Lawler early life: Lawler family materials, prepared by William Kizer; Anderson Lawler scrapbook, NYPL.

107 Lawler-Lydell Peck in college: Washinton & Lee University, Special Collections.

107 Peck, DeMille: Letter from Lydell Peck, printed in the Washington & Lee alumni magazine, June 1927; Paramount publicity biographies of Anderson Lawler.

107 Andy's mother: William Kizer, interview with the author.

107 "very safe": Geist, Kenneth. *Pictures Will Talk: The Life and Films of Joseph L. Mankiewicz* (NY: Scribner's), p. 125.

109 Parsons quote on backgammon: unsourced clip, circa 1932, Anderson Lawler scrapbook. NYPL.

108 arrives with Akins and Francis: *New York Telegraph,* February 16, 1930.
108 Francis, Haines, Goulding party: *Hollywood Reporter,* March 26, 1935.
108 David Manners: unsourced clip, March 1934, Anderson Lawler scrapbook, NYPL.
108 Akins telegram: July 22, 1930, Anderson Lawler scrapbook. NYPL.
108 "Ilk and Zoo . . .": Letter from Lilyan Tashman to George Cukor, undated, circa 1930, Cukor Collection.
108 clique to Andy's for dinner: *Hollywood Reporter,* June 21, 1932.
108 Dietrich admirers: *Movie Mirror,* April 1938.
109 "three gay months": *Bachelor,* October 1937.
110 Gill on DiFrasso party: Zerbe and Gill, *Happy Times.*
110 Cal York and wax disks: *Photoplay,* May 1936.
111 "I'm not one . . .": See Anthony Slide, "The Silent Closet."
111 "With his short . . .": Emlyn Williams, *George* (New York: Random House, 1961).
111 "handsomest page-boy": Paramount studio biography, circa 1929.
112 "bad little boys . . .": *Los Angeles Examiner,* undated 1930, NYPL.
112 "She goes where . . .": *Silver Screen,* January 1931.
112 "When Lilyan had . . .": Paris, *Garbo,* p. 233.
112 Tashman and Taylor: Information comes courtesy of Anthony Slide, who is editing Starr's memoirs.
112 "Ever since she . . .": *Silver Screen,* 1931.
113 Tashman family: U.S. Census, 1900, King's County, New York.
113 Lil at 17: This according to sister Jennie Tashman, unsourced clip, Lilyan Tashman file, NYPL.
113 Tashman-Lee marriage date: Notice of separation, *Zit's Magazine,* February 12, 1921, NYPL.
113 "pretty fresh": Tashman to Gladys Hall, Gladys Hall Collection, AMPAS.
113 "Sables, Rollses . . .": Tashman to Gladys Hall, Gladys Hall Collection, AMPAS.
114 Tashman-Lee divorce: *New York Review,* February 12, 1921, NYPL.
114 Tashman-Lowe meeting: clippings, Robinson Locke Collection, NYPL.
114 Chu Chin Chow ball: undated clip, *New York American,* and *Detroit Free Press,* February 28, 1920, Lilyan Tashman Collection, NYPL.
114 Lowe and Tashman on getting married: *Photoplay,* August 1925.
115 Haines-Shields: See Mann, *Wisecracker.*
115 Cornell, McClintic, Lunt, Fontanne: see Schanke and Marra, *Passing Performances.*
116 "supremely happy . . .": *Silver Screen,* January 1931.
116 Lowe-Tashman assets: Los Angeles County Superior Court, Lilyan Tashman probate file.
116 "Sophistication . . .": Lilyan Tashman to Gladys Hall, Gladys Hall Collection, AMPAS.
116 "Eddie Goulding's journey . . .": *New York Daily News,* November 26, 1931.
116 "unhorsed": *New York Telegraph,* November 28, 1931.
117 Brooks on Goulding: *Focus on Film,* March 1978.
117 Marjorie Goulding death: *New York Telegraph,* February 5, 1935.
117 "going out of . . .": *Variety,* December 8, 1931.
117 "Julie" and "Alice": Lilyan Tashman to George Cukor, undated, circa 1930, Cukor Collection.
117 "Sex, oddly . . .": unsourced clipping, Lilyan Tashman file, NYPL.
117 "I am fortunate . . .": *Photoplay,* August 1925.
117 "Every woman . . .": *Photoplay,* March 1933.
117 "Lowe's roles . . .": *New York Times,* May 18, 1930.
118 Tashman-Marlowe row: *Los Angeles Evening Herald,* May 9, 1931; May 12, 1931.
118 Tashman tips: *Motion Picture Classic,* December 1929.
119 "If you have . . .": *Collier's,* November 19, 1932.
119 "It seems odd": Edmund Lowe to Gladys Hall, April 30, 1934, Gladys Hall Collection, AMPAS.
119 "Hysterical women . . .": *New York Sun,* March 23, 1934.
119 "People have said . . .": Edmund Lowe to Gladys Hall, April 30, 1934, Gladys Hall Collection, AMPAS.

WILD PANSIES

122 "The revulsion . . .": Chauncey, *Gay New York.*

122 Depression-era view of homosexuality: See Mann, *Wisecracker.*

122 The Catholic Church crusade against the film industry: See Black, *Hollywood Censored;* Leff, *The Dame in the Kimono;* Veira, *Sin in Soft Focus.*

123 "What emerged . . .": Black, *Hollywood Censored.*

123 Production Code: See Jowett, *Film: The Democratic Art;* Black, *Hollywood Censored.*

124 "an exposé of . . .": RKO press sheets, *Our Betters,* 1933, NYPL.

124 "Surely one can . . .": quoted in a letter from Maurice McKenzie, assistant to Will Hays, to James Wingate, February 25, 1933, Production Code Administration (PCA) files, AMPAS.

125 "Nobody out there . . .": Joseph Breen to Wilfrid Parsons, October 10, 1932, Will Hays papers.

125 "It may be noted . . .": Martin Quigley to Will Hays, February 25, 1933, Will Hays papers.

125 "Effeminate boys . . .": *Variety,* February 2, 1932.

125 "Sexual perversion . . .": Joseph Breen to Wilfrid Parsons, October 10, 1932, Will Hays papers.

125 "In the last . . .": James Wingate to Merian C. Cooper, February 20, 1933, PCA files, AMPAS.

126 "As you already . . .": James Wingate to Will Hays, February 23, 1933, PCA files.

126 "At the finish . . .": *Variety,* February 28, 1933.

126 FILMS TOO WISE and "panz stuff": *Variety,* February 28, 1933.

126 "There is a story . . .": Will Hays to James Wingate, March 1, 1933, PCA files, AMPAS.

127 "was a sin": Black, *Hollywood Censored,* p. 64.

127 "Their seminude . . .": Vieira, p. 106.

128 "I think the . . .": Sidney Kent to Winfield Sheehan, March 7, 1933, PCA files, AMPAS.

128 "Only he-men . . .": *Variety,* June 11, 1930.

128 "lousy Jews . . .": Joseph Breen to Wilfrid Parsons, October 10, 1932, Will Hays papers.

129 "one of the . . .": Marion, *Off With Their Heads,* p. 189.

129 "Mother was a Scot . . .": ABC-TV press release, February 24, 1970, Horton Collection, AMPAS.

130 "I was an . . .": 20th Century Fox press release, circa 1942, Horton File, NYPL.

130 "I played all . . .":*Focus on Film,* No. 1, 1970.

131 "The audience figures . . .": *Motion Picture Classic,* May 1929.

131 "It pays to . . .": 20th Century Fox press release, 1942, Horton file, NYPL.

131 "scrubbed on . . .": Russo, *The Celluloid Closet,* p. 36.

131 "I have often . . .": 20th Century Fox press release, 1942, Horton file, NYPL.

132 "home and sex . . .": *Silver Screen,* March 1935.

132 Grady Sutton: interview with Robert Wheaton by the author; see also Maltin, *The Real Stars.*

133 Horton and Gordon: The publicist Herb Sterne was reportedly aware of the relationship, and told the historian Anthony Slide. Courtesy Slide.

133 "the suave, sophisticated . . .": undated clip, Rex O'Malley file, NYPL.

133 Leisen on O'Malley: Chierichetti, *Hollywood Director,* p. 123.

133 Pangborn early life: U.S. Census, 1900, Newark, NJ.

133 "To mention the . . .": *Detroit News,* undated clip, circa 1914, Pangborn file, NYPL.

134 Pangborn's kerchiefs: *Detroit Free Press,* May 25, 1917, Robinson Locke Collection, NYPL.

134 Pangborn in World War I: military records, National Personnel Records Center.

134 Pangborn's wartime entertainments: *Motion Picture,* July 1928.

135 "I've never quite . . .": and "always faultlessly . . .": *New York Daily Mirror,* November 30, 1938.

135 Lesbian character actresses: Despite the dearth of anecdotal evidence, these women may indeed have been lesbians. In her will, Moorehead left bequests to a number of female friends. Her close friendship with Debbie Reynolds gave rise during her lifetime to the rumor that the two were lovers. (Reynolds even acknowledged the rumor in her autobiography.) Moorehead chose to cloak her private life in almost fanatical secrecy, even going so far as to pretend her two (possibly three) marriages had never taken place. Yet Dick Sargent, her costar on the 1960s television show "Bewitched," who came out very publicly as gay, was unable to say for sure whether Moorehead was in fact a lesbian.

   Marjorie Main left her home and jewelry to a Mrs. Claire Flint. Curiously, both Moorehead and Main also left money in their wills to conservative universities: Moorehead to Bob Jones and Main to Pepperdine. Both were known as deeply religious women. Both had early marriages that produced no children, although Moorehead had an adopted son she specifically ignored in her will, stating she had no children, "natural or adopted." (Probate files, Los Angeles Superior Court.)

   Spring Byington, however, left two daughters, three grandchildren, and two great-grandchildren at her death. (*Variety* obituary, September 7, 1971).

   For more on the lesbian "representability" of these actresses, see Patricia White, *Uninvited.*

137 Ona Munson letters to Hedda Hopper: undated postcard, circa 1950; May 15, 1951; May 23, 1951. Hedda Hopper Collection.

137 Lindsay and Gaynor: *New York American,* December 21, 1935; *New York World-Telegram,* July 27, 1936.

137 "grin and bear . . .": *Motion Picture,* July 1934.

137 Lindsay and marriage: *New York Post,* December 30, 1935; unsourced clipping, 1937, NYPL;

138 Patsy and Malin: *New York Times,* August 11, 1933; *Hollywood Studio Magazine,* February 1982.

138 "I'm having too . . .": *Motion Picture,* January 1937.

138 "If we'd had . . .": *New York Daily News,* February 14, 1971.

138 "There was almost . . .": *Silver Screen,* March 1936.

139 Patsy Kelly New York career: *New York Times,* December 23, 1928; June 29, 1930.

139 "Even the plainest . . .": *Silver Screen,* March 1936.

139 "She seldom gets . . .": unsourced Skolsky "Tintypes" column, August 12, 1941.

139 "Funny Patsy . . .": *New York Post,* October 2, 1936.

139 "fix madam . . .": *Hollywood Studio Magazine,* February 1982.

140 studio and movie attendance statistics: Jowett, *Film the Democratic Art.*

141 "I was convinced . . .": Carl Milliken to Walter T. Pearcy, November 19, 1934, Will Hays papers.

141 "fairly feminine voice . . .": Joseph Breen to Maurice Pivar, August 26, 1940, PCA files.

141 "was never intended . . .": Edward F. Cline to Joseph Breen, August 29, 1940, PCA files.

142 "This characterization . . .": Joseph Breen to Mat O'Brien, February 15, 1940, PCA files.

142 Breen on *Bride of Frankenstein:* James Whale to Joseph Breen, December 7, 1934, PCA files.

142 "As written . . .": Joseph Breen to Mat O'Brien, February 22, 1940, PCA files.

143 *Turnabout* rating: Letter from Rev. John T. McClafferty, Legion of Decency, to Joseph Breen, June 14, 1940, PCA files.

143 "if Pangborn plays . . .": Joseph Breen to Maurice Pivar, April 17, 1941, PCA files.

143 "Jean Malin and . . .": Chauncey, *Gay New York,* p. 329.

144 "While the whoops . . .": *Variety,* September 27, 1932.

144 Jimmy's Back Yard: Harry Hay, interview with the author. Hay had originally believed that actor-director Lowell Sherman had been among the first-night crowd. Later questioning, however, indicated he meant Edmund Lowe.

144 Rae Bourbon background: programme for "Catherine Was Great," August 1944, NYPL. See also Slide, *Encyclopedia of Vaudeville.*

145 "He has a wealth . . .": undated *Variety* clipping, Rae Bourbon file, NYPL.
145 David Hanna remembrances: Hanna, "The Watering Holes," *The Harvard Gay and Lesbian Review*, Summer 1996, and Strong, Lester, "A Talk With David Hanna," *Journal of Gay, Lesbian & Bisexual Identity*, April 1999.
145 B.B.B.'s hammers: *The Hollywood Reporter*, September 25, 1932.
145 "a mean rumba . . .": *Variety*, October, 4, 1932.
145 Malin background: *New York Daily News*, April 2, 1931; *New York Times*, August 11, 1933. See also Chauncey, *Gay New York*.
145 "Wisecracks . . .": *Variety*, October 4, 1932.
146 "Polly Moran's companion . . .": *New York Graphic*, September 28, 1931.
146 "The fears for . . .": Loughery, p. 58.
146 "drive on the Nance . . .": *Variety*, October 4, 1932.
146 "That killed the . . .": *Variety*, November 21, 1933.
146 Eltinge at Rendezvous: Slide, *The Great Pretenders*, p. 29.
147 "For some reason . . .": Hanna, "The Watering Holes."
147 Bourbon fate: See his letter published in *Variety*, June 3, 1970; also obituary, July 19, 1971.
147 "There was a . . .": Fred Frisbie, interview included in the Los Angeles Gay & Lesbian History Project, conducted by the One Institute/International Gay & Lesbian Archives, University of Southern California, Los Angeles.
147 "The elegant nightclub . . .": Blackwell, *From Rags to Bitches*, p. 105.
148 "Poor old thing . . .": Frank Lysinger, interview with the author.
148 "there tended to be . . .": Walter Plunkett, interview with David Chierichetti, courtesy Chierichetti.
149 Loos and Talmadge: Loos, *The Talmadge Girls*.
149 "We are watching . . .": *Los Angeles Evening Herald*, April 23, 1931.
150 "latent sadism": Walker, *The Shattered Silents*.
150 Haines press: See Mann, *Wisecracker*.
150 Allison interview with Novarro: *Photoplay*, April 1933.
151 Albert, Novarro, Loy: *Modern Screen*, May 1933.
151 "Before Mr. Quirk . . .": Memo from Maude Lathem to Frances Kish, July 22, 1930, Photoplay Collection, Museum of Modern Art, New York.
152 "to pass on . . .": *Cinema Digest*, January 9, 1933.
152 "The history of . . .": John Moffitt, *Kansas City Star*, reprinted in *Cinema Digest*, January 9, 1933.
152 "I would rather . . .": Gabler, *Winchell*, p. 158.
153 "A massive barrel . . .": Slide, Anthony, "Hedda Hopper," *Stallion*, June 1986.
153 "In half an . . .": *Time*, July 28, 1947.
154 "the big laugh . . .": *Los Angeles Examiner*, June 4, 1936.
154 "Whom does he think . . .": Hedda Hopper to Mike Cowles, Hedda Hopper Collection, AMPAS, courtesy Anthony Slide. Also see Slide, "Hedda Hopper," *Stallion*, June 1986.
154 "mincing minion . . .": Unsigned note to Hedda Hopper, August 25, 1952, Hopper Collection, AMPAS.
155 "She was very . . .": Robert Shaw, interview with the author.
155 "She seemed to . . .": Eells, *Hedda and Louella*.
156 Baxter contract: AMPAS
156 Haines' moral clause: Contract between William Haines and MGM, September 18, 1928. Courtesy of Turner Entertainment.
156 Haines' contracts: Contract between William Haines and MGM, dated September 25, 1931; Off Pay Roll Notices, August 13, 1931; August 15, 1932; August 14, 1933. See also Mann, *Wisecracker*, for detailed discussion of the end of Haines' career.
157 "empty bridal suite": *Photoplay*, June 1941.
158 "he-man": *Motion Picture*, September 1935.
158 "I'm no ladies . . .": *Motion Picture*, October 1935.
158 "loved the ladies . . .": Cesar Romero, oral history, DeGolyer Library, Southern Methodist University.

158 Tyrone Power: See Blackwell, *From Rags to Bitches;* Acre, *The Secret Life of Tyrone Power.*
159 "Tyrone would never . . .": Robert Wheaton, interview with the author.
159 "He felt it . . .": Charles Williamson, interview with the author.
159 Cherrill in divorce court: *Los Angeles Evening Herald Express,* March 26, 1935.
159 "three-gay month": *Bachelor,* April 1937.
159 Zerbe affairs with Grant and Scott: See Brendan Gill, "Pursuer and Pursued," *New Yorker,* June 2, 1997.
159 "deeply, madly . . .": Blackwell, *From Rags to Bitches,* pp. 54–56.
160 Grant, Scott holding hands: Higham and Moseley, *Cary Grant: The Lonely Heart.*
160 "In three previous . . .": *Brooklyn Daily Eagle,* December 18, 1938.
160 "implant five hard . . .": undated publicity department release, RKO Radio Pictures.
160 Lindsay and Romero: *Photoplay,* January 1941.
160 "developed a certain . . .": *New York Times,* June 19, 1938

AUTEUR THEORIES

162 "great films . . .": David O. Selznick to Spyros Skouras, January 16, 1962, quoted in Vertrees, *Selznick's Vision.* Vertrees offered a detailed discussion of the role Selznick played as a creative producer.
162 "It was the producer": Lewis, *The Creative Producer.*
162 "represents a meeting . . .": Bodeen, *More from Hollywood,* p. 55.
162 Robert Taylor and Jack Moore: Frank Lysinger, interview with the author.
162 "Who is that . . .": McGilligan, p. 120.
163 "I get annoyed . . .": Kevin Thomas, interview with the author.
163 Walters, "Madeleine Carroll": Ehrenstein, *Open Secret,* p. 83.
163 "too much like . . .": Curtis, *James Whale,* p. 349.
163 "Very nice pictures": David Chierichetti, interview with the author.
163 "For the most . . .": Gavin Lambert, interview with the author.
164 "Coming of professional . . .": Lambert, *Mainly About Lindsay Anderson,* p. 96.
165 Murnau-Rollins: Slide, "The Silent Closet."
165 James Vincent: Robert Wheaton, a close friend of Cukor's who also knew Vincent, remembered hearing of Vincent's early cohabitation with an important gay film star. However, the James Vincent of *Romeo and Juliet* was born in South Africa; according to the 1920 Census, the Vincent who lived with Kerrigan was born in Massachusetts. Still, the census often contains such errors. Both are the same age, and the Los Angeles City Directories seems to bear out the idea that both are the same man. Vincent disappears from the directories at a time we know James Vincent was in New York, becoming lovers with Guthrie McClintic and stage manager for McClintic's wife Katharine Cornell. He reappears in Los Angeles in 1930 living with Kerrigan, at a time Cornell's Vincent was still working for her, although there may have been a break. He is gone from Kerrigan's address, in fact, the next year. But we know he was back in Hollywood, working with Cukor, by 1935. Vincent's body was found floating in the Hudson River in New York on June 10, 1953. Cornell believed it was suicide; Cukor thought he'd been killed by a hustler. Making identification even more tricky is the existence of several other James Vincents, one of whom was a (married with children) silent movie and stage director (died 1957) who apparently was confused in some obituaries with the Cornell stage manager. See Cukor Collection AMPAS; *Los Angeles Examiner* June 11, 1953; Tad Mosel, *Leading Lady: The World and Theatre of Katharine Cornell* (Boston: Little, Brown, 1978).
165 Cukor's parties: For more details on the gay social scene that revolved around Cukor, William Haines, Cole Porter, and others, see Mann, *Wisecracker;* McGilligan, *George Cukor: A Double Life;* and McBrien, *Cole Porter.*
166 "very gay . . .": unsourced clipping, Anderson Lawler scrapbook, NYPL.
166 "They had lovely . . .": Lambert, *On Cukor.*
166 "a private promotional . . .": Pandro S. Berman to Charles Higham, in Higham, *Kate,* p. 75.

166 "He was fascinated . . .": Don Bachardy, interview with the author.

167 "It is difficult . . .": Joseph Breen to B. B. Kahane, August 5, 1935, PCA files, AMPAS.

167 "We suggest that . . . " Joseph Breen to B. B. Kahane, August 12, 1935, PCA files, AMPAS.

167 "Previewed our little love child": Telegram from George Cukor to Katharine Hepburn, December 9, 1935, George Cukor Collection, AMPAS.

168 "is its subtlety . . .": Scott F. Stoddart, "George Cukor's 'Take' on the Literacy Narrative: Hollywood Style," *Cineaction*, No. 50, September 1999.

168 "You should never . . .": Bogdanovich, *Who the Devil Made It?*, pp. 444–45.

168 "The whole auteur . . .": Lambert, *On Cukor*, pp. 13–14.

168 Cukor criticism: For more on Cukor's disinterest in the formal details of filmmaking, see "Notes on the Long Take in George Cukor's *A Life of Her Own*," *Cineaction*, No. 50, September 1999.

169 Karen Morley: McGilligan, *Tender Comrades*, p. 472.

169 "a homosexual piece," Pandro Berman, oral history, American Film Institute, August 4, 1972.

169 "flattened . . . much of . . .": McGilligan, p. 291.

169 Haines-Shields attack: See Mann, *Wisecracker*.

170 "It took a mere . . .": George Cukor to John Collier, George Cukor Collection, AMPAS.

170 "The important thing . . .": Gavin Lambert, interview with the author.

170 "If you view . . .": Michael Bronski, interview with the author.

171 "Why, the tear jerker . . .": *New York Herald Tribune*, June 28, 1942.

171 "He probably walked . . .": *Los Angeles Times*, December 30, 1959.

171 "chemistry, or a . . .": *New York Herald Tribune*, June 28, 1942.

171 "The sight of . . .": Unsourced, undated clip by Robert L. Wheeler, 1943, Goulding file, NYPL.

172 "Mr. Goulding wanted . . .": Spada, *More Than a Woman*, p. 155.

172 "Mitchell Leisen is outranking . . .": undated, unsourced clip, Hedda Hopper column, 1944.

172 "I learned photography . . .": Chierichetti, pp. 51–52.

173 "I don't consider . . .": *New York Times*, April 8, 1945.

173 "tower over that . . .": Drabelle, Dennis, "Swing High, Swing Low: Mitchell Leisen in Perspective," *Film Comment*, September–October, 1994.

173 "Sometimes when things . . .": *New York Times*, April 8, 1945.

173 "I think Leisen . . .": David Chierichetti, interview with the author.

173 hormone shots: Eleanor Broder to David Chierichetti, see *Hollywood Director*, p. 10.

174 "He got so . . .": David Chierichetti, interview with the author.

174 "leave his sex . . .": Hedda Hopper Collection, AMPAS, see Slide, "Hedda Hopper."

174 "Part of Leisen's . . .": Chierichetti, p. 12.

174 "There were lots . . .": David Chierichetti, interview with the author.

174 "He was coming . . .": Chierichetti, p. 287.

175 "You look at . . .": Gavin Lambert, interview with the author.

175 "this half-pint . . .": Joseph Breen to Luigi Luraschi, Paramount, June 5, 1942, PCA files, AMPAS.

176 "Bette Davis had . . .": Irving Rapper to Charles Higham, *The Celluloid Muse*, p. 199.

176 "I'd sometimes begin . . .": *Celluloid Muse*, p. 200.

176 "It was supposed . . .": *Celluloid Muse*, p. 203.

177 "If I'd stayed . . .": *Films in Review*, August–September, 1986.

177 Rapper as child outside theater: Warner Brothers studio biography, undated, circa 1941, AMPAS.

177 Rapper and McClintic: *Films in Review*, August–September, 1986.

178 Rapper's Soviet invitation: *New York Herald Tribune*, March 8, 1934; undated clip, *New York Sun*, circa 1938, Irving Rapper file, NYPL.

178 "the most sympathetic . . .": *Celluloid Muse*, p. 199.

178 "She's a very . . .": *Films in Review*, August–September, 1986.

178 Rapper, Davis, *The Corn is Green:* Spada, *More Than a Woman,* p. 228.
178 "I have a rule . . .": *Celluloid Muse,* pp. 201, 203.
179 "My agent begged . . .": *Films in Review,* August–September, 1986.
179 "deciding whether they . . .": Murray, *Images in the Dark,* p. 193.
179 Lesbian read of *Now, Voyager:* see Patricia White, *Uninvited.*
179 "It was Irving . . .": Robert Wheaton, interview with the author.
179 Rapper's attempt to seduce Gilmore: Gilmore, *Laid Bare,* pp. 31–32.
180 Rapper very much . . .": Robert Wheaton, interview with the author.
180 "kindly, efficient . . .": Schickel, *Clint Eastwood,* p. 67.
180 "I think working . . .": Arthur Lubin oral history, conducted by James Desmarais for the Directors' Guild of America, December 1976–January 1977, AMPAS.
181 pictorial spread: *Los Angeles Herald-Express,* March 10, 1963.
181 Lubin data: His personal worth and the sharing of his home with Frank Burford comes from his probate file and will, filed in Los Angeles County Superior Court. On January 24, 1992, Lubin put the house in Burford's name; both were listed as "unmarried men."
181 Lubin birth: Probate file; death certificate; U.S. Census, 1910, San Diego County, CA.
182 Lubin New York career: Paramount studio biography, circa 1935; *New York Times,* March 5, 1934.
182 "I've never considered . . .": Lubin oral history, AMPAS.
183 "I tried to get . . .": *Classic Images,* No. 166, April 1989.
183 "Clint was working . . .": Arthur Lubin oral history, AMPAS.
184 Clint calls Lubin: Schickel, *Clint Eastwood,* p. 83.
184 "I have done . . .": Arthur Lubin oral history, AMPAS.
184 "Most likely, Whale . . .": Curtis, *James Whale,* p. 185.
184 "a homosexual joke . . .": Monika Morgan, "Sexual Subversion: The Bride of Frankenstein," *Bright Lights,* No. 11, Fall 1993.
185 "Cukor didn't approve . . .": Ehrenstein, *Open Secret,* p. 72.
185 "Everybody in Hollywood . . .": Curtis, p. 185.
185 Phil Berg question to Lewis: Lewis, *The Creative Producer,* p. 84.
185 "became absorbed . . .": *New York Herald-Tribune,* December 3, 1944.
185 "I was sorry . . .": David Lewis to James Curtis, see *James Whale,* p. 133.
185 "flamboyantly gay": Benshoff, *Monsters in the Closet,* p. 43.
187 "a frail ex-prisoner . . .": *Times* (London), May 31, 1957.
187 "He was camp . . .": Slide, *Eccentrics of Comedy,* p. 146.
187 "Anyone fancy . . .": Anthony Slide, *Stallion,* p. 31.
187 "Whale's magical rendering . . .": Morgan, "Sexual Subversion: The Bride of Frankenstein," *Bright Lights,* No. 11, Fall 1993.
187 James Whale's later career: For a full discussion of Whale's industry decline, see James Curtis, *James Whale.*
188 "That kind of . . .": Lambert, *Mainly About Lindsay Anderson,* p. 221.
188 MGM meeting of producers after Paul Bern's death: Samuel Marx to Charles Higham, in Higham, *Merchant of Dreams.*
189 "When I hire . . .": Curtis, *James Whale,* p. 187.
189 "Men marry whores . . .": Lewis, p. 84.
189 David Lewis family background: U.S. Census, 1920, King County, WA.
189 "My father was . . .": Lewis, *The Creative Producer,* p. 3.
190 [Montagne] said I had . . .": David Lewis to James Curtis, *James Whale,* p. 82.
191 "I feel that . . .": *New York Sun,* October 3, 1944.
191 "Mr. Lewis is . . .": *New York Sun,* October 3, 1944.
191 "A former art . . .": Lewis, *The Creative Producer,* p. 196.
192 "I became friendly . . .": Arthur Laurents, interview with the author.
192 "It had become . . .": David Lewis to George Lovett, quoted in Curtis, *James Whale,* p. 290.
193 "If you believe . . .": *Los Angeles Times,* August 25, 1977.
193 "For someone as . . .": *Hollywood Studio Magazine,* October 1982, Vol. 15, No. 12.
193 new women producers: *New York Times,* January 7, 1945.

194 "The studio didn't . . .": *Hollywood Studio Magazine,* October 1982, Vol. 15, No. 12.
194 "The first thing . . .": *Films in Review,* October 1954.
194 Bodeen and Parsons on *The Enchanted Cottage: Films in Review,* June-July 1963.
195 "They were very . . .": Charles Higham, interview with the author.
195 "Even when I . . .": *Hollywood Studio Magazine,* October 1982, Vol. 15, No. 12.
195 Harriet on phone books: *Los Angeles Times,* July 6, 1980.
195 "I suppose there . . .": *Hollywood Studio Magazine,* October 1982, Vol. 15, No. 12.
195 "Despite the male . . . " *Films in Review,* October 1954.

QUEER WORK

197 "I got to . . .": Frank Lysinger, interview with the author.
197 "Oh, my, yes . . .": Elliot Morgan, interview with the author.
198 "like so many . . .": Schatz, *Genius of the System,* p. 20.
198 "Calling Grace Moore": Elliot Morgan, interview with the author.
198 "queer work": I am indebted to historian Allan Berubé for helping me understand and apply this concept to this study. See Berubé, *Coming Out Under Fire,* for further discussion. Berubé points out that within the armed forces during World War II, medical officers often generalized about the "special talents" of gay men and lesbians, assigning them jobs accordingly. While obviously gays played roles in all aspects of the war, the more overt ones were often segregated into queer work. One report said they could be found in the military as hospital corpsmen, yeomen, and chaplain's assistants; another listed stenographic, musical, and entertainment services (pp. 57–58). See also Gluckman and Reed, *Homo Economics.*
198 "The sexual division . . ." and labor statistics: Matthaei, Julie, "The Sexual Division of Labor, Sexuality and Lesbian/Gay Liberation," in Gluckman and Reed, *Home Economics.*
198 "save for a . . .": Helms, *Young Man From the Provinces,* p. 74.
199 "[Some homosexuals] openly admit . . .": Maurice Leznoff and William A. Westley, "The Homosexual Community," *Social Problems,* No. 3, 1956, 257–63.
199 "You couldn't be . . .": McGilligan, *Tender Comrades,* p. 285.
199 "A gay cameraman . . .": Alan Cahan, interview with the author.
199 Rosten's statistics: Rosten, *Hollywood,* p. 399.
200 Donald Vining: See Vining, *A Gay Diary, 1933–1946.*
200 Statistics on film editors: Rosten, *Hollywood,* p. 399.
201 Robert Seiter: Robert Wheaton, interview with the author. See McGilligan, *George Cukor: A Double Life;* Seiter obituary, *Variety,* January 12, 1986.
201 "I very quickly . . .": *Millimeter,* November 1984.
201 "Keep it simple": *American Cinemeditor,* Summer 1991.
201 "I valued Bill's . . .": and "one of the quiet . . .": *Los Angeles Times,* July 18, 1997.
202 "The editor's object . . .": *Millimeter,* November 1984.
203 Statistics on screenwriters: Rosten, *Hollywood,* pp. 325, 399. Rosten's data on screenwriters appear contradictory, with one page giving a figure of 71.3 percent married and another closer to 88 percent.
203 "inbred and insular . . .": Oppenheimer, *The View From the Sixties,* p. 104.
203 Oppenheimer and Harry Hay: Timmons, *The Trouble With Harry Hay,* pp. 70–71.
203 "Poor young . . .": Gabler, pp. 322–23.
204 "Going to a . . .": Davis, *The Glamour Factory,* p. 179.
204 "If I were . . .": Schwartz, *The Hollywood Writers' Wars,* p. 108.
204 "I think it . . .": Oppenheimer, *The View From the Sixties,* p. 105.
205 Charles Brackett being gay: In addition to confirmations by Gavin Lambert and Don Bachardy, nearly everyone else interviewed knew Brackett was homosexual, albeit deeply hidden. Alan Cahan, a former publicist, frequently played bridge with Brackett and his wife. It was an accepted fact, he said, although Brackett rarely alluded to it.
205 "It was a . . .": Gavin Lambert, interview with author.

205 James Larmore: See the Christopher Isherwood *Diaries;* also James Larmore file, NYPL.
205 "It was an . . .": Don Bachardy, interview with the author.
205 *American Colony:* Published in New York by Horace Liveright, 1929. Quotation is from pp. 86–87.
206 "the belief that . . .": Corliss, *Talking Pictures,* p. 143.
206 "I don't think . . .": Arthur Laurents, interview with the author.
206 "I suppose there . . .": Gavin Lambert, interview with the author.
207 Colton in drag: *Photoplay,* May 1936.
207 "a wild . . .": Harmetz, *The Making of the Wizard of Oz.*
208 "Remember, a [film] . . .": Gavin Lambert, interview with the author.
208 Gore Vidal on *Ben-Hur:* Kaplan, *Gore Vidal,* p. 443; see also Vidal's interview in the film *The Celluloid Closet.*
208 "Someone who feels . . .": Gore Vidal, interview with the author.
209 Bodeen on *Cat People:* Bodeen, *More From Hollywood.* Also see Telotte, *Dream of Darkness:* Robert Wise has said a "community of creators" was responsible for Lewton's films.
209 "Indeed, [Irena] seems . . .": Telotte, *Dreams of Darkness,* p. 34.
209 "weary, dreary" and "the wonderful city": DeWitt Bodeen to Anthony Slide, February 14, 1976; March 8, 1976, Anthony Slide Collection.
209 Bodeen family background: U.S. Census, 1910, 1920, Fresno County, CA.
210 "the boy could be . . .": *Rob Wagner's Script,* January 18, 1947.
210 "deconstructing widely . . .": *The Gay and Lesbian Review,* Spring 2000.
210 "Of all the . . .": Bodeen, *More From Hollywood,* p. 92.
210 "If there was . . .": James Robert Parish, interview with the author.
211 "Leave the old . . .": Bodeen, *More From Hollywood,* p. 317.
211 "Writing an original . . .": *Films in Review,* June–July 1963.
211 "DeWitt told me . . .": Anthony Slide, correspondence with the author.
212 "He had felt . . .": Charles Higham, interview with the author.
212 "doors open and . . .": *Daily News,* February 9, 1949.
212 Five Guys Club: Memorial service tribute to Leonard Spigelgass, published in *WGAw News,* April 1985.
212 "Just by being . . .": *WGAw News,* April 1985.
212 "He lived for . . .": Miles White, interview with the author.
213 "I wouldn't say . . .": Don Bachardy, interview with the author.
213 Spigelgass, Runyon, and Cohen: Marshall, *Blueprint on Babylon,* p. 174.
213 Spigelgass family background: U.S. Census, 1900, 1920, Kings County, NY.
213 Spigelgass' Jewishness: various interviews, NYPL and AMPAS files; also *WGAw News,* April 1966.
213 "Anyone who tells . . .": Marshall, p. 166.
213 Levien and Hitler: Associated Press wire report, several sources, June 23, 1936.
213 "The real problems . . .": Marshall, p. 169.
214 Spigelgass military service: U.S. Military Personnel Records.
214 "I had a . . .": Marshall, p. 170.
215 "I'm sure you've . . .": Henry Grace speech, A. I. D., AMPAS file.
215 "At first they . . .": Elliot Morgan, interview with the author.
215 "The set decorator, . . .": Arthur Krams to Mike Steen in Steen, *Hollywood Speaks,* pp. 241–42.
215 "pretty sad affairs": Speech given by Henry Grace to American Institute of Decorators (A.I.D.), May 15, 1951, AMPAS file.
216 "Set decorators [were] . . .": Unpublished manuscript memoir by Henry Grace, in possession of Michael Grace, quoted courtesy Michael Grace, hereafter referred to as Grace manuscript. Portions of this memoir were edited for an undated article in the trade publication *Interior Design and Decoration,* circa 1942, "The Interior Design Influence in the Motion Picture Industry," by Henry Grace. I have occasionally used the slightly revised wording from this article.

216 "You didn't pay . . .": Hal Gausman, interview with the author.

216 Straight set decorators: Information gleaned from studio biographies as well as their *Variety* obituaries. To name just a few others: George Sawley, Edward Boyle, Dave Milton, and Ray Moyer, all married with children, started out as property masters—Sawley and Boyle at the old Tiffany studios, Milton and Moyer at Warner Bros.

216 "That's how you . . .": Hal Gausman, interview with the author.

217 1942 set decorators contract: dated April 27, 1942, MGM Property Department Records, AMPAS.

217 Samuel Comer: Paramount studio biography, AMPAS; death certificate; Elliot Morgan, interview with the author.

217 "the character sets . . .": Frank Lysinger, interview with the author.

217 "Knowing these men . . .": Frank Lysinger, interview with the author.

218 Hopkins on *Casablanca:* Hopkins manuscript.

218 Hopkins on *Streetcar: Production Design,* September 1952.

219 Moore on *Oz* and *Conquest:* Unsourced speech given by Jack Moore, AMPAS, received by the library May 1, 1980.

219 "Movies had great . . .": Grace manuscript.

219 "A flood of . . .": *Interior Design and Decoration.*

219 "Then Norma Shearer . . .": *Home Furnishings Daily,* May 3, 1967.

219 "I was fascinated . . .": Frank Lysinger, interview with the author.

220 Pefferle background: U.S. Census, 1910, 1920, Shelby County, OH; Frank Lysinger, interview with the author.

220 Grace background: U.S. Census, 1910, San Bernardino County, CA; 1920, Los Angeles County; interview with Henry Grace, January 1979, unsourced, AMPAS.

220 Grace family and Henry's early career: In addition to the above sources, I am indebted to Michael Grace for sharing background as well as Henry's memoir.

221 Moore background: Unsourced Moore speech, AMPAS; unsourced clipping by Ruth Elgutter, from unnamed Toledo newspaper, Jack Moore file, AMPAS; Frank Lysinger, interview with the author.

221 Set decorators' dates of hire: MGM Property Department Records, AMPAS.

221 Keogh Gleason divorce: *Los Angeles Herald-Examiner,* April 13, 1963; Frank Lysinger, interview with the author.

222 "I don't think . . .": Michael Grace, interview with author.

222 war ruined marriage chances: 20th Century Fox publicity release, 1961.

222 Howard Bristol assault: *Los Angeles Examiner,* February 4, 1953; *Los Angeles Times,* February 4, 1953; March 10, 1953; *Los Angeles Daily News,* February 3, 1953; March 6, 1953.

223 Elliot Morgan background: Elliot Morgan, interview with the author.

223 "Everybody in research . . .": George Schoenbrunn, interview with the author.

224 "Many of the . . .": Southern Methodist University oral history collection, quoted in Davis, *The Glamour Factory,* p. 227.

224 Make-up departments: See *New York Times,* July 21, 1935; August 6, 1939; *Sunday Mirror Magazine,* October 15, 1939; *New York World Telegram,* June 3, 1939.

224 "Dawn was a . . .": Davis, *The Glamour Factory.*

224 "All the make-up . . .": Steen, *Hollywood Speaks,* p. 284.

225 Guilaroff memoir: Guilaroff, *Crowning Glory: Reflections of Hollywood's Favorite Confidant.*

225 "I think even . . .": Michael Logothetis, interview with the author.

225 Guilaroff adoptions: See *Crowning Glory;* also *Look,* May 9, 1939.

226 "He hated me . . .": Bangley, Jimmy, "Sydney Guilaroff," *Classic Images.*

226 "to make with . . .": *New York Times,* August 8, 1943.

226 "I knew Sydney . . .": Michael Logothetis, interview with the author.

226 "We were all . . .": Michael Logothetis, deposition to Los Angeles Superior Court, *Guilaroff v. Logothetis,* Case No. C721435, January 9, 1990. Logothetis succeeded in having Guilaroff evicted from the property.

226 Kobal interview: See *Films and Filming,* July 1986.
227 "Guilaroff has always . . .": *Interview,* September 1985.
227 "We were friends . . .": Michael Logothetis, interview with the author.
227 "I'd say Walter . . .": Don Bachardy, interview with the author.
227 "They were very . . .": Satch LaValley, interview with the author.
227 Plunkett background: *New York Evening Journal,* February 4, 1937; MGM studio biography, 1952; LaVine, *In a Glamorous Fashion.* Curiously, Plunkett's family does not turn up in the U.S. Census for Alameda County, California, in 1900, 1910, or 1920. But we know they lived there during this time, as the birth of a brother is recorded in the California birth index in 1911.
228 "inability to act": *Velvet Light Trap,* Spring 1978.
228 "No one with . . .": *California Monthly,* June–July 1981.
229 "It was hysterical . . .": Walter Plunkett to David Chierichetti, quoted in *Hollywood Costume Design,* p. 136.
229 "Everything at MGM . . .": *Velvet Light Trap,* Spring 1978.
229 "That's true . . .": Satch LaValley, interview with the author.
229 "They were both . . .": Don Bachardy, interview with the author.
229 Plunkett death, estate: Death certificate, State of California; Probate file, Los Angeles Superior Court.
230 "I can't believe . . .": Satch LaValley, interview with the author.
230 "Orry-Kelly was . . .": Robert Shaw, interview with the author.
230 Orry-Kelly background: Birth records, Kiama, New South Wales, Australia; see also Higham, *The Lonely Heart.* His birthdate has been erroneously reported as December 1, 1897; January 1, 1897; and January 1, 1898.
230 Orry-Kelly early career: "Film and Stage News," unsourced clipping, 1938, Orry-Kelly file, NYPL.
231 "lecherous frogs": Program for Orry-Kelly's one-man show at I. Magnin, Los Angeles, August 1963; Orry-Kelly file, AMPAS.
231 Priscilla Lane on *Arsenic and Old Lace:* Priscilla Lane to Roy Moseley, see Higham and Moseley, *Cary Grant: The Lonely Heart.*
231 "Queen for a Day": Hopkins manuscript.
231 "I used to . . .": LaVine, p. 219.
232 Orry-Kelly war anecdote: *Saturday Home Magazine, New York Journal American,* December 8, 1945.
233 "And M'Lord . . .": Hedda Hopper column, March 16, 1960.
233 Orry-Kelly vs. Noel Coward: *Hollywood Reporter,* May 11, 1961; *New York Herald-Tribune,* May 17, 1961.
233 Orry-Kelly will: Probate files, Los Angeles Superior Court.
233 "He did the . . .": Jack Warner's eulogy is among the papers in the Orry-Kelly file in the Hedda Hopper Collection at AMPAS. It is marked up with edits, apparently made by Hopper.
234 "Adrian has gone . . .": *Los Angeles Daily News,* July 29, 1938.
234 "Adrian has never . . .": *Photoplay,* November 1939.
234 "having no illusions . . .": Anthony Slide, correspondence with the author.
234 "One day Adrian . . .": *Vanity Fair,* June 2000.
234 "Oh, no, I'll . . .": Lambert, *Mainly About Lindsay Anderson.*
234 Adrian poll: *MGM Studio News,* April 16, 1940.
235 "no lace . . .": *New York American,* January 14, 1934.
235 "none of the night . . .": Travis Banton to Hedda Hopper, 1941, Hedda Hopper Collection.
235 Banton marriage in Hopper column: *Los Angeles Times,* June 20, 1942.
235 "You might like . . .": Margaret Banton to Hedda Hopper, July 1942, Hedda Hopper Collection, AMPAS.
235 "He could think . . .": *Los Angeles Daily News,* July 4, 1944.
237 "If a woman . . .": *New York Times,* September 19, 1958.

WAR SPIRIT

239 Shoup and Ball: Anecdote courtesy of David Chierichetti.

240 "Howard's truest . . .": Eulogy by Donald C. Shoup, June 6, 1987, Howard Shoup file, AMPAS.

241 "a secret opportunity . . .": Kaiser, *The Gay Metropolis,* p. 37.

241 Drag in World War II and the gay experience: See Berubé's groundbreaking study, *Coming Out Under Fire: Gay Men and Women in World War II.*

241 "conventional thing . . .": George Sylvester Viereck, in *American Aphrodite,* vol. 4, no. 5, 1954, quoted in Berubé, p. 273.

241 "Why in hell . . .": Jim Kepner to Jerry Watson, April 21, 1943, Kepner correspondence, One Institute/International Gay & Lesbian Archives, University of Southern California.

241 "People sort of . . .": Kaiser, p. 39.

242 Shoup family background: U.S. Census, 1910, 1920, Dallas County, TX; Warner Bros., studio biography.

242 "I hear that . . .": Sarah Barnwell Elliott to Mary Shoup, 1910, quoted in Eulogy by Donald C. Shoup, June 6, 1987, Howard Shoup file, AMPAS.

243 "Very gay": David Chierichetti, interview with the author.

243 Adrian recommends Anderson: *Los Angeles Times,* August 19, 1983.

243 "Economic times were . . .": David Hanna and Lester Strong, "The Watering Holes: Los Angeles Gay Bars During Hollywood's Golden Age," *Harvard Gay and Lesbian Review.*

244 "They are a . . .": *Los Angeles Evening News,* April 13, 1937.

244 Donald Vining: See Vining, *A Gay Diary, 1933–1946.*

244 "open season . . .": Strong, "A Talk With David Hanna," p. 185.

244 "Homosexuality in that . . .": Grafton, *Red, Hot & Rich! An Oral History of Cole Porter.*

245 "I'll never forget . . .": Miles White, interview with the author.

245 "the exceptional ones . . .": Mortimer and Jack Lait, *Washington Confidential,* pp. 90–91.

246 "At least I . . .": Miles White, interview with the author.

247 "I knew nothing . . .": Laurents, *Original Story By,* p 79.

247 "The first time . . .": Arthur Laurents, interview with the author.

248 "You have been . . .": *New York Times,* September 1, 1947.

248 "By revealing that . . .": D'Emilio, *Sexual Politics, Sexual Communities,* p. 37.

248 "domestication of masculinity": For a full discussion of the social dynamics of the post-war period, see Corber, *Homosexuality in Cold War America.*

248 "It didn't matter . . .": Kaiser, p. 60.

249 "These writers . . .": Corber, p. 4, 18.

249 "Mr. Belvedere of . . .": *Life,* May 30, 1949.

249 Leff on Clifton Webb: Leonard Leff, "Queer Mr. Belvedere," unpublished manuscript. I am grateful to Leff for allowing me to quote from this excellent article.

250 "He flies": The story is told in two slightly different versions by Preminger, once in his autobiography and again in Pratley, *The Cinema of Otto Preminger.*

250 "fine suede glove:" *New York Times,* October 22, 1944.

250 "a combination of . . .": *Chicago Tribune,* June 4, 1944.

250 "any movie that . . .": Naremore, *More Than Night,* p 262.

250 "so thoroughly . . .": *The Hartford Courant Magazine,* July 25, 1948.

251 "Not all mothers . . .": "What It Means to Be a Homosexual," *New York Times Magazine,* January 17, 1971.

251 Skolsky column: *New York Post,* March 1, 1959.

251 Claim that Jacob Hollenbeck was a lawyer: press release, circa 1920, Robinson Locke Collection, NYPL.

251 Jacob Hollenbeck family: Indianapolis City Directories, 1877–1904; Indiana Vital Records.

251 Mabelle background: U.S. Census, 1880, Marion County, IN.

251 Mabelle's ambitions: *New York Herald Tribune,* June 24, 1934.

251 Webb birth: Although he'd give conflicting accounts of his age, the 1900 Census con-
firms the 1889 date, which also appears on his death certificate.
251 Webb childhood photos: Clifton Webb Collection, Boston University.
252 "I loathe the . . .": undated column, Lucius Beebe, *New York American,* circa 1939,
Clifton Webb file, NYPL.
252 "If you stick . . .": *New York Herald Tribune,* June 24, 1934.
252 Jacob Hollenbeck later life: Missouri marriage and death records.
252 Green Raum: U.S. Census, 1900, New York County, NY.
252 "threw his stepfather . . .": *Los Angeles Times,* October 19, 1960.
253 Webb autograph book: Clifton Webb Collection.
253 Webb arrest, Maurel, and Maybelle at Folies Marigny: *New York Telegraph,* October 22,
1914.
253 "He is known . . .": unsourced press release, circa 1917, Robinson Locke Collection,
NYPL.
253 "Dr. Reiland says . . .": Clifton Webb statement, issued March 9, 1917, Robinson
Locke Collection, NYPL.
254 "Clifton Webb's debut . . .": *New York Evening Journal,* June 25, 1935.
254 Cal York on Webb and Crawford: *Photoplay,* July 1937.
254 "It's stupid . . .": *New York Evening Journal,* August 15, 1936.
255 "Everyone knew about . . .": quoted in Kaiser, p. 16.
255 "stiff and erect . . .": *Coronet,* July 1954.
255 Webb photo: Clifton Webb Collection.
255 "I've destroyed their . . .": *Life,* May 30, 1949.
255 "This violated all . . .": *Cosmopolitan,* June 1953.
255 "There was novelty . . .": *New York Sun,* April 21, 1949.
256 "I may not . . .": *Los Angeles Herald Express,* April 5, 1950.
256 "the only man . . .": *Coronet,* July 1954.
256 Skolsky interview: *Hollywood Citizen-News,* April 22, 1948.
256 "Ernest's chi-chi . . .": *Chicago Tribune,* June 4, 1944.
256 "When it's that . . .": Arthur Laurents, interview with the author.
256 Gladys Hall's draft: "Jeannette" at 20th Century-Fox to Gladys Hall, May 26, 1949,
Gladys Hall Collection, AMPAS.
257 "his eyes laugh . . .": unsourced clip, circa 1945, Clifton Webb file, AMPAS.
257 "I remember Clifton . . .": Robert Wheaton, interview with the author.
257 "very kind . . .": Robert Wagner, interview with the author.
257 "As you might . . .": undated postcard, Clifton Webb to Hedda Hopper, Hedda Hopper Collection, AMPAS.
258 "his enormous cock . . .": Stricklyn, *Angels and Demons,* p. 112.
258 Webb and Kubie: This was told to the historian Charles Kaiser by an actor who said
he'd been sent to Kubie by Webb. For more on Kubie's "treatment" of gays, see
Kaiser, *The Gay Metropolis,* and Donald Spoto's biography of Tennessee Williams, *The
Kindness of Strangers.*
258 Ron Ely and Webb: Stricklyn, p. 111.
258 Truth is . . .": undated, circa 1954, 20th Century Fox press release, AMPAS.
259 Flyte on Webb: *Los Angeles Examiner,* February 17, 1950.
259 Clift: See Bosworth, *Montgomery Clift,* p. 154.
260 Eythe background: U.S. Census, 1920, Butler County, PA; *Modern Screen,* March 1945;
Fox studio biography; Barrie Roberts, "The Man From Mars," *Films of the Golden
Age,* Fall 1999.
260 Eythe and Lawler: This is presumed due to correspondence between them found in
Lawler's papers. A photograph of Eythe is inscribed: "For Andy, with fond remem-
brance and real appreciation and go to hell, thanks really, Bill." I thank William Kizer
for sharing this information.
260 "a wonderful catch": *Photoplay,* March 1944.
261 "I'm going to . . .": *Photoplay,* November 1944.
261 "He's a fresh . . .": *Modern Screen,* March 1945.

261 "intense and serious": *Silver Screen,* May 1945.

261 "wasn't too happy": Stricklyn, p. 65.

261 Eythe divorce: *Los Angeles Times,* January 10, 1949; *Los Angeles Daily News,* September 4, 1950; *New York Times,* September 6, 1950.

262 Eythe arrests: *Los Angeles Examiner,* June 4, 1952.

262 "Bill's too fat . . .": *Mirror-News,* August 17, 1955.

262 Goldwyn and Granger: Pela, Robrt, "Goldenboy," *The Advocate,* August 20, 1996.

263 "It didn't last . . .": John Dall to Gladys Hall, undated notes for a proposed article, Gladys Hall Collection, AMPAS.

263 "But something was . . .": *The Advocate,* August 20, 1996.

263 Hurd Hatfield: *Silver Screen,* July 1945; *After Dark,* December 1974; interview with Robert Wheaton.

263 Vincent Price: See Victoria Price, *Vincent Price: A Biography.*

263 "an anguished . . .": Mank, *The Hollywood Hissables,* p. 197.

263 Harry Hay on Cregar: Timmons, *The Trouble With Harry Hay,* p. 60; Harry Hay, interview with the author.

263 Cregar background: Studio biographies, *Hollywood Hissables; American Classic Screen,* Fall 1982.

264 "I used to . . .": quoted in *Hollywood Hissables,* p. 198.

264 "Pleasingly plump . . .": Laird Cregar to Gladys Hall, September 7, 1942, notes for proposed article, Gladys Hall Collection, AMPAS.

264 "I knew Laird . . .": *Hollywood Hissables,* p. 199.

265 "Laird Cregar . . .": *Focus on Film,* Summer 1975.

265 Cregar as chorus boy: *Hollywood Hissables,* p. 219.

265 David Bacon: *Los Angeles Examiner,* September 14, 1943.

265 "on this subject . . .": *Silver Screen,* January 1944.

265 "He was like . . .": *Hollywood Hissables,* p. 217.

266 "Some actors who . . .": *Hollywood Hissables,* p. 235.

266 "ever-present friend": Laird Cregar to Gladys Hall, September 7, 1942, notes for proposed article, Gladys Hall Collection, AMPAS.

266 "Dishonesty is a . . .": *New York Times,* April 5, 1942.

267 "a certain anxiety, . . .": See Richard Dyer in E. Ann Kaplan (ed.), *Women in Film Noir,* British Film Institute, 1980.

267 "traumatized or . . .": See Frank Krutnick, *In a Lonely Street: Film Noir, Genre, Masculinity,* London: Routledge, 1991, p. 91.

267 "a modernist . . .": See Naremore, *More Than Night,* pp. 222–23.

267 "The people who . . .": Dorothy B. Jones, "Is Hollywood Growing Up?," *The Nation,* February 3, 1945.

267 *Gentleman's Agreement* study: *Journal of Psychology,* Vol. 26, 1948, pp. 525–36.

268 Cukor and Schary: Note dated February 1956, Cukor Collection, AMPAS.

268 "It's understood . . .": *New York World-Telegram,* October 25, 1939.

268 "When these people . . .": *New York Herald Tribune,* July 10, 1949.

268 "With Hollywood's . . .": Leff and Simmons, *The Dame in the Kimono,* p. 179.

268 "I made her": Joseph Breen to Jason Joy, 20th Century Fox, November 2, 1943, PCA files, AMPAS.

269 "The actual word . . .": Laurents, pp. 124, 127.

270 "Plain and simple . . .": Arthur Laurents, interview with the author.

271 "Roger *was* the . . .": Lela Simone, oral history conducted by Rudy Behlmer, AMPAS.

272 "You have to . . .": *Sight and Sound,* Spring 1958.

272 "Professionally, Roger . . .": Luft, *Me and My Shadows,* p. 31.

272 "I loved Roger . . .": Luft, p. 80.

272 "He was a . . .": Silverman, p. 89.

272 "very civilized . . .": Lela Simone, oral history conducted by Rudy Behlmer, AMPAS.

273 "That was a . . .": J. C. Edens, interview with the author.

273 Edens family background: U.S. Census, 1910 and 1920, Hills County, TX; J. C. Edens, interview with the author.

274 "Mr. and Mrs.": *Los Angeles Herald Express,* November 14, 1934.
274 "She was not . . .": Silverman, pp. 90–91.
274 Roy Yoneda: Interview with the author.
274 Michael Morrison: Interview with the author.
274 Edens and Lysinger: Frank Lysinger, interview with the author.
275 "Lennie's work was . . .": Oral History with Lela Simone, interviewed by Rudy Behlmer, AMPAS Oral History Program, 1994.
275 Gershe in will: Last Will and Testament, Roger Edens, Los Angeles Probate Court.
275 "clunky backstage . . .": Silverman, p. 79.
276 camp sensibility of Freed unit films: See Matthew Tinkcom, "Working Like a Homosexual: Camp Visual Codes and the Labor of Gay Subjects in the MGM Freed Unit," *Cinema Journal,* Winter 1996.
276 "Take away his . . .": Gavin Lambert, interview with the author.
276 Minnelli's homosexuality: See Gerald Clarke, *Get Happy,* for further discussion.
277 "Minnelli was a . . .": Oral History with Lela Simone, interviewed by Rudy Behlmer, AMPAS Oral History Program, 1994.
277 "The antithesis . . .": Fordin, *MGM's Greatest Musicals: The Arthur Freed Unit,* p. 101.
277 "Connie was very . . .": Frank Lysinger, interview with the author.
277 "It conveyed . . .": Fordin, p. 102.
278 Salinger death: *Hollywood Reporter,* June 19, 1962; *Boston Globe,* June 20, 1962.
278 "Choreography, a much . . .": *Films and Filming,* August 1970.
278 "in dance and . . .": Arthur Laurents, interview with the author.
279 Walters background and quotes: Oral History with Charles Walters, interviewed by Ronald Davis, Southern Methodist University Oral History Project, 1980.
279 Robert Alton background: U.S. Census, 1900, Bennington County, VT; 20th Century Fox studio biography; Robert Alton file, NYPL. Curiously, the 1900 Census lists a Robert Hart among his older siblings, suggesting that Alton, like Roger Edens, appropriated an older brother's name at some point.
279 "a brunette Duke . . .": *New York Journal-American,* undated clipping, Charles Walters file, NYPL.
279 Walters New York press: *New York World Telegram,* January 15, 1938; *New York Herald Tribune,* January 23, 1938.
280 "finished with chocolate . . .": *New York Herald Tribune,* July 10, 1938.
280 "I have watched . . .": *New York Herald Tribune,* March 28, 1937.
280 "The studio liked . . .": Oral History with Charles Walters, interviewed by Ronald Davis, Southern Methodist University Oral History Project, 1980.
281 "If the word . . .": *Film Culture,* Spring 1963.
281 "I begged Arthur . . .": Fordin, p. 217.
282 "Darrow always wanted . . .": Alan Cahan, interview with the author.
282 "a relaxed . . .": Douglas McVay, "Charles Walters: A Case for Reassessment," *Focus on Film,* No. 27, 1977.
282 "Jack changed musical . . .": Gwen Verdon, interview with the author.
283 "queen bees": Fordin, p. 438.
283 "I have this . . .": Miles White, interview with the author.
284 "tried to capture . . .": *Dance,* May 1956.
284 "energetic, angular . . .": *Dance,* January 1956.
285 "He understood how . . .": Loney, *Unsung Genius,* p. 219.

PINKOS, COMMIES, QUEERS

287 "Here we were . . .": Elliot Morgan, interview with the author.
287 Gays and Communism: For a detailed discussion, see Stephanie Coontz, *The Way We Never Were: American Families and the Nostalgia Trap* (New York: Barricade Books, 1992).
288 "The SMPID has . . .": *The Hollywood Reporter,* May 29, 1940.
288 1942 set decorators contract: dated April 27, 1942, MGM Property Department Records, AMPAS.

288 "It's interesting . . .": Michael Grace, interview with the author.

288 "everything that IATSE . . .": Friedrich, *City of Nets*, p. 247.

289 "As far as . . .": Schwartz, *The Hollywood Writers' Wars*, p. 223.

289 "This is not . . .": *Variety*, March 14, 1945.

289 Chronology of the strike: *New York Times*, March 13, March 15, March 16, March 19, 1945; *Variety*, March 14, March 21, 1945. For background, I am also grateful to Allan Berubé.

289 property men at Warners: *Variety*, March 21, 1945.

290 George Gibson: Letter dated June 15, 1945, MGM Art Department Records, AMPAS. Gibson was later reinstated after insisting he'd never written the letter.

290 "Save for . . .": *The Nation*, October 20, 1945.

290 "It is obvious . . .": *The Peoples' Daily World*, July 24, 1945, courtesy Allan Berubé.

291 NLRB vote: *Variety*, October 17, 1945.

291 Edward Mussa as straight: His obituary in the *Hollywood Citizen-News*, January 12, 1968, lists a widow and three sons.

291 White during strike: Miles White, interview with the author.

291 Hopkins during strike: Hopkins manuscript.

292 Decorators' post-strike contracts: Contracts for Henry Grace, Richard Pefferle, Jack Moore, Keogh Gleason, April 12, 1946; terminated January 28, 1947; MGM Property Department Records, AMPAS.

292 "What the strike . . .": McGilligan, *Tender Comrades*, p. 477.

293 "The committee members . . .": Bernstein, *Inside Out*, p. 11.

293 "The real function . . .": Richard Hofstadter, *Anti-Intellectualism in American Life*, New York: Knopf, 1963, p. 41.

293 "What actors didn't . . .": Oral History with Will Geer, interviewed by Ronald L. Davis, Southern Methodist University Oral History Project, 1975.

293 "post-war crisis of masculinity": For detailed discussion, see Corber, *Homosexuality in Cold War America*.

294 "swing tremendous . . .": *Los Angeles Mirror*, March 13, 1953.

294 "Don't sell the . . .": *Confidential*, May 1954.

295 "sexual perverts who . . .": *New York Times*, April 19, 1950.

295 "dominated by an . . .": quoted in Von Hoffman, *Citizen Cohn*, pp. 127–28.

295 3,500 deviates: *New York Times*, May 20, 1950.

295 "There should be . . .": *Washington Post*, July 17, 1950.

295 "You can't separate . . .": quoted in Von Hoffman, p. 130

295 "Three decades . . .": Loughery, p. 204.

295 425 employees: *New York Times*, April 13, 1953.

295 "Of course, it . . .": Don Bachardy, interview with the author.

296 "I knew gays . . .": Harry Hay, interview with the author.

296 "It's hilarious . . .": Gavin Lambert, interview with the author.

297 McCarthy family background: U.S. Census, 1920, Henrico Co., VA; obituary of Frank J. McCarthy Sr., *Richmond Times-Dispatch*, June 13, 1927.

297 "the West Point . . .": Frank McCarthy to Sylvia Shorris, complete, unpublished interview notes later edited for *Talking Pictures With the People Who Made Them*.

297 "Bill Keighley . . .": McCarthy to Shorris.

298 McCarthy and Abbott: *Richmond News-Leader*, April 15, 1938; September 3, 1938; *Variety*, May 31, 1939; *New York Daily News*, May 19, 1940.

298 McCarthy early military career: Military records, National Personnel Records Center, St. Louis, MO; *Current Biography*, 1945.

299 McCarthy at State Department: *New York Times*, August 22, 1945; September 19, 1945; October 9, 1945; October 12, 1945.

299 "He is of modest . . .": *New York Times Magazine*, September 9, 1945.

299 McCarthy name floated: *New York Times*, January 20, 1947; January 23, 1945.

299 "I didn't stay . . .": McCarthy to Shorris.

300 "the gag around . . .": Lait and Mortimer, *Washington Confidential*, pp. 96–97.

300 McCarthy nomination: *Congressional Record,* 79th Congress, 1st Session, September 19, 1945, p. 8767; *Congressional Quarterly,* Vol. I, 1945.

301 McCarthy FBI file: *Frank McCarthy, 62-HQ-79782,* Federal Bureau of Investigation.

302 McCarthy 1951 FBI investigation: *Frank McCarthy, 123-HQ-11578,* Federal Bureau of Investigation.

302 "When Brigadier General . . .": *Los Angeles Mirror,* November 17, 1960.

302 McCarthy on *Let's Make Love:* McCarthy to Shorris.

303 "Frank was rather . . .": Gavin Lambert, interview with the author.

303 "It was typical . . .": Lambert, *Mainly About Lindsay Anderson,* p. 135.

303 "I listen systematically . . .": *California Living,* magazine of *Los Angeles Herald-Examiner,* October 27, 1968.

304 "[She] took it . . .": Davis, *The Glamour Factory,* p. 350.

304 "The motion picture . . .": Davis, p. 351.

304 Joseph McCarthy and army gays: *New York Times,* March 13, 1954.

305 Gays among blacklisted names: Some eighteen pages of names are listed in Vaughn, *Only Victims.* Most are writers, producers, and actors; the craft unions are represented by strike leaders like Frank Drdlik and Ralph Smith.

305 "I knew a . . .": Timmons, *The Trouble With Harry Hay,* p. 109.

305 "I can't think . . .": Don Bachardy, interview with the author.

306 "It was obvious . . .": Katz, *Gay American History,* p. 408.

306 "ever really far . . .": Robert Wheaton, interview with the author.

306 Hay and Geer: Harry Hay, interview with the author: Timmons, pp. 63–70.

306 "biggest shock": Alan Cahan, interview with the author.

306 "the ingenue": *The Michigan Daily,* October 7, 1962.

306 Geer later life: *New York Times,* December 17, 1972; *Newsweek,* October 14, 1974.

306 "the word Communist . . .": *New York Times,* April 12, 1951.

307 "exceptional . . . dull, dumb . . .": Lait and Mortimer, pp. 90–91.

308 Freed films: See Tinkcom, "Working Like a Homosexual."

308 "the people who . . .": Speech by Leonard Spigelgass, Chicago Conference of Motion Picture Industry Organizations, August 30, 1949, AMPAS.

309 "dedicated to flipping . . .": Steve Govoni, "Now It Can Be Told," *American Film,* February 1990.

310 "a weird-looking . . .": Conrad, *Dear Moffo,* p. 96.

310 Harrison background: See Tom Wolfe, "Public Lives," *Esquire,* April 1964.

310 "a curious preoccupation . . .": *American Film,* February 1990.

310 Hudson and Calhoun: See Ehrenstein, *Open Secret,* p. 100.

310 Paul Gregory: *Confidential,* May 1956.

311 "It wasn't seen . . .": Ehrenstein, p. 94.

311 Hunter and Perkins: See Winecoff, *Split Image: The Life of Anthony Perkins.*

311 "I hate frilly . . .": *Silver Screen,* August 1945.

311 "bypasses romance . . .": *Los Angeles Times,* October 14, 1951.

312 "Could that name . . .": *Confidential,* September 1955.

312 "private life [was] . . .": *Uncensored,* march 1956.

312 "I'm puzzled . . .": *Film Fan Monthly,* December 1971.

313 *Time* and *Newsweek:* See Lisa Bennett, "Fifty Years of Prejudice in the Media," *The Gay & Lesbian Review,* Spring 2000.

313 homosexuality in gossip columns: *The Nation,* October 13, 1956.

313 Dick Williams: clippings from *One* magazine, March 1957, One Institute/International Gay & Lesbian Archives USC.

313 Liberace: See *Los Angeles Times,* June 9, 1959.

313 Raymond Burr known to be gay: Bob Thomas, interviewed on A&E *Biography* series, March 2, 2000.

313 "Dear Ray . . .": Hedda Hopper to Raymond Burr, September 16, 1963, Hedda Hopper Collection, AMPAS.

314 "After every binge . . .": *Inside,* June 1955.

314 "He'd never do . . .": Silverman, p. 210.
314 "offbeat Manhattan . . .": *Confidential,* January 1957.
315 "How the hell . . .": Conrad, p. 110.
315 Dailey avoids subpoena: *New York Daily News,* August 12, 1957.
315 "his basic problem . . .": undated, unsourced clipping, Dan Dailey file, NYPL.
315 End of *Confidential:* See *American Film,* Fenruary 1990.
316 "What *Confidential* proved . . .": Goodman, *The Fifty-Year Decline and Fall of Hollywood.*
317 "Both of us . . .": Hudson and Davidson, *Rock Hudson: His Story,* p. 52.
318 "Dear John": *New York Post,* April 10, 1955.
318 George Nader career: I am indebted to background information provided by Nader's partner, Mark Miller.
318 "proving their dates . . .": *Filmland,* July 1955.
318 "Like Gregory Peck . . .": *Photoplay,* June 1955.
318 Beefcake photo: *After Dark,* June 1978.
318 "You're losing parts . . .": Davidson, *Rock Hudson: His Story,* p. 98.
318 "I could give . . .": transcribed interview with George Nader, undated, Hedda Hopper Collection, AMPAS.
319 "I like ladies": *American Weekly,* July 22, 1956.
319 "The studio let . . .": *New York Post,* November 12, 1957.
319 "Do I think . . .": Stricklyn, *Angels and Demons,* p. 276.
320 Perkins and Hunter: For a detailed account of Anthony Perkins, including his relationship with Hunter, see Winecoff, *Split Image: The Life of Anthony Perkins.*
320 Helms and Perkins: Helms, *Young Man From the Provinces,* pp. 96–97.
320 "He was so . . .": Tucker Fleming, interview with the author.
320 "for fear we'd . . .": Don Bachardy, interview with the author.
321 "had no conclusions . . .": For this quote and a thorough discussion of Dean's life and work, including his sexuality, see Holley, *James Dean: The Biography.*
321 Ray and Mineo: Vidal, *Palimpsest: A Memoir.*
321 Lambert and Ray: Lambert, *Mainly About Lindsay Anderson,* p. 90.
322 "Rock was about . . .": Ehrenstein, p. 135.
322 "I don't wonder . . .": Kevin Thomas, interview with the author.
323 "Yes, there sure . . .": Alan Cahan, interview with the author.
324 Allan and Princess Grace: Lee Lacey, *Grace,* and Spada, *Grace: The Secret Life of a Princess.*
324 "On the face . . .": Gabler, *Winchell,* pp. 243, 247.
325 "Will you still . . .": Kevin Thomas, interview with the author.
325 Asher, Combs, Sterne: *Variety* obituaries; Alan Cahan and Anthony Slide, interviews with the author.
325 "Their influence is . . .": *Newsweek,* February 22, 1954.
325 "I lived in . . .": Strong, "A Talk With David Hanna."
325 Monroe and Newcomb: See Wolfe, *The Last Days of Marilyn Monroe.*
326 "the most important . . .": *Newsweek,* February 22, 1954.
326 Charles Pierce: Letter to the editor, *Classic Images,* April 1998.
326 Liz Smith: See Smith, *Natural Blonde.*
327 "Willson stared up . . .": *New York Times Magazine,* February 16, 1958.
327 "He had a . . .": Stricklyn, p. 66.
328 "I knew what . . .": Jonathan Gilmore, interview with the author.
328 "Henry was a . . .": Gates, p. 24.
328 "not an infrequent . . .": Stricklyn, p. 97.
329 "Whether it was . . .": Gates, p. 121.

THE BOLD ONES

331 Jack Larson in New York: *New York Times,* May 15, 1998; *Films of the Golden Age,* Winter 1997–98.
332 "Where the old-time . . .": *Time,* May 13, 1957.

332 TV programming shift to L.A.: See William Boddy, "Building the World's Largest Advertising Medium: CBS and Television, 1940-60," in Balio (ed.), *Hollywood in the Age of Television,* pp. 165–83.

332 "Almost overnight . . .": Memoir of Robert J. Shaw, Pewaukee Area Historical Society, Pewaukee, WI.

332 TV production stats: *Time,* May 13, 1957.

332 "It's like a . . ." and "There has never . . .": *Newsweek,* December 16, 1957.

333 "The rise of . . .": *Time,* May 13, 1957.

334 Stricklyn career: Stricklyn, *Angels and Demons.*

334 "That whole freer . . .": Charles Williamson, interview with the author.

335 "Television opened . . .": Robert Shaw, interview with the author.

335 "to the sensible . . .": Shaw memoir.

336 TV gay art directors: *Variety* obituaries; interviews with Robert Wheaton, Robert Shaw, Curtis Harrington, Alan Cahan.

336 "There seemed to . . .": Joe Armetta, interview with the author.

336 Quiroga: *Variety* obituary; Christopher Isherwood *Dairies.*

336 "[Movie] producers are . . .": *The Morning Telegraph,* September 3, 1958.

336 Stricklyn on TV: Stricklyn, p. 276.

337 Yarborough murder: *Variety,* September 4, 1962.

337 "never publicly labeled . . .": *Inside Story,* September 1964.

337 "the gay guys . . .": *Whisper,* November 1964.

338 "the president of . . .": *San Francisco Chronicle,* September 22, 1996.

338 Dick Sargent: *People Weekly,* December 2, 1991.

339 "Is a fag . . .": Merle Miller, "What It Means to be a Homosexual," *The New York Times Magazine,* January 17, 1971.

340 "His idea of . . .": Don Bachardy, interview with the author.

340 "As far as . . .": *Art and Understanding,* February 1998.

340 Evelyn Hooker: Hooker, "A Preliminary Analysis of Group Behavior of Homosexuals," *Journal of Psychology* (1956), 42, pp. 217–25.

340 Hay and Isherwood: Timmons, p. 163.

341 Coming out: see Loughery p. 70.

341 "Which was a . . .": Gavin Lambert, interview with the author.

342 "an open secret": Lambert, *Mainly About Lindsay Anderson,* p. 96.

342 "Zubie was a real . . .": Robert Wheaton, interview with the author.

342 "The spics are . . .": Arthur Miller to Charles Higham, courtesy Higham.

342 "The older generation . . .": Chase, *Filmmaking,* p. 127.

343 "Cinematography is all . . .": Steven Katz, interview with the author.

343 GGRC memories: Curtis Harrington, interview with the author; Robert Wheaton, interview with the author; Don Bachardy, interview with the author; Gavin Lambert, interview with the author; Ron Anderegg, correspondence with the author, Bill Dawson, correspondence with the author; Billy Williams, correspondence with the author.

344 "That's where the . . .": Marshal Kendzy, interview with the author.

344 "Each year Ray . . .": Ron Anderegg, correspondence with the author.

344 "I was always . . .": unsourced clipping, James Crabe file, AMPAS.

346 "A visit to . . .": David Hanna, "The Watering Holes," *Harvard Gay & Lesbian Review,* Summer 1996.

346 Willson, Rapper, Gallery Room: Charles Higham, interview with the author.

347 "Let Vincent Canby . . .": *New York Times,* May 28, 1972.

348 "I'm not a . . . " Publicity release, Allied Artists, 1964.

348 Movie attendance: U.S. Bureau of Census, chart in Balio, *The American Film Industry.*

349 "Hollywood had become . . .": Davis, *The Glamour Factory,* p. 356.

349 "I would like . . .": Davis, p. 381.

349 "His films are . . .": Kevin Thomas, interview with the author.

349 "sick nigh . . .": undated Hedda Hopper column, circa 1960.

349 "You might just . . .": *Show,* August 1962.
350 "but Lana knew . . .": *Los Angeles Herald-Examiner,* May 27, 1960.
350 "You guys give . . .": *Show,* August 1962.
350 "A producer has . . .": Stephen Rebello, "Beautiful Dreamer," *Movieline.*
350 "*Hiroshima, Mon Amour* . . .": *New York Times,* October 16, 1960.
350 "It's the oldest formula . . .": *The American Weekly,* September 1, 1963.
351 "The kind of . . .": Alpert, p. 81.
351 "When I met . . .": Alpert, p. 83.
351 Hunter birth: Various accounts list his birth year as either 1916, 1920, or 1925. The U.S. Census for 1920 does not list him among the family, seeming to invalidate the 1916 date.
351 Cleveland Jewish history: "The History of Jewish Life in Cleveland," Cleveland Public Library.
351 Fuss family: U.S. Census, 1910 and 1920, Cuyahoga County, OH.
351 Mutual Cloak and Suit: Cleveland city directories, 1934–1960.
352 "I come from . . .": *Show,* August, 1962.
352 Hunter background: *Movieland,* June 1946; *Motion Picture,* undated clip, circa 1946.
352 "he would rather . . .": *Cleveland Plain-Dealer,* March 10, 1944.
353 "Bruce Foos": *Movieland,* June 1946.
353 "couldn't even . . .": *Show,* August 1962.
353 "terrible, terrible . . .": *Movieline.*
353 Hunter marriage claim: *Show,* August 1962.
353 Leonard Goldstein: Alpert, p. 88; *Variety* obituary, July 28, 1954.
354 *Tumbleweed:* Alpert, p. 89.
354 "At Universal, [Ross] . . .": L. Sirk, *Sirk on Sirk,* p. 106.
355 "I hate poor . . .": *New York Mirror,* August 21, 1960.
355 "When they'd . . .": Alan Cahan, interview with the author.
355 "Ross could be . . .": Tucker Fleming, interview with the author.
356 The European producers . . .: Ross Hunter to Hedda Hopper, July 9, 1963, Hedda Hopper Collection, AMPAS.
356 "put stars in . . .": *Christian Science Monitor,* August 18, 1959.
356 "that exists in . . .": Alpert, p. 80.
356 Jack Navaar: Davidson, pp. 72–73.
357 "The woman is . . .": *Show,* August 1962.
357 "Many people have . . .": *The Washington Post,* October 11, 1961.
357 "This house is . . .": *New York Post,* September 24, 1966.
358 "Abe, it's absolutely . . .": *Hollywood Citizen News,* April 7, 1967.
358 "He is not . . .": Alpert, p. 80.
358 "Fringe producers . . .": address by Ross Hunter, accepting a citation for excellence from the Center of American Living, Biltmore Hotel, New York, September 16, 1968, Collection of Charles Champlin, NYPL.
359 "My last few . . .": Turner, Lana. *The Lady, The Legend, The Truth.* (New York: Dutton, 1982).
360 "I never thought . . .": Elliot Morgan, interview with the author.
360 "an ancient dowager . . .": Davis, *The Glamour Factory,* p. 378.
360 "swarm of able . . .": Drabelle, *Film Comment.*
361 "he was never . . .": Lambert, *Mainly About Lindsay Anderson,* p. 220.
361 "I'm quite a . . .": *New York Herald-Tribune,* November 11, 1958.
362 Kelly brawl: *New York Mirror,* September 1, 1963.
362 "For those of . . .": Kevin Thomas, interview with the author.
363 "a complete . . .": Lambert, *Mainly About Lindsay Anderson,* p. 221.
363 "My own experience . . .": Michael Everett, correspondence with the author.
363 "Set decorating": undated clip, *Los Angeles Times,* courtesy Michael Grace.
364 "You learned not . . .": Robert Shaw, interview with the author.
364 "Sometimes the toads . . .": Joe Armetta, correspondence with the author.
365 "Universal was the . . .": Michael Kearns, interview with the author.

BIBLIOGRAPHY

•

This is a general list of books; for articles and other sources, published and un-published, see Notes. Books used for more specific reference will also be cited in the Notes.

Acker, Ally. *Reel Women: Pioneers of the Cinema,* 1896 to the Present. New York: Continuum, 1991

Alexander, Diane. *Playhouse.* Los Angeles: Dorleac-Macleish, 1984

Alexander, Paul. *Boulevard of Broken Dreams: The Life, Times, and Legend of James Dean.* New York: Viking, 1994

Alpert, Hollis. *The Dream and the Dreamers.* New York: Macmillan, 1962

Arce, Hector. *Gary Cooper: An Intimate Biography.* New York: William Morrow, 1979

————. *The Secret Life of Tyrone Power.* New York: William Morrow, 1979

Balio, Tino. *The American Film Industry.* Madison: University of Wisconsin Press, 1985

————. *Grand Design: Hollywood as a Modern Business Enterprise 1930–1939.* Berkeley: University of California Press, 1993

Balio, Tino (ed.) *Hollywood in the Age of Television.* Boston: Unwin Hyman, 1990

Beauchamp, Cari. *Without Lying Down: Frances Marion and the Powerful Women of Early Hollywood.* New York: Scribner, 1997

Benshoff, Harry M. *Monsters in the Closet: Homosexuality and the Horror Film.* Manchester: Manchester University Press. 1997

Bernstein, Walter. *Inside Out: A Memoir of the Blacklist.* New York: Knopf, 1996

Berubé, Allan. *Coming Out Under Fire: The History of Gay Men and Women in World War II.* New York: Penguin, 1990

Billingsley, Kenneth Lloyd. *Hollywood Party: How Communism Seduced the American Film Industry in the 1930s and 1940s.* Rocklin: Prima Publishing, 1998

Black, Gregory D. *Hollywood Censored.* Cambridge, Cambridge University Press, 1994

Blackwell, Mr. *From Rags to Bitches: An Autobiography.* Los Angeles: General Publishing Group, 1995

Bodeen, DeWitt. *From Hollywood.* Cranbury, NJ: A. S. Barnes and Co., 1976

———. *More from Hollywood.* New York: A. S. Barnes and Co., 1977

Bogdanovich, Peter. *Who the Devil Made It: Conversations with Legendary Film Directors.* New York: Random House, 1998

Bosworth, Patricia. *Montgomery Clift: A Biography.* New York: Harcourt Brace, 1978

Bourne, Stephen. *Brief Encounters: Lesbians and Gays in British Cinema 1930–1971.* London: Cassell, 1996

Brian, Denis. *Tallulah Darling.* New York: Pyramid Books, 1992

Brode, Douglas. *Crossroads to the Cinema.* Boston: Holbrook, 1975

Bronski, Michael. *Culture Clash: The Making of Gay Sensibility.* Boston: South End Press, 1984

———. *The Pleasure Principle: Sex, Backlash, and the Struggle for Gay Freedom.* New York: St. Martin's, 1998

Brooks, Louise. *Lulu in Hollywood.* New York, Knopf, 1982

Brown, Susan Jenkins. *Robber Rocks: Letters and Memoirs of Hart Crane, 1923–1932.* Middletown, CT: Wesleyan University Press, 1968

Brownlow, Kevin. *Hollywood: The Pioneers.* New York: Knopf, 1979

———. *The Parade's Gone By.* New York: Knopf, 1968

Bucknell, Katherine (ed.). *Christopher Isherwood Diaries, Vol. One: 1939–1960.* London: Methuen, 1996

Buhle, Paul, and Patrick McGilligan. *Tender Comrades: A Backstory of the Blacklist.* New York: St. Martin's, 1997

Calistro, Paddy. *Edith Head's Hollywood.* New York: Dutton, 1983

Callow, Simon. *Charles Laughton: A Difficult Actor.* London: Methuen, 1987

Chase, Donald. *Filmmaking: The Collaborative Art.* Boston: Little, Brown, 1975

Chierichetti, David. *Hollywood Costume Design.* New York: Harmony, 1976

———. *Mitchell Leisen: Hollywood Director.* Los Angeles: Photoventures Press, 1995

Clark, Tom. *Rock Hudson: Friend of Mine.* New York: Pharos Books, 1990

Clarke, Gerald. *Get Happy: The Life of Judy Garland.* New York: Random House, 2000

Cogley, John. *Report on Blacklisting, Volume 2.* New York: Arno Press, 1972

Conrad, Harold. *Dear Moffo: 35 Years in the Fast Lane.* New York: Stein and Day, 1982

Corber, Robert J. *Homosexuality in Cold War America: Resistence and the Crisis of Masculinity.* Durham: Duke University Press, 1997

Corliss, Richard. *Talking Pictures: Screenwriters in the American Cinema.* Woodstock: Overlook Press, 1974

Curtin, Kaier. *"We Can Always Call Them Bulgarians": The Emergence of Lesbians and Gay Men on the American Stage.* Boston: Alyson, 1987

Curtis, James. *James Whale: A New World of Gods and Monsters.* London: Faber and Faber, 1998

Custen, George F. *Twentieth Century's Fox: Darryl F. Zanuck and the Culture of Hollywood.* New York: BasicBooks, 1997

Davidson, Sara, and Rock Hudson. *Rock Hudson: His Story.* New York: Morrow, 1986

Davis, Ronald L. *The Glamour Factory: Inside Hollywood's Big Studio System.* Dallas: Southern Methodist University Press, 1993

de Acosta, Mercedes. *Here Lies the Heart.* New York: Morrow, 1960

D'Emilio, John. *Intimate Matters: A History of Sexuality in America.* New York: Harper & Row, 1988

———. *Sexual Politics, Sexual Communities.* (2nd ed.). Chicago: University of Chicago Press, 1998

Doherty, Thomas. *Pre-Code Hollywood.* New York: Columbia University Press, 1999

Duberman, Martin, et al. (ed.). *Hidden from History: Reclaiming the Gay and Lesbian Past.* New York: Meridian Books, 1990

Duberman, Martin. *Left Out: The Politics of Exclusion*. New York: BasicBooks, 1999

Durham, Weldon B. *American Theatre Companies*. New York: Greenwood Press, 1987

Dyer, Richard. *Heavenly Bodies: Film Stars and Society*. New York: St. Martin's Press, 1986

———. *Now You See It: Studies of Lesbian and Gay Film*. New York: Rutledge, 1990

Eells, George. *Ginger, Loretta and Irene Who?* New York: G. P. Putnam's Sons, 1976

———. *Hedda and Louella*. New York: G. P. Putnam's Sons, 1972

Ehrenstein, David. *Open Secret: Gay Hollywood 1928–1998*. New York: William Morrow, 1998

Ellenberger, Allan. *Ramon Novarro*. Jefferson, NC: McFarland and Company, 1999

Erté. *My Life, My Art: An Autobiography*. New York: Dutton, 1989

———. *Things I Remember*. New York: Quadrangle, 1975

Eyman, Scott. *The Speed of Sound: Hollywood and the Talkie Revolution*. New York: Simon & Schuster, 1997

Fordin, Hugh. *MGM's Greatest Musicals: The Arthur Freed Unit*. New York: Da Capo Press, 1996

Friedrich, Otto. *City of Nets: A Portrait of Hollywood in the 1940s*. New York: Harper & Row, 1986

Gabler, Neal. *An Empire of Their Own: How the Jews Invented Hollywood*. New York: Crown, 1988

———. *Winchell: Gossip, Power and the Culture of Celebrity*. New York: Knopf, 1994

Gates, Phyllis, and Bob Thomas. *My Husband Rock Hudson*. Garden City: Doubleday, 1987.

Gilmore, John. *Laid Bare*. Los Angeles: Amok Books, 1997

Gluckman, Amy, and Betsy Reed. *Homo Economics: Capitalism, Community and Lesbian and Gay Life*. New York: Routledge, 1997

Golden, Eve. *Vamp: The Rise and Fall of Theda Bara*. Vestal, NY: Emprise Publishing, 1996

Goldman, Herbert G. *Fanny Brice: The Original Funny Girl*. New York: Oxford University Press, 1992

Goodman, Ezra. *The Fifty Year Decline and Fall of Hollywood*. New York: Macfadden, 1962

Grafton, David. *Red, Hot & Rich! An Oral History of Cole Porter*. New York: Stein and Day, 1987

Gray, Lois S., and Ronald L. Seeber. *Under the Stars: Essays on Labor Relations in Arts and Entertainment*. Ithaca: Cornell University, 1996

Greer, Howard. *Designing Male*. New York: G. P. Putnam's Sons, 1951

Guilaroff, Sydney. *Crowning Glory: Reflections of Hollywood's Favorite Confidant*. Santa Monica: General Publishing Group, 1996

Guiles, Fred Lawrence. *Tyrone Power: The Last Idol*. New York: Doubleday, 1979

Hambley, John. *The Art of Hollywood: 50 Years of Art Direction*. London: Thames Television, 1979

Hammer, Langdon, and Brom Weber (eds.). *O My Land, My Friend: Selected Letters of Hart Crane*. New York: Four Walls Eight Windows, 1997

Harmetz, Aljean. *The Making of the Wizard of Oz*. New York: Hyperion, 1998

Hay, Peter. *MGM: When the Lion Roars*. Atlanta: Turner Publishing, 1991

Head, Edith, and Jane Kesner Ardmore. *The Dress Doctor*. Boston: Little, Brown, 1959

Heimann, Jim. *Sins of the City: The Real Los Angeles Noir*. San Francisco: Chronicle Books, 1999

Heisner, Beverly. *Hollywood Art: Art Direction in the Days of the Great Studios*. Boston: Faber and Faber, 1995

Helms, Alan. *Young Man from the Provinces: A Gay Life Before Stonewall*. Boston: Faber and Faber, 1995.

Higham, Charles. *Hollywood Cameramen: Sources of Light*. Bloomington: Indiana University Press, 1970

Higham, Charles, and Roy Moseley. *Cary Grant: The Lonely Heart*. New York: Avon, 1989

Higham, Charles. *The Celluloid Muse: Hollywood Directors Speak*. Argus and Robertson, 1969

———. *Kate: The Life of Katharine Hepburn*. New York: W. W. Norton, 1975

———. *Merchant of Dreams: Louis B. Mayer, MGM and the Secret Hollywood*. New York: Dell, 1993

Holley, Val. *James Dean: The Biography*. New York, St. Martin's, 1997

Hopper, Hedda. *From Under My Hat.* New York: Macfadden Books, 1964
———. *The Whole Truth and Nothing But.* Garden City, NY: Doubleday, 1963
Jackson, Carlton. *Hattie: The Life of Hattie McDaniel.* Lanham, MD: Madison Books, 1990
Janis, Elsie. *So Far So Good.* New York: E. P. Dutton, 1932
Johnston, Claire (ed.). *The Work of Dorothy Arzner: Toward a Feminist Cinema.* London: British Film Institute, 1975
Jowett, Garth. *Film: The Democratic Art.* Boston: Little, Brown & Co., 1976
Kaiser, Charles. *The Gay Metropolis.* New York: Harcourt Brace, 1998
Kaplan, Fred. *Gore Vidal.* New York: Doubleday, 2000
Katchmer, George A. *Eighty Silent Film Stars.* Jefferson, NC: McFarland, 1991
Katz, Jonathan Ned. *Gay American History: Lesbians and Gay Men in the USA.* New York: Meridian, 1992
Kennedy, Matthew. *Marie Dressler.* Jefferson, NC: McFarland, 1999
Kerrigan, J. Warren. *How I Became a Successful Moving Picture Star.* Los Angeles: Kellow and Brown, 1914
Knight, Arthur. *The Hollywood Style.* London: Macmillan, 1969
Lacey, Robert. *Grace.* New York: G. P. Putnam's Sons, 1994
LaGuardia, Robert. *Monty: A Biography of Montgomery Clift.* New York: Avon, 1978
Lahue, Kalton C. *Winners of the West: The Sagebrush Heroes of the Silent Screen.* South Brunswick, NJ: A.S. Barnes, 1970
Lait, Jack, and Lee Mortimer. *New York Confidential.* New York: Crown, 1951
———. *Washington Confidential.* New York: Crown, 1951
Lambert, Gavin. *Mainly About Lindsay Anderson.* New York: Knopf, 2000
———. *Nazimova: A Biography.* New York: Knopf, 1997
———. *On Cukor.* New York, G. P. Putnam's Sons, 1972
Laurents, Arthur. *Original Story By.* New York: Knopf, 2000
LaVine, W. Robert. *In a Glamorous Fashion: The Fabulous Years of Hollywood Costume Design.* New York: Scribner's, 1980
Lawton, Stephen. *Santa Barbara's Flying A Studio.* Santa Barbara: Fithian Press, 1997
Lee, Betty. *Marie Dressler: The Unlikeliest Star.* University Press of Kentucky, 1997
Lee, Sarah T. (ed.). *American Fashion: The Life and Times of Adrian, Mainbocher, McCardell, Norrell and Trigeve.* New York: Quadrangle, 1975
Leff, Leonard J., and Jerold L. Simmons. *The Dame in the Kimono: Hollywood Censorship and the Production Code.* New York: Doubleday, 1990
Leiter, Samuel L. (ed.). *The Encyclopedia of the New York Stage.* Westport, CT: Greenwood Press, 1985
Levy, Emmanuel. *George Cukor: Master of Elegance.* New York: William Morrow, 1994
Lewis, David. *The Creative Producer: A Memoir of the Studio System.* Metuchen, NJ: Scarecrow Press, 1993
Lobrutto, Vincent. *By Design: Interviews with Film Production Designers.* Praeger, 1992
Loney, Glenn. *Unsung Genius: The Passion of Dancer-Choreographer Jack Cole.* New York: Franklin Watts, 1984
Loughery, John. *The Other Side of Silence: Men's Lives and Gay Identities.* New York: Henry Holt, 1998
Luft, Lorna. *Me and My Shadows.* New York: Pocket Books, 1998
Lyons, Timothy J. *The Silent Partner: The History of the American Film Manufacturing Company 1910–1921.* New York: Arno Press, 1974
Maas, Frederica Sagor. *The Shocking Miss Pilgrim.* Lexington: University Press of Kentucky, 1999
Maltin, Leonard. *The Real Stars: Articles and Interviews on Hollywood's Great Character Actors.* New York: Curtis, 1973
Mank, Gregory William. *The Hollywood Hissables.* Metuchen, NJ: Scarecrow Press, 1989
Mann, William J. *Wisecracker: The Life and Times of William Haines.* New York: Viking, 1998
Marion, Frances. *Off With Their Heads.* New York: Macmillan, 1972
Marmor, Judd. *Sexual Inversion: Multiple Roots of Homosexuality.* New York: Basic, 1985
Marshall, J. D. *Blueprints on Babylon.* New York: Phoenix House, 1978

Martin, W. K. *Marlene Dietrich*. (*Lives of Notable Gay Men and Lesbians* series, ed. Martin Duberman). New York: Chelsea House, 1995

Mayne, Judith. *Directed by Dorothy Arzner*. Bloomington: Indiana University Press, 1994

McBrien, William. *Cole Porter: A Biography*. New York: Knopf, 1998

McClure, Arthur F., and Ken D. Jones. *Star Quality: Screen Actors from the Golden Age of Films*. South Brunswick, NJ: A. S. Barnes, 1974

McDonald, Boyd. *Cruising the Movies*. New York: Gay Presses of New York, 1985

McGilligan, Patrick. *Backstory: Interviews with Screenwriters of Hollywood's Golden Age*. University of California Press, 1986 (vols 1-2)

———. *A Double Life: George Cukor*. New York: St. Martin's, 1991

Meyer, William. *Warner Brothers Directors*. New York: Arlington House, 1978

Mikotowicz, Thomas J. *Theatrical Designers: An International Biographical Dictionary*. New York: Greenwood Press, 1992

Miller, Neil. *Out of the Past: Gay and Lesbian History from 1869 to the Present*. New York: Vintage Books, 1995

Morris, Michael. *Madam Valentino: The Many Lives of Natacha Rambova*. New York: Abbeville Press, 1991

Morsberger, Robert E. (ed.). *American Screenwriters (Volume 26, Dictionary of Literary Biography)*. Detroit: Gale Research, 1984

Mosley, Leonard. *Zanuck*. Boston: Little, Brown & Co., 1985

Naremore, James. *More Than Night: Film Noir in Its Contexts*. Berkeley: University of California Press, 1998

Navasky, Victor S. *Naming Names*. New York: Viking, 1980

Nielsen, Mike, and Gene Mailes. *Hollywood's Other Blacklist: Union Struggles in the Studio System*. London: British Film Institute, 1995

Oppenheimer, George. *The View From the Sixties: Memories of a Spent Life*. New York: McKay, 1966

Oppenheimer, Jerry, and Jack Vitek. *Idol: Rock Hudson, the True Story of an American Film Hero*. New York: Villard, 1986

Owen, Bobbi. *Costume Design on Broadway*. New York: Greenwood Press, 1987

———. *Scenic Design on Broadway*. New York: Greenwood Press, 1991

Paris, Barry. *Garbo: A Biography*. London: Pan Books, 1996

———. *Louise Brooks*. New York: Knopf, 1989

Parsons, Louella O. *Tell It to Louella*. New York, Lancer 1962

Payne, Graham, and Sheridan Morley (eds.). *The Noel Coward Diaries*. Boston: Little, Brown, 1982

Peters, Margot. *The House of Barrymore*. New York: Alfred A. Knopf, 1990

Pratley, Gerald. *The Cinema of Otto Preminger*. New York: A. S. Barnes, 1971

Preminger Otto. *Preminger: An Autobiography*. New York: Doubleday, 1977

Price, Victoria. *Vincent Price*. New York: St. Martin's Press, 1999

Quirk, Lawrence. *Norma: The Story of Norma Shearer*. New York: St. Martin's Press, 1988

Ralston, Esther. *Someday We'll Laugh*. Metuchen, NJ: Scarecrow Press, 1985

Ramsaye, Terry. *A Million and One Nights*. New York: Simon & Schuster, 1926

Riva, Maria. *Marlene Deitrich*. New York: Knopf, 1993

Rollyson, Carl. *Marilyn Monroe: A Life of the Actress*. New York: Da Capo Press, 1993

Rosenberg, Bernard, and Harry Silverstein. *The Real Tinsel*. New York: Macmillan, 1971

Ross, Steven J. *Working-Class Hollywood: Silent Film and the Shaping of Class in America*. Princeton: Princeton University Press, 1998

Rosten, Leo. *Hollywood: The Movie Colony and the Movie Makers*. New York: Harcourt Brace, 1941.

Russo, Vito. *The Celluloid Closet*. New York: Harper & Row, 1987

Scarfone, Jay. *The Wizardry of Oz*. New York: Random House, 1999

Schanke, Robert A., and Kim Marra (eds.). *Passing Performances: Queer Readings of leading Players in American Theater History*. Ann Arbor: University of Michigan Press, 1998

Schatz, Thomas. *The Genius of the System: Hollywood Filmmaking in the Studio Era*. New York: Henry Holt, 1996

Schickel, Richard. *Clint Eastwood: A Biography.* New York: Knopf, 1996

Schmidgall, Gary. *Walt Whitman: A Gay Life.* New York: Dutton, 1997

Schwartz, Nancy Lynn. *The Hollywood Writers' Wars.* New York: Knopf, 1982

Sedgwick, Eve Kosofsky. *Epistemology of the Closet.* University of California Press, 1992

Sennett, Ted. *Hollwood Musicals.* New York: Harry Abrams, 1981

Sennett, Robert S. *Hollywood Hoopla: Creating and Selling Movies in the Golden Age of Holly-wood.* New York: Billboard Books, 1998

————. *Setting the Scene: The Great Hollywood Art Directors.* New York: Harry Abrams, 1994

Server, Lee. *Screenwriter: Words Become Pictures.* Pittstown, NJ: Main Street Press, 1987

Shorris, Sylvia, and Marion Abbott Bundy. *Talking Pictures with the People who Made Them.* New York: New Press, 1994

Sikov, Ed. *On Sunset Boulevard: The Life and Times of Billy Wilder.* New York: Hyperion, 1998

Silverman, Stephen M. *Dancing on the Ceiling: Stanley Donen and His Movies.* New York: Knopf, 1996

Sirk, Douglas. *Sirk on Sirk.* Boston: Faber and Faber, 1997

Slide, Anthony. *The American Film Industry.* New York: Greenwood Press, 1986

————. *The Big V: A History of the Vitagraph Company.* Metuchen, NJ: Scarecrow Press, 1987

————. *Early American Cinema.* Cranbury, NY: A.S. Barnes, 1969

————. *Eccentrics of Comedy.* Lanham, MD: Scarecrow Press, 1998

————. *Encyclopedia of Vaudeville.* Westport, CT: Greenwood Press, 1994

————. *The Great Pretenders: A History of Female and Male Impersonation in the Performing Arts.* Lombard, IL: Wallace Homestead, 1986

————. *The Silent Feminists: America's First Women Directors.* Lanham, MD: Scarecrow Press, 1996

Smith, Liz. *Natural Blonde, A Memoir.* New York: Hyperion, 2000

Spada, James. *More Than a Woman: An Intimate Biography of Bette Davis.* New York: Bantam, 1993

————. *Peter Lawford: The Man Who Kept the Secrets.* New York: Bantam, 1991

Spoto, Donald. *Blue Angel: The Life of Marlene Dietrich.* New York, Doubleday, 1992

————. *The Kindness of Strangers: The Life of Tennessee Williams.* Boston: Little Brown, 1985

————. *Rebel: The Life and Legend of James Dean.* New York: Harper Collins, 1996

Staiger, Janet. *The Studio System.* New Brunswick: Rutgers University Press, 1995

Steen, Mike. *Hollywood Speaks.* New York: G. P. Putnam's Sons, 1974

————. *A Look at Tennessee Williams.* New York: Hawthorne Books, 1969

————. *Clara Bow: Runnin' Wild.* New York: Doubleday, 1988

————. *Bombshell: The Life and Death of Jean Harlow.* New York: Doubleday, 1993

Stephens, Michael L. *Art Directors in Cinema: A Worldwide Biographical Dictionary.* Jefferson, NC: McFarland, 1998

Stricklyn, Ray. *Angels and Demons: One Actor's Hollywood Journey.* Los Angeles: Belle Publishing, 1999

Summers, Anthony. *Goddess: The Secret Lives of Marilyn Monroe.* New York: MacMillan, 1985

Swenson, Karen. *Greta Garbo: A Life Apart.* New York: Scribner, 1997

Swindell, Larry. *The Last Hero: A Biography of Gary Cooper.* Garden City, NY: Doubleday, 1980

Telotte, J. P. *Dreams of Darkness: Fantasy and the Films of Val Lewton.* Chicago: University of Illinois Press, 1985

Thomson, David. *Showman: The Life of David O. Selznick.* New York: Knopf, 1992

Timmons, Stuart. *The Trouble With Harry Hay.* Boston: Alyson, 1990

Torrence, Bruce T. *Hollywood: The First Hundred Years.* New York: Zoetrope, 1982

Vaughn, Robert. *Only Victims: A Study of Show Business Blacklisting.* New York: Limelight Editions, 1996

Vertrees, Alan David. *Selznick's Vision: Gone With the Wind and Hollywood Filmmaking.* Austin: University of Texas Press, 1997

Vickers, Hugo. *Cecil Beaton: A Biography.* New York: Donald I. Fine, 1985

Vidal, Gore. *Palimpsest.* New York: Penquin, 1995

Vieira, Mark. *Sin in Soft Focus.* New York: Harry Abrams, 1999

Vining, Donald. *A Gay Diary 1993–1946.* New York: Hard Candy, 1996

Von Hoffman, Nicholas. *Citizen Cohn.* New York: Doubleday, 1988

Walker, Alexander. *The Shattered Silents.* New York: William Morrow, 1979

Walker, Danton. *Danton's Inferno: The Story of a Columnist and How He Grew.* New York: Hastings House, 1955

Webb, Michael. *Hollywood: Legend and Reality.* Boston: Little, Brown, 1986

White, Patricia. *Uninvited: Classical Hollywood Cinema and Lesbian Representability.* Bloomington: Indiana University Press, 1999

Whiteside, Jonny. *Cry: The Johnnie Ray Story.* New York: Barricade Books, 1994

Winecoff, Charles. *Split Image: The Life of Anthony Perkins.* New York: Dutton, 1996

Wolfe, Donald H. *The Last Days of Marilyn Monroe.* New York: William Morrow, 1998

Zerbe, Jerome, and Brendan Gill. *Happy Times.* New York: Harcourt Brace, 1973

INDEX